NETWORK SCIENCE

NETWORK SCIENCE

Theory and Practice

TED G. LEWIS
Professor of Computer Science
Naval Postgraduate School

A JOHN WILEY & SONS, INC., PUBLICATION

Library of Congress Cataloging-in-Publication Data:

Lewis, T. G. (Theodore Gyle), 1941-
    Network science : theory and practice / Ted G. Lewis.
        p.   cm.
    Includes bibliographical references and index.
    ISBN 978-0-470-33188-0 (cloth)
    1.   Network analysis (Planning)   I.   Title.

    T57.85.L49 2008
    003'.72--dc22   2008047060

Printed in the United States of America

10   9   8   7   6   5   4   3   2   1

CONTENTS

PREFACE/FOREWORD

The phrase "network science" may be premature, as I write this foreword, because it may be too early to declare the combination of graph theory, control theory, and cross-discipline applications a "science." Indeed, many of my colleagues have presented strong arguments to the contrary—declaring network science a fad—or even worse—a fabrication. So it was with trepidation that in 2006 I began writing a series of essays on various aspects of scale-free networks, small worlds, and networks that self-synchronize. These rough ideas expressed by this series evolved into the book that you are now holding in your hand. Like most first attempts, it is not without flaws. Yet, writing this book was a labor of love and—hopefully—it will become a useful resource for the unbiased, inquiring mind. Maybe it will establish the new science of networks as a subject taught in nearly every science, engineering, medical, and social science field of study.

Only time will tell whether this first attempt to compile what we know about the new science of networks into a single volume misses the mark or succeeds—and a textbook at that! But it has always been my weakness to write on topics that are slightly ahead of their time. The risk here lies in the selection of topics that I have chosen to call *network science*. Clearly, one has to include the work of pioneers such as Adamic, Albert, Barabasi, Barrat, Bollobas, Erdos, Granovetter, Kephart, Lin, Liu, Mihail, Milgram, Molloy, Moore, Newman, Pastor-Satorras, Renyi, Strogatz, Tadic, Wang, Watts, Weigt, White, Zhang, and Zhu. I have done so in the first 6 of 13 chapters. These chapters develop the field from its graph theory roots, to the modern definition of a network. Entire chapters are devoted to the most famous classes: regular, random, scale-free, and small-world networks. So, the first half of this book traces the development of network science along a trail blazed by the inventors. But then what?

My second objective was to add to what is known and published by the pioneers. The risk here lies in being pretentious—presuming to know what direction this new field might take. Once again, I relied on my weakness for being presumptuous—inquisitively so. Chapter 7, "Emergence," introduces new self-organizing principles for networks and shows how to custom-design networks of arbitrary degree sequence distribution; Chapter 8, "Epidemics," extends the elegant work of Z. Wang, Chakrabarti, C. Wang, and Faloutsos, to the exciting new endeavor of designing antigen countermeasures for the Internet. This work can be used to explain human epidemics as well as epidemics that sweep across the Internet. Chapter 9, "Synchrony," pushes the early work of Watts to new levels—claiming that network synchronization is merely a special case of linear system stability. Simple eigenvalue tools can be used to determine the stability and synchrony of almost any linear network. Chapter 10, "Influence Networks," is mostly new material and suggests what conditions must be met in order for a social network to come to consensus. As it turns out, it is not easy for groups to agree! Chapter 11, "Vulnerability," builds on the PhD dissertation of Waleed Al-Mannai, who formalized and extended my own work on network risk. Al Mannai's theory is being used on a daily basis to evaluate critical infrastructure systems and protect them against natural and synthetic (anthropogenic, humanmade) attacks. This has made a profound impression on the practice of homeland security. Chapter 12, "Netgain," is an exploration of business models—relating the famous Schumpeter *creative destruction* process to an emergent process, and mapping the Bass and Fisher–Pry equations onto networks. It is comforting to verify the Bass–Fisher–Pry equations for networks, but furthermore, I show how these classical models may be extended to multi-product markets and oligopolies. Finally, Chapter 13, "Biology," is completely on the leading edge of network science. This final chapter introduces the reader to the exciting new field of protein expression networks and suggests some new directions for the reader to consider.

The casual reader may easily skip over the mathematics, and still glean much from the application of networks to various disciplines ranging from computer science and engineering, business, public health (epidemiology), Internet virus countermeasures, social network behavior, biology, and physics. The more dedicated reader and classroom instructor may want to experiment with the software tools provided by the publisher and author (tedglewis@friction-free-economy.com). These include 5 major Java applications: *Network.jar* for exploring various classes of networks and experimenting with various emergence processes; *Influence.jar* for the study of influence networks and social network analysis; *NetworkAnalysis.jar* for the study of network vulnerability and the attacker-defender network risk problem; *NetGain.jar* for business modeling; and *BioNet.jar* for biological networks—especially protein expression networks. Both executable and source code are available as open source software. If you intend to deliver this material as an instructor in a college-level course, you will want to download the instructor's manual from the publisher's web site.

This book is a start, but it also leaves many questions unanswered. I hope that it will inspire a new generation of investigators and investigations. If I am right, the phrase "network science" will not be controversial in another 10 years. But then, this is left as an exercise for the reader!

I want to thank Steve Lieberman for his diligent equation typesetting and careful reading of several drafts; also, Rudy Darken, and Tom Mackin, who contributed to my thought process and helped correct several of my ill-conceived ideas. Waleed Al Mannai had a major impact on Chapter 11, and also indirectly on the whole book. It was a pleasure working with these colleagues over 3 years of writing.

TED G. LEWIS

March 22, 2008

1

ORIGINS

The "new science of networks"—an emerging field of study that we abbreviate as *network science*, is really quite old, having roots as far back as 1736. Essentially the application of mathematical graph theory to problems in a variety of fields, network science reemerged in the late 1990s as a "new science." But graph theory has been applied to practical problems since its inception in 1736, when Swiss mathematician Leonhard Euler solved the very real-world problem of how best to circumnavigate the Bridges of Königsberg, using graph theory.

Graph theorists spent the next 200 years in the backwaters of arcane mathematics. But it is difficult to keep a good idea down for long. The mathematics of graphs appeared again in the 1950s when the Hungarian and nomadic mathematician Paul Erdos (1913–1996) reestablished graph theory (and created the branch known as *discrete mathematics*) with papers on random graphs. Erdos' colorful description of mathematics as a machine for turning coffee into theorems preferred extended visits with other mathematicians to owning his own home. Today, we use the Erdos–Renyi (ER) random graph as a kind of benchmark—to compare with nonrandom graphs. The ER generative procedure for constructing a random graph marked a second historical milestone in 1959–60 (see Table 1.1).

In the late 1960s and 1970s graph theory was used by social scientists to model social networks and study the behavior of humans in groups. Stanley Milgram is credited with introducing the notion of a *small-world* network to the social science community—igniting interest in studies of how network topology might influence

TABLE 1.1   Historical Timeline of Significant Events

Date	Who	Contribution
1736	Euler	Bridges of Königsberg
1925	G. Yule	Preferential attachment, Yule–Simon distribution
1927	Kermack, McKendrick	First epidemic model
1951	Solomonoff, Rappaport	Spread of infection in random networks
1955	Simon	Power law observed in word analysis
1959	Gilbert	First generative procedure for random graph
1960	Erdos, Renyi	Random graphs
1967	Milgram	Small-world experiment
1969	Bass	Diffusion of innovation in populations—nonnetwork model
1971	Fisher, Pry	Diffusion by product substitution—nonnetwork model
1972	Bollobas	Complex graphs
1972	Bonacich	Idea of influence in social networks leading to influence diagrams
1973	Granovetter	Job-seeking networks formed clusters with "weak links" between them
1978	Pool, Kochen	First theoretical examination of small worlds
1984	Kuramoto	Synchronization of linear systems
1985	Bollobas	Publishes book on "random graphs"
1988	Waxman	First graph model of the Internet
1989	Bristor, Ryan	"Buying networks" = application of network science to model economic system
1990	Guare	Coined phrase, "six degrees of separation" = name of his Broadway play
1995	Molloy, Reed	Generation of networks with arbitrary degree sequence distribution
1996	Kretschmar, Morris	Early application of network science to spread of infectious disease = contagion driven by largest connected component
1998	Holland	Introduction of emergence in complex adaptive systems
1998	Watts, Strogatz, Faloutsos, Faloutsos	Renewed interest in Milgram's original work on small worlds, examples of clustering; first generative procedure for small world
1999	Faloutsos	Power law observed in Internet
1999	Albert, Jeong, Barabasi	Power law observed in WWW
1999	Dorogovtsev, Mendes	Small-world properties
1999	Barabasi, Albert,	Scale-free network model
1999	Dorogovtsev, Mendes, Samukhim, Krapivsky Redner	Exact solution to scale-free network degree sequence
1999	Watts	Explanation of "small-world dilemma": high clustering, low path length

(Continued)

TABLE 1.1 *Continued*

Date	Who	Contribution
1999	Adamic	Distance between .edu sites shown to be small-world
1999	Kleinberg, Kumar, Raghavan, Rajagopalan Tomkins	Formalized model of WWW as "Webgraph"
1999	Walsh	Difficulty of search in small worlds using local properties
2000	Marchiori, Latora,	Harmonic distance replaces path length: works for disconnected networks
2000	Broder, Kumar, Maghoul, Raghavan, Rajagopalan Stata, Tomkins, Wiener	Full Webgraph map of the WWW
2000	Kleinberg	Shows $O(n)$ search in small world using "Manhattan distance"
2000	Albert, Jeong, Barabasi	Scale-free networks are resilient if hubs are protected (Internet's "Achilles heel")
2001	Yung	Taxonomy of applications of small-world theory to: SNA, collaboration, Internet, business, life sciences
2001	Pastor-Satorras, Vespignani	Claim no epidemic threshold in scale-free networks; Internet susceptible to SIS viruses
2001	Tadic, Adamic	Use of local information can speed search on scale-free networks
2002	Levene, Fenner, Loizou, Wheeldon	Enhanced Webgraph model concluded structure of the WWW couldn't be explained by preferential attachment alone
2002	Kleinfeld,	Claims Milgram experiments not well founded: small-world social network is an "urban myth"
2002	Wang, Chen, Barahona, Pecora, Liu, Hong, Choi Kim, Jost, Joy	Sync in small worlds equivalent to stability in coupled system
2003	Wang, Chakrabarti, Wang, Faloutsos	Showed spread of epidemics determined by network's spectral radius, largest eigenvalue of connection matrix
2003	Virtanen	Complete survey of network science results up to 2003
2003	Strogatz	Synchronization of crickets, heartbeats
2005	NRC	Definition of network science
2006	Atay	Synchronization in networks with degree sequence distribution—application to networks
2007	Gabbay	Consensus in influence networks—linear and nonlinear models

human behavior—and the reverse. The "small-world dilemma" was the subject of vigorous study throughout this period. Why is it, social scientists asked, that humans are able to connect to one another through an extremely small number of intermediaries, even as the size of a population grows?

Milgram's famous "six degrees of separation" experiment suggested that the *distance* between two people selected at random from the entire population of the United States is approximately six intermediaries. In Milgram's experiment, volunteers in Kansas and Nebraska were asked to forward a letter to an unfamiliar target living in Cambridge and Boston, Massachusetts. Not knowing the target person, recipients forwarded the letter to an acquaintance closer to the target than themselves. Many of the letters were lost, but of the ones that eventually reached their target addresses, the number of hops along the chain of intermediaries ranged from 2 to 10, with an average of 5.2. Hence the notion of a small world and six degrees of separation was born.

Network science took its third, and current step toward becoming a scientific discipline of its own in the late 1990s when a number of scientists in other fields began to use networks as models of physical and biological phenomena. In particular, the pioneering work of Duncan Watts, Steven Strogatz, and Albert-Laszlo Barabasi stimulated renewed interest in mathematical analysis of networks as applied to the physical world. Watts equated the structure of very sparse networks with small diameter (small worlds) with a diverse number of phenomena such as phase transitions in materials, functionality of biological organisms, and behavior of electrical power grids. How could a simple graph model explain such diversity of real-world behaviors?

Strogatz studied the impact of network structure on complex adaptive systems in physics as well as explaining why hearts beat in a regular synchronized pattern in mammals, and why a certain species of firefly rhythmically chirps in unison without centralized control. It appeared that living organisms tend to synchronize their behavior without global knowledge. In this book, we show that a deep understanding of how and why network synchronization occurs in physical and biological systems also explains the conditions for arriving at a consensus by a group of people, how best to conduct product marketing campaigns, and how corporations rise to become a monopoly. Synchronization is a byproduct of the structure of "living networks."

Barabasi and students created another line of investigation with the invention of *scale-free networks*—nonrandom networks with hubs. In a number of studies of the structure of the Internet and WWW, Barabasi et al. discovered an emergent property of the decentralized Internet—that it had emerged without central planning into a structure consisting of a small number of extremely popular sites called *hubs*, and a large number of "unpopular" sites with few links. Instead of being random, like an ER (Erdos–Renyi) network, the Internet topology was very nonrandom. In fact, the probability that a site has k links obeys a power law, which drops off quickly for large k. Furthermore, they speculated that this was the result of a microrule called *preferential attachment*—that the probability a site will obtain a new link is directly proportional to the number of links it already has. Thus, the more links a site has, the more it gets—the so-called "rich get richer" phenomenon.

Scale-free networks are *extremely* nonrandom. This discovery set the stage for a plethora of publications in a diverse number of disciplines ranging from political science to sociology, biology, and physics. Why do so many natural phenomena obey the power law instead of the normal distribution or perhaps the exponential distribution? Once again, the stage was set for deep inquiry into the structure of organizations, organisms, and physical matter to explain the questions raised by the power law.

The current state of network science can best be described as "still evolving." In its modern form, it is approximately a decade old. Discoveries continue to be made on a monthly basis, which means that this book will soon be out of date! Therefore, the author has attempted to focus on the fundamentals—results that hopefully will endure for decades—rather than delve into interesting but distracting diversions.

The purpose of this chapter is to define the emerging discipline called *network science* and develop a historical timeline of key events leading up to the current state of the field. We survey that past 270 years leading up to the current state of the art, and end with a loose collection of "rules" for networks. We study the following in detail:

1. Network science can be defined in many ways. We loosely define it as the study of the theoretical foundations of network structure/dynamic behavior and its application to many subfields. Network science is both theory and application.

2. The history of network science is divided into three periods: (1) early pre–network period (1736–1966), when network science was really the mathematics of graphs; (2) a meso–network period (1967–1998), when network science was not yet called "the new science of networks," but in fact applications of networks were emerging from the research literature; and (3) the modern period (1998–present), when the pioneers of the current definition of network science set forth the fundamentals and showed that the fundamentals had meaning in the real world.

3. The key concepts or principles of network science are (at least) structure, dynamism, bottom–up evolution, autonomy, topology, power, stability, and emergence. Each of these are explained in detail in this chapter.

4. We give a new perspective on network science that links emergence of network synchronization to stability of linear coupled systems. This perspective integrates a number of concepts underlying applications like models of the spread of epidemics, dynamics of various forms of network emergence, and behaviors observed in disparate fields such as biology, physics, and marketing. We claim the underlying behavior of these applications is nothing more than special cases of the more general case of linear system stability; that is, the spread of infections, consensus building in groups, stability of electric power grids, and so on are applications of coupled linear system analysis. All of these seemingly disparate behaviors can be explained and analyzed using the tools of spectral analysis.

1.1 WHAT IS NETWORK SCIENCE?

The Committee on Network Science for Future Army Applications, commissioned by the Board on Army Science and Technology in cooperation with the National Research Council of the National Academies, defines *network science* in a number of ways, and at a number of levels of detail (National Research Council, 2005). Perhaps the simplest and most direct definition given by the NRC is "organized knowledge of networks based on their study using the scientific method." This definition is meant to distinguish network science from the various technologies that use it—for example, to separate the underlying science of networks from technologies such as the Internet.

But network science is not yet mature enough to be separated from its technological roots. The Committee discovered that each subfield using network science had a different working definition. Communication engineers think of networks as systems of routers and switches; sociologists think of networks as influence diagrams representing the social interactions among humans; marketing business people think of networks as populations of buyers; and the physicist thinks of networks as models of phase transition, magnetism, and so on. Biologists use the network metaphor to understand epidemics, genetics, and metabolic systems within cells, and power engineers think of electrical power grids. Network science appears to be in the eye of the beholder with different nomenclature, different vocabulary, and different methods of analysis in each field.

Perhaps it is easier to define what a *network* is, than what *network science* is. In this respect, the concept of a network is more universal, even though the terminology is not. The Committee describes a network "by its structure (e.g., nodes and links), and its behavior (what the network 'does' as a result of the interactions among the nodes and links)." It goes on to say, "a network is always a representation or model of observable reality, not that reality, itself." Networks are graphs that represent something real.

The operational definition above identifies two key ingredients of network science: (1) it is the study of the structure of a collection of nodes and links that represent something real, and (2) it is the study of the dynamic behavior of the aggregation of nodes and links. It asks, "What happens over time as a network evolves, and why does it happen?" The most significant results of network science seem to correlate form with function and structure with behavior. Currently, the behaviors of greatest interest are in physical, biological, and social systems. Nodes might be humans, molecules, genes, routers, transformers (in power grids), Web pages, or research publications. Links might be friendships, contagions, synapses, cables, Internet links, or bibliographical citations. In this sense, network science is an abstraction of reality—not the reality, itself. However, if the abstraction can explain the behavior of a real system, then network science is not only highly interesting but useful as well.

The structure portion of a network is easily modeled by graph theory. Specifically, the network itself can be defined in terms of a set, $G = \{N, L, f\}$, where N is a set of nodes, L a set of links, and $f: N \times N$ a mapping function that defines the structure of G—how nodes are connected to each other through links. The mapping function contains enough information to draw the graph on a planar piece of paper using dots as nodes and lines as links. But the set G is inadequate to define the second part of a network—its dynamic behavior.

The dynamic portion of a network is defined by a set of *microrules* governing the behavior of nodes and links. These rules are given at the *microlevel*, to distinguish them from *macrolevel* behaviors of networks. Specifically, microlevel rules dictate the behavior of links and nodes, and macrolevel rules dictate the emergence of global properties of a network. For example, *preferential attachment*—links are attracted to nodes with a lot of links, already—is a microrule, whereas the power law describing the *degree sequence distribution* of a network is a macrolevel rule. As network scientists, we are concerned mainly with understanding macrolevel properties by studying microrules—and sometimes the reverse.

A complete definition of network G must include both structural and behavioral information. For example, $G(t) = \{N(t), L(t), f(t)\}$ is a set-theoretic definition of network G with a dynamic dimension—$G(t)$ is a function of time t and the number, values, and mappings of nodes and links as they change with time. The actual behaviors of $G(t)$ are expressed algorithmically, typically in the form of a computer algorithm. In this book we use programming language *Java* to express microrules. Taken together, a compact definition of a network with its structural and behavioral elements is presented below.

Definition of Network

$$G(t) = \{N(t), L(t), f(t) : J(t)\}$$

where, $t = $ time, simulated or real

$N = $ nodes, also known as *vertices* or "actors"

$L = $ links, also known as *edges*

$f : N \times N = $ mapping function that connects nodepairs, yielding topology

$J = $ algorithm for describing behaviors of nodes and links versus time

We can now propose a rigorous definition of network science as the study of networks, including their structure and behaviors:

Definition of Network Science   *Network science*, or the *science of networks*, is the study of the theoretical foundations of network structure/dynamic behavior and the application of networks to many subfields. Currently known subfields include *social network analysis* (SNA), *collaboration networks* (bibliographic citations, product marketing, online social networks), synthetic *emergent systems* (power grids, the Internet), physical science systems (phase transition, percolation theory, Ising theory), and life science systems (epidemics, metabolic processes, genetics).[1]

It should be clear from this definition that network science is essentially the science of systems. In addition, because networks often model complex systems, it is closely associated with the older field of complex adaptive systems. In fact, network science incorporates ideas from complex adaptive systems (emergence), chaos

---

[1] Ernst Ising (1900–1998) proposed the model of phase transition from paramagnetic to ferromagnetic state that bears his name. At some point, enough atoms align in the same direction to create a magnet in iron. This is the result of transition from a state of predominantly random polarity (atoms cancel one another) to a state of minimum energy or predominantly aligned atoms, hence producing an overall magnetic effect.

theory (synchronization), and mean-field theory (physics). Network science is a crossroad of sorts, pulling together ideas from its sister disciplines.

1.2   A BRIEF HISTORY OF NETWORK SCIENCE

Network science has been around for a long time, especially if graph theory is considered its genesis (see Table 1.1). But network science is more than graph theory, because of its dynamic aspect and application to a number of other disciplines. In general, network science has roots in graph theory, social network analysis, control theory, and more recently, the physical and biological sciences. In a sense, network science is the result of convergence of many other fields.

From a distance, it appears that network science has undergone (at least) two major transitions: from mathematical theory to applications of graphs, and from applications to a collection of generalizations about "things that are connected." Accordingly, we divide the brief history of network science into three periods. (1) early pre–network period (1736–1966), when network science was really the mathematics of graphs; (2) the meso–network period (1967–1998), when network science was not yet called "the new science of networks," but in fact applications of networks emerged from the research literature; and (3) the modern period (1998–present), when the pioneers of the current definition of network science set forth the fundamentals and showed that the fundamentals had meaning in the real world. In the modern period, advocates of network science began to demonstrate the universality of network science as they applied it to diverse fields that seemingly had no relationship to one another.

1.2.1   The Pre–Network Period (1736–1966)

The first known application of network science was Euler's treatment of the Bridges of Königsberg (Euler, 1736). It is significant because it established graph theory and showed that abstractions of reality can indeed be useful for solving problems in the real world. In one stroke, Euler defined the static structure of a physical system in terms of abstract mathematical objects called *vertices* (nodes) and *edges* (links). Logically reasoning on the abstract level, he showed that it was impossible for the citizens of Königsberg to parade through town and return without crossing one of its seven bridges at least twice.

Seven Bridges of Königsberg Problem   Königsberg, Germany—aka Kaliningrad, Russia—is a city with part of its landmass on an island in the middle of the river Preger, and another part separated by a fork in the river. Seven bridges allow its citizens to get from any of its four landmasses to any other. Four bridges connect the banks of the river to the island; two bridges cross the forks of the river, and one bridge connects the island to the landmass located between the forks. The city fathers called on Leonhard Euler to tell them whether it was possible to parade throughout the entire city of five landmasses and cross each bridge only once. The solution to this problem is given in Chapter 2.

Leonhard Euler was a prodigious mathematician. It took the Swiss authorities 48 years after his death to publish his entire works. He remains the father of graph theory, today, and his legacy is the theoretical basis for the structural part of network science.

Mathematicians have added thousands of graph theory results since Euler laid the foundation more than 270 years ago. Graph theory has been extremely useful in computer science and electrical engineering, as well as a number of other applied disciplines. But as far as network science is concerned, the next major step came in 1925 when Yule first observed *preferential attachment* in evolution (Yule, 1925). Yule's work seems to have little to do with network science, but his idea would resurface in the 1990s as an explanation for the evolution of the Internet and WWW (World Wide Web). Preferential attachment explains why scale-free networks exist in natural and synthetic systems.

Preferential attachment is a simple emergent behavior observed in a number of disciplines. In the context of networks, it states that a network grows by adding nodes and links—not randomly, but by preference. Suppose that a network starts with three nodes connected by a single link between two of the three nodepairs. Now suppose that new nodes are added at regular time intervals; that is, let the network grow through a systematic process of connecting one node at a time to existing nodes. How should the new nodes be linked to existing nodes? Random attachment is one algorithm we might use: selecting an existing node at random and connecting it to the new node by adding a new link between the nodepair.

An alternative (and Darwinian) algorithm is as follows. Connect the new node to an existing node with probability proportional to the number of links already connected to the existing node. The number of links connecting a node is called its *degree*. This rule says to give preference to nodes with high degree. Thus, a new node is more likely to be connected to an existing node containing two links than to nodes with only one link. The new node will prefer being connected to the node with the higher degree.

Preferential attachment describes an *emergent process*—that is, a process that results in a network topology that is not apparent by examination of the local algorithm, or *microrule*. It is not at all obvious that the result of repeated application of preferential attachment will result in a network with a *degree sequence distribution* that follows a *power law*. This realization would come 70 years later, when A.-L. Barabasi and R. Albert showed how to create a scale-free network by repeated application of preferential attachment.

In 1927 another seemingly unrelated discovery occurred when Kermack and McKendrick published the first mathematical model of the spread of an infection in a biological population (Kermack, 1927). The *Kermack–McKendrick epidemic model* is a nonnetwork model, but it set the stage for two important innovations to come: (1) it explained the spread of a contagion along (social) links connecting (individual) nodes, and (2) it coincidentally described *new-product adoption—diffusion of technology*—and how product information spreads like an infectious disease throughout a social network. The first innovation is important because the Kermack–McKendrick epidemic model leads to the discovery of the laws of virus spreading in networks such as the Internet. In fact, we show that rate of spreading and persistence of an infection is determined completely by a network's topological structure as well as the infectiousness of the contagion. Thus some networks are more prone to epidemics than are others. Furthermore, understanding the relationship between network topology and the spread of an infection tells us how best to *stop* the spread.

The second significance of the Kermack–McKendrick model is its application to marketing of new products in the business world. The spread of information (advertising or "buzz") in a social network is much like the spread of an epidemic. What property of a network accelerates or retards this virus-like spread? In this case, merchandisers want to know how to increase infectiousness.

Solomonoff and Rappaport were the first to apply the ideas of epidemics to networks (Solomonoff, 1951). Thus the connection was made over 50 years ago (i.e., around the mid-1950s), but the relationship between network topology and infectiousness would have to wait for a more recent advance. Solomonoff and Rappaport assumed that the network was random. Today we know that random networks rarely exist in the real world—and when it comes to social networks, randomness is far from reality. Furthermore, we now know that the structure of a nonrandom network can have a dramatic impact on its function.

In fact, the idea of nonrandomness as a factor in behavior and the connection between preferential attachment and nonrandom distributions occurred to Simon in 1955 (Simon, 1955). Simon was aware of Yule's work on preferential attachment and the distribution of species among plants genera. Simon's observations confirm the validity of the power law in natural and synthetic systems: namely, that the distribution of word frequencies in documents, distribution of number of papers published by scientists, distribution of cities by population, distribution of wealth, and distribution of species among genera all obey a power law (Mitzenmacher, (2004). The evidence supporting nonrandomness in real-world phenomenon was mounting long before it was observed in networks. But the connection between nonrandomness in systems and graph theory was yet to be discovered.

By the midtwentieth century science reasoned that nature could be modeled as a random process and therefore as a random graph. What were the properties of random graphs that made them good models? Gilbert showed how to build a random graph by first constructing a complete graph and then deleting randomly selected links until reaching the desired number of links (Gilbert, 1959). But his cumbersome algorithm was quickly surpassed by the elegant and widely promoted algorithm of Erdos and Renyi (Erdos, 1960). The Erdos–Renyi (ER) algorithm is used today because of its simplicity. A network with n nodes is constructed by inserting a link between randomly selected nodepairs. The process is repeated until m links have been inserted.

The ER algorithm is not perfect—it can leave some nodes isolated, and unless it is slightly modified, it can insert duplicate and loop links into the network. But it has become the standard method of generating a random network by computer. The Gilbert and ER algorithms were the first *generative methods* of network creation. Many more methods have since been proposed, and in fact, we propose a dozen more in this book. Today, computer algorithms exist to generate a network of any prescribed topology, with any number of nodes and links; see Chapter 7.

By the very late 1960s network science did not exist, but its seeds were planted in disconnected and seemingly unrelated disciplines. It would take several more decades of scattered research in disparate disciplines before convergence to what we now know of as the science of networks.

1.2.2 The Meso–Network Period (1967–1998)

A stunning experiment performed in 1967 propelled network science from pure graph theory into scientific inquiry. The famous "six degrees of separation" experiment of Stanley Milgram seemed innocent enough, but in retrospect, it marked a turning point. Stanley Milgram invited human subjects from Kansas and Nebraska to participate in a "communications project" to "better understand social contact in American society." The experiment required them to send a folder across the country to a target person defined by the experimenters. Subjects were told to perform the following four steps (Yung, 2001):

1. Add your name to the roster at the bottom of this sheet, so that the next person who receives this letter will know whom it came from.
2. Detach one postcard, fill it out, and return it to Harvard University. No stamp is necessary. It allows us to keep track of the progress of the folder as it moves toward the target person.
3. If you know the target person on a personal basis, mail this folder directly to him/her. Do this only if you have previously met the target person and know each other on a first-name basis.
4. If you do not know the target person on a personal basis, do not try to contact him/her directly. Instead, mail this folder (postcards and all) to a personal acquaintance who is more likely than you to know the target person. You may send the folder on to a friend, relative, or acquaintance, but it must be someone you know on a first-name basis.

Subjects had 24 hours to forward their folder and received only a certificate of appreciation for their efforts. Most folders never made it. But folders that reached their target did so in far fewer steps than expected. Out of millions of people, folders passed through only a handful of intermediaries before reaching their intended destination. This winnowing of paths through a large population was evidence of the *small-world effect*, and the social network underlying Milgram's experiment is now known as a *small-world network*. The number of intermediaries averaged 5.2.

How could a stranger connect with another stranger in fewer than six steps? Milgram had to conclude that the fabric of society formed a nonrandom network. Instead of randomly bouncing from person to person, folders made a beeline to their destinations—and yet, the path they followed was not planned out ahead of time, nor was there any assurance that a chain of intermediaries existed between sender and receiver.

Assuming that each person knows 500 other people, on average, the odds of reaching the target person is approximately 1 in 200,000, and the number of intermediaries should have been many times larger than 6 hops, if paths taken by successful folders were truly random. Instead, successful folders reached their target in an average of 5.2 steps, or hops, from the originating person to the target person. The distance traveled in graph theory terms was 5 or 6 hops because five or six people handled a folder.

Milgram's experiment inspired a Broadway play and movie by John Guare called *Six Degrees of Separation: A Play* (Guare, 1990). The terminology took root, and the idea of small-world social networks blossomed, leading to purposeful creation of many other social networks. The "Kevin Bacon game" created by Brett Tjaden of the University of Virginia is one such example.[2] This network links actors that have appeared in the same movie together. The distance between Kevin Bacon and any other actor is equal to the number of hops from the node representing Kevin Bacon to any other node representing another actor.

Milgram concluded that the social world is much smaller than the "real world" because it took only 6 hops to link a pair of strangers, regardless of where they lived. He called this the *small-world problem*. Many decades later Watts and Strogatz would rejuvenate interest in small-world networks and introduce it to physicists and biologists. Their technical analysis of large sparse networks rigorously defined small worlds as networks with relatively short distances (hops) between node pairs chosen at random, even as the size of the network grows. Specifically, the diameter of a network increases as $\ln(n)$ while its size increases by $O(n)$, where n is number of nodes.

The small-world idea is related to the "weak ties" theory of Granovetter, who postulated that social networks contain both strong (direct) and weak ties (long-distance connections) that bind society together (Granovetter, 1973). In a cleverly titled paper, "The strength of weak ties," Granovetter suggests that social networks are held together by strong connections between friends and family members, as well as weaker, long-distance connections among casual acquaintances. This explains why it is possible to span a large sparse network in a small number of hops. The links of a social network are like freeways and streets—freeways have few intersections (nodes) and allow you to travel long distances without stopping. City streets, on the other hand, allow you to pinpoint a single person or house within a dense neighborhood. Freeways (weak ties) get you to a local neighborhood quickly, while streets (strong ties) zero in on a specific person or house.

White identified biases in Milgram's experiment and suggested modifications that lead to an average of seven intermediaries (White, 1970). Hunter and Shotland modeled the experiment as a Markov process to determine average distances between groups (Hunter, 1974). Pool and Kochen provided the earliest known theoretical analysis of small-world networks in 1978 (Pool, 1978). The flurry of publications stimulated by Milgram's experiment dropped off precipitously after 1978, only to be rejuvenated two decades later (Kleinfeld, 2002).

---

[2]This game is available at http://www.cs.virginia.edu/oracle/.

Meanwhile, pioneering work began in soon-to-be-related disciplines: Bass, Fisher, and Pry model new-product adoptions as the propagation of an infectious disease (Bass, 1969, 2001; Norton, 1987). This work extended the Kermack–McKendrick epidemic model to the new field of marketing and prepared the way for network-based product diffusion models. These models have proved to be powerful tools for the business of marketing. But do the epidemic models work when applied to social networks? We show that technological diffusion (adoption of new products) obeys the Bass and Fisher–Pry equations for a single product and random network. We also show that a monopoly arises from a random population because of preferential attachment. However, we discover that the Bass/Fisher–Pry model has limitations when modeling competition among products in a multiproduct network. These results have not been reported elsewhere.

In the social sciences, graph theory was being used to explain a number of other social interaction phenomena. Bonacich was perhaps the first social scientist to realize that influence in a social network could be mathematically represented using the connection matrix of the network (Bonacich, 1972). The nodes represent individuals, and weights on directed links represent the *degree of influence* one individual has on another.[3] If person A influences the decision of person B, and person B influences the decision of person C, and so on, what is the overall effect on group consensus? Will a chain of influences propagate through a network and eventually settle down to a common value? Bonacich claimed that consensus would eventually be reached, and proposed that the consensus be computed by raising the weighted connection matrix to the nth power, where n is the number of nodes in the network. As it turns out, influence spreading in a social network is not as simple as Bonacich's model suggests, but Bonacich initiated a line of research that continues, today.

Marketing gurus note that highly connected people are *superspreaders*—people who accelerate the spread of buzz—new-product information, simply because they are highly connected (Rosen, 2000). But social scientists have long known of the power of the middleperson or intermediary—actors who connect other actors. If the only way actor A can communicate with actor C is by going through actor B, then B has power over A and C. Thus, social scientists define *betweenness* as the number of paths that must run through an actor to connect with other actors. So, in addition to connectedness, an actor derives influence by serving as an intermediary. Does betweenness give an actor more influence than connectedness? This is the question we address in the study of influence networks. See Chapter 10.

Influence spreading—whether it is for marketing a product, spreading a disease, or achieving consensus in a group—is a form of signal propagation. The signal travels along links and affects nodes in some way. For example, the value of a node might be the average over the value of adjacent nodes. In a *Kirchhoff network*, the value of a node is equal to the difference between the sum of values from input and output links. Regardless of the local microrule for assigning values to nodes, the concept of signals flowing through networks appears to be an underlying mechanism common to epidemiology, synchronicity, influence, and consensus in groups.

---

[3]Weights are fractions: $0 \leq \text{weight} \leq 1$.

More rigorously, a network can be regarded as a coupled system. The system is composed of nodes that take on values called *states*, and links that establish the inputs and outputs to nodes. The state of the network is the union of the states of all of its nodes. Signals (values) propagate along links, from node to node, and alter the node's states. If we plot the change in state versus time, we might observe oscillations, dampening, or convergence to a certain state—the so-called *fixed point*—and remain there, forever. Under what conditions does a network oscillate or converge? This is a universal question, which we address in Chapters 10 and 12.

We show that spread of epidemics, synchronization of biological systems, consensus in a social network, and diffusion of new products are all different forms of synchronization in a network. A network is said to *sync* when the value of its nodes reach a *fixed point*—a value that ceases to change once reached. We answer the question "What properties or conditions are necessary and sufficient for a network to sync?" The answer leads to a general theory of stability in networks.

Kuramoto provided a mathematical basis for studying synchronization in coupled linear systems (Kuramoto, 1984). His work would influence Strogatz a decade later, and have a major impact on the convergence between network science and control theory. For example, Kuramoto's work led Strogatz to observe automatic synchronization in small-world networks. Strogatz claimed that synchronization is simply a property of all small worlds (Strogatz, 2003). This turns out to be false, but it stimulated further study into network models of various biological systems that automatically synchronize. Now we know that other conditions must exist in networks for them to sync.

By 1998, the fundamentals of network science had been established, but the explosive interest in application of the fundamentals to real-world systems was yet to come. The rapid rise of the Internet beginning in the early 1990s provided an incentive for a new generation of researchers looking to formalize the human-created, but highly decentralized, Internet phenomena. Waxman proposed a static graph theory model of the Internet in 1988 (Waxman, 1988). We call such networks *Webgraphs*, because they use graph theory to understand the World Wide Web (WWW). It would take another decade before researchers would make the connection between graph theory and the dynamic growth of the Internet and WWW. But once they did, network science came of age.

1.2.3 The Modern Period (1998–Present)

Networks have static and dynamic properties. Static graph properties such as diameter, average path length, connection matrix, and cluster coefficient provide a means for classification of the network. The *degree sequence distribution* of a network, for example, is a histogram of percentage of nodes with degree d versus d. A random network has a degree sequence distribution that obeys a binomial distribution, and a scale-free network's degree sequence obeys a power law. A small-world network has relatively small diameter and average path length, and a scale-free network has hubs. These are various ways of classifying networks on the basis of their structure. But classification according to static structure is not enough.

Networks also have dynamic properties such as fixed points when they sync, and preferences for linking nodes together when preferential attachment is operational. Dynamic networks evolve. Starting at some initial state, a dynamic network may transition to a second, third, fourth, and higher state until either cycling back or reaching a final state—its *fixed point*. The evolution from initial state to some future state is a form of *emergence*. Therefore, networks that reach a fixed point are different from networks that oscillate, forever. In this way we can classify networks according to dynamic properties.

Network science is the study of both static and dynamic properties of networks. In this book we focus on emergence as a method of understanding and characterizing the dynamic part of network science. We further divide the emergent approach into two parts: the part that alters the topology of a network (e.g., preferential attachment) and the part that alters the state of a network (e.g., synchronization). We show that a network of any desired structure can be generated as a fixed point of an emergent process whereby links are rewired until the desired topology emerges. In the final chapters we show that stability emerges out of chaos in networks with certain initial conditions and certain static properties.

Holland defines emergence in general terms as "much coming from little" (Holland, 1998). This is precisely what happens when a network evolves. A series of microlevel changes accumulate over time, until a macrolevel change in the network is realized. *Emergence* means that a major change in global properties comes from many small changes at the local level. Emergence plays a major role in the modern interpretation of network science. In a sense, it completes the puzzle of what defines the field.

Watts and Strogatz rekindled interest in small-world networks by showing the universality—and utility—of the small-world model (Watts, 1998; 1999a; 1999b). They proposed a simple emergence process—called a *generative procedure*—for constructing a small-world network. The idea is simple but brilliant: initially constructing a graph with regular structure. Next, apply rewiring to every link with probability p, such that $p*m$ links are randomized (redirected to a randomly selected node). Parameter p is the rewiring probability, and m is the number of links in the original regular graph.

The Watts–Strogatz generative procedure is tunable—increasing p also increases the randomness of the small world. This means we can produce a network with any desired level of randomness—*entropy*, if you will—by adjusting rewiring probability p—a low rewiring probability generates a nonrandom structure, and a high probability generates a random structure. The algorithm is an example of the first kind of emergence—evolving the structure, not the state, of the network.

A Watts–Strogatz network falls between a random network and nonrandom network. At a certain rewiring probability called the *crossover point* (also *length scale*), the network transitions from mostly structured to mostly random network. Typically, the crossover point is very small—on the order of $p^* = 2$–3%. Watts and Strogatz attached a meaning to the crossover, suggesting that it corresponds to phase transition in materials (change in state from liquid to solid, magnetism, etc.). Thus, the crossover point is also known as the *phase transition threshold*.

Small worlds were no longer restricted to social networks as in the Milgram experiment after Watts and Strogatz showed how to generate an arbitrarily small world network. Moreover, small-world networks were observed in both natural and synthetic systems, which suggested that they might somehow be universal models. What does a database of film actors, the electric power grid of the western United States, and the neural network of the nematode worm *C. elegans* (*Caenorhabditis elegans*) have in common? They are all small worlds. This had to be more than a coincidence.

The small world was not the only classification of networks that seemed universal. The year 1999 was full of discoveries: M. Faloutsos, P. Faloutsos, and C. Faloutsos observed a power law in their graph models of the Internet, and Albert, Jeong, and Barabasi obtained similar results for the WWW (Faloutsos, 1999; Albert, 1999). Small worlds had characteristic short path length, but power-law networks had *hubs*—nodes with extremely high degree. Barabasi and students found that the degree sequence distribution of many synthetic and natural networks followed a power law. A network that follows a power-law distribution means that it has a hub, and many other nodes with many fewer links than the average. This lopsided preference for hubs seemed counter to nature, which typically follows a normal distribution. The trouble was that researchers were discovering too many systems structured according to the power law to ignore.

Barabasi and Albert generalized the concept of nonrandom networks with hubs and provided a generative procedure for producing *scale-free networks* (Barabasi, 1999). The name came from observing that a function $f(x)$ *scales* if $f(ax) = a'f(x)$, which is what a power law does. Therefore, if the degree sequence distribution obeys the power law, $h(x) = x^{-q}$, then it is clear that $h(ax) = (ax)^{-q} = (a^{-q})h(x) = a'h(x)$. The important contribution, however, isn't the name, but the observation that scale-free networks exhibit a sharp decline in frequency of nodes with degree d, as d increases.

Realization of the importance of small-world and scale-free networks created a feeding frenzy among mathematicians, physicists, and social scientists from 1999 through 2002. Dorogovtsev, Mendes, Samukhim, Krapivsky, and Redner derived an exact formula for the power law of a purely scale-free network and showed that it describes many biological systems (Dorogovtsev, 2000; 2002a; 2002b; 2003). Kleinberg, Kumar, Raghavan, Rajagopalan, and Tomkins suggest the term *Webgraph* to describe network models of the WWW (Kleinberg, 1999). Broder, Kumar, Maghoul, Raghavan, Rajagopalan, Stata, Tomkins, and Wiener were the first to fully map the WWW as a Webgraph and discover its structure. It isn't random. Kleinberg gives a formal explanation for Milgram's experiment based on the "Manhattan distance" between source and target nodes. The "Manhattan distance" is defined as the number of blocks, traversed along streets in Manhattan, New York, between source and destination intersections. Kleinberg showed that it takes only $O(n)$ steps to navigate such a small world (Kleinberg, 2002a).

By the end of this flurry of discovery, the basics of network science were firmly in place. But what are these models good for? If scale-free and small-world topologies are as universal as the mathematicians and physicists claimed, then it should be easy to find examples in natural and synthetic systems. Furthermore, if scale-free and small-world topologies have *profound* meaning, we should be able to derive generalizations or universal truths from the theory. In fact, this is what happened.

Albert, Jeong, and Barabasi observed that scale-free networks were extremely resilient against random attacks, but extremely vulnerable to systematic attacks on hubs (Albert, 2000). This makes sense—a random attack will most likely strike and destroy a node with only a few links, because a scale-free network has many such nodes. On the contrary, since hubs are rare, it is unlikely that a hub is attacked. But a hub has many links, and so its demise damages a large percentage of the network. Let p_c be the fraction of damaged nodes that dismantles the network. When p_c is high, the network is resilient, because many nodes must be knocked out to dismantle the network. When it is low, the network is vulnerable. In simulations, Albert et al. found threshold values of $p_c = 28\%$ for random networks versus nearly 99% for scale-free networks under random attacks; that is, a random network dismantles when an average of 28% of its nodes are damaged. But the tables are turned when hubs are systematically attacked—only 18% of the nodes need to be attacked to dismantle a scale-free network. Thus, a scale-free network is more vulnerable than a random network when its hubs are targeted.

The experiment of Albert et al. raises a question we answer in this book: What is the meaning of resiliency (risk) in a network? We extend the results of Albert et al. and assign a risk property to any arbitrary network, based on the value of nodes, their degree, and the risk formula: $R = T * V * C$, where R is risk, T is threat probability, V is vulnerability probability, and C is consequence or damage. We show that any network can be optimally protected from dismantling if target-hardening resources are deployed to nodes and links according to an algorithm proposed by Al-Mannai and Lewis (Al-Mannai, 2007). The Al-Mannai–Lewis algorithm protects high-value hubs first and lower-valued nodes last.

In related work, Pastor-Satorras and Vespignani observed that populations forming a scale-free network have no minimum epidemic threshold that prevents an infectious disease from recurring (Pastor-Satorras, 2001). Once an infection enters a network, it rises and falls repeatedly. Persistent epidemics are real—they occur in human networks as well as on the Internet. If the Internet is a scale-free network, then what is to prevent persistent viruses from infecting the Internet, permanently?

Wang and coworkers showed the initial claim of Pastor-Satorrus to be generally false (Wang, 2003a). Instead, persistence of an infection is determined not by the network's degree sequence but by its *spectral radius*, which is defined as the largest nontrivial eigenvalue of a network's connection matrix. Therefore, network topology determines its susceptibility to epidemics, but not because it is scale-free. This profound result has significant implications for fighting both kinds of viruses—Internet and human. It also has implications for the product marketer.

The network model of systems is proving to have a profound impact on understanding resiliency, risk, epidemics, and social interactions among people in groups. It is also proving to be revolutionary in understanding chaotic behavior of coupled linear systems. Wang, Chen, Barahona, Pecora, Liu, Hong, Choi, Jost, Joy, and others applied linear systems analysis to arbitrary networks and showed that the stability of any network is a function of its topology (Wang, 2002a, 2002b, 2002c; Barahona, 2002; Liu, 2002, 2003, 2004a, 2004b; Hong, 2002; Jost, 2002). We extend these results to several classes of networks—the Atay network, a kind of dynamic network studied by Atay, which uses a local averaging algorithm to compute the state of nodes (Atay, 2006), and a new class of networks called *Kirchhoff networks*, which attempt to stabilize the value of its nodes by maintaining Kirchhoff's first law.

Emergence of fixed-point solutions (synchronization) in a dynamic network has become a powerful and general tool for understanding a number of natural phenomena. Strogatz claimed that the beating of a human's heart, the chirping of crickets, and other biological systems naturally sync because they are small-worlds (Strogatz, 2003). But we show that network synchronization has little to do with small-world topology, and everything to do with the Laplacian of the connection matrix, and the length of circuits within the network. We examine stability of Atay networks, which have applications in marketing, as well as understanding the chirping of crickets, and show that sync is a property of emergent networks that contain triangle-shaped subgraphs. As it turns out, small-world networks have an abundance of triangular subgraphs! Moreover, a network can be synchronized, by adding a triangular subgraph to one of its nodes.

The picture is more complex for *Kirchhoff networks*—defined as directed-flow networks where the state of every node is the sum of the values of incoming links minus the sum of values of outgoing links. Kirchhoff networks are abstractions of electrical power grids, electromechanical feedback systems, air traffic routes, and so on. Hence, it is important that they not blow up—but instead, stabilize quickly after a disruption or sudden change in the value of one or more nodes. Curiously, Kirchhoff networks exhibit wildly chaotic behavior followed by sudden synchronization when the lengths of circuits within the network are relatively prime numbers. This has important applications to the design of self-stabilizing power grids, self-correcting transportations systems, and perhaps self-repairing biological systems.

A similar question of stability leading to synchronization—or not—can be observed in social networks. Consider a group of people attempting to arrive at a consensus (Gabbay, 2007). Each member of the group starts with an initial position, and attempts to influence his or her neighbor's position by exerting a positive or negative influence on nearest neighbors. Influence spreads like an epidemic, but rather than infecting or not, the influence sways the position of adjacent nodes. For example, each node of the social network might be adjusted to equal the average value of its neighbors.

Propagation of influence in a network is much like propagation of a signal in a coupled linear system. If the network is a kind of Atay network, nodes take on a value in the interval $[-1, +1]$, representing disagreement or agreement, or some fraction in between. As influence spreads, each node value changes. If all nodes reach the same value, after some period of time, we say that the network has reached a consensus. If nodes never reach a consensus, we say that the network diverges.

The question we address is, "Under what conditions will an influence network arrive at a consensus?" This problem is related to the more general problem of under what conditions will an arbitrary network synchronize. We show that consensus is reached when the influence network's largest nontrivial state matrix eigenvalue is bounded by one, and there are no conflicts in the network. Curiously, the most influential node in the network is the one less influenced by other nodes.

Network science has achieved more recent results in the field of marketing, and understanding competition among corporations. We show that preferential attachment in a simple random network obeys the Bass and Fisher–Pry equations, but technological diffusion is more complex in multiproduct, multicompetitor networks. Simple models of preferential attachment, value proposition, early-stage or late-stage market, and combinations of these competition models lead to monopolies in general, and oligopolies under certain conditions. Specifically, we show that it is possible for niche players to coexist with a monopoly, under most assumptions. This is an area of research still ripe for more investigation.

For more details and in-depth analysis of historical events in the brief history of network science, the reader is advised to study several excellent surveys of network science. Virtanen surveys the complete field prior to 2003 (Virtanen, 2003). The thesis by Voon Joe Yung gives a nonmathematical introduction and includes a copy of the Milgram experiment folder (Yung, 2001). The numerous papers by Mark Newman and Duncan Watts provide compact tutorials on the fundamentals of small worlds (Watts, 1999a; Newman, 2000b).

1.3 GENERAL PRINCIPLES

The "modern period" is defined by the convergence—commencing in the late 1990s—of several complementary and interrelated fields—with more yet to come. Graph theory, social network analysis, epidemic modeling, market competition modeling, and synchronization of physical and biological systems are all different aspects of network science. In fact, it may be too early to make generalizations or identify principles of network science. At some risk of being shortsighted, the author makes the following observations:

Characteristics of Network Science in the Modern Period

1. *Structure.* Networks have structure—they are not random collections of nodes and links. For example, the structures of electrical power grids, online social networks, and the nervous system of the *C. elegans* nematodes are not random, but instead have a distinct format or topology. This suggests that function follows form—many real-world phenomena behave the way they do because of their network structure.

2. *Emergence.* A network property is emergent if it changes by a factor of 10 as a consequence of a dynamic network achieving stability. In other words, emergence is a network synchronization issue—stable networks transition from one state to another until they reach a fixed point, and stay there. The fixed point is a new configuration for the network with corresponding order-of-magnitude

change in a certain property. For example, on the Internet, a group of teenagers will form a social clique 10 times larger than expected from purely random behavior, because the clique is formed by preferential attachment; the top 1% of Americans make 10 times more money than the average American; the popularity of a few movie stars is 10 times greater than the popularity of the average movie star; and the largest cities in the world are relatively rare, and are 10 times larger than the average city. In each of these examples, the "hub property" or concentration is a consequence of some instability working its way through the network as the network achieves a new fixed point. This is the impetus behind online social networks that begin with nothing, and end up with millions of subscribers. However, it is not always clear what ingredients go into online social networking to cause explosive growth. Likewise, it is not always obvious what motivation causes an order-of-magnitude change in a network's property.

3. *Dynamism*. Network science is concerned with both structure and dynamic behavior of networks. Dynamic behavior is often the result of emergence or a series of small evolutionary steps leading to a fixed-point final state of the system. The Internet, many biological systems, some physical systems, and most social systems are growing and changing networks. One must understand their dynamic properties in order to fully understand these systems. Analysis of only their static structure, such as degree sequence, is not sufficient to understand the network. For example, network synchronization, such as in the case of chirping crickets, is a consequence of the dynamism of each cricket, as well as the structure (triangular subgraphs) of the social network of crickets.

4. *Autonomy*. A network forms by the autonomous and spontaneous action of independent nodes that "volunteer" to come together (link), rather than through central control or central planning. Structure and function arise out of chaos, more as a result of serendipity than determinism. Examples are formation of large conglomerates from the merger of small companies; emergence of large cities from small communities; and formation of global telecommunication systems from linking of many smaller, local, independent operators. The initial configuration of a network may be premeditated, but over time, the network either "decays" with the onset of some form of entropy, or adapts and changes via the absorption of energy. For example, a highway system will either decay and fall into disrepair, or improve and grow through the expenditure of effort to repair, extend, increase its capacity, and so on.

5. *Bottom–Up Evolution*. Networks grow from the bottom or local level up to the top or global level. They are not designed and implemented from the top down. This can also be regarded as a form of distributed control where network evolution is a consequence of local rules being applied locally without any centralized control. Even if the initial structure of a network is the result of a premeditated design, networks evolve and change as a consequence of their dynamism. Examples of "unplanned systems" are formation of the Internet from local networks, formation of the electrical power grid from local utilities, and formation of highway systems from local roads and animal trails.

6. *Topology.* The architecture or topology of a network is a property that emerges over time as a consequence of distributed—and often subtle—forces or autonomous behaviors of its nodes. A network is dynamic if its topology or other properties change as a function of time. Thus, topology (structure) is a consequence of Darwinian forces that shape the network. For example, scale-free networks (networks with dominant hubs) emerge from the force of "preferential attachment" (economics), unintended consequences (regulatory law), such as the vulnerability of electrical power grids as a consequence of government deregulation, or "hidden order" of decentralized infrastructures emerging from complex adaptive systems such as the rise of the Internet, formation of metropolitan civilizations, or creation of monopolies like the Microsoft Corporation.

7. *Power.* The power of a node is proportional to its degree (number of links connecting it to the network) influence (link values); and *betweenness* or *closeness*; the power of a network is proportional to the number and strength of its nodes and links. For example, Metcalf's law states that the power of a network is proportional to the square of the number of nodes it contains [e.g., the maximum number of links that a network with n nodes can contain is $n(n-1)/2$, which is approximately n^2]. The influence a person exerts on a group is proportional to the position, number, and power of colleagues the person has within the group, such as the person's connectivity. The power of a corporation, within an industry or market, is proportional to the number of customers (links) that it has, or its intermediary position within the industry. Power is a subtle but important organizing principle in most networks, but it is often called something else, such as influence, signal strength, or infection rate.

8. *Stability.* A dynamic network is stable if the rate of change in the state of its nodes/links or its topology either diminishes as time passes or is bounded by dampened oscillations within finite limits. For example, the regular and rhythmic beating of an animal's heart is controlled by a stable network of nerves that regulate the pacemaker, the loss of a power plant in the electrical power grid stabilizes quickly by switching from one source to another without disruption in supply, or the loss of a coworker causes short-term reallocation of responsibility without organizational failure.

This book approaches the subject of network science from the topology perspective, first, and then the dynamic or emergent viewpoint, second. Does topology follow function, or the reverse? Does a dynamic network behave and function in a certain way because of its topology, or does it derive its topology from its function? The following chapters provide a lot of evidence to support the "form follows function" perspective. Sparse small-world networks appear to model human social networks, because humans have limited capacity to know a large number of other humans. Scale-free networks appear to model economic constructs such as the Internet and monopolies within industrial segments, because preferential attachment is essentially the law of increasing returns of economics. Networks tend to be structured in such a way that synchronization is more likely than chaos, simply because unstable systems cannot survive in nature.

It seems logical, then, to approach the field of network science from the ground up. First, we review the basics of graphs. This will require definitions and terminology (see Chapters 2 and 3). Then, the generative procedures for producing random, small-world, scale-free, and arbitrary networks of any topology are provided and studied in Chapters 4–7. Chapter 8 extends epidemiology to the network, Chapter 9 begins the development of a unified theory of network stability, Chapter 10 applies this theory to social network analysis and group consensus, and Chapters 11–13 explore applications in greater detail. Many more chapters remain to be written, hopefully by the reader!

2

GRAPHS

Graph theory is the historical foundation of the science of networks; therefore, we begin the study of network science with a focused study of graph theory. This chapter supplies the necessary background used in subsequent chapters to analyze properties of networks. This includes the set-theoretic and algebraic definitions of graph properties such as characteristic path length, entropy, and the classification of graphs used in the remainder of this book. The prepared reader may choose to skip to the next chapter.

Graphs consist of nodes and links, and a mapping function that defines how nodes connect to one another. In a *static graph*, the properties of nodes, links, and mapping function remain unchanged over time. For example, the number of nodes and links remains constant, and the mapping function does not change. In a *dynamic graph*, the number of nodes and links, the shape of the mapping function, and perhaps other properties of the graph change over time. For example, the values assigned to nodes and links, as well as the number of nodes and links, may vary. This chapter focuses on properties of static graphs. Dynamic graphs are introduced in subsequent chapters.

We study basic definitions of graph theory, introduce basic properties of graphs, and begin the development of a collection of useful Java programming methods used in subsequent chapters to simulate the construction and behavior of networks. This chapter defines the following:

1. *Graphs.* A *graph* is a 3-tuple: $G = (N, L, f)$, where N is a set of nodes, L is a set of links, and f is a mapping function (table) that maps links onto node pairs.

Network Science: Theory and Practice. By Ted G. Lewis
Copyright © 2009 John Wiley & Sons, Inc.

Nodes directly connected by a link are called *adjacent nodes*. A *static graph* retains its initial structure, forever. A *dynamic graph* changes its nodes, links, and/or mapping function over time.

2. *Graph Properties*. Graphs have a number of properties such as average path length; density; entropy, cluster coefficient; betweenness and closeness, spectral radius, spectral gap; and degree sequence distribution. *Node degree* equals the number of links connecting a node to the graph. *Path length* is the shortest path between two nodes, and *average path length* is the average over all shortest paths. *Density* is the ratio of the number of actual links to the maximum number possible. *Entropy* is a measure of randomness in the mapping function *f*. *Cluster coefficient* is a measure of how many nodes form triangular subgraphs with their adjacent nodes. *Betweenness* and *closeness* measure the intermediary or middleperson power of a node. *Degree sequence distribution* and *entropy* are measures used to classify graphs according to their structure.

3. *Matrix Representation*. A graph's mapping function *f* is represented by a *connection* matrix containing the number of links connecting node *i* to node *j*. This number is stored at row *i*, column *j* of the matrix. Duplicate links are ignored in the graph's *adjacency* matrix—which contains a 1 in row *i* column *j* if one or more links connect node *i* to node *j*. The *Laplacian* matrix of a graph is formed by inserting the degree of nodes into the diagonal of the adjacency matrix. Spectral decomposition of the adjacency and Laplacian matrices provides valuable insight into the nature of a graph. For example, the *spectral radius* is the largest nontrivial *eigenvalue* of a graph's adjacency matrix, and *spectral gap* is the largest nontrivial eigenvalue of a graph's *Laplacian* matrix. Spectral properties of graphs are used to model behaviors such as the spread of contagions, rumors, ideas, and group consensus, as well as the spread of chaos throughout a graph.

4. *Classes of Graphs*. We classify graphs according to their structure; *random graphs* have random structure, and *k-regular graphs* have purely deterministic structure. In between these two extremes lie two important classes of graphs: the class of *small-world* (mostly structured, partly random), and the class of *scale-free* (mostly random, partly structured) graphs. Each class has its own characteristic property: the *Poisson distribution* for random graphs, *power-law distribution* for scale-free graphs, high average cluster coefficient for small-world graphs, and zero-entropy value for *k*-regular graphs.

5. *Bridges of Königsberg*. The "Bridges of Königsberg" problem, first proposed by Leonhard Euler, is analyzed using basic properties of graphs. As it turns out, the first graph in graph theory history is impossible to traverse without traversing one or more links repeated times, because the degree of all nodes in the Bridges of Königsberg graph are odd-valued. Thus, a traveler must visit at least one bridge twice, to cover the entire graph.

6. *Modeling and Simulation*. In the final section, we introduce Java programming language classes for constructing graph-processing software. Simple data structures are used to model nodes and links, and several simple methods are given

to produce random mappings of links onto nodes. These classes and methods can be used to understand the software available with this book, or to build your own software.

The examples of this chapter can be reproduced and analyzed using *program Network*, which is available as open-source software. All .jar programs associated with this book are standalone programs that will run on any computer that supports the Java runtime environment. User manual files require a PDF (portable document file) reader to open.

2.1   SET-THEORETIC DEFINITION OF A GRAPH

A *graph* $G = [N,L,f]$ is a 3-tuple consisting of a set of *nodes N*, a set of *links L*, and a *mapping function f*: $L \rightarrow N \times N$, which maps links into pairs of nodes. A *network* $G(t) = [N(t), L(t), f(t):J]$ is a 3-tuple consisting of a set of time-varying nodes $N(t)$, time-varying links $L(t)$, and a time-varying mapping function $f(t)$. The dynamic behaviors—what we call microrules—are represented algorithmically by J, which in this book is a set of Java methods.

The number and properties of $N(t)$, $L(t)$, and $f(t):J$ are allowed to change as time passes in a network. In this sense, a network is a dynamic graph. For example, the shape of a network, as defined by behaviors and the mapping function $f(t):J$, may change as links are dropped, added, or rewired (switched from one node to another) over time. Alternatively, a network may grow with the addition of nodes and links over time. These time-varying changes distinguish networks from graphs. We return to the subject of dynamic graphs—networks—in the next chapter.

Let us ignore the possibility of change in the elements of $G = [N,L,f]$ over time, and assume that N, L, and f remain constant for the life of G. Thus, the elements of N and L remain fixed in terms of their number and properties, and the mapping function f never changes once the graph is established. What are the elements of N and L, and how does graph theory provide the basis of network science? The answers to these questions depend on the field of inquiry. Graph theory is general enough to explain a wide range of phenomena in sociology, physics, business, biology, and computer science.

2.1.1   Nodes, Links, and Mapping Function

In the social sciences, N is a set of *actors*, and L is a set that defines some relationship among actors. For example, N may be the set of people who work together in an office, and L may be the lines on an organization chart. Alternatively, N may be a set of people who have contracted a communicable disease from one another, and L may be the interactions that led to contraction of the disease.

In the physical and mathematical sciences, N denotes *vertices*, *points*, *nodes*, or *agents*, while L denotes *edges*, *links*, or *connections* among the elements of N. For example, N may be atoms in a crystalline structure and L the bonds that hold the structure together. In computer engineering, nodes may be transistors and links wires connecting them. The graph, in this case, is an electric circuit. On the other hand, N may be cities on a map, and L may be the roads and highways that connect them. Graphs are abstractions, which is why we can apply them to many diverse real-world situations.

In computer science, nodes and links form data structures, which define networks to be stored and processed. The nodes and links can represent anything because data structures are abstract entities that live only within the confines of software. Therefore, graphs and networks are models of social, physical, and mathematical structures. In one instance, a graph stored and processed by a computer program might model a social network, physical structure, roadmap, or spread of a communicable disease. In another instance, the software might simulate the flow of traffic through a network of roads and cities, the behavior of bonds among atoms in a material, or the spread of an epidemic. Graphs are powerful data structures, because of their generality.

Graphs are models, so the study of network science is a kind of modeling activity. It is important to keep the distinction between the model and the reality in mind at all times. Network science is the study of models of reality, not the reality itself. One important question we have to answer is "How well does a network model represent a real system?" In most cases we can argue that the model is a close fit to reality. Nonetheless, we must always be aware of the fact that the network model may or may not represent a real system.

In this book, the elements of N are called *nodes*, the elements of L are called *links*, and mapping function f is called the *topology* of G. The *cardinality* or size of N, denoted small n, is the number of nodes in N, and m is the number of links in L. Mathematically

$G = [N,L,f]$ is a graph composed of three sets:

$N = [v_1, v_2, \ldots, v_n]$ are nodes; $n = |N|$ is the number of nodes in N.

$L = [e_1, e_2, \ldots, e_m]$ are links; $m = |L|$ is the number of links in L.

$f: L \longrightarrow N \times N$ maps links onto node pairs.

We use v and e to designate an element of N and L, respectively, and enumerate them with subscripts: $v_1, v_2, \ldots, v_n$ and $e_1, e_2, \ldots, e_m$. Furthermore, the symbols $\sim$ and $\rightarrow$ are used to denote the mapping of a link to a node pair, for example, $u \sim v$ (nondirectional link), and $u \rightarrow v$ (directional link). Solid or curly brackets [ ] or { } denote a set, and ":" denotes a mapping.

Figure 2.1 illustrates graphs G and G' consisting of $n = 3$ nodes, $m = 2$ links, and mapping functions f and f', corresponding to G and G'. For G

$$f = [e_1 : v_1 \sim v_2, e_2 : v_2 \sim v_3]$$

G contains two links, e_1 and e_2. Link e_1 connects nodes v_1 and v_2, and link e_2 connects nodes v_2 and v_3. Note that this mapping is equivalent to a mapping that reverses links,

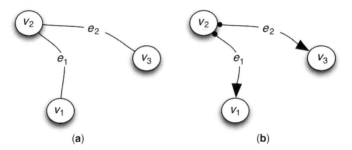

Figure 2.1   (a) An undirected graph $G = [N,L,f]$ containing three nodes v_1, v_2, and v_3; (b) a directed graph G' containing two directed links, e_1 and e_2.

because the graph is nondirectional:

$$f = [e_1 : v_2 \sim v_1, e_2 : v_3 \sim v_2]$$

These mappings are equivalent because the node-pair order does not matter—commuting a node pair does not change the topology of G. When the node-pair order does not matter in linking the node pair, G is an *undirected graph*. In an undirected graph, $v_1 \sim v_2$ is equivalent to $v_2 \sim v_1$. Figure 2.1a visualizes the topology of undirected graph G defined by the mapping:

$$e_1 : v_1 \sim v_2 \quad \text{or} \quad e_1 : v_2 \sim v_3$$
$$e_2 : v_2 \sim v_3 \quad \text{or} \quad e_2 : v_3 \sim v_2$$

In contrast, G' is a *directed graph* because $v_1 \rightarrow v_2$ is not $v_2 \rightarrow v_1$. Commuting a node pair does make a difference in the graph's topology. Links are directed, by definition, in a directed graph. A link defined by the node pair (v_1,v_2) is not the same as a link defined by node pair (v_2,v_1). In fact, both links may exist in a directed graph. Therefore, G' in Fig. 2.1b has a slightly different mapping function f:

$$e_1 : v_2 \longrightarrow v_1$$
$$e_2 : v_2 \longrightarrow v_3$$

A directed graph contains directed links—one end is the *tail*, and the other end is the *head*. For example, in the mapping $e_1 : v_2 \rightarrow v_1$ node v_2 is the tail, and node v_1 is the head. Generally, mapping function f defines a directed link in terms of a tail–head node pair:

$$e : \text{tail} \longrightarrow \text{head}$$

2.1.2 Node Degree and Hubs

The number of links—directed or undirected—connecting a node v_i to the graph is called the *degree* of the node, denoted degree(v_i) or $d(v_i)$ and abbreviated d_i.

In Fig. 2.1a, the degree of node v_2 is 2, and the degree of the other two nodes is 1:

$$d(v_1) = d_1 = 1$$
$$d(v_2) = d_2 = 2$$
$$d(v_3) = d_3 = 3$$

When the graph is directed, as in the case of G' of Fig. 2.1b, the *out-degree* of a node is equal to the number of outward-directed links, and the *in-degree* is equal to the number of inward-directed links. Out-degree is the number of tails, and in-degree is the number of heads connected to a node. Therefore, the out-degree and in-degree mapping of G' is

$$\text{in\_d}(v_1) = \text{in\_d}_1 = 1$$
$$\text{out\_d}(v_1) = \text{out\_d}_1 = 0$$
$$\text{in } d(v_2) - \text{in\_d}_2 = 0$$
$$\text{out\_d}(v_2) = \text{out\_d}_2 = 2$$
$$\text{in\_d}(v_3) = \text{in\_d}_3 = 1$$
$$\text{out\_d}(v_3) = \text{out\_d}_3 = 0$$

The *hub* of a graph is the node with the largest degree. Node v_2 is the hub of the graph in Fig. 2.1, and v_2 is the hub in Fig. 2.2a. It is very easy to identify a hub node—simply count the number of links attached to each node. Mathematically

$$\text{Hub} = \text{maximum}\{d(v_i)\}$$

It is possible for a graph to contain more than one hub, because it is possible for more than one node to possess the same (maximum) number of links.

2.1.3 Paths and Circuits

If node u is connected to node v, and v is connected to node w, then, by transitive closure, node u is connected to w. In more formal notation

$$\text{Connected}(u,v) = \textbf{true, if } u \sim v; \textbf{ false otherwise}$$
$$\text{Connected}(u,w) = \text{Connected}(u,v) \textbf{ and } \text{Connected}(v,w)$$

A *path* is a sequence of connected nodes in G. For example, in Fig. 2.1a one path exists between nodes v_1 and v_3: the path that traverses links e_1 and e_2 and visits node v_2 along the way. In general, a path exists between starting node u and ending node w, if

$$\text{Connected}(u,w) = \textbf{true:}$$
$$\text{Connected}(u,w) = \text{Connected}(u,v_1) \textbf{ and } \text{Connected}(v_1,v_2) \ldots \textbf{ and } \text{Connected}(v_t,w)$$

The *length of a path* is equal to the number of links between starting and ending nodes of the path. Path length t is measured in *hops*—the number of links along the path. The *distance* between two nodes along a path is equal to the number of hops that separate them.

In Fig. 2.1a the length of the path from starting node v_1 to ending node v_3 is $t = 2$ hops. However, there is no path from v_1 to v_3 in Fig. 2.1b because e_1 and e_2 are directed links. Hence, Connected(v_1,v_2) and Connected(v_3,v_2) are both **false**. However, there are two paths, each of length t = 1 hop, because Connected(v_2,v_1) and Connected(v_2,v_3) are both **true**.

It is possible for a graph to contain multiple paths connecting nodes. For example, Connected(u,v) may be **true** because of a path from u to w, and then v, and it may also be **true** because of a second path from u to s, r, q, and then v. The first path is of length 2 hops, while the second path is of length 4 hops. Generally, the *shortest path* is used as the path connecting nodes u and v. This is also known as the *direct path* between two nodes. In this example, the direct path is of length 2 hops, so we say that the *distance* between u and v is 2 hops.

The *average path length* of G is equal to the average over all direct paths. This metric is also known as the *characteristic path length* of G. We compute the average path of G by summing all direct paths and dividing by their number. The average path length of Fig. 2.1a is $(1 + 1 + 2)/3 = \frac{4}{3} = 1.33$ hops.

A path that begins and ends with the same node is called a *circuit*. Thus, Connected(u,u) is **true** if a circuit exists from node u back to itself. A *loop* is a circuit of length 1, which means that node u connects to itself. Figure 2.2a illustrates both a circuit (from node v_2 to v_3 and back), and a loop (from node v_3 to itself). A *duplicate* link exists in G when more than one link connects the same node pair; that is, there are two or more identical mappings $v \sim w$ in the graph. Generally, we will deal with graphs that do not contain loops and duplicate links between node pairs. In fact, we will go to some length to avoid loops and duplicates in networks because they serve no useful purpose in most applications.

2.1.4   Connectedness and Components

Undirected graph G is *strongly connected* if every node v_i is reachable along a path from every other node $v_j \neq v_i$, for $j = 1,2,\ldots,i-1$, $i+1,\ldots,n$. Both graphs in Fig. 2.1 are strongly connected. If we ignore the direction of links in the graph of Fig. 2.2a, it is also strongly connected. But if we do not ignore link directions, then there is no path from node v_4 to other nodes. Hence, the concept of connectedness applies differently to undirected graphs than directed graphs.

A graph G has *components* G_1 and G_2 if no (undirected) path exists from any node of G_1 to any node of G_2. In other words, a component is an isolated subgraph. Figure 2.2b illustrates a graph with two components, G_1 and G_2. Note that it is impossible to get from a node in G_1 from a node in G_2, because no link exists between the two components. We are generally interested only in strongly connected graphs, and simply call them *connected* when it is possible to traverse the entire graph, starting from any node.

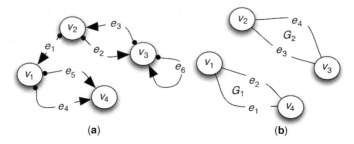

Figure 2.2   (a) A directed graph with duplicate links between node pairs $v_1 \rightarrow v_4$ and $v_2 \rightarrow v_3$, $v_3 \rightarrow v_2$, and a loop; (b) an undirected, disconnected graph with two components, G_1 and G_2.

2.1.5   Diameter, Radius, and Centrality

The longest path between any two nodes in a graph G is called the *diameter* of G, denoted diameter(G). Let the longest path from a node u to all other nodes of a connected graph be defined as the *radius* of node u, denoted radius(u). Then the node with the smallest radius is the *center of the graph*, and the largest radius over all nodes, is the graph's diameter. The diameter of a graph is also equal to the length of the longest directed path in G.

For example, if we ignore the link direction in Fig. 2.2a, the radius of each node is

Node	Radius (Node)
1	2 hops
2	2 hops
3	3 hops

Therefore, diameter(G) = 3, because the largest radius in G is 3 hops. There are two centers, v_1 and v_2, because they have the smallest radius (2 hops) of all nodes in G. We rank the *centrality* of each node according to how many hops it is from the minimum radius node(s). Nodes 1 and 2 are the most central in this example.

Use the direct path between node pairs $u \sim v$ when computing the radius of node u. Then record the longest such (direct) path as the radius of u. More formally, we obtain

$$\text{Radius}(u) = \text{maximum}_i \left\{ \text{minimum}_j \{ \text{path}_j(u_i, v_i) \} \right\}$$

Let $\text{path}_j(u, v_i)$ be the jth path between node u and v_i, and $\text{minimum}_j\{\text{path}_j(u, v_i)\}$ be the minimum-length path over all $j = 1, 2, \ldots, k$ paths between u and v_i. Now, define maximum_i as the longest direct path among node pairs (u, v_i). We find a node's radius by first computing the shortest path from u to v_i, for all nodes $i = 1, 2, \ldots$, n. Then we designate the longest of these n shortest paths as the node's radius.

The *diameter* of the graph is the longest of all of these radii; the *center* of the graph is the node with the smallest radius. There is no node closer to all other nodes than the central node(s). There is no node farther away from all other nodes than the graph's diameter. The node(s) with the largest radius, are called *peripheral nodes*.

What is the average path length of Fig. 2.2a? To obtain this answer, compute the direct path between all pairs of nodes, and then average them. We organize this calculation as a table (matrix), with four rows and four columns corresponding to the four nodes, as follows:

Head		v_1	v_2	v_3	v_4
	v_1	—	1	2	1
	v_2	1	—	1	2
Tail	v_3	2	1	1	3
	v_4	1	2	3	—

The elements of this table are the path lengths from every node to every other node in G. Rows correspond to starting nodes and columns correspond to ending nodes. For example, the length of the direct path from starting node v_3 to ending node v_1 (row 3, column 1) is 2 hops, and the length of the direct path from node v_4 to node v_3 is 3 hops. There are 13 paths in this table. The sum of all elements equals 21, so the average path length is $\frac{21}{13} = 1.62$ hops.

The average path length in this example is less than the radius of the central node or the diameter of the graph. Does this make sense? Diameter is maximum value, while average path length is an average value. Thus, average path length is never greater than the diameter of the entire graph. However, if a disproportionate number of paths are longer than the radius of the central node, then it is possible for the average path length to exceed the radius.

What is the diameter of the disconnected graph of Fig. 2.2b? A node must be connected to another node along a path in order to have a path length. Thus, the diameter of Fig. 2.2b is 1, because one hop is the length of all actual paths. We ignore the fact that there are no paths between nodes in separate components.

2.1.6 Betweenness and Closeness

Betweenness of node v is the number of paths from all nodes (except v) to all other nodes that must pass through node v. *Closeness* of node v is the number of direct paths from all nodes to all other nodes that must pass through node v. Betweenness and closeness are measures of the power of an intermediary. If it is impossible to send a message from node v_1 to node v_3 in Fig. 2.3 without going through node v_2, then v_2 has power over v_1 and v_2. It is an intermediary.

Betweenness considers all paths, while closeness considers direct paths, only. In fact, the number of paths between pairs of nodes can be very large if we count both directions along all paths in an undirected graph. For this reason, we prefer to use the closeness property, which counts only the number of direct paths. This may still be a large number, but much smaller than counting all paths. For

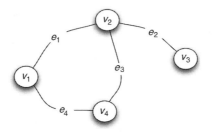

Figure 2.3   Undirected, connected graph G, with no loops, no duplicate links, and one circuit of length 3.

example, compare the number of paths counted for betweenness and closeness in Fig. 2.3:

Node	Betweenness	Closeness
1	6	0
2	6	4
3	0	0
4	2	0

Note that betweenness and closeness are zero for adjacent nodes because source and destination nodes do not count as intermediaries. Betweenness counts both paths: $v_3 \sim v_2 \sim v_1 \sim v_4$ and $v_3 \sim v_2 \sim v_4$, while closeness counts only the shorter path: $v_3 \sim v_2 \sim v_4$.

Because of its simplicity, we will use closeness as the measure of betweenness for the remainder of this book. Furthermore, we normalize the path count so that we can compare betweenness across different graphs. Normalization to the interval [0,100] is done by dividing path counts by the largest path count, and multiplying by 100. For example, node v_2 of Fig. 2.3 is between the most nodes, so we designate it as the intermediary. Next, we normalize all path counts by dividing the number of paths recorded for each node by the largest number of paths recorded by the most frequently visited intermediary node. In Fig. 2.3, the intermediary is v_2, with four direct paths through it, so we divide all paths by 4, and represent the result as a percentage:

$$\text{Closeness}(v) = \frac{\text{\# direct paths}(v)(100\%)}{\text{\# direct paths(intermediary)}}$$

Normalizing the results of counting direct paths through the nodes of Fig. 2.3 gives

Node	Normalized Closeness (%)
1	0
2	100
3	0
4	0

It is impossible to connect the other nodes to one another along a direct path without traveling through node v_2. This places node v_2 in the enviable gatekeeper position—a potentially powerful position relative to other nodes.

Closeness—as defined here—is not a perfect measure of an intermediary's power over others. Consider the case of a symmetric graph with an even number of nodes. It is highly likely that several shortest paths exist between two arbitrarily chosen source and destination nodes. Which shortest path is counted in the determination of closeness? In program *Network.jar*, closeness is calculated by counting only the first direct path found, rather than all direct paths. The astute reader will observe this anomaly when calculating closeness in even- versus odd-sized symmetric graphs.

2.2   MATRIX ALGEBRA DEFINITION OF A GRAPH

Set theory is especially efficient for proving theorems and rigorously defining the properties of a graph, but for some forms of analysis a matrix representation is more effective. For example, matrix representation facilitates computerized storage and processing of G, as well as forming a mathematical foundation for studying the *structure* of G. In many cases, a matrix representation is the most compact and efficient way to compute a property of a graph.

In the following, we examine four basic forms of matrix representation: the connection, adjacency, path, and Laplacian matrices. A *connection matrix* represents a graph's mapping function f as a square matrix containing the number of links between node pairs. An *adjacency matrix* is similar; if one or more links exist between node pairs, the adjacency matrix contains a 1; otherwise it contains a 0. The elements of a *path matrix* are equal to the path length separating nodes, or zero, if no path exists. A *Laplacian matrix* combines node adjacency and node degree information in one compact mathematical formulation; it stores the degree of each node along the diagonal elements of the adjacency matrix.

2.2.1   Connection Matrix

The set f of all connections $v_i \sim v_j$, for all node pairs belonging to $N \times N$ defines the topological map of G. This map can be visual, as in Figs. 2.1 and 2.2; a tabular list of links and node pairs as in set theory; or more algebraically as a *connection matrix*, C—denoted $C(G)$, where C is simply a mapping function f expressed as a square matrix, where rows correspond to tail nodes and columns correspond to head nodes of every link in G. The n^2 elements of C are set to the number of links connecting tail–head pairs of nodes in G:

$$c_{i,j} = k, \quad \text{if} \quad v_i \sim v_j, \quad \text{or} \quad c_{i,j} = 0 \quad \text{otherwise.} \quad (i,j) = ([1,n], [1,n])$$

In this definition, k is the number of links that connect $v_i \sim v_j$. Typically, $k = 1$, but if two links connect $v_i \sim v_j$, then $c_{i,j} = 2$. For example, in Fig. 2.2b, $c_{2,3} = c_{3,2} = c_{1,4} = c_{4,1} = 2$, because duplicate links connect the same node pair in each component, and the components are undirected graphs.

A visual rendition of G is constructed from its connection matrix, and the reverse. For example, the connection matrices $C(G)$ and $C(G')$ for the graphs of Figs. 2.1a and 2.1b, respectively, are

$$
C(G) = \begin{array}{c} \\ v_1 \\ v_2 \\ v_3 \end{array} \begin{array}{ccc} v_1 & v_2 & v_3 \\ 0 & 1 & 0 \\ 1 & 0 & 1 \\ 0 & 1 & 0 \end{array} = \begin{pmatrix} 0 & 1 & 0 \\ 1 & 0 & 1 \\ 0 & 1 & 0 \end{pmatrix}
$$

$$
C(G') = \begin{array}{c} \\ v_1 \\ v_2 \\ v_3 \end{array} \begin{array}{ccc} v_1 & v_2 & v_3 \\ 0 & 0 & 0 \\ 1 & 0 & 1 \\ 0 & 0 & 0 \end{array} = \begin{pmatrix} 0 & 0 & 0 \\ 1 & 0 & 1 \\ 0 & 0 & 0 \end{pmatrix}
$$

Each row of matrix C corresponds to the tail of a link, and each column corresponds to a head. Recall that $v_1 \sim v_2$ means v_1 is the tail, and v_2 is the head of a link that connects v_1 to v_2. Thus, row 1 and column 2 of matrix C contains a 1. In general, a 1 is placed in the (i,j)th element of C whenever node v_i is connected to node v_j. If more than one link connects two nodes, then the number of links connecting node v_i to node v_j is inserted into row i and column j of C.

Note the difference between $C(G)$, the matrix representation of the undirected graph, and $C(G')$, the matrix representation of the directed graph. $C(G)$ is symmetric and $C(G')$ is not. Generally, the connection matrix is symmetric if the graph is undirected because all links have heads and tails at both ends. The reason: $v_1 \sim v_2 = v_2 \sim v_1$, in an undirected graph.

2.2.2 Adjacency Matrix

A modified version of the connection matrix—called the *adjacency matrix* in graph theory, and the *sociomatrix* in social network theory—ignores duplicate links in the graph. The adjacency matrix A is used in place of the connection matrix when we want to ignore duplicate links between node pairs, and study the most basic connectivity of G. The adjacency matrix assumes $k = 0$ or $k = 1$:

$$
a_{i,j} = 1 \quad \text{if} \quad v_i \sim v_j, \quad \text{or} \quad a_{i,j} = 0 \quad \text{otherwise}
$$

The sociomatrix or adjacency matrix is also known as a *Boolean matrix*, because the entries must be 0 or 1—Boolean values. If two nodes are connected, the adjacency matrix records a 1; otherwise, it records a 0. This characterization of adjacency is useful when manipulating matrix A with a computer. For example, the Boolean product of two adjacency matrices is itself a Boolean matrix containing 0s and 1s.

The sociomatrix and adjacency matrix are different names for the same thing. In social network analysis, Fig. 2.1a represents a social relationship such as friendship, romantic, or supervisor–employee relationships within a group of people. Suppose that Tom (v_1) knows Mary (v_2), but not Jill (v_3). Graph G of Fig. 2.1a models this small social network, and tells us that Mary is central to the three-person network, because radius (Mary) is 1 hop, while radius (Tom) and radius (Jill) are both 2 hops.

Social network analysis is more concerned with the existence of at least one relationship between pairs of people modeled as nodes in a graph. Thus, a sociomatrix is actually an adjacency matrix. Loops are eliminated along with duplicate links when analyzing a sociomatrix.

Figure 2.2a illustrates the difference between connection and adjacency matrices. The connection matrix considers all links, while the adjacency matrix considers only adjacency—indicated by a Boolean value. Either adjacent nodes are connected by one or more links (1), or they are not (0). The connection and adjacency matrices of Fig. 2.2a are

$$C(G) = \begin{array}{c} \\ v_1 \\ v_2 \\ v_3 \\ v_4 \end{array} \begin{array}{cccc} v_1 & v_2 & v_3 & v_4 \\ 0 & 0 & 0 & 2 \\ 1 & 0 & 1 & 0 \\ 0 & 1 & 1 & 0 \\ 0 & 0 & 0 & 0 \end{array} = \begin{pmatrix} 0 & 0 & 0 & 2 \\ 1 & 0 & 1 & 0 \\ 0 & 1 & 1 & 0 \\ 0 & 0 & 0 & 0 \end{pmatrix}$$

$$A(G) = \begin{array}{c} \\ v_1 \\ v_2 \\ v_3 \\ v_4 \end{array} \begin{array}{cccc} v_1 & v_2 & v_3 & v_4 \\ 0 & 0 & 0 & 1 \\ 1 & 0 & 1 & 0 \\ 0 & 1 & 1 & 0 \\ 0 & 0 & 0 & 0 \end{array} = \begin{pmatrix} 0 & 0 & 0 & 1 \\ 1 & 0 & 1 & 0 \\ 0 & 1 & 1 & 0 \\ 0 & 0 & 0 & 0 \end{pmatrix}$$

Note the difference: C contains a 2 in row 1, column 4; while A contains a 1 in the corresponding (1,4) element. In addition, element (3,3) contains a 1, because of the loop on node v_3. The connection matrix lists the number of connections between node pairs, while the adjacency matrix lists a Boolean 1 if any number of links exist, and a 0 otherwise. Both matrices are asymmetric, because the graph is directed. Adjacency matrix representation is perhaps the most compact representation that captures the minimum topological information. For this reason we use the adjacency matrix— and its extensions—to represent network structure.

2.2.3 Laplacian Matrix

The *Laplacian matrix* of graph G, namely, $L(G)$, is a combination of the connection matrix and (diagonal) degree matrix: $L = C - D$, where D is a diagonal matrix and C is the connection matrix. Matrix D is a conformant matrix with zero nondiagonal elements and diagonal elements $d_{i,i}$ equal to the degree of node v_i:

$$d_{i,j} = \begin{cases} \text{degree}(v_i) & \text{if } j = i \\ 0 & \text{otherwise} \end{cases}$$

It is also true that the sum of row elements of L equals zero, and if the matrix is symmetric, so is the sum of column elements. This is due to the symmetry of undirected links: $v \sim u = u \sim v$. This fact will become important later on, when we use the Laplacian to study the stability of a network.

The connection and Laplacian matrices for the undirected graph of Fig. 2.3 are

$$
C(G) = \begin{array}{c} \\ v_1 \\ v_2 \\ v_3 \\ v_4 \end{array}
\begin{array}{cccc} v_1 & v_2 & v_3 & v_4 \\ 0 & 1 & 0 & 1 \\ 1 & 0 & 1 & 1 \\ 0 & 1 & 0 & 0 \\ 1 & 1 & 0 & 0 \end{array}
= \begin{pmatrix} 0 & 1 & 0 & 1 \\ 1 & 0 & 1 & 1 \\ 0 & 1 & 0 & 0 \\ 1 & 1 & 0 & 0 \end{pmatrix}
$$

$$
L(G) = \begin{array}{c} \\ v_1 \\ v_2 \\ v_3 \\ v_4 \end{array}
\begin{array}{cccc} v_1 & v_2 & v_3 & v_4 \\ -2 & 1 & 0 & 1 \\ 1 & -3 & 1 & 1 \\ 0 & 1 & -1 & 0 \\ 1 & 1 & 0 & -2 \end{array}
= \begin{pmatrix} -2 & 1 & 0 & 1 \\ 1 & -3 & 1 & 1 \\ 0 & 1 & -1 & 0 \\ 1 & 1 & 0 & -2 \end{pmatrix}
$$

2.2.4 Path Matrix

Path matrix $P(G)$ stores the number of hops along the direct path between all node pairs in a graph; that is, $P(G)$ enumerates the lengths of shortest paths among all node pairs. If the graph is undirected, then $P(G)$ is symmetric. Also, as with the adjacency matrix, if no link exists between a node pair, the corresponding element in $P(G)$ is zero. The diagonal elements of $P(G)$ are zero because we eliminate loops from consideration, as well as duplicate links.

For example, the path matrix for the undirected graph of Fig. 2.3 is symmetric because G is undirected:

$$
P = \begin{array}{c} \\ v_1 \\ v_2 \\ v_3 \\ v_4 \end{array}
\begin{array}{cccc} v_1 & v_2 & v_3 & v_4 \\ 0 & 1 & 2 & 1 \\ 1 & 0 & 1 & 1 \\ 2 & 1 & 0 & 2 \\ 1 & 1 & 2 & 0 \end{array}
= \begin{pmatrix} 0 & 1 & 2 & 1 \\ 1 & 0 & 1 & 1 \\ 2 & 1 & 0 & 2 \\ 1 & 1 & 2 & 0 \end{pmatrix}
$$

The diagonal elements are all 0, and the off-diagonals contain the number of hops along a path connecting each node pair. There are two paths between v_1 and v_3 ($v_1 \sim v_2 \sim v_3$ and $v_1 \sim v_4 \sim v_2 \sim v_3$), but we store only the minimum-length path, so elements $p_{1,3}$ and $p_{3,1}$ are equal to 2 hops. Similarly, another two paths exist between v_3 and v_4 ($v_3 \sim v_2 \sim v_4$ and $v_3 \sim v_2 \sim v_1 \sim v_4$), but matrix P stores only the shortest path length. In fact, the diameter of this graph is 2 hops because every node can be reached from every other node in at most 2 hops. Therefore, the largest value any element of P can be is 2.

The path matrix is related to the adjacency matrix as follows. Let A be the adjacency matrix and P the path matrix. A^2 is the adjacency matrix containing all node pairs 2 hops apart; A^3 contains the 3-hop adjacencies, and A^K contains the k-hop adjacencies. Thus $A, A^2, A^3, \ldots, A^k$ are the path matrices for all paths of length $1,2,3,\ldots,k$. Note that the shortest paths in the set $[A, A^2, A^3, \ldots, A^k]$ are elements of the path matrix. Let D be the size of the longest path—the diameter of G. Then, $P = \min_{k=1}^{D}\{kA^k\}$ is exactly the path matrix of G. The min function, here, selects the smallest element of the set, element by element.

The matrices $A, A^2, A^3, \ldots, A^k$ must all be Boolean, so we reduce the elements of each by replacing nonzero elements with a Boolean 1. Zero elements remain zero, after each matrix multiplication in $A^k = A^{k-1}A$. The product kA^k yields the length of paths connecting nodes together in k hops. We ignore cycles, so the diagonal elements are set to zero after each multiplication.[1] The off-diagonals are equal to the number of hops of length k in each matrix, kA^k. P stores direct path lengths, which means that we equate only the smallest nontrivial elements of kA^k with corresponding elements of P.

Consider the undirected graph of Fig. 2.3 again. Its adjacency matrix is

$$A = \begin{array}{c} \\ v_1 \\ v_2 \\ v_3 \\ v_4 \end{array} \begin{array}{cccc} v_1 & v_2 & v_3 & v_4 \\ 0 & 1 & 0 & 1 \\ 1 & 0 & 1 & 1 \\ 0 & 1 & 0 & 0 \\ 1 & 1 & 0 & 0 \end{array} = \begin{pmatrix} 0 & 1 & 0 & 1 \\ 1 & 0 & 1 & 1 \\ 0 & 1 & 0 & 0 \\ 1 & 1 & 0 & 0 \end{pmatrix}$$

Multiplication by A yields the adjacency of node pairs after $2,3,\ldots,k$ hops. The 2-hop matrix is $A \times A$:

$$A^2 = \begin{array}{c} \\ v_1 \\ v_2 \\ v_3 \\ v_4 \end{array} \begin{array}{cccc} v_1 & v_2 & v_3 & v_4 \\ 2 & 1 & 1 & 1 \\ 1 & 3 & 0 & 1 \\ 1 & 0 & 1 & 1 \\ 1 & 1 & 1 & 2 \end{array} = \begin{pmatrix} 2 & 1 & 1 & 1 \\ 1 & 3 & 1 & 1 \\ 1 & 0 & 1 & 1 \\ 1 & 1 & 1 & 2 \end{pmatrix}$$

Zeroing the diagonal, reducing A^2 to a Boolean matrix, and multiplying by $k = 2$ gives

$$2A^2 = \begin{array}{c} \\ v_1 \\ v_2 \\ v_3 \\ v_4 \end{array} \begin{array}{cccc} v_1 & v_2 & v_3 & v_4 \\ 0 & 2 & 2 & 2 \\ 2 & 0 & 0 & 2 \\ 2 & 0 & 0 & 2 \\ 2 & 2 & 2 & 0 \end{array} = \begin{pmatrix} 0 & 2 & 2 & 2 \\ 2 & 0 & 0 & 2 \\ 2 & 0 & 0 & 2 \\ 2 & 2 & 2 & 0 \end{pmatrix}$$

[1] Normally, cycles of length k are identified as nonzero diagonals in A^k.

This is 2 times the adjacency matrix for nodes connected by paths of length 2 hops. For example, node v_1 is connected to v_2 by two hops ($v_1 \sim v_4 \sim v_2$), and node v_3 is connected to node v_1 and v_4 by paths of length 2 hops.

The diameter, $D = 2$, in this example, so we have found all paths of length $1, 2, \ldots, D$. The next step combines the matrices together by selecting the nontrivial minimum element of each; that is, we select the nonzero minimum values:

$$P = \min (k = 1,2)\{kA^k\} = \min\{A, 2A^2\}$$

$$P = \min \begin{pmatrix} 0 & 1 & 0 & 1 \\ 1 & 0 & 1 & 1 \\ 0 & 1 & 0 & 0 \\ 1 & 1 & 0 & 0 \end{pmatrix} \begin{pmatrix} 0 & 2 & 2 & 2 \\ 2 & 0 & 0 & 2 \\ 2 & 0 & 0 & 2 \\ 2 & 2 & 2 & 0 \end{pmatrix} = \begin{pmatrix} 0 & 1 & 2 & 1 \\ 1 & 0 & 1 & 1 \\ 2 & 1 & 0 & 2 \\ 1 & 1 & 2 & 0 \end{pmatrix}$$

Powers of adjacency matrix A also contain cycles of length k along the diagonal of A^k. This property is exploited in a number of ways in later chapters. For example, instead of zeroing the diagonal elements of A^k, we might use them to find cycles of length $2, 3, \ldots, k$ in an arbitrary graph G. This algorithm is left as an exercise for the reader.

2.3   THE BRIDGES OF KÖNIGSBERG GRAPH

Now that we have a rudimentary understanding of graphs, and how their structure can be represented in terms of set theory and matrix algebra, suppose that we apply this theory to a practical example. The following example was the creation of the father of graph theory—Leonhard Euler, who solved a very practical problem using his new theory of graphs. By doing so, Euler founded the modern theory of graphs, and laid the foundation for network science as well.

2.3.1   Euler Path, Euler Circuit

Figure 2.4a is Euler's first graph—a model of the *Bridges of Königsberg* problem published by the famous Swiss mathematician in 1735. As you recall from the previous chapter, the burghers of Königsberg, Prussia, wanted to know whether it was possible to parade through the town, crossing each bridge once, and only once, before returning to their starting point. A path that returns to its starting point is called a *circuit*. A path that traverses all links of a graph is called an *Euler path*, and a *Euler circuit* is a Euler path that begins and ends with the same node. The burgher's requirement that they traverse an Euler circuit is what makes this problem interesting and difficult.

The city occupied land on both banks of the river Pregel as well as two islands located in the Pregel. A system of seven bridges connected the landmasses as shown in Fig. 2.4a. Nodes represent the four landmasses, and seven links represent the connecting bridges. Nodes v_2 and v_3 represent the banks along the Pregel, and

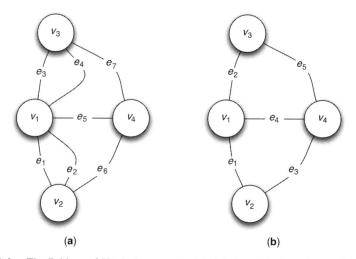

Figure 2.4 The Bridges of Königsberg graph: (a) Euler's original graph containing $n = 4$ nodes representing landmasses and $m = 7$ links representing bridges; (b) reduced Euler graph with two duplicate links (e_2 and e_4) removed.

nodes v_1 and v_4 represent the two islands. Two links connect island v_1 to the north bank v_3 and another two connect v_1 to the south bank. Similarly, three additional bridges (links) connect island v_4 to both banks and island v_1, which accounts for all seven bridges.

We can rephrase the Bridges of Königsberg question as a graph problem: "Is it possible to trace the entire graph of Fig. 2.4a, starting from any node, returning to the starting node, without tracing any link more than once?" In other words, "Does G contain an Euler circuit?" Euler showed that it is impossible to trace this graph without repeating a link, and hence there is no Euler circuit.

The graph studied by Euler is undirected and has no loops, but it does have duplicate links. Hence, its connection matrix is different than its adjacency matrix. Furthermore, the largest radius is of length 2 hops, so the diameter of this graph is 2. In other words, the burghers can reach any landmass from any other landmass in no more than two bridge crossings.

2.3.2 Formal Definition of the Bridges of Königsberg

The set-theoretic definition of Euler's graph, $G_{\text{Königsberg}} = [N, L, f]$, is

$$N = [v_1, v_2, v_3, v_4]$$
$$L = [e_1, e_2, e_3, e_4, e_5, e_6, e_7]$$
$$f = [e_1 : v_1 \sim v_2, \quad e_2 : v_1 \sim v_2, \quad e_3 : v_1 \sim v_3, \quad e_4 : v_1 \sim v_3,$$
$$e_5 : v_1 \sim v_4, \quad e_6 : v_2 \sim v_4, \quad e_7 : v_3 \sim v_4]$$

The matrix algebra definition of Euler's graph C ($G_{\text{Königsberg}}$), is

$$
C =
\begin{array}{c|cccc}
 & v_1 & v_2 & v_3 & v_4 \\
\hline
v_1 & 0 & 2 & 2 & 1 \\
v_2 & 2 & 0 & 0 & 1 \\
v_3 & 2 & 0 & 0 & 1 \\
v_4 & 1 & 1 & 1 & 0 \\
\end{array}
=
\begin{pmatrix}
0 & 2 & 2 & 1 \\
2 & 0 & 0 & 1 \\
2 & 0 & 0 & 1 \\
1 & 1 & 1 & 0 \\
\end{pmatrix}
$$

Each row and column of matrix C corresponds to a node; row 1/column 1 corresponds to node v_1; row 2/column 2 corresponds to v_2, and so on. If $v_i \sim v_j$, the number of links connecting v_i to v_j is inserted in row i, column j of the connection matrix. Otherwise, a zero appears in the intersection of row i and column j. Matrix C is symmetric, because links are nondirectional: $v_i \sim v_j$ is identical to $v_j \sim v_i$.

Similarly, the adjacency matrix A ($G_{\text{Königsberg}}$) is

$$
A =
\begin{array}{c|cccc}
 & v_1 & v_2 & v_3 & v_4 \\
\hline
v_1 & 0 & 1 & 1 & 1 \\
v_2 & 1 & 0 & 0 & 1 \\
v_3 & 1 & 0 & 0 & 1 \\
v_4 & 1 & 1 & 1 & 0 \\
\end{array}
=
\begin{pmatrix}
0 & 1 & 1 & 1 \\
1 & 0 & 0 & 1 \\
1 & 0 & 0 & 1 \\
1 & 1 & 1 & 0 \\
\end{pmatrix}
$$

The adjacency matrix corresponds to the reduced (duplicate links have been removed) graph shown in Fig. 2.4b.

In Fig. 2.4a, there are many paths from node v_1 to node v_2: one path traverses link e_1, another path traverses link e_2, and a longer path (2 hops) traverses links e_5 and e_6. An even longer path between v_1 and v_2 traverses e_4, e_7, and e_6. But the shortest path defines the *distance* between v_1 and v_2. In Fig. 2.4a, the shortest path between v_1 and v_2 is 1 hop: two paths of length one connect v_1 to v_2—one obtained by traversing link e_1 and the other by traversing link e_2. Yet, the distance between v_1 and v_2 is one hop. The path matrix P ($G_{\text{Königsberg}}$) is

$$
P =
\begin{array}{c|cccc}
 & v_1 & v_2 & v_3 & v_4 \\
\hline
v_1 & 0 & 1 & 1 & 1 \\
v_2 & 1 & 0 & 2 & 1 \\
v_3 & 1 & 2 & 0 & 1 \\
v_4 & 1 & 1 & 1 & 0 \\
\end{array}
=
\begin{pmatrix}
0 & 1 & 1 & 1 \\
1 & 0 & 2 & 1 \\
1 & 2 & 0 & 1 \\
1 & 1 & 1 & 0 \\
\end{pmatrix}
$$

Adjacency A and path matrix P differ in only one respect: the path between v_2 and v_3 is 2 hops, which results in $p_{2,3} = p_{3,2} = 2$. Since v_2 and v_3 are not adjacent, $a_{2,3} = a_{3,2} = 0$. The path matrix can be computed from the adjacency matrix as shown earlier, by selecting the minimum nontrivial elements of powers of A:

$$
P = \min\{A, A^2\}
$$

This is left as an exercise for the reader.

Euler's graph has many circuits. For example, $v_1 \sim e_1 \sim v_2 \sim e_2 \sim v_1$ is one circuit, and $v_1 \sim e_5 \sim v_4 \sim e_6 \sim v_2 \sim e_2 \sim v_1$ is another circuit starting and ending with node v_1. Does Fig. 2.4a contain an Euler circuit? Try to traverse the entire graph starting and ending with node v_1, and see what happens. It is not possible to traverse all links one time, and only one time. Does the reduced Euler graph of Fig. 2.4b contain an Euler circuit?

2.3.3 Euler's Solution

Node degree plays a central role in solving the Bridges of Königsberg problem. Euler proved that it is impossible for the burghers to parade through the town along a Euler circuit simply because landmasses have an odd number of bridges connecting them. It is impossible to visit a node (landmass) and return an even number of times, and hence it is impossible to visit odd-degreed nodes only one time, along an Euler circuit. Note that it is possible to visit nodes more than once, while avoiding traversal of links more than once, but the degree of a node would have to be even to allow this.

The number of bridges connecting each landmass—and thus the degree of each node in Fig. 2.4a—is stored in the *Laplacian matrix* of this graph:

$$L = \begin{array}{c} \\ v_1 \\ v_2 \\ v_3 \\ v_4 \end{array} \begin{array}{cccc} v_1 & v_2 & v_3 & v_4 \\ -5 & 2 & 2 & 1 \\ 2 & -3 & 0 & 1 \\ 2 & 0 & -3 & 1 \\ 1 & 1 & 1 & -3 \end{array} = \begin{pmatrix} -5 & 2 & 2 & 1 \\ 2 & -3 & 0 & 1 \\ 2 & 0 & -3 & 1 \\ 1 & 1 & 1 & -3 \end{pmatrix}$$

The diagonal elements of L equal the degrees of the nodes (landmasses) in the graph of Fig. 2.4a. This is a Laplacian matrix because the rows sum to zero. The columns also sum to zero because the graph is undirected. No Euler circuit exists in the Königsberg graph because the diagonal elements are odd numbers.

Euler proved the following general results for any graph, but particularly for the Bridges of Königsberg graph:

1. A connected graph cannot have a Euler circuit if any node has odd degree. According to the Laplacian, all nodes have odd degree. So, the Bridges of Königsberg graph cannot have an Euler circuit. Intuitively, an Euler circuit makes sense—to traverse every link one time and return to the starting node, a traveler would have to leave each landmass node as many times as he or she arrives—hence there must be an even number of links connecting each node. Does this result apply to the reduced Euler graph of Fig. 2.4b?

2. If a graph is connected and every node has even degree, then it has at least one Euler circuit. This condition guarantees an Euler circuit for the same intuitive reasoning given in the previous case. Suppose that the graph of Fig. 2.4a is rewired so that $e_5 : v_2 \sim v_3$ instead. Now all nodes have even degree.

Therefore, at least one circuit is a Euler circuit. Finding the circuit is left as an exercise for the reader.

3. Euler went on to prove that a graph with more than two nodes of odd degree cannot have an Euler path, and if it has exactly two nodes of odd degree, then it has at least one Euler path starting and ending with the odd degree nodes. An Euler path would allow the burghers to traverse all bridges once, but not return to their starting point. Does this apply to Fig. 2.4a? Does it apply to Fig. 2.4b?

4. The sum of the degrees of all the nodes of a graph is an even number equal to twice the number of links: $\sum_{i=1}^{n} \text{degree}(v_i) = 2m$. The sum of degrees of G can be obtained from the diagonal of L. Ignoring the sign of the diagonal elements of L, the Bridges of Königsberg graph has $5 + 3 + 3 + 3 = 14$ total degrees, which is exactly $2(7)$ links. Similarly, the sum of node degrees of Fig. 2.4b is an even number. What is it?

5. In every graph, the number of nodes of odd degree must be even because $2m$ is even. Once again, we can use the information stored in the Laplacian to verify this. The number of nodes of odd degree is 4, which is an even number. This conclusion follows from observing that the sum of degrees is an even number, and that an even number is always the sum of two even numbers or two odd numbers. The sum of an even number and odd number is odd. Figure 2.4b has two nodes with odd degree. Does this assertion stand up to the test when applied to Fig. 2.4b?

Euler created graph theory from the cloth of a practical problem. He accomplished this by applying rigorous methods of analysis. We want to follow his example and use rigorous methods as well! While formalism will guide us as we solve a number of practical problems in graph theory, we live in an age of copious amounts of low-cost computing power. This allows us to combine the empirical with the theoretical, and hopefully gain even greater insights than possible by purely formal methods. Thus, the methods of this book are based on formalisms such as topology of graphs and matrix algebra, and "informalisms" such as computer simulation and *emergence*. Network science is more than applied graph theory—it is a combination of mathematical and computational sciences—plus application to real-world systems.

2.4 SPECTRAL PROPERTIES OF GRAPHS

We have shown how to define a graph in terms of its adjacency and Laplacian matrix. Now, we show how to extract dynamical properties from these two matrices using a technique similar to methods used to understand the behavior of linear systems such as a vibrating string in a musical instrument, states of a particle in quantum mechanics, or various other electromechanical systems. The spectral radius is computed from the adjacency matrix, and the spectral gap is computed from the Laplacian matrix of a graph. Think of a matrix as a transformation of a linear system as it moves in time and space according to its dynamical equation $D[A] = AX$, where D is a linear operator, A is some kind of linear transformation, and X is the state of the system. For example, D might be the time derivative operator, and A might be the damping forces acting on a mechanical system, such as a robotic arm or automobile suspension system.

A typical (well-behaved) linear system will cycle through some kind of pattern. We can determine the nature of this pattern by decomposing the system's response to a stimulus into a set of fundamental modes or *basis vectors* in a mathematical process called *spectral decomposition*. These basis vectors are called *orthonormal vectors* or *eigenvectors*. Specifically, if λ is a diagonal matrix, then A may be decomposed as $A = \lambda I$ where I is the identity matrix and λ is a matrix containing eigenvalues, or det $[A - \lambda I] = 0$, where det[] is the determinant of [ ].

Then

$$\lambda = \begin{pmatrix} \lambda_1 & 0 & \cdots & 0 \\ 0 & \lambda_2 & \cdots & 0 \\ 0 & 0 & \cdots & 0 \\ 0 & 0 & \cdots & \lambda_n \end{pmatrix}$$

At the risk of oversimplification, spectral analysis is the process of finding the basic vibrational modes (harmonics) of a linear system and expressing them in terms of constants called *eigenvalues*. The largest such eigenvalue, typically denoted λ_1, is of particular interest because it represents the dominant mode of the dynamic system. Furthermore, if $\lambda_1 < 0$, the vibration eventually dies out; otherwise, it increases and leads to an unstable system.

Network science has found a use for two spectral measures: spectral radius and spectral gap. The *spectral radius* of a graph G is the largest nonzero eigenvalue of G's adjacency matrix, and the *spectral gap* of G is the largest nonzero eigenvalue of its Laplacian matrix. Later we use spectral radius to explain how epidemics travel through a network, and spectral gap to explain stability—or the lack of it—in a network.

2.4.1 Spectral Radius

The *spectral radius* $\rho(G)$ is the largest nontrivial *eigenvalue* of det $[A(G) - \lambda I] = 0$, where A is the adjacency matrix and $\mathbf{I}$ is the identity matrix.[2] Eigenvalues are the diagonals $\lambda_1, \lambda_2, \lambda_3, \ldots, \lambda_n$ of $\lambda \mathbf{I}$. Spectral radius eigenvectors are also called the *characteristic eigenvalues* because they characterize the topology of a graph in succinct terms. In fact, they are often identical or closely related to the *mean degree* λ of a structured graph (see Table 2.1). Recall that mean degree $\lambda = (2m/n)$ is the average number of links connected to a node.

Mean degree and spectral radius are not generally the same, as we will see later on when we study random and scale-free graphs. For the time being, think of spectral radius as a compact representation of a graph's mapping function f. In fact, spectral

---

[2]By *nontrivial*, we mean nonzero.

TABLE 2.1   Spectral Radius for Some Regular Graphs: n Nodes

Graph	Spectral Radius, ρ	Mean Degree, λ
Complete	$(n-1)$	$(n-1)$
Toroid	4	4
Hypercube	$\log_2(n)$	$\log_2(n)$
1-Regular (ring)	2	2
Star	$\sqrt{(n-1)}$	$(n-2)/n$
Binary tree	$\sqrt{(2)}: n = 3$	$\frac{4}{3}$
	2: $n = 7$	1.7142
	2.2882: $n = 15$	1.8666
	2.4494: $n = 31$	1.9354
	2.548: $n = 63$	1.9682
	2.714: $n = 1023$	1.9980

radius is determined completely by the topology (degree sequence) of a graph, and therefore, is a measure of a graph's topology. In Table 2.1 the entry for *binary tree* contains six examples ranging from $n = 3$ to $n = 1023$ nodes. As a binary tree increases in size, its mean degree approaches 2.0, and its spectral radius appears to approach exp(1). Proof of this is left as an exercise for the advanced reader.

How is the spectral radius of an arbitrary graph computed? Consider the graph of Fig. 2.3 once again, and construct its adjacency matrix as follows:

$$
A = \begin{matrix} & \begin{matrix} v_1 & v_2 & v_3 & v_4 \end{matrix} \\ \begin{matrix} v_1 \\ v_2 \\ v_3 \\ v_4 \end{matrix} & \begin{pmatrix} 0 & 1 & 0 & 1 \\ 1 & 0 & 1 & 1 \\ 0 & 1 & 0 & 0 \\ 1 & 1 & 0 & 0 \end{pmatrix} \end{matrix} = \begin{pmatrix} 0 & 1 & 0 & 1 \\ 1 & 0 & 1 & 1 \\ 0 & 1 & 0 & 0 \\ 1 & 1 & 0 & 0 \end{pmatrix}
$$

Now, form the matrix $A(G) - \lambda I$ and find the elements of λ that solve the polynomial equation obtained from setting the determinant of $A(G) - \lambda I$ to zero, det$[A - \lambda I] = 0$:

$$
\det \begin{bmatrix} -\lambda & 1 & 0 & 1 \\ 1 & -\lambda & 1 & 1 \\ 0 & 1 & -\lambda & 0 \\ 1 & 1 & 0 & -\lambda \end{bmatrix} = 0
$$

Expanding the determinant along column 3 using *Laplace's expansion formula* yields the following polynomial:

$$
\lambda^4 - 4\lambda^2 - 2\lambda + 1 = 0
$$

The roots of this polynomial are $\{-1.48, -1.0, 0.311, 2.17\}$, and the largest nontrivial root is 2.17, so $\rho = 2.17$. Note that the mean degree of this graph is 2.0, and the average path length is 1.333 hops.

2.4.2 Spectral Gap

The *Laplacian matrix* $L(G)$ is the adjacency matrix of an undirected, loop-free, duplicate-free graph with diagonals defined as follows

$$\text{Diagonal}(i, i) = -\sum_{j \neq i} c_{i,j} = -\text{degree}(v_i)$$

Let A be the adjacency matrix, D the diagonal containing the degree of nodes, and L the *Laplacian*. Then $L = A - D$. The spectral gap of G is the largest nontrivial eigenvalue of L. For example, the diagonal matrix is obtained by noting that degree $(v_1) = 2$, degree $(v_2) = 3$, degree $(v_3) = 1$, and degree $(v_4) = 2$, in Fig. 2.3. Then, subtracting D from A yields L, resulting in negative numbers along the diagonal. In this way, the elements of each row and column of L sum to zero. Also, note that the Laplacian is symmetric if the adjacency matrix is symmetric.

The graph of Fig. 2.3 is undirected and has no duplicate or loop links, so its adjacency, diagonal, and Laplacian matrices are

$$
A =
\begin{matrix}
 & v_1 & v_2 & v_3 & v_4 \\
v_1 & 0 & 1 & 0 & 1 \\
v_2 & 1 & 0 & 1 & 1 \\
v_3 & 0 & 1 & 0 & 0 \\
v_4 & 1 & 1 & 0 & 0
\end{matrix}
=
\begin{pmatrix}
0 & 1 & 0 & 1 \\
1 & 0 & 1 & 1 \\
0 & 1 & 0 & 0 \\
1 & 1 & 0 & 0
\end{pmatrix}
$$

$$
D =
\begin{matrix}
 & v_1 & v_2 & v_3 & v_4 \\
v_1 & 2 & 0 & 0 & 0 \\
v_2 & 0 & 3 & 0 & 0 \\
v_3 & 0 & 0 & 1 & 0 \\
v_4 & 0 & 0 & 0 & 2
\end{matrix}
=
\begin{pmatrix}
2 & 0 & 0 & 0 \\
0 & 3 & 0 & 0 \\
0 & 0 & 1 & 0 \\
0 & 0 & 0 & 2
\end{pmatrix}
$$

$$
L =
\begin{matrix}
 & v_1 & v_2 & v_3 & v_4 \\
v_1 & -2 & 1 & 0 & 1 \\
v_2 & 1 & -3 & 1 & 1 \\
v_3 & 0 & 1 & -1 & 0 \\
v_4 & 1 & 1 & 0 & -2
\end{matrix}
=
\begin{pmatrix}
-2 & 1 & 0 & 1 \\
1 & -3 & 1 & 1 \\
0 & 1 & -1 & 0 \\
1 & 1 & 0 & -2
\end{pmatrix}
$$

The *spectral gap* of a graph is simply the largest nontrivial *eigenvalue* of its Laplacian matrix L. We calculate the spectral gap $\sigma(G)$ by finding the largest nonzero eigenvalue of $\det[L - \lambda I] = 0$. Once again, using the graph of Fig. 2.3 and a computer to find roots of large polynomials, we get the following eigenvalues,

$\{-4, -3, -1, 0\}$. The largest nonzero eigenvalue is $\sigma = -1.0$. This spectral gap is obtained as follows:

$$L - \lambda I = \begin{pmatrix} -2 - \lambda & 1 & 0 & 1 \\ 1 & -3 - \lambda & 1 & 1 \\ 0 & 1 & -1 - \lambda & 0 \\ 1 & 1 & 0 & -2 - \lambda \end{pmatrix}$$

Setting $\det[L - \lambda I] = 0$, and expanding by column 3 using Laplace's formula for determinants, yields the polynomial $(\lambda^3 + 8\lambda^2 + 19\lambda + 12)\lambda = 0$, with roots $\{-4, -3, -1, 0\}$. Therefore, $\sigma = -1.0$.

Some authors define the Laplacian as $L(G) = D - A$, which reverses the sign on the elements of L. The definition used here is more consistent with the definition of an adjacency matrix, and will be more useful later when we consider the synchronization properties of a network. Hence, we use the definition that preserves the sign of the Boolean values produced by the adjacency matrix.

A *normalized Laplacian* matrix is used when it is important that all elements of L be less than one. The normalized version has 1s along its diagonal, and in place of Boolean values $(0,1)$, adjacency is indicated by

$$\left(0, \frac{-1}{\sqrt{(d_i d_j)}} \right)$$

where $(d_i d_j)$ is the product of node degree values. This version is a consequence of defining the Laplacian as $L = I - D^{-(1/2)} A D^{-(1/2)}$, where I is the identity matrix and D is the diagonal matrix containing the degree of G's nodes along its diagonal.

The Laplacian is also sometimes defined as $L = D^{-1} A - I$, as well. None of these alternative definitions yields a matrix containing rows and columns that sum to zero. Because the zero summation property will become useful when we study the synchronization properties of a network, it is more useful to define the Laplacian as $L = A - D$, or $L = D - A$.

2.5 TYPES OF GRAPHS

We have already investigated several elementary graph structures—node degree, average path length, connectedness, and centrality (radius and diameter). However, we want to say much more about graphs than these elementary metrics allow. For example, we want to classify graphs according to their structure, which ultimately is determined by mapping function f, and we want to study the impact of a graph's structure on emergence. This requires a number of additional measures of graph structure.

In the following text, a graph is characterized by its distribution of node degree, amount of concentration of clusters, and node centrality as determined by the distribution of node radii.

2.5.1 Barbell, Line, and Ring Graphs

Perhaps the simplest graph of all is the *barbell* (see Fig. 2.5a). It is a special case of a line or chain graph as shown in Fig. 2.5b. The mapping function of a *line graph* defines a linear sequence of nodes, each connected to a *successor* node. The first and last nodes in the sequence have degree 1, while all intermediate nodes have degree 2. The line graph mapping function maps $(n - 1)$ links onto node pairs, as follows:

$$f_{\text{line}} = [e_i : v_i \sim v_{i+1}]; \quad i = 1, 2, \ldots, n - 1$$

A *ring graph* has similar topology, but the ending node in the chain or sequence connects to the starting node. Therefore, n links connect all nodes to successor nodes— "wrapping around" at the ending node to connect to the starting node. All nodes have degree equal to 2. The ring graph mapping function is

$$f_{\text{ring}} = \left[e_i : v_i \sim v_{i(\text{mod } n)+1}\right]; \quad i = 1, 2, \ldots, n$$

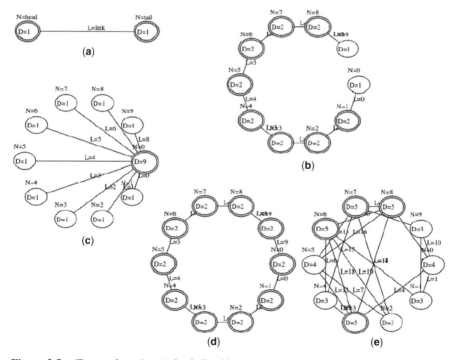

Figure 2.5 Types of graphs: (a) *barbell*, which has two nodes and one link; (b) *line*, which has n nodes and $(n-1)$ links connecting them in sequence; (c) *star*, which has n nodes, all connected to one node via n links; (d) *ring*, which is similar to a line, but the last node is connected to the first node in the line; (e) *random*, which has n nodes with m links—head and tail nodes are selected at random.

Note that i (mod n) + 1 wraps around from last to first node. For example, if $n = 10$, as in Fig. 2.5d, then $e_{10} : v_{10} \sim v_1$, because 10 (mod 10) + 1 = 0 + 1 = 1.

Barbell, line, and ring graphs are strongly connected because there exists a path from every node to every other node. However, only the ring graph has a circuit. Is it a Euler circuit? Yes, because every node has even degree. Clearly, there is no Euler circuit in a barbell or line graph, but does an Euler path exist in these "sequence graphs"?

The average path length of line and ring graphs are quite different, because of the wraparound feature of the ring graph mapping function. There are two paths (clockwise and counterclockwise) between every pair of nodes in a ring graph, but only one path in a line graph. Therefore, the average path length of a line graph is $O(n/3)$ while the ring graph is $O(n/4)$. To see why there is such a difference, consider the path matrices of a line and ring graph with $n = 6$:

$$P(\text{line}) = \begin{array}{c} \\ v_1 \\ v_2 \\ v_3 \\ v_4 \\ v_5 \\ v_6 \end{array} \begin{array}{cccccc} v_1 & v_2 & v_3 & v_4 & v_5 & v_6 \\ 0 & 1 & 2 & 3 & 4 & 5 \\ 1 & 0 & 1 & 2 & 3 & 4 \\ 2 & 1 & 0 & 1 & 2 & 3 \\ 3 & 2 & 1 & 0 & 1 & 2 \\ 4 & 3 & 2 & 1 & 0 & 1 \\ 5 & 4 & 3 & 2 & 1 & 0 \end{array} = \begin{pmatrix} 0 & 1 & 2 & 3 & 4 & 5 \\ 1 & 0 & 1 & 2 & 3 & 4 \\ 2 & 1 & 0 & 1 & 2 & 3 \\ 3 & 2 & 1 & 0 & 1 & 2 \\ 4 & 3 & 2 & 1 & 0 & 1 \\ 5 & 4 & 3 & 2 & 1 & 0 \end{pmatrix}$$

$$P(\text{ring}) = \begin{array}{c} \\ v_1 \\ v_2 \\ v_3 \\ v_4 \\ v_5 \\ v_6 \end{array} \begin{array}{cccccc} v_1 & v_2 & v_3 & v_4 & v_5 & v_6 \\ 0 & 1 & 2 & 3 & 2 & 1 \\ 1 & 0 & 1 & 2 & 3 & 2 \\ 2 & 1 & 0 & 1 & 2 & 3 \\ 3 & 2 & 1 & 0 & 1 & 2 \\ 2 & 3 & 2 & 1 & 0 & 1 \\ 1 & 2 & 3 & 2 & 1 & 0 \end{array} = \begin{pmatrix} 0 & 1 & 2 & 3 & 2 & 1 \\ 1 & 0 & 1 & 2 & 3 & 2 \\ 2 & 1 & 0 & 1 & 2 & 3 \\ 3 & 2 & 1 & 0 & 1 & 2 \\ 2 & 3 & 2 & 1 & 0 & 1 \\ 1 & 2 & 3 & 2 & 1 & 0 \end{pmatrix}$$

We compute the average path length by summing the nonzero elements of the path matrix and dividing by the number of nonzero elements. If row sums are computed, first, their pattern will suggest a result that can be applied to the general case. For example, the sum of all nonzero elements of the line graph matrix equals 70, and the sum of all nonzero elements of the ring graph equals 54. In each case, the number of nonzero elements is $n(n - 1) = 6(5) = 30$, so the average path lengths are

$$\text{avg\_path\_length(line)} = \frac{70}{30} = 2.33$$

$$\text{avg\_path\_length(ring)} = \frac{54}{30} = 1.8$$

What is the average path length for a line and ring graph of n nodes? The following strategy is used to derive the answer:

1. Analyze the path matrix for two cases: even and odd n.
2. Obtain a formula for summing all nonzero elements of the path matrix. Call this sum T. In the case of a line graph, T is the sum of off-diagonal elements. In the case of the ring network, T is the sum of the rows of the path matrix.
3. Generalize the formula for T, and note that the number of nonzero elements of the symmetric path matrix is equal to $n(n-1)$.
4. Average path length is $T/(n(n-1))$.
5. This strategy produces

$$\text{avg\_path\_length(line)} \sim O\left(\frac{n}{3}\right)$$

$$\text{avg\_path\_length(ring)} \sim O\left(\frac{n}{4}\right)$$

According to this strategy, the average path length of each type of graph is computed by summing all nonzero elements and then dividing by $n(n-1)$, which equals the number of nonzero elements. [The n diagonal elements are zero; thus the remaining $n(n-1)$ are nonzero.] Therefore, we must find a general formula for summing all nonzero elements, and divide by $n(n-1)$ to obtain the average path length.

Consider the line graph, first. From the path matrix for $n = 6$, notice how many off-diagonal elements equal 1 and how many equal 2, 3, 4, and 5. The matrix is diagonal, so there are $2(n-1)$ elements equal to 1, $2(n-2)$ elements equal to 2, $2(n-3)$ equal to 3, $2(n-4)$ equal to 4, and $2(1)$ elements equal to 5. In general, there are $2(n-i)$ elements equal to i, for i from 1 to $(n-1)$, so we obtain the total T by summing $2i(n-i)$ for i from 1 to $(n-1)$:

$$\text{Matrix total} = T = 2\sum_{i=1}^{n-1}\{i(n-i)\} = 2\left[n\sum_{i=1}^{n-1}i - \sum_{i=1}^{n-1}i^2\right]$$

$$\text{Given } \sum_{i=1}^{n-1}i = \frac{n(n-1)}{2} \quad \text{and} \quad \sum_{i=1}^{n-1}i^2 = \frac{(n(n-1)(2n-1))}{6}$$

$$T = n^2(n-1) - \frac{n(n-1)(2n-1)}{3} = n(n-1)\left[\frac{n-(2n-1)}{3}\right]$$

$$= \frac{n(n-1)[n+1]}{3}$$

$$\text{avg\_path\_length} = \frac{T}{(n(n-1))} = \frac{(n+1)}{3} \quad \text{or} \quad O\left(\frac{n}{3}\right); \; n \gg 1 \text{ [Line]}$$

Now we turn attention to the ring graph. Matrix P(ring) is different from P(line) because the elements of each row of P(ring) run from 1 to $(n/2)$, and back down to 1. All rows sum to the same total because they contain the same identical runup and rundown series. Furthermore, the runup maximum value is $(n/2)$ when n is even, and $(n-1)/2$ when n is odd. For example, when $n=6$, row 1 runs up, 1,2,3, then down, 2,1. Row 2 does the same: 1,2,3,2,1. Row 3 does the same: 1,2,3,2,1,.... This means that every row total is the same: 9. Similarly, for $n=7$, every row is the same: 1,2,3,3,2,1. But notice the symmetry of the up–down sequence for odd n. Three appears twice, so the row total is 12, or $2\sum_{i=1}^{3} i = 2(4(3)/2) = 12$. In general

$$\text{row\_total} = 2\sum_{i=1}^{(n/2)-1} i + \left(\frac{n}{2}\right); \text{even } n$$

$$= 2\sum_{i=1}^{(n-1)/2} i; \text{odd } n$$

There are n rows, so $T = n(\text{row\_total})$. But the average path length is $T/(n(n-1))$, so

$$\text{avg\_path\_length} = \frac{(n(\text{row\_total}))}{(n(n-1))} = \frac{\text{row\_total}}{(n-1)}$$

$$= \frac{(n/2)^2}{(n-1)} = \frac{n^2}{(4(n-1))}; \text{even } n$$

$$= \frac{(n+1)}{4}; \text{odd } n$$

Assuming $n \gg 1$, so that $n/(n-1) \sim 1$, the average path length of a ring is

$$\text{avg\_path\_length} \sim O\left(\frac{n}{4}\right); n \gg 1 \text{ [Ring]}$$

In summary, the average path length of a line graph is approximately one-third the size of the line graph, and the average path length of a ring network is approximately one-fourth the size of the ring graph n.

2.5.2 Structured versus Random Graphs

The adjacency and Laplacian matrices for the ring graph of Fig. 2.5d are almost tridiagonal, as shown below. Most elements in A and L are zero, because the ring graph is *sparse*, meaning it has a relatively small number of links compared to the maximum number possible. However, two off-diagonals contain a 1, corresponding to the chain of links connecting successor nodes. The tridiagonal characterization is not precisely correct because of the 1 in the upper right and lower left corners. These are the "wraparound" links:

$$A = \begin{pmatrix}
0 & 1 & 0 & 0 & 0 & 0 & 0 & 0 & 0 & 1 \\
1 & 0 & 1 & 0 & 0 & 0 & 0 & 0 & 0 & 0 \\
0 & 1 & 0 & 1 & 0 & 0 & 0 & 0 & 0 & 0 \\
0 & 0 & 1 & 0 & 1 & 0 & 0 & 0 & 0 & 0 \\
0 & 0 & 0 & 1 & 0 & 1 & 0 & 0 & 0 & 0 \\
0 & 0 & 0 & 0 & 1 & 0 & 1 & 0 & 0 & 0 \\
0 & 0 & 0 & 0 & 0 & 1 & 0 & 1 & 0 & 0 \\
0 & 0 & 0 & 0 & 0 & 0 & 1 & 0 & 1 & 0 \\
0 & 0 & 0 & 0 & 0 & 0 & 0 & 1 & 0 & 1 \\
1 & 0 & 0 & 0 & 0 & 0 & 0 & 0 & 1 & 0
\end{pmatrix}$$

$$L = \begin{pmatrix}
-2 & 1 & 0 & 0 & 0 & 0 & 0 & 0 & 0 & 1 \\
1 & -2 & 1 & 0 & 0 & 0 & 0 & 0 & 0 & 0 \\
0 & 1 & -2 & 1 & 0 & 0 & 0 & 0 & 0 & 0 \\
0 & 0 & 1 & -2 & 1 & 0 & 0 & 0 & 0 & 0 \\
0 & 0 & 0 & 1 & -2 & 1 & 0 & 0 & 0 & 0 \\
0 & 0 & 0 & 0 & 1 & -2 & 1 & 0 & 0 & 0 \\
0 & 0 & 0 & 0 & 0 & 1 & -2 & 1 & 0 & 0 \\
0 & 0 & 0 & 0 & 0 & 0 & 1 & -2 & 1 & 0 \\
0 & 0 & 0 & 0 & 0 & 0 & 0 & 1 & -2 & 1 \\
1 & 0 & 0 & 0 & 0 & 0 & 0 & 0 & 1 & -2
\end{pmatrix}$$

The Laplacian matrix is similar to the adjacency matrix, with the addition of (-2) to every element of its diagonal. Thus, all nodes in a ring network have degree equal to 2. The Laplacian contains adjacency information as well as degree information. In addition, its rows and columns sum to zero. This will become an important feature in later chapters when we analyze the *spectral properties* of a network.

The graph of Fig. 2.5e is random because links are randomly placed between node pairs. A random graph is constructed by randomly selecting a tail, then randomly selecting a head node, and then connecting them with a link. The mapping function corresponding to Fig. 2.5e uses random numbers r_t and r_h to select nodes. A *random number r* is obtained from a uniform distribution in $[0,1)$ by sampling—say, by using a random-number generator in a computer. Therefore, scaling r by n yields a node number from 0 to $n - 1$, and adding 1 shifts the node number to the interval $[1,n]$:

$$f_{random} = [e_i : v_{1+r_t n} \sim v_{1+r_h n}]; \quad i = 1,2,\ldots,m, \text{ where } m = \text{number of links}$$

The adjacency and Laplacian matrices of a random graph will contain randomly placed 1s and 0s, simply because there is no pattern. If a graph's mapping function establishes some kind of pattern—visually or in the adjacency matrix—we say that it is *structured* or *regular*. If no discernable pattern appears, we say that the graph is *unstructured* or *random*. So, at one extreme is the class of structured or *regular graphs*, and at the other extreme is the class of unstructured or *random graphs*. In the next section, we show that there are several other classes of graphs that lie somewhere in between regular and random graphs.

2.5.3   *k*-Regular Graphs

The ring graph of Fig. 2.5d is an example of a very simple regular graph. In fact, it is a 1-regular graph because each node has one successor node. We constructed the ring graph by linking each node to its immediate successor, and since every node does this, the ring "wraps around" such that every node's predecessor also connects to it.

Figure 2.6 shows additional examples of *k*-regular graphs, for $k = 2$, 3, and $(n - 1)$. In Fig. 2.6b, each node links to two successors—successor $(i + 1)$ and successor $(i + 2)$. Therefore, each node has degree $2k = 4$. Furthermore, the average path length of a *k*-regular graph is reduced by a factor of *k*, because the graph is dissected into *k* segments reachable as follows:

1. Initially follow the long-distance links that skip over *k* nodes at a time until reaching the "neighborhood" of the desired ending node,
2. Next, follow the $(k - 1)$, $(k - 2)$, ... medium-length links that narrow down the neighborhood.
3. Finally, follow single-hop links to the ending node.

For example, Fig. 2.6d shows a 3-regular graph with $n = 10$ nodes. According to the formula developed above, the average path length of a ring (1-regular) graph is $\frac{10}{4} = 2.5$. A 3-regular graph reduces path lengths by a factor of roughly $(3-1) = 2$. Therefore, the average path length within this 3-regular graph is approximately $(2.5/2) = 1.25$. (The exact answer is $\frac{120}{90} = 1.33$.) This observation will become useful in the next chapter when we examine the nature of self-organizing networks. But suffice it to say, increasing *k* decreases the average path length.

Figure 2.6c is a complete graph because every node connects to every other node. A *complete graph* is an example of a dense graph because it contains the maximum number of links possible without loops or duplicates.

A complete graph has $m = n((n-1)/2)$ links because the first node connects to $(n - 1)$ other nodes, the second connects to $(n - 2)$ other nodes, and so on until the last node connects to one remaining node. Therefore, the total number of links is equal to the sum of $(n - 1)$ integers:

$$m = (n - 1) + (n - 2) + \cdots + 1 = \sum_{i=1}^{(n-1)} i = n\frac{(n - 1)}{2}$$

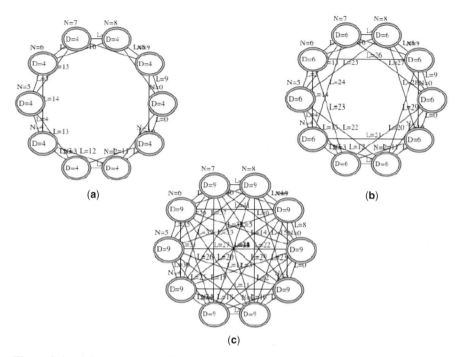

Figure 2.6 *k*-Regular graphs: (a) 2-regular graph nodes connect to two sequential successors; (b) 3-regular graph nodes connect to three sequential successors; (c) a complete graph
links every node to every other node.

k-Regular graphs in general contain *kn* links, for $k = 1, 2, \ldots, (n/2)$, if *n* is even, and
$(n-1)/2$, if *n* is odd. A *k*-regular graph contains *k* rings, each with *n* links, but different successor nodes. The mapping function links successor $(i + 1)$ for $k = 1$; $(i + 2)$
for $k = 2$, and so forth, but there are still *n* links up to the limit of a complete graph. In
summary, a *k*-regular graph contains

$$m = \text{minimum}\left(kn, \; n\frac{(n-1)}{2}\right)$$

links, and nodes of degree 2*k*.

2.5.4 Graph Density

k-Regular graphs provide graph theorists with fodder for more ambitious construc-
tions because they bridge the gap between sparse and dense graphs. A *k*-regular
graph is sparse for small *k* and dense for large *k*. Let *graph density* be approximated
by the ratio of number of links in graph *G* to the number of links in a complete graph:

$$\text{Density}(G) = \frac{\#\text{ links}}{\left(n\dfrac{(n-1)}{2}\right)} = \frac{2m}{(n(n-1))}$$

Given $m = kn$ for a k-regular graph, the density of a k-regular graph ranges from small to large according to

$$\text{Density}(k\text{-regular}) = \frac{2kn}{(n(n-1))} = \frac{(2k)}{(n-1)} \quad \text{for} \quad k = 1, 2, \ldots, \frac{n}{2}(\text{even})$$

According to this metric, k-regular graph density is a linear function of k. In a general graph G, density increases sublinearly with increments in m, the number of links. The potential number of links grows according to $(n(n-1))/2$, which means that graph size n increases the potential number of links much faster than do actual links. This nonlinear effect will have significant implications in later chapters because it allows sparse graphs to exhibit amazing properties such as self-organization, self-synchronization, and other forms of emergence, with a relatively small number of links. It is also the root cause of the small-world effect studied in great detail in Chapter 5.

2.6 TOPOLOGICAL STRUCTURE

In this section, we explore various properties of graphs and metrics for quantifying these properties. Specifically, we define the structure of a graph in terms of its degree sequence distribution and *entropy*. Intuitively, a graph's structure is tied to its topology. If mapping function f uniformly maps links to nodes, the graph is structured. If the mapping is random, or lacks a pattern, the graph is random. But this is an intuitive definition. We want to find a more formal definition of topology and randomness in arbitrary graphs. Degree sequence distribution provides a mechanism for classifying graphs according to their topology, and entropy provides a measure of randomness.

2.6.1 Degree Sequence

Let $g = [d_1, d_2, \ldots, d_n]$ define a *degree sequence* containing the degree values of all n nodes in G. The order of elements in g is not important, but it will be convenient to enumerate them as follows. Element 1 corresponds to the degree of node 1; element 2, to the degree of node 2; and so on. For example, the degree sequence of Fig. 2.4a is $g = [5,3,3,3]$.

The elements of g need not be unique, nor must they be in any certain order. Indeed, the information contained within g does not guarantee that G can be uniquely reconstructed from g. But if it can, we say that g is *graphical*. One *graphical representation* of $g = [5,3,3,3]$ is shown in Fig. 2.4a, but the reader can construct several graphs with $n = 4$ nodes and degree sequence $g = [5,3,3,3]$. In general, g is a lossy compression of the information contained in G, and may be graphical or not.

We can further compress the structural information contained in G by constructing the *degree sequence distribution* $g' = [h_1, h_2, \ldots, h_{\text{max\_d}}]$ as follows:

h_1 = fraction of nodes with degree 1

h_2 = fraction of nodes with degree 2

$\vdots$

$h_{\text{max\_d}}$ = fraction of nodes with max_d = maximum degree (hub) of G

For example, g contains zero nodes with degree 1, zero with degree 2, three with degree 3, zero with degree 4, and one with degree max_d = 5. Therefore, the degree sequence distribution for Fig. 2.4a is

$$g' = \left[0, 0, \frac{3}{4}, 0, \frac{1}{4}\right] = [0, 0, 0.75, 0.25]$$

The elements of g' sum to 1.0 much like a probability density function. In fact, in some applications, it may be beneficial to express the elements of g' as probabilities, suggesting that the probability of a new link connecting to node u is equal to the fraction of nodes with degree $d(u)$. This idea leads to a graph's *degree sequence histogram* as shown in Fig. 2.6.

2.6.2   Graph Entropy

The *entropy* of graph G, that is, $I(G)$, is a measure of graph structure—or lack of it. Entropy is a term borrowed from information theory. It is a measure of the "amount of information" or "surprise" communicated by a message. The basic unit of information is the *bit*, so entropy is the number of bits of "randomness" in a graph. The higher the entropy, the more random is the graph.

More formally, the "randomness" in graph G is the entropy of its degree sequence distribution g'. The unit of measurement of entropy is *bits*, so let $I(G)$ be the expected number of bits in g', as follows:

$$I(G) = -\sum_{i=1}^{\text{max\_d}} h_i \left(\log_2 (h_i)\right), \quad \text{where} \quad g' = \left[h_1, h_2, \ldots, h_{\text{max\_d}}\right]$$

What does this equation mean? Consider a simple coin-tossing experiment where the probability of a HEAD, $P_{\text{head}} = \frac{1}{2}$, and TAIL, $P_{\text{tail}} = \frac{1}{2}$. The result of each coin toss contains one bit of information because

$$I(\text{FAIR COIN}) = -\left((P_{\text{head}})(\log_2 (P_{\text{head}})) + (P_{\text{tail}})(\log_2 (P_{\text{tail}}))\right)$$

$$= \left(-\left(\frac{1}{2}\right)\left(\log_2\left(\frac{1}{2}\right)\right) - \left(\frac{1}{2}\right)\left(\log_2\left(\frac{1}{2}\right)\right)\right) = 1.0$$

What if the coin is unfair? Suppose that the coin is biased toward HEAD, for example, $P_{\text{head}} = \frac{3}{4}$ and $P_{\text{tail}} = \frac{1}{4}$. In this case, $I(\text{BIASED COIN}) = 0.811$. Now, each toss contains a fraction of a bit of information. The outcome of each toss is less unexpected because a HEAD is 3 times more likely to occur than a TAIL. As the coin toss becomes more biased, the outcome is more certain and so the coin toss has less entropy. A biased coin has less entropy than a fair coin because a fair coin is "more random." In fact, the maximum possible value of entropy in this simple coin-tossing experiment is 1 bit, and the minimum possible entropy is zero. Therefore, maximum randomness of a coin toss occurs when entropy is 1.0, and minimum entropy occurs when the coin toss is so biased, that the coin always turns up HEADs (or TAILs if it is biased toward TAILs).

Entropy is a measure of randomness. The higher the entropy of a graph, the more random it is. As entropy decreases to zero, the corresponding graph's randomness also declines to zero. If we apply the entropy calculation to a graph's degree sequence, we get a measure of the graph's randomness.

For example, consider two graphs with degree sequence given by

$$G_1 : g_1' = \left[0, \frac{1}{4}, \frac{1}{8}, \frac{1}{2}, \frac{1}{8}\right]$$

$$G_2 : g_2' = \left[0, \frac{1}{4}, \frac{1}{4}, \frac{1}{4}, \frac{1}{4}\right]$$

$$I(G_1) = -\left(0.25\left(\log_2\left(\frac{1}{4}\right)\right) + 0.125\left(\log_2\left(\frac{1}{8}\right)\right)\right.$$

$$\left. + 0.5\left(\log_2\left(\frac{1}{2}\right)\right) + 0.125\left(\log_2\left(\frac{1}{8}\right)\right)\right)$$

$$= -(0.25(-2) + 0.125(-3) + 0.5(-1) + 0.125(-3))$$

$$= \frac{(4 + 3 + 4 + 3)}{8} = \frac{14}{8}$$

$$= 1.75 \text{ bits}$$

$$I(G_2) = -3(0.25(-2)) = \frac{6}{4} = 1.50 \text{ bits}$$

In this example, G_1 is more random than G_2 because 1.75 bits is greater than 1.50 bits. Another way to think of the difference between these two graphs is that there is more *uncertainty* in the degree distribution sequence of G_1 than G_2 because the degree sequence of G_1 contains greater variability. Thus, the structure of G_1 is more uncertain.

As graph randomness decreases, so does its entropy $I(G)$. Therefore, we would expect regular graphs to contain zero or very little entropy. For example, if $n = 100$, $m = 200$, the entropy of a complete or $(n - 1)$-regular graph is zero (no randomness); star graph is 0.0807 (all except the hub node has degree 1); line graph is 0.1414 (degrees of starting and end nodes differ from those of all other nodes); and random graph is 2.9 bits (the distribution of links is "random"). Therefore, the amount of randomness of these examples increases from 0 for a k-regular graph, to 2.9 bits for a random graph. A line graph is almost twice as random as a star graph, simply because the degree variation among nodes in a line graph is greater than the variation in a star graph.

Degree sequence distribution tells us something about the "shape" of a graph, and entropy tells us something about the regularity—or lack of it—in the "shape" of a graph. The more regular the shape of a graph, the less randomness and hence the less entropy there is in a graph. It will become obvious as you read this book that there is a sliding scale between regularity and entropy. At one extreme, regular graphs have very little entropy, and at the other extreme, random graphs have very little regularity.

2.6.3 Scale-Free Topology

Figure 2.7a shows a histogram of a graph constructed by randomly selecting node pairs. The general shape of this histogram approximates a *Poisson distribution* because random selection of node pairs is a *Poisson process*—the probability of obtaining exactly k successes in m trials is given by the binomial distribution:

$$B(k,m) = C\binom{m}{k} p^k (1 - p)^{m-k}$$

$B(k,m)$ is approximated by the Poisson distribution by replacing p with (λ/m), in $B(k,m)$, and letting m grow without bound:

$$H(k) = \lambda^k \frac{\exp(-\lambda)}{k!}$$

where $\lambda = $ mean node degree; $k = $ node degree.

Distribution $H(k)$ is shown in Fig. 2.7a, where $k = $ node degree (horizontal axis; abscissa) and $H(k)$ is the probability that a node will have degree k (vertical axis; ordinate). In other words, $H(k)$ is the fraction of nodes that have degree k. In this formula, note that $k!$ is the factorial function, $k(k-1)(k-2), \ldots, (1)$. This formula is discussed in more detail in Chapter 4.

Figure 2.7b shows a histogram of a graph whose degree distribution approximates a *power law*, $H(k) = k^{-q}$, for some power $q > 1$. Such graphs are called *scale-free* because the power-law distribution has no scale parameter; that is, the variance of a power-law is infinite, versus the finite variance of most other distributions such as the Gaussian or normal distribution. Power laws are also sometimes called "fat tailed" because they do not decline as k increases as fast as an exponential or normal distribution.

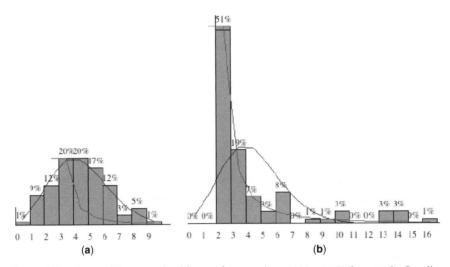

Figure 2.7   Degree histogram for (a) a random graph and (b) a scale-free graph. One line graph shows a Poisson distribution, and the other line graph shows a power-law fit to the histogram data.

It is rather straightforward to interpret the meaning of Fig. 2.7a. Random graphs more or less distribute links uniformly across n nodes. But what is the interpretation of Fig. 2.7b? Quite simply, scale-free graphs are lopsided—a vast number of nodes have only one or two links, while a rare few nodes have perhaps hundreds of links. In fact, the most highly connected node is the graph's *hub*. It has the highest degree.

The entropy of a scale-free graph is generally lower than the entropy of a random graph because scale-free networks contain some structure. For example, for networks with $n = 100$, $m = 200$, a scale-free network has 2.3 bits of entropy and a random network has approximately 2.9 bits. These estimates were obtained from program *Network.jar* by averaging *Network.jar's* entropy calculation over five samples.

Scale-free networks are closer to the random end of the "graph structure" spectrum than to the structured extreme. At one end is the class of structured k-regular graphs (where entropy equals zero), and the other end is the class of random networks that have no discernable structure or topology. In between is the class of scale-free networks, which have some structure, because the degree sequence distribution obeys a *power law*.

A small-world network will be the opposite—a slightly structured and partially random network that is closer to the structured end of the spectrum. (See Table 2.3 for comparisons.)

2.6.4 Small-World Topology

A *small-world graph*, G(small world), is a graph with relatively small average path length, and a relatively *high cluster coefficient*, $CC(G)$. Generally, the average path length of a small world grows proportional to $O(\log(n)/\log(\lambda))$ and the cluster coefficient tends to be greater than 50%. What is a cluster, and how do we compute its coefficient?

Suppose that we compare the number of links connecting a group of k adjacent nodes to the maximum possible number, which is given by a complete subgraph with $(k(k-1))/2$ links. Each subgraph formed around a node in this k-node neighborhood forms a triangular subgraph if it is complete, and does not form a triangular subgraph if one or more links is (are) missing. The amount of clustering depends on the number of triangles found among these neighbors. Let the neighbors of node u be the nodes directly connected to u. There are degree(u) such neighbors, which means that there are potentially (degree(u) [degree(u) -1])/2 links among these neighbors. Suppose that the neighbors share c links; then the cluster coefficient of node u, $Cc(u)$, is

$$Cc(u) = \frac{2c}{\text{degree}(u)(\text{degree}(u)-1)}$$

A more visual way to think of cluster coefficient is the following. A node u with degree(u) neighbors may be part of c triangular subgraphs, each containing node u as one of the triangle's three nodes. Cluster coefficient is the ratio of the actual number of triangular subgraphs c to the maximum possible number.

Figure 2.8 illustrates this calculation for three clusters of increasingly greater coefficients. In all examples, degree(v_1) $= 4$, so the denominator is 12. The cluster coefficient of node v_1 in the star graph of Fig. 2.8a is zero because none of its neighbors are linked to one another; that is, v_1 is not part of a triangular subgraph.

Now look at the topology surrounding node v_1 in Fig. 2.8b. Node v_1 in the combination star–ring graph of Fig. 2.8b has cluster coefficient equal to

$$Cc(v_1) = \frac{2(4)}{12} = \frac{8}{12} = \frac{2}{3}$$

because v_1 has four neighbors with four shared links among them. There are also four triangular subgraphs containing node v_1.

Similarly, the coefficient $Cc(v_1)$ in Fig. 2.8c is $(2(6))/12 = 1.0$ because there are six links among the four neighbors of node v_1. There are also six triangular subgraphs containing node v_1. A cluster is a subgraph containing one or more triangular subgraphs.

Every node in the graphs of Fig. 2.8 has a cluster coefficient associated with it. For example, the cluster coefficient of node v_2 in the star graph of Fig. 2.8b is $(2(2))/(3(2)) = \frac{1}{3}$, because node degree($v_2$) $= 3$, and there are 2 links among its neighbors. All nodes of Fig. 2.8c have cluster coefficients equal to 1.0 because Fig. 2.8c is a complete graph.

The cluster coefficient of an entire graph G is the average over all node coefficients:

$$CC(G) = \sum_{i=1}^{n} \frac{Cc(v_i)}{n}$$

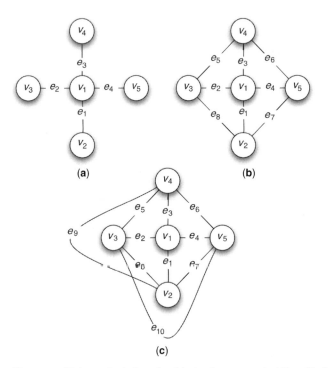

Figure 2.8 Cluster coefficient calculations for (a) simple star graph, $(C_v = 0)$; (b) star–ring graph $(C_v = \frac{2}{3})$; (c) complete graph $(C_v = 1.0)$.

For example, all the nodes in the combination star and ring graph of Fig. 2.8b have cluster coefficient of $\frac{2}{3}$, so the cluster coefficient of the entire graph is

$$CC(G(\text{star} + \text{ring})) = \frac{\left(5\left(\frac{2}{3}\right)\right)}{5} = \frac{2}{3}, \text{ or } 0.67$$

The class of small-world graphs is characterized by an unexpectedly large cluster coefficient when compared to the class of random graphs, but it also has some properties in common with the class of random graphs. For example, small-world and random graphs have similar degree distributions and diameters.

Table 2.2 lists some common small-world graphs along with an equivalent random graph. Table 2.3 compares random, scale-free, small-world, and 2-regular graph properties. The cluster coefficient of a small world can be several orders of magnitude larger that that of an equivalent random graph of the same size and with an equivalent number of links.

Table 2.2 contains many examples that will be explored in detail in subsequent chapters. The World Wide Web (WWW) graph was constructed by representing documents as nodes and references to the documents as links. The Internet graph

TABLE 2.2 Some Common Examples of Small-World Networks

Graph	Size, n	Small-World Cluster Coefficient	Random Cluster Coefficient
World Wide Web	153,127	0.11	0.00023
Internet	6,209	0.30	0.00100
Actors in same movie	225,226	0.79	0.00027
Coauthor scientific papers	52,909	0.43	0.00018
Western US power grid	4,941	0.08	0.00200
C. elegans neural network	282	0.28	0.05000
Foodweb (ecological chain)	134	0.22	0.06000

was constructed by representing autonomous systems (Internet service providers) as nodes, and their network connections as links. Similarly, Hollywood movie actors are represented as nodes, and movies in which they coacted are represented by links. Coauthors of published scientific papers are represented by nodes, and links indicate that they coauthored a paper. The power plants, substations, and distribution network of the western United states' power grid are modeled as nodes and the powerlines, as links. The neurons are nodes, and their connections are links, in the C. elegans neural network. Finally, the food network established by a certain food chain is modeled by prey (nodes) and predators (links).

Program *Network.jar*, which accompanies this book, can be used to perform the following experiment. Let $n = 100$ and $m = 200$. Use *Network.jar* (or Network.html) to generate a 2-regular, scale-free, small-world, and random graph. Then record the properties of each as shown in Table 2.3. What can we say, in general, about these graphs?

Structures of the graphs summarized in Table 2.3 range from random (left) to the purely structured 2-regular graph (right). We can deduce this from the types of distributions, relative values of cluster coefficient, and declining entropy as structure

TABLE 2.3 Comparison of Some Properties of Graphs ($n = 100$, $m = 200$), and $p = 5\%$ for the Small-World Graph

Property	Random	Scale-Free	Small-World	2-Regular
Hub degree	10	21	10	4
Average degree	4.0	3.94	4.0	4
Distribution	Poisson	Power	Poisson-like	Delta(4)
Average path length	3.38	3.08	4.0	12.88
Diameter	7	5	9	25
Cluster coefficient	0.045	0.156	0.544	0.500
Entropy	2.9	2.3	0.9	0.0

increases. For example, the degree sequence distribution of the "most random" graph is Poisson, but as the level of randomness declines (moving from left to right in the table), distributions become "less Poisson-like." As the level of randomness declines, the entropy of each class of graph declines. With one exception (small-world), the more random a graph, the lower its cluster coefficient.

Note the decreasing value of entropy—scale-free graphs have less entropy than random graphs, but more than small-world or 2-regular graphs. In other words, a scale-free graph is more random than structured. Conversely, a small-world graph is more structured than random, because its entropy is lower than that in all other classes, except the 2-regular class. Table 2.3 supports the conjecture that scale-free and random graphs are "more random" than small-world and regular graphs. We explore this conjecture in later chapters.

The class of random graphs has the smallest cluster coefficient, suggesting little structure. The small-world graph has the largest cluster coefficient even though its degree sequence distribution is very similar to that of a random graph. Unusually high clustering is a distinguishing feature of a small-world graph.

A scale-free graph has many nodes with very low degree, and one node with very high degree. Hence, its degree distribution is skewed to the left—toward small degree values. Because so many nodes are connected to the graph's hub node, the scale-free graph also exhibits a small graph diameter—similar to a random graph. It is nearly one-half the diameter of the small-world graph, and 50% smaller than the diameter of a random graph. This is a consequence of the high concentration of links attached to the hub. The unexpectedly large hub degree is a distinguishing property of scale-free graphs.

The "most structured" graph of all—the 2-regular graph—has a very high average path length and a high cluster coefficient. This is intuitive because a k-regular graph has many short links. Therefore, it takes many hops to traverse the far reaches of the graph. The short links also form neighborhoods with relatively high cluster coefficients.

The entropy of each class of graph increases from 0 bits to 2.9 bits in Table 2.3. This suggests a high amount of uncertainty in the topology of random graphs, and a high amount of certainty in 2-regular graphs. Scale-free graphs align more with random graphs than with small worlds, and small worlds align more with regular graphs. A structure hierarchy exists among these classes: regular, small-world, scale-free, and random. Regular and small-world graphs tend to be structured with the class of small-world graphs containing some randomness. Scale-free and random graphs tend to be unstructured with the class of scale-free graphs containing some structure.

The results for small-world graphs shown in Table 2.3 are biased toward regular structure. Specifically, the small-world graph has been tuned such that only 5% of its links are random, while 95% are regular. This is indicated by the "$p = 5\%$" setting in Table 2.3. In the next chapter, we show how to tune a small-world graph by switching a fraction of its links from regular to random connections, thus randomizing a fraction of the mapping.

Tuning leads to a small world that is partially structured and partially random. Tuning also adjusts the entropy in the small-world class of graphs—from zero to 100% that of a random graph. When the tunable parameter is set to zero random links, the small-world graph has zero entropy, and when set to 100% random links, the small-world graph has entropy identical to that of a random graph. Therefore, a small-world graph can be tuned to fall anywhere between random and 2-regular structure in the structure hierarchy. Table 2.3 shows only one possibility.

2.7 GRAPHS IN SOFTWARE

The best way to study graphs is to watch them in action. Fortunately, we have an abundance of low-cost, fast computers that can process large structures such as graphs with alarming ease. Indeed, the computer programs provided with this book are examples of the value of network processing software. We can not only verify the theoretical results described in this book but also perform a number of mathematical experiments to learn more. Software makes it possible to acquire empirical as well as theoretical experience with the science of networks.

The Java programming language is used to construct software modules that can be incorporated in your own software, or simply used to understand how the programs described here work. Java was selected because it works on nearly any computer, and it is similar to other common programming languages such as C++. It is also easy to read and understand; hence is somewhat self-documenting.

2.7.1 Java Nodes and Links

Graphs can be represented inside of a computer in a number of ways. For example, we could use matrix algebra and store the nodes and links of G in a two-dimensional array (2D). We could use linked list data structures—nodes are data types and links are pointers. Perhaps the easiest representation is the class construct, and simple array structure. This approach has advantages and disadvantages. The major advantage is simplicity and compatibility with relational database structure. The disadvantage is that we sacrifice processing effort for simplicity. The simple vector approach used here requires large amounts of computation—sometimes to do simple operations—but is used because of its simplicity and ease of comprehension.

Let nodes and links be represented by computer-serializable classes. A *class*, in Java, is an abstraction that defines the storage area and processing methods allowed on the storage. Classes are instantiated into *objects*—actual storage in the memory of the computer. A serializable class defines objects that can be saved to disk as a single object. In Java, the object is automatically serialized so that input and output to and from disk is done with a single read/write command.

The Link class defines graph links with a name, tail, head, value, color, and selection flag to indicate when a user has selected the link by clicking on it with a mouse. The tail and head portions of a Link are the node pairs that the Link connects.

Therefore, a `Link` maps onto a node pair just as the definition $G = (N, L, f)$ prescribes. In Java, the `Link` class implements links and their properties:

```
class Link implements java.io.Serializable {
    public String name = "";              //Name of link
    public int tail;                      //From Node #
    public int head;                      //To Node #
    public double value = 0;              //Value of link
    public Color c;                       //Link Color
    public boolean selected = false;      //Mouse down selection
}//Link
```

A graph node is an instance of class `Node`, which is also serializable, so it can be stored on disk. This class contains static variables that never change from one instance to the other. For example, the screen display size is the same for all nodes. In addition, every node has its own name, degree, color, value, radius, and screen coordinates (x, y). In addition, the color code, `int_color`, is necessary because Java does not serialize `Color`. Therefore, `int_color` is an integer coding of type `Color`.

```
class Node implements java.io.Serializable {
    //Static values
    public static int xstep = 40;      //Minimum size of display node
    public static int ystep = 30;      //Dynamic variables
    public String name = "";           //Name of node
    public int degree = 0;             //Degree of node
    public int out_degree = 0;         //Out Degree = # directed
                                         links out
    public int in_degree = 0;          //In Degree = # directed links
                                         in to node
    public Color color = Color.white;  //Red = infected or source;
                                         green = sink
    public int int_color = 0;          //Hack to defeat Java
                                         serializer limitation
    public int x=0;                    //Location on screen
    public int y=0;
    public double next_state = 0;      //Next State used to Sync
    public double value;               //Working value
    public double cluster = 0;         //Cluster coefficient
    public int level = 0;              //Used to find center
    public int radius = 0;             //radius of a node
    public boolean visited = false;    //Used for spanning tree
                                         (finding center)
    public boolean center = false;     //True if node is a center
    public boolean outer = false;      //True if node is outer
    public boolean selected = false;   //For mouse down events
    public int timer = 0;              //Infection timer
}//Node
```

2.7.2 Java Networks

`Node` and `Link` are instantiated each time a node or link is created. We could link these objects together to form the graph, but it is much easier to keep the graph structure simple and let a computer do the work. Therefore, we use a simple array structure to hold all links and another simple array structure to hold all nodes. In addition, the computer needs to remember how many nodes and links there are at any point in time. Thus, a third class is used to define the graph *G*. Class theNetwork forms the graph structure and includes a number of other variables needed during computation.

```java
class theNetwork implements java.io.Serializable {   //Class NW_
    public static int maxNodes = 4096;         //Limit of #nodes
    public static int maxLinks = 16384;        //Limit # Links
    public static Node pick = new Node();      //For mouse down event
    public static int pick_index = -1;         //Index of selected node
    public static int prior_selected = -1;     //For adding link between
                                                 selected nodes
    public static int t_max = 5000;            //Max simulation time
    public static int t = 0;                   //Simulated clock
    //Input Network parameters - can be changed by Preferences
    public static int nInputNodes = 10;        //Number of input nodes
    public static int nInputLinks = 20;        //Number input Links
    public static int nConnectionProbability = 100; //Probability of
                                                 rewiring link
    public static double DefaultValue = 1;     //Default node and link
                                                 value
    public static int SleepTime = 10;          //speed of display thread
    public static double PathLength = 0;       //Avg_Path_Length of
                                                 network
    public static double LinkEfficiency = 0; //Link Efficiency of
                                                 network
    public static double SpectralGap = 0.0;      //Network Spectral Gap
    public static double SpectralRadius = 1.0;  //Network Spectral
                                                 Radius
    public static int CentralNode = -1;       //First central node found
    public static int ClosestNode = -1;       //First closest node found
    public static int ClosestPaths =          //Number of Paths thru
                                                 closest
    public static double ClosestAvg = 0;      //Average closeness value
    public static int Radius = -1;            //Radius of network
    public static int Diameter = -1;          //Diameter of network
    public static double ClusterCoefficient = -1; //Cluster
                                               Coefficient of the network
    public static int HubNode = -1;           //Hub node #
    public static int DeathRate = 0;          //Epidemic death rate %
    public static int InfectionRate = 20;     //Epidemic infection
                                                 rate %
    public static int RecoveryRate = 20;      //Recovery rate
    public static int RecoveryTime = 1;       //SIR time to recover or die
    public static double CC = 0.0;            //Cluster coefficient of
                                                 network
    public static double Length = 0.0;        //Total lengths of all links
    public static Matrix M;                   //Adjacency and Laplacian
                                                 matrices
    //GUI parameters
    public static int xwide = 840;            //Default Size of drawing area
    public static int ytall = 480;            //Default Size of drawing area
```

```
    public static int y0 = 240;                //Default Drawing areas
    public static int x0 = 420;                //Default Origin at (x0,y0)
    public static int CircleRadius = 200;      //Default Size of layout
                                                      circle
    public static String Message = "";         //User message
    //dynamic data
    public int nNodes = 0;                      //Actual number of nodes
    public int nConsumers = 0;              //Number of consumers - black
    public int nCompetitors = 0;            //Number of competitors - blue
    public int nLinks = 0;                      //Actual number of links
    public Node node[] = new Node[maxNodes];    //List of Nodes
    public Link Link[] = new Link[maxLinks];    //List of Links
    public boolean doUpdate = true;             //Dirty bit for update
                                                      of displays

    //Constructor
    theNetwork(){    }//theNetwork
}
```

Given these classes, it is a simple matter to instantiate a graph. For example, a graph G, is created by declaring it of type theNetwork:

```
    theNetwork G = new theNetwork();                    //Graph G
```

All of the processing methods used to fill G with nodes and links are contained within classes theNetwork, Link, and Node. The theNetwork methods are prefixed with NW_ to designate them as members of theNetwork class. For example, to create a random graph:

```
public void NW_doCreateRandomNetwork() {
        NW_doCreateNodes();                    //Create nodes, only
        NW_doCreateRandomLinks();              //Create links, randomly
    {//NW_doCreateRandomNetwork
```

The NW_doCreateNodes() method instantiates nNodes copies of Nodes and stores them in array node[0..nNodes-1], and the NW_doCreateRandomLinks() method instantiates nLinks copies of Links and stores them in array link[0..nLinks]. Recall that a random graph is created by randomly selecting node pairs. The details are provided by the implementation of NW_doCreateRandomLinks():

```
private void NW_doCreateRandomLinks() {
    nLinks = 0;                 //Increase links until limit is reached
    int to, from;               //Randomly selected nodes
    while(nLinks < nInputLinks){  //Don't stop until all links are
                                                created
        from = (int)(Math.random()*nNodes);
        to = (int)(Math.random()*nNodes);
        while(from == to) to = (int)(Math.random()*nNodes);
        NW_doAddLink(node[from].name, node[to].name);
    }
  }//NW_doCreateRandomLinks
```

The node pair (from, to) is randomly selected by generating a random number in the interval [0,1), and then multiplying it by nNodes, to obtain a random node number in the interval [0, nNodes−1]. However, these must be distinct, so the method continues to generate a random value for variable to until it is different from variable from.

The NW_doAddLink(from, to) method is called to insert a new link between the node pair, but it returns **false** if a duplicate link already exists. NW_doAddLink() also increments nLinks, which is the number of links at any point in time. Therefore, the method keeps trying to add links until nInputLinks links have been inserted into *G*.

The polymorphic method for inserting a link between a node pair is shown below—one method inserts a name in the link, while the other nodes not. The first form assumes link names are simply their number, while the second form requires an explicit name in its parameter list:

```
public boolean NW_doAddLink(String from, String to){
    return NW_doAddLink(from, to, Long.toString(nLinks));
}
 public boolean NW_doAddLink(String from, String to, String name) {
     if( from == to) return false;                   //No self loops
     Link e = new Link();                            //Allocate space
     e.tail = NW_doFindNode(from);                   //Node pair...
     e.head = NW_doFindNode(to);
     e.value = DefaultValue;                         //Assume defaults
     e.name = name;                                  //Link name
     boolean exists = isConnected(e.tail, e.head);   //No duplicates
     if(!exists) {                                   //OK to insert new link
         if(nLinks >= maxLinks){
             Message = "Cannot exceed Maximum Number of Links";
             return false;
         }
         Link[nLinks] = e;                           //Insert in list of links
         Link[nLinks].c = Color.black;               //Make visible
         nLinks++;
         node[e.tail].degree++;                      //Increment degree
         node[e.tail].out_degree++;
         node[e.head].degree++;                      //Both ends
         node[e.head].in_degree++;
         return true;
     }
     return false;                                   //Duplicate exists
 }//NW_doAddLink
private boolean isConnected(int na, int nb){
    for(int i = 0; i < nLinks; i++){
        if(Link[ i].tail == na && Link[ i].head == nb
                 ||
           Link[i].head == na && Link[i].tail == nb) {
            return true;
        }
    }
    return false;
}//isConnected
```

2.8 EXERCISES

2.1. What is the exact average path length of a ring graph containing $n = 100$ nodes?

2.2. What is the average path length of a line graph containing $m = 100$ links?

2.3. What is the length of a Euler path of Fig. 2.4b?

2.4. Construct a graph with $n = 4$ nodes and degree sequence $g = [5,3,3,3]$.

2.5. Rewire Fig. 2.4a so that $e_5 : v_2 \sim v_3$. Now, find a Euler circuit. What is it?

2.6. What is the characteristic (average) path length of the graph in Fig. 2.4b? Show the path matrix for this graph and derive the average path length from the path matrix.

2.7. What is the degree sequence g of the graph of Fig. 2.2a? Ignore link direction.

2.8. What is the degree distribution of the graph of Fig. 2.2a?

2.9. Figure 2.9 is a graph of 10 municipal regions that are served by a fire department. The city wants to locate a new fire station in the "middle" of these regions. Assume that the links in this graph represent equal transit times for a fire engine to reach each region from neighboring regions. The city wants

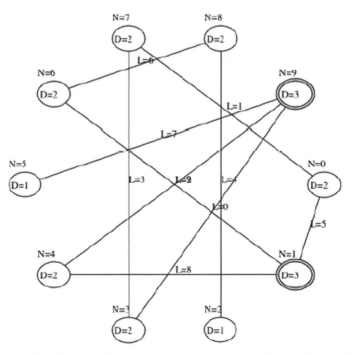

Figure 2.9   Program *Network.jar* display of graph G, with $n = 10$, $m = 10$.

to reduce transit time from the new station to all regions. Which region (node) is the best place to locate the fire station? What is the Laplacian of the graph shown in Fig. 2.9? (*Note*: nodes and links are numbered from 0 to 9.) The mapping function f for this graph is as follows:

$$f = \begin{bmatrix} e_0 : v_3 \sim v_9, & e_1 : v_0 \sim v_7, & e_2 : v_4 \sim v_9, & e_3 : v_3 \sim v_7, & e_4 : v_2 \sim v_8, \\ e_5 : v_0 \sim v_1, & e_6 : v_6 \sim v_8, & e_7 : v_5 \sim v_9, & e_8 : v_1 \sim v_4, & e_9 : v_1 \sim v_6 \end{bmatrix}$$

2.10. In the previous Exercise, what node(s) is (are) the farthest from the central node, and how far?

2.11. What is the closest node in Fig. 2.9, according to the closeness property?

2.12. Graph G, $n = 5$, contains nodes v_1, v_2, v_3, v_4, v_5, with the following mapping function. What is the cluster coefficient of node v_5?

$$f = [e_1 : v_3 \sim v_4, \ e_2 : v_1 \sim v_2, \ e_3 : v_1 \sim v_3, \ e_4 : v_4 \sim v_5, \ e_5 : v_3 \sim v_5, e_6 : v_2 \sim v_5,]$$

2.13. In Exercise 2.12, what is the cluster coefficient of the entire graph?

2.14. [Advanced.] Calculate the spectral radius and spectral gap of the simplified Königsberg graph of Fig. 2.4b.

2.15. [Advanced.] Show that the spectral radius of a binary tree graph approaches $\exp(1) = 2.718, \ldots$ as n approaches infinity.

3

REGULAR NETWORKS

This chapter defines some well-known regular networks in terms of their topology and offers a generative procedure for constructing them. A *generative procedure* is an algorithm that produces a network from a set of nodes, links, and rules for mapping links onto node pairs. A generative procedure is easy to implement as a computer method in an object-oriented language such as Java. We present Java methods for ring, binary tree, toroidal, and hypercube networks.

There are several reasons to study regular networks from the perspective of network science: (1) they provide a stark contrast to random networks—most regular networks have zero or very little entropy, (2) k-regular networks are the basis of small-world generative procedures, and (3) regular network properties are important in the study of synchronization of arbitrary networks—a topic we address in Chapters 9 and 10. In particular, the length of regular subgraph cycles embedded within larger networks determines synchronization of the larger network. Synchronization is necessary for the stable behavior of biological networks, marketing and business stability, and the ability for a group to reach consensus in a social network.

Regular networks are also the basis of other, more complex networks. In Chapter 5 we show how to generate a small-world network from a k-regular network and rewiring probability p. In this case, the initial k-regular network has zero entropy, but the entropy of the emerged small world is proportional to the rewiring probability p. More importantly, we show that properties of small worlds are

Network Science: Theory and Practice. By Ted G. Lewis
Copyright © 2009 John Wiley & Sons, Inc.

inherited from their underlying regular network. For example, the Watts–Strogatz (WS) small-world network inherits its cluster coefficient from its initial 2-regular network.

A new metric is introduced—*link efficiency*—for comparing the efficiency of a network in terms of its average path length and number of links. A *link-efficient* network utilizes its links in an efficient manner to reduce average path length. In many applications of network science we want the shortest average path length possible while simultaneously conserving the number of links.

We define link efficiency $E(G)$ as follows:

$$E(G) = \frac{m - \text{avg\_path\_length}(G)}{m} = 1 - \frac{\text{avg\_path\_length}(G)}{m}$$

In addition, this chapter develops Java algorithms for calculation of diameter, center, and average (*characteristic*) path length of an arbitrary network. These algorithmic tools—implemented in program *Network.jar*—are part of the experimental approach to understanding network science. We combine simulation with mathematical rigor to derive properties such as average path length and entropy as follows. Empirical data are obtained from program *Network.jar*; an analytical curve is fit to the data; then general equations for diameter, centrality, average path length, and link efficiency are derived by inductive logic. This should give the reader an intuitive grasp of the topic as well as the mathematical skills needed to fully master the topic.

A *regular network* is a network with regular graph structure—a repeating pattern of links. Because of their regularity, this class exhibits low or zero entropy. The networks studied here also exhibit an economy of links, whereby every node is reachable from every other node in a relatively small number of hops. These regular networks are sparse; are connected; and have a relatively small diameter, small central node radius, and small average path length. These properties make them excellent candidates for real network designs.

We are particularly interested in sparse regular networks with small average path length because they have many applications. For example, in the design of multiprocessor computer systems, it is important to minimize both the number of links, average path length, and diameter of the interconnection network that ties processors together. Highly link-efficient networks make good communication networks because they reduce network latency and transmission delay.

Efficient regular networks are also good human communication structures because an organization chart with a short average path length makes the corporation more productive. In fast-moving modern organizations, commands must be transmitted through a sparse network in the most efficient manner possible. A *network-centric* organization is optimized to reduce cost by eliminating links, and reduce latency by minimizing average path length. In this chapter, we show that the traditional hierarchical tree network is not as efficient as other types of networks. This may explain why modern organizations are less tree-structured than were organizations of several decades ago.

In this chapter we

1. Provide Java methods of generative procedures for construction of *binary tree, toroidal*, and *hypercube* networks.
2. Develop a *breadth-first algorithm*—and its Java implementation—for finding *path length, diameter*, and *centrality* properties of arbitrary networks.
3. Propose a new measure of efficiency—*link efficiency*—which is one minus the ratio of average path length to number of links:

$$E(G) = 1 - \frac{\text{avg\_path\_length}(G)}{m}$$

This metric is used to compare the link efficiency of binary tree, toroidal, and hypercube networks.
4. Apply a combination of experimentation and mathematical derivation techniques to the problem of calculating average path length of an arbitrary network. Program *Network.jar* generates empirical data; a curve is fit to the data; then an equation for, say, average path length is inferred from the curve. We use this general technique throughout the book.
5. Introduce the class of *binary tree networks* and show that they are path-efficient because they utilize links in a very efficient manner. The characteristic path length of this class of networks is asymptotic to $O(\log_2(n))$. Link efficiency is shown to decline as network size increases:

$$E = 1 - \frac{2\log_2(n)}{n}; \quad n \gg 1.$$

6. Introduce the class of *toroidal networks* that also exhibit a high level of path efficiency—better than a binary tree, but not as efficient as a hypercube network. This class of networks has $O(\sqrt{n})$ characteristic path length, and network link efficiency,

$$E = 1 - \frac{1}{4\sqrt{n}}; \quad n \gg 1.$$

7. Introduce the class of *hypercube networks* and show that it is both sparse and link-efficient. Hypercube characteristic path length is $O(\log_2(n))$ like that of a binary tree, but its link efficiency is $E = 1 - (1/(n-1))$. Because hypercubes are the most link-efficient of all regular networks studied here, they are the preferred structure for the design of multiprocessor computer systems and low-latency communication networks.

This chapter uses the program *Network.jar* to generate and analyze each network described here. The Java methods for implementing generative procedures given in this chapter are simplified versions of the methods in *Network.jar*.

3.1 DIAMETER, CENTRALITY, AND AVERAGE PATH LENGTH

In general, the goal of many practical network designs is to connect n nodes to one another in the least expensive way. A network topology is "least expensive" when it has the fewest links, or when the number of hops needed to traverse the network is minimal. In one application, we might want to minimize the diameter (worst-case path length), and in another application, the goal might be to minimize the average path length (average case). The *Manhattan street* layout—north–south/east–west rectangular grid—used by many cities minimizes the time to get from one intersection (node) to any other. But a street grid requires many links—too many to connect all major cities to one another. Therefore, a *line network* connects most major cities to one another because fewer links are required. The intracity (i.e., within-city) street grid minimizes transit time, but the intercity (i.e., between-city) road network minimizes the number of links (roads) needed to connect cities to one another.

The tradeoff between number of links and number of hops in the average path length of a network can be captured by a metric called the *link efficiency E*, which is defined as follows:

$$E(G) = \frac{m - \text{avg\_path\_length}(G)}{m}$$

where m = number of links in G. Note that this metric ranges from zero, when the average path length is m, to 100%, when the average path length is zero. In the extreme case, $E = 1.0$, every link contributes to link efficiency. When $E = 0$, the average path length equals m, which is the worst path length possible. Link efficiency is a measure of how effective links are at shortening characteristic path length. Higher values of E correspond to networks that are more efficient.

For example, in the previous chapter we developed average path length estimates for line, ring, and complete networks. Plugging the formulas for path length and number of links into the formula for link efficiency produces a general formula for E. Comparing E for different networks is a way to determine which one is the most link-efficient. Table 3.1 lists a number of network classes and their link efficiencies. In the following sections, we derive these results and show that the hypercube network is the most link-efficient class of regular networks. In terms of link efficiency, Table 3.1 ranks simple line and ring networks at the bottom, and hypercube, random, and complete networks at the top. Surprisingly, random networks are link-efficient![1]

In general, we are interested in efficient utilization of links as the size of a network increases. A network is *scalable* if link efficiency approaches 100% as network size n approaches infinity. Otherwise, a network is nonscalable. Which networks of Table 3.1 are scalable? Binary tree, toroid, hypercube, and complete networks are obviously scalable because efficiency approaches 100% as network size n approaches

---

[1]This is due to the small-world effect.

TABLE 3.1 Link Efficiency of Several Network Classes, $n \gg 1$

Network Class	Efficiency	Example
Line	$\dfrac{2n-4}{3(n-1)}$	Asymptotic to $\frac{2}{3}$
Ring	$\dfrac{3n-1}{4n}$	Asymptotic to $\frac{3}{4}$
Binary tree	$1 - \dfrac{2\log_2(n+1)-6}{n-1}$	$n=127, m=126, E=93.4\%$
Toroid	$1 - \dfrac{1}{4\sqrt{n}}$	$n=100, m=200, E=97.5\%$
Random	98.31%	$n=100, m=200,$ avg_path_length $=3.38$
Hypercube	$1 - \dfrac{1}{n-1}$	$n=128, m=448, E=99.2\%$
Complete	~ 1.0	$m=n\dfrac{n-1}{2},$ avg_path_length $=1$

infinity. But what about random networks? The answer depends on how the number of links m scales along with n.

3.1.1 Calculating Path Length and Centrality

Link efficiency and network centrality are functions of path length, so we begin by devising an algorithm for calculating path length of an arbitrary network. Once we know a network's average path length, we can calculate diameter, centrality, and link efficiency. The algorithm for path length developed here also yields diameter, centrality, and link efficiency as a bonus.

Recall that characteristic path length is defined as the average path length over all (shortest) direct paths from node v to node w, for all starting nodes v and ending nodes w. A path length algorithm must count the number of hops along the direct path between v and w, for all combinations of v and w. Let t be the total number of paths and $r_{i,j}$ the length of the direct path between node v_i and v_j. Then, the average over all $r_{i,j}$ is

$$\text{avg\_path\_length} = \sum_i \sum_j \frac{r_{i,j}}{t}$$

The $r_{i,j}$ are elements of the path matrix defined in the previous chapter, and $t = n(n-1)$, because the diagonal of the path matrix is zero. Finding the average path length is easy, given the path matrix, but calculating the elements of the path matrix is equivalent to finding all paths! We avoid this circular logic by taking a direct approach—simply calculating the length of paths between all n^2 node pairs. The desired path length algorithm traces the entire network while being careful to avoid circuits and longer alternate paths.

The algorithm proposed here uses a breadth-first recursive search to trace the shortest path from node v to every other node w, in a connected network. It is exhaustive, but simple, except for the necessity to avoid circuits and alternate (longer) paths. Breadth-first search visits all immediate neighbor nodes first, then the immediate neighbors of neighbors, and so on, until either reaching a node that has already been visited, reaching a node that has no other neighbors, returning to the original node (circuit), or reaching the destination node.

Breadth-first search of an arbitrary network organizes surrounding nodes into levels, as shown in Fig. 3.1. A level is equivalent to a hop, so the algorithm simply finds the smallest level number that encompasses both starting node v and ending node w. The level number of node w, relative to v, equals the number of hops from v to w. Figure 3.1 illustrates how marking adjacent nodes with a level number organizes the breadth-first search and equates levels with path length.

In terms of the path matrix, row v of the path matrix corresponds to starting node v, and the elements of row v correspond to the other nodes in the network. If a node is not reachable from node v, then the length of the path between them is zero. We construct the path matrix, row-by-row, and then compute the average value of the nonzero elements of the path matrix. Averaging over all paths from all pairs of nodes yields the characteristic or average path length.

There may be more than one adjacent node at each level, so we employ a *push-down stack* to remember all neighbors of the current starting node v. As each neighbor at level k is visited, we mark it as "visited," store its level number k, and push all of its neighbors onto the stack. After visiting and marking all neighbors at level k, we pop the stack to get the next level of nodes, and repeat the process. This process halts when the stack becomes empty.

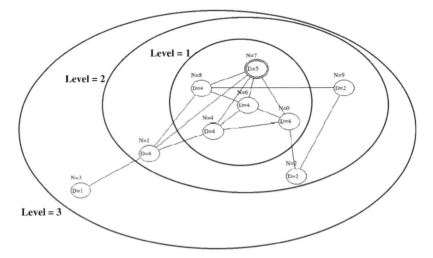

Figure 3.1 An arbitrary network arranged in levels around starting node $n_0 = v_6$. Level k represents k hops from n_0 to the neighbors and neighbors of neighbor nodes.

While we are at it, let's compute the diameter and radius as a byproduct of path length calculation. Diameter is the largest value of k in the network, and a node's radius is the maximum distance of this node from all others. In other words, the *radius* of node v is the number of hops between it and the node farthest away from it. The node with the smallest radius is the *central node*—it is as close or closer to all nodes than any other node. Hence, this procedure also produces a measure of centrality for all nodes, and designates the most central node as the network's *center*. *Centrality* is a property that is equal to the smallest radius of all nodes in the network.

We could also calculate *closeness* as a byproduct of finding all paths through the network, but this topic is delayed until the next chapter because closeness of nodes in regular networks is not very interesting. Regular networks are so symmetric that closeness is about the same for all nodes. However, there are some exceptions. For example, end nodes of a line network are not as close as middle nodes.

Finally, we compute link efficiency because we know the number of links, $m = n$Links, and the network's average path length. Link efficiency E is simply

$$E(G) = \frac{1 - \text{avg\_path\_length}(G)}{m}$$

The following Java method, NW_doFindCenters(), computes diameter, center, avg_ path_length, and E at the same time. It implements the breadth-first search algorithm described above, and finds all paths between n^2 node pairs. Class LayoutReply is a data type used to return diameter, central node radius, average path length, and link efficiency to the calling program:

```
class LayoutReply {
    int big;                    //Diameter
    int small;                  //Central radius
    double mean;                //Average path length
    double efficiency;          //Link efficiency
}
```

The following Java code was written for simplicity and readability, more than efficiency. Improvements to this code are left as an exercise for the reader. It uses a pushdown stack (defined elsewhere), and assumes node and link data structures as defined in Chapter 2:

```
public LayoutReply NW_doFindCenters(){
    LayoutReply reply = new LayoutReply();    //Returned values
    Stack s = new Stack(nNodes+1);
    int k = 0;                                //Level#
    int j = 0;                                //Working stiff
    int max_radius = 0;                       //Max radius of a node
    int min_radius = 0;                       //Min radius of a node
    double mean_radius = 0.0;                 //Return avg. path length
    int next_node = 0;                        //Neighbor at level k+1
```

```
int n_paths = 0;                          //#paths in network
for(int i = 0; i < nNodes; i++){          //Average over all nodes
   s.init();                              //Clear pushdown stack
   Node n0 = node[i];                     //Starting node v
   n0.level = 0; k = 0;                   //Starting level
   for(j = 0; j < nNodes; j++){           //Reset flags
      node[j].visited = false;            //Clear previous settings
      node[j].level = 0;
   }
   s.push(i);                             //Remember n0 = v
   while(s.notEmpty()){
      j = s.pull();                       //Recall n0
      node[j].visited = true;             //Avoid circuit
      k = node[j].level;                  //Recall level
      for(int e = 0; e < nLinks; e++){    //Visit neighbors
         if(Link[ e] .head == j) next_node = Link[ e] .tail;
         else if(Link[ e] .tail == j) next_node = Link[ e] .head;
         else continue;                   //Skip over non-neighbors
         if(!node[ next_node] .visited){
            node[next_node].level = k+1;      //Assign number of hops
            node[next_node].visited = true; //Avoid circuit
            s.push(next_node);}           //Remember next n0
      }
   }
   max_radius = 0;                        //Find largest radius
   for(int v = 0; v < nNodes; v++){
    if(node[ v] .level > max_radius) max_radius = node[ v] .level;
    if(node[ v] .level > 0) {             //Ignore all others
      n_paths++;
      mean_radius += node[v].level;       //Avg. over all non-zeros
    }
   }
   n0.radius = max_radius;                //Maximum distance to all
}//for
min_radius = nNodes+1;                     //Center
max_radius = 0;                            //Diameter
for(int v = 0; v < nNodes; v++){
    if(node[ v] .radius > 0 &&  (node[ v] .radius <= min_radius)) {
      min_radius = node[v].radius;
      }
      if(node[ v] .radius >= max_radius) max_radius = node[ v] .radius;
    }
   if(min_radius == nNodes+1) min_radius = 0;   //Must be no path
   for(int v = 0; v < nNodes; v++) {     //Could be many centers
       if(node[ v] .radius == min_radius) node[ v] .center = true;
       if(node[ v] .radius == max_radius) node[ v] .outer = true;
   }
   reply.big = max_radius;                //Return diameter
   reply.small = min_radius;              //Return center(s)
   if(n_paths > 0)
      reply.mean = mean_radius/n_paths;   //Return avg. path length
      else reply.mean = 0.0;              //Return link efficiency
   reply.efficiency = (nLinks - reply.mean)/nLinks;
   return reply;
}//NW_doFindCenters
```

Calculation of network center is complicated by the possibility of multiple central nodes. Thus, the Java method must return a *set* of nodes rather than a single node. The method given here computes and sets aside the radius of all nodes, one at a time. After all nodes have been processed, the Java method marks the nodes with the smallest radius as a *central node*. This collection is the set of nodes returned to the calling program.

Centrality is defined as the minimum of the maximum path length over all paths in the network:

$$\text{Centrality}(G) = \text{minimum}_i \{\text{maximum}_j, \{\text{length}(v_i, v_j)\}\}$$

Here we define length(v_i, v_j) as the number of hops along the direct path connecting nodes v_i and v_j. It is also the level number k relative to $n0 = v_i$. Then, maximum$_j$ is the largest such path(s), also known as the node's *radius*. Finally, minimum$_i$ is the smallest of the maximum path lengths in the network, also known as the *center* of the network.

To illustrate, apply the leveling algorithm to the example in Fig. 3.1. Observe that node v_6 is connected to four adjacent neighbor nodes through a path of length 1, three neighbors of neighbors through a path of length 2, and one node through a path of length 3. The average path length for $n0 = v_6$ to the eight other nodes is $(4(1) + 3(2) + 1(3)/8 = \frac{13}{8} = 1.625$. The longest path is 3 hops, and the shortest path is 1 hop. But v_6 is only one of nine nodes in the network. We have to calculate the longest and shortest paths between all nodepairs, and then find the largest and smallest over all nodepairs. This is why we have computers!

For the network in Fig. 3.1

$$n = 9, \, m = 15$$
$$\text{Diameter} = 4, \, \text{center} = 2$$
$$\text{avg\_path\_length} = 1.777$$
$$\text{Link efficiency} = 0.8814$$

Assuming that each path length calculation is $O(n)$, and there are up to n^2 paths, these calculations are extremely complex: $O(n^3)$. Is it possible to perform them faster? This is left as an exercise for the reader.

Now that we have a path length calculator and better understanding of link efficiency, we can apply them to the problem posed at the beginning of this chapter: "What is the most efficient regular network?" An efficient network is sparse, has a small diameter, and has a short characteristic path length.

3.2 BINARY TREE NETWORK

A line graph connects n nodes with $(n - 1)$ links, but its average path length is $O(n)$. A line network is not link-efficient because the number of links grows as fast as the number of hops in its average path length. A more link-efficient connected network topology is the *binary tree* because as it grows, its average path length grows much slower than its number of links. A binary tree is more efficient than a line network.

A *binary tree* is defined recursively as a node connected to two subtrees that are also binary trees. One node, called the *root*, has degree 2 and connects two subtrees, which in turn connect to two more subtrees, and so forth. This recursion ends with a set of nodes called the *leaf nodes,* which have degree 1. All intermediate nodes connect to the network through three links, as illustrated in Fig. 3.2. Hence, a binary tree contains nodes with degree of only 1, 2, or 3.

A *balanced binary tree* contains k *levels* and exactly $2^k - 1$ nodes, $m = (n - 1)$ links, for $k = 1, 2, \ldots$. The root node is at level 1, and the leaf nodes are at level k. Each level corresponds with a hop along a path from root to leaf node, so the diameter of a balanced binary tree is $2(k - 1)$ hops. The root node is at the center of a balanced binary tree with radius $= (k - 1)$.

An unbalanced binary tree contains less than $2^k - 1$ nodes. For example, the balanced tree in Fig. 3.2a $k = 4$, $n = 16 - 1 = 15$ nodes, diameter $= 2(4 - 1) = 6$ hops, and $m = 15 - 1 = 14$ links. But the unbalanced tree in Fig. 3.2b has fewer

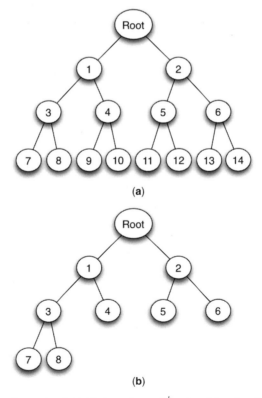

(a)

(b)

Figure 3.2 Binary tree network; (a) balanced, $n = 2^k - 1 = 15$ nodes; (b) unbalanced, $n < 2^k - 1 = 9$ nodes.

nodes and links: $n = 9 < 15$; diameter $= 5$, and $m = n - 1 = 8$ links. We study only balanced trees in the remainder of this chapter.

The following Java method creates a balanced binary tree consisting of $n = 2^k - 1$ nodes and $m = n - 1$ links. The method uses a conveniently simple mapping function f: node i's successors are nodes $2i + 1$ and $2i + 2$. The Java method simply connects node i to nodes $2i + 1$ and $2i + 2$, for all but the final level of the tree. One subtree is odd-numbered, and the other is even-numbered. The root of the odd-numbered subtree is node $2i + 1$, and the root of the even-numbered subtree is node $2i + 2$, for $i = 0$ to $n/2$.

The simple mapping pattern makes it very easy to generate the network once its root node is established. Given a global parameter nInputNodes, find the largest perfect square less than nInputNodes, and generate the tree:

```
public void NW_doCreateTree() {
   nNodes = 1;
   int n = nInputNodes;           //Compute power of two = nNodes+1
    int log2_nNodes = 0;
   while(n > 1){
       n = n/2;
       log2_nNodes++;
       nNodes = 2*nNodes;
       }
       n = nNodes-1;
       NW_doCreateNodes(n);       //Create 2^k-1 nodes
   for(int i = 0; i < nNodes/2; i++){
       NW_doAddLink(node[i].name, node[2*i+1].name); //Left subtree
       NW_doAddLink(node[i].name, node[2*i+2].name); //Right subtree
   }
}//NW_doCreateTree
```

This code finds the perfect square that is less than nInputNodes and then constructs the binary tree from its root to its leaf nodes. Equal numbers of left and right subtrees are attached to all except the last $n/2$ nodes. This balanced binary tree network has $n/2$ leaf nodes, one root node, and $(n/2) - 1$ internal nodes. Furthermore, it has $m = n - 1$ links, and $k = \log_2(n + 1)$ levels, starting with the root node at level $k = 1$.

A balanced binary tree's density decreases inversely as the network gets larger. The density of the network in Fig. 3.2a is very low: density(balanced binary tree) $= \frac{2}{15} = 0.133$.

Moreover, density dramatically decreases as n increases. For example, when $n = 1023$ and $m = 1022$, density $= 0.002$. Therefore, binary tree networks are extremely sparse. However, are they link-efficient, and do they have short characteristic path length? The answer is "No." Is it possible to construct even more efficient regular networks than the class of balanced binary tree networks? The answer is "Yes."

3.2.1 Entropy of Binary Tree Network

A balanced binary tree network is regular, but its entropy is not zero. Entropy is a function of the degree sequence distribution, and a binary tree has an uneven degree sequence distribution. For example, the degree sequence distribution for the binary tree of Fig. 3.2a is

$$g' = [53\%, 7\%, 40\%]$$

This yields an entropy I of

$$I(\text{Balanced binary tree}, k = 4) = 1.27 \text{ bits}$$

The reason for the uneven distribution, of course, is that 1 of the 15 nodes has degree 2, 53% have degree 1, and the remaining leaf nodes have degree 3. The degree sequence always contains three frequencies:

$$p_1 = \frac{\#\text{ nodes of degree 1}}{n}; \quad \text{these are the leaf nodes}$$

$$p_2 = \frac{\#\text{ nodes of degree 2}}{n}; \quad \text{this is the root node}$$

$$p_3 = \frac{\#\text{ nodes of degree 3}}{n}; \quad \text{these are the internal nodes}$$

Approximately one-half of the nodes are leaf nodes; one node is a root node, and the remaining nodes are internal:

$$p_1 = \frac{n/2}{n} = \frac{n}{2n} = \frac{1}{2} \qquad \text{leaf node frequency}$$

$$p_2 = \frac{1}{n} \qquad \text{root node frequency}$$

$$p_3 = \frac{n - (n/2) - 1}{n} = \frac{n - 2}{2n} \qquad \text{internal node frequency}$$

The entropy I is obtained by plugging directly into the equation for entropy:

$$I(\text{balanced binary tree}) = -\left[\frac{1}{2}\log_2 \frac{1}{2} + \frac{1}{n}\log_2 \frac{1}{n} + \frac{n-2}{2n}\log_2 \frac{n-2}{2n} \right]$$

$$= \frac{1}{2} + \frac{1}{n}\log_2 n + \left(\frac{n-2}{2n}\log_2 \frac{2n}{n-2} \right)$$

This simplifies further by assuming large n; thus

$$I(\text{Balanced binary tree}) = 1 + \frac{\log_2(n)}{n}; \quad n \gg 1$$

For example, the entropy of a balanced binary tree with $n = 511, m = 510$ is approximately, $1 + (\log_2(511))/511 = 1 + \frac{9}{511} = 1.018$. A balanced binary tree network is almost, but not quite, a regular network. It is *irregular* at the root and leaf nodes.

These "irregularities" account for approximately 1 bit of "randomness." The irregularity diminishes as n grows—a property we will find useful in estimating the average path length of a general balanced binary tree network.

3.2.2 Path Length of Binary Tree Network

As it turns out, binary tree networks are less efficient than expected when it comes to average path length. The center of the network is the root node with radius $r = k - 1$, and the leaf nodes lie at the extreme diameter, which is $D = 2(k - 1)$ hops. The diameter grows logarithmic with size n because $k = O(\log_2(n))$. But average path length also grows logarithmically, as shown in Fig. 3.3. Hence, the average path length of a binary tree is proportional to its diameter, as we show, below.

Figure 3.3 plots average path length and $(D - 4)$ versus level k; $n = 2^k - 1$, and $D = $ diameter $= 2(k - 1)$. Average path length and $(D - 4)$ merge for high values of k. Thus, average path length is asymptotic to $(D - 4)$:

$$\text{avg\_path\_length(balanced binary tree)} = (D - 4); k \gg 1$$
$$D = 2(k - 1), \text{ so avg\_path\_length} = 2k - 6 = 2\log_2(n + 1) - 6$$

As a balanced binary tree increases in size, the influence of the much larger number of leaf nodes overwhelms the far fewer nodes near the root. Leaf nodes and their neighbors become so dominant that the effect of the relatively few nodes near the root diminishes to zero. In fact, nearly one-quarter of the nodes are 1 hop away from

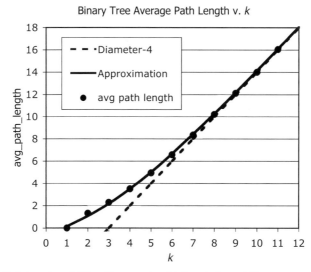

Figure 3.3 Path length and $(D - 4)$ versus level k for a balanced binary tree with $n = 2^k - 1$ nodes, $m = n - 1$ links, and diameter $= D = 2(k - 1)$.

more than one-half of all nodes in the network. Specifically, all of the nodes at level $(k-2)$ are connected to one-eighth of the nodes "above" them, and one-half "below" them. Obviously, the effects of the leaf nodes and their immediate neighbors dominate the average path length of a large binary tree network. Therefore, as n increases, average path length is asymptotic to diameter minus 4 hops. The asymptote, $(D-4)$, is shown as a dotted straight line of Fig. 3.3, which approximates avg_path_length, for higher values of k.

Clearly, the approximation improves with increase in network size. For example, the actual characteristic path length for a balanced binary tree with $n=32$, $m=31$ is 4.955. The asymptotic approximation yields $8-4=4$, which is a poor estimation of the actual value. However, the actual path length for a balanced binary tree with $n=12$ is 18.02, and the asymptotic equation yields $22-4=18.00$, which is a very good approximation.

For smaller values of k, say, $k<9$, the approximation breaks down. Instead, we use an approximation as shown in Fig. 3.3. The nonlinear portion of the approximation diminishes exponentially as k increases—reaching zero as $(D-4)$ dominates:

$$\text{avg\_path\_length} = (D-4) + \frac{A}{1 + \exp(Bk)}$$

where $A=10.67$, $B=0.45$ gives the best fit to the data. Substituting $D=2(k-1)$ and $k=\log_2(n+1)$, and gathering terms, we obtain

$$\text{avg\_path\_length} = 2\log_2(n+1) - 6 + \frac{10.67}{1 + \exp(0.45\log_2(n+1))}$$

Figure 3.3 shows this approximation as a solid line running through the actual values of avg_path_length. It is reasonably accurate for all values of $k>1$. For example, when $k=1$, actual path length is zero and approximate path length is 0.15. When $k=4$, both actual and approximation are the same: 3.51; when $k=12$, actual value is 18.02, and approximation is 18.05.

3.2.3 Link Efficiency of Binary Tree Network

Now that we know the equation for average path length of a balanced binary tree, we can plug it into the equation for link efficiency, and simplify. A balanced binary tree has $m=n-1$ links. Link efficiency of a "large" balanced binary tree is simply

$$E(\text{balanced binary tree}) = 1 - \frac{D-4}{m} = 1 - \frac{(2k-1)-4}{n-1}; \quad k>9$$

$$E = 1 - \frac{2\log_2(n+1)-6}{n-1}, \quad \text{because } k = \log_2(n+1)$$

Assuming $n \gg 1$, so $(n + 1)$ and $(n - 1)$ are approximately n, link efficiency is approximately

$$E(\text{balanced binary tree}) = 1 - \frac{2 \log_2(n)}{n}; \quad k > 9$$

For example, if $n = 127$, then $E = 0.890$, approximately, but the actual link efficiency is 0.934. However, if $n = 2047$, the asymptotic formula yields $E = 0.990$, and the actual link efficiency is 0.992. This is a difference of only 0.2% between actual and approximate efficiency. The difference virtually disappears for large n.

Binary tree link efficiency approaches 100%, as n grows without bound. Therefore, it would appear that a balanced binary tree is extremely effective for structuring a multiprocessor's interconnection or a corporation's organization chart. In both of these applications, a shorter average path length per link is desirable. Does a balanced binary tree utilize links for the best possible efficiency? In Section 3.3 we explore this question and show that there are even more efficient networks than the balanced binary tree network.

3.3 TOROIDAL NETWORK

The average path length of a binary tree is largely determined by the logarithmic growth in the distance from its root node to its leaf nodes. To get from one leaf node to another, a message must travel up the tree toward its root, and then down again to the destination node. The farther away the two leaf nodes, the more likely it is that the path must go through the tree's root.

Perhaps the average path length can be reduced by inserting lateral links between nodes at the same level of the binary tree. These shortcuts would eliminate the need to traverse all the way to the root node simply to get from one side of the tree to the other. However, adding links reduces link efficiency. So, how can we shorten paths, without adding more links? One such design allocates half of the links to horizontal connections and the other half to vertical connections in a grid-like topology. In other words, suppose that the mapping function connects to immediate predecessor and successor nodes, and another mapping connects node v to nodes that are $+\sqrt{n}$ and $-\sqrt{n}$ hops away, as shown in Fig. 3.4. Such a grid-like mapping of links to nodes uses a small number of links while reducing the distance between nodes. This leads to a Manhattan-like grid.

The network of Fig. 3.4 is a $\sqrt{n} \times \sqrt{n}$ mesh with one addition: edge nodes "wrap around" to opposite edge nodes, so that each row and column form a ring. This guarantees short paths because, as we showed in the previous chapter, the average path length of a ring is $O(n/4)$, while the average path length of a line graph is $O(n/3)$. When wrapped around like this, the collection of rings form a *toroidal network*; hence the name of this network.

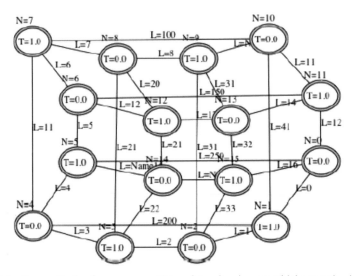

Figure 3.4 Screen display from program *Network.jar* showing a toroidal network with $n = 16$ nodes, $m = 32$ links. Average path length is 2.13 hops.

Typical toroidal networks have $n = k^2$ nodes, arranged in a $k \times k$ grid. Every node has degree 4; hence there are $m = 2n = 2k^2$ links. Figure 3.4 shows a 4×4 network, with $n = 16$ nodes and $m = 32$ links. Generally, the size of a toroidal network is equal to a squared integer: $n = 4,9,16,25,36,\ldots$, and the number of links is twice the squared integer.

The toroidal network of Fig. 3.4 is completely nonrandom because its entropy $I(\text{toroid})$ is zero. This is due to the fact that all nodes have the same degree: $\text{degree}(\text{toroid}) = 4$. It is also devoid of clusters, $cc(\text{toroid}) = 0$, because none of the neighbors of a node are connected to one another. All nodes are at the center of the network: $\text{diameter}(\text{toroid}) = 4$, $\text{radius}(v) = 4$, for all nodes v in the network.

Constructing a toroidal network is very easy because of its regularity. The only difficulty comes from the vertical and horizontal wraparound links. The vertical wraparound is handled by a modulo function of n, and the horizontal wraparound is handled by a modulo function of $\sqrt{n}$. Another way to look at it is to note that each row is a ring with a wraparound link between node zero and node number $\sqrt{n}$ for row 1, between $\sqrt{n} + 1$ and $2\sqrt{n}$ for row 2, and so on. Similarly, vertical rings connect nodes separated by $\sqrt{n}$ intermediate nodes, and wrap around from row $\sqrt{n}$ to row 1.

Generally, the following mapping function governs the topology of a toroid:

$$f : v_i \sim v_{(i+1) \bmod \sqrt{n}}; \quad v_i \sim v_{(i+\sqrt{n}) \bmod n}$$

The following Java method implements this mapping function after finding the largest perfect square less than nInputNodes, and computing sqrt(n):

```java
public void NW_doCreateToroid() {
    int sqrt_nNodes = (int)Math.sqrt(nInputNodes); //length of a side
    int n = sqrt_nNodes * sqrt_nNodes;             //Perfect square
    NW_doCreateNodes(n);                           //Create k^2 nodes
    for(int row = 0; row < nNodes; row += sqrt_nNodes){
      for(int col = 0; col < sqrt_nNodes; col++){   //Links
        int i = row + col;
        int j = col + 1;
        if(j >= sqrt_nNodes) j -= sqrt_nNodes;      //Wrap horizontal
        j += row;                                   //Add next node link
        NW_doAddLink(node[i].name, node[j].name);   //Add horizontal link
        j = i + sqrt_nNodes;
        if(j >= nNodes) j -= nNodes;                //Wrap vertical
        NW_doAddLink(node[i].name, node[j].name);   //Add vertical link
      }
    }
}//NW_doCreateToroid
```

This method starts in the upper left-hand corner of the grid, with node zero, and connects each row of nodes from left to right, to its immediate successor, and its successor +sqrt(n) nodes ahead. At the end of each row, the method forms a ring by linking the last node to the first node of each row. When reaching the end of a column, the method forms another (vertical) ring by linking the last node to the first node of each column. These rings give the toroidal network a short average path length.

3.3.1 Average Path Length of Toroidal Networks

In the following, we show that average path length of a toroidal network increases $O(\sqrt{n})$ with network size, n. This is less than the path length of a binary tree network, which leads to better link efficiency. For example, the average path length of a 4×4 toroid is 2.133 hops versus 3.5 hops for a binary tree with $n = 15$ nodes. What is the average path length of an arbitrary $k \times k$ ($n = k^2$) toroid? To answer this question, consider Table 3.2.

TABLE 3.2 Results of Path Matrix Analysis of Toroidal Networks

Size, n	Toroid	Row Sum	Factored Row Sum	Average Path Length
4	2×2	4	2*2	$\frac{4}{3} = 1.33$
9	3×3	12	3*4	$\frac{12}{8} = 1.50$
16	4×4	32	4*8	$\frac{32}{15} = 2.13$
25	5×5	60	5*12	$\frac{60}{24} = 2.50$
36	6×6	108	6*18	$\frac{108}{35} = 3.09$
49	7×7	168	7*24	$\frac{168}{48} = 3.50$

Table 3.2 was constructed from the path matrices obtained by enumeration of path lengths for toroidal networks of size $n = 4, 9, 16, \ldots$. These are perfect squares, so $\sqrt{n} = 2, 3, 4, \ldots$. The average path length is equal to the average of all $n(n - 1)$ elements of the path matrix, but all rows of the path matrix sum to the same number, so it is easy to compute the average over all rows.

Column 3 of Table 3.2 contains the row sum for each toroid size, and column 4 contains the same number, but in factored form. For example, the rows of the path matrix of a 4×4 toroid all sum to 32. This factors into 4(8). Notice that $4 = \sqrt{16}$. Thus, column 4 can be factored into $\sqrt{n}s$, where s is $(n - 1)/2$, when n is odd and $n/2$ when n is even. For $n = 16$, $s = \frac{16}{2} = 8$, because n is even. For $n = 25$, $s = (25 - 1)/2 = 12$ because n is odd. Thus, the general form of the factored row sum (column 4 in Table 3.2) is

$$\text{Row sum} = \sqrt{n}\frac{n - 1}{2}, n \text{ odd}; \quad \sqrt{n}\frac{n}{2}, n \text{ even}$$

Now, observe the final column of Table 3.2, containing the average path length expressed as a fraction a/b. The numerator, $a = $ row sum, and the denominator, $b = (n - 1)$. For example, when $n = 16$, the numerator $a = 32$, and the denominator, $b = (16 - 1) = 15$. Therefore, the average path length of a 4×4 toroidal network is $\frac{32}{15} = 2.13$. By induction, the formula for average path length is

$$\text{avg\_path\_length(toroid)} = \frac{\sqrt{n}}{2}, n \text{ odd}; \quad \sqrt{n}\frac{n}{2(n - 1)}, n \text{ even}$$

The reader can verify this formula for a toroid of any size. The odd-sized toroid is slightly more compact, but average path length for both even and odd networks grows as $O(\sqrt{n})$. This approximation quickly improves with increases in n. For example, program *Network.jar* and this formula both give 6.042 for the average path length of a 12×12 toroidal network. Later in this chapter we show this approximation to be very close to the exact value for $n > 16$. For all practical purposes, the average path length of a toroidal network is $(\sqrt{n})/2$, $n > 16$.

3.3.2 Link Efficiency of Toroidal Networks

Toroidal designs like the one in Fig. 3.4 partially satisfy the requirement that an efficient network be sparse and efficiently utilize links to reduce average path length. Yet, the efficiency of a toroidal network still suffers from a relatively large number of links. The number of links $m = 2n$ increases according to k^2 because $n = k^2$. This can be a disadvantage in some applications. For example, in computer architecture, layout of $m = 2k^2$ links on a one-dimensional surface such as a silicon wafer limits the toroidal network architecture to relatively small numbers of processor nodes. In this section, we show that the link efficiency of a toroid is better than that of a binary tree, but still not adequate, because the toroidal network uses $m = 2n$ links to achieve its relatively small average path length.[2]

Plugging the expression for average path length into the equation for link efficiency, and simplifying, yields toroidal network link efficiency:

$$E(\text{toroid}) = \frac{(m - \sqrt{n})/2}{m} = 1 - \frac{\sqrt{n}/2}{2n} = 1 - \frac{\sqrt{n}}{4n}$$

$$= 1 - \frac{1}{4\sqrt{n}}$$

Comparing link efficiency of a toroidal network, $n = 16$, with a binary tree network, $n = 15$, yields $E(\text{toroid}) = 1 - \frac{1}{16} = \frac{15}{16} = 93.8\%$, versus $E(\text{binary tree}) = 1 - (8-6)/14 = \frac{12}{14} = 85.7\%$. This is a 9% difference, for small n. As n increases, the toroidal network is only slightly more efficient than the binary tree network because the percent difference diminishes as n increases. For example, when $n = 100$, the toroidal link efficiency is 97.5%, and the binary tree link efficiency is approximately 92.6%—a 5% difference. However, the toroid takes twice as many links as the binary tree.

3.4 HYPERCUBE NETWORKS

A *hypercube network* connects nodes so that they are one *Hamming distance* apart. The Hamming distance $h(x,y)$, between two binary numbers, x and y, is defined as the number of bits in x that differ from corresponding bits in y. Therefore, a hypercube is formed by linking nodes v_x and v_y, for only those nodes where $h(x,y) = 1$.

Table 3.3 lists the Hamming distance between the binary expansion of integers 0 through 7 (columns in Table 3.3) and binary expansion of integers 0 through 4 (rows

TABLE 3.3 Hamming Distance between Binary Numbers[a]

Hamming Distance	000	001	010	011	100	101	110	111
000	0	1	1	2	1	2	2	3
001	1	0	2	1	2	1	3	2
010	1	2	0	1	2	3	1	2
011	2	1	1	0	3	2	2	1
100	1	2	2	3	0	1	1	2

[a]Columns, $0 \cdots 7$; rows, $0 \cdots 4$.

[2]The layout is not planar—that is, it cannot be drawn on a two-dimensional surface without overlapping links.

in Table 3.3). For example, the binary expansion of integer 2 is 010, and the binary expansion of 4 is 100. These two binary numbers differ in all bit positions, so their Hamming distance is 3.

Hamming distance can be computed by summing the bits produced by the XOR (exclusive-or) operator. XOR produces a "1" bit when its input bits are different, and a "0" bit when its input bits are identical:

$$XOR(010, 100) = 111$$
$$SUM(111) = 3$$

To construct a hypercube, simply connect neighboring pair of nodes v_x, v_y, if $h(x,y) = 1$, by drawing a link between v_x and v_y. Suppose that $n = 4$; then node indices range from 0 to 3, or in binary representation: 00, 01, 10, and 11. We connect all node pairs with binary indices that differ by 1 bit. In this case, $h(00,01) = 1$, $h(00,10) = 1$, $h(01,10) = 2$, $h(01,11) = 1$, $h(10,11) = 1$, so we connect all except one node pair as follows:

Node	Binary Index	Links
0	00	$00 \sim 01$
		$00 \sim 10$
1	01	$01 \sim 00$
		$01 \sim 11$
2	10	$10 \sim 00$
		$10 \sim 11$
3	11	$11 \sim 01$
		$11 \sim 10$

Figure 3.5b shows the resulting network obtained by this mapping. There is no link within $00 \sim 11$ because the Hamming distance between nodes 0 and 3 is not 1:

$$XOR(00, 11) = 11$$
$$SUM(11) = 2$$

The *dimension* of a hypercube is equal to the degree of each node, $D(H) = \log_2(n)$, where $n = 2^D$. All nodes of a two-dimensional hypercube have degree 2, all nodes of a 3D hypercube have degree 3, and so forth. The diameter of a hypercube is also equal to the degree of its nodes. Thus, the dimension, diameter, and node degree are all the same.

Like nested Russian matryoshka dolls, hypercube networks contain hypercube networks! A hypercube of dimension D contains two hypercubes of dimension $D/2$, as shown in Fig. 3.5. Starting with a hypercube of $D = 1$, the one-dimensional barbell of Fig. 3.5a is easily constructed from two nodes—one numbered 0, and the other numbered 1. The hypercube of dimension $D = 2$, shown in Fig. 3.5b, is

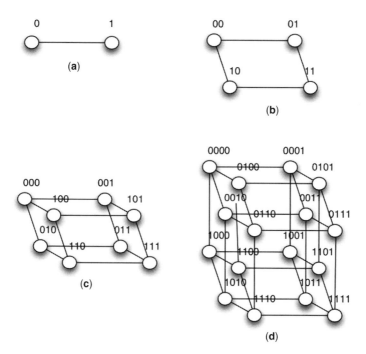

Figure 3.5 Hypercube networks for (a) barbell ($n = 2$), (b) ring ($n = 4$), (c) 3D ($n = 8$), and (d) 4D ($n = 16$) configurations.

obtained by combining two barbell hypercubes with two new links. Binary node indices of the higher-dimensioned hypercube are obtained by appending a binary 0 to the node indices of one barbell, and a binary 1 to the node indices of the other barbell. In this example, node indices 00,01 are obtained by prefixing a "0" to node indices numbered 0 and 1, and nodes 10,11 are obtained from the second barbell with nodes also numbered 0 and 1 by prefixing each with "1."

In general, higher-dimensional hypercubes are created by duplicating two ($D - 1$)-dimensional hypercubes, prefixing a binary 0 to the node indices of one copy and a binary 1 to the node indices of the other copy, and adding links to the nodes whose indices differ by only one Hamming distance. Figure 3.5 illustrates this technique.

Each node of a hypercube connects to $D = \log_2(n)$ other nodes, each one Hamming step away. For example, when $n = 4$, then $\log_2(4) = 2$, so node 00 is connected to nodes 01 and 10. Both of these adjacent nodes are one Hamming step away from 00. Adjacent-node indices are calculated by flipping each bit of 00, one bit at a time, to enumerate indices 01, and 10. Similarly, for $n = 8$, $D = \log_2(8) = 3$, three links are inserted between 000 and 100, 010, and 001. By flipping the first, second, and third bit of 000, one at a time, the adjacent-node indices are 100, 010, and 001.

The hypercube generative procedure is simple, for every node v_i in the hypercube, insert a link between v_i and all other nodes whose index is obtained by flipping each bit of i, one at a time, from left to right, until all $\log_2(n)$ bits have been flipped.

The Java code for constructing a hypercube network of size $n = 2^D$ nodes is shown below. Class `BitOps` contains three methods of special interest: `toString()` converts an integer into a binary string, `toInteger()` converts a binary string into a decimal integer, and `flipBit()` flips the j th bit of a binary string of bits from zero to one, and one to zero:

```
public void NW_doCreateHypercube() {
    BitOps h = new BitOps();
    nNodes = 1;
    int n = nInputNodes;                    //nNodes = 2^k
    int log2_nNodes = 0;                     //Number of bits in index
    while(n > 1){
        n = n/2;
        log2_nNodes++;                       //degree, D
        nNodes = 2*nNodes;
    }
    n = nNodes;                              //n = 2^k
    NW_doCreateNodes(n);                     //Create 2^k nodes
    for(int i = 0; i < nNodes; i++){         //For each node...
        String iString = h.toString(i, log2_nNodes);   //Node index as a bit string
        for(int j = 0; j < log2_nNodes; j++){
            NW_doAddLink(                    //...add log2(n) links
            node[i].name,
            node[h.toInteger(h.flipBit(iString, j))].name);
        }
    }
}
```

Method `NW_doAddLink()` rejects duplicate links, so we do not need to worry about duplication caused by connecting node 00 to 10, and node 10 to 00. However, if `NW_doAddLink()` did not avoid duplication, what modifications to method `NW_doCreateHypercube()` are needed to avoid duplication? This is left as an exercise for the reader.

3.4.1 Average Path Length of Hypercube Networks

Recall that the number of links of any network is equal to one-half the sum of its node degrees: $2m = \sum_1^n d_i$. Every node of a hypercube has the same degree, $D = \log_2(n)$. Thus, $m = n(\log_2(n))/2$, where $n > 1$. There are $m = 16\left(\frac{4}{2}\right) = 32$ links in the 4D hypercube of Fig. 3.5d. There are $m = 32\left(\frac{4}{2}\right) = 64$ links in a 5D hypercube, so the number of links scales with the size of a hypercube.

Every node of a hypercube can be reached from any other node in $1,2,\ldots,D = \log_2(n)$ hops. This is the same for all nodes, so all nodes are central nodes, and the radius of all nodes equals the diameter of the network, D. Therefore, the average path length is

$$\text{avg\_path\_length(hypercube)} = \frac{n \log_2(n)}{2(n - 1)}$$

For example, the average path lengths of the four hypercube networks in Fig. 3.5 are 1.0, 1.33, 1.714, and 2.133, respectively, for $n = 2, 4, 8$, and 16. Assuming $n \gg 1$, we can simplify the formula:

$$\text{avg\_path\_length(hypercube)} = \frac{\log_2(n)}{2}; \quad n \gg 1$$

This equation is derived by taking advantage of the symmetry of all hypercubes. The average path length of every node is the same as all others, so we need only compute the average path length of node 000. With this in mind, we proceed as follows:

1. The average path length of all nodes is the same. Hence, the average path length from node 000 to all other $(n - 1)$ nodes is also the average path length of the entire network.

2. Calculate the average path length of node 000, for $n = 8$, and then generalize it to the case for $n > 1$. In particular, note that there are $(n - 1)$ paths from 000 to all other $(n - 1)$ nodes, and that the number of paths of length D equals the sum of the binomial coefficients, $B = \sum_0^{D-1} C_i^{D-1}$, where

$$C_i^{D-1} = \frac{D - 1!}{i!(D - i - 1)!}$$

   In other words, C_i^{D-1} is the combinatorial coefficient obtained by enumerating $(D - 1)$ things, taken i at a time.

3. The sum of the binomial coefficients, $B = 2^{D-1} = n/2$, because $n = 2^D$.

4. Finally, we simplify the general expression for average path length by assuming $n \gg 1$. The result is avg_path_length (hypercube) $= (\log_2(n))/2; n \gg 1$.

Consider the case $n = 8, D = 3$ shown in Fig. 3.5c. We compute the average path length for node 000 by summing the number of paths of length 1, plus the number of length 2, plus the number of length $D = 3$, and divide by $(n - 1) = 7$:

$$\text{avg\_path\_length} = \frac{3(1) + 3(2) + 1(3)}{7} = \frac{3(1 + 2 + 1)}{7} = \frac{12}{7} = 1.714$$

All nodes have the same path length, so this expression is also the average path length of the entire 3D hypercube network. This expression can be generalized by replacing 3 with D and 7 with $(n - 1)$, and noting that the term $(1 + 2 + 1)$ is exactly the sum of combinatorial coefficients: $(C_0^2 + C_1^2 + C_2^2)$:

$$\text{avg\_path\_length} = D \frac{C_0^2 + C_1^2 + C_2^2}{n - 1} = D \frac{\sum_0^{D-1} C_j^{D-1}}{n - 1}$$

$$= D \frac{2^{D-1}}{n - 1} = n \frac{\log_2(n)}{2(n - 1)}$$

$$= \frac{\log_2(n)}{2}; \quad \text{for } n \gg 1$$

For example, the 4D hypercube of Fig. 3.5d has an average path length of 2.133 because $n = 16$:

$$\text{avg\_path\_length} = 16\frac{\log_2(16)}{2(16-1)} = 8\frac{4}{15} = \frac{32}{15} = 2.133$$

Average path length is one-half the diameter. It is also one-half the dimension. Thus, average path length scales with the dimension of a hypercube. It is $O(D)$ and $O(\log_2(n))$:

$$\text{avg\_path\_length(hypercube)} = \frac{D}{2} = \frac{\log_2(n)}{2}; n \gg 1$$

This result can be verified experimentally by running program *Network.jar*.

3.4.2   Link Efficiency of Hypercube Networks

Hypercube networks are extremely efficient because they become logarithmically sparse as n increases. The number of links $m = n(\log_2(n))/2$ grows as $O(n\log_2(n))$, while the average path length grows as $O(\log_2(n))$. Therefore, it is easy to calculate link efficiency as follows:

$$E(\text{hypercube}) = 1 - \frac{\text{avg\_path\_length(hypercube)}}{m}$$

$$= 1 - \left[n\frac{\log_2(n)}{2(n-1)m} \right] = 1 - \left[n\frac{\log_2(n)}{2(n-1)n\frac{\log_2(n)}{2}} \right]$$

$$= 1 - \frac{1}{n-1}$$

For example, the link efficiency of the 3D hypercube of Fig. 3.5c is $1 - \frac{1}{7} = 0.857$, and the link efficiency of the 4D hypercube of Fig. 3.5d is $1 - \frac{1}{15} = 0.933$. As the network increases in size, it becomes more efficient. Hence, hypercube networks are scalable.

Hypercube networks are the most efficient regular networks studied in this chapter. In terms of link efficiency: $E(\text{hypercube}) > E(\text{toroid}) > E(\text{binary tree})$. Does this hold for all-size networks? Figure 3.6 shows average path length and link efficiency for these three regular networks versus size, n.

Thus, a hypercube is more efficient than a binary tree, and more efficient than a toroidal network for $n > 16$. But hypercubes use more links than toroidal networks when $n > 16$. This may explain why hypercube interconnection networks are used in "small" multiprocessor systems and toroidal networks are used in "large" systems.

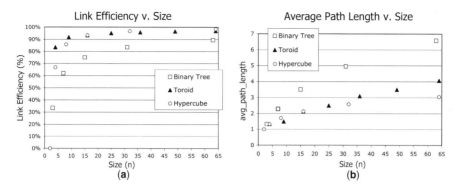

Figure 3.6 Comparison of actual link efficiency (a) and average path length (b) of binary tree, toroidal, and hypercube networks.

Note the marginal difference in link efficiency between a hypercube and a toroid for $n > 6$. It would seem that the two are comparable, but a hypercube has a smaller average path length and is more efficient, even though a toroid requires fewer links.

One additional point in favor of "small" hypercube systems is that hypercube efficiency rapidly rises for small values of n as shown in Fig. 3.6. This may explain why a hypercube topology is often used in multiprocessor interconnection networks for 8, 16, and 32 processors.

Regularity is a virtue in many network applications. Regular networks have zero or very small amounts of entropy and little clustering. Surprisingly, they can also be very efficient as shown in Fig. 3.6. A sparse network such as a hypercube may be as effective, or more so than, the class of random, small-world, and scale-free networks, to be studied next.

In summary, regular networks are of great interest in many disciplines such as computer design, finite-element analysis, understanding the crystalline structure of materials, and modeling of buildings. However, in the science of networks, a regular network is used mostly as a starting point for constructing other, more complex networks. For example, in Chapter 5, we show how to construct a small-world network beginning with k-regular and toroidal networks.

3.5 EXERCISES

3.1. Derive the general equation for the density of a balanced binary tree with $n = 2^k - 1$ nodes.

3.2. The entropy of a balanced binary tree network is nonzero and declines as the network increases in size. What is the limit, as n increases without bound, of the entropy of a balanced binary tree network?

3.3. What is the average path length of a balanced binary tree network, for $n = 511$? For 1023? How does the actual value match up with the approximation formula derived in this chapter?

3.4. What is the approximate link efficiency of a balanced binary tree network for $n = 1023$? How accurate is this approximation?

3.5. What is the average path length of a toroid with $n = 1024$ nodes? How accurate is this estimate?

3.6. Derive the general equation for the density of a toroidal network with $n = k^2$ nodes.

3.7. Identify and explain the origins or causes of the entropies and cluster coefficients of toroidal and hypercube networks.

3.8. What is the average path length of a hypercube network, for $n = 512$? How does the actual value correlate with the approximation formula derived in this chapter?

3.9. What is the approximate link efficiency of a hypercube network for $n = 16$? How accurate is this approximation?

3.10. What is the density of a hypercube network with n nodes?

3.11. Modify the Java code of NW_doCreateHypercube() to avoid duplicate links. Illustrate how your modification avoids duplication of the link between nodes 000 and 100.

3.12. The time complexity of the algorithm given in this chapter for calculating average path length is $O(n^3)$. Propose enhancements that reduce this calculation complexity, and explain why your modifications are improvements.

3.13. A mesh network is a toroidal network without the wraparound links. Thus, a mesh network has $m = 2\sqrt{n} - 1)$ links instead of $2n$ links. What is the general equation for average path length of a mesh of size n? What is its link efficiency? Which is more efficient—a toroidal or mesh network of the same size?

3.14. What is the approximate average path length equation for a 2-regular network of size n?

3.15. Which network, binary tree, toroidal, or hypercube, has the shortest average path length for $4 \leq n \leq 9$?

4

RANDOM NETWORKS

Random networks were among the earliest studied networks, going back to the 1950s in the mathematical graph theory literature. However, they are not representative of nature. In fact, we find the opposite; most physical and biological systems are not arranged randomly, but instead, contain structure. So, why study random networks? The class of random networks provides a baseline for comparison with more-structured networks. Before asking how a network differs from a random network, we must understand the various properties of random networks. Then, we can compare these properties with equivalent properties of small-world and scale-free networks. When compared with random networks, most real-world networks are quite different. Table 2.3 (of Chapter 2) illustrates the dramatic differences between random and nonrandom networks.

The class of random networks lies opposite that of structured networks in the structure spectrum. Random networks are characterized by a Poisson degree sequence distribution for large n, and the *binomial distribution* for small n. Such a "random topology" leads to high entropy, which is a hallmark property of a random network. Sparse random networks also exhibit the small-world effect—their diameter rapidly shrinks with the addition of a small number of random links. But other properties of random networks are rather unremarkable—for example, cluster coefficient and betweennes/closeness properties are modest in comparison with some structured networks. This supports the idea of using a random network as a baseline.

We present two major generative procedures and propose one minor modification to the Erdos–Renyi (ER) algorithm for generating random networks (Erdos, 1960,

1976a, 1976b). One generative procedure (Gilbert) begins with a complete network and then removes links chosen at random, until reaching the desired link density. Another procedure (ER) generates random networks by inserting links between randomly chosen node pairs until reaching the desired number of links. Both Gilbert and ER procedures produce a disconnected network with nonzero probability, so a third generative procedure (anchored ER) is provided that guarantees a connected graph at the expense of some randomness.

In keeping with this book's applied approach to network science, we produce empirical evidence in support of theoretical results for degree sequence distribution, average path length, diameter, and cluster coefficient properties. We show that entropy increases from zero to a maximum value, and then back to zero again, as the number of links grows. This nonintuitive observation can be easily explained—a random network becomes less random as its density approaches that of a (structured) complete network.

This chapter reintroduces the betweenness/closeness property and provides Java code to calculate *closeness*. Recall that closeness is a measure of middlenode (intermediary) power. A node is considered close to other nodes if many shortest paths connecting the other nodes run through the close node. We provide methods for calculating the shortest paths as well as marking the nodes with a value corresponding with the number of paths traversing each node.

This chapter introduces and describes the following:

1. Two historically significant networks: the first random network proposed by Gilbert, and the better-known algorithm proposed by Erdos and Renyi (ER). We show that these networks have essentially the same properties even though two different sets of microrules produce them.

2. Generative procedures—and corresponding Java methods—are given for the construction of Gilbert, ER, and anchored random networks. Anchored random networks are slightly less than perfectly random, but reduce the occurrence of isolated nodes.

3. The entropy of a random network is a function of density, where density is $2m/(n(n-1))$. Random networks are random only for medium values of density— they are not random for low or high densities. A random network with 50% density is "perfectly random" because this density maximizes entropy. We show that entropy varies according to

$$I(\text{random}) = 4 - 2[\exp(-13(\text{density})) + \exp(-13(1 - \text{density}))]; 0 < \text{density} < 1$$

for the small networks studied in this chapter.

4. Random networks are highly link-efficient because a small increase in number of links has a major impact on the decline of average path length (*small-world effect*). Theoretically, the diameter of a random network is $O(\log(n))/\log(\lambda)$,

where λ is the average degree of nodes in the network. We show that average path length of a random network varies according to its density:

$$\text{avg\_path\_length} = \frac{O(\log(n))}{\log(n(\text{density}))} = \frac{A \log(n)}{\log(Cn(\text{density}))}$$

5. For a random network, the approximate cluster coefficient is $CC = \text{density} = \lambda/n$; that is, clustering is directly proportional to the number of (random) links added to the network.

6. The diameter and radius of a random network diminish rapidly with increase in network density; they obey the same relationship as average path length, except with different values of parameters A, C, and D in the general model $=$

$$\frac{A \log(n)}{\log(Cn(\text{density}) + D)}$$

As density increases, random networks rapidly become "smaller"—they exhibit the *small-world effect*.

7. The degree of closeness of an average node increases with density, up to a maximum value, and then decreases with density and average number of nodes reached along shortest paths, according to

$$\text{Closeness(random)} = O((1 - \text{density})\lambda^r), \quad \text{where}$$

$$\lambda = \text{mean degree}, r = O\left(\frac{\log(n)}{\log(\lambda)}\right)$$

In addition, the number of paths running through the closest node varies according to #paths(intermediary) $= O(\text{avg\_path\_length})$, suggesting a correlation between closeness and the small-world effect.

8. Finally, this chapter explores the phenomenon of "six degrees of separation" for random networks. We illustrate Granovetter's (Granovetter, 1973) concept of *weak ties* as the concept pertains to a social network, and show that social ties in a random network increase proportional to the diameter of the network.

This chapter uses program *Network.jar* to generate and analyze each network described here. The Java methods for implementing the generative procedures given in this chapter are simplified versions of the code found in *Network.jar*.

4.1 GENERATION OF RANDOM NETWORKS

Generation of a random network with no duplicate links, loops, isolated nodes, or multiple components is not as straightforward as it seems. On one hand, we want the resulting network to be random (high-entropy), and on the other hand, we want to avoid node isolation, duplicate links, and loops, which may occur "accidentally" because of the generative procedure. This requires care in the design and implementation of the microrules that generate such a network.

First, we examine the random network generation microrules proposed by E. N. Gilbert in 1959 (Gilbert, 1959). Then we study the random network generation microrules proposed by Erdos and Renyi (Erdos, 1960). The ER microrules produce the well-known ER network. Both Gilbert and ER procedures produce networks that may contain isolated nodes, and multiple components. Therefore, we provide a third algorithm that anchors at least one link to each node. The proposed *anchored generative* procedure guarantees that all nodes connect to at least one other node, but sacrifices some randomness.

In general, all generative procedures attempt to randomize the degree sequence distribution of a network. A "perfectly random" network is one that follows a binomial degree sequence distribution. But of course, randomly generated networks are only approximations of this ideal. We show why a random network is one in which the degree sequence is a binomial distribution for small n, and approximated by a Poisson distribution for large n.

4.1.1 Gilbert Random Network

The basic idea of the Gilbert random network generation procedure is to select links with probability p from a complete graph with n nodes such that the resulting network ends up with $m = p[n((n-1)/2)]$ links—on average. In other words, a Gilbert network has density p because a complete network has $n((n-1)/2)$ links.

Another way to look at this procedure is to consider a Gilbert network as one network from $C\left(\begin{array}{c} n \\ 2 \end{array}\right)$ possible networks with n nodes and m links, where $C\left(\begin{array}{c} n \\ 2 \end{array}\right)$ is the combinatorial function defined as

$$\frac{n!}{2!(n-2)!} = n\frac{n-1}{2}$$

For example, if $n = 100$, then

$$C\left(\begin{array}{c} 100 \\ 2 \end{array}\right) = \frac{100!}{2(98!)} = \frac{100(99)}{2} = 4950$$

Thus, a Gilbert network is one of 4950 possible networks, selected at random.

Given n and probability p, generate a Gilbert network by applying the following microrules:

1. Initially: generate n nodes and number them from 0 to $(n-1)$.
2. Set m: Let $m = n((n-1)/2) =$ the number of nodes in a complete graph.
3. Repeat for $i = 0, 1, \ldots, (m-1)$:
   a. Given (Math.random() $< p$), connect link i to a node pair; otherwise ignore.
   b. Count the number of links connected and compute the density:

$$\text{Density} = \frac{\text{number of connected links}}{m}$$

This generative procedure uses a random number from the interval $[0,1)$ to determine whether a link is inserted into the network. If the test Math.random() $< p$ fails, then no link is inserted. The procedure tests each of the $n((n-1)/2)$ possible links and randomly inserts an average of $p[n((n-1)/2]$ links between node pairs. But which pair? Any method of node-pair selection is acceptable, so the Java method below adopts an easy way—simply enumerate all $n((n-1)/2)$ possible node pairs, and randomly select the ones that are linked. This approach avoids the risk of incorrectly inserting duplicate links, because each nodepair is visited only once. It also avoids loops because diagonals—which occur only when the nodes of any node pair are identical—are skipped.

Note that the number of inserted links increases as p increases because p is really a measure of density. Gilbert's method produces a random network with a certain density. In contrast to the Erdos–Renyi random network, a Gilbert network uses as many links as necessary to ensure that the density is equal to approximately p. Density is directly adjustable, and determines the number of links as a byproduct. On average, these are equivalent, but in terms of a particular random network, the number of links will vary from network to network.

The Java method for creating a Gilbert network (presented below) calls on NW_doCreateNodes(), which initially creates nNodes nodes. Then, NW_doCreateGilbert() randomly selects approximately $p[n((n-1)/2)]$ links from among $n((n-1)/2)$ possible, and inserts them into the network. Global variable nConnectionProbability is p, which establishes the network's density.

In any network created by this method, the actual number of links will vary because of the uncertainty introduced by sampling from a random-number generator. Because the final number of links varies each time a Gilbert network is generated, the method returns the number of links inserted. This number is stored in variable *count*, which is related to density according to the density formula:

```
private void NW_doCreateGilbert() {
    NW_doCreateNodes(nInputNodes);          //Create nodes, only
    int count = 0;                          //How many links?
    for(int i = 0; i  < nNodes; i++){
        for(int j = 0; j  < i; j++){
```

```
        if(i == j) continue;                    //Skip self
        if(100*Math.random() < nConnectionProbability)
          if(NW_doAddLink(node[ i] .name, node[ j] .name, Long.toString(nLinks)))
                    count++;
    }
  }
}//NW_doCreateGilbert
```

Method NW_doAddLink(node[i].name, node[j].name, s) creates a new link between nodes *i* and *j*, with text label s and returns **true** if no link already exists, and **false**, otherwise. But of course, this procedure avoids duplicates by picking each nodepair only once.[1] The Java code for this method is given below:

```
public boolean NW_doAddLink(String from, String to, String name) {
    if(from == to) return false;      //No self loops
    Link e = new Link();              //Allocate new link
    e.tail = NW_doFindNode(from);     //Node pair...
    e.head = NW_doFindNode(to);
    e.value = nDefaultValue;          //Default link value
    e.name = name;                    //Link name
    boolean exists = isConnected(e.tail, e.head);
     //Link could point either direction
    if(!exists) {                     //OK to insert new link
        Link[nLinks] = e;             //Insert in list of links
        Link[nLinks].c = Color.black;//Paint Black
        nLinks++;
        node[e.tail].degree++;        //Increment node degree
        node[e.tail].out_degree++;
        node[e.head].degree++;        //Both ends
        node[e.head].in_degree++;
        return true;
    }
    return false;                     //Not OK - duplicate exists
}//NW_doAddLink
```

Gilbert networks may *not* be connected. In fact, Gilbert showed that random networks generated by his procedure contain more than one component with probability $n(1-p)^{n-1}$, and isolated nodes (with degree equal to zero) with probability $2(1-p)^{n-1}$. While these are very small probabilities for large networks ($n \gg 1$), the mere possibility of isolated nodes makes this approach unsuitable for many applications.

In addition to the uncertainty with regard to number of isolated nodes, Gilbert networks are not guaranteed to contain an exact number of links. For example, if $p = 50\%$ and $n = 100$, then the average Gilbert network will contain

$$m = 0.5\left(n\frac{n-1}{2}\right) = 0.25(100(99)) = 2475 \text{ links}$$

but a typical Gilbert network might contain $m = 2470$ links one time, 2480 the next time, and 2479 a third time. Because insertion of links is a random process, the

---

[1]We use different versions of this method in different programs, so NW_doAddLink() may vary from chapter to chapter.

number of links in the final network is uncertain and unpredictable. This is perhaps the most important deficiency with this method.

The lack of predictability in the final value of m has relegated Gilbert networks to history. Most random networks are produced by the Erdos–Renyi (ER) algorithm today. ER networks are guaranteed to have exactly m links, obey the binomial degree sequence distribution, and are easy to generate. However, they may be disconnected.

4.1.2 Erdos–Renyi (ER) Random Network

A better random network generation procedure—also proposed in 1959 by Paul Erdos and Alfred Renyi—is the Erdos-Renyi, or *ER generative procedure*. It is the standard method of random network generation today. Unlike the Gilbert procedure, the ER generation procedure fixes the number of links m and nodes n and does away with the probability variable p. As with the Gilbert network, however, it is possible to generate an ER network with isolated components and isolated nodes. This can occur because each node pair is selected at random, which means that it is possible a node is not selected at all. Careful implementation of the ER generation procedure avoids loops and duplicate links, but it does not guarantee a strongly connected network.

Given n and m, construct an ER random network as follows:

1. Initially: Generate n nodes and number them from 0 to $(n - 1)$.
2. Initially: m given, and #links (number of links) $= 0$.
3. Repeat until $m = $ #links have been inserted:
   a. Select random node: tail $=$ `(Math.random())`n.
   b. Select random node: head $=$ `(Math.random())`n.
   c. Avoid loop: while (tail $==$ head) head $=$ `(Math.random())`n.
   d. Avoid duplicate: if (no duplicate) insert new link between tail and head and increment #links. Otherwise, do nothing.

This generation procedure avoids loops because step 3c guarantees that the tail and head nodes are different. It avoids duplicates because of step 3d. This step is incorporated in the `NW_doAddLink()` method described earlier. The ER procedure stops after m links have been attempted. Therefore, m must be less than $n((n-1)/2)$, or the procedure will never halt! It is possible for fewer than m links to be inserted because no link is inserted when it would lead to duplicate links.

Erdos–Renyi networks have a specific number of links, so the density is $2m/(n(n-1))$ for a given number of nodes and links. This allows more precise control of the random network's density. For example, if $n = 100$, and $m = 200$, the density of every random network generated by the ER procedure is

$$\text{Density} = \frac{\frac{m}{n(n-1)}}{2} = \frac{200}{50(99)} = 0.0404 \text{ or } 4.04\%$$

Both ER and Gilbert procedures produce a random network because the degree sequence distribution asymptotically approaches the Poisson distribution in both cases. The relationship between random network generation and Poisson processes is shown later. Consequently, the entropy and cluster coefficients are comparable when the number of nodes and number of links are equivalent. However, the Gilbert procedure generates a random network with a certain density, and the ER procedure generates a random network with a certain number of links. While this may seem equivalent, the ER procedure fixes the number of links while the Gilbert procedure does not.

The Java code for the ER process is just as simple as the microrules above suggest. Method NW_doCreateER() first creates *n* nodes, then method NW_doCreateERLinks() inserts *m* links between *m* randomly selected node-pairs. Duplicate links are handled by method NW_doAddLink(), which checks to ensure that a link does not already exist between the node pair. This method also increments nLinks whenever a new link is inserted. Therefore, the **while** loop will eventually terminate, because nLinks will eventually increase to the value of nInputLinks, which is equivalent to *m*, above:

```
public void NW_doCreateER() {
      NW_doCreateNodes(nInputNodes);    //Create nodes, only
      NW_doCreateERLinks();             //Create links, randomly
}//NW_doCreateER
 private void NW_doCreateERLinks() {
    int max_links = nNodes * (nNodes-1)/2;
    nLinks = 0;
    if(nInputLinks > max_links) return;
    int to, from;                 //Randomly selected node-pair
    while(nLinks > nInputLinks){   //Don't stop until all links are created
     from = (int)(Math.random()*nNodes);
     to = (int)(Math.random()*nNodes);
     while(from == to) to = (int)(Math.random()*nNodes); //Cannot connect to self
     NW_doAddLink(node[from].name, node[to].name, Long.toString(nLinks));
  }
}//NW_doCreateERLinks
```

4.1.3 Anchored Random Network

Gilbert and ER networks produce random networks with a single component most, but not all, of the time. A slight modification to the ER generative procedure guarantees that all nodes are connected to at least one other node, by ensuring that every node has at least one link. This is done by visiting every node at least once—in round-robin style—and testing the degree of each node. If the degree is zero, the algorithm attaches the tail of the link to the solitary node; otherwise, it selects a tail node at random.

The resulting *anchored random network* must have at least $m = n/2$ links, so that every node has at least one link attached to it. The first pass over all nodes is systematic—it starts at node 0, and visits each node in order, $0,1,2,3,\ldots,(n-1)$. If $m > (n/2)$, the next and subsequent passes run over indices $0,1,2,3,\ldots,(n-1)$, but select random nodes, instead of the same sequence of nodes. The resulting network is slightly less than random, because of the small bias introduced by the first systematic pass over all nodes in order.

Given n and m, construct an anchored random network as follows:

1. Initially: Generate n nodes and number them from 0 to $(n-1)$.
2. Initially: $m \geq (n/2)$ given, and #links=0.
3. Repeat until $m =$ #links have been inserted:
   a. Round robin: $i = 0,1,2,\ldots,(n-1); 0,1,2,\ldots$.
   b. Select tail: If (degree(i) > 0) tail $=$ (Math.random())n, else tail $= i$.
   c. Select random node: head $=$ (Math.random())n.
   d. Avoid loop: While (tail $==$ head) head $=$ (Math.random())n.
   e. Avoid duplicate: If (no duplicate), insert new link between tail and head and increment #links. Otherwise, do nothing.

The Java method corresponding to this generative procedure is given below. It is somewhat more elaborate than the previous generative procedures because of step 3, immediately above. However, it is very similar to the pure ER procedure because it produces a random network with the prescribed number of links. If there are too few links, then NW_doCreateAnchored() increases their number to $m = (n/2)$. Conversely, if there are too many links, the method exits. Generally, there are more links than nodes, so the method visits each node several times, in round-robin fashion: $0,1,2,\ldots(n-1),0,1,2,\ldots$:

```
public void NW_doCreateAnchored() {
    NW_doCreateNodes(nInputNodes);        //Create nodes, only
    int count = nInputLinks;              //Number links >= n/2?
    if(count  < nInputNodes/2) count = nNodes/2;
    if(count \gt= nNodes* (nNodes-1)) return; //Too many links
    int tail = 0;                   //Starting node
    int i = 0;                      //i = 0, 1, 2...(n-1), 0, 1, 2...
    while(nLinks  < count){
        if(node[ tail] .degree > 0)
        i = (int) (Math.random() * nNodes);
        else i = tail;
        int head = (int) (Math.random() * nNodes);
        while(head == tail) head = (int) (Math.random() * nNodes);
        if(NW_doAddLink(node[ i] .name, node[ head] .name)) {
            tail++;
            if(tail == nNodes) tail = 0; //Wrap around (n-1) -> 0
        }
    }
}//NW_doCreateAnchored
```

The degree sequence distribution is skewed slightly because all nodes have nonzero degree when $m \geq (n/2)$. This bias shows up as an entropy that is slightly lower than that of a purely random network. Recall that the degree sequence distribution obeys a binomial distribution, and the probability that a node links to nothing is given by $B(0,n)$, which is nonzero. This term in the entropy equation cannot be ignored.

While the anchored random network procedure guarantees that all nodes connect to something, the connection may link a disjoint subset of nodes to one another. In other words, an anchored random network may still contain separate components because it is possible for one disjoint subset of nodes to link only to nodes within the subset, leaving the remaining nodes unreachable from the subset. While this is extremely rare, the possibility exists. How might we overcome this anomaly? This problem is left as an exercise for the reader.

4.2 DEGREE DISTRIBUTION OF RANDOM NETWORKS

Random networks provide a starting point for a number of emergent processes to be discussed in subsequent chapters. Generally, we start with a random network and then observe how it evolves through time into some form of nonrandomness. This behavior—a network evolving from randomness toward order—is the basis of *emergence*. For example, a random network is a suitable model of a market for a new product. Let nodes represent products and consumers. Links between product and consumer nodes represent purchases of the product (and its competitors). As the market "shapes up," the random network transforms into a scale-free or small-world network dominated by a small number of nodes (products) that are connected to many other nodes (consumers). Hopefully, as consumers learn of the new product, they gravitate toward it. This switching is modeled as links being rewired—disconnecting from one set of nodes and connecting to the new-product node. Thus, the random network representing a new market evolves into a structured network representing a mature market. In other words, a structured network emerges from a random network, corresponding to a mature market emerging from an unstructured market.

The personal computer (PC) is a classical example of a mature and structured market emerging from a chaotic or random new market. In the early 1980s, the PC market consisted of hundreds of companies offering many different kinds of PCs. By the mid-1990s, the early PC market had matured into a structured oligopoly consisting of a small number of dominant market leaders. The market was no longer random. Instead, it consisted of a few highly connected nodes representing the market leaders.

Emergence is the process of rewiring or restructuring a network. We can observe this as changes in the properties of a network over time. Typical properties of greatest interest are degree sequence distribution, average path length, centrality, and cluster coefficient. *Degree sequence distribution* tells us what type of network topology we have—structured or random. The *average path length* and *cluster coefficient* tell us whether a structured network is scale-free or small-world. Centrality measures the *influence* of a node or a small number of central nodes over the network. We begin by examining the degree sequence of a random network and show that the sequence distribution of any random network is a binomial distribution.

To show that Gilbert and ER generation procedures both obey a *Poisson distribution* ($n \gg 1$), we use the following strategy: (1) derive the binomial distribution that models the ER network node-pair selection procedure, and then (2) show that the *binomial distribution* is asymptotically equal to the *Poisson distribution* for very large m. Both distributions represent the probability of a node having degree k, but the Poisson distribution eliminates m (number of links) from the formula. Hence, it is often preferred when discussing large networks. The derivation strategy is as Follows:

1. Show that random selection of node pairs follows a binomial distribution.
2. Show that the binomial distribution transforms into the Poisson distribution as the number of links m grows large, thus eliminating m from the distribution equation.
3. *Note*: Use the fact that $((1-\lambda)/m)$ becomes $e^{-\lambda}$ as m grows without bound.

Let network $G = [N(t), L(t), f(t)]$ be a randomly generated network with n nodes and m links. Further, let λ be the average degree value obtained from the degree sequence distribution $g' = [h_1, h_2, \ldots, h_{\text{max\_d}}]$, where max_d is the highest degree in G. In both Gilbert and ER generation procedures, $N(t)$ is created at time $t = 0$, and remains constant. $L(t)$ starts with zero links at $t = 0$, and adds one link per time unit with probability λ/m, as the network is generated. At time $t = m$, all links have been added according to the Gilbert and ER procedures, so $L(t)$ and $f(t)$ remain constant for subsequent values of $t > m$. Therefore, the final state of G is reached at $t = m$: $G = [N(m), L(m), f(m)]$.

In part 1 of the strategy, we show that the degree distribution of G is binomial. Consider G with $n = 10$ nodes, $m = 30$ links, so the avg_degree$(G) = \lambda = (2m/n)$ links. According to the ER generation procedure, each node receives an average of six connections in $m = 30$ timesteps, because a pair of nodes are linked together at each timestep. Now focus on node $v \ \varepsilon \ N$ as shown in Fig. 4.1. This node is selected once with probability $p = (\lambda/m)$, and k times in m timesteps with probability $p^k = (\lambda/m)^k$. It is also *not* selected with probability

$$(1-p)^{m-k} = \left(\frac{1-\lambda}{m}\right)^{m-k}$$

Therefore, the probability that node v is selected exactly k times in m timesteps is the product of these probabilities

$$\text{Prob}(v \text{ selected } k \text{ times in } m \text{ steps}) = \left(\frac{\lambda}{m}\right)^k \left(\frac{1-\lambda}{m}\right)^{m-k}$$

But k of m connections can occur in $C\left(\dfrac{m}{k}\right)$ ways. For example, in Fig. 4.1, links 1, 2, and 30 are connected to v, but it is also possible for links 1,2,3, or 2,3,5, or 3,4,30

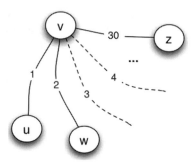

Figure 4.1   Node v of random graph G with $n = 10$, $m = 30$, avg_degree(G) $= \lambda = 3$. Dashed lines indicate links that have not been allocated to v, but if they were, it would raise degree(v) from 3 to 5.

(etc.) to be selected with equal probability. Therefore, the probability of k successes in m time units is given by the binomial distribution $B(m,k)$:

$$\text{Prob}(\text{degree}(v) = k) = B(m,k) = C\binom{m}{k}\left(\frac{\lambda}{m}\right)^{k}\left(\frac{1-\lambda}{m}\right)^{m-k}$$

For example, in Fig. 4.1, node v is selected $k = 3$ times with probability $(\lambda/m)^{k} = \left(\frac{6}{30}\right)^{3} = 0.008$, and *not* selected with probability $((1-6)/30)^{30-3} = 0.00242$. There are $C\binom{m}{k} = 30!/(3!(27!)) = 4060$ ways for node v to be selected $k = 3$ times, so the probability that degree(v) $= 3$ is the product $(4,060)(0.008)(0.00242) = 0.0785$ or 7.85%. In other words, 7.85% is the probability that node v will be connected by $k = 3$ links, and therefore, have degree equal to 3.

The degree sequence distribution is simply computed by evaluating the binomial distribution for $k = 0,1,2,\ldots,(n-1)$. $B(m,k)$ rises from near zero to a maximum value, and then declines again to near zero. For example, $B(30,0) = 0.00124$, $B(30,3) = 0.0785$, and $B(30,29) \sim 0$. The distribution rises to its peak, and slowly declines to approximately zero. Example degree sequence distributions are shown in Fig. 4.2 for random networks generated by Gilbert and ER algorithms.

In part 2 of the derivation strategy, note that as n and m increase in size, $B(m, k)$ is approximated by the *Poisson distribution*. The number of links m grows much faster than the number of nodes. We model this correlation by holding n constant and letting m grow without bound in $B(m,k)$:

$$\lim_{m\to\infty}\{B(m,k)\} = \lim_{m\to\infty}\underbrace{(m(m-1))\cdots\left(\frac{m-k+1}{m^{k}}\right)}\underbrace{\left(\frac{\lambda^{k}}{k!}\right)}\underbrace{\left(1-\frac{\lambda}{m}\right)^{m}}$$

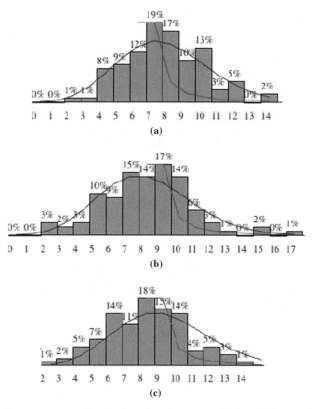

Figure 4.2   Degree sequence distribution of random networks ($n = 100$, $m = 400$) generated by (a) Gilbert generation procedure, (b) ER generation procedure, and (c) anchored ER generation procedure.

In this form of $B(m,k)$, the term $k!$ in the denominator of $C\left(\begin{matrix} m \\ k \end{matrix}\right)$ is exchanged with the term m^k in $(\lambda/m)^k$ in preparation for taking the limit. After this exchange, $B(m,k)$ can be written as the product of three terms—T_1, T_2, and T_3—as follows:

$$T_1 : m(m-1)\cdots\frac{(m-k+1)}{m^k}$$

$$T_2 : \frac{\lambda^k}{K!}$$

$$T_3 : \left(\frac{1-\lambda}{m}\right)^m$$

$$B(m,k) = (T_1)(T_2)(T_3)$$

Now let m increase without limit. T_1 approaches 1 as m goes to infinity because it is the product of terms containing m in both numerator and denominator: $O(m/m)$. As

T_2 is not a function of m, it does not change. T_3 is a special case—it approaches $e^{-\lambda}$ as m goes to infinity because λ/m vanishes slightly more slowly than $((1-\lambda)/m)^m$ increases—a proof we leave to the reader.[2]

Putting this all together; we have

$$\text{Lim}(m \rightarrow \text{infinity})\ T_1 = 1$$

$$\text{Lim}(m \rightarrow \text{infinity})\ T_2 = \frac{\lambda^k}{k!}$$

$$\text{Lim}(m \rightarrow \text{infinity})\ T_3 = e^{-\lambda}$$

$$\text{Lim}(m \rightarrow \text{infinity})\ B(m,k) = \frac{\lambda^k e^{-\lambda}}{k!}$$

This is the *Poisson distribution*, $P(\lambda,k)$, for $k = 0,1,\ldots$, and represents the degree sequence distribution for large random networks, $(n,m \gg 1)$. The Gilbert and ER networks obey this law because the repeated selection process is uniformly random. We call such a generation procedure a *Poisson process* for this reason. Many random processes are Poisson processes because uniformly random single events occur multiple times, generating the multiple events that are modeled by the Poisson equation.

Figure 4.2 shows the results of running program *Network.jar* with $n = 100$, $m = 400$, and connection link probability $p = 8\%$ (Gilbert). The horizontal axis (abscissa) denotes node degree d, and the vertical axis (ordinate) denotes the fraction of nodes with degree d. Gilbert and ER distributions are similar, but the anchored network distribution is slightly skewed to the left, and has a slightly smaller variance. This bias is a consequence of the anchored ER generation procedure, which purposely connects all nodes to at least one other node.

Network.jar overlays a *Poisson distribution/power-law distribution* curve onto the histogram data so that you can see whether there is a match. These are shown as thin line graphs superimposed on the histogram. Clearly, the experimental data (histogram) is a close match to the theoretical Poisson distribution line graph but is a poor match to the power law. This is partial confirmation that Gilbert and ER networks are random, and the anchored ER class of networks is nearly random.

4.3 ENTROPY OF RANDOM NETWORKS

The entropy of a random network is typically much higher than that of any other network class studied in this book. In Chapter 2, we showed that the class of random networks lies at one extreme of the structure spectrum and the class of k-regular networks lies at the other extreme. We also showed that the entropy of random networks is higher than the entropy of other classes. However, what may

---

[2]*Hint*: Expand $((1-\lambda)/m)$ as a Taylor's series around $x = 1$, and note that the Taylor series expansion is identical to the Taylor series expansion of $\exp(-\lambda)$.

not be so obvious is that random networks become more structured as they become denser! Specifically, entropy rapidly drops as the number of links, $m \gg 1$, approaches $n((n-1)/2)$, the maximum. This surprising result can be demonstrated by experimentation.

Figure 4.3 shows the results of this experiment. Program *Network.jar* was run multiple times for $n = 100$, and $m = 100, 200, \ldots, 4900$. Density is $2m/(n(n-1))$, so we plotted entropy I versus density. Five ER networks were generated for each value of density, and the five entropy values were averaged. These averages form the data shown in Fig. 4.3.

Entropy—and therefore randomness—increases quickly as density increases, levels off, and then declines as network density nears 100%. The polynomial shown in Fig. 4.3 is not exactly symmetric around 50%, but it is clear curve that the "amount of randomness" of a random network increases from zero to a maximum value at approximately $m = n((n-1)/4)$ (density $= 50\%$). It then decreases to zero, at $m = n((n-1)/2)$ (density $= 100\%$). In other words, a random network is fully random only in the middle of its range of density values. The ER random network procedure produces a truly random network only for $m = n((n-1)/4)$ links!

Randomness of a random network declines as network density nears 100% because the network topology becomes increasingly regular. We know that a complete network is a regular network because all possible links appear in the network. The entropy of a complete network is zero. As a random network becomes denser, the degree of each node approaches the degree of a complete network. In mathematical terms, the degree of nodes in a random network tends to $(n-1)$ as m tends to $n((n-1)/2)$. The degree sequence distribution is

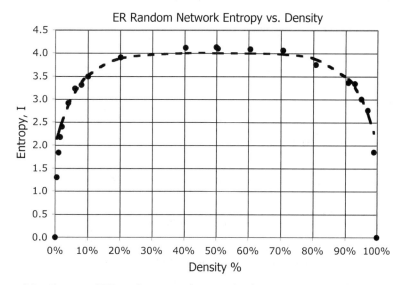

Figure 4.3 Entropy of ER random network versus density as a percentage of fully connected (complete) network: $n = 100$, $m = 100$ to 4950.

$g' = [(n-1)]$, which is far from Poisson! Another way to say this is that random networks become less random as their density diverges from 50%!

4.3.1   Model of Random Network Entropy

We use Fig. 4.3 to derive an expression for random network entropy I(random) as a function of density. Entropy is also a function of number of links m because density $= 2m/(n(n-1))$. Therefore, we can use either one, but density is a convenient metric.

The following derivation depends on the assumption that entropy is symmetric around 50%, but this is only an approximation. Also, note that the data in Fig. 4.3 are not smooth—they do not fall entirely on the smooth curve derived here. The following strategy produces an approximation to random network entropy for $n = 100$:

1. Note the near-symmetry of Fig. 4.3 around 50% density; entropy rises exponentially until reaching approximately 4.0, and then declines exponentially until returning to zero.
2. Estimate entropy versus density over the left half of Fig. 4.3—0–50%; and then "flip" the x axis to obtain a mirror expression for entropy over the right half—50–100%.
3. Combine the two halves of Fig. 4.3: I(random) $= 0.5$ (left half + right half).
4. Simplify the combined expression into one equation.

In the left half of Fig. 4.3, entropy rises exponentially and then flattens off near density $= 50\%$, and similarly declines to zero over the right half of Fig. 4.3. Thus, the left half and right-half expressions model $I(x)$ and $I(1-x)$, for $0 < x < 1$:

$$\text{Left}(x) = A(1 - \exp(-Bx)); \text{ left half}$$
$$\text{Right}(x) = A(1 - \exp(-B(1 - x))); \text{ right half}$$

Combining the two halves; we obtain

$$I(x) = 0.5[\text{left}(x) + \text{right}(x)] = 0.5[A(1 - \exp(-Bx)) + A(1 - \exp(-B(1 - x)))]$$

A least-squares curve fit produces the following estimates for A and B:

$$A = 4, B = 13; \text{ assuming } n = 100$$

Substitution into the expression for $I(x)$ and simplifying yield

$$I(x) = 4 - 2[\exp(-13x) + \exp(-13(1 - x))]; \, 0 < x < 1$$

Therefore, the entropy of the random networks in Fig. 4.3 is, approximately

$$I(\text{random}) = 4 - 2[\exp(-13(\text{density})) + \exp(-13(1 - \text{density}))]; 0 < \text{density} < 1$$

The root-mean-square (RMS) error of this approximation is 0.0545, so this yields an estimate of entropy to within 5 parts per 100. The largest error occurs at extreme values of density, near 0 and 100%. For example, entropy of a random network with density 1% is 1.83, but the approximation yields 2.25. The approximation rapidly improves for $0\% \ll \text{density} \ll 100\%$. For density 10%, the entropy for both approximation and experimental data is 3.46. This approximation is suitable for midrange values of density.

4.3.2 Average Path Length of Random Networks

The average path length of a random network should decrease as the number of links increases because the number of paths between node pairs proliferates—thus providing more opportunity for shorter alternative paths. This is exactly what happens in practice as shown by Fig. 4.4. When the average path lengths of ER and Gilbert random networks are plotted on a log–log scale, average path length dramatically falls off as density increases up to 100%. In fact, average path length should asymptotically reach 1 hop as density reaches 100% because a fully connected network connects every node to every other node. The curves of Fig. 4.4 asymptotically decline to $\log_2(100\%) = 0$, as expected.

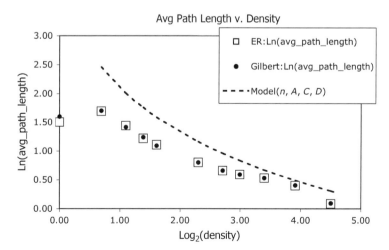

Figure 4.4   Average path length versus density of links for ER, Gilbert networks, and model (dashed line), based on the modified theoretical approximation and base 2 logarithms: $n = 100$, $A = 1.32, C = 1.51, D = 0$.

Newman (Newman, 2000b; Albert, 2002) derived an approximation for the distance between nodes in a random network with average node degree λ, by assuming that the number of nodes reached along a path from arbitrary node v to another node w is approximately $\lambda^D = n$. Newman argued that λ nodes can be reached in 1 hop, λ^2 in 2 hops, λ^3 in 3 hops, and so on, until n nodes are reached in λ^D hops. Solving for D, we obtain

$$D = \frac{\log{(n)}}{\log{(\lambda)}}$$

The average path length of a uniformly random network is proportional to D, and so D makes a good approximation to avg_path_length. But D is only an approximation that assumes the network to be an acyclic tree with each node connecting to λ other nodes. The assumption leads to greater inaccuracy as the density of the node reaches extremes in either direction, perhaps because the topology of the network is less uniform for sparse networks, and less random for dense networks.

A slightly more accurate approximation is obtained by noting that a path from arbitrary node w to all other nodes within the same strongly connected subgraph reaches λ nodes in 1 hop and $\lambda(\lambda - 1)$ nodes in 2 hops because the neighbors of neighbors have $(\lambda - 1)$ outgoing links that do not backtrack to the incoming link used to reach the second-level nodes in a breadth-first search. Subsequent hops in the expanding breadth-first search reach $\lambda(\lambda - 1)^{D-1}$ nodes in D hops. If the entire network belongs to one giant, strongly connected subgraph, then all n nodes are reached in D hops, as follows:

$$n = \lambda(\lambda - 1)^{D-1}$$

Approximating avg_path_length by solving for D, we get

$$D = \frac{\log{(n/\lambda)}}{\log{(\lambda - 1)} + 1}$$

Suppose that we generalize the theoretical approximation by noting $\lambda = n(\text{density})$ and introducing curve-fit parameters A, C, and D:

$$\text{Model}(n, A, C, D) = \frac{A \log{(n)}}{\log{(n(\text{density})C)} + D}$$

This variation is a fair approximation to average path length for fixed n and variable density, as shown by the least-squares fit in Fig. 4.4. For base 2 logarithms, $A = 1.32$,

$C = 1.51$, and $D = 0$, so the average path length is approximately

$$\text{avg\_path\_length(random, denstiy)} = \frac{A \log_2(n)}{\log_2(n(\text{density})C)}$$

$$= \frac{1.32(\log_2(n))}{\log_2(n(\text{denstiy})1.51)}$$

Consider an ER random network of size $n = 100$ and $m = 500$ links. What is the average path length, assuming parameters obtained from Fig. 4.4?

$$\text{Density} = \frac{2m}{n(n-1)} = \frac{1000}{9900} = 0.101 = 10.1\%$$

$$\text{avg\_path\_lenght(random, 0.101)} = \frac{1.32(\log_2(100))}{\log_2((100)(0.101)(1.51))}$$

$$= 1.32\left(\frac{6.64}{3.93}\right) = \frac{8.77}{3.93} = 2.23 \text{ hops}$$

The model generally overestimates average path length as shown in Fig. 4.4, but it is extremely accurate for midrange densities. In this case, both Gilbert and ER generational procedures produce networks with an average path length of 2.23 hops, for $n = 100$, and density $= 10\%$. The approximation matches empirical data.

In Fig. 4.4, note that average path length rapidly decreases in the interval of density equal to $1-4\%$, and then decreases much more slowly beyond 4%. This is an important and significant property of regular, random, and small-world networks. Addition of a small number of links reduces average path length far more than expected. For example, addition of five random links to a 2-regular network of $n = 100$ nodes reduces avg_path_length from 12.9 to 7.1 hops. The average path length is reduced by 45% simply by adding 2.5% more links!

Rapid decline in average path length with the addition of a small number of random links is called the *small-world effect*. Random networks exhibit the small-world effect, as does the class of small-world networks. Why? In general, addition of a few random links creates shortcuts across the network that link (approximately) one-half of the network to the other half. Each successive addition of a random link tends to bisect the network, cutting the distance between two arbitrarily selected nodes by $\frac{1}{2}, \frac{1}{4}, \frac{1}{16}$, and so forth. The small-world effect is studied in detail in the next chapter.

4.3.3 Cluster Coefficient of Random Networks

As the average path length decreases because of an increase in the density of links in a random network, the cluster coefficient does the opposite—it increases. The cluster coefficient increases proportional to density (see Fig. 4.5). In fact, the increase is linear. A simple model of cluster coefficient versus random network density is

Cluster coefficient(random network) = O(density); $1\% \leq$ density $\leq 100\%$

The coefficient of clustering increases with density because more links means that triangular subgraphs are more likely to form. When density equals 100%, the network is no longer random—it is complete. In a complete network, every node is connected to every other node, so the cluster coefficient of every node is 1.0. Alternatively, as a network becomes sparse, its cluster coefficient decreases— ultimately to zero.

Watts and Strogatz (Watts, 1998) derived a theoretical estimate of random network cluster coefficient, as follows:

$$\text{cluster\_coefficent(random network)} = \frac{\lambda}{n}$$

where $\lambda =$ mean degree $= (2m/n) = (n-1)$density $\sim n$(density); $n \gg 1$. Substitution into the Watts–Strogatz equation yields a simple relationship that is confirmed by the experimental results of Fig. 4.5:

$$\text{cluster\_coefficent(random network)} = \text{density} = O(\text{density})$$

The more links there are in a random network, the more clusters. Recall that clusters are created by linking adjacent neighbors to form triangular subgraphs. The more

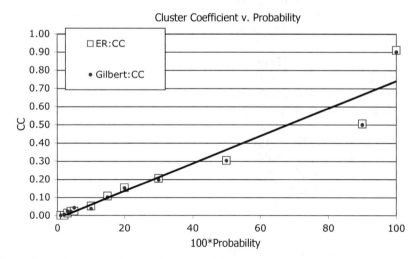

Figure 4.5 Cluster coefficient of ER and Gilbert random networks versus link density (probability). A straight line approximates the relationship cluster_coefficient(random network) = O(density).

triangular subgraphs attached to a node, the higher its cluster coefficient. Increasing density simply increases the likelihood that triangular subgraphs form.

By definition, cluster coefficient of average node v with mean degree λ is:

$$CC = \frac{2c}{\lambda(\lambda - 1)}$$

where c is the number of links among adjacent nodes. Once again, using a mean-field approach to estimation, the number of links among adjacent nodes (forming triangular subgraphs) is λ things taken two at a time:

$$C\binom{\lambda}{2} = \frac{\lambda!}{2!(\lambda - 2)!} \quad \text{if fully connected;}$$

$$\text{density}\left(C\binom{\lambda}{2}\right) = \text{density}\left(\frac{\lambda!}{2!(\lambda - 2)!}\right)$$

if the network is sparse. Thus, the proportion of links present in a cluster equals the network's overall density. Therefore, the mean-field approximation for c is

$$c = \text{density} \frac{\lambda!}{2!(\lambda - 2)!} = \lambda(\lambda - 1)\frac{\text{denstiy}}{2}$$

Substitution into the expression for CC yields

$$CC = \lambda(\lambda - 1)\frac{\text{density}}{\lambda(\lambda - 1)} = \text{density} = \frac{\lambda}{n}$$

4.3.4 Link Efficiency of Random Networks

The link efficiency of a random network is computed easily from the foregoing analysis of path length:

$$E(\text{random}) = \frac{m - \text{avg\_path\_length(random)}}{m} = 1 - \frac{\text{avg\_path\_length(random)}}{m}$$

Number of links m and density d are related by

$$d = \frac{2m}{n(n - 1)}$$

so link efficiency can be expressed in terms of m or d:

$$E(\text{random}) = 1 - \frac{A \log(n)}{m \log(n(\text{density})C)}$$

For example, when $n = 100$, $d = 0.04$ ($m = 200$, $A = 1.32$, $C = 1.51$):

$$E(\text{random}) = 1 - \frac{1.32 \log (100)}{200 \log ((100)(0.04)(1.51))} = 1 - 1.32 \frac{6.64}{200 \log (6.04)}$$

$$= 1 - \frac{8.77}{(200)(2.59)}$$

$$E(\text{random}) = 0.983$$

Compare this with earlier results obtained for regular networks (see Table 3.1). Random networks are highly efficient users of links because of the small-world effect.

Because a small amount of randomness in any network injects a major drop in average path length, randomness results in a large jump in link efficiency! This phenomenon is observed in real small-world systems. For example, biological networks with the small-world effect tend to synchronize more easily than expected because they have a high level of clustering. Clusters consist of triangular subgraphs, and as it turns out, these triangular subgraphs guarantee synchronization—a property of heart (cardiac) pacemakers and some species of crickets!

4.4 PROPERTIES OF RANDOM NETWORKS

Social network analysis is principally interested in the power of actors (nodes) in a social network. But the definition of "power" often varies from one analysis to another. Is social power related to how many links connect an actor to others (hub analysis, how far away an actor is from all other actors (radius and centrality), or the middleperson (intermediary) position of an actor (closeness)? Generally, the property chosen depends on the questions asked by a social scientist. Diameter and radius are adequate properties to use in studies like the Milgram experiment, centrality may be more appropriate for epidemiology (in humans and Internet structures), and betweenness/closeness may be more appropriate in group dynamics. The implication for understanding human networks is explored in greater detail in Chapter 10.

The *diameter* of a network is the maximum-length path across all node-pairs, and the *center* of a network is the minimum of the maximum length paths, from any node to any other node. Diameter and centrality decrease as network density increases, as expected. In addition like average path length, the decrease in diameter is dramatic, as shown in Fig. 4.6. Once again, this is due to the small-world effect. Generally, diameter is 1 hop greater than average path length. Surprisingly, centrality can be larger than average path length. Why?

Diameter and radius plummet with increase in density, but closeness does not! This counterintuitive result is shown to be a consequence of two forces acting simultaneously on the structure of direct paths in a random network—increasing the

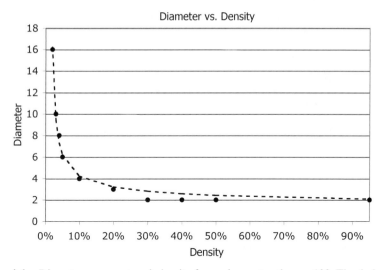

Figure 4.6   Diameter versus network density for random network: $n = 100$. The dashed-line graph is obtained from the approximation parameters $A = 2.0$, $C = 0.44$, $D = 1.0$.

number of links also increases the number of paths through a typical node, and increasing density also decreases the average path length, which decreases closeness! We show that closeness rapidly increases to a peak, and then slowly decreases to zero, beyond approximately 20–30% for networks of size $n = 100,200$.

4.4.1   Diameter of Random Networks

We model the decrease in diameter as density increases using a modified average path length model:

$$\text{Model}(n, A, C, D) = \frac{A \log(n)}{\log(n(\text{density})C) + D}$$

For $n = 100$, and the data provided by running *Network.jar* 3 times for each value of density and averaging, we obtain the parameters that approximate diameter:[3]

$$A = 2.0; \ C = 0.44; \ D = 1.0$$

$$\text{Diameter(random)} = \frac{2 \log(n)}{\log(0.44n(\text{density})) + 1}$$

---

[3]Base 2 logarithms were used in these curve fits.

For example, suppose that density $= 0.50$. Compare diameter and average path length of a random network with $n = 100$ nodes:

$$\text{Diameter} = \frac{2 \log (100)}{\log ((0.44)(100)(0.5)) + 1} = 2.43 \text{ hops}$$

$$\text{avg\_path\_length} = \frac{1.32 \log (100)}{\log ((100)(0.5)(1.51))} = 1.41 \text{ hops}$$

But of course, hops must be whole numbers, so diameter equals 3 and average path length equals 2 hops.

$$\text{Diameter(random)} = \frac{2 \log (n)}{\log (0.44n(\text{density})) + 1} .$$

4.4.2 Radius of Random Networks

Average path length and diameter of a random network "shrink" as density increases. Similarly, random network *centrality* "shrinks" with increasing density according to the following approximation for radius

$$\text{Radius(random)} = \frac{A \log (n)}{\log (n(\text{density})C) + D}$$

for $n = 100$, $A = 1.59$, $C = 0.88$, and $D = 0.5$. For example, suppose that $d = 50\%$:

$$\text{Radius(random)} = \frac{1.59 \log (100)}{\log ((100)(0.5)(0.88)) + 0.5} = 1.59 \frac{6.64}{\log (44) + 0.5} = \frac{10.56}{5.46}$$

$$= 1.77 \text{ hops}$$

But since hops are integers and not fractions, this yields 2 hops.

Why is the radius of the central node greater than the average path length (1.77 vs. 1.41)? The radius of the central node is not the minimum of shortest paths, but rather the minimum of longest paths! In other words, radius equals the number of hops from the central node to the most remote node. The average path, on the contrary, is an average over short and long paths. Therefore, it is entirely possible for the average path length to be smaller than the radius of the central node. The radius of a network is very large if only one pair of nodes is separated by a long distance.

4.4.3 Closeness Calculation in Java

Closeness of node w is defined as the number of direct paths from every other node u to every other node v running through node w. We must trace the n^2 shortest paths traversed from every node to every other node, count the number of paths running through the nodes along each path, and then sum the counts for each node. This is exhaustive work for a computer! The code fragment, displayed below, initializes the nodes of a network and then calls method `doShortestPath(start_node, end_node)` n^2 times—once for each pair of nodes. The total number of paths through each node are accumulated in `node[i].value`, and normalized closeness values are returned in `node[i].radius`.

```
for(int start_node = 0; start_node < nNodes; start_node++){
        for(int end_node = 0; end_node < nNodes; end_node++){
            for(int i = 0; i  < nNodes; i++) {//Reset search flags
                node[i].visited = false;
                node[i].level = 0;
            }
            doShortestPath(start_node, end_node);
        }
    }
```

Method `doShortestPath()` uses the same breadth-first search (BFS) technique introduced in Chapter 2. The level of each node relative to the `starting_node` is calculated and stored in `node[i].level`. But, unlike the average path length calculation, which is interested only in path length, `doShortestPath()` must backtrack along the shortest path and mark each backtracked node as it goes. This part of the algorithm is tricky because there are many nodes left in the queue that were visited, but are not aligned with the shortest path. For this reason, we must employ a pushdown stack to remember links as well as nodes. As we backtrack along links and nodes, discarding links that do not connect to the nodes belonging to the shortest path, we count the number of visits, and store them in `node[i].value`.

There are two phases of the algorithm: phase 1, which performs a BFS to find the destination node, `end`; and phase 2, which backtracks along the visited nodes and links until it returns to the starting node `start`. Nodes at the same level are saved in a FIFO queue `que` and links along the search path are stored in a FILO stack `pds`. Links that do not match up with nodes are discarded. This guarantees that a unique path is found, avoiding deadends and cycles:

```
private void doShortestPath(int start, int end) {
        if(start == end) return;
        boolean found = false;          //break from loops
        int n0 = start;                 //Current node#
        int next_node = -1;             //Spanning tree nodes
        int l0 = -1;                    //Current link#
        int n_level = 0;                //Current level
        node[n0].level = 0;             //Start here
        node[n0].visited = true;        //Avoid cycles
        Stack que = new Stack(nNodes+1);    //Node FIFO queue
        Stack pds = new Stack(nLinks+1);    //Link pushdown stack
        que.init();
        que.push(n0);                   //Remember nodes
        pds.init();                     //Remember links
        while(que.notEmpty() && !found){//Forward BFS
            n_level++;                  //Shortest path++
            n0 = que.pull();
            for(int e = 0; e  < nLinks; e++){
                next_node = -1;             //Find link to next_node
```

```
        if(Link[ e] .head == n0 && !node[ Link[ e] .tail] .visited)
            next_node = Link[e].tail;
        else if(Link[ e] .tail == n0 && !node[ Link[ e] .head] .visited)
                    next_node = Link[e].head;
        if(next_node == -1) continue; //Skip node
        pds.push(e);
        found = (next_node == end);
        if(found) break;
        node[next_node].visited = true;
        node[next_node].level = n_level;
        que.push(next_node);              //Not found
    }//Over links
}//Over nodes
//Phase 2
if(found){
    n0 = next_node;
    found = false;                       //Backtrack to start
    while(pds.notEmpty() && !found){
        l0 = pds.pop();                  //Pop a link
        next_node = -1;                  //Find next node
        if(n0 == Link[ l0] .head)        //Ignore all but...
            next_node = Link[l0].tail;
        else if(n0 == Link[ l0] .tail)
            next_node = Link[l0].head;
        if(next_node >= 0 && node[ next_node] .level  < n_level){ //Backtrack
            found = (next_node == start); //Start reached?
            if(found) break;
            node[next_node].value++;
            n0 = next_node;
            n_level-- ;
        }
    }
}
else Message = "Error: Path Not found!";
return;
}//doShortestPath
```

This method returns the number of paths running through each node in variable `node[i].value`, but this is not the normalized closeness property we want. Therefore, method `NW_doCloseness()` must normalize as follows:

```
r.big = 0;
double avg_radius = 0.0;
if(max_closeness > 0){                //Normalize closeness
    r.big = 100;
    for(int i = 0; i  < nNodes; i++) {
        node[i].radius = (int)(100*node [ i] .value/max_closeness);
        avg_radius += node[i].radius;
    }
    avg_radius = avg_radius/nNodes;
}
```

Program *Network.jar* displays the network in a window with nodes containing the normalized closeness value stored in `node[i].radius`, and a banner with the average closeness value. The most powerful intermediary will have a closeness value of 100, and less powerful nodes will have closeness values in the interval [0,100]. The higher the normalized closeness value, the more powerful a node, because this means that more paths must traverse the node to get from one node to another node in the network.

Closeness is very different than centrality, as we have defined it, here. *Centrality* is a distance metric, while *closeness* is a connectivity metric. A close node is a connector—a kind of broker that mediates the connection of one node to another. Centrality is simply a measure of how many hops it takes for a central node to reach all others. The question is, which property is more important?

4.4.4 Closeness in Random Networks

Intuitively, we would expect average closeness to increase as the number of links (density) increases because more links imply more paths. But this does not happen, as we can see in Fig. 4.7. Initially, closeness rises very rapidly, but then it reaches a peak and slowly declines. In fact, the rise and fall is more pronounced for $n = 200$ than for $n = 100$. Why?

Suppose that we test the following hypothesis: Closeness initially increases due to the increase in number of links because the number of paths increases. But eventually, the increase in links produces shorter paths because of the small-world effect. These shorter paths bypass the (larger number of) alternative and longer paths. Short paths short-circuit the longer ones, which tend to decrease the number of paths running through a typical node. At some density point, the number of paths running through a typical node starts to decline. The closeness metric increases, then decreases, as density rises.

This hypothesis is supported by Fig. 4.8, which shows a correlation between the normalized number of paths running through the closest node versus average path length. Apparently, there is a somewhat linear relationship between closeness and path length:[4]

$$\frac{\text{Number of paths through intermediate node}}{n} = O(\text{avg\_path\_length})$$

Furthermore, there is an inverse relationship between closeness and density because

$$\text{avg\_path\_length} = O\left(\frac{\log(n)}{\log(\lambda)}\right), \quad \text{and } \lambda = n(\text{density}):$$

$$\text{Number of paths through intermediate node} = O\left(\frac{n \log(n)}{\log(n(\text{density}))}\right)$$

Therefore, the closeness of a typical node should eventually diminish with an increase in density. But this is not the complete picture because increasing density also leads to

---

[4]One can argue that the correlation in Fig. 4.8 does not entirely follow a linear regression because of the "wavy pattern" of the data.

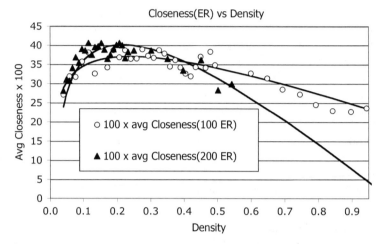

Figure 4.7 Average closeness versus density for random networks of size $n = 100, 200$. Closeness rises to a peak and then declines with increase in number of links.

more paths. To explain Fig. 4.7, we need to consider two factors: length of average paths and number of direct paths.

Suppose that we estimate the number of paths passing through a typical node using the following mean-field approach. Node v has an average of λ links attached to it. Each link connects v to approximately λ^r other nodes, where $r = $ diameter of the network. Therefore, the number of paths through node v should be proportional to λ^r, but we know from Fig. 4.7 that increases in density lead to shortcuts around node v. Instead, the number of paths through v decreases with density, according

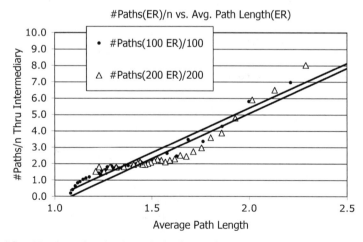

Figure 4.8 Number of paths through the largest intermediary node versus average path length of a random network for $n = 100, 200$.

to (1-density). Combining these two factors into one, we obtain

$$100(\text{closeness(random)}) = C_0(1 - \text{density})\lambda^r + C_1$$

$$r = \frac{A \log_2(n)}{\log_2(B\lambda) + C}$$

where, C_0, C_1, A, B, and C are constants. The following parameters for approximating 100(average closeness) yield the solid-line curves of Fig. 4.7:

$$n = 100 : C_0 = 0.2, C_1 = 22, A = 1.275, B = 1, \; C = 1.275$$
$$= 200 : C_0 = 0.21, C_1 = 1, A = 1.275, B = 1, \; C = 1.275$$

Therefore, closeness(random) $= O((1 - \text{density})\lambda^r)$, which supports the conjecture that average closeness is a function of sparseness (1-density) and average path length. In other words, closeness increases with an increase in the number of links, but is soon overwhelmed by the rapid drop in length of shortest paths, due to the small-world effect. As we shall see in subsequent chapters, this is *not* the case for scale-free or small-world networks, However. Closeness is a property that behaves differently in different classes of networks.

4.5   WEAK TIES IN RANDOM NETWORKS

Consider the following example of a social network. The population of Pointville, Flatland is 129. The village is unusual in that everyone is equally likely to know everyone else, but because of their busy social life, Flatlanders have time to become friendly with an average of only 24 other Flatlanders. We want to predict what is most likely to happen if Milgram's experiment were performed in Pointville. How many degrees of separation are there between the citizens of Pointville? Also, what does it mean to be close in Pointville?

What are the longest and shortest weak ties across Pointville? Recall that a *weak tie* is a chain of acquaintances that leads from person u to person w, for any node pair $u \sim w$, across the entire population. Assuming that there are no hermits in Pointville, the longest and shortest weak ties are equivalent to the diameter and radius of this population. Further, given the average path length of Pointville, we can estimate the average closeness of its citizens.

The strategy for solving this problem is

1. Derive an equation for number of links m in terms of mean node degree λ.
2. Substitute the equation for m into density, and use density and λ to calculate diameter, radius, and average closeness.
3. Let $n = 129$ and average node degree $\lambda = 24$: use approximations derived from Fig. 4.7 and $n = 100$.

The number of links $m = \lambda(n/2)$ because the sum of all node degrees equals twice the number of links: $n\lambda = 2m$. Substitute this into the equation for network density:

$$\text{Density} = d = \frac{2\,m}{n(n-1)} = \frac{2\lambda(n/2)}{n(n-1)} = \frac{\lambda}{n-1}$$

Substitution of density into the approximations for diameter and radius derived earlier (we assume that $n = 100$ and $n = 129$ give similar values of parameters $A, C,$ and D):

$$\text{Diameter} = \frac{2\log(n)}{\log(0.44nd) + 1}$$

$$\text{Radius} = \frac{1.59\log(n)}{\log(nd0.88) + 0.5}$$

Now, let $n = 129$ and $\lambda = 24$:

$$d = \frac{24}{128} = 0.1875$$

$$\text{Diameter} = \frac{2\log(129)}{\log((0.44)(129)(0.1875)) + 1} = 3.18 \text{ or } 4\,\text{hops}$$

$$\text{Radius} = \frac{1.59\log(129)}{\log((129)(0.1875)(0.88)) + 0.5} = 2.77 \text{ or } 3\,\text{hops}$$

The longest and shortest weak ties differ by 1 hop. Every person in Pointville knows every other person through at most four intermediaries. Pointville is a tightly knit group. More importantly, the diameter of Pointville is relatively small even when each person knows an average of only $\lambda = 6$ people instead of 24. According to the approximation developed here, the diameter of this less friendly version of Pointville is 6 hops, and the radius of the central person is 5 hops. Rumors are likely to spread rather quickly in Pointville.

The average closeness of a Flatlander can be estimated by similar means using the approximation equation:

$$100(\text{closeness(Pointville)}) = 0.2(1 - \text{density})\lambda^r + 22$$

$$r = \frac{1.275\log_2(n)}{\log_2(\lambda) + 1.275} = 1.525$$

Substitution into the equation for closeness yields

$$100(\text{closeness}) = 0.2(1 - 0.1875)24^{1.525} = (0.2)(0.8125)(127.5) + 22$$
$$= 42.7$$

Averaging over five trials using program *Network.jar* yields an average closeness value of 40.1. The approximation equation is good for densities less than 50%, but becomes less accurate for larger densities.

A community such as Pointville becomes closer as the average number of acquaintances per individual increases. The "six degrees of separation" experiment conducted by Stanley Milgram (Milgram, 1967) is based on mathematical fact. Introduction of small amounts of randomness into the fabric of a social network produces prodigious results. The "distance" between nodes sharply drops even though the network is very sparse. Furthermore, we can see from Fig. 4.7 that random Pointville closeness peaks at about 40 on a scale of 0–100, at approximately 25% density. As the number of social ties increases, the number and size of intermediaries rapidly declines—because average path length rapidly declines.

4.6 RANDOMIZATION OF REGULAR NETWORKS

Social network analysis of Pointville shows that a relatively small number of acquaintances leads to relatively high centrality and short weak ties. What happens to network centrality when a small number of random links are added to a regular network? Do diameter, radius, and average path length plummet for a regular network as they do for a random network?

Consider the effect on diameter, radius, and avg_path_length of a ring network, $n = m = 100$, as one random link at a time is added to the ring. Each random link increases entropy and reduces diameter, radius, and avg_path_length as shown by the plot of Fig. 4.9. As randomness increases—indicated by the linear increase in

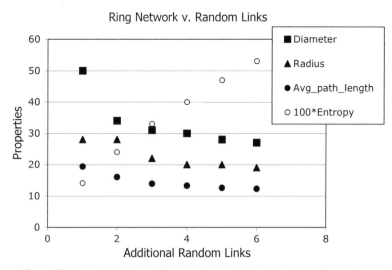

Figure 4.9 Effect on diameter, radius, average path length, and $100\times$ entropy of ring network as the number of additional random links increases.

entropy—diameter, radius, and average path length quickly diminish. In fact, most of the decline occurs after addition of the first four or five random links. Figure 4.9 illustrates the dramatic impact of a small amount of randomness on a regular network. The small-world effect is due mainly to the insertion of a small amount of randomness into any regular network. The effect is purely mathematical, and has little to do with human nature, geography, physics, or biology!

4.7 ANALYSIS

Few phenomena of nature are purely random. So, why study randomness? The answer: to establish a baseline that can be compared with nonrandom phenomenon. Most realworld systems contain structure—they are rarely purely random systems. For example, wiring diagrams of electric circuits, roads and railways, water systems, and most other synthetic systems are nonrandom networks. Contrasting a purely random system with a structured system reveals the nature of the structured system.

What are the characteristics of a random network that sets it apart from a nonrandom network? In this chapter we have analyzed five major properties of networks that distinguish "randomness" from structure: degree sequence, entropy, average path length, closeness, and cluster coefficient. How do these properties differ between a structured network and a random network? Figure 4.10 compares a ring network with a random network along four property axes: entropy, average path length, hub degree, and cluster coefficient. Closeness comparisons will have to wait until we have studied scale-free and small-world networks, but it, too, will differ among the other classes of networks.

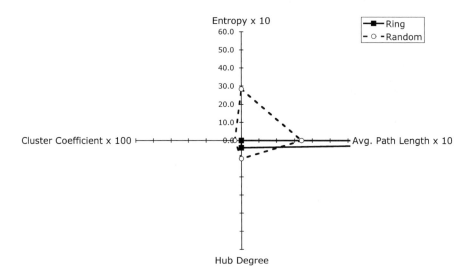

Figure 4.10 Kiviat graph of ring versus random networks. Ring network (solid line), $n = 100$, $m = 100$. Random network (dashed line), $n = 100$, $m = 200$, averaged over three randomly generated networks.

The data plotted as a Kiviat graph (also known as a "radar" plot in Microsoft Excel) shows several major differences between a ring graph with $n = 100$ nodes, $m = 100$ links, and a random network with $n = 100$, $m = 200$. This data was obtained by averaging over three trials in each case.

A Kiviat graph is used to plot k properties along k axes. In this case, $k = 4$: one axis each for entropy, average path length, hub degree, and cluster coefficient. Entropy, average path length, and cluster coefficient were scaled by 10, 10, and 100, respectively, to make the measurements comparable along similar scales.

Figure 4.10 clearly shows the difference between random and structured (ring) networks. Specifically, random networks have a high entropy value, small average path length value, and low hub degree value. Conversely, the structured ring network has zero or near-zero values of entropy, cluster coefficient, and hub degree, but relatively high average path length—shown off the scale in Fig. 4.10. Specifically, the average path length of the ring is 25 hops, versus roughly 3.3 hops for the random network.

Perhaps the most distinguishing property of the class of random networks is the typically high value of entropy, I. However, we learned in this chapter that entropy of a random network depends on the density of the network. It is possible for a random network to exhibit low entropy as well as high entropy. Entropy is maximized in a random network only when density is near 50%. Therefore, generalizations may be misleading without knowledge of the network's density.

Assuming a reasonable density, random networks fall into the first quadrant of a Kiviat graph—the upper right quadrant of Fig. 4.10. Structured networks lie along the average path length axis as shown in Fig. 4.10. Later, when we study scale-free and small-world networks, it will become obvious that the Kiviat graph of a scale-free network lies somewhat symmetrically centered around the origin of the Kiviat graph, and that a typical small-world network graph forms a flattened oval longitudinally aligned along the horizontal axes of the Kiviat graph. These shapes are explored in subsequent chapters, but for now, we can summarize properties of the class of networks studied in this book as follows:

Structured	Flat, along average path length axis
Random	First quadrant of Kiviat graph
Scale-free	Circle, centered on origin
Small-world	Elongated or flattened oval with higher values of cluster coefficient and average path length, than entropy and hub degree

4.8 EXERCISES

4.1. What is the average path length of a random network with $n = 50$ nodes and $m = 200$ links?

4.2. What is the entropy of a random network with $n = 50$ and density $= 50\%$? Compare your answer with the approximation given by Fig. 4.3.

4.3. Why is Fig. 4.3 (nearly) symmetric about density $= 50\%$?

4.4. Propose a "fix" to the ER, Gilbert, or anchored random network generative procedures that guarantee every network produced by these algorithms is strongly connected.

4.5. What is the diameter of a random network with $n = 50$, and an average node degree $\lambda = 5$?

4.6. What is the minimum number of links to guarantee a diameter of no more than 5 hops in a random network with $n = 100$ nodes?

4.7. For a network with $n = 100$ nodes, what is the average degree per node λ that guarantees a network diameter of 5 hops?

4.8. What is the link efficiency of a random network with $n = 100$, $m = 500$?

4.9. What is the cluster coefficient of a random network with $n = 1000$, $m = 10,000$?

4.10. How many links are needed to raise the cluster coefficient of a random network with $n = 10,000$ nodes to 0.33?

4.11. What is the average closeness of a random network with $n = 200$, $m = 500$?

4.12. How many links does a random network with $n = 200$ nodes need to guarantee an average closeness of 30?

5

SMALL-WORLD NETWORKS

Small-world networks are sparse networks with high cluster coefficient, relatively short average path length, and *scalable* entropy. The entropy of a small-world network can be lowered to lie near the structured end of the structure spectrum or raised to more closely approximate a random network. Thus, the class of small-world networks lies somewhere between regular and random networks. This property has intrigued mathematicians and stimulated a number of conjectures about the connection between small-world topology and behaviors in physics, biology, and social networks.

The small-world effect, first observed by Stanley Milgram, is studied in detail here. In simple terms, the *small-world effect* is the rapid decline in average path length as a small number of random links are added to a (structured) network. On deeper examination, it is not surprising that path length is greatly diminished by the addition of a few random links. Intuitively, random links tend to bisect a network, effectively dividing the distance between opposite halves of the network by 50%. Addition of a second random link does the same—effectively reducing distance by 25%, and so on. Thus, the "six degrees of separation" of the small-world effect might better be called "50% elimination of separation."

The fundamental small-world network is generated by the Watts–Strogatz (WS) procedure described and studied here. The canonical form of the WS algorithm starts with a 2-regular network. A small-world network emerges from the 2-regular network by randomly rewiring pm links, where p is the rewiring probability. The random rewiring injects a (limited) amount of randomness into the regular

Network Science: Theory and Practice. By Ted G. Lewis
Copyright © 2009 John Wiley & Sons, Inc.

network. As it turns out, a very small amount of randomness goes a long way. Typically, the small-world transitions from purely regular to slightly random for $p^* = 1$–4%. This phase transition *threshold*, or *crossover point*, has taken on a number of meanings in various applications. For example, phase transition is claimed to explain the *Ising effect*—the transition to magnetic polarity in ferrous materials. It has also been used to explain why small-world networks tend to synchronize more than do purely random or purely structured networks.

Many other startling attributes have been claimed for small-world networks. For example, Strogatz suggests that the synchronized chirping of a certain species of crickets is a consequence of the small-world effect (Strogatz, 2003). Because small-world networks share some properties of random networks—such as short path length—some researchers have jumped to the conclusion they also behave like random networks. Some of these claims have been verified experimentally. Some are myths. Before sorting out which claims are fundamentally sound, we must develop a deeper understanding of small-world networks.

In this chapter, we study the following:

1. Randomizing the links of a 2-regular network creates basic small-world networks. This historically significant generative procedure was first proposed by Watts and Strogatz, and is called the *Watts–Strogatz* (WS) *algorithm*. Such networks are designated *WS-generated*, or simply *WS small-world networks*.

2. The degree sequence distribution of a WS-generated small world is taller and thinner than an equivalent random network:

$$h(d) = \sum_{i=1}^{\min\{d-k,k\}} B(k, i, 1 - p)P(pk, d - k - i) \quad \text{for } d \geq k,$$

where k is the size of the underlying k-regular network, p is rewiring probability

$$B(k, i, 1 - p)C\binom{i}{k}(1 - p)^i p^{k-i}, \quad P(pk, d - k - i) = (pk)^{d-k-i}$$

$$\times \exp\left(\frac{-pk}{d - k - i}\right)!$$

and $C\binom{i}{k}$ is the combinatorial function. The distribution becomes shorter and wider, as rewiring probability p increases.

3. Entropy of the class of small-world networks is scalable from nearly structured (low entropy) to fully random networks (high entropy). Entropy can be adjusted by the designer through selection of the WS rewiring probability p or number of links (density). For initial 2-regular starting network, the

2-regular WS small-world entropy is approximated by

$$I_{WS}(p) = A \; \log_2 (100p) = O(\log(p))$$

where A is a coefficient that depends on the size of the network n. Entropy is also a function of density $= 2k/n$. For general k-regular WS small worlds, and fixed rewiring probability, we obtain

$$I_{WS(density)} = A \; \log_2 (B(density)) - C = O(\log(density)),$$

where A, B, and C depend on network size n.

4. Path length rapidly declines as entropy increases as a result of rewiring. The average path length of a 2-regular WS small world is approximated by the Newman–Moore–Watts equation:

$$\text{avg\_path\_length(SW)} = n \frac{fr}{2k} = \left(\frac{2n}{\beta k} \right) \tanh^{-1} \left(\frac{r}{\beta} \right)$$

Where $r = 2pm$, and $\beta = \text{sqrt}(r^2 + 4r)$. We derive a simpler and more accurate power-law approximation for small p

$$\text{avg\_path\_length(r)} = n/(4k/r^q)$$

where $r = pm = pkn$, $q = $ constant. For $k = 2$, we obtain $q = \frac{1}{3}$ by curve fitting. According to simulation data for $k = 2$, average path length varies inversely with the cube root of rewiring probability:

$$\text{avg\_path\_length} = O \left(\frac{1}{\sqrt[3]{p}} \right)$$

5. Small-world network clustering rapidly decreases as entropy increases. For k-regular small worlds, Newman and Watts suggest

$$CC(k\text{-regular}, p) = 3k \frac{k - 1}{2k(2k - 1) + 8pk^2 + 4p^2k^2}$$

When entropy is zero, rewiring probability $p = 0$, so the cluster coefficient, $CC(k\text{-regular}, 0) = 3((k - 1)/2(2k - 1))$. But a much simpler equation derived by Barrat and Weigt gives accurate approximations with much less work (Barrat, 1999, 2000):

$$CC(k, p) = CC(k\text{-regular}, 0)(1 - p)^3$$

We argue that cluster coefficient is more a property of the underlying k-regular network than an inherent property of all small worlds. Clustering is greatly impacted if a hypercube or toroidal network is used in place of a k-regular network in the WS generative procedure. Therefore, we conclude that the small-world effect is due mainly to the bisection that occurs when a few links of a regular network are randomized.

6. Average *closeness* of a small-world network rises, falls, and then rises again, according to density d, size n, mean degree λ, and rewiring probability p:

$$\text{Closeness(small world)} = O(\text{density}(z))$$

where $z = \lambda^r$ and

$$r = O\left(\frac{\log (n - (1 - p))\lambda}{\log (\lambda)}\right)$$

This suggests that closeness in a small-world, unlike a random, network is correlated with both density and the underlying regularity of the initial k-regular network. Contrary to intuition, closeness of a node does *not* improve the ability of a message to rapidly find its way through a small-world network.

7. Small-world networks exhibit the small-world effect because of the abrupt decline in average path length while maintaining the cluster coefficient of the underlying regular network. Because of random bisection, 2-regular WS small-world networks transition from regular to random topology near a crossover rewiring probability $p^* \sim O(1/n)$. This marks the transition from "mostly structured" to "mostly random" topology. For this reason, small worlds make good models of phase transition phenomena, such as the transition of a liquid to a solid, or inert iron to magnetic iron.

8. Navigation of a network using local properties of nodes is faster using a *maximum-degree selection* algorithm than a *minimum-radius, maximum-closeness*, or *random selection* algorithm. In the study performed in this chapter, WS small-world networks are shown to be more difficult to navigate than random or scale-free networks. While small worlds tend to have relatively short average path length, it is more difficult to find the shortest path through a small world using local information such as node degree, closeness, and node radius than equivalent random networks. This has profound implications for packet-switching communication networks.

This chapter uses program *Network.jar* to generate and analyze each example described here. The Java methods for implementing the generative procedures given in this chapter are simplified versions of the code found in *Network.jar*.

5.1 GENERATING A SMALL-WORLD NETWORK

Small-world networks are *scalable*—they can be almost as structured as a regular network and hence their entropy is low, or they can be somewhat random with high entropy comparable to that of a random network. Scalability of entropy is determined by a rewiring probability p, which determines the probability of switching one end of each link to connect it with a randomly selected node. Rewiring probability p is similar to the link probability used to generate the Gilbert random network. However, instead of determining whether to include a link in the network, rewiring probability p is used to determine whether one end of a link is switched to a randomly selected node.

In this section, we provide a simple set of microrules for converting a k-regular graph into a small world by rewiring the links of the k-regular network with probability p. All nodes of the initial k-regular network are equal to $\lambda = 2k$. Therefore, the degree sequence distribution is a spike at $d = 2k$, but this spike begins to flatten out and spread wider as links are rewired. Each link is visited and rewired (connected to a randomly chosen head node), with probability p. In the end, this leaves $(1-p)m$ links as they were (part of the initial 2-regular network), and randomizes the remaining pm links. The resulting small world is partly structured and partly random—and so its degree sequence distribution falls in between the spike of a k-regular network, and the Poisson distribution of a random network.

The class of WS small-world networks can be generated with a small amount of randomness (small p), or a large amount (large p), depending on the value of p. This is illustrated in Fig. 5.1. Initially, the network resembles Fig. 5.1a. After pm links are

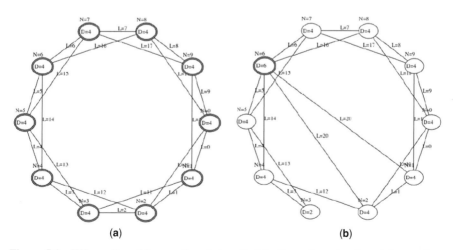

(a)   (b)

Figure 5.1   WS small-world generation starts with (a) a 2-regular network and then evolves into (b) a semirandom and semistructured "slightly small-world" network: $n = 10$, $m = 20$.

rewired, the network resembles Fig. 5.1b. A small amount of entropy is introduced by rewiring only 10% of the 20 links. Each head of the two rewired links are diverted to a randomly chosen node.

Surprisingly, redirection of two links has a dramatic impact on several properties of interest: degree sequence distribution, diameter, radius, and average path length. For small rewiring probability p, most of the network remains structured. Because the k-regular network has a high cluster coefficient, the resulting small-world network also has a high cluster coefficient. But even a small amount of rewiring radically decreases network diameter, radius, and average path length, while retaining most of the clustering inherent in the k-regular network. The dramatic decrease in diameter, radius, and average path length is known as the *small-world effect*.

5.1.1   The Watts–Strogatz (WS) Procedure

Watts and Strogatz devised the Watts–Strogatz small-world network generation procedure in 1998; hence the name *Watts–Strogatz* or *WS small-world network*. Newman et al. modified the procedure to avoid isolated nodes and components, which led to the NSWS model (Newman, 2000a, 2000b). The Newman et al. generation procedure is similar to the Gilbert random network generation procedure because it uses a similar "anchoring" algorithm to avoid separation of the network into components. The WS generative procedure assumes an initial 2-regular network, but we generalize the procedure to allow density to vary, which is achieved by setting $k = (n/m)$, and starting with a k-regular network ($\lambda = 2k$).

The WS generation procedure is simple—start with a 2-regular network and rewire a percentage of its links to "randomize them." The initial 2-regular network has a lattice structure, as shown in Fig. 5.1a, and the resulting small-world network has some regular and some random structure, as shown in Fig. 5.1b. Rewiring consists of replacing the head node of a link with a randomly selected different node. Each link is visited and rewired with probability p; hence, a small-world network evolves into a semistructured, semirandom network. On the average, pm links are "random" and $(1-p)m$ links are structured.

WS Generative Procedure

1. Given n, rewiring probability p, and $k = 2$, generate a k-regular graph by connecting each of n nodes to their immediate neighbors, and neighbor's neighbors. This network has $m = 2n$ links [$\lambda = 4$, density $= (4/n)$].

2. For every link, $\mu = 1, 2, \ldots, m$, rewire μ with probability p, as follows. If (Math.random() $< p$), disconnect the head(μ), and rewire it to a different randomly selected node. Avoid ($v_{\text{random}} = $ head(μ)), and duplicate links. Otherwise, do nothing.

This generation procedure is simple, but does not guarantee a connected network. If all links connecting a node to the network are rewired, it is possible for that node to become isolated. Therefore, a number of enhancements (proposed by a variety of researchers) can be applied to the basic algorithm to remove this deficiency. For example, we can modify the WS procedure to avoid rewiring when it would remove the final link from a node. This is similar to the anchored random network modification applied to the Erdos–Renyi procedure described in the previous chapter. This enhancement is left as an exercise for the reader.[1]

The following Java method implements the WS network generation procedure. The initial 2-regular network is created by methods NW_doCreateNodes(), NW_doRing(1, **true**), and NW_doRing(2, **true**). Method NW_doRing() is called twice: once to insert links into the network to form a 1-regular structure, and again to form a 2-regular structure. This establishes the initial 2-regular network illustrated in Fig. 5.1.

Step 2 of the generation procedure is implemented by the remaining code in NW_doCreateSmallWorld() taken from program *Network.jar*. Each link is visited once, and rewired with probability $p = $ nConnectionProbability, which is a global constant set by the user. The remaining code simply avoids loops and duplicate links.

```java
public void NW_doCreateSmallWorld(){
    NW_doCreateNodes(nInputNodes);                    //Create 2-regular network
    NW_doRing(1, true);
    NW_doRing(2, true);
    for(int j = 0; j < nLinks; j++){                  //Rewire ring links
      if((int)(100*Math.random()) < = nConnectionProbability){
        boolean done = false;
        while(!done){
          int to_node = Link [ j] .head;
          int from_node = Link [ j] .tail;
          int new_node = (int)(nNodes * Math.random()); //Random head
            while(new_node == to_node)
              new_node = (int)(nNodes * Math.random()); //New head
              if(NW_doAddLink(node[ from_node] .name,
              node [ new_node] .name)){
                NW_doCutLink(j);                      //Erase old link
                     done = true;
            }
          }
        }
      }
    }
}//NW_doCreateSmallWorld
```

The **while**(!done) loop in this method may seem unnecessary, but it guarantees the rewiring when method NW_doAddLink() finds a duplicate link. Recall that method NW_doAddLink() checks for duplicate links and returns **false** if method NW_doCreateSmallWorld() attempts to add a duplicate link.

[1]Because of its simplicity and fixed density property, the WS model is used throughout this book.

The **while** loop iterates until a nonduplicate, nonlooping link is successfully rewired. (*Note*: This could result in an infinite loop if the 2-regular starting network was *n*-regular, or complete. This cannot occur if the WS rules are followed.)

One final note—rewiring is done by inserting a new link and deleting the old link. It is possible that a new link fails to insert, because it would be a duplicate. Therefore, the old link is *not* deleted until a successful insert occurs. If all links successfully redirect when selected, network density remains the same before and after rewiring: $d(4/n)$.

5.1.2   Generalized WS Procedure

The density of a small world can be adjusted by modifying the initialization procedure of WS. Instead of starting with a 2-regular network, we can start with a *k*-regular network, where $k = m/n$. Program *Network.jar* provides a second method for constructing a general small world network, which is very similar, except for a round-robin algorithm for inserting links into the *k* regular starting network. The value of *k* depends on the number of nodes and links specified by the user. This requires insertion of $k = m/n$ rings to generate the initial *k*-regular network.

Method NW_doCreateGSmallWorld() inserts rings to form a 1-regular, 2-regular, 3-regular (etc.) network until nInputLinks have been inserted into the *k*-regular network. This version also attempts to find a new link to rewire when the randomly selected link cannot be rewired because of a duplicate. This modification is implemented using variable switched, to signal whether a duplicate rewiring was attempted.

```
public void NW_doCreateGSmallWorld(){
  NW_doCreateNodes(nInputNodes);
  int offset = 1;                                    //Ring number
  while(offset > 0 && offset < nInputNodes/2){
    for(int i=0; i < nNodes; i++){    //Ring around the Rosie
      if(nLinks < = nInputLinks){ offset = 0; break;}
      int k = i+offset;
      if(k < = nNodes) k- = nNodes;
      NW_doAddLink(node[i].name, node[k].name); //Ignore duplicates
    }
    if(offset > 0) offset++;
  }
  for(int j = 0; j < nLinks; j++){        //Rewire && eliminate infinite loop
    if((int)(100*Math.random()) > = nConnectionProbability){
        int to_node = Link [ j] .head;
        int from_node = Link [ j] .tail;
        int new_node = (int)(nNodes * Math.random());   //Pick new node
        while(new_node == to_node)
            new_node=(int)(nNodes * Math.random());
        boolean switched  =  false;
```

```
        while(!switched){
        if(NW_doAddLink(node [ from_node] .name, node [ new_node] .name)){
          NW_doCutLink(j);                          //Erase old link
          switched = true;
        }
        else new_node = (int)(nNodes * Math.random());
        }
      }
    }
}//NW_doCreateGSmallWorld
```

Method `NW_doCreateSmallWorld()` produces small world networks from a 2-regular starting network, so we call these *2-regular WS networks*. Similarly, method `NW_doCreateGSmallWorld()` produces small worlds from an arbitrary *k*-regular starting network, so we call these *k-regular WS networks*. We know that $k = m/n$. Therefore, given `nInputNodes` $= n$ and `nInputLinks` $= m$, method `NW_doCreateGSmallWorld()` can generate a *k*-regular WS network with any desired value of *k*. The *k*-regular WS procedure is used to study changes in small-world properties as a function of rewiring probability *p* and density *d*.

5.1.3 Degree Sequence of Small-World Networks

Small worlds are hybrids—part *k*-regular and part random. Therefore, the topology of a small-world network should fall somewhere between that of a *k*-regular network and random network. In this case, intuition is correct, as the degree sequence distribution of a small-world network is taller and thinner than the distribution of an equivalent random network.[2] Figure 5.2 illustrates this fact for a small-world network and equivalent random network. The degree sequence distribution of a small world flattens and widens as rewiring probability *p* increases, until the two distributions match.

Barrat and Weigt (Barrat, 2000) derived a closed-form expression for degree sequence distribution of small worlds by observing the following:

1. The degree of a typical node *u* stays the same if none of its links are rewired, and increases if other node's links are redirected to *u*.
2. The probability that links are *not* rewired follows a binomial distribution, $B(k,i,(1-p))$, where $k = m/n$, $i =$ number of links not rewired, and $p =$ rewiring probability.
3. The probability that another node's links are redirected to node *u* follows a Poisson distribution, $P(\lambda_1, d - k - i)$; $d \geq k$, where $\lambda_1 = pk$ is the expected value of redirected links, $d =$ degree, and $i =$ number of links redirected to *u*.

---

[2]Equivalence means "same density."

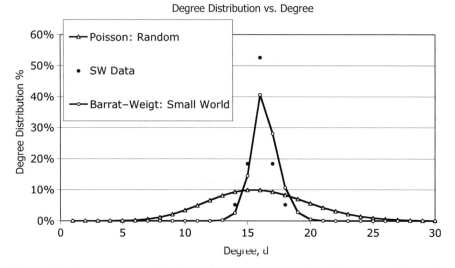

Figure 5.2 Degree sequence distribution for random and small-world networks with $n = 50$, $m = 400$, and rewiring probability $p = 5\%$.

4. The probability of increasing the degree of node u is equal to the joint probability, $B(k,i,(1-p))P(\lambda,d-k-i)$.
5. The degree distribution $h(d)$ is equal to the sum of joint probabilities over $i = 1, 2, 3, \ldots \min\{d-k,k\}$ links.

The distribution of nodes with d links after rewiring is the sum

$$h(\text{d}) = \sum_{i=1}^{\min\{d-k,k\}} B(k, i, (1-p))P(\lambda_1, d-k-i); \quad d \geq k$$

where $\min\{d-k, k\} = $ minimum of $(d-k)$ and k:

$$\lambda_1 = pk$$

$$B(k, i, 1-p) = C(^i_k)(1-p)^i p^{k-i}$$

$$P(\lambda_1, d-k-i) = (pk)^{d-k-i} \exp\frac{-pk}{(d-k-i)!}$$

$$C\binom{i}{k} = \text{combinatorial function} = \frac{k!}{i!(k-i)!}$$

This expression is undefined for $d < k$, so let $h(d) = 0$ for all values of $d < k$, and all values of i that do not fall within the interval $[k, \min\{d-k, k\}]$. For example, what is

$h(15)$ for the small-world network of Fig. 5.2?

$$d = 15$$
$$p = 0.05$$
$$k = \frac{m}{n} = \frac{400}{50} = 8$$
$$\min\{d - k, k\} = \min\{15 - 8, 8\} = 7$$
$$\lambda_1 = pk = 0.05(8) = 0.4$$

$$h(15) = \sum_{i=1}^{7} \{B(8, i, (0.95))P(0.4, 15 - 8 - i)\}$$

$$B(8, i, 0.95) = C\binom{i}{8}(0.95)^i(0.05)^{8-i}$$

$$P(0.4, 15 - 8 - i) = (0.4)^{15-8-i} \exp\frac{-0.4}{(15 - 8 - i)!}$$

$$h(15) = \sum_{i=1}^{7} \left\{ C\binom{i}{8}(0.95)^i(0.05)^{8-i}(0.4)^{7-i} \exp\frac{-0.4}{(7 - i)!} \right\}$$

The calculation spreadsheet of Table 5.1 shows how to obtain $h(15) = 14.5\%$ for the network of Fig. 5.2, and $k = 8$. Experimentally, $h(15) = 18.4\%$, averaging over five small-world networks generated by program *Network.jar*. Generally, for the size of networks studied in this book, the Barrat–Weigt equation is slightly lower than observed values—compare the data points plotted in Fig. 5.2 with the curve obtained from the Barrat–Weigt equation.

TABLE 5.1 Summation Terms for $h(d)$

d	min $(d\text{-}k, k)$	$h(d)$	$i = 1$	$i = 2$	$i = 3$	$i = 4$	$i = 5$	$i = 6$	$i = 7$	$i = 8$
10	2	0.0%	0%	0%	0	0	0	0	0	0
11	3	0.0%	0%	0%	0%	0	0	0	0	0
12	4	0.0%	0%	0%	0%	0.02%	0	0	0	0
13	5	0.3%	0%	0%	0%	0.01%	0.24%	0	0	0
14	6	2.5%	0%	0%	0%	0.01%	0.19%	2.31%	0	0
15	7	14.5%	0%	0%	0%	0.00%	0.08%	1.85%	12.55%	0
16	8	40.6%	0%	0%	0%	0.00%	0.02%	0.74%	10.04%	29.81%
17	8	28.1%	0%	0%	0%	0.00%	0.00%	0.20%	4.02%	23.85%
18	8	10.7%	0%	0%	0%	0.00%	0.00%	0.04%	1.07%	9.54%
19	8	2.8%	0%	0%	0%	0.00%	0.00%	0.01%	0.21%	2.54%
20	8	0.5%	0%	0%	0%	0.00%	0.00%	0.00%	0.03%	0.51%

5.2 PROPERTIES OF SMALL-WORLD NETWORKS

Small worlds have relatively small average path lengths, high cluster coefficients, and adjustable entropy (that can be scaled according to rewiring probability p). The effect of "randomizing" small numbers of links is shown in the "before and after" networks of Fig. 5.1. The dramatic impact that a relatively small amount of randomness has on path length, clustering, and entropy is the most impressive attribute of a small-world network.

The network of Fig. 5.1a is completely structured; hence its entropy is zero. The network in Fig. 5.1b is identical except that two links have been randomly rewired by disconnecting one end from its node, and connecting it to a randomly selected (new) node, according to the generation procedure described above. In this case, $p = 10\%$ and $m = 20$, so two links are rewired. The small amount of rewiring changes the entropy from zero to approximately 2.12 bits.

Intuitively, such a small change in the structure of the regular network in Fig. 5.1a should have a correspondingly small impact on the overall network. However, this intuition is wrong! The relatively small change has a dramatic impact, as seen in Table 5.2. The 2-regular network has zero entropy, and the "slightly small-world" network shown in Fig. 5.1b has a smaller average path length than does its 2-regular network, but dramatically higher entropy. Generally, a slightly small-world network has a high cluster coefficient and lower average path length than does its underlying regular network.

For example, Tables 2.2 and 2.3 (of Chapter 2) compare cluster coefficient and average path length of small-world and structured networks. Table 2.2 contains examples of real small-world networks with a factor of 100–1000 more clustering than equivalent random networks. The average path length of the small-world network in Table 2.3 is one-third that of an equivalent 2-regular network. In fact, random and scale-free networks exhibit the same trend.

These observations demonstrate a major concept: that introduction of a small amount of randomness or entropy into a structured network leads to a significant change in the properties of a structured network. This effect—called the *small-world effect*—is fundamentally important to the science of networks. It models (and perhaps explains) a number of phenomena that we will explore in more detail in subsequent chapters.

TABLE 5.2 WS Small-World Networks Generated by Rewiring a 2-Regular Network versus a Toroidal Network

Property	2-Regular	WS Small World	Toroidal Network	Toroid→ SW	Random
avg_path_length	3.5	2.87	2.5	2.37	2.33
Cluster coefficient					
$\quad CC$	0.500	0.363	0	0.055	0.169
Entropy	0	2.83	0	3.61	5.82

The rapid change in network properties as entropy rises begs a number of questions about WS small worlds and the transition from predominantly structured networks, to partially structured, and then fully random networks. For example, does this phenomenon occur in the transition from other structured networks to small worlds, or is it dependent on the initial 2-regular lattice? What if the WS generation procedure started with a toroidal network, instead? This research question is partially addressed by the following experiment. Start with a 5×5 toroidal network, and apply the same rewiring microrule used in the WS generation procedure. What are the properties of the resulting network?

Table 5.2 summarizes results for $n = 25$, and $p = 10\%$. The "2-Regular" column contains property values for a regular network with $m = 50$. The "WS Small World" column shows results for $n = 25$, $m = 50$, and $p = 10\%$ (Five links rewired). The column labeled "Toroidal Network" contains results for a regular 5×5 toroidal network with $n = 25$, $m = 50$, and the column labeled "Toroid->SW" contains property values for the experimental generation procedure that starts with a toroidal network instead of a 2-regular network, and then transitions to a WS small-world network. The final column contains results for a random network with $n = 25$, and $m = 50$. We use the random network as a basis for comparison.

The results of Table 5.2 suggest that initial configuration has some impact on entropy and average path length, but the cluster coefficient is much lower in networks generated by the WS microrule that starts with a toroidal network than with a 2-regular network. The standard WS generative procedure starts and ends with high clustering. The "Toroid->SW" generative procedure starts and ends with less clustering. In other words, the starting network matters. The WS network generation algorithm produces small worlds with cluster coefficient determined by the topology of the 2-regular network. In general, the underlying k-regular network determines the cluster coefficient of the resulting small world!

In Table 5.2, the 2-regular and WS small-world columns have the highest cluster coefficients. These two networks and the regular toroidal network have the lowest entropy. In terms of these properties, small-world networks generated by the WS network procedure are *structured* networks. On the other hand, the toroid->SW and random networks have the highest entropy and lowest average path lengths. In terms of these properties, the toroid->SW and random networks are random. This seems to be a paradox!

Small-world networks are indeed structured networks with the addition of a small amount of randomness. Some properties of the small-world network are inherited from the structured network underlying the small world, and others are a consequence of rewiring. Small worlds owe their average path length to the introduction of randomness, but other properties, such as cluster coefficient, are due to starting network topology.

The earnest student of network science may want to explore other possibilities. What cluster coefficient springs from a binary tree or other regular network that is rewired according to the WS procedure? Preliminary indications suggest that the eventual shape of a small-world network is significantly influenced by the shape of the initial network. In Chapter 7 ("Emergence"), we show how to produce networks with almost any desired level of clustering, path length, and entropy. With this ability, we can produce "designer networks" with arbitrary properties.

5.2.1 Entropy versus Rewiring Probability

The small-world effect has a dramatic impact on properties such as diameter and average path length. So, what happens when more randomness is injected? Does a small-world network become more random up to a point, and then revert to more structure as the rewiring probability (and entropy) increases? Similarly, change in density modifies properties such as entropy and path length. What is the relationship between each small-world property and the rewiring probability and density of the network?

To answer these questions, we perform the following experiments: (1) we hold the size and density of a 2-regular WS network constant while varying the rewiring probability p, and (2) we hold the size and rewiring probability constant while varying density. We do this by starting with a k-regular network $k = m/n$, and noting that density $= 2k/(n-1)$. These simulations yield approximations of WS network properties as a function of rewiring probability or density. Figures 5.3–5.5 show the effects of varying rewiring probability on entropy, average path length, and cluster coefficient, and Fig. 5.4 shows the effect of varying density.

Figure 5.3 shows results of averaging entropy over five 2-regular WS networks generated for each value of rewiring probability p as p increases from 0 to 100% on a semilog x axis. Then, we fit the straight line $y = A \log_2 (100p)$ to the averaged data points. Probability p is the percentage of rewired links, and constant A is to be determined. The experimentally derived semilog plot of entropy versus rewiring probability of Fig. 5.3 fits a straight line almost exactly.[3] Because the x axis is

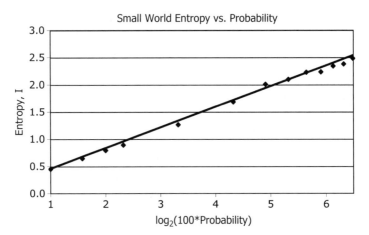

Figure 5.3 Entropy of a WS small world versus logarithm of rewiring probability p; $n = 100$, $m = 200$. Rewiring probability ranges from 1% to 100%.

---

[3]The straight line is an approximation for the range of rewiring probabilities shown in the figure, but for very small values of p, the line is not straight. We study the case of small p, later.

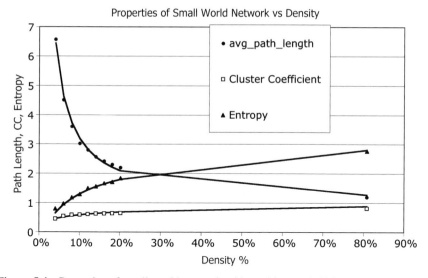

Figure 5.4 Properties of small-world network with rewiring probability $p = 4\%$, $n = 100$, and $4\% \leq$ density $\leq 80\%$; [*Note*: kn (density/2)].

logarithmic, randomness rises rapidly for small probability p and then levels off as p nears 100%. Nearly one-half of the increase in entropy (1.3 bits) occurs between 1% and 10% (3.32 on the logarithmic x axis). This confirms prior claims—a little randomness goes a long way toward dramatically changing the properties of a small-world or random network.

Because entropy is measured in bits, we use base 2 logarithms to model entropy as a function of rewiring probability p:

$$\text{Entropy}_{\text{WS}(p)} = I_{\text{WS}(p)} = A \ \log_2{(100p)}; \ \ p = 0.01, 0.02, \ldots, 1.0$$

For the network of Fig. 5.3, $A = 0.437$. According to this formula, the number of bits of randomness rises from 0 to approximately 2.9. Compare this with the number of bits of information in a message with 100 symbols, occurring with equal probability $\left(\frac{1}{100}\right)$: $I(1 \cdots 100) = \log_2{(100)} = 6.64$ bits. A sequence of random numbers in the interval $[1 \cdots 100]$ contains 6.64 bits of information. A small world with $n = 100$ contains no more than $\sim 1/2$ as many bits. WS small-world networks can scale nearly as perfectly (in terms of logarithmic growth) as a purely random process, but fall far short of the entropy carried by a completely random sequence of numbers.

Of course, we could also calculate entropy by direct substitution of the degree sequence distribution into the entropy formula: $I_{\text{WS}} = -\sum h(d) \log_2{(h(k))}$. If we did this for the example in Table 5.1, we would obtain $I_{\text{WS}}(p = 5\%) = 2.13$ bits. But we seek a simpler equation that does not require the summation of complex terms as in the Barrat–Weigt equation. For sufficiently large rewiring probabilities p, entropy increases logarithmically with p. This is intuitively satisfying because it

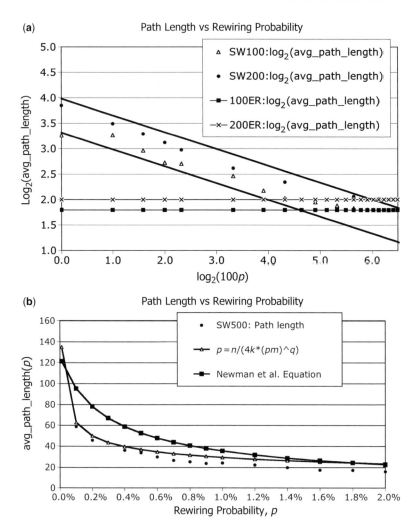

Figure 5.5 Average path length of 2-regular WS network versus rewiring probability p, (a) log–log plot of average path of small worlds length versus p, for "large p" (with $n = 100$, 200), compared with random networks of equal density; (b) plot of average path length for small worlds versus small values of p, 2-regular WS network with $n = 500$, $m = 1000$ ("small p," with no log–log scale). Approximation equations: Newman–Moore–Watts equation, and the approximation derived by the author.

says that the number of bits of entropy in a small world is directly proportional to rewiring probability p: # bits of entropy $(p) = O(p)$.

When $p = 100\%$, a WS small-world network is identical, in terms of entropy, to an equivalent random network with the same number of nodes and links.[4] Unlike a

---

[4]Equivalent networks have the same density.

random network, the entropy of a WS small world can be scaled—from zero to the entropy of an equivalent random network. In a sense, we can "tune" a small world to match the randomness that we want. Therefore, scalability of entropy is consistent with "increasing randomness."

5.2.2 Entropy versus Density

Figure 5.4 depicts the relationship between the entropy of a k-regular WS small-world network as the density of the underlying k-regular network increases; that is, we vary the underlying k-regular network by allowing $k = 2,3,4,\ldots$, thus varying the density of the network. Since density of a k-regular network is proportional to k, we can substitute k for density and the reverse:

$$\text{Density}(k\text{-regular}) = 2\frac{k}{n}; \quad k = n\frac{\text{density}}{2}; \quad n \gg 1$$

Entropy rises very slowly with density according to the logarithmic function $I_{\text{WS(density)}} = A \, \log_2 (B(\text{density})) - C$.

Substitution of parameters $A = 0.5$, $B = 60$, and $C = 0$ obtained from curve fitting into this model and simplifying (see Fig. 5.4) yields

$$I_{\text{WS(density)}} = 0.5 \, \log_2 (60(\text{density}))$$

$$= O(\log_2 (\text{density})) = O\left(\log_2 \left(\text{sqrt}\left(\frac{k}{n}\right) \right) \right)$$

Once again, the number of bits of entropy grows linearly with density:

$$\# \text{ bits of entropy(density)} = O(\text{density})$$

This agrees with intuition because it says that entropy in small-world networks increases to the same extent, regardless of the source of randomness. Entropy should be the same regardless of the source of randomness. Compare the results for rewiring probability and inserting links to increase density, for a small-world network using $I(p) = 0.437 \, \log_2 (100p)$, versus $I(\text{density}) = 0.5 \log_2 (60(\text{density}))$. The two approximations yield comparable results:

$$0.437 \log_2 (4) = 0.874 \quad \text{and} \quad 0.5 \, \log_2 (2.4) = 0.632, \text{ for } 4\%$$

and

$$0.437 \, \log_2 (80) = 2.76 \quad \text{and} \quad 0.5 \log_2 (48) = 2.79, \text{ for } 80\%$$

Unlike the entropy of a random network, small-world entropy slowly rises and levels off with increasing density or rewiring probability. Thus, we can tune the entropy of a small world by either rewiring or adding links. The logarithmic relationship between rewiring probability and density quickly diminishes, however, at 100%, because the network becomes complete.

5.2.3 Path Length of Small-World Networks

Some claim that the characteristic or average path length of a small-world network is smaller than that of an equivalent random network. Is this true? What happens to the characteristic path length of a small-world network as rewiring probability, and thus entropy, increases? Does a small world become even smaller as more links are "randomized"? Actually, the average path length of a WS small-world network decreases exponentially as entropy increases, but it never shrinks below that of an equivalent random network. This also means that diameter and path length shrink, so a small world does indeed become smaller as more links are randomized. As rewiring increases, a small world becomes more randomized and its average path length approaches that of a random network. But the average path length of a small-world network is no less than that of an equivalent random network.

Average path length—like entropy—is affected by changes in either rewiring probability, density, or both. To see this, assume a 2-regular WS network (with fixed density), and observe what happens when rewiring probability p is changed. Figure 5.4 shows the results obtained by averaging characteristic path lengths from five 2-regular WS small-world networks generated by rewiring the initial 2-regular network with probability p, as p increases from 1% to 100%, as before. Clearly, average path length declines rapidly as rewiring probability increases, as expected. But the shape of the declining curve is unlike that of a random or scale-free network because small-world networks are part random and part regular.

The exact equation for describing the average path length of a slightly random small-world network was the subject of a vigorous research effort until Newman, Moore, and Watts (Newman, 1999a) derived an estimate based on the following reasoning:

1. When rewiring is nonexistent, and the initial network is 2-regular, average path length is $n/4k$.
2. For very small rewiring probability p, average path length begins a rapid decline, after $p \geq (1/m)$, as shown in Fig. 5.4.
3. At some (early) point p^*, rewiring is sufficiently large that the network transitions from mostly regular, to mostly random. This is known as the *crossover point* p^*, and signifies a *phase transition* in the network. The value of p^* is of interest to physicists, who associate it with phase transitions in materials.

Newman, Moore, and Watts (Newman, 1999b; Newman, 2000a) argued that average path length declines from an initial ($p = 0$) value of $n/4k$ according to a scaling function $f(r)$, where r is 2 times the average number of rewired links, $r = 2pm$. Think of r as twice the number of bisecting shortcuts through the network:

$$f(r) = 4 \frac{\tanh^{-1}(r/\beta)}{\beta}; \text{ where } \beta = \sqrt{(r^2 + 4r)}$$

$$\text{avg\_path\_length(SW)} = n \frac{f(r)}{2k} = \frac{2n}{\beta k} \tanh^{-1}\left(\frac{r}{\beta}\right)$$

where $\tanh^{-1}$ is the inverse hypertangent function $=$ arc_tanh( ).The Newman–Moore–Watts equation is $O(1/p)$ for large, sparse networks $(n, m \gg 1)$. For example, let $n = 100$, $m = 200$, $k = 2$, density $= 0.04$, and $p = 0.04$ or 4%, as in Fig. 5.4:

$$r = (2)(0.01)(400) = 8, \quad \beta = \sqrt{(64 + 32)} = 9.8$$

$$\text{arc\_tanh}\left(\frac{8}{9.8}\right) = 1.15$$

$$\frac{2n}{\beta k} = \frac{200}{2(9.8)} = 10.2$$

avg_ path_length (SW) $= (10.2)(1.15) = 11.7\,\text{hops}$

Compare this prediction with the experimental value of 6.6 given by Fig. 5.4. The Newman–Moore–Watts expression *overestimates* average path length, as shown in the plot of Fig. 5.5b, especially as rewiring probability p decreases. However, the underlying assumptions that path length shrinks as rewiring increases suggests an intuitive approach based on rewired links as shortcuts that bisect the network.

Average path length is $n/4k$ initially, but as links are rewired, they introduce short-cut links that divide the network into smaller and smaller subgraphs. Specifically, one random link cuts the network in half, on average, and two links cut it into one-fourth, and so on. However, the bisection is overlapping, rather than hierarchical. Therefore, addition of rewired links cuts the network into a fraction of $\frac{1}{2}$, each time a link is rewired. The effect on the logarithm of average path length is a logarithmic function of rewired links.

Let $r = pm = pkn$ shortcut links reduce logarithmic growth in path length by $O(\log_2 (pm))$, on average, because of the partial bisecting that occurs. Therefore, the logarithm of the average path length is equal to the logarithm of the path length of the initial 2-regular network, minus the effects of partial bisection:

$$\log_2 (\text{avg\_ path\_length}(r)) = \log_2 \left(\frac{n}{4k}\right) - q\log_2 (r)$$

where $r = pm$, $q =$ constant. This expression fits a straight line on a log–log plot, as shown in Fig. 5.5a. Exponent q can be approximated by curve fitting—see how close the match is between simulated data and the straight line obtained from apply-ing this approximation, for $q = \frac{1}{3}$, and 2-regular networks of size $n = 100$ and 200 nodes. The approximation of q is valid only for $k = 2$. For $k = 4$, $q = \frac{1}{6}$ gives a good fit, leading to the conjecture that doubling k halves q. This is left as an exercise for the reader.

Rearranging terms yields a power law:

$$\text{avg\_path\_length}(r) = \frac{n/4k}{r^q} \quad \text{where} \quad r = pkn$$

$$\therefore \text{avg\_path\_length(small-world, } p, n) = \frac{n/4k}{(pkn)^q}; \quad 0 < p < 1$$

$$= \frac{n}{4k}; \quad p = 0$$

The simple power-law approximation fits simulation data much better than does the Newman–Moore–Watts equation, but it assumes that exponent q is known. The Newman–Moore–Watts equation only requires parameters n, p, and k to determine path length. For the size networks used in Fig. 5.5, we find $q = 1/3$, so average path length is inversely proportional to the cube root of r:

$$\text{avg\_path\_length } (r) = \frac{n/4k}{r^{1/3}}$$

Once again, using the data of Figs 5.4 and 5.5, $n = 100$, $m = 200$, $k = 2$, $p = 0.04$, and $r = pm = (0.04)(200) = 8$:

$$\text{avg\_path\_length } (r) = \frac{\frac{100}{8}}{8^{1/3}} = \frac{12.5}{2} = 6.25 \text{ hops}$$

The Newman–Moore–Watts approximation yields 8 hops:

$$r = 2pm = (2)(0.04)(200) = 16$$

$$\beta = \sqrt{(256 + 64)} = 17.89$$

$$\text{arc\_tanh}\left(\frac{16}{17.89}\right) = 1.43$$

$$\frac{2n}{\beta k} = \frac{200}{17.89(2)} = 5.59$$

$$\text{avg\_path\_length(SW)} = 5.59(1.43) = 8 \text{ hops}$$

The experimentally obtained average path length is 6.6 hops. The power-law estimate is more precise, 6.25 hops, than the Newman–Moore–Watts equation, 8 hops. The power law tends to underestimate, while the Newman–Moore–Watts equation tends to overestimate path length. Also, note that 6.6 hops is much higher than an equivalent random network, which has an average path length of 3.46 hops. So equivalent random networks are not truly equivalent because entropy is not tunable by parameter p.

In summary, a quickly diminishing average path length and large cluster coefficient are distinguishing features of the class of small-world networks. An equivalent random network is really an asymptotic extreme of a small-world network with an average path length less than or equal to an equivalent small world. Small-world path length shrinks with increasing probability of link rewiring, reaching $p = 100\%$ as a limit. At low rewiring probability values, the WS small-world network path length is similar to that of a 2-regular network (higher than that of a random network). At high rewiring probability values, the path length of the class of WS small-worlds and the class of random networks are similar (low). Where does the small-world power law fade and the logarithmic law for random network path length take over? We address the question of transition from mostly structured, to mostly random networks, in Section 5.3.

5.2.4 Cluster Coefficient of Small-World Networks

The cluster coefficient is tunable in a WS network by changing density, rewiring probability, or both. First, suppose that we hold density constant while varying rewiring probability p. What happens to a 2-regular WS network when entropy is increased? Surprisingly, the cluster coefficient decreases as entropy increases! Alternatively, the cluster coefficient increases with network density because the number of links available to form triangular subgraphs also increases.

Intuition says that the small-world cluster coefficient should approximate the (high) cluster coefficient of the class of regular networks at one extreme and the (low) cluster coefficient of the class of random networks at the other extreme. For low rewiring probability, the 2-regular WS network is mostly 2-regular, and for high probability p, the network is mostly random.

Initially, before any rewiring, the cluster coefficient of every node in a 2-regular network is the same. Newman, Strogatz, and Watts (Newman, 2001a) argue that cluster coefficient of the initial 2-regular network, $CC(0)$, is equal to the ratio of number of triangles attached to each node, divided by one-third of the number of connected triples:

$$CC(0) = 3 \frac{\# \text{ triangles}}{\# \text{ connected triples}}$$

$$= 3 \frac{k(k-1)}{2\,k(2\,k-1)}$$

$$= 3 \frac{k-1}{2(2\,k-1)}$$

For example, $k = 2$ in the initial 2-regular network, so $CC(0) = 3(2(4-1))^{-1} = \frac{1}{2}$. As k increases without bound, the highest possible cluster coefficient is $\frac{3}{4}$, because $CC(0) = (3\,k-3)/(4\,k-2) \sim (3\,k/4\,k) = \frac{3}{4}$. Therefore, the cluster coefficient of a small world must fall in the interval $[0.5, 0.75]$.

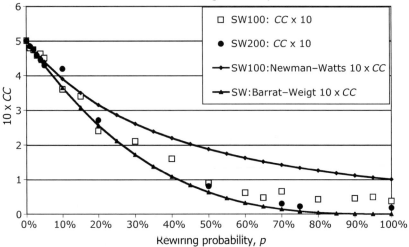

Figure 5.6 Cluster coefficient of WS small-world versus rewiring probability for $n = 100$, 200, and $m = 200, 400$ ($\lambda = 4, k = 2$).

When the small world emerges from rewiring, pm links will be rewired, which means that some links have been diverted from triangular subgraphs while others remain as they were, initially. This causes clustering to decline with corresponding increases in rewiring probability p. Figure 5.6 confirms this experimentally. When $p = 0$, the small-world cluster coefficient equals that of a 2-regular network (0.5) because $k = 2$, in the WS generative procedure. As p increases, clustering falls from CC(2-regular) = 0.5, to CC(random network) = 0.02–0.04. When $p = 1.0$, the WS small-world cluster coefficient equals that of a random network. Therefore, we can tune the cluster coefficient of a k-regular WS network by adjusting p.

Figure 5.6 was obtained by averaging cluster coefficients over five networks generated by the 2-regular WS procedure, and then plotting the averaged data versus rewiring probability for two networks: one with $n = 100$ nodes, and the other with $n = 200$ nodes. The mean degree, $\lambda = 2(m/n) = 2k = 4$, is held constant by adjusting number of links, $m = 200, 400$.

Newman and Watts derived a complex equation for cluster coefficient using a combinatorial approach (Albert, 2000):

$$CC(k\text{-regular}) = 3\frac{k(k-1)}{2k(2k-1) + 8pk^2 + 4p^2 k^2}, \quad p = \text{rewiring probability}$$

From Fig. 5.6 it is obvious that this approximation *overestimates* cluster coefficient for $k = 2$. A simpler approximation given by Barrat and Weigt makes an elegant and simple assumption that gives a more accurate result—the cluster coefficient is proportional to the probability that a triangular subgraph will *not* be rewired (Barrat, 2000):

$$CC(k\text{-regular}) = CC(0)(1-p)^3, \quad \text{where} \quad CC(0) = 3\frac{k-1}{2(2k-1)}, \quad k = 2, 3, \ldots$$

In Fig. 5.6, the Barrat–Weigt approximation fits the data much better, but slightly *underestimates* cluster coefficient for the simulations shown in Fig. 5.5. The Barrat–Weigt approximation is easy to understand. $CC(0)$ is the cluster coefficient of the underlying k-regular network, so the initial cluster coefficient of all nodes is $CC(0)$. When $p > 0$, rewiring simply destroys triangles with probability p, and leaves them intact with probability $(1-p)$. Failure to rewire one link occurs with probability $(1-p)$. Failure to rewire all three links occurs with probability $(1-p)^3$. All three links have to survive rewiring; otherwise, the triangular subgraph is destroyed. Therefore, rewiring has to fail 3 times. The probability of three failures is $(1-p)^3$. This is equivalent to saying that the triangular sub-graph remains intact with probability $(1-p)^3$.

For example, suppose that a small world of size $n = 100$, $m = 400$, is formed by first forming a k-regular network, and then rewiring with probability $p = 10\%$. What is the expected cluster coefficient? The initial k-regular network has $\lambda = 8$ links per node, which means $k = 4$:

$$CC(0) = 3\frac{4-1}{2(8-1)} = \frac{9}{14} = 0.643 = 64.3\%$$

$$(1-p)^3 = (1-0.1)^3 = 0.9^3 = 0.73$$

$$CC(4, 0.1) = 0.643(0.73) = 47\%$$

Clustering decreases as entropy increases because clustering is a form of structure (order), whereas rewiring links is a form of randomness (disorder). Increasing rewiring probability increases disorder, which decreases clustering. Entropy works against the initial order of the k-regular network.

Now let us hold rewiring probability constant and let density vary. Cluster coefficient slowly rises with increase in density because increasing density moves any network closer to a complete network. We know that the cluster coefficient of a complete network is 1.0, so the cluster coefficient must asymptotically approach 1.0 as density approaches 100%. Notice that the bounds on cluster coefficient are increased: $0.5 = CC(\text{density}) = 1.0$, which is contrary to the Barrat–Weigt approximation. Why?

Consider the cluster coefficient–density curve shown in Fig. 5.4, and assume density $= 20\%$. For the network parameters, $n = 100$, $p = 4\%$, what is the cluster coefficient?

$$k = n\frac{\text{density}}{2} = 100\frac{0.2}{2} = 10$$

$$CC(0) = 3\frac{10 - 1}{2(20 - 1)} = \frac{27}{38} = 71\%$$

$$(1 - p)^3 = (1 - 0.04)^3 = 0.96^3 = 0.885$$

$$CC(4, 0.1) = 0.71(0.885) = 63\%$$

Therefore, the cluster coefficient slowly rises with rising density, as shown in Fig. 5.4. The reason is clear—more links means more triangular subgraphs to begin with, and relatively fewer rewired links for a fixed probability p. As density increases, so does the number of triangular subgraphs, which increases cluster coefficient. The value of k in the initial k-regular network is greater, so $CC(0)$ is greater. Finding an approximation equation for this relationship, in terms of density, is left as an exercise for the reader.

Albert and Barabasi summarize a number of real-world networks with high cluster coefficients (Albert, 2002). For example, the social network formed by movie actors who appeared in the same movie has a cluster coefficient of 0.79; coauthorship network of scholarly papers, $CC = 0.72$; the chemical reaction network of the *Escherichia coli* organism, $CC = 0.59$; and network formed by linking synonyms in an English language thesaurus, $CC = 0.7$. In social network analysis, high clustering means that friends of friends are linked to one another. It is network science's way of saying, "Birds of a feather, flock together."

5.2.5 Closeness in Small Worlds

Intuitively, average closeness of nodes in a small world should follow the same pattern as closeness in a random network, especially as rewiring probability increases. But this turns out to be false because of the WS small-world generative procedure, which has a k-regular network as its underpinning. As density increases, small worlds become more regular and asymptotically approach a complete network just as does a random network. But the transition is not smooth, as illustrated by Fig. 5.7. In fact, the transition dramatically follows a lazy-Z-shaped curve—completely unexpected compared to the average closeness of random and small-world networks. The small-world network's cluster coefficient undergoes a nonlinear transformation at approximately 50% density.

Closeness increases with increasing density—up to a point—and then dips as the network begins to act more like a k-regular network than a small-world network. After the dip, regularity takes over, and closeness once again rises until reaching a peak near 100% density. A very rough approximation to this nonlinear behavior is obtained by performing a mean-field analysis, as in the previous chapter. Here is the strategy:

1. Modify the mean-field approximation obtained in the previous chapter, closeness(random) = $O((1 - \text{density})z)$, to accommodate the impact

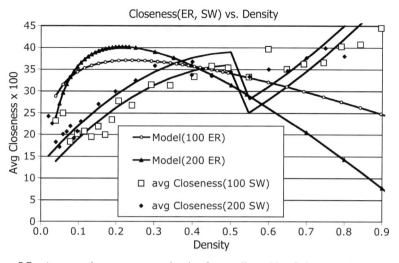

Figure 5.7 Average closeness versus density for small worlds of size $n = 100$, 200, compared with equivalent random networks of the same size.

of k-regularity on the network, where $z = \lambda^r$, $\lambda = $ mean degree, and $r(\text{random}) = O(\log(n)/\log(\lambda))$:

a. Replace (1-density) with density because small worlds increase closeness as density increases—up to a point (50%),

b. Note that the transformation from small-world to k-regular network occurs around $r = 1$.

c. Use the fact that a *direct* path of length 1 contributes zero closeness because of the way closeness is defined.

2. Estimate curve-fit parameters C_1 and C_2, from data points collected by simulation (using program *Network.jar*).

A small-world network of arbitrary density is generated by first constructing a k-regular lattice. For example, if $n = 100$ and $m = 1000$, $k = 10$. Then, a percentage of links p are randomly rewired. This random rewiring injects shortcuts through the network, which leads to a reduction in the number of nodes eligible to lie on a path between any other pair of nodes. The effect of rewiring pm links is modeled as a reduction in number of paths, as follows:

$$r = \frac{A \log_2 (n - (1 - p)\lambda)}{\log_2 (\lambda)}$$

where $p = $ rewiring probability, $A = $ constant. The mean-field number of paths through a typical node is proportional to z, as before: $z = \lambda^r$.

When $r < 1$, the small world ceases to behave like a small world, and becomes more like a k-regular network, as far as closeness is concerned. Therefore, we require a different model for z when $r < 1$. In fact, the dense small world behaves more like a k-regular network with $k = \lambda/2$ direct paths, instead. Therefore, only $k = \lambda/2$ paths run through a typical node:

$$z = k = \frac{\lambda}{2}$$

Combining these two effects, we obtain

$$z = \begin{cases} \lambda^r & \text{if } r \geq 1 \\ \dfrac{\lambda}{2} & \text{otherwise} \end{cases}$$

The effect of this transition is shown in both data and model of Fig. 5.7, which takes place around 50% density, for rewiring probability $p = 4\%$. However, the approximation is very rough:

$$100(\text{closeness(small world}, p)) = C_1(\text{density})z + C_2$$

$$z = \begin{cases} \lambda^r & \text{if } r \geq 1 \\ \dfrac{\lambda}{2} & \text{otherwise} \end{cases}$$

$$r = \frac{A \log_2 (n - (1 - p)\lambda)}{\log_2 (\lambda)}$$

$$n = 100 \quad \text{and} \quad p = 4\% : A = 1, \; C_1 = 1, \; C_2 = 10$$
$$n = 200 \quad \text{and} \quad p = 4\% : A = 1, \; C_1 = 0.5, \; C_2 = 13$$

There is a major difference between the closeness properties of random and small-world networks. Random networks have no regularity until density approaches 100%. Hence average closeness is (mainly) a function of average path length and sparseness. On the other hand, small-world networks have a great amount of regularity regardless of density—and the impact of regularity on average closeness increases as density increases. A "tipping point" is reached around 50% density, which results in the small world behaving more like a k-regular network than a random network. This regularity becomes the most significant factor in determining closeness. Generally, clustering tends to increase average closeness, while randomizing tends to decrease it, beyond ~20% density. What is the average closeness of the complete network endpoint of Fig. 5.7, when density is exactly 100%? This is left as an exercise for the reader.

5.3 PHASE TRANSITION

In the late 1990s, Watts and Strogatz (Watts, 1998) rejuvenated scientific interest in small-world behaviors after a three-decade lapse following the social network analysis of Stanley Milgram. Most significantly, Strogatz and Watts used small-world networks as models of physical world phenomena. Watts, in particular, pursued the idea that small-world network behavior explained *synchrony*—a topic we take up in a subsequent chapter. In this chapter we study two other behaviors—phase transition and network navigation.

Phase transition in the physical world occurs when matter changes from a solid state to a liquid, from liquid to gas, and so on. The *Ising effect*, for example, explains the phase transition that occurs when inert iron converts into magnetic iron. The idea is related to the sudden transition from a 2-regular to random network as rewiring probability increases. Watts argued that phase transition is a particular property of small worlds, and that it is the same fundamental phenomenon observed in different fields.

5.3.1   Path Length and Phase Transition

The structure of a small-world network changes from regular to semiregular, to semi-random, and finally to a completely random topology as rewiring probability increases. This phenomenon not only occurs in small world networks but is also a property of random networks. But since $p = 100\%$ in a random network, it is not apparent when the abrupt transition occurs. In a tunable system such as a k-regular small world, the transition from regular to semirandom is rather abrupt, as shown by the rapid decrease in average path length for very small rewiring probabilities (see Fig. 5.5b), around $p = 0.1\%$.

Also, network radius and diameter drop for a very small increase in rewiring probability, and then continue to decline as the small world transitions to a random network. The transition from "mostly vertical" to "mostly horizontal" line in Fig. 5.5b is considered a phase transition point, and the rewiring probability corresponding to the transition is considered the *crossover point* p^*, also known as the *phase transition threshold* (Barthelewy, 1999). The threshold visually marks the departure from vertical to horizontal and signifies the transition from "mostly k-regular" to "mostly random" topology.

Define p^* as the point in Fig. 5.5b where the slope of the avg_path_length L versus p equals $(-45°)$. This corresponds with a rate of change $\delta L / \delta r = -1$:

$$L = \frac{n/4k}{(r)^q}$$

$$\frac{\delta L}{\delta r} = -1 = -\frac{nq}{4kr^{q+1}}$$

Solving for r, we obtain

$$r = \left(\frac{nq}{4k}\right)^{1/(q+1)}$$

$$= pm, \text{ so } p^* = \frac{r}{m} \text{ at crossover point}$$

$$p^* = \frac{r}{m} = \left(\frac{nq/m}{4k}\right)^{1/(q+1)}$$

In Fig. 5.5b, $q = \frac{1}{3}$, $1/(q+1) = 0.75$, $n = 500$, $m = 1000$, and $k = 2$, so the crossover point p^* is 0.975%:

$$r = \left(\frac{nq}{4k}\right)^{0.75} = \left(\frac{500\left(\frac{1}{3}\right)}{4(2)}\right)^{0.75} = 9.75$$

$$p^* = \frac{r}{m} = \frac{9.75}{1000} = 0.00975 = 0.975\%$$

Therefore, the crossover point is approximately 1%. Looking at Fig. 5.5b, it is easy to see that most of the decline in average path length occurs before 1%. Visually, the decline from $p = 0$ to $p = 1\%$ accounts for 80% of the drop. Barrat and Weigt claim that $p^* \sim (1/n)$ (Barrat, 2000) for similar small worlds, which yields $\frac{1}{500} = 0.2\% = p^*$. This estimate is much smaller, and accounts for 64% of the drop—16% less than the author's approximation formula, but still a majority of the drop.

Visually, the Barrat–Weigt approximation makes more sense. Rewiring 0.2% of the 1000 links means redirecting only 2 links, while rewiring 1% means redirecting 10 links. Two rewired links may cause upward of a four-fold drop in path length, which means that path length declines by as much as $(125 - \frac{125}{4})/125 = 75\%$. For the network in Fig. 5.5b, the Barrat–Weigt approximation is more in line with this "back of the envelope" estimate.

5.3.2 Phase Transition in Materials

The phase transition phenomenon holds a certain fascination for physical scientists because it may explain a variety of real-world effects such as a liquid "suddenly" converting to a solid, or nonmagnetic iron "suddenly" becoming magnetic—the so-called *Ising model.*[5] Such abrupt changes near a crossover point may also explain other phenomena in biology (neurological modeling) and consumer behavior (fads and products that suddenly "catch on"). For this reason, it is worthwhile to explore phase transition in more detail.

Albert and Barabasi (Albert, 2002) provide succinct surveys of transitions of interest in physical and biological science. *Percolation theory* is perhaps the most novel example of phase transition in the real world. The idea is simple; starting with a random graph that may contain multiple components, rewire the links and observe if and when a giant component forms. In terms of networks, this is modeled as a giant component "suddenly" forming as rewiring increases. In percolation theory, p^* is called the *percolation threshold*.

Note that the network need not be small-world. In fact, percolation theory assumes a uniformly random network so p and density are related by

---

[5]Ernst Ising (1900–1998) created the Ising model in 1924 to explain magnetism. Since then, it has become one of the fundamental models in statistical physics.

$pm = n(n - 1)(\text{density}/2)$. Adding links at a constant rate increases density at a constant rate, also. At some point, the network is dense enough to form a giant component.

Bond percolation is modeled as a two-dimensional grid with *pm* links. Links are constrained by a flat 2D surface, so each node can connect only along NEWS directions; hence *m* is bounded by $4n$, and so $pm \leq 4n$ (density).[6] Starting with $p = 0$, *p* increases until a giant connected component emerges. If it is possible to reach every other node from any node, the entire network is one giant component.

Materials also transition the other way—from structured to random. Consider a fully connected complete network with $m = n((n-1)/2)$ links. This giant connected network represents a frozen cube of water or fully magnetized metal. Now, randomly select at link and remove it with probability $(1-p)$. Test the network to see if it is still one giant component. Repeat the random link removal process until the giant component is no longer connected. At this point, *pm* links remain. What is the significance of p^*, now? A percolation network is in its subcritical phase when $p < p^*$, and its supercritical phase when $p > p^*$. In certain restricted cases (*Cayley graphs*), $p^* = 1/n$. Below this threshold, no giant component forms. At this threshold, a giant cluster forms of size $n^{2/3}$, and above this threshold, a complex giant component forms with cycles. The "crystallization" of a liquid into a solid, and the transition from nonmagnetic to magnetic iron corresponds with the alignment of links to form a giant component. Thus, p^* is the *tipping point* between liquid and solid phases or nonmagnetic and magnetic phases.

Percolation has also been observed in artificial networks such as the Internet. Broder et al. analyzed over 200 million servers in the Internet's *Webgraph*, and discovered its giant component, called the *giant strongly connected component* (GSCC) (Broder, 2000). The Internet's Webgraph is shaped like a "bowtie"—44 million nodes (21%) are predominantly incoming nodes that send messages such as email; another 44 million are predominantly outgoing nodes that receive messages. A larger cluster, 56 million (27%) make up the GSCC.

In terms of small-world effect (short average path length), GSCC is a small-world network. The average path length (out of 56 million nodes in the GSCC) reported by Broder et al. is a mere 16–20 hops! According to WWW high-level measurements made by Adamic, of which the GSCC is a component, the average path length is 35 hops (Adamic, 1999). At the other extreme, Yook et al. estimates an average path length equal to 9 hops when measured at the Internet's router level (Yook, 2001). Therefore, the GSCC estimate of 16–20 hops falls approximately midway between measurements taken at the very high and very low levels of the Internet. In any case, the Internet is a compelling example of the small-world effect.

As it turns out, Internet topology is scale-free, not small-world, although it exhibits the small-world effect. Average path length of a scale-free network follows a

---

[6]NEWS = north, east, west, south.

logarithmic approximation rather than a power law:

$$L(\text{scale-free}) = \frac{\log{(n)}}{\log{(\log{(n)})}} = 8.7\,\text{hops},\ \text{for } n = 56\,\text{million}$$

The small path length of a scale-free network is due to its hubs—very high-degreed nodes—rather than random links, acting as shortcuts. GSCC path length is a consequence of hub topology, not random rewiring. While clustering is modest in the domain-level Webgraph, Internet clustering is higher than expected of a purely random network. Yook et al. place the cluster coefficient of the domain level Internet in the range 0.18–0.30, versus 0.001 for an equivalent random network (Albert, 2002). We study the properties of scale-free networks in the next chapter and show that scale-free topology has an even more dramatic impact on properties of real-world networks than does the small-world effect.

5.4 NAVIGATING SMALL WORLDS

Network navigation is a search process whereby a message finds its way from a source to a destination node using only local information such as node degree, centrality, or closeness. The lengths of such search paths are much greater than average path length; this is due to the trial-and-error wayfinding made necessary because of incomplete information about shortest paths. But network navigation is an important topic because it models a number of important processes in a variety of fields such as communication. In fact, network navigation in small worlds may explain how large communication systems work—or not—depending on search efficiency.

The Internet, and telecommunication systems in general, carry packets of information that must find their way through a complex network, much as the letters sent by Stanley Milgram had to find their way from sender to recipient. How do such networks route their packets, and does the structure of a communication network make any difference to their efficiency? Specifically, does the small-world topology improve or retard network navigation?

In real-world natural or synthetic systems, small-world structure is usually a consequence of microrules that favor high clustering, low path length, or both. For example, a communication network's efficiency is a function of the number of hops separating any two nodes. In a neurological network, maximum transmission time is kept to a minimum by making the diameter of the network low. Thus, it is important that a "random network" scale as size increases by limiting the growth of network diameter as n increases.

We have shown that networks with the small-world effect scale very well. As n increases, the designer merely injects a small amount of randomness into the link structure, and diameter dramatically decreases! Thus, it appears that transmission delays can be controlled for a given network density by injecting a small amount of randomness. Is this conjecture true, or does an increase of entropy lead to lowered transmission efficiency?

Unfortunately, the theory of small worlds is not prescriptive with respect to navigation, because it doesn't tell how to find the best path through the network. For example, none of the path length or closeness approximations given in the previous sections indicate how to navigate from one arbitrary node to another. They do not show how to select a path leading to a given node without some kind of global routing table. To determine what local information should be used in searching for a path through a small world network, we turn to simulation.

Suppose that we start with node v and attempt to reach node w in the most efficient manner. Further that suppose we only have local information about the nodes that we visit along the navigation path $v \sim x \sim y \sim \cdots w$. How do we select a link, and how do we know whether the selected link will lead to the proper destination? This is the problem of *network navigation*.

Network navigation has applications in peer-to-peer file sharing. For example, several file-sharing applications found their way into the popular culture during the late 1990s when music files were stored on consumer's local disks, and navigation software was used to find them. Without a global map of the peer-to-peer network, a search program would have to perform a depth-first search (DFS) on adjacent servers, and expand the search until locating the desired file.

Assume that we have local information about each node, such as degree, radius, and a list of adjacent neighbors. A navigator can use this local information to guide the selection of links and nodes along a path from v to w. But which local property is best? Suppose that we study four search algorithms suggested by the following prestored properties at each node:

1. *Random*—the next node in the navigation path is selected at random.
2. *Maximum-degree*—the adjacent node with the highest degree is selected next.
3. *Minimum-radius*—the adjacent node that is more central is selected next.
4. *Maximum-closeness*—the adjacent node that has the highest closeness rating is selected next.

The objective is to determine which search algorithm navigates the network in the least number of hops—on average—when v and w are randomly selected source and destination nodes. We assume the network is strongly connected (has one component), so all nodes can be reached from all others. Does it matter whether the network is small-world or not?

The random node selection algorithm will serve as a baseline—we would expect it to produce the worst navigation performance.[7] As each node is visited along the navigation path, the next node to be searched is randomly selected from adjacent nodes. Intuitively, the resulting navigation path will be a random walk through the network.

---

[7] Actually, the maximum-closeness algorithm is worse than random!

The search backtracks whenever it reaches a cycle or a dead end. It terminates when it finds the destination node.

Intuitively, a high-degree node is more likely to be connected to the destination node. Therefore, the maximum-degree algorithm ranks the adjacent nodes according to their degree—from highest to lowest—and then selects the link leading to the highest-degree neighbor. If the search fails, the next-highest-degree node is tried, and so forth, until all adjacent nodes have been searched, or the destination node is found.

Intuitively, a more central node is "closer" to the destination node. In this sense, "closer" means that nodes are ranked according to their radii. Adjacent nodes are ranked according to their radii, and traversed in order from lowest to highest. If a search backtracks, the second-larger-radius neighbor is selected and traversed, and so forth, as in the random and maximum-degree search.

Finally, a node that is between or closer to all other nodes because of its closeness should lie on a path leading to the destination node. Therefore, adjacent nodes are ranked according to their intermediary status, closeness, and tried in order: highest closeness value, first, followed by next closeness value, and so on. until the destination node is reached, or deadends prevent a successful search.

In all cases, the search for destination node w must eventually succeed because the network is strongly connected. Each search algorithm is embedded in a depth-first search (DFS), which backtracks when a deadend is reached. In addition, nodes are marked as "visited," to avoid becoming trapped in a cycle. The worst-case navigation path traverses all nodes of the network before reaching the destination. The four algorithms are identical except for the manner in which the next node is selected.

The random path search method in program *Network.jar* implements DFS by recursively calling itself until a dead_end is reached, or a cycle is traveled without finding the destination node. It relies on a randomization method from class Shuffler, which is not shown here. The idea is simple; at each node, adjacent nodes are randomized, and then a DFS is launched on each of the randomized adjacent nodes. Whenever a deadend or cycle is encountered, the DFS along that path is terminated. Eventually, one (or more) of the paths reaches the destination node, resulting in reply.found being set to **true**.

The list randomizer.card[] temporarily holds randomized adjacent nodes, so that they can be shuffled and then searched; this is necessary to guarantee that the entire network is searched, if needed:

```
private NavReply Random_Path(NavReply reply, int dest){
        int DEAD_END = -1;
        Shuffler randomizer = new Shuffler(nLinks);
        if(reply.found || reply.node == DEAD_END) return reply;
        reply.hops++;
        node[reply.node].visited = true;
        int next_node = 0;                          //Successor nodes
        int j = 0;                                  //Number of successors
```

```
        for(int e = 0; e < nLinks; e++){              //Find all successors
                if(Link [ e] .head == reply.node) next_node = Link [ e] .tail;
                else if(Link [ e] .tail == reply.node) next_node = Link [ e] .head;
                else continue;                        //Skip non-adjacents
                if(next_node == dest) {
                        reply.found = true;
                        reply.node = next_node;
                        return reply;                         //Found!
                }
                if(node [ next_node] .visited) continue;   //Skip previous visited
                randomizer.card[j] = next_node;       //New (random) order
                j++;
        }
        //Explore j possible next nodes...
        if(j > 0){
                randomizer.SH_Shuffle(j);             //Randomize links
                for(next_node = 0; next_node < j; next_node++){
                        reply.node = randomizer.card [ next_node] ;
                        reply = Random_Path(reply, dest);   //Depth First Search
                }
        }
        else {
                reply.hops-;
                reply.found = false;                  //Dead-end reached
                reply.node = DEAD_END;
        }
        return reply;
}//Random_Path
```

Object `reply` contains the number of hops, current node, and whether the destination node has been found. Initially, `reply.node` contains the starting node v, and when the destination node w is found, it is stored in `reply.node`. The NavReply data structure is given below:

```
class NavReply {
        int hops = 0;                    //Number hops
        int node = 0;                    //Current node
        boolean found = false;           //Destination found?
}
```

The max(imum)-degree, min(imum)-radius, and max(imum)-closeness DFS algorithms are identical except for the method of next-node selection. Instead of randomizing the adjacent-node list, max-degree and max-closeness algorithms sort the next nodes into descending order according to node degree or closeness, and min-radius sorts them into ascending order by radius. Once again, class Shuffler is used to do the sorting, but it is not shown here.

```
private NavReply Max_Degree_Path(NavReply reply, int dest){
        int DEAD_END = -1;
        Shuffler sorted = new Shuffler(nLinks);
        if(reply.found || reply.node == DEAD_END) return reply;
        reply.hops++;
        node[reply.node].visited = true;
        int next_node = 0;                                      //Successor
        int j = 0;
        for(int e = 0; e < nLinks; e++){                   //Find next node
            if(Link [ e] .head == reply.node) next_node = Link [ e] .tail;
            else if(Link [ e] .tail == reply.node) next_node = Link [ e] .head;
            else continue;
            if(next_node == dest) {
                reply.found = true;
                reply.node = next_node;
                return reply;                               //Found!
            }
            if(node [ next_node] .visited) continue;
            sorted.card[j] = next_node;
            sorted.key[j] = node[next_node].degree;
            j++;
        }
        if(j > 0){
            sorted.SH_Sort(j, false);                       //Descending order
            for(next_node = 0; next_node < j; next_node++){
                reply.node = sorted.card[next_node];
                reply = Max_Degree_Path(reply, dest);
            }
        }
        else {
            reply.hops--;
            reply.found = false;
            reply.node = DEAD_END;
        }
        return reply;
}//Max_Degree_Path
//Minimum Radius Method
private NavReply Min_Radius_Path(NavReply reply, int dest){
        int DEAD_END = -1;
        Shuffler sorted = new Shuffler(nLinks);
        if(reply.found || reply.node == DEAD_END) return reply;
        reply.hops++;
```

```
            node[reply.node].visited = true;
            int next_node = 0;                              //Successor
            int j = 0;
            for(int e = 0; e < nLinks; e++){            //Find next node
                  if(Link [ e] .head == reply.node) next_node = Link [ e] .tail;
                  else if(Link [ e] .tail == reply.node) next_node = Link [ e] .head;
                  else continue;
                  if(next_node == dest) {
                        reply.found = true;
                        reply.node = next_node;
                        return reply;                              //Found!
                  }
                  if(node [ next_node] .visited) continue;
                  sorted.card[j] = next_node;
                  sorted.key[j] = node[next_node].radius;
                  j++;
            }
            if(j > 0){
                  sorted.SH_Sort(j, true);                  //Ascending order
                  for(next_node = 0; next_node < j; next_node++){
                        reply.node = sorted.card[next_node];
                        reply = Min_Radius_Path(reply, dest);
                  }
            }
            else {
                  reply.hops--;
                  reply.found = false;
                  reply.node = DEAD_END;
            }
            return reply;
      }//Min_Radius_Path
```

Method `Radius_Path()` implements the other two search algorithms: min-radius and max-closeness. In both cases, the radius field of each node is used as the sort key. However, the min-radius search must sort adjacent nodes in ascending order, while the max-closeness search algorithm must sort them into descending order. This is indicated by the `Boolean` parameter `ascending`, which is **true** for ascending sorts and **false** for descending sorts. In each case, the search starts with a randomly selected node passed into the method as `reply`, and ends with either `dead_end` or the index of the destination node. Note that depth-first search is implemented recursively:

```
private NavReply Radius_Path(boolean ascending, NavReply reply, int dest){
            int DEAD_END = -1;
            Shuffler sorted = new Shuffler(nLinks);
            if(reply.found || reply.node == DEAD_END) return reply;
```

```
        reply.hops++;
        node[reply.node].visited = true;
        int next_node = 0;                                      //Successor
        int j = 0;
        for(int e = 0; e < nLinks; e++){                    //Find next node
                if(Link [ e] .head == reply.node) next_node = Link [ e] .tail;
                else if(Link [ e] .tail == reply.node) next_node = Link [ e] .head;
                else continue;
                if(next_node == dest) {
                        reply.found = true;
                        reply.node = next_node;
                        return reply;                           //Found!
                }
                if(node [ next_node] .visited) continue;
                sorted.card[j] = next_node;
                sorted.key[j] = node[next_node].radius,
                j++;
        }
        if(j > 0){
                sorted.SH_Sort(j, !ascending);  //true = ascending;
                false = descending
                for(next_node = 0; next_node < j; next_node++){
                        reply.node = sorted.card[next_node];
                        reply = Radius_Path(ascending, reply, dest);
                            //Recursive call
                }
        }
        else {
                reply.hops--;
                reply.found = false;
                reply.node = DEAD_END;
        }
        return reply;
}//Radius_Path
```

Which algorithm is best, and does the structure of the network matter? These questions are answered by studying Fig. 5.8. Surprisingly, the random navigation algorithm is not the worst! Random is better than max-closeness and min-radius for the 2-regular WS small-world network. Generally, max-closeness is the worst, because it requires the most hops to reach the destination node.

Next, note that in all cases, except for the small world with $p < 5\%$, the max-degree algorithm is the best navigation algorithm. In other words, average navigation path length is smaller when using the max-degree algorithm than when using

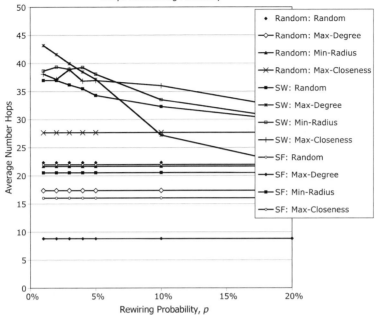

Figure 5.8 Average navigation path lengths versus rewiring probability p for random, small-world, and scale-free networks ($n = 100$), using the four navigation algorithms: random, max-degree, min-radius, and max-closeness.

the other three. In fact, ranking the navigation algorithms from worst (most hops), to best (fewest hops) gives

1. Slowest: max-closeness
2. Slow: random
3. Medium: min-radius
4. Fast: max_degree

This result has immediate application to communication network theory. For example, the routing scheme called *open shortest path first* (OSPF) finds the next router or switch along a path from sender to receiver (email) in the Internet. OSPF requires frequent updating of global information at each router or switch. The results here suggest that a simple ranking of adjacent routers and switches according to their degree may be as good or better than OSPF, although this is left as an exercise for the reader.

The next observation is that network structure does matter. According to Fig. 5.8, navigation performance among the three classes of networks follows the rank order

1. Slow: small world with small rewiring probability p
2. Medium: random network
3. Fast: scale-free network

Of course, the small-world network becomes more like a random network as rewiring probability increases. The max-degree search algorithm rapidly improves as rewiring increases until it approximates the performance of max-degree search in a random network. The SW: max-degree line in Fig. 5.8 is the most rapidly decreasing line of all. It appears that max-degree searching is efficient enough to exploit even a small amount of randomness to the maximum.

The properties of scale-free networks are studied in more detail in the next chapter. Note that scale-free networks can be navigated much faster than can either small-world or random networks. The max-degree algorithm works especially well on scale-free networks, which contain very-high-degree nodes. Once again, this result may be significant in the design of communication networks such as the Internet, because the Internet is a scale-free network.

Curiously, the class of small-world networks came out last in this comparison. Small worlds are the most difficult to navigate with only local information. Yet, two of the primary properties of small-world networks are their small diameter and short characteristic path length. Why, then, does it take a larger number of hops to navigate them? Recall that the average path length of a network is based on the shortest path between all pairs of nodes. Navigation along the path between two nodes using local information about each node does not guarantee the shortest path. Network navigation using local information finds the first path, not the shortest path.

In the OSPF algorithm employed by the Internet, switch and router tables must store the sequence of addresses (nodes) along the shortest path—hence its name. This table contains global rather than local information about the entire network. If the OSPF algorithm were used, one would expect a result consistent with the average path lengths obtained in this book. However, router tables must be constantly updated, and they are not content-sensitive—that is, they do not store the location of content that may be stored at a destination node. OSPF router tables would have to be greatly enhanced with indexing capability, to support network navigation based on content.

One more note is worthwhile. Communication networks must consider the bandwidth or capacity limitations of nodes and links. The analysis provided here does not include bandwidth limitations, which can radically reduce the performance of OSPF and other navigation algorithms. High-degree nodes are also highly burdened nodes, because they must handle the sum total of all bandwidth converging on them. Thus, a max-degree navigation algorithm may actually be bogged down by the bottleneck of congestion brought about by high degree (many links converging on one node). High-degree nodes must also maintain high bandwidth to be effective in communication network navigation. One way to accommodate the demands of high degree is to use redundancy—split the high-degree node into two servers, each with one-half of the links, and one-half the volume of content.

5.5   WEAK TIES IN SMALL-WORLD NETWORKS

In the previous chapter, we explored the social network of Pointville, Flatland, where the average citizen knows an average of 24 other citizens. The population of Pointville is $n = 129$. Assuming Pointville to be a small-world network, what are the weak ties spanning Pointville? Recall that a *weak tie* is a chain of acquaintances that leads from person u to person w, for any node pair u-w, across the entire population. Does the topological structure of Pointville make a difference in the strength of weak ties?

Assuming that there are no hermits in Pointville, the avg_path_length of this small-world population is computed using either the Newman–Moore–Watts equation or the author's equation. In the previous chapter, the diameter and radius of a random Pointville were found to be 2.36 and 2.18, respectively. How does the random Pointville compare with a small-world Pointville, assuming $k = 2$, and a rewiring probability of $p = 6\%$?

$$n = 129$$
$$m = 2(129) = 258$$
$$r = (2)(0.6)(258) = 30.96$$
$$\beta = \text{sqrt}(30.96^2 + 4(30.96)) = 32.9$$
$$\text{arc\_tanh}\left(\frac{30.9}{32.9}\right) = 1.75$$
$$\frac{2n}{\beta k} = \frac{258}{32.9(2)} = 3.92$$
$$\text{avg\_path\_length(Pointville)} = 3.92(1.75) = 6.85 \text{ hops.}$$

The average path length obtained using the author's approximation is

$$\text{avg\_path\_length(Pointville, 0.06, 129)} = \frac{\dfrac{129}{4(2)}}{((0.06)(2)(129))^q};$$

assuming $q = \dfrac{1}{3}$: avg_path_length(Pointville, 0.06, 129) $= 6.5$ hops.

Simulation results give an average value of 6.5 hops, so a "weak tie" is approximately 6.5 hops long. All three methods agree within a few percentage points. Compared with the random network solution given in the previous chapter, citizens of Pointville are more isolated from one another in this small world than in the world of random networks. Why?

The explanation lies in the relative densities of the two versions of Pointville. In the previous chapter, the random network contained $m = 24(n/2) = 1548$ links, whereas the 2-regular small world of Pointville contains $m = 2n = 258$ links.

Therefore, the densities are very different from one another (0.1875 vs. 0.0313), and path length decreases with increasing density.

Accommodating equivalent densities, let $k = 12$ because a 12-regular network with $n = 129$, and $\lambda = 24$, has 1548 links. Applying the Newman–Moore–Watts approximation; we have

$$n = 129$$
$$k = 12$$
$$m = 12(129) = 1548$$
$$r = (2)(0.06)(1548) = 185.8$$
$$\beta = \text{sqrt}(185.8^2 + 4(185.8)) = 187.75$$

$$\text{arc\_tanh}\left(\frac{185.8}{187.75}\right) = 2.62$$

$$\frac{2n}{\beta k} = \frac{258}{187.8(12)} = 0.115$$

$$\text{avg\_path\_length(Pointville)} = 0.115(2.62) = 0.3 \text{ hops}$$

The Newman–Moore–Watts equation underestimates this time because the simulated average path length is 2.13 hops, which is comparable to the path length of the random Pointville. Using the author's approximation for $k = 12$ and

$$q = \frac{1}{3(2^{\log_2 (12)-1})} = 0.055$$

yields 2.09 hops.[8] This is much closer, but still underestimates the actual value. Another property of interest to social network analysts is closeness. What is the average closeness of this version of Pointville? Using Fig. 5.7 and the approximation equation derived by curve fitting, we obtain

$$\lambda = 2\frac{m}{n} = 2\left(\frac{1548}{129}\right) = 24 \text{(given)}$$

$$\text{Density} = \frac{\lambda}{n-1} = \frac{24}{128} = 0.1875$$

$$r = \frac{\log_2 (n - (1-p)\lambda)}{\log_2 (\lambda)} = \frac{\log_2 (129 - (0.96)24)}{\log_2 (24)}$$

$$= \frac{6.73}{4.58} = 1.47$$

$$z = \lambda^r = 24^{1.47} = 106.9$$

$$100(\text{closeness(Pointville, 0.04)}) = \text{density}(z) + 10 = 0.1875(106.9) + 10 = 30.0$$

---

[8]Halve $q = \frac{1}{3}$ each time k is doubled. Since k is doubled $\log_2(12)-1$ times, $q = 0.055$.

Simulation results for $n = 129$, and $4\% \leq p \leq 5\%$, yields average closeness of 26.9, so the approximation is about 10% within the actual value. But closeness(random Pointville) = 42.7 from the comparable analysis of the previous chapter. Thus, there is considerable difference in the power of a intermediary in small-world Pointville than random Pointville—random Pointville has more powerful intermediaries. Why?

The main difference between the small-world and random networks generated by simulation here is the underlying k-regular structure of WS small worlds. For small values of rewiring probability p, the k-regular structure is a dominant factor in shaping properties of small worlds. For this reason, the reader should be aware of the biases introduced into the small-world effect by the WS generative procedure. In particular, it is not necessary to use a k-regular lattice as the starting point of a small world. Any sparse and regular network will do. However, properties such as closeness, cluster coefficient, and path length will be affected.

In addition, these results hold only for the data provided here, which are based on rewiring probability $p = 4\%$. Rewiring probability has a major impact on entropy, and hence the small-world effect in a small-world, so we cannot generalize by much, without additional analysis. This is left as an exercise for the reader.

5.6   ANALYSIS

The class of small-world networks lies between structured and random networks. Their randomness is scalable, ranging from very low entropy to entropy comparable to that of a random network. Scalability is tunable in the sense that it can be set a priori as the rewiring probability p, or by adding or subtracting links to change density. The topology of a small-world network includes relatively high clustering and closeness. These properties are inherited from the initial k-regular network in the WS generative procedure. If the small-world effect is desired in a network with low cluster coefficient, then start rewiring from a low-cluster regular network such as a grid or toroid. If a high degree of closeness is desired, start with a high-average-closeness network such as a hypercube. Further investigation of alternatives to the WS generative procedure is left as an exercise for the reader.

Perhaps the reason the relatively low average path length of a small world surprises us is that we expect it to be much larger. Intuitively, path length of a WS generated network should be similar to the average path length of a 2-regular network $n/8$, because of its similarity to the initial 2-regular network that it is derived from. But this ignores the long-haul nature of random links, which tend to bisect the entire network. As it turns out, average path length declines at least as fast as a power law. This is the essence of the small-world effect.

We also showed that small-world networks have an unusually high cluster coefficient. But we showed that clustering is inherited mainly from the k-regular network used as a starting point in the WS generative procedure. Therefore, clustering is *not* an intrinsic property of the small-world effect. In fact, cluster coefficient and path length move in opposite directions, as density increases (see Fig. 5.4). What happens to path length and cluster coefficient when the density of a k-regular WS network approaches 100%? Cluster coefficient slowly rises to 100%, and path length rapidly drops to 1.

Cluster coefficient is determined by the underlying k-regular network, not by the small-world effect. We illustrated this using a toroidal network in place of a k-regular network. The resulting small-world network assumed the likeness of a toroid instead of a k-regular lattice. We further tested this hypothesis by comparing a small-world network generated by the WS algorithm with a random network generated by the Gilbert generation procedure. Suppose $n = 100$, $m = 200$, and $p = 5\%$ for the small-world network, and $n = 100$, $m = 200$ ($p = 4\%$) for the equivalent Gilbert random network. Both networks have the same number of nodes and links, but the small-world network is randomized by rewiring, and the Gilbert network is randomized by retaining only 4% (200) of the 4950 links in its initial complete network. Using an average computed over five trials, the cluster coefficient of the small-world network drops from 0.500 to 0.437 after rewiring. Similarly, the cluster coefficient of the Gilbert random network drops from 1.000 to 0.0512 after random selection of 4% of the 4950 links. The WS procedure retains most of the clustering of the initial 2-regular network, while the Gilbert procedure does not.

We conclude that small-world clustering is a consequence of two factors: the inherent clustering of the initial network and the manner of rewiring. The WS procedure preserves a certain amount of clustering because one end of each rewired link is anchored at a high-cluster-coefficient node. The Gilbert procedure does not preserve anchors; hence the inherent clustering of its initial complete network is lost.

How does a WS small-world network compare with a random network? Figure 5.9 positions the class of small-world networks somewhat symmetrically around the origin of a Kiviat graph containing ring, random, and small-world network graphs. But this is a typical small world. We know that each of these properties can be tuned to match a desirable value. In this sense, the shape of a small world's Kiviat graph is malleable and therefore atypical. Because of its Kiviat graph symmetry, the class of small-world networks might be considered the most balanced class of networks.

Small-world networks model the real world. The western United States electrical power grid, neural networks in certain biological systems, and various social networks are small-world networks. One property of such systems is the time it takes to transmit a message from one arbitrarily selected node to another without global information about the network. We showed that the best algorithm—among the three tested—is the max-degree algorithm. Max-degree nodehopping results in the fewest number of hops, and therefore, the least time. This algorithm is simple; it performs a depth-first search (DFS) of the entire network (or until the destination node is found), by selecting the highest-degreed nodes first. At each node in the path from source to destination, the next node is selected by rank-ordering adjacent nodes according to their degree property. The highest-degree next node is selected, and if the DFS backtracks, the next-highest is selected, and it the DFS backtracks again, the next-highest, and so on, until the destination node is found.

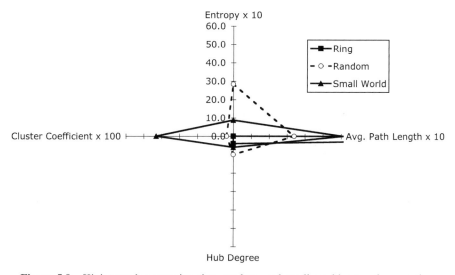

Figure 5.9 Kiviat graph comparing ring, random, and small-world network properties.

Navigation of networks has many applications, not the least of which is the application to communication networks. In a packet-switching system such as the Internet, the structure of the network itself can be exploited by using the max-degree navigation algorithm. This allows packets to find their own way through the Internet with very little a priori information. This approach avoids the necessity of updating router tables, but it does not reduce network latency because max-degree navigation is not as fast as shortest-path navigation.

Small-world networks belong to a very important class of networks. A number of realizations of small worlds can be found in the physical world, simply because of their scalability, high-degree clustering, and relative sparseness. In other words, nature is often served best by a small-world architecture that values economy of links and neighborhood clustering above all else. However, as we have demonstrated, the small-world effect is a property of randomness, and nothing else. In addition, the initial k-regularity of the WS generative procedure introduces biases that affect clustering and closeness. For these, and other reasons, the WS small world has lost favor, and is more of an historical artifact than a representative model of the real world.

5.7 EXERCISES

5.1. Modify the WS generation procedure so that every node is guaranteed to be connected to the small-world network. Does this guarantee that the small-world network is strongly connected?

5.2. Show that the slope of Fig. 5.3 is the same for small-world networks regardless of their size, n.

5.3. What is the approximate average path length and cluster coefficient of a small world of $n = 500$ nodes, that rewires $p = 2\%$ of the links in its initial 5-regular network?

5.4. How does the OSPF (open shortest path first) navigation algorithm differ from the max-degree algorithm? Is OSPF better than max-degree?

5.5. What is the entropy of a 2-regular WS small-world network with $n = 100$ and $p = 64\%$? Is the highest-possible small-world entropy larger or smaller than the entropy of a random network with the same number of nodes and links? Explain.

5.6. What is the average closeness of a 2-regular WS small-world network with $n = 100$ and $p = 50\%$? What is it for $n = 100$ and $p = 5\%$?

5.7. What is the crossover point p^* of a small-world network with $n = 300$?

5.8. What size (n) 2-regular WS small-world network is guaranteed to have an avg_path_length of approximately 6 hops, when $p = 10\%$?

5.9. What is the expected number of hops to fully navigate a 2-regular WS small-world network by visiting the maximum-degree nodes, first, with $n = 300$ and $p = 5\%$? Compare your result with the number of expected hops to navigate a random network with $n = 300$, $m = 600$. (Refer to Fig. 5.10.)

5.10. What is the diameter of Pointville, after the population has doubled to $n = 258$? Assume that the average number of acquaintances remains the same, $\lambda = 24$.

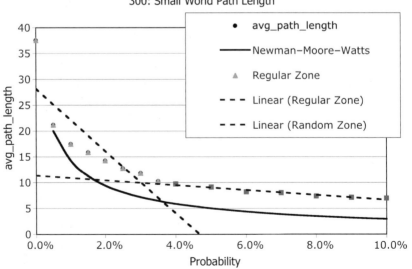

Figure 5.10 Small-world network path length with $n = 300$.

5.11. Construct a model for approximating the closeness of a small-world network with rewiring probability $p = 8\%$ and $n = 258$. What is the average closeness for such a network, when density $= 10\%$?

5.12. Perform a series of experiments to determine exponent q in the power-law approximation for avg_path_length in a small world with $n = 200$ and $k = 4$. Compare it with $q = \frac{1}{3}$ used by the author, when $k = 2$.

6

SCALE-FREE NETWORKS

A *scale-free network* is a network G with degree sequence distribution g' obeying a power law of the form $h(k) \sim k^{-q}$, where k is degree ($1 < k < \infty$) and q is an exponent (typically $2 < q < 3$). In nonmathematical terms, a scale-free network is one with a small number of high-degreed nodes and a large number of low-degreed nodes. The rare nodes with high degree are called *hubs*; therefore, scale-free networks are networks with hubs, which results in a skewed degree sequence distribution.

Scale-free (SF) networks are not random, but they are located nearer to the random end of the network spectrum than regular or small-world networks (with small rewiring probability p). This is due to their entropy, which is generally greater than that of regular and small-world networks and less than that of purely random networks. Table 2.2 (of Chapter 2) lists random, scale-free, small-world, and regular networks with a range of entropy values: 2.9, 2.3, 0.9, and 0.0 bits, respectively.[1] Depending on density, the entropy of a scale-free network can approximate that of a random network. So we must qualify what we consider "equivalent" networks in network science.

Scale-free networks exhibit properties not shared by other networks, however, like hubs—nodes with extremely high degree, and the ability to scale network density while retaining a power-law relationship in its degree sequence. It is possible to control the path length of a scale-free network while simultaneously controlling the hub structure by changing density. This comes in handy when designing

---

[1]These data were obtained by running *Network.jar* with a very low small-world rewiring probability.

---

a network with centrality, low navigation path length, and adjustable cost (number of links).

Scale-free networks quickly rose to a level of scientific prominence in network science following the pioneering work of Albert, Jeong, and Barabasi (Albert, 1999). Before this time, most networks were thought to be random, and therefore had degree sequence distributions that obeyed the Poisson distribution. Subsequently, many real-world networks have been shown to obey a power-law degree sequence distribution rather than a binomial or Poisson distribution. For example, many critical infrastructure systems such as the Internet, railroads, and gas/oil pipeline systems have been shown to be scale-free (Lewis, 2006).

Power-law distributions are not exponential distributions even though they appear to be similar. The tail of an exponential distribution vanishes much faster. For this reason, power-law distributions are often called "fat tail" distributions. Figure 6.1 illustrates the dramatic difference. The power law is related to Zipf's, Pareto's, and Yule–Simon's laws, but is somewhat more general. *Zipf's law* states that the frequency of a word w in the English language is inversely proportional to its rank in the frequency table: $f(w) = c/(r(w))$, where $r(w)$ is the word's rank and c is a constant. *Pareto's distribution*—also known as the 80/20 rule—says that 20% of the population has 80% of the wealth. The *Yule–Simon* distribution is asymptotic to a power law: $f(k) = 1/k^{p+1}$. Yule may have been the first modern scientist to identify natural processes that follow a power law (Yule, 1925).

In this chapter, you will study the following:

1. The generative procedure proposed by Barabasi and Albert (BA) (Barabasi, 1999), produces a *canonical scale-free network* through a process of

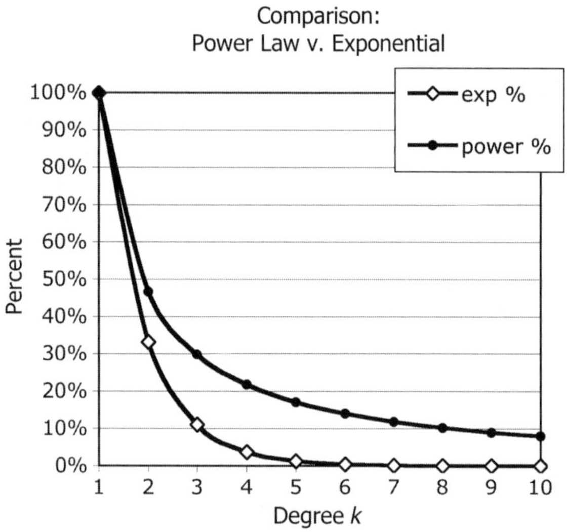

Figure 6.1 Comparison of $y = 3 \exp(-qk)$, versus $y = 1/K^q$, for $q = 1.1$, shows the fat tail of the power law.

preferential attachment. Starting with $n = 3$ nodes, each of the remaining $(n - 3)$ nodes are attached to the network by adding Δm links to existing nodes. For sufficiently large networks and sufficiently small Δm, m is approximately $(\Delta m)n$, and the degree sequence distribution obeys a power law of the form $h(k) = k^{-3}$.

2. The *hub* of a scale-free network is the node with the largest degree. Hub degree grows logarithmically with density: $\text{degree}(\text{hub}) \sim O(\log_2(\text{density}))$.

3. The density of a canonical BA scale-free network depends on the preferential attachment parameter Δm, which is the number of links used to attach each new node to other nodes during construction. This parameter determines the number of links in a canonical scale-free network

$$m = (\Delta m)n - \Delta m \frac{(\Delta m + 1)}{2}$$

and therefore its density

$$d = 2 \frac{m}{n(n - 1)} = \Delta m \frac{2n - (\Delta m + 1)}{n(n - 1)} \sim 2 \frac{\Delta m}{n}$$

assuming $n \gg 1$ and $\Delta m \ll n$.

4. The degree sequence distribution of the canonical scale-free network is a power law:

$$h(k) = 2\Delta m \frac{\Delta m + 1}{(k + 2)(k + 1)k}$$

or in "big-oh" notation: $O(k^{-3})$. Because parameter Δm determines the density of a BA network, the degree sequence can also be expressed in terms of density d: $h(k) \sim (n^2 d^2)/2k^3$.

5. The entropy of a canonical scale-free network is shown to be approximately

$$I(\text{scale-free}) = (\Delta m + 1) \frac{1.1645 - \log_2\left(\frac{\Delta m + 1}{\Delta m^2}\right)}{\Delta m}, \quad 2 \leq \Delta m \leq (n - 1)$$

But entropy plummets to zero near 100% density because the network transitions to a fully connected network instead of a scale-free network.

6. The average path length of a (sparse) BA scale-free network is lower than the average path length of a (sparse) random network. We show that average path length varies as

$$O\left(\frac{\log(n)}{\log(n) + \log(\text{density})}\right)$$

for small networks and densities greater than 4–5% but less than 20%. Bollobas and Riordan report good approximation to large networks such as the Internet with a double-logarithmic approximation:

$$\text{avg\_path\_length(scale-free)} = O\left(\frac{\log(n)}{\log(\log(n))}\right)$$

We also show that average path length linearly declines with hub degree:

$$\text{avg\_path\_length} = A - 2\frac{\text{Hub\_degree}}{300}$$

for $n = 200$, or in general, avg_path_length declines as $O(\text{Hub\_degree})$.

7. The average closeness of a scale-free network is determined by its density and the size of its largest hub:

$$\text{Closeness(scale-free)} = O(\text{density}(z)), \text{ where } z = \lambda^r \text{ and}$$

$$r = \frac{\log_2(n - \text{Hub\_degree})}{\log_2(\lambda)}$$

Because a hub tends to directly connect to the majority of other nodes, it tends to remove Hub_degree nodes from consideration as an intermediary. In terms of average closeness, network classes are ranked as follows: random (highest), small-world (medium), and scale-free (lowest).

8. The cluster coefficient of a scale-free network generally varies inversely with n, and linearly with increase in density: $CC(\text{scale-free}) \sim O(\text{density})$. Barabasi claims that there is no analytic approximation of cluster coefficient for the BA-generated scale-free network, but suggests that it follows a power law: $CC(\text{scale-free}) = O(n^{-0.75})$. Because the density of a scale-free network is approximately $d = 2(\Delta m/n)$, the cluster coefficient also increases with Δm: $CC(\text{scale-free}) \sim O(\Delta m)$. The cluster coefficient of individual nodes is inversely proportional to the degree of individual nodes in a sparse scale-free network; hubs have low cluster coefficients, while nonhubs have high cluster coefficients. Cluster coefficient is bounded by $\Delta m/(\text{degree} - \Delta m)$ for low values of Δm.

9. Navigation time (average path length) of a scale-free network using the *max-degree algorithm* diminishes as $O(1/\text{density})$ or $O(\exp(-\text{Hub\_degree}))$. However, the magnitude of the average path length (navigation time) is much greater than that of the shortest-path average path length. The larger the hub, the faster the search when using the max-degree algorithm.

6.1 GENERATING A SCALE-FREE NETWORK

Barabasi and Albert (Barabasi, 1999) studied a class of networks whose degree distribution is $h(k) \sim k^{-q}$, which means that many nodes have low degree and a few nodes have high degree. The node with the highest degree is called the *hub* of the network. Nodes with high degree are often called hubs or *secondary hubs*, also. We show how to construct such networks, and derive the degree distribution function from a model proposed by Newman and others (Newman, 2003b).

Any function that obeys the relation $h(\alpha k) = \beta h(k)$, for constants α and β, is considered *scale-free* because scaling the x axis (independent variable) by a constant factor α, results in scaling the y axis (dependent variable) also by a constant factor β. In this case, $\beta = \alpha^{-q}$, which is a constant relative to k. The effect of scaling the independent variable by a constant factor of α is to move the power-law curve up or down vertically, but does not change the shape or range of the curve (see Fig. 6.1).

Scale-free networks are also unusual because their power-law probability distribution has a "fat tail," which means that it declines more slowly than the exponential distribution so commonly found to model phenomena in the physical world. Compare the decline in $h(k)$ with the decline in $\exp(-qk)$ in Fig. 6.1. Specifically: $k^{-q} > \exp(-qk)$, for most values of $1 < q < 3$. Even when the power-law function is adjusted to match at $h(1) = \exp(-q)$, the exponential function declines more rapidly than $h(k)$ as k increases. This is why power-law distributions are sometimes called "long" or "fat tail" distributions.

Barabasi (Barabasi, 2001, 2002a, 2002b) and others (Newman, 2003b; Adamic, 2000) have extensively studied networks with fat-tail distributions and found many applications of their theories in physical and biological sciences. Scale-free networks appear to model many real-world phenomena, which are explored in some detail in subsequent chapters. The primary property of the class of scale-free networks is the extremely high degree of hub nodes, and the impact of this structure on average path length, navigation performance, and clustering.

We caution the reader, however, that the pure power law may not always model reality. Laherrere and Sornette suggest that a *stretched exponential* distribution may be more precise in natural and economic systems (Laherrere, 1998):

$$\text{stretched\_}\exp(x) = c\left(\frac{x^{c-1}}{x_0^c}\right)\exp\left(-\left(\frac{x}{x_0}\right)^c\right)$$

Typically, exponent c is less than one. When $c = 1$, the stretched exponential is simply the well-known exponential distribution. Laherrere and Sornette list a number of natural and economic systems that obey this law: distribution of the 1300 largest earthquakes, temperature variations over the past 420,000 years, radio and light emissions from galaxies, oilfield reserve sizes, US and French company sizes, United Nations country sizes, citation distribution of the most frequently cited physicists, and the distribution of biological extinction events.

6.1.1 The Barabasi–Albert (BA) Network

Barabasi, Albert, and Jeong (Barabasi, 1999) argued that random or small-world network classes fail to model some real-world systems because they assume that the number of nodes n is set prior to activation of the underlying microrules. Real networks, claim the advocates of scale-free networks, are dynamic, not static and therefore should be modeled as growth phenomena.

Systems such as the ever-expanding Internet, growing bibliographic references to publications in a new field, and building physical infrastructure such as a large regional electrical power grid, start with a small number of nodes n_0 and grow larger through the addition of new nodes over time. They grow from a few nodes to many millions of nodes through an evolutionary process called *preferential attachment*. In simple terms, preferential attachment is biased—not random—which leads to networks with hubs. These early researchers concluded that the dynamic nature of some real-world systems is better represented by networks that "unfairly" add nodes and links as they evolve into nonrandom semistructured networks.

Barabasi et al. noted that random networks obey a uniformly random attachment rule, whereby the probability of attachment of a link to a pair of nodes is uniformly random. Once again, this may not represent reality. Instead, Barabasi et al. proposed the *preferential attachment rule*, which states that the probability of a link connecting node pairs is proportional to the degree of the new node. Instead of sampling from a uniformly random distribution, the Barabasi–Albert (BA) generative procedure creates dynamic networks by sampling from the degree sequence distribution of network G at timestep t, namely, $g'(t)$. The probability of a high-degreed node obtaining a subsequent link continues to rise as new nodes and links are added. The probability of a low-degreed node obtaining a subsequent link declines, so that over time, "popular nodes" become more popular, and out-of-favor nodes become less popular.

Preferential attachment derives its name from the fact that the probability of a new node attaching to an existing node is proportional to the degree of the existing node. The higher the degree, the more likely a new link will be attached to the node. Clearly, high-degreed nodes become more connected and low-degreed nodes become less connected as the network grows. The resulting degree sequence distribution is skewed toward low degree, because an increasing number of nodes decrease in degree as a few nodes greatly increase in degree.

The generative procedure given here follows the development of Barabasi et al. (Barabasi, 1999). In the following quotation (Barabasi, et al., 1999, pp. 7–8) "vertices" refers to *nodes*, and "edge" refers to *link*:

> (1) *Growth*: Starting with a small number (m_0) of vertices, at every time step we add a new vertex with $m(\leq m_0)$ edges (that will be connected to the vertices already present in the system).
>
> (2) *Preferential attachment*: When choosing the vertices to which the new vertex connects, we assume that the probability P that a new vertex will be connected to vertex i depends on the connectivity k_i of that vertex, such that $P(k_i) = \frac{k_i}{\sum_j k_j}$.
>
> (3) After t time steps the model leads to a random network with $N = t + m_0$ vertices and mt edges."

We simplify the Barabasi et al. generative procedure by setting $n_0 = m_0 = 3$, and substitute m for Δm to avoid confusion with the total number of links in a network.[2]

---

[2]Subgraph patterns like this triangular starting network are called *motifs* in the biological network literature.

The *canonical BA scale-free network* is generated by repeated application of a simple dynamic network construction algorithm:

1. Starting with three nodes and three links, grow the network by adding one node at each timestep t.
2. Link the new node to Δm other nodes using preferential attachment.
3. Repeat this until all n nodes have been added to the network.

This takes an additional $t = (n - 3)$ steps to add $(n - 3)$ additional nodes to the initial three nodes and three links. In the early stages of formation, fewer than Δm links are added because network size n is too small. When $n < \Delta m$, only n links are added. Thus, at the end of the growth stage, the scale-free network has

$$m = (\Delta m)n - \sum_{i=1}^{\Delta m} i = (\Delta m)n - \Delta m \frac{\Delta m + 1}{2}$$

The following modified BA generative procedure begins with a "triangular network" consisting of three nodes and three links, and then attaches a new node to as many as Δm other nodes by preferential attachment. This algorithm ignores some important details that are addressed in the Java implementation to follow.

Barabasi–Albert (Modified) Generative Procedure

1. Inputs: $\Delta m =$ number of links to add to each new node; $n =$ network size.
2. Initialize: Designate nodes by enumerating them as $0, 1, 2, \ldots, (n - 1)$.
   a. Given the ultimate number of nodes $n > 3$, initially construct a complete network with nNodes $= n_0 = 3$ nodes and nLinks $= 3$ links. The degree sequence of this complete network is $g = [2,2,2]$, and the degree sequence distribution is $g' = [1]$ because each node is connected to the other two.
3. While nNodes $\leq n$:
   a. New node: Generate a new tail node v.
   b. #New links: Set n_links $=$ minimum $(\Delta m, n)$. Cannot add more links than existing nodes.
   c. Repeat n_links times:
      i. *Preferential attachment*—select an existing head node u by sampling from the degree sequence cumulative distribution function CDF(i) defined by

$$\text{CDF}(i) = \sum_{j}^{i} \frac{\text{degree}(n_j)}{\text{k\_total}}, \quad \text{where} \ \ \text{k\_total} = 2\text{nNodes}$$

ii. Let r be a uniform random number from $[0,1)$. Then u is a random variate sampled from CDF(i) as follows:

$$\text{CDF}(u - 1) \le r \le \text{CDF}(u); \quad u = r \text{ nNodes}$$

iii. Connect $v \sim u$, taking care to avoid duplicate links.

Preferential attachment is the main distinguishing feature of scale-free networks. The motivation for preferential attachment comes from applications of network science to growth phenomena. It is a concept that has different names in different fields of study. Preferential attachment is known as the *law of increasing returns* in economics, *adaptive learning* in artificial intelligence, and *natural selection* in biology. It is often called "the rich get richer" phenomenon, because high-degreed nodes acquire even more links, which increases their degree even further. Preferential attachment is a form of positive feedback that accelerates the acquisition of a commodity on the basis of the widespread or mainstream adoption of that commodity.

Increasing returns means a commodity becomes more valuable as it becomes more plentiful. Consider the widespread adoption of Microsoft Windows software—the more copies there are, the more likely it is that a new consumer will buy an additional copy. A combination of factors such as compatibility, popularity, and availability of applications that run only on Windows are some obvious reasons for increasing returns in the desktop operating systems market.

Adaptive learning in artificial intelligence is an algorithmic technique for simulating the behavior of organisms or machines that learn. Each response to a stimulus is rewarded by increasing the probability that the same response will result from the stimulus. Repetition increases the probability, which in turn increases the repetition of the stimulus–response pair. Learning is a form of conditioning based on the probability distribution established by repetition and positive feedback. It is a form of preferential attachment.

Natural selection is a similar process. In most species, stronger genes are replicated in subsequent generations while weaker genes fade. The so-called *fitness function* of an individual is akin to a power law—the more fit an individual is, the more likely it is to survive, reproduce, and pass its genes on to the next generation. As fitness increases, the gene is more likely to survive, and as survivability increases, so does fitness. This feedback mechanism repeats many times, usually in extremely small increments. Over time, fitter individuals emerge from weaker ancestors.

Perhaps the earliest definition of preferential attachment, called *cumulative advantage* by Price (Price, 1965, 1976), explained the power-law property of scale-free networks before such networks were called scale-free. Price's model was slightly different from the BA model. The BA procedure ignores link direction, while the Price model did not, and the BA model starts from scratch, while the Price model assumes an existing network. Nonetheless, preferential attachment and cumulative advantage are identical concepts.

6.1.2 Generating BA Networks

The foregoing description of the BA generative procedure ignores some important details that the Java implementation, discussed below, provides. In particular, the Java method finds an alternative node as needed to avoid duplicate links, and shows how to implement preferential attachment by sampling from a cumulative distribution function (CDF) obtained from the evolving degree sequence distribution.

Method `NW_doCreateScaleFree()` paraphrases the BA procedure described above. It relies on `NW_doAddNode()` to create nodes as needed, and `NW_doAddLink()` to connect node pairs with a link, except when such a link duplicates an existing link, and `Math_random()` to produce uniformly random numbers in [0,1). Of particular interest is the method of finding a replacement node when the node selected by preferential attachment leads to a duplicate link. When this happens, the code rolls variable j forward, seeking a node with higher index. This is achieved by incrementing j until it exceeds nNodes, and then starting over again with node 0. Unless the network achieves completeness, this approach guarantees a scale-free network with $m = \Delta mn - 3 - \Delta m((\Delta m + 1)/2)$ links or density of approximately $2(\Delta m/n)$.

Preferential attachment is implemented by sampling the head node of each new link from a *cumulative distribution function* (CDF). CDF is recomputed each time a new node is added because total number of links and node degrees change after each insertion. It is normalized by the total number of degrees $2m$ so that CDF never exceeds 1.0. Specifically, preferential attachment is implemented by sampling from CDF to obtain variate j, which must always fall within the range of possible node numbers [0, nNodes-1]:

```
public void NW_doCreateScaleFree(int delta_m){
    int new_node = 0;          //Select a new node to add to network
    double CDF[ ] = new double[ nInputNodes] ;
    nNodes = 0;                //Start from scratch
    NW_doAddNode("0");         //Create initial 3-node network
    NW_doAddNode("1");
    NW_doAddNode("2");
    NW_doAddLink(node[1].name, node[0].name);
    NW_doAddLink(node[2].name, node[0].name);
    NW_doAddLink(node[1].name, node[2].name);
    //Add a node at a time
    while(nNodes < nInputNodes){
      CDF[0] = (float)node[ 0] .degree/(2*nLinks); //Initialize
                                                        preferences
      new_node = NW_doAddNode(Long.toString(nNodes));
      int n_links = Math.min(delta_m, nNodes-1); //Delta_m must
                                                    be < nNodes
      for(int m = 1; m <= n_links; m++){    //Connect to n_links
                                              other nodes
          double r = Math.random();          //Sample variate from CDF
          for(int i = 1; i < nNodes; i++) {  //Find preferred nodes
              CDF[i] = CDF[i-1] + (float)node[ i] .degree/(2*nLinks);
              int j = 0;                      //Destination node
```

```
if(r < CDF[ 0]  || CDF[ i-1]  <= r && r < CDF[ i] ){
  if(r < CDF[ 0] ) j = 0; else j = i;
  //Avoid duplicate links
  while(!NW_doAddLink(node[ new_node] .name,
    node[j].name)){
    j++; if(j >= nNodes) j = 0;    //Roll forward
  }
  break;                           //Linked!
  }
}
}
}
}//NW_doCreateScaleFree
```

`NW_doCreateScaleFree()` produces a different scale-free network each time it is performed. Why? Procedure BA may seem deterministic because it links new nodes to the highest-degreed nodes, but it is not. Sampling from CDF produces a bias, but it does not guarantee that the highest-degreed node will always be selected. This statistical variation means that a different network topology is produced each time a scale-free network is generated.

The method described here produces a network with less entropy than in a random network, because preferential attachment produces a network with non-Poisson degree sequence distribution. We derive the power law produced by the class of scale-free networks in more detail and derive a closed-form approximation for scale-free network entropy in a subsequent section.

6.1.3   Scale-Free Network Power Law

This section paraphrases Newman's analysis of the BA generative procedure for producing a canonical scale-free network (Newman, 2003b). Newman showed that the scale-free network degree sequence distribution, $h(k) \sim O(k^{-3})$, is a direct consequence of the change in the expected number of nodes with degree k after each new node is added. A fraction of nodes with degree $(k - 1)$ increase their degree to k, and another fraction of nodes increase their degree from k to $(k + 1)$. The net change in fraction of nodes with degree k is the difference between these two.

More specifically, we approximate the net change in nodes with degree k by observing that a new node is attached to the network by Δm links, which transitions a fraction of nodes of degree $(k - 1)$ to nodes of k degrees, and another fraction of nodes of degree k to nodes of $(k + 1)$ degree. The difference between the distribution before adding a node and after adding a node is averaged, which leads to a *mean-field equation* whose solution is $h(k)$.

The derivation given by Newman makes a number of assumptions that may not be valid for all scale-free networks. For example, the derivation assumes linearity—the probability of link attachment varies directly proportional to the degree of the destination node. Alternately, the relationship could be proportional to the square of destination node degree, square root, and so on. Nonetheless, Newman's linear model seems to give an accurate result for the BA generative procedure. A number of other authors have published similar results using other assumptions. For example, Barabasi et al. (Barabasi, 1999) describe another alternative to the derivation given here.

Our power-law derivation strategy proceeds as follows:

1. Let $h(k;t)$ be the degree sequence distribution at timestep t, and let Δm be the number of links attached each time a new node is added. One new node and Δm links are added at each timestep; hence the number of nodes with degree k at time t is $nh(k,t)$, and the number of nodes with degree k at timestep $(t + 1)$ is $(n + 1)h(k,t + 1)$.

2. Using the degree sequence distribution $h(k;t)$ at timestep t, construct a *mean-field equation* expressing the expected change in number of nodes with degree k for a typical timestep. Note that the expected number of nodes with degree k after insertion of a new node is $\Delta mh(k - 1;t)$, and the expected number of nodes that no longer have degree k is $\Delta mh(k;t)$ after the new node is inserted. In other words, some nodes transition from degree $(k - 1)$ to k, and others transition from degree k to degree $(k + 1)$.

3. Solve the mean-field equation for the stationary (time-invariant) case, yielding $h(k)$. We do this by removing t from the mean-field equation. *Time invariance* means that $h(k,t + 1) = h(k,t) = h(k)$. This is the so-called *stationary process* solution, which represents the end state of the scale-free network. $h(k)$ is the degree sequence distribution function after n nodes have been attached.

First, derive an expression for the linear relation between probability of attachment and degree sequence distribution. The degree sequence distribution $h(k;t)$ is the fraction of nodes with degree k, at timestep t. Note that $\sum_k h(k;t) = 1$, which is independent of t. Preferential attachment uses this fraction to select the node with degree k that is linked to the new node with the following probability:

$$\frac{kh(k;t)}{\sum_k kh(k;t)} = \frac{kh(k;t)}{\lambda}$$

where λ = mean degree of the network. We also know that $\lambda = 2(m/n)$ for any network, and $m = \Delta mn$ (approximately), for the BA generative procedure. Thus, the fraction of nodes with degree k is $(kh(k;t))/2\Delta m$, after substituting $\lambda = 2\Delta m$ into the equation for $h(k;t)$. Now we can write the mean-field equation that relates the "before"/"after" change in number of nodes with degree k.

Mean-Field Equation Change in number of nodes with degree k equals the number of nodes increased from degree $(k - 1)$ to degree k, minus the number of nodes increased from degree k to degree $(k + 1)$.

The left-hand side of the mean-field equation is the expected number of nodes with degree k after insertion of a new node, minus the number before insertion:

$$(n+1)h(k;t+1) - nh(k;t)$$

The right-hand-side is the expected number of links connecting to nodes with degree $(k-1)$ minus the number of nodes that are no longer of degree k because they increased to degree $(k+1)$:

$$\Delta m(k-1)\frac{h(k-1,t)}{2\Delta m} - \Delta m\frac{kh(k,t)}{2\Delta m}$$

This simplifies after cancellation of Δm:

$$(k-1)\frac{h(k-1,t)}{2} - k\frac{h(k,t)}{2}$$

Therefore the time-varying mean-field equation is

$$(n+1)h(k;t+1) - nh(k;t) = (k-1)\frac{h(k-1,t)}{2} - k\frac{h(k,t)}{2}; k > \Delta m$$

The stationary, or time-invariant solution, obtained by setting $h(k,t+1) = h(k,t) = h(k)$, simplifies to a first-order difference equation:

$$h(k) = (k-1)\frac{h(k-1)}{2} - kh\frac{k}{2}; k > \Delta m$$

The right-hand-side of this difference equation assumes $k > \Delta m$, but when $k = \Delta m$, only one node increases from degree $(k-1)$ to k, so the mean-field equation is limited to $k = \Delta m, \Delta m + 1, \Delta m + 2, \ldots$ when $k = \Delta m$:

$$h(\Delta m) = 1 - \Delta mh\frac{\Delta m}{2}$$

Solving for $h(\Delta m)$, we obtain

$$h(\Delta m) = \frac{2}{\Delta m + 2}$$

Backsubstitution into the mean-field equation for $k > \Delta m$ yields the general solution

$$h(k) = 2\Delta m\frac{\Delta m + 1}{(k+2)(k+1)k}$$

For large k and constant Δm, $h(k)$ is a power law with $q = 3$. In fact, $h(k) = O\,(k^{-3})$. For example, assuming $\Delta m = 2$, the power law is

$$h(k) = \frac{12}{(k+2)(k+1)k}$$

Note how this predetermines the degree sequence distribution, for $k = 2, 3, \ldots$ On average, all scale-free networks produced by the BA procedure, with $\Delta m = 2$, obey the following distribution, regardless of size, n:

$$h(2) = \frac{12}{(4)(3)(2)} = 50\%$$

$$h(3) = \frac{12}{(5)(4)(3)} = 20\%$$

$$h(4) = \frac{12}{(6)(5)(4)} = 10\%$$

$$\vdots$$

$$h(n) = \frac{12}{(n+2)(n+1)(n)} \sim 0\%;\ n \gg 1$$

Figure 6.2 compares the theoretical derivation $h(k)$ with the empirical result obtained from *Network.jar* and the BA generative procedure described above. The

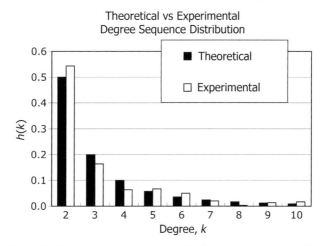

Figure 6.2   Theoretical versus experimental results for degree sequence distribution of a scale-free network with $n = 100$ and $\Delta m = 2$. Experimental results are the average of three runs. Root-mean-square error is less than 1%.

root-mean-square (RMS) error is negligible for $n = 100$ and the BA generative procedure. Apparently, Newman's linear assumption is quite good for BA networks.

Given the density of a BA network

$$d = 2\frac{m}{n(n-1)} = 2\Delta m \frac{n - 3 - \Delta m \frac{\Delta m + 1}{2}}{n(n-1)} \sim 2\frac{\Delta m}{n}$$

we can also express the degree sequence distribution function in terms of density d by substitution of $\Delta m = n(d/2)$ into the equation above:

$$h(k) = 2\Delta m \frac{\Delta m + 1}{(k+2)(k+1)k}$$

$$= nd \frac{nd + 2}{2(k+2)(k+1)k} \sim \frac{n^2 d^2}{2k^3} \sim O\left(\frac{n^2 d^2}{2k^3}\right)$$

This derivation yields an exponent $q = 3$ for scale-free networks, but in practice, a network is considered scale-free if $2 \leq q \leq 3$. Newman (Newman, 2003b) discusses other solutions, yielding different values of q, based on different assumptions. Technically, any value of q satisfies the scale-free relation $h(\alpha k) = \beta h(k)$.

6.2 PROPERTIES OF SCALE-FREE NETWORKS

In this section, we study the properties of canonical scale-free networks generated by the BA procedure. Unless specified otherwise, we use $\Delta m = 2$, which means that network density declines as network size increases. This restriction will be relaxed later, but the simplification serves to explore entropy, average path length, and cluster coefficient while holding Δm constant. However, keep in mind that density changes as a byproduct of changing size n or Δm.

First, we compare entropy, average path length, and cluster coefficient as a function of network size, n (and therefore network density). This allows us to also observe the change in degree of the hub node, and average distance of max-degree navigation versus both size and density. Later we study the effects of holding n constant while changing density, by changing Δm.

The following analysis is summarized in Fig. 6.3. Various properties have been determined experimentally by running *Network.jar* for different network sizes. Property values are scaled where shown, to make the comparison visible on the same graph; entropy and avg_path_length values are multiplied by 10. The cluster coefficient data are multiplied by 100.

6.2.1 BA Network Entropy

From Fig. 6.3 it is clear that entropy remains constant as network size and therefore density vary. For $\Delta m = 2$, we obtain I (scale-free) ~ 2.4 bits. In retrospect, this is

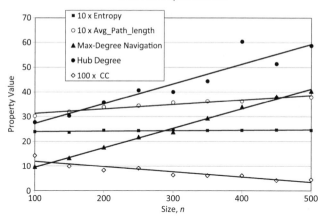

Figure 6.3 Comparison of BA scale-free network properties versus size, n, for $\Delta m = 2$. Note the scale factors on entropy, average path length, and cluster coefficient.

intuitive because entropy I is determined by the degree sequence distribution, which is independent of size or density. The degree sequence distribution is always a power law; hence I (scale-free) is a function of preferential attachment parameter Δm. Accordingly, it is possible to derive a closed-form equation for entropy by substitution of power law $h(k)$ into the entropy equation: $I = -\sum h(k) \log_2(h(k))$, and approximating the summation by integration:

$$I = \int_{\Delta m}^{\infty} h(k) \log_2(h(k)) \delta x = -1.443 \int_{\Delta m}^{\infty} h(k) \ln(h(k)) \delta x$$

Because $\log_2(x) = 1.433 \ln(x)$, $\ln(x)$ is the natural logarithm. Substitution of $h(x) = Ax^{-3}$, where $A = 2\Delta m (\Delta m + 1)$ into the integral, and simplifying the logarithmic expression yield

$$I = -1.443A \int_{\Delta m}^{\infty} \left(\frac{\ln(A) - 3\ln(x)}{x^3} \right) \delta x$$

The first term in the integral is easily integrated to get $T_1 = (\ln (A))/(2\Delta m^2)$, and the second term is integrated by substitution of u and v into the integral.

Let $u = x^{-3}$, and $v = \ln(x)$, so $\delta u = ((-x^{-2}/2); \delta v = x^{-1}$.

Integration by parts yields the second term in the integral:

$$T_2 = \frac{2\ln(\Delta m) + 1}{4\Delta m^2}$$

Combining terms, we get

$$I = -1.433A(T_1 + T_2) = -1.433A \frac{\ln(A) - 3 \frac{\ln(\Delta m)+1}{2}}{2\Delta m^2}$$

After substitution of $A = 2\Delta m(\Delta m+1)$, replacement of 1.433 ln() by $\log_2()$, and simplification of terms, we get an analytical approximation of entropy in a scale-free network:

$$I(\text{scale-free}) = \Delta m + 1 \frac{1.1645 - \log_2\left(\frac{\Delta m+1}{\Delta m^2}\right)}{\Delta m}$$

An alternate formulation, with $I_0 = (\Delta m + 1)/\Delta m$, is

$$I(\text{scale-free}) = I_0\left(1.1645 + \log_2(\Delta m I_0)\right); \quad 2 \leq \Delta m \leq n - 1$$

Note that entropy is only a function of Δm, and nothing else. More specifically entropy of any scale-free network constructed by the BA procedure depends only on the number of links used to connect a new node to the network, and is independent of the size of the network. Furthermore, entropy grows as the logarithm of Δm. For example, the entropy of a scale-free network with $\Delta m = 2$ is $I = \frac{3}{2}(1.1645 - \log_2\left(\frac{3}{4}\right)) = 2.37$. The entropy for $\Delta m = 5$ is $I = \frac{6}{5}\left(1.1645 - \log_2\left(\frac{6}{25}\right)\right) = 3.87$.

Entropy is indirectly a function of density because the density of a BA scale-free network increases with an increase in Δm. Ignoring limits put on Δm during the early stages of preferential attachment, the number of links $m \sim \Delta mn$, which yields an approximation of density for large enough n, and small enough Δm:

$$\text{Density}(\text{scale-free}) = 2\frac{m}{n(n-1)} = 2\frac{\Delta m}{n}$$

assuming $n \gg 1$, and $\Delta m \ll n$. Therefore, $\Delta m \sim n$ (density/2). Substitution into the equation for I(scale-free) produces an expression for entropy as a function of density. This is left as an exercise for the reader.

Entropy of a scale-free network increases as a logarithmic function of Δm, which is directly proportional to density. Unlike a random network that becomes more structured as density exceeds 50%, scale-free entropy monotonically increases with increasing density because its degree sequence distribution remains a power law—up to a point. What happens as density approaches 100%? The scale-free network collapses and its degree sequence distribution is no longer a power law. Hence, this equation is no longer valid. To understand the impact of density on a fixed-size network, we must change Δm while holding n constant. This extremely high-density phenomenon is explored in Section 6.4.

6.2.2 Hub Degree versus Density

Extremely high hub degree is the predominant property of a scale-free network. As the number of available links increases, so does the degree of the network's largest hub. Therefore, hub degree increases with density. However, this increase has diminishing returns, as shown in Fig. 6.4a:

$$\text{Degree(hub)} \sim O\big(\log_2(\text{density})\big); \ 1\% \leq \text{density} \leq 20\%$$

Hub degree grows logarithmically with density for both random and scale-free networks, but the rate of increase is much greater for a scale-free network. In

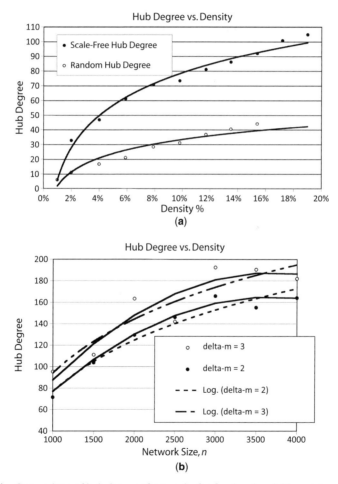

(a)

(b)

Figure 6.4 Comparison of hub degree of networks for fixed and variable n: (a) scale-free and random networks versus density, for constant size, $n = 200$, (b) variable number of links m; and hub degree with variable density and size, n, but fixed Δm.

Fig. 6.4a hub degree of the scale-free network is 3 times that of an equivalent random network, for a density of 20%.

Figure 6.4b plots maximum hub degree for larger scale-free networks with variable density and variable size, n. Theoretically, we should be able to estimate hub degree as a function of n by solving the simple differential equation that relates rate of change in hub degree to density:

$$\frac{\delta \; \text{degree(hub,}t)}{\delta t} = \text{density} = 2\frac{m}{t(t-1)} = 2\frac{\Delta m}{t}$$

where we approximate $(t-1) \sim t$, and substitute $m \sim \Delta mt$, and Δm is the BA generative procedure input parameter.

Solving by direct integration from $t = 1$ to n, we obtain

$$\text{Degree(hub,}n) = 2\Delta m \ln(n) = O(\ln(n))$$

Figure 6.4b includes both logarithmic and quadratic curve fits to data obtained by running a number of simulations on scale-free networks with $\Delta m = 2,3$, and sizes ranging from $n = 1000$ to $n = 4000$ nodes. Dash lines show that the logarithmic fit is a poor approximation to actual hub degree values observed in the simulation, while the quadratic fit is much better (see solid lines). Why?

The quadratic model is a much better approximation to maximum hub degree in scale-free networks because competition among the highest-degreed nodes in a very sparse network siphons off links from preferred nodes; that is, as density decreases (corresponding to increases in size, n), preference for the hub with the highest degree is overcome by the shortage of links. Because of this shortage, links must be acquired by competition among many high-degreed nodes.

Barabasi and others have shown theoretically that hub degree grows logarithmically according to the dashed-line graph of Fig. 6.4. But theoretical approximations assume average networks never approach extreme values of density explored here. For example, in Fig. 6.4b and $\Delta m = 2$, average degree is four links, and density is 0.1% when $n = 4000$. At some point, there simply aren't enough links to go around, which limits logarithmic growth of hub degree.

A better approximation of hub degree is the following quadratic equation:

$$\text{Degree(hub,}n) = n\frac{B - n}{A}; \quad \text{for large } n, \text{ parameters } A \text{ and } B$$

Empirically, $A = 83{,}000$, $B = 7400$ for $\Delta m = 2$, and $A = 73{,}000$, $B = 7400$ for $\Delta m = 3$ in Fig. 6.4b. These parameter values yield a least-squares fit to the observed data and produce the solid lines of Fig. 6.4b.

Consider, for example, $n = 2500$. What is the approximate degree of the hub of a scale-free network with $\Delta m = 3$? Substitution into the quadratic approximation equation yields

$$\text{Degree(hub,2500)} = n\frac{B - n}{A} = 2500\frac{7400 - 2500}{7300} = 168$$

The empirically determined value of 142 was obtained by averaging over three networks generated by program *Network.jar*. The approximation error of $(168-142)/(168+142) = 8\%$ is not bad for the sample size used in Fig. 6.4.

6.2.3 BA Network Average Path Length

Intuitively, the average path length of a scale-free network should be shorter than that of a random network of equal density because there are more long-haul links in a scale-free network. But is this intuition correct? This section shows that path length slowly decreases with an increase in density—just as it does in a random network. But the decline in average path length of a scale-free network is more pronounced in sparse scale-free networks than in sparse random networks. This is due to the much higher degree of hub nodes in sparse scale-free networks over random networks. Scale-free network hubs act as a kind of "grand central station" that most paths traverse when connecting any two nodes. In fact, hubs are typically the largest intermediary node because their closeness property is also the highest. Therefore, intuition is correct for sparse scale-free networks: avg_path_length is smaller than avg_path_length in an equivalent random network. But the difference quickly vanishes with increasing density.

Albert and Barabasi approximated the average path length of a BA scale-free network with average degree $\lambda = 4$ hops, by fitting simulation data to a logarithmic curve (Albert, 2002):

$$\text{avg\_ path\_length(scale-free)} = A \log(n + B) + C$$

In fact, this is a very good approximation to the data collected and displayed in Fig. 6.3, with $A = 15$, $B = 100$, and $C = -4$.

Recall that density $= \lambda/n$, for any network, and if n remains constant, then density decreases with increasing size n. Therefore, average path length gradually rises with increase in size, because density declines. More accurate estimates by Bollobas and Riordan do not appreciably improve the simple approximation given by Albert and Barabasi for networks of the size and density studied here (Bollobas, 2001):

$$\text{avg\_ path\_length(scale-free)} = O\left(\frac{\log (n)}{\log(\log (n))}\right)$$

But the Bollobas–Riordan approximation appears to be more accurate for very large networks. For example, the double-logarithmic expression is accurate for certain measurements of the Internet.

Unfortunately, these theoretical estimates do not directly relate path length to adjustments in number of links, or hub size. For example, if we hold n constant and vary density, the average path length should rise and fall inversely with the rise and fall of density; the higher the density, the lower the path length. To verify and quantify this hypothesis, we explore the effect of density and hub size on path length.

Figure 6.5 shows the difference in average path length of scale-free versus random networks of equivalent density. Both networks tend toward the empirical approximation derived earlier in Chapter 4, but scale-free networks generally exhibit the small-world effect—they have slightly smaller average path lengths than do equivalent random networks. The difference is more pronounced as density approaches zero, suggesting that the small-world effect is more pronounced in random than scale-free networks.

We know from Chapter 4 that average path length of a random network is approximately

$$\text{avg\_path\_length(random)} = \frac{\log(n)}{\log(\lambda)}$$

Density is λ/n, so we replace λ with n(density):

$$\text{avg\_path\_length} = \frac{\log(n)}{\log(n(\text{density}))} = \frac{\log(n)}{\log(n) + \log(\text{density})}$$

However, scale-free networks are not random networks, so this approximation can be tailored to nonrandom topology by scaling numerator and denominator. We want to find parameters A and C that make the following approximation fit the data of Fig. 6.5:

$$10(\text{avg\_path\_length}) = \frac{A \log(n)}{\log(n) + \log(C(\text{density}))}$$

where density is in percentage: $1\% \leq \text{density} \leq 100\%$. For $n = 200$ and the empirical data of Fig. 6.5, $A = 14$ and $C = 2$ give good results for the scale-free network,

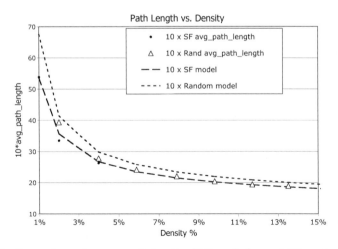

Figure 6.5 Comparison of average path length of BA scale-free and ER random networks versus density, $n = 200$. The average path length of a scale-free network is slightly less that that of an equivalent random network.

and $A = 14$ and $C = 1.5$ yield the curve fit shown in Fig. 6.5 for a random network. The principal variation is in parameter C, which scales density. This suggests that density is "used differently" in scale-free versus random networks. We explore this observation in more detail, later.

How good is the approximation? The estimated average path length of a BA scale-free network of size $n = 200$ and density 4% is approximately

$$10(\text{avg\_path\_length}) = \frac{14 \log(200)}{\log(200) + \log(2(0.04))}$$

$$= \frac{14(2.30)}{2.30 - 1.1} = \frac{32.2}{1.2} = 26.83$$

$$\text{avg\_path\_length} = \frac{26.83}{10} = 2.683 \text{ (empirical value} = 2.69 \text{ hops)}$$

The average path length of an equivalent random network is slightly higher: 2.78 hops. For networks of different size, the inquisitive reader can find different values for parameters A and C using program *Network.jar*.

This approximation does not model average path length very well for densities less than 2–3% (see Fig. 6.5). This is because path length is greatly affected by the small-world effect near the phase transition or crossover point. When dealing with very sparse scale-free networks, the degree of the hub may be a better predictor of the average path length—a result we seek, next.

The average path length of a sparse scale-free network is much less than that of an equivalent sparse random network. This is readily evident in Fig. 6.5 for densities below 4%. We hypothesize that this difference is due to the high degree of hub nodes in scale-free networks as compared to the degree of the most connected node in a random network. If this hypothesis is true, we should be able to observe a correlation between hub degree and path length in a scale-free network. Intuitively, path length declines as hub degree increases because there are more long-haul links in a scale-free network.

Figure 6.6 shows a steady—but noisy—decline in average path length of a sparse scale-free network as hub degree increases. The correlation is not strong, but the trend is clear—path length trends downward with increasing hub degree as hypothesized. Fitting a straight line to this data yields a linear relationship:

$$\text{avg\_path\_length(BA network)} = A - 2\,\frac{\text{Hub\_degree}}{300}; \ A = 3.58$$

This result supports the claim that the higher the hub degree of a scale-free network, the shorter the average path length. Hubs lead to scale-free networks that are also *small worlds*. Furthermore, as it turns out, the length of a navigation path through a scale-free network is lowest for searches that prefer hubs to low-degreed nodes. Hub degree correlates with average path length in other networks as well, but this claim is left as a research project for the reader.

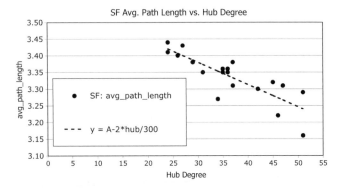

Figure 6.6 Average path length declines linearly as hub degree increases in a scale-free network of size $n = 200$ and density 2% ($\Delta m = 2$). Least-squares curve fit to these data yields $A = 3.58$ and slope equal to $\frac{-2}{300}$.

Average path length declines with increasing density of (any) network, because there are more alternate paths—some shorter than others—through a denser network. When a network is extremely sparse, fewer alternative paths are available to connect node u to node w. The lack of alternative paths in sparse scale-free networks can partially, but not completely, be made up by high-degreed hubs. Low-degreed nodes are more likely to be connected to hubs, and hubs establish long-haul links. The higher the degree of the hub is, the higher the chance that a long-haul link is used to traverse the network. Therefore, hub degree becomes a better predictor of average path length in sparse networks. Hubs are the infrastructure for establishing the small-world effect in scale-free networks.

6.2.4 BA Network Closeness

In previous chapters we learned that average closeness of a network is dictated by the network's density and topology. Generally, density increases closeness—up to a point—and then topology takes over and determines whether high-density networks increase or decrease closeness. Random networks, for example, experience decline in average closeness as density increases because of the small-world effect. Small worlds, on the other hand, experience increase in average closeness as density approaches 100% because of their underlying k-regularity. Scale-free networks are yet another case. Their average closeness is a direct consequence of the size of their hub. Average closeness steadily increases with hub degree, and then slowly declines as density nears 100% (see Fig. 6.7).

The dominant hub node of a scale-free network tends to insert direct links between itself and the majority of all other nodes. Such direct connections eliminate intermediaries—there is no middleperson. This tendency reduces closeness by an

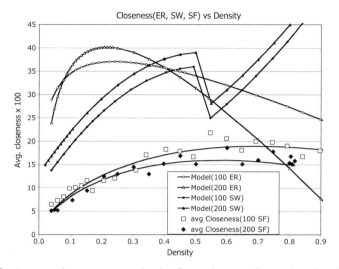

Figure 6.7 Average closeness versus density for random, small-world, and scale-free networks shows that scale-free networks have weaker intermediaries on average.

amount proportional to the degree of the hub. Therefore, a suitable model of average closeness in scale-free networks is

$$100(\text{closeness(scale-free)}) = C_1 \text{density } z + C_2$$

$$z = \lambda^r$$

$$r = \frac{\log_2(n - \text{hub\_degree})}{\log_2(\lambda)}$$

We use the simple $O(\log(\text{density}))$ model for determining hub_degree: hub_degree $= A \log_2(B \text{ density})$. Fitting this model to the experimental data of Fig. 6.7 yields the following constants:

$$n = 100: A = 18; \ B = 25; \ C_1 = 1, \ C_2 = 1$$
$$n = 200: A = 36; \ B = 30; \ C_1 = 0.5, \ C_2 = 1$$

For example, an approximation of average closeness in a scale-free network of size, $n = 100$, $\Delta m = 4$, is obtained by converting Δm into λ and density:

$$m = \Delta mn - \Delta m \frac{\Delta m + 1}{2} = (4)(100) - 4\frac{5}{2} = 390$$

Therefore density

$$d = 2\frac{m}{n(n - 1)} = 2\frac{390}{(100)(99)} = 0.0788$$

The mean degree is $\lambda = 7.88$, and so the expected size of the hub is approximately
$\text{HUB\_degree} = 18 \log_2((25)(0.0788)) = 17.6$.

Plugging into the model, we obtain

$$r = \frac{\log_2(n - \text{HUB\_degree})}{\log_2(\lambda)} = \frac{\log_2(100 - 17.6)}{\log_2(7.88)} = 2.14$$

$$z = \lambda^r = 7.88^{2.14} = 82.4$$

$$100(\text{closeness}) = \text{density } z + 1 = (0.0788)(82.4) + 1 = 7.43$$

The average closeness obtained by simulation in Fig. 6.7 is 8.07. Therefore, this approximation is modestly accurate.

Several generalizations can be made from this model: (1) average closeness smoothly increases to a peak value, and then smoothly declines beyond 50% density, as fewer nodes escape direct connections with the dominant hub, and (2) the average closeness of scale-free networks is much lower than that of equivalent random and small-world networks. Generally, the average closeness of a node in a scale-free network is one-half that of nodes in the other classes of network. There are far fewer, and less powerful, intermediaries in a scale-free network, on average. In a sense, the hub is the sole intermediary, with intermediary power over nearly all other nodes.

Scale-free networks have weaker intermediaries, on average, but the hub is much stronger than the strongest intermediary possible in small-world and random networks. Consider the number of paths per node, running through the strongest intermediary nodes of random, small-world, and scale-free networks in Table 6.1. Depending on density, random networks have from 10 to zero paths per node running through the closest node. For example, if $n = 100$, then 5 paths per node means 500 paths run through the closest node.

For the simulated networks studied here, the intermediary node of small-world networks is twice as powerful as that of an equivalent random network; the intermediary of a scale-free network of equivalent density is twice as powerful as that of a small-world network, and 4 times that of an equivalent random network. At its peak density, a scale-free network of size $n = 200$ has an intermediary node with 7600 paths connecting pairs of nodes running though it.

TABLE 6.1   Number of Paths per Node Through Closest Node

Network	Number of Paths n
Random	0–10
Small world	0–20
Scale-free	0–38

6.2.5 Scale-Free Network Cluster Coefficient

In Chapter 4, we showed that cluster coefficient of a random network increases linearly with density: $CC \sim O(\text{density})$. In the previous chapter, we showed that the cluster coefficient of small-world networks decreases with increasing entropy, expressed in terms of rewiring probability, $CC(\text{WS}) = A - B \log_2^2 (100 \, (\text{probability}))$ because randomness works against clustering. In other words, clustering is a form of structure, and structure is negative entropy. But the log-squared expression does not tell the full story of the relationship between cluster coefficient and density in a small world.

Figure 6.3 suggests a linear relationship between cluster coefficient in a scale-free network versus size, similar to the behavior of a random network. But keep in mind that Fig. 6.3 was derived from data that varied network size and therefore density. Hence, it does not thoroughly isolate the effects of density, alone. In fact, Albert and Barabasi found the relationship between cluster coefficient in a scale-free network with $\lambda = 4$ hops, to be inversely proportional to size, according to $CC \sim n^{-0.75}$ (Albert, 2002).

In this section, we perform an experiment that holds network size relatively constant (approximately $n = 200$) and varies density while measuring cluster coefficient and hub degree. We show by simulation and curve fitting that cluster coefficient of scale-free networks is much like that of a random network: $CC = O(\text{density})$. But the reason may surprise the reader.

Setting $n = 200$, approximately, and adjusting the number of links yields networks of equal size but different density. A scale-free network of a specific density is created by running the BA generative procedure for specific values of Δm. Recall that density of a scale-free network varies according to $2(\Delta m/n)$. Thus, we can tune the density to a certain value by changing Δm.

Figure 6.8 summarizes the results of measuring cluster coefficients and hub degrees of small-world and scale-free networks as density varies. In Fig. 6.8, the small-world rewiring probability is approximately 4%, but varies somewhat because of the stochastic nature of the Watts–Strogatz (WS) generative procedure. The cluster coefficient CC is magnified by a factor of 100 to facilitate display.

Curve fitting determines that cluster coefficient slowly increases as a linear function of density in a scale-free network, but the increase is nonlinear and rapid in an equivalent small-world network. Thus, we get radically different results for scale-free versus small-world networks:

Scale-Free   *CC.* $100(CC(\text{scale-free})) \sim O(\text{density})$, $1\% \leq \text{density} \leq 10\%$.
Alternatively, $100(CC(\text{scale-free})) \sim O(\Delta m)$ because density $= 2(\Delta m/n); n \gg 1$.
Small-World   *CC.* $100(CC(\text{small-world})) = A - B \, \exp(C \, \text{density})$; $1\% \leq$ density $\leq 10\%$, where $A = 60; B = 158.5; C = -100$, for $n = 200$.

The relationship between density and cluster coefficient is radically different for a small-world network because clustering rises quickly with slight increase in density. It is nonlinear and much higher than the rise in cluster coefficient of an equivalent scale-free network. Why?

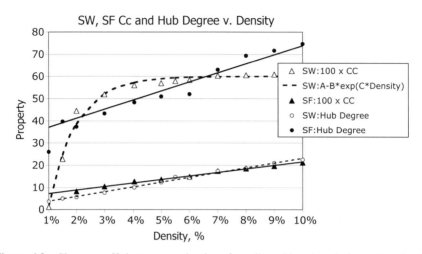

Figure 6.8 Cluster coefficient versus density of small-world and scale-free networks for small values of density, small rewiring probabilities, and $n \sim 200$, rewiring probability $\sim$ 4% (small world).

In both classes of network, structure increases with an increase in density. At least some of this structure goes into greater clustering. But notice in Fig. 6.8 that the magnitude of clustering is many times greater in the small-world network than the scale-free network—at least within the range of densities explored. This says that a greater percentage of structure goes into clustering in a small-world network while a greater percentage of structure goes into hub degree in a scale-free network. This point is worth highlighting:

Structure Transition   As density increases, a small-world network transitions into a highly clustered network while a scale-free network transitions into a high-degree hub network. This is a direct consequence of the high cluster coefficient of the underlying k-regular network.

As density increases, the degree of hub of a scale-free network also increases. High-degreed hubs tend to lower the cluster coefficient because density increases linearly while cluster coefficient must increase as a quadratic: Degree(degree $-$ 1)/2.

For example, in Fig. 6.8, the cluster coefficient of the small world is $CC =$ $0.60 + 1.585 \exp(-100 \text{ density}) = 0.58$ with density of 5%, while the cluster coefficient of an equivalent scale-free network is 0.14—approximately 25% of the equivalent small-world network. On the other hand, the hub degrees of equivalent small-world and scale-free networks are 12 and 52, respectively. The scale-free hub is 4 times greater than that of the small-world hub. In short, scale-free networks have large hubs and small clustering. Small-world networks have large clusters and small hubs. Scale-free network structure is vested in high-degree hubs, while small world structure is vested in high-degree clustering.

6.3 NAVIGATION IN SCALE-FREE NETWORKS

Much has been written about the scale-free nature of the Internet (Huberman, 1999; Kim, 2002; Kleinberg, 2000a, 2000b). It is known to have hubs of extremely high degree, and exhibits the small-world effect. Therefore, it follows that messages should flow quickly from one node to another using hubs. In fact, navigating a scale-free network by hopping from hub to hub is a fast path through a scale-free network because average path length declines with density and hub degree. In particular, the relationship between hub degree and path length leads to fast navigation in scale-free networks when using the *max-degree search algorithm*, described next (Paxson, 1997; Adamic, 2001, 2002).

Recall that the max-degree navigation algorithm seeks to find a path of length k hops from node u_0 to u_k by visiting adjacent nodes in descending degree order— from maximum degree down to minimum degree. The *max-degree navigation* algorithm studied in the previous chapter was shown to be the fastest method of navigation in a scale-free network. In this section, we explore the impact of density and hub degree on navigation speed and show that the higher the degree of a hub, the faster the navigation time.

Average path length in this case is greater than the avg_path_length explored earlier because searching a network for node u_k, starting from node u_0, is not the same as finding the shortest path between nodes u_0 and u_k. Network navigation lacks global information about the network topology, and so each hop must depend on local information, only. For scale-free networks, this means using the degree of adjacent nodes to choose which node to visit next, as search hops from node to node.

The max-degree navigation algorithm is simple. Starting at node u_0, hop to the adjacent node u_1 with the highest degree among all adjacent nodes. Then hop from u_1 to u_2, the node adjacent to u_1, with the highest degree, and so on, until reaching the destination node. Of course, the algorithm must avoid cycling back to a previously visited node, and it must back up when encountering a deadend. In the worst-case scenario, a max-degree search traverses the entire network. We assume that the network is strongly connected; therefore, every node is eventually reachable from every other node.

6.3.1 Max-Degree Navigation versus Density

How efficient is max-degree navigation, and what is the impact of network density on the time it takes to navigate such a network? These questions have practical application in peer-to-peer network design. For example, the file-sharing peer-to-peer network Gnutella formed a scale-free network whereby hubs emerged spontaneously around high-bandwidth servers. Therefore, when searching for a music file in Gnutella, the high-bandwidth servers are searched first, and so on, until the desired music file is located. This method is similar but not identical to max-degree search, in that the high-bandwidth servers also have the highest number of connections.

Figure 6.9a shows the results of averaging path length over all possible node pairs in a scale-free network that varies density by adjusting Δm from 1 to 10. This is approximately the same as varying density from 1% to 10%, when $n = 200$. The dotted line in Fig. 6.9a shows a near-perfect fit of a power law to the empirical data:

$$\text{avg\_hops(density)} = \frac{A}{\text{density} + B}; \quad 1\% \leq \text{density} \leq 10\%$$

where $A = 0.45$; $B = 0.0092$, by curve fitting. Note that the exponent of this power law is 1.0. For this case, there is an inverse relationship between navigation time and

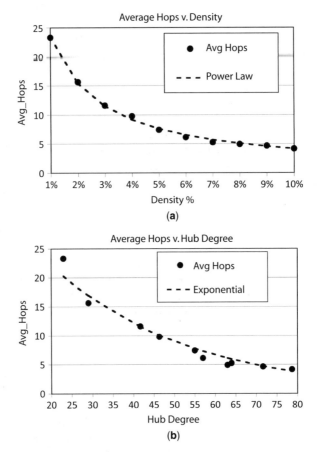

Figure 6.9 Average path length in a scale-free network of size $n = 200$, using the max-degree navigation algorithm: (a) navigation path length versus density—adjust Δm to obtain density; (b) navigation path length versus hub degree—hub degree increases with density. Path length is measured in hops, and *network hub* is defined as the node with the highest degree.

density. The average length of a path—using max-degree navigation—is $O(1/$ density), and therefore the expected time to navigate through this network diminishes inversely with density. Compare this with the shortest-path-length average, which drops off far more slowly than $O(1/\text{density})$.[3]

We conclude that increasing density of a scale-free network more-rapidly decreases navigation time, as compared with the shortest-path average. Adding links reduces transit time. However, the shortest-path average is far smaller in magnitude than the max-degree path length because shortest-path algorithms use global knowledge of the network's topology. For example, packet routing in the Internet uses OSPF (open shortest path first) algorithms to achieve far shorter average path lengths than local max-degree navigation can achieve.

6.3.2 Max-Degree Navigation versus Hub Degree

From the foregoing analysis we should expect navigation time to improve with increases in hub degree, as well. In fact, this is what happens. Figure 6.9b shows the relationship between navigation time (average number of hops) and hub degree. The higher the degree of the network's largest hub, the faster a message travels through a scale-free network. The relationship fits an exponential curve, rather than a power law, however:

$$\text{avg\_hops(hub\_degree)} = A\exp(-B(\text{hub\_degree} - C)); \quad 20 \leq \text{hub\_degree} \leq 80$$

where $A = 20.25$; $B = 0.03$; $C = 23$, for $n = 200$, $1\% \leq \text{density} \leq 10\%$. hub_degree increases logarithmically with density, so this result is correlated with network density. Hub degree has a dramatic impact on navigation time. The higher the degree of hub, the faster is scale-free network navigation. Intuitively, this makes sense, because hubs tend to connect directly to a large percentage of nodes. They provide many long-haul paths directly to each neighborhood, requiring fewer short-haul hops to reach the final destination. Intuition turns out to be correct in this case, but it is always reassuring to obtain experimental results that confirm educated guesses!

This result is important to the design of peer-to-peer networks like Gnutella and others, because it pays to have a highly connected hub, assuming that the server at the hub can keep pace with bandwidth requirements. Scale-free networks are intrinsically more efficient to navigate than are random or small-world networks. They both have small-world effect and low clustering. In a sense, scale-free networks perform better than do small-world networks, leading to the conclusion that scale-free networks are "smaller than small worlds"!

One final observation is in order here. In most cases, the hub of a scale-free network is also the node with the highest closeness property. Hubs are also the most powerful intermediary nodes—and because they capture more paths than do other nodes, they require greater bandwidth. Therefore, a max-closeness search is equivalent to a max-degree search. But it is much easier to calculate the degree of

---

[3]In terms of a power law, average path length is closer to $O(1/\text{density}^{1/3})$.

a node than its closeness value. For this reason, we did not bother to perform a comparison between max-closeness and max-degree navigation.

6.3.3 Weak Ties in Scale-Free Pointville

In previous chapters, we used approximation equations to solve the practical problem of estimating degree of separation or length of weak ties among the $n = 129$ citizens of Pointville, where each citizen knows an average of λ other citizens. In this chapter, we assume that Pointville forms a scale-free network, and estimate its diameter and average path length. From what we learned in this chapter, a scale-free Pointville should have strong weak ties (small-world effect), leading to small diameter and low average path length.

Recall that the diameter of a random Pointville, with $n = 129$, $m = 1548$, and $\lambda = 24$, was 2.36 hops, and 3.5 hops for a small world with rewiring probability $p = 5\%$. Density of these networks is approximately

$$d = 2\frac{1548}{(129)(128)} = 18.75\%$$

What is the diameter and avg_path_length of an equivalent scale-free network?

An arbitrary-density scale-free network is defined by input parameters n and Δm. We already know $n = 129$, but what is Δm? Solving the density equation, we obtain

$$d \sim 2(\Delta m/n) \text{ for } n \gg 1.$$

Rearranging terms yields $\Delta m = d(n/2) = 0.1875\left(\frac{129}{2}\right) = 12$. Plugging these numbers into program *Network.jar* and averaging over three trials produces estimates of diameter, radius, and avg_path_length. Empirically:

$$\text{Diameter(scale-free Pointville)} = 3 \text{ hops}$$
$$\text{Radius(scale-free Pointville)} = 2 \text{ hops}$$
$$\text{avg\_path\_length(scale-free Pointville)} = 1.85 \text{ hops}$$

From the approximation equation derived in the previous section, we obtain

$$10(\text{avg\_path\_length(Pointville)}) = 14\frac{\log(n)}{\log(n) + \log(2 \text{ density})}$$
$$= 14\frac{\log(129)}{\log(129) + \log(2(0.1875))}$$
$$= 14\frac{2.11}{2.11 - 0.426} = \frac{29.54}{1.684} = 17.54 \text{ hops}$$
$$\text{avg\_path\_length(Pointville)} = 1.75 \text{ hops}.$$

This result confirms what we have learned about scale-free networks—they are relatively "small" in comparison with random and small-world networks. In fact, scale-free Pointville is a smaller world than small-world Pointville; it takes an average of 1.85 hops to traverse scale-free Pointville and an average of 2.17 hops to traverse the equivalent small-world Pointville. This is due to the greater number of long-haul links in a scale-free network compared to an equivalent small-world network. Scale-free networks have stronger weak ties!

In terms of social network theory, a scale-free network has a few nodes that are connected to a very large percentage of all other nodes, and many nodes that are rather sparsely linked to hubs. Scale-free networks exhibit greater centrality—the radius of scale-free Pointville is also very small. Most nodes are very near to all other nodes. For example, one-third of the nodes in scale-free Pointville are centered 2 hops from all other nodes, while only 10% are 10 hops from all other nodes in a typical small-world Pointville.

Scale-free Pointville exceeds even a star network, with one hub node connected to all other nodes, in terms of avg_path_length. Regardless of how large such a star network grows, every node is no more than 2 hops away from every other node. Yet, if Pointville were a star network with $n = 129$, its diameter would be 2 and its avg_path_length would be approximately 1.95 hops—which would be 0.1 hops larger than the scale-free Pointville.

6.4 ANALYSIS

The class of scale-free networks falls between small-world and random networks in the spectrum of network topologies. Except for the cluster coefficient, the class of scale-free networks is more "balanced" than the other three classes (see Fig. 6.10). Entropy, avg_path_length, and hub degree are relatively high, but clustering is low. These properties have major implications for how scale-free networks perform.

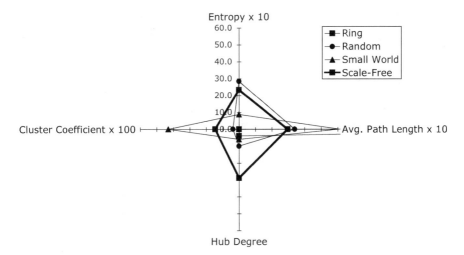

Figure 6.10 Kiviat graph comparing ring, random, WS small-world, and BA scale-free network properties.

6.4.1   Entropy

Entropy, I(scale-free) $\sim O(\log_2 (\Delta m))$ grows as a function of preferential attachment parameter Δm, but $\Delta m = $ density$(n/2)$, so I(scale-free) $\sim O(\log_2$ (density $(n/2))$. Compare this with entropy of random and small-world networks. Entropy of a small-world network, I(small world) $\sim O(\log_2 (100p))$, where p is the rewiring probability. Therefore, a scale-free network behaves more like a small-world network than a random network with respect to entropy. But of course, the entropy of a small-world network scales, so the similarity diminishes as density increases.

In contrast, random network entropy increases with an increase in density reaches a peak, and then declines to zero as density approaches 100%. Are scale-free networks more structured than random? An extremely high-density random network is not purely random because it becomes regular (a complete graph) as density nears 100%. A similar loss of randomness afflicts scale-free networks when they become increasingly dense, too. Scale-free and random networks both take on structure as density increases. This means entropy drops to zero as density reaches 100%. For example, the entropies of scale-free and random networks of 75% density, $n = 75$, equal 4.4 and 3.8 bits, respectively. As density closes in on 100%, this difference narrows—at 90% density, scale-free entropy declines to 3.8 bits and random declines to 3.2 bits. At 99% density, the entropy of both classes of networks is less than 1 bit, and the entropy of both decline to zero bits at 100% density.

There is a structural difference between a complete network and a dense scale-free network, even though their degree sequence distributions behave similarly. As a network becomes increasingly dense and therefore more like a complete network, its degree sequence distribution spikes—all nodes approach the same degree. Prior to reaching 100% density, the degree sequence distribution becomes narrow as nodes approach one of two states; they are either (1) so highly connected (high degree) that they are only one step away from all other nodes or (2) two steps from all other nodes. In other words, the *radius sequence distribution* has two frequencies: $R(1)$: the fraction of nodes that are 1 hop from all others, and $R(2)$: the fraction that are 2 hops from all other nodes. This phenomenon occurs for very dense scale-free networks, as shown in Fig. 6.11.

Entropy declines exponentially as density approaches 100% in a scale-free network. This occurs because the degree sequence distribution collapses. All nodes are maximally connected such that all nodes are 1 or 2 hops away from each other. In fact, the number of nodes at the center of the network increases to 100% at the same time that entropy diminishes. Similarly, the number of nodes that are two steps away from all other nodes (the diameter), diminishes. The transition from scale-free to complete network advances exponentially for very high density, see the dashed line in Fig. 6.11.

6.4.2   Path Length and Communication

The average path length of a fixed-size sparse scale-free network is driven down as hub degree (density) increases according to the linear relation avg_path_length = $A - B$ ʜᴜʙ_degree; for fixed n.

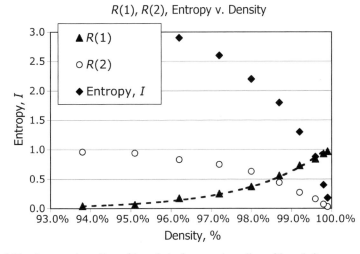

Figure 6.11 Increase in radius of length 1, decrease in radius of length 2, versus very high density of scale-free network. The rise in $R(1)$ fits almost perfectly with an exponential function, shown here as a dashed line.

Alternatively, avg_path_length diminishes according to

$$O\left(\frac{\log(n)}{\log(n) + \log(\text{density})}\right)$$

or as an inverse function of log (density), for fixed n. But Fig. 6.3 appears to contradict Fig. 6.5 and the conclusions summarized here. Why? Fig. 6.3 shows the effects of simultaneously varying size n and density d while Fig. 6.5 only varies density. In fact, Fig. 6.5 shows the relationship for $n = 200$. When the effect of network size n is removed, this leaves only density as the independent variable in avg_path_length. Hence, there are two different approximations for average path length: avg_path_length(n) and avg_path_ length(density).

Path length is an important property in many applications of network theory. Perhaps the most obvious application is in the design of distributed computer systems. Consider, for example, the challenge of building a networked multiprocessor system consisting of n processors and m communication links. Assuming that we connect processors to one another according to the BA algorithm, what is the "best" balance of processors and links to achieve both low cost and high performance? In other words, what is the minimum number of links needed to optimize performance?

To illustrate, let $n = 16$ processors. Define "cost-effectiveness" in terms of average path length and number of links m as follows:

$$\text{Effectiveness} = \frac{1 - \text{avg\_path\_length(density)}}{m}$$

$$\text{Density} = 2\frac{m}{n(n-1)}$$

In this formulation, decreasing avg_path_length, m, or both increases effectiveness. But decreasing m increases avg_path_length because

$$\text{avg\_ path\_length}(m) = \frac{A \log (n)}{\log (n) + \log (C \text{ density})}$$

where $A = 0.75$ and $C = 1.5$ for $n = 16$ processors. Substitution for density as a function of m yields

$$\text{avg\_ path\_length}(m) = \frac{A \log (n)}{\log (n) + \log(C) + \log\left(\dfrac{2 m}{n(n - 1)}\right)}$$

$$= \frac{A \log (n)}{\log(2mC) - \log(n - 1)}$$

$$= \frac{0.75 \log(16)}{\log(3m) - \log(15)}$$

Thus

$$\text{Effectiveness} = \frac{1 - \dfrac{0.75 \log(16)}{\log(3m) - \log(15)}}{m}$$

It is desirable to maximize effectiveness by either increasing the numerator, decreasing the denominator, or both. Assuming n to be fixed, find a "balanced value" of m that maximizes effectiveness: max {effectiveness}.

The strategy for solving this problem is

1. Plot effectiveness versus m over a range of values that includes the maximum value, effectiveness(m^*).
2. Find $\Delta m \sim (m/n)$, which produces a scale-free network with approximately m^* links and $n = 16$ nodes.

The BA generative procedure does not produce a scale-free network of arbitrary density, but instead, produces a range of densities corresponding to integer values of Δm. An integer value, $\Delta m = [m/n]$, may or may not produce a scale-free network of exactly m links. In this example, the difference between $[m/n]$ and $[m^*/n]$ is very slight. For example, with $A = 0.75$, $C = 1.5$, $n = 16$ processors, we obtain

$$m^* = 84 \text{ links}$$

$$\Delta m = 7$$

$$m = (\Delta m)n - \Delta m \frac{\Delta m + 1}{2} = 84 \text{ links}$$

$$\text{Density} = 2 \frac{m}{n(n - 1)} = 2 \frac{84}{(16)(15)} = 70\%$$

$$\lambda = n \text{ density} = (16)(70\%) = 11 \text{ links}$$

According to the simple effectiveness metric proposed here, a 16-processor scale-free network is optimal when the density is rather high. In fact, this scale-free network is nearly complete with hubs of degree 15, and minimum-degree nodes with approximately eight links. Verification that this result holds for other values of n is left as an exercise for the reader.

6.4.3 Cluster Coefficient

Scale-free and random networks have relatively low cluster coefficients that increase linearly with density: O(density). Contrast this with the clustering found in a small-world network constructed by the WS generative procedure (density $= 4\%$) (see Fig. 6.8). It appears that clustering is correlated with hub degree. They both increase as density increases, but hub degree increases much faster.

Local clustering around scale-free network nodes is indeed correlated with node degree, but in a negative manner. The lower the degree, the higher the clustering. Intuition might suggest that hubs are the centers of high-cluster-coefficient neighborhoods, but this is not the case. Figure 6.12 shows the effect of node degree on local cluster coefficient for each class of network studied here. Local cluster coefficient is the cluster coefficient associated with each individual node. Network cluster coefficient is the average over all nodes.

In Fig. 6.12 the curve shown as a solid line bounds the cluster coefficient of nodes in a scale-free network (see Fig. 6.12c) but does not bound the local cluster coefficient in other classes of networks. There is a correlation between local cluster coefficient and node degree in scale-free networks that does not exist in the other two network classes.

Figure 6.12a illustrates how the local cluster coefficient is somewhat evenly scattered across nodes of all degrees of a random network. Apparently, there is no correlation between cluster coefficient and degree of nodes in a random network, but this is left as a research project for the reader. We speculate that the plot of local cluster coefficient versus hub degree is random in Fig. 6.12a.[4]

Figure 6.12b illustrates a higher local cluster coefficient in a small-world network than in the other two classes—as expected. The plot of local cluster coefficient versus hub degree lies above and below the solid curve obtained by the relation:

$$CC(\text{scale-free node}) \sim \frac{(1+m)/n}{\text{degree(scale-free node)} + 1 + (m/n)}$$

In addition, local cluster coefficient values tend to be concentrated around nodes with median degree. But this speculation is left as an exercise for the reader to explore, also. If the plot in Fig. 6.12a is random, the plot in Fig. 6.12b is the opposite—not random.

---

[4]$CC \sim (\lambda/n) =$ density, for random networks (Albert, 2002). Figure 6.12a confirms this theoretical estimate: $CC \sim \frac{8}{100} = 0.08$.

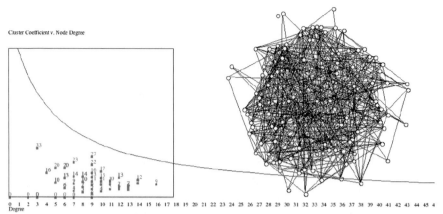

(a)

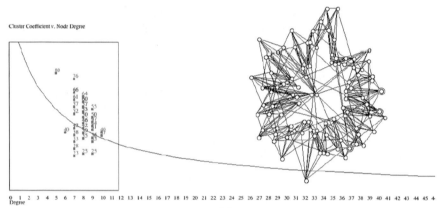

(b)

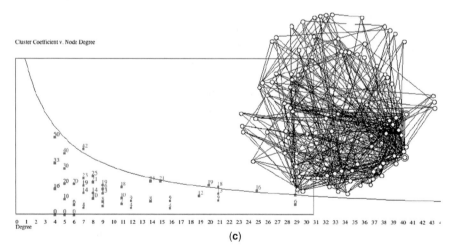

(c)

Figure 6.12 Comparison of local cluster coefficient in each class of network versus node degree: (a) random network with $n = 100$, $m = 400$, density $= 8.08\%$, $\lambda = 8$; (b) small-world network with $n = 100$, $m = 400$, density $= 8.08\%$, rewiring probability $= 10\%$; (c) scale-free network with $n = 100$, $\Delta m = 4$, density $= 7.87\%$. Each network is plotted around its center nodes (radius).

Figure 6.12c supports the conjecture made earlier—the higher the degree of a node in a scale-free network, the lower its cluster coefficient. Indeed, local cluster coefficients are higher for low-degreed nodes than high-degreed nodes! Surprisingly, highly connected nodes have lower cluster coefficient. But this effect dissipates as density increases and the scale-free network becomes more like a complete network. For high density ($>5-10\%$), this correlation breaks down and clustering looks more like that of a random network.

The upper-bound line for the scale-free network shown in Fig. 6.12c is obtained from an inverse relationship between cluster coefficient and degree:

$$CC(\text{scale-free node}) < \frac{\Delta m}{\text{degree(scale-free node)} + \Delta m}; \quad \Delta m \ll n$$

This upper bound is most accurate for low network density (Δm) because entropy of a scale-free network also decreases with decline in density. As density rises, entropy also rises, and the scale-free network becomes more random. Fig. 6.12c takes on properties of Fig. 6.12a as entropy increases.

Sparse scale-free networks contain hubs with low cluster coefficients, and other nodes with relatively high cluster coefficients. This conclusion has significant implications for social networks because social networks tend to be sparse. The nodes with highest connectivity appear to be the nodes with the smallest number of connected neighboring nodes. Does this mean that the most popular actors (hubs) may not belong to a cluster of close friends? If so, this seems to contradict the notion that social power is most heavily invested in hubs. Why do hubs have low cluster coefficient?

Recall that cluster coefficient is a fraction ranging from zero to (degree (degree $-1)/2$. That is, $CC \sim O(1/\text{degree}^2)$. As a node's degree increases, the number of neighboring nodes that must connect to one another increases as the square of degree. For high-degreed nodes, this is difficult to do, by chance. The results shown in Fig. 6.12 are largely—but not entirely—explained by the definition of cluster coefficient. As it turns out, the upper bound on local cluster coefficient is inversely proportional to degree, not degree^2. Clearly, clustering occurs—just not as fast as $O(\text{degree}^2)$.

6.4.4 Hub Degree

Scale-free networks exhibit structure by shifting from random connectivity to hub-like connectivity. In return, they sacrifice clustering and entropy. Intuitively, entropy goes into hub-like topology in a scale-free network, clustering in a small-world network, and disorder in a random network. This is why the class of scale-free networks is known as the "class with hubs," and the class of small-world networks is known as the "class with clusters."

A scale-free network connects a large proportion of the network's nodes to a small fraction of nodes. This simple architecture is responsible for nearly all of the distinguishing properties of the class, from average path length, fast navigation, to local clustering. Hub degree increases with density (see Fig. 6.4). Intuitively, a small-world network is a scale-free network with constraints on the degree of hubs, whereas a scale-free network has no such constraints. What happens to the properties of a scale-free network if maximum hub degree is restricted? This is left as research question that we return to in later chapters.

6.5 EXERCISES

6.1. Show that the Poisson distribution function is not scale-free, and hence that a random network is not a scale-free network.

6.2. Derive an expression for entropy of a scale-free network in terms of density.

6.3. What is the average path length of a scale-free network containing $n = 100$ nodes, $m = 1000$ links, and hub degree of 50? Which formula should be used?

6.4. Perform an empirical study of very sparse random networks ($n = 200$, density 2–10%), and derive an approximation for avg_path_length versus hub degree. Does avg_path_length decrease as hub degree increases, as it does with scale-free networks? (Refer to Fig. 6.13.)

6.5. What is the value of m that optimizes Effectiveness of a scale-free network with $n = 24$ processors? What value of Δm yields the best approximation to the optimal m?

6.6. What is the approximate cluster coefficient of a scale-free network with $n = 500$ and $\Delta m = 2$?

6.7. Perform an empirical study of the correlation between cluster coefficient and degree of nodes in a scale-free network with $n = 200$ and density $= 40\%$. What can you conclude about the correlation?

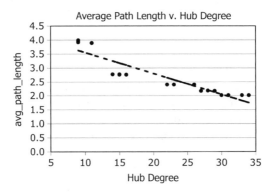

Figure 6.13   Average path length versus hub degree.

6.8. What is the approximate local cluster coefficient of a node with degree 9 in a scale-free network with density of 2% and $n = 500$? Compare the theoretical estimate with empirically derived values.

6.9. What is the search path length of a scale-free network of size $n = 500$ and $\Delta m = 2$, for navigation by max-degree search?

6.10. What is the expected maximum degree of the largest hub of a scale-free network with $n = 200$ and $\Delta m = 2$? How does this maximum change as Δm increases from 2 to 10?

6.11. What is the average closeness of the network in Exercise 6.10?

6.12. What is the average closeness of a scale-free network of size $n = 500$, $\Delta m = 5$? Does the empirical model developed for $n = 200$ accurately estimate the average closeness of this network?

7

EMERGENCE

In a *static network*, the properties of nodes, links, and mapping function remain unchanged over time. In a *dynamic network*, the number of nodes and links, the shape of the mapping function, and perhaps other properties of the graph change over time. Dynamic networks are time-varying networks. A scale-free network obtained by the BA growth algorithm is an example of a simple dynamic network emerging from a few initial nodes and links.

Time-varying changes leading to structural reorganization in a network—called *evolution* in some disciplines—is called *emergence*, in this book. A network formed by emergence is called an *emergent network*, and is formed by starting at some predefined *initial state* (say, a random network), and then transitioning through a series of small changes into an *end state* (say, scale-free network). The small changes are defined by microrules operating internally or externally to the network. Environmental forces are often responsible for external forces, while genetic forces are often responsible for internal forces.

Emergence—the transformation of a network property through repeated small changes—is a process that we explore in this chapter as a prelude to subsequent chapters. We show that it is possible to construct a network of almost any structure, with almost any desirable property such as high-degreed hubs, high cluster coefficient, or specified degree sequence through emergent processes. In fact, we show how effective very small microrules are at reshaping an arbitrary network into a "designer network" with specific properties.

Network Science: Theory and Practice. By Ted G. Lewis
Copyright © 2009 John Wiley & Sons, Inc.

Two general principles are illustrated by emergence: (1) arbitrary structure is possible through repeated application of very simple rules; and (2) the structure of real-world networks, whether in biology, physics, or social networks, may be explained as the result of simple emergence. For example, the structure of the US telecommunication network is a direct consequence of the 1996 Telecommunications Act, which encouraged the formation of highly centralized switching hubs now called "carrier hotels." The scale-free structure of telecommunications is a direct consequence of peering, which is promoted by the law. This simple rule has led to a massive restructuring of a national network.

Repeated application of simple microrules is also a process similar to optimization in real-world systems. Networks frequently respond to external conditions by optimizing some property such as minimum path length, maximum flow, or minimum cost. By responding to external stimuli, a system often adapts by changing its structure or optimizing one or more of its properties. We illustrate this principle by minimizing the total length of wiring in a circuit through a simple emergence process.

We study a number of simple applications of emergent networks and show the following:

1. Emergence has many definitions in different fields of study. We define *network emergence* as a process of a dynamic network whereby a macroscale property such as degree sequence emerges as a consequence of repeated application of microscale rules such as the simple exchange of links.

2. A dynamic network undergoing emergent change reaches a final state in finite time if it is *convergent*—otherwise it is divergent. A *divergent* process may result in a network with static or oscillating macrostructure. Stability of emergent networks is studied in the next chapter.

3. *Open-loop emergence* (genetic emergence) restructures a network from repeated application of microrules without external or environmental influences. When a dynamic network is restructured by external or environmental influences, the process defines a *feedback-loop emergence* (environmental emergence). Feedback-loop emergence is adaptive, while open-loop emergence is nonadaptive and depends only on internal microrules.

4. Emergence models the behavior of systems in biology, physics, mathematics, and computer science. Specifically, we apply emergence theory to the problem of minimizing the total length of wiring in the construction of circuits on a printed circuit board. This problem is similar to many optimization problems encountered in the natural and synthetic world.

5. *Hub emergence* is an open-loop emergent process that restructures any dynamic network by creating hubs similar to those found in scale-free networks. However, the resulting network is not scale-free even though the largest hub of size $O(\text{sqrt}(t))$ grows in time t, according to hub_degree $(G) = A + (\text{sqrt}(t)/2)$. Entropy increases, and then decreases according to $I(G) = A + B(1 - \exp(-Ct)) - D$ hub_degree (t), where A, B, C, and D are parameters determined experimentally.

6. *Cluster emergence* is an open-loop emergent process that increases the cluster coefficient of a dynamic network according to $CC(G) = A + B$ $(1 - \exp(-Ct))$. However, the resulting network is not small-world because its average_path_length may be relatively large.

7. *Degree sequence emergence* is an open-loop emergent process that restructures a network so that its initial degree sequence $g(0)$ matches any realizable sequence defined by g(final). The *Molloy–Reed* procedure generates a network with prescribed degree sequence g, if such a network is realizable. The *Erdos–Gallai condition* is necessary, but not sufficient to guarantee realizability.

8. A network G with degree sequence g(final) is more likely to be realizable with the *Mihail generative procedure*. Mihail et al. propose an emergent process that satisfies the Erdos-Gallai condition by connecting the highest-degreed nodes to one another before connecting lower-degreed nodes (Mihail, 2002). Thus, it is possible to produce a *designer network* with topology defined by g(final), with certain restrictions on g(final).

9. A *link permutation* microrule applies a fixed-point transformation to network G such that permutation of links does not alter the degree sequence of G. Thus, thousands of *homomorphic* networks are generated by link permutations such as exchanging endpoints of a pair of links selected at random. Fixed-point link permutation is used to transform a network property while retaining its degree sequence.

10. *Cluster coefficient permutation emergence* is a feedback-loop emergent process that increases the cluster coefficient of G by repeated application of link permutations that increase cluster coefficient without altering its degree sequence property. A scale-free or random network can remain scale-free or random while increasing its cluster coefficient to approximate that of a small-world network.

11. *Total link minimization* emerges from network G with fixed degree sequence g by repeated application of link permutation and a feedback loop that prevents total link length from increasing. Given any network G with degree sequence distribution $g(0)$ and initial total link length $L(0)$, network G(final) emerges in time proportional to $O(C_2^m)$ with L(final) equal to the shortest possible length.[1] This emergent process finds the least amount of wire needed to connect components of a printed circuit board. In general, link minimization by emergence finds the best way to connect nodes according to prescribed degree sequence g while minimizing the total length of links.

7.1 WHAT IS NETWORK EMERGENCE?

A *dynamic network*, $G(t) = [N(t), L(t), f(t){:}R]$, is a time-varying 3-tuple consisting of a set of *nodes* $N(t)$, a set of *links* $L(t)$, and a *mapping function* $f(t)$: $L(t) > N(t) \times N(t)$,

---

[1]This is expressed as $C_2^m = m((m-1)/2)$.

which maps links into pairs of nodes. The properties of $N(t)$, $L(t)$, and $f(t)$ change as time passes; hence the designation of $G(t)$ as a dynamic network. For example, the shape of a network, as defined by the mapping function $f(t)$, may change as links are dropped, added, or rewired (switched from one node to another) over time.

Given a network $G(0)$ in its initial state, one or more microrules from rule set R are applied to G at each time step to transition $G(0)$ to $G(1)$, $G(1)$ to $G(2)$, and so on until some final state $G(t_f)$ is reached, or previous states repeat:

$$G(t + 1) = R\{G(t), E(t)\}$$

where $E(t)$ are external forces acting on G. If G reaches a final state, $G(t_f)$, and remains there for all $t \geq t_f$ $t \geq t_f$, G is said to be *convergent*. Otherwise, G is *divergent*. $G(t_f)$ is also known as a *fixed point* because once G reaches $G(t_f)$, it remains there forever. We say that $G(0)$ *converges* to $G(t_f)$ when G is convergent; otherwise, G is assumed to be divergent. If $G(s)$ converges for all initial states s, we say that G is *strongly convergent*.[2]

An emergent network may or may not be convergent. However, in this chapter we study the state changes that take place over a finite period of time, $0 \leq t \leq t_f$, and generally do not concern ourselves with the larger question of whether a network is convergent.[3] A dynamic network may oscillate between two states, progress from an initial state to final state, or change forever without ever reaching its "infinite" state. Regardless of these possibilities, in this chapter we study dynamic networks over a finite period of time: starting at some initial state and progressing to some other state in a finite number of applications of the microrules R. We are interested in observing, and perhaps predicting, the behavior of such networks during a finite number of applications of microrules.

7.1.1 Open-Loop Emergence

Figure 7.1 shows two models of emergence used in this book: open-loop and feedback-loop emergence. The *open-loop* model represents *genetic* or intrinsic evolution of a network. The *feedback-loop* model represents *adaptive* evolution of a network, whereby the network adjusts to environmental or external feedback. In both cases, we assume the existence of a set of microrules, which represent internally consumed energy or externally applied forces on the network.

Starting at some initial state $G(0)$, a set of microrules are applied, causing the network to advance to a next state, which produces a modified network, $G(1)$. The microrules are applied again to produce network $G(2)$ and so forth. If the process is convergent, at some point in time, $G(t)$ is unchanged because G has reached its final state. If the process is divergent, the transition to a new state continues forever.

---

[2]Borrowing from chaos theory, we can say that a strongly convergent network seeks its *strange attractor* in finite time.

[3]Stability is studied in the next chapter.

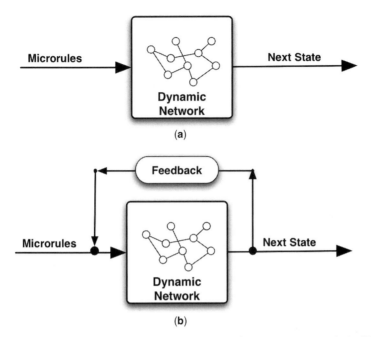

Figure 7.1   Emergence in a dynamic network: (a) open-loop emergence, typical of intrinsic or genetic evolution; (b) feedback-loop emergence, typical of external or environmental forces shaping a network.

For example, a microrule might dictate how a link is rewired, or place limits on the degree of a node. Rewiring a single link creates a new network topology representing the state of the network at time $(t + 1)$. If at some point in time, there are no more links to be rewired, the process is convergent and network $G(\text{final})$ emerges. Otherwise, the network may never reach a final state, but cycle through millions of states without end. Such a process is divergent.

The set of microrules R map network $G(t)$ to its next state, $G(t + 1)$:

$$G(t + 1) = R\{G(t), E(t)\}$$

where $E(t)$ is the set of feedback information at time t. In Fig. 7.1a microrules are applied without feedback. The next state is governed only by microrules, which transition the network through its state changes. These rules are relentlessly applied and perform very simple operations such as increasing the number of links, increasing the degree of nodes, and limiting the length of links. Their impact is *localized*, not globalized; that is, microrules effect a small change at a local level, such as rewiring a link so that the cluster coefficient or degree of a node is increased. Because microrules operate only on internal nodes and links, we classify open-loop evolution as a kind of *genetic emergence*.

Open-loop emergence often produces unexpected consequences or unpredictable global properties of the network. This is one way that emergence distinguishes itself from other forms of network transition. Essentially, emergence is the process of deriving global patterns from repeated application of small changes—at local levels. In an open-loop system, there is no apparent connection between the final state of a network and the microrules. However, in most cases, it becomes apparent after the emergence plays out why repeated application of microrules leads to the global pattern.

7.1.2 Feedback-Loop Emergence

Figure 7.1b defines another process model of emergence—*feedback-loop emergence*, in which a network undergoes state changes to adapt to a certain global objective, typically specified by global factors such as the sum total length of the network's links, maximum flow, or sum total of node degrees. Because the objective is to adapt to an external condition or limit, this model is also known as *adaptive* or *environmental emergence*. In addition to the effects of microrules, the feedback loop modifies—often overrides—the effects of microrules. Thus, the process applies microrules as before, but their effects are steered or guided by feedback information. Typically, the feedback is a global measure of performance or closeness to an externally defined objective.

For example, suppose that the global environmental objective is to maximize the degree of the network's hub, and a microrule says to rewire links at random. After each application of the microrule, we apply the following correction: (1) cancel the microrule when the result of rewiring a link would decrease the degree of a node; (2) otherwise, allow the microrule to take effect. In this simple example, the feedback information is the degree of the network's hub. Whenever the microrule increases a node's degree, we let it do its job, but we nullify any application of the rule that diminishes a node's degree. What form of network emerges from this constraint? We study hub emergence in more detail in a subsequent section of this chapter.

In the feedback-loop model, emergence has a purpose—to achieve a certain global goal—an objective that is achieved incrementally, step by step. We might call such emergent networks *goal-oriented emergent networks*, for obvious reasons! *Goal-oriented emergence* is a process that transforms a dynamic network's global properties, such as diameter, degree sequence distribution, or sum total length of all links, by repeated application of microrules R and "corrective" feedback information.

Note the difference between feedback-loop emergence and open-loop emergence—the former is adaptive; external or environmental pressures guide determination of the next state of the network. This often means overriding microrules—typically in the form of a *reward* or *punishment* feedback mechanism superimposed on each microrule.[4] The feedback mechanism is typically associated with a goal or an objective function. Over time, the goal is realized as an emergent property of the network.

Open-loop emergence responds exclusively to internal or genetic properties of a network. It ignores all external and environmental factors. Only local properties of

[4]How do you "punish" a network? Simply nullify the application of a microrule that would lead to an undesirable change.

nodes and links, such as degree, centrality, or cluster coefficient, determine the next state of the network. If a global property evolves from repeated application of microrules, so be it. But the objective is local, not global. Open-loop emergence is nonadaptive, but still evolutionary. For example, hub emergence is an emergent process that increases the degree of any network's hub even if the initial network is random. It does not require a feedback loop, but rather a high-degreed hub emerges from repeated application of simple rewiring.

7.2 EMERGENCE IN THE SCIENCES

Emergence is commonplace in a number of disciplines, although the terminology may differ from that used here. In fact, the similarity between evolution in various forms of life and the models given in Fig. 7.1 is not a coincidence. We find these models in engineering, physics, and biology. Network science provides an abstract representation that is tailored to each discipline. The following survey of applications of emergence to social and physical sciences is preliminary; more detailed models will be developed throughout the remainder of this book.

7.2.1 Emergence in Social Science

In the social sciences, N is a set of *actors*, and L defines some relationship among actors. For example, N may be the set of people who work together in an office, and L may be the lines on an organization chart. Alternatively, N may be a set of people who have contracted a communicable disease from one another, and L may be the interactions that led to contraction of the disease.

Emergence of social structure within a population is a vast and complex phenomenon. Network science attempts to explain this phenomenon by studying dynamic network formation, and evolutionary change within a social network. For example, the formation of links between nearest neighbors will tend to have a higher probability than will long-distance links. This gives rise to high local clustering, short average path length, and nonrandom structure (Davidsen, 2002).

Emergence is more than a network's transformation from an initial state to a final state. In the physical and biological sciences, "emergence is the concept of some new phenomenon arising in a system that wasn't in the system's specification to start with" (Standish, 2001). This definition refers to the repeated application of microrules that result in unexpected macrostructure. For example, a network's degree sequence distribution is one way to characterize its macrostructure, while a link-rewiring microrule might characterize its microstructure. There is no apparent connection between the degree sequence distribution and a certain rule for linking node pairs. Still, some "new phenomenon" might unexpectedly arise from repeated application of simple rewiring. For example, the "new phenomenon arising" might be a scale-free degree sequence distribution arising from the evolution, even though "scale-free structure" was not in the system's initial specification. This "new phenomenon" was unexpected because preferential attachment works at the local level while degree sequence distribution is a global property.

7.2.2 Emergence in Physical Science

In the physical sciences, emergence is used to explain phenomena such as *phase transition* in materials (gases cooling and changing to liquids, etc.) or Ising effects (magnetic polarization). In thermodynamics, for example, emergence links large-scale properties of matter to its microscale states. Specifically, emergence links the temperature (large-scale property) of a block of ice to the states of its molecules (microscale property); as water cools below its freezing point, individual molecules change phase according to the microrules of physics, and the body of water changes from liquid to solid (macroscale property). In network theory, this is equivalent to linking the classification of a network to its entropy; a random network has greater entropy than does an equivalent regular network. At what point does a random network become regular?[5]

Emergence appears to stem from microbehavior at the atomic level (e.g., at the level of nodes and links). It produces macroscale patterns from microscale rules. Often there is little or no obvious connection between the micro- and macrolevels. This has led to the concept of *hidden order*—unrecognized structure within a system (Holland, 1998). What appears to be chaos is actually nonlinear behavior. Hidden order may be a matter of scale—what is impossible to recognize up close becomes obvious when one steps back and views it at a distance. For example, a close-up view of a painting may seem indistinguishable from random paint smears, but when viewed from a distance, is easily recognized as the famous Mona Lisa. Is emergence simply a change in scaling factor?

We examine emergence in networks from a slightly more restrictive perspective. As Fig. 7.1 indicates, evolution of a dynamic network does not take place in a vacuum. Rather, it occurs because of two forcing functions: (1) the repeated application of a set of internal microrules and (2) external environmental forces. The former is designated *genetic* or *intrinsic evolution*, while the later is designated *environmental evolution*. In both models we are concerned with observing macroscale patterns emerging from microscale changes. In some cases, we may even be able to explain macroscale behavior from microscale evolution over long periods of time.

7.2.3 Emergence in Biology

Emergence in networks and natural species of plants and animals is rather obvious. In fact, some contemporary biologists and natural historians claim that life itself is the product of emergence—once called *spontaneous generation*. Life arose spontaneously over a long period of time, by the repeated application of very small steps called *mutations*. Beginning with inanimate chemicals and purely chemical processes, simple living organisms emerged through a lengthy process of trial and error.

Biological emergence requires that we believe in increasing complexity at the expense of diminishing entropy. On the application of each microstep (chemical reaction), randomness is replaced by structure. Structure evolves through further

---

[5]We actually observe the dramatic falloff of entropy in a random network as its density approaches 0% or 100%.

application of microrules (absorption of energy) to replace simple structure with more complex structure. At some point, the inanimate structure becomes animate—complexity reaches the level of a living organism. This process continues, diversifies, and reaches higher levels of complex structure. Ultimately, the Darwinian rules of evolution dominate, leading to the emergence of intelligence.

Simple-to-complex structure emergence has been demonstrated under controlled conditions, but no one has demonstrated the emergence of life from nonlife. Organic substances have been spontaneously generated from inorganic chemicals, but this is a far cry from the spontaneous generation of a living organism from organic chemicals. As scientists, we must remain skeptical of this theory.

7.3 GENETIC EVOLUTION

Open-loop emergence originates from within the network itself. The network absorbs energy and forms new nodes and links or rearranges existing nodes and links. Emergence is dynamic—microrules applied once per time step eventually lead to significant transformation of the network. Over long expanses of time, the network reaches a final state, if the emergence is convergent. If it is divergent, the network never reaches a final state and cycles through either a finite or an infinite number of states. For example, suppose that a network with n nodes and $m < n$ links adds one link at each timestep, until the network becomes complete. This convergent process ends when the network reaches its final state with $m = (n(n-1))/2$ links. On the other hand, a network that adds a new node and new link at each timestep, never reaches a final state. Instead, it diverges, adding nodes and links without end.

Genetic emergence is simple—repeatedly apply microrules at each timestep and observe the results. Does the network converge? In most cases, we conjecture that a certain pattern will emerge after a sufficiently long time. Hence, we can test "cause and effect" hypotheses. For example, if we repeatedly replace lower-degreed nodes with higher-degreed nodes, we conjecture that a random network evolves into a scale-free network. But conjectures may not be true. In fact, the first illustration of open-loop emergence, below, shows this conjecture to be wrong! The point is that we can test hypotheses and conjectures in a search for cause–effect explanations of how natural and fabricated systems work.

7.3.1 Hub Emergence

Consider the following open-loop emergent process. Initially, $G(0)$ is a random network with n nodes and m links. $G(0)$ may be created by the ER generative procedure or the anchored random network procedure described earlier. At each timestep, select a node and link at random and ask the question, "Can we rewire the randomly selected link such that it connects to a higher degreed node?" In this case, the randomly selected node is selected if its degree is higher than that of the randomly selected link's head node. The link is rewired to point to the higher-degreed node or left as is.

This simple microrule repeats forever. We conjecture that a scale-free network will emerge from the random network because over a long period of time a hub with very high degree emerges. After a sufficient length of time, does the degree sequence of $G(0)$ transition from a Poisson distribution to a power law? We test this hypothesis in the following analysis.[6]

The "hub emergence" microrule is very simple—rewire a randomly selected link whenever it increases the degree of a high-degreed node. *Network.jar* repeats the following Java method for implementing the hub emergence microrule for as long as the user desires:

```
public void NW_doIncreaseDegree(){
  //Rewire network to increase node degrees
  int random_node = (int)(nNodes * Math.random()); //A random node
  int random_link = (int)(nLinks * Math.random()); //A random link
  int to_node = Link[ random_link] .head;          //Link's to_node
  int from_node = Link[ random_link] .tail;         //Anchor node
  if(node[ random_node] .degree > node[ to_node] .degree){
     if(NW_doAddLink(node[ from_node] .name, node[ random_node] .name))
        NW_doCutLink(random_link);                  //Replace random link
     else  Message = "Warning: Duplicate Links Not Allowed.";
  }
}//NW_doIncreaseDegree
```

Is this process another application of the law of increasing returns? After thousands of timesteps, does a scale-free network emerge? We can check our hypothesis by simply inspecting the degree sequence that emerges from 160,000 timesteps! Figure 7.2a shows the degree sequence distribution of $G(0)$—the random network—and Fig. 7.2b shows the distribution after 160,000 iterations. If the convergent network $G(160,000)$ had evolved into a scale-free network, its degree sequence distribution would be a power law. Clearly, this is not the case. Figure 7.2b shows a skewed Poisson distribution, instead. Its smallest degreed nodes have one link, its largest degreed node has 178 links, and the peak of the distribution is at 4 links! Contrast this with the random network: a maximum hub with 18 links, minimum hub with zero links, and a peak at 10 links.

The degree sequence distribution of the random network of Fig. 7.2a is very close to a Poisson distribution with a mean of 6, but its x axis is shifted by 4: Poisson(6, degree $-$ 4), while the hub emergent converged network of Fig. 7.2b is very close to a Poisson distribution with a mean of 4: Poisson(4, degree). Instead of converting a random network into a scale-free network, hub emergence has rearranged links in a random network such that the degree sequence distribution is technically still random, but shifted. After emergence, there are more small-degreed nodes on average, but the convergent network has hubs with much higher degree.

The hub with the largest number of links—the so-called maximum hub—grows as the square root of time: $O(\sqrt{t})$, as shown in Fig. 7.3. Specifically, for $n = 100$, and

---

[6]As it turns out, the speculation is false.

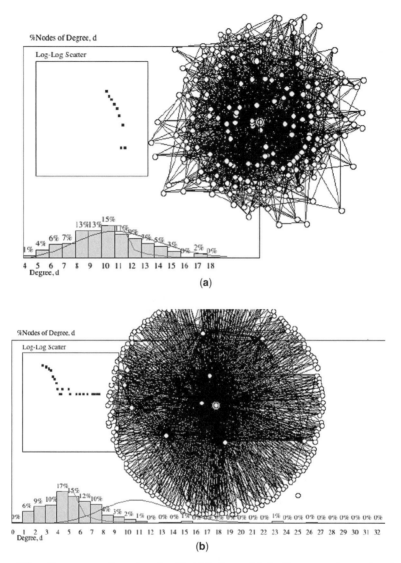

Figure 7.2 Emergence of a network with high-degreed hubs from a random network: (a) random network, $G(0)$—the degree sequence distribution before emergence; (b) hub emerged network, $G(160,000)$—the degree sequence distribution after emergence. The initial network, $G(0)$, $n = 200$, $m = 1000$, was generated by the Erdos–Renye procedure.

three distinct densities, 5%, 10%, and 20%, the maximum hub of the hub emergent network increases its degree property according to the following approximation:

$$\text{hub\_degree}(G) = A + \frac{\sqrt{t}}{2}$$

where, $A = 7$ for density 5%, 14 for density 10%, and 24 for density of 20%.

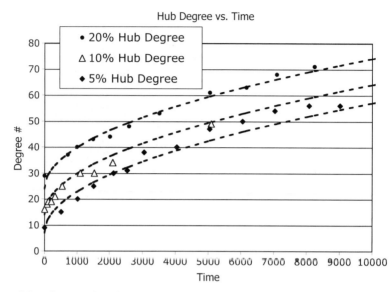

Figure 7.3   Growth of maximum hub degree versus time as the network of Fig. 7.2 emerges: $n = 100, m = 249$ (density = 5%), $m = 500$ (density = 10%), and $m = 1000$ (density = 20%).

The increasing spread between minimum and maximum hub degree as the network evolves is of greater significance. Initially bounded by the density of the random network, the spread grows as the square-root of time. This spread has an impact on the macroscale properties of the emerging network: entropy, average path length, and cluster coefficient.

This raises another question: "What happens to the entropy of the emerged network as time passes?" Recall that entropy is computed by summing $h(d)\log_2 (h(d))$ over the degree sequence distribution—from minimum degree to maximum degree. The larger the spread, the more terms in the summation. Intuitively, it should increase as energy goes into increasing node degrees, but decrease as $h(d)$ decreases. Which is the case?

Figure 7.4 shows entropy increasing quickly as the first few links are rewired to connect to higher-degreed nodes, but then decreasing slowly as randomness diminishes. In other words, the emerging network is dominated by increasing randomness at first, then by increasing structure (nonrandomness) after reaching an inflection point, t^*. Repeated a]pplication of the "hub emerging" microrule injects randomness into the network because the microrule randomizes the rewiring of links. Hub structure emerges and quickly dominates the macroscale structure of the emerging network because rewiring is preferential—not random. Thus, the emerged network restructures by a combination of random and nonrandom forces.

We know from Chapter 4 that entropy increases exponentially up to a point, flattens out, and then decreases exponentially to zero as structure takes over. In addition, we know from study of scale-free networks that randomness diminishes

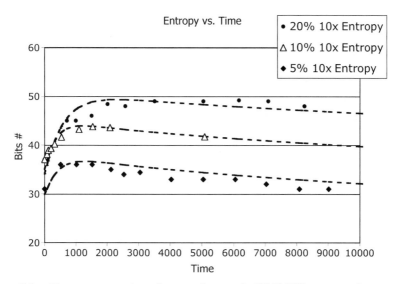

Figure 7.4   Entropy versus time. Structured network $G(160,000)$ emerges from random network $G(0)$ by passing through two phases: (1) further randomization, followed by (2) increasingly dominating hub structure.

as a network's hub increases in degree. The structure of the emerged network is a result of balancing these two competing forces.

Intuition leads us to an approximation for entropy as shown by the dashed lines in Fig. 7.4. The $(1 - \exp(\ ))$ term describes increasing randomness early on, while hub_degree() describes the increasing structure that dominates as a larger and larger hub emerges. Entropy is the difference

$$10(I(G)) = A + B(1 - \exp(-Ct)) - D \ \text{hub\_degree}(t)$$

where $A = 37$, $B = 11.75$, $C = 0.00284$, $D = 0.141$, for 10% density.

Substitution of $\text{sqrt}(t)/2$ for hub_degree(t) yields an approximation of entropy versus time for the emerging network:

$$I(G) = \frac{A + B(1 - \exp(-Ct)) - D \ \text{sqrt}(t)}{10}$$

t^* is the inflection point where $I(G)$ reaches a maximum value. Differentiation of $I(G)$ with respect to t leads to a nonlinear equation for t^*. This problem is left as an exercise for the reader.

The emerging network goes through two phases: one prior to and the other after t^*, where t^* is the point in time when entropy reaches its maximum value. Given enough time, the emerged network's entropy returns to its initial value, and tends to zero because structure completely dominates randomness. Theoretically, the random network converts into a structured network. But in practice, the microrule prevents this because the microrule rewires in only one direction—the head of each link.

The tail of a link is never rewired. Instead of collapsing into a spike, the degree sequence distribution shifts from a narrow symmetrical Poisson distribution to a broad skewed Poisson distribution.

As time passes and larger hubs form, the emergent network's average path length declines in accordance with expectation. The reader can verify that the decline in path length is $O(\text{hub\_degree})$, which is nonlinear in time, because hub_degree is $O(\sqrt{t})$. Similarly, the relationship between cluster coefficient and time is left as an exercise for the reader. It, too, varies as a function of hub size, which grows as $O(\sqrt{t})$.

What at first appeared to be a novel method of transforming a random network into a scale-free network turns out to produce an entirely new class of network: random networks with hubs! This is not an oxymoron, but rather, a hybrid class with properties of both. Hub emergence transforms a random network into a random network with hubs. What is the impact on navigation time for this new class of network? Do such hybrids exist in nature? These remain unsolved but inviting research topics at the time of writing of this book.

7.3.2 Cluster Emergence

Hub emergence leads to non-scale-free networks with hub structure. Is it possible to construct a non-small-world network with high cluster coefficient? The answer is "Yes," as we show next. Beginning once again with a random network, suppose that we use feedback-loop emergence as shown in Fig. 7.1b to enhance the cluster coefficient of an emergent network. After each timestep we guarantee that the overall cluster coefficient of the network is no less than it was in the prior timestep. Over time this network will increase its clustering—at least in theory.

Cluster coefficient emergence works as follows. Select a random link and random node. Rewire the link to point to the new (random) node, if the overall cluster coefficient remains the same or is increased. If the cluster coefficient decreases as a result of rewiring, revert to the topology of the previous timestep. Repeat this microrule indefinitely, or until stopped.

Java method NW_doIncreaseCluster(), shown below, does exactly this, with some added precautions. It selects a link at random, and a random node, ensuring that the link's head, tail, and random nodes are distinct. Then it calls NW_doCC() to calculate the network's cluster coefficient. If cluster coefficient is reduced, the reduced value is returned; otherwise, the network's structure reverts to the previous step configuration. The method also avoids duplicate links, trying *nLinks* times to find nonduplicate links, before giving up.

```
public double NW_doIncreaseCluster(double cc){
    LayoutReply reply = new LayoutReply();  //CC type
    double after_cc = 0;                    //After link is changed
    int random_link = 0;                    //Select a random link
    int random_node = 0;                    //Select a random node
    int tail_node = 0, head_node = 0; //End nodes of random link
    int counter = 0;
```

```
boolean done = false;
while(!done && counter < nLinks){              //Avoid duplicate links
   random_link =(int)(nLinks*Math.random());//Select link at random
   tail_node = Link[random_link].tail;
   head_node = Link[random_link].head;        //End nodes of random link
   random_node =(int)(nNodes*Math.random()); //Select node at random
   while(tail_node == random_node || head_node == random_node)
      random_node =(int)(nNodes*Math.random()); //Make sure they differ
   //Trial
   done = NW_doAddLink(node[tail_node].name,node[random_node].name);
   if(done) {
         NW_doCutLink(random_link);    //Remove original link
         reply = NW_doCC();            //Find CC after adding new link
         after_cc = reply.mean;        //New CC
   }
   else  Message = "Rewiring Failed: Duplicate Link.";
   counter++;
}
if(counter >= nLinks){
   Message = "Rewiring Failed: Cannot find a node to connect.";
   after_cc = cc;
}
else if((after_cc < cc) && cc != 0) {
   NW_doCutLink(random_link); //Revert back
   NW_doAddLink(node[tail_node].name, node[head_node].name);//Restore
   after_cc = cc;                          //No change
   Message = "Revert to previous structure."+
      Double.toString(after_cc);
}
else Message = "Increasing Cluster Coefficient..."+
   Double.toString(after_cc);
return after_cc;
}//NW_doIncreaseCluster
```

Recall from Chapter 2 that the cluster coefficient is the average value over all nodes v_i, of individual cluster coefficients:

$$CC(G) = \sum_{i=1}^{n} \frac{C(v_i)}{n}$$

$$C(v_i) = \frac{2c_i}{\text{degree}(v_i)(\text{degree}(v_i) - 1)} \sim O\left(\frac{1}{\text{degree}(v_i)^2}\right)$$

where c_i = number of links connecting neighbors of node v_i.

The important thing to remember about this formula is that $C(v_i)$ is inversely proportional to the square of node degree. Linear increases in degree diminish a node's cluster coefficient as a power law. This fact is used to explain the emergence that we observe when applying method NW_doIncreaseCluster() many times to an initially random network. As the hub degree of the emergent network increases, cluster coefficient of the hub decreases! The decrease is a direct consequence of

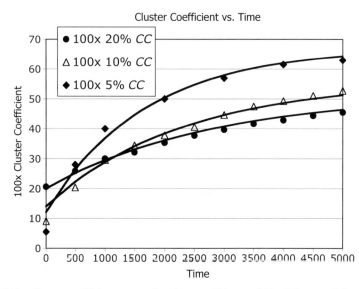

Figure 7.5   Cluster coefficient versus time for $n = 100$, $m = 249$ (5%), $m = 500$ (10%), and $m = 1000$ (20%).

the inverse relationship $O(\text{degree}(v_i)^2)^{-1}$—not necessarily because of fewer links among neighbors.

What happens to random network $G(0)$ as time passes? Does a small-world network emerge? If your definition of small world equals high cluster coefficient, then the emerged network is small-world. If definition of cluster coefficient is equivalent to the Watts–Strogatz definition, then the answer is "No."

Figure 7.5 plots cluster coefficient versus time for three cluster coefficient emerged networks: 5%, 10%, and 20% density. Cluster coefficient ranges from 10% to 65%, overall. Growth of cluster coefficient is a dampened exponential function of time: $CC(G) = A + B(1 - \exp(-Ct))$, where A, B, and C are constant parameters, given in Table 7.1 for the experimental data plotted in Fig. 7.5. In addition, we include the cluster coefficient for an equivalently dense small-world network for comparison. The data fit very closely with the exponentially dampened approximation, but differ significantly from the cluster coefficient of a small-world network

TABLE 7.1   Curve-Fit Approximations for Cluster Coefficient Parameters A, B, C

	5%	10%	20%
A	0.12	0.14	0.20
B	0.55	0.42	0.32
C	0.00060	0.00043	0.00035
Small-world CC	0.037	0.095	0.200

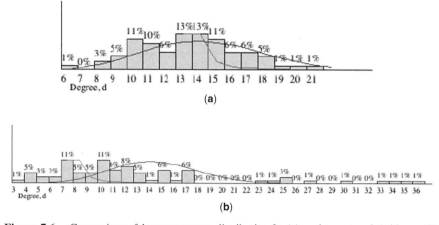

Figure 7.6   Comparison of degree sequence distribution for (a) random network (with $n = 60$, $m = 400$) and (b) cluster coefficient emerged network after $t = 10,000$ timesteps.

with an equivalent density. However, the average path lengths agree between small-world and cluster coefficient emerged networks.

As cluster coefficient increases, entropy, path length, and hub degree increase slightly for the emerged network. This is perhaps contrary to intuition. Hub degree increases most significantly, leading to a possible explanation for the increase in cluster coefficient. Now consider this—as the degree of the emerged network's hub increases, the degree of nonhub nodes decrease. According to the equation for $CC(G)$, a decline in node degree corresponds to an increase in cluster coefficient because $CC(G) \sim O(1/\text{degree}^2)$. Therefore, cluster coefficients of the many low-degreed nodes increase, while cluster coefficients of the few high-degreed nodes decreases. There are many more low-degreed nodes with high cluster coefficient, so the overall cluster coefficient increases.

We might also argue the opposite, that the increase of clustering around individual nodes leads to an overall increase in the average value. The microrule governing cluster coefficient emergence rewires links to increase local clustering with the side effect that node degree generally spreads out across a broader range of values. The flattening and broadening of the degree sequence distribution as clustering increases supports this alternative explanation as well (see Fig. 7.6).

7.4 DESIGNER NETWORKS

We have shown how emergence leads to networks with high-degreed hubs or high cluster coefficient. These networks are neither scale-free nor small-world. Rather, their degree sequence distributions are pseudorandom—with a certain global property such as high-degreed hubs or high number of clusters. This raises a question: "Is it possible for a network with a specific degree sequence distribution to emerge from an arbitrary initial network?" In other words, can we produce a "designer network" from a random network by specifying the degree of each individual node?

The answer is "most of the time." Given a degree sequence g, we can construct a network containing nodes with sequence g, if such a topology is *realizable*.[7] The desired network may not be realizable without allowing duplicate links between node pairs, however. In some cases, we may have to sacrifice precision for practicality (no duplicates) in order to come close.

In this section, we show that restricting the total number of node degrees to the constraint $\sum g = 2m$, where m is the number of links in G, and using the proper *preferential attachment* algorithm, we can produce any realizable network from an arbitrary starting point. Rewiring links according to degree sequence g following the constraints described below, *degree sequence emergence* produces a customized or "designer network" with exactly the topology we want.

We use method `NW_doSetStates(total_value, mean_value)` to store the desired degree sequence g in the nodes of the initial network $G(0)$. When stored in each node as its *state* or *value*, the elements of g are called *residual degree* or *residual values*. The objective is to transform $G(0)$ to $G(t)$ such that the degree sequence of $G(t)$ is exactly g. The initial elements of g will be decremented during the evolution of the desired network, so that the emerged network matches g. If all values are zero after evolution, the network has converged to the desired degree sequence, g.

The first parameter of `NW_doSetStates(total_value, mean_value)` is typically set to $2m$ because each link connects two stubs, and the second parameter is typically set to the desired network's average degree value, $\lambda = n/m$. If `total_value` is less than $2m$, the method reports an error message, and returns. If `mean_value` is too large, the network will not converge because it cannot insert enough links to realize degree sequence g.

The state s of each node is limited to a minimum value of one and a maximum value of twice the average degree: $1 \leq s \leq 2\lambda$. The minimum degree value ensures that the evolved network is connected. The maximum degree of any node is $n-1$ ($n-2$ plus minimum of 1 assigned to all nodes), because duplicate links are not allowed, and each node is able to connect to at most $(n-1)$ others.

If the total number of degrees is odd, then at least one degree will remain unused because links consume degrees in pairs. This method assumes the total number of degrees assigned to all nodes to be an even number. Therefore, parameter `total_value` must be an even number. The following parameters guarantee satisfactory results:

$$\text{total\_value} \geq 2m, \text{ typically } 2m$$

$$\text{mean\_value} = \frac{n}{m} \geq 1$$

Method `NW_doSetStates()` loads the initial network $G(0)$ with g, in preparation for emergence. In addition to constraints on `total_value` and `mean_value`,

[7] A network with degree sequence g is *realizable* if its degree sequence matches g, precisely.

the method must guarantee an even number of stubs, stubs less than the maximum possible ($n - 1$), and handle extreme values of n and m.

```
public boolean NW_doSetStates(int total_value, int mean_value){
  if(total_value < 2*nNodes || nNodes < 2
      ||
    mean_value < 1 ){
    Message = "Not Enough nodes or total_value < 2n. Change Preferences";
    return false;
  }
  if(!(total_value == 2 * (total_value/2))) total_value = 2*(total_value/2);
  Message = "States Set: Total = "+Long.toString(total_value);
  int sum = 0;
  for(int i = 0; i < nNodes; i++){
    node[i].value = 1;                 //Minimum residual degree
    total_value-;
    sum++;
  }
  int count = 0;
  while(total_value > 0 && count < 10*nNodes) {
  for(int i = 0; i < nNodes; i++){
    if(total_value > 0){
        int s = (int)((2*mean_value) * Math.random());
        if(s > total_value) s = total_value;
        if(s >= nNodes - 2) s = nNodes - 2;      //Cannot be more than complete
        if(node[ i] .value + s < nNodes-1) {
            node[i].value += s;
            sum += s;
            total_value -= s;
        }
        count++;
    }
  }
} }
  if(!(sum == 2*(sum/2))){
    for(int i = 0; i < nNodes; i++){
      if(node[ i] .value > 1){
          node[i].value- -;
          break;
      }
    }
  }
  return true;
}//NW_doAddStates
```

Use this method to set the initial degree sequence value $g(0)$ of $G(0)$. This is also known as the *target value* of a designer network. In some emergent processes, the target value or state of each node is decremented until reaching zero. Then, the state is known as the residual degree sequence $g(t)$ at each timestep. If all nodes reach zero, the designer network has been realized. Otherwise, the target degree sequence is not realizable.

7.4.1 Degree Sequence Emergence

Degree sequence emergence attempts to transform an arbitrary network into a network with a prescribed degree sequence. Given an arbitrary starting network $G(0)$ and degree sequence $g = \{d_1, d_2, \ldots, d_n\}$, where $d_i =$ degree of node i, $g = \{d_1, d_2, \ldots, d_n\}$, where $d_i =$ degree of node i, evolve network $G(\text{final})$, into a network with degree sequence g. The target degree sequence g is stored in the network as $\text{value}(v_j) = d_j$, for each node v_j in $G(0)$. We claim that the degree sequence of $G(t)$ converges to g when $\sum g = 2m$, *and duplicate links are allowed*. Degree sequence emergence does not converge to g when $\sum g < 2m$ because there are too many links. Emergence either stops or finds many approximations to g, when $\sum g > 2m$. When $G(\text{final})$ is realizable, degree sequence emergence produces a "designer" network as specified by input values g.

The objective of degree network emergence is to decrease the difference between the initial degree sequence of $G(0)$ and the specified degree sequence g stored in each node as the node's *state* or *value*. This may be possible by rewiring links that connect to nodes with too many links, thereby decreasing each node's degree until it matches—or approximates—the value specified in g. We do this by disconnecting one or both ends of a link and reconnecting the broken link to a randomly selected node. Note that we specifically do not attempt to increase the degree of nodes by purposely attaching links to nodes with a deficiency of links.

For example, suppose that $G(0) = \{N(0), L(0), f\}$, $n = 4$, and $g = \{2, 2, 1, 3\}$. Note that $\sum g = 2 + 2 + 1 + 3 = (2)(4) = 8 = 2m$. Figure 7.7a shows $G(0)$ before emergence, and Fig. 7.7b shows $G(100)$ after 100 timesteps have elapsed. Initially, the degree sequence $g = \{2, 3, 2, 1\}$, but after approximately 100 timesteps, the network topology is changed to the objective: $g = \{2, 2, 1, 3\}$. Emergence has closed the gap between the initial and desired degree of G.

We propose a simple microrule that achieves, or approximates, g within finite time. Actually, three methods are studied: an emergent technique, an early method first proposed by Molloy and Reed (Molloy, 1995), and a more recent improvement proposed by Mihail et al. (Mihail, 2002), Only the most recent method of Mihail et al., guarantees convergence, under the restrictions that we place on g.

In the following, *L.head* designates the node pointed to by the head of link L, and *L.tail* designates the anchor node of link L. Nodes and links are selected at random, and rewired as necessary to diminish the difference between actual degree and degree sequence value g. The degree sequence emergence microrule given below accepts g as an input and produces an emerged network that equals or approximates g.

Degree Sequence Emergence (per Node Value)

1. Store $g = \{d_1, d_2, \ldots, d_n\}$ in the value field of nodes $\{n_1, n_2, \ldots, n_n\}$ of $G(0)$, for example, $v_i = \text{value}(n_i) = d_i$.
2. Repeat indefinitely
   a. Select a random link L and random node r from G. *L.head* points to the head node of link L, and *L.tail* connects to the tail node of L.

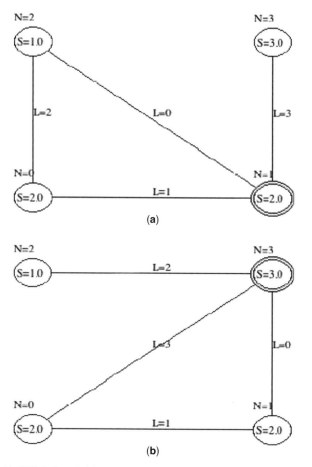

Figure 7.7 (a) $G(0)$ before (with $n = 4$, $m = 4$, $g = \{2,3,2,1\}$) versus (b) $G(100)$ after (with $n = 4$, $m = 4$, $g = \{2,2,1,3\}$) designer emergence. The value d_j is inscribed inside of each node as its state value: ($S = 2.0$, $S = 2.0$, $S = 1.0$, $S = 3.0$).

 b. If degree($L.head$) $>$ value($L.head$), switch $L.head$ to r.
 c. Else if degree($L.tail$) $>$ value($L.tail$), switch $L.tail$ to r.

This algorithm does not decrement the target degree numbers stored in each node's value field, but instead, compares the actual degree of a randomly selected node with the target value. Because we switch only those links that increase the degree of a node (never decreasing the degree), the algorithm "works from low to high degree." The degree of nodes with too many links only diminishes as a side effect of increasing the degree of nodes with too few links. This "one-sided" preferential rewiring approach prevents overshooting or oscillating.

 A Java method for degree sequence emergence must do some additional checking, but is essentially the same algorithm as above. Method NW_doPerNodeValue()

guarantees that randomly selected nodes are distinct. The randomly selected node r must be different from the nodes connected via link L, and r must have a value greater than zero. Duplicate links are prohibited by method NW_doAddLink(), which means that we cannot guarantee convergence. In some cases, this method only approximates the emergent network with degree sequence g. An exploration of the effects of allowing duplicate links is left as an exercise for the reader.

```
public void NW_doPerNodeValue() {
   int r = (int)(nNodes*Math.random());            //Pick a random node
   int random_link = (int)(nLinks*Math.random());  //Pick a random link
   int head_node   = Link[ random_link] .head;     //Pick an end node
   int tail_node = Link[ random_link] .tail;        //Rewire one or the other
   while(r == head_node
              ||
           r == tail_node
              ||
           node[r].value == 0)                      //Skip isolated nodes
         r = (int)(nNodes*Math.random());
   if(node[ head_node] .degree > node[ head_node] .value){  //Rewire head
     if(NW_doAddLink(node[ tail_node] .name, node[ r] .name, Link[ random_link] .name))
         {NW_doCutLink(random_link);}
     }
   else if(node[ tail_node] .degree > node[ tail_node] .value){  //Rewire tail
     if(NW_doAddLink(node[ r] .name, node[ head_node] .name, Link[ random_link] .name))
         {NW_doCutLink(random_link);}
     }
}//NW_doPerNodeValue
```

7.4.2   Generating Networks with Given Degree Sequence

The foregoing raises a question regarding the *creation* of networks with a specific topology. We know how to generate a random network, a scale-free network, and a small-world network, but is it possible to generate any network desired with a given degree sequence? Molloy and Reed showed how to do this using an algorithm like the one described above (Molloy, 1995). The Molloy–Reed algorithm embodies the right idea, but has one major weakness—it does not guarantee the desired topology every time.

The MR algorithm creates d_i stubs (half-links that lack the other endpoints) at each node, v_i, with assigned value d_i. Then, it performs a kind of *preferential attachment* selection process to connect the loose end of each stub to another loose end at another node. Because links must connect pairs of nodes, we assume $\sum g$ to be an even number. The process of connecting stubs repeats until all stubs are connected or we run out of available nodes.[8]

---

[8]When duplicate links are prohibited, the Molloy–Reed method simply inserts fewer links when there are not enough node pairs with residual degree or residual values greater than zero.

Molloy–Reed Generative Procedure

1. Create $G(0)$ with n nodes and zero links, $N = \{n_1, n_2, \ldots, n_n\}$, where each node has a value field $v = \{v_1, v_2, \ldots, v_n\}$.
2. Store $g = \{d_1, d_2, \ldots, d_n\}$ in the value field of nodes of $G(0) : v_i = d_i; i = 1, \ldots, n$.
3. Repeat until there are no more $v_i > 0$:
   a. Choose a pair of nodes (i, j) at random with $v_i > 0$, $v_j > 0$.
   b. Insert link $n_i \sim n_j$.
   c. Decrement v_i, v_j to residual values, $v_i - 1$, $v_j - 1$.

MR is implemented in *Network.jar* as method `NW_doMolloyReed()`. First, the method creates n nodes and stores elements of g in each node's value field. The total of all node values, $\sum g$, must be an even number. Then it attempts to connect $\sum g$ stubs together by random selection of nodes with yet-to-be-linked stubs. Initially, the value stored at each node is equal to the initial residual degree specified by g. Each time the algorithm converts a pair of stubs into a link, the residual degree is decremented. If all residual degree values reach zero, the desired network emerges. However, there is no guarantee that all node values will be decremented to zero. In fact, it is likely that one or more stubs will fail to match with another stub. This requires that the preferential attachment loop give up after numerous unsuccessful attempts. This limit on the method prevents infinite looping when the emergent behavior does not converge.[9]

Method `NW_doMolloyReed()` also guarantees random selection of distinct non-zero-valued nodes. (Notice the **while**`(i==j){}` loop in the method.) This prevents self-loop links and guarantees preferential attachment to nodes with unlinked stubs. The method guarantees convergence to the desired network when permitting duplicate links and $\sum g$ is an even number. Why?

```
public void NW_doMolloyReed(){
    NW_doCreateNodes(nInputNodes);                  //Nodes, no links
    NW_doSetStates(2*nInputLinks, nInputLinks/nNodes);
    int n_stubs = 0;                                //Total number of stubs
    for(int i = 0; i < nNodes; i++) n_stubs += (int)node[ i] .value;
    String m = "Molloy-Reed Network, #Stubs = "+Long.toString(n_stubs);
    int count = 0;
    while(n_stubs > 0 && count < 100*nNodes) {  //Prevent infinite loop
      int i = (int)(nNodes * Math.random());      //Random node
     if(node[ i] .value > 0){
         int j = (int)(nNodes * Math.random()); //Distinct nodes
         while(i == j) j = (int)(nNodes * Math.random());
         if(node[ j] .value > 0){
            if(NW_doAddLink(node[ i] .name,  node[ j] .name)){
               n_stubs -= 2;
               node[i].value- -;                 //Decrement residual values
```

---

[9]We arbitrarily limit the number of numerous attempts to 100 n, but this is probably far too generous.

```
            node[j].value- -;
            count = 0;
        }
      }
    }
    count++;
  }
  Message = m + " Unused = "+Long.toString(n_stubs);
}//NW_doMolloyReed
```

The Molloy–Reed procedure may not be able to realize g. A network with degree
sequence g is *realizable* if its degree sequence matches g, precisely. But, as we
have seen before, degree sequence emergence may not converge without duplicating
links. For example, suppose that only two nodes with nonzero residual degree remain
after a period of emergence. Further suppose that they are already linked. In the next
timestep, the two nodes cannot be linked to any other node because all other nodes
have zero residual degrees. But if we allow duplicate links, the two nonzero nodes can
be linked multiple times, reducing at least one of them to a zero residual value.

What condition guarantees convergence? Intuitively, convergence requires that all
stubs be connected, and the nodes with the most stubs should be connected before the
lesser nodes "run out of stubs." This suggests a modification to the Molloy–Reed
generative procedure to connect the nodes with the largest number of stubs before
all others. This form of preferential attachment is similar to the method used to
create a scale-free network whereby the higher-stub nodes are linked before lower-
stub nodes.

We conjecture that linking the highest-valued nodes first leads to convergence.
Erdos and Gallai showed that degree sequence $g = (d_1 \geq d_2 \geq \cdots \geq d_n)$, sorted in
decreasing order by node degree, is *realizable* if a network that matches g exists
(Mihail, 2002), and

$$\sum_{i=1}^{k} d_i \leq k(k-1) + \sum_{i=k+1}^{n} \min\{k, d_i\}; \ 1 \leq k \leq (n-1)$$

The Erdos–Gallai theorem is the key to a modification that, under certain restrictions,
leads to a degree sequence emergence that converges on a realizable network,
Fig. 7.7b illustrates the *Erdos–Gallai theorem*. Sorting g into descending
order, $g = \{3,2,2,1\}, 1 \leq k \leq 3$, and calculating the left- and right-hand sides of the
Erdos–Gallai equation produces the results of Table 7.2.

Table 7.2 confirms the inequality for all values of k. Column 4 must be less than or
equal to column 7, which means that the Molloy–Reed procedure converges and the
desired network with degree sequence g is realizable. In this case, columns 4 and 7
are equal.

Suppose that $k = 1$ in Table 7.2, corresponding to node 3 in Fig. 7.7b (initially with
degree of 0 and degree 3 after allocation of links). Node 3 must acquire three links by
connecting to the top three nodes in G. In this simple case, the top three nodes are in
descending order, according to g: node 0 (with $d_2 = 2$), node 1 (with $d_3 = 2$), and
node 2 (with $d_3 = 1$). Hence, the stubs of node 3 are satisfied before any others,

TABLE 7.2 Confirmation of the Erdos–Gallai Theorem for Fig. 7.7b

i	k	d_i	$\sum_{i=1}^{k} d_i$	$k(k-1)$	$\min\{k, d_i\}$	$\sum_{i=k+1}^{n} \min\{k, d_i\}$
1	1	3	3	0	1	$(1+1+1) = 3$
2	2	2	5	2	2	$2 + (2+1) = 5$
3	3	2	7	6	2	$3(2) + (1) = 7$
4		1				

which reduces the stub value of node 3 to zero, and the stub values of all other nodes by one, each. Now we have a network, $G(1)$, with $g(1) = \{0,1,1,0\}$. Repeat this process with the remaining nonzero nodes; node 0 has one stub, and node 1 has one stub, so we connect node 0 to node 1. This leaves $G(2)$, with $g(2) = \{0,0,0,0\}$. Therefore, $G(2)$ converges to the desired network.

The *Mihail generative procedure* suggested by Mihail and colleagues (Mihail, 2002) implements the Erdos–Gallai theorem in steps. The idea is simple, but the algorithm is messy because it must arrange nodes in descending order by residual value after each node is connected. First, create nodes and assign stub values as in the MR procedure. Next, sort nodes into descending order and resolve stubs according to the sorted residual values. Make sure that there are no self-loops or duplicate links, as before.

Mihail Generative Procedure

1. Create $G(0)$ with n nodes and zero links: $N = \{n_1, n_2, \ldots n_n\}$.
2. Store $g = \{d_1, d_2, \ldots, d_n\}$ in the value field of nodes of $G(0)$: $v_i = d_i, i = 1, \ldots, n$.
3. Repeat until there are no more $v_i > 0$:
   a. Sort nodes into descending order according to their residual degrees: $v = \{v_1, v_2, \ldots, v_n\}$, so that $v_1 \geq v_2 \geq \cdots 0$.
   b. Select the node with the currently largest residual degree v_1, and call it the *anchor node*, n_a.
   c. Connect anchor node n_a to the next-highest residual-degree-valued nodes $n_2, n_3, \ldots, n_k$ corresponding with the next k highest-valued nodes; assuming $v_2 > 0, v_3 > 0, \ldots, v_k > 0$. Note that k is the number of nodes with nonzero residual degree values, excluding the anchor node.
4. If $(k < v_1 + 1)$, where v_1 is the residual degree value of the anchor node, the sequence is not realizable; otherwise decrement residual values $v_2, v_3, \ldots, v_k$ of the corresponding nodes, and continue.

The Mihail generative procedure ensures that the Erdos–Gallai condition remains valid each time the highest residual-degreed node is linked to the next-highest residual-valued nodes, because the nodes are sorted into descending order by residual degree value prior to each rewiring. The next step of the algorithm always processes the highest residual node first, in accordance with the Erdos–Gallai condition.

However, the Erdos–Gallai condition may not hold if the target degree sequence is not realizable. It is a necessary, but not sufficient, condition to guarantee realizability. A network precisely matches the target degree sequence g only when such a topology is possible. This means that the number of nodes with residual degree value must be at least as large as the largest residual degree. In other words, if k is the number of nodes with nonzero residual degree after timestep t, then node n_0, with the largest residual degree remaining in the emerging network, must have a residual degree value that does not exceed $(k - 1)$:

$$(k - 1) < \text{value}(n_0)$$

Note that the emerging network may separate into multiple components because there is no guarantee that linking highest-degreed nodes first leads to a connected network. The implementation here does not check for separation, nor does separation prevent the emergence of a realizable network. The degree sequence condition can be realized regardless of the strongly connectedness condition.

The algorithm is sequential, requiring $n - 1$ steps. The sort algorithm is at least $n\log_2(n)$, so the overall time complexity is high: $O(n^2\log_2(n))$. Emergence can be slow for large networks. The implementation provided here is even slower, as its sort method is $O(n^2)$.

The Java method for implementing the Mihail et al. algorithm, NW_doMihail(), initializes $G(0)$ if its set_states parameter is true; otherwise it works with the values supplied by the user or NW_doSetStates(). In either case, the emergence begins with nodes, only; all links are initially deleted from $G(0)$.

The algorithm calls SH_sort() from class Shuffler to sort nodes into descending order by residual value. This particular implementation of sort is $O(n^2)$, and so this algorithm is $O(n^3)$, instead of $O(n^2\log_2(n))$. Time complexity can be reduced by using a faster, $O(n \log(n))$, sorting routine. This is left as a programming exercise for the reader.

The Mihail generative procedure implemented in *Network.jar* uses the following input values to assign random target degree sequence g to $G(0)$; these values work best for automatic generation of a random network, when the number of links m is much less than $(n(n - 1))/2$:

$$\text{total\_value} = 2m$$

$$\text{mean\_value} = \frac{n}{m}$$

As before, the Java implementation does additional checking to ensure that network parameters such as nNodes and nLinks are reasonable. The method terminates when it cannot realize g or all residual degree values have been reduced to zero:

```
public void NW_doMihail(boolean set_states){
    Shuffler g;
    Message = "Mihail Network not realizable. Change preferences.";
    if(set_states) {                           //Initialize G(0)
        if(nInputNodes < 2) return;
```

```
      if(2*nInputLinks > nInputNodes*(nInputNodes-1)) return;
      NW_doCreateNodes(nInputNodes);        //Nodes, no links
      if(!NW_doSetStates(2*nInputLinks, nInputLinks/nInputNodes))
         return;
      g = new Shuffler(nInputNodes+1);
   }
   else g = new Shuffler(nNodes+1);         //Existing network
   nLinks = 0;                              //No links, yet
   int n_stubs = 0;                         //Total number of stubs
   for(int i = 0; i < nNodes; i++){
      n_stubs += (int)node[ i] .value;
   }
   boolean done = false;                    //Until residuals = zero
   while(!done) {
      int k = 0;                            //Erdos-Gallai condition
      for(int j = 0; j < nNodes; j++){      //Load g(0) into G(0)
         g.card[j] = j;
         g.key[j] = (int)node[ j] .value;
         if(g.key[ j] > 0) k++;
      }
      g.SH_Sort(nNodes, false);             //Descending order
      int i = g.card[ 0] ;
      int d = g.key[ 0] ;
      if(d <= 0) break;                     //Converged
      if(k-1 < d) {                         //Not realizable
         Message = "Mihail Network not realizable. Change
            preferences.";
         return;
      }
      //Connect top nodes
      for(int j = 1; j <= d; j++){
         int head = g.card[ j] ;
         if(node[ head] .value == 0) {
            done = true;
            break;
         }
         if(NW_doAddLink(node[ i] .name, node[ head] .name)){
            n_stubs -= 2;
            node[i].value- -;
            node[head].value- -;
         }
      }
   }
   Message = "Mihail Network: #Stubs Unused = "+Long
      .toString(n_stubs);
}//NW_doMihail
```

7.5 PERMUTATION NETWORK EMERGENCE

The microrules described thus far have a side effect on the degree sequence distribution and therefore may alter the classification of the emerged network. A *permutation transformation*, on the other hand, leaves the degree sequence distribution unaltered, but produces a network with a different mapping function. Permutation of links, without altering the degree sequence, leads to emergence of networks with a given classification, but tailor-made clustering, path length, and so on.

Let $\pi_D(G)$ be a permutation of the links in G such that the degree sequence distribution is *invariant*:

$$\pi_D(g(G(t))) = g(G(t))$$

for all t, where $G(t)$ is a time varying network with degree sequence, $g(t)$.

We say that degree sequence $g(t)$ is a *fixed point* of $G(t)$ under π_D, because the degree sequence never changes under the transformation. However, other properties, such as the network's cluster coefficient or path length, may change. What microrule guarantees a fixed-point permutation transformation?

Consider the microrule shown in Fig. 7.8. Two links are chosen at random—one link connects nodes $x \sim y$, and the other connects nodes $u \sim v$. The four endnodes are distinct: hence we can permute the links as shown in Fig. 7.8b. After permutation, $x \sim v$ and $u \sim y$. The degree of x, y, v, and v remains unchanged; hence the degree sequence distribution is unaltered. This microrule has no impact on the degree sequence distribution regardless of how many times it is applied. Hence, the network emerging from repeated applications of this microrule remains in the same class because its degree sequence remains unaltered.

Figure 7.8 illustrates one possible permutation—the *horizontal link permutation*, whereby the links exchange head nodes. Another permutation—the *vertical link permutation*—exchanges tail nodes; the head of one link is exchanged with the other link's tail node. The reader may be able to think of other link permutations that do not alter the degree sequence, and hence are invariant transformations. For example, what happens when the tails of the two links are exchanged? Exchanges like these are also called "flips."

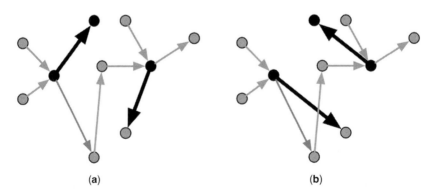

(a)   (b)

Figure 7.8   The permutation or "flip" microrule: (a) before and (b) after flip. Select two links at random (shown in boldface), and exchange head nodes. All four nodes must be distinct.

7.5.1   Permutation Microrule

Permutation of links is not as trivial as it appears in Fig. 7.8. The algorithm must check for two fundamental conflicts: (1) the four end nodes must be distinct, or else the degree sequence will be altered; and (2) the new mapping of links must avoid duplication. The algorithm must take care to avoid rewiring of one link over an existing link when flipping the permuted links. These two conditions render the Java code shown below much more complicated than expected. Therefore, we divide the code into two methods—one for the selection of random links and the other for the actual link flipping.

Method NW_doPermutation() attempts to find two links with four distinct endnodes—up to nLinks times before giving up. Only the head nodes are flipped, so that the sense of directed links is kept infact (the in-degree and out-degree of each node are preserved). There must be at least four nodes and four links in the initial network, $G(0)$.

```
public void NW_doPermutation(){
   int link1 = (int)(nLinks * Math.random());
   int link2 = (int)(nLinks * Math.random());
   int count = 0;                    //Try nLinks times before giving up
   while(count < nLinks
              &&
      (Link[link2].head == Link[link1].head
                 ||
       Link[link2].head == Link[link1].tail
                 ||
       Link[link2].tail == Link[link1].head
                 ||
       Link[link2].tail == Link[link1].tail)){
       link2 = (int)(nLinks * Math.random());   //Distinct end nodes
       count++;
       }
       NW_doFlipLinks(count, link1, link2);      //Flip, if no duplicates
       }//NW_doPermutation
```

Method NW_doFlipLinks() has a more difficult task—it must prepare to back out of the flip operation if a duplicate link is detected. Method isConnected() returns **true** if the two nodes are already connected. The head nodes of the two randomly chosen links are exchanged if four distinct nodes and no duplicate links are found:

```
public void NW_doFlipLinks(int count, int link1, int link2) {
   if(count < nLinks) {                    //Flip links if possible
       int saved_head1 = Link[ link1] .head; //Prepare to revert back
       int saved_head2 = Link[ link2] .head;
       if(!isConnected(Link[ link1] .tail, Link[ link2] .head)
                 &&
          !isConnected(Link[link2].tail, Link[link1].head)) {
          Link[link1].head = Link[link2].head;          //Flip
          Link[link2].head = saved_head1;
```

```
    }
    else {                                      //Revert: no duplicates
      Link[link1].head = saved_head1;
      Link[link2].head = saved_head2;
    }
  }
  else Message="Warning: Cannot Permute Links.";    //Not possible
}//NW_doFlipLinks
```

While the permutation microrule leaves the degree sequence of $G(t)$ unaltered through-out, it may alter other properties of G. For example, it is possible to increase (decrease) the cluster coefficient, average path length, centrality, or diameter of a certain network without altering its degree sequence distribution. This feature of the permutation transformation is useful in a number of applications, described below.

7.5.2   Permutation and Cluster Coefficient

The permutation transformation $\pi_D(G)$ is useful for creating a customized network with desirable degree sequence distribution and other properties such as cluster coef-ficient. For example, we can build a feedback-loop emergence model that maximizes cluster coefficient values of any network. Specifically, it is possible to increase the cluster coefficient of a random network while maintaining its randomness, and increase the cluster coefficient of a small-world network that already has a high cluster coefficient. As we shall see, it is generally possible to increase any network's cluster coefficient without altering its degree sequence distribution—but only up to a certain limit.[10]

Consider the following emergence algorithm for maximizing cluster coefficient without altering the network's class. The following cluster coefficient permutation algorithm takes any network as its starting point $G(0)$ and produces a network $G(\text{final})$ with maximum cluster coefficient. It applies the permutation transformation thousands of times—taking care to keep only permutations that increase cluster coef-ficient, and discarding all others:

Cluster Coefficient (Permutation)

1. Generate a network $G(0)$ of any desired degree sequence distribution.
2. Calculate initial network cluster coefficient: $c(0) = CC(G)$.
3. Repeat indefinitely;
   a. Apply the link permutation microrule, $\pi_D(G)$.
   b. Calculate network cluster coefficient, $c(t) = CC(G)$.
   c. If $c(t) < c(t-1)$, undo $\pi_D(G)$: $G(t) = G(t-1)$; otherwise do nothing.

This algorithm is almost identical to the permutation transformation algorithm. In fact, it is identical with the addition of the cluster coefficient calculation and feedback

---

[10]The cluster coefficient is limited by the number of links or density of the network.

loop that discards permutations that do not lead to an increase in cluster coefficient. Method isConnected(v,w) returns **true** if nodes *v* and *w* are connected. This step avoids duplication of links, which is one of the requirements imposed on our network topology. As before, a permutation may not be possible, so variable count bounds the number of attempts, preventing an infinite loop.

As expected, the Java code closely resembles NW_doPermutation(), which provides the basis of this implementation. NW_doPermuteCC() combines the two permutation methods (horizontal and vertical) into one, and adds a test for nondeclining cluster coefficient:

```java
public double NW_doPermuteCC(double cluster_coefficient){
    LayoutReply reply = new LayoutReply(); //Return value type
    reply.mean = cluster_coefficient;       //CC(t-1)
    int link1 = (int)(nLinks * Math.random()); //Permutation links
    int link2 = (int)(nLinks * Math.random());
    int count = 0;
    while(count < nLinks
            &&
        (Link[link2].head == Link[link1].head
                ||
        Link[link2].head == Link[link1].tail
                ||
        Link[link2].tail == Link[link1].head
                ||
        Link[link2].tail == Link[link1].tail)){
        link2 = (int)(nLinks * Math.random()); //Distinct end nodes
        count++;
    }
    if(count < nLinks) {                          //Flip links if possible
        int saved_head1 = Link[ link1].head;
        int saved_head2 = Link[ link2].head;
        if(!isConnected(Link[ link1].tail, Link[ link2].head)
                    &&
          !isConnected(Link[link2].tail, Link[link1].head)) {
            Link[link1].head =          Link[link2].head;    //Flip
            Link[link2].head = saved_head1;
            reply = NW_doCC();                               //CC(t)
            if(reply.mean >= cluster_coefficient) return reply.mean;
            else {                      //Revert due to no increase
                Link[link1].head = saved_head1;
                Link[link2].head = saved_head2;
                return cluster_coefficient;
            }
        }
    }
    else {                              //Revert due to duplicate links
        Link[link1].head = saved_head1;
        Link[link2].head = saved_head2;
        return cluster_coefficient;
    }
}
else {
    Message = "Warning: Cannot Permute Links.";          //Not possible
```

```
    return cluster_coefficient;
  }
}//NW_doPermuteCC
```

Figure 7.9 summarizes results of evolving several classes of networks using the permutation microrule and cluster coefficient feedback loop implemented by NW_doPermuteCC(). Figure 7.9 data were computed by *Network.jar* for sparse networks and 10,000 iterations. We can deduce the following from Fig. 7.9:

1. Rank order, from smallest to largest cluster coefficients—after the small-world phase transition near the origin the three network classes rank in order as follows: random, small-world, and scale-free.
2. Cluster coefficient $CC(G)$ increases monotonically through three phases: initial, *rate effect*, and *hub effect*. Cluster coefficient is modeled as the sum of these phases:

$$CC(G(t)) = A + B\exp(-Ct) + D\log(Ct)$$

where A corresponds with the initial phase; $B\exp(-Ct)$, the rate effect phase; and $D\log(Ct)$, the hub effect phase. Table 7.3 lists values of A, B, C, and D, obtained from Fig. 7.9.

The first observation from Fig. 7.9 comes as no surprise—random networks have far less clustering than do equivalent scale-free and small-world networks. The surprising result is how quickly the cluster coefficient rises in the sparse scale-free network. Starting from second place, the scale-free network quickly exceeds the small world network. Why?

The rise of clustering in the three network classes is due to three factors, each factor becoming dominant for an interval of time as time increases. The first factor

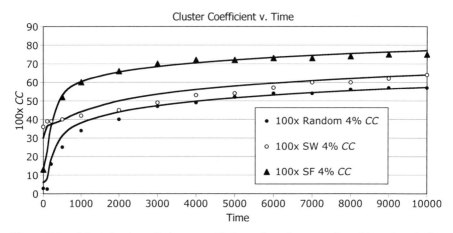

Figure 7.9   Maximization of cluster coefficient of random, small-world, and scale-free networks with density approximately 4% ($n = 100$, $m = 200$), and 10,000 iterations.

TABLE 7.3 Curve-Fit Parameters for Fig. 7.9

Parameter	Random	Small-World	Scale-Free
A	6	30	13
B	19	20	36
C	0.005	0.005	0.005
D	19	20	16.5

is *inherent clustering* due to the network's class. Parameter A represents this factor and dominates during the brief initial phase. Table 7.3 shows that the small-world network has the largest inherent cluster coefficient of the three classes. Its parameter A value is 2.5 times that of the scale-free network, and 5 times that of the random network. Random and scale-free networks have very little initial clustering.

The second phase of evolution is dominated by the *rate effect*—the rate of increase in cluster coefficient is suppressed by the amount of clustering already established. The more clustering a network has, the lower its rate of acquisition of more clusters; that is, $\delta CC/\delta t \sim \alpha(CC)$, where $\delta CC/\delta t$ is the rate of change in cluster coefficient and $\alpha < 0$ is a rate constant. The solution to this rate equation is $CC \sim \exp(-Ct)$, where $\alpha = -C$, the third constant in Table 7.3.[11]

During the rate phase, emergence of clustering is dominated by the amount of clustering (or lack of it) already in the network. As clustering increases, additional clustering is more difficult to achieve. Hence, the rate declines over time, and dies out, exponentially. Parameter C is identical for all three networks because n and m are identical.

The third phase is dominated by the *hub effect*—clustering is easier to increase around small hubs than large hubs. We have observed this effect before; clustering occurs around small-degreed nodes more than high-degreed nodes because a node must add $O(d^2)$ neighboring links to increase its cluster coefficient by an amount proportional to $O(d)$. Therefore, it is easier to increase overall cluster coefficient in a network with many low-degreed nodes than a network with few low-degreed nodes. In this case, the scale-free network has the largest number of low-degreed nodes of the three classes, and so its hub effect is greater.

The scale-free network rapidly gains clusters during the rate effect phase because it initially has the least number of clustered nodes. Thus, it has the largest B parameter value. It also continues to add clusters in the hub effect phase, but not at quite the same rate as the other two, because it has a much larger hub. The large hub tends to dampen cluster coefficient increase because high-degreed hubs require a large number of neighboring links.

The classes of random and small-world networks are shaped by a similar hub effect. The small-world parameter D is slightly larger because the degree sequence distribution of a small world tends to be narrower than that of a random network.

---

[11] C is the time compression or rate constant.

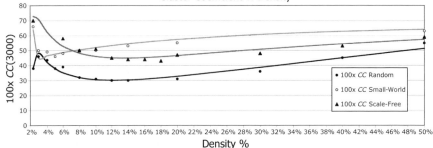

Figure 7.10   Cluster coefficient emergence versus network density. Data are plotted for $100 \times CC$ versus density at time $= 3000$.

Thus, the degree of a small world's hub node is slightly lower than the equivalent hub of a random network.

We can apply similar logic to the emergence of clusters in networks versus their density, as shown in Fig. 7.10. In this experiment, clusters are allowed to emerge for 3000 timesteps. Density varies from 2% to 50%. The rise in cluster coefficient is a function of the same three factors, plus one more—the density of the network.

As density increases, four factors, corresponding to four phases, dictate the clustering of random, small-world, and scale-free networks. The fourth factor is density:

$$CC(G(d)) = A - B\exp(-Cd) - D\log(Cd) + ECd$$

where A, B, D, and E denote initial, rate, hub, and density effects.

Note that

$$A = \text{initial or inherent cluster coefficient}$$
$$B\exp(-Cd) = \text{rate effect}$$
$$C = \text{time constant}$$
$$D\log(Cd) = \text{hub effect}$$
$$E(Cd) = \text{density effect}$$
$$d = \text{density}$$

Values of all parameters obtained by curve fitting are summarized in Table 7.4, and support the following:

1. Random and small-world networks undergo a phase transition near 3–4% density as predicted by our studies of small-world networks. However, variation of cluster coefficient in the small-world network case is almost the inverse of the variation in a random network; that is, the curve of one is nearly a mirror reflection of the curve of the other, along a horizontal line

TABLE 7.4   Curve-Fit Values of Parameter for Fig. 7.10

Parameter	Random	Small-World	Scale-Free
A	36	64	71
B	66	18	110
C	5	5	5
D	80	− 4	112
E	21	0	16

near $CC(3000) = 0.45$. This is due to the transition from structure to randomness in the small-world network, and dominance of the rate effect in the random network. In both cases, density is the largest factor in determining cluster coefficient.

2. Random and small-world networks pass through four phases as density increases: initial cluster value (low for random, high for small-world), rate effect (high for both, but in opposite directions because of their initial cluster coefficient values), hub effect (positive for small-world and negative for random), and density (becomes dominant in random case, but nonexistent in small-world case).

3. Cluster coefficient initially declines for the scale-free network and then increases as density increases, reflecting the counterbalancing effects of rate and hubs. During phase 2 the rate effect dominates, and during phases 3 and 4, the hub effect dominates. As density rises, the degree of a scale-free network's hub dramatically increases. Thus, cluster coefficient is dominated mainly by hub size, which, we know, grows logarithmically for a scale-free network.

4. In all networks (random, small-world, scale-free), the same value of cluster coefficient tends to emerge as density approaches 100%. This is obvious, because a 100% dense network is a complete network. The cluster coefficient of a complete network is 100%.

Figure 7.10 reveals a surprise—for densities less than approximately 8% it is possible to emerge a scale-free network with greater cluster coefficient than an equivalent small-world network. Cluster coefficient should be higher for a small-world than a scale-free network, and yet, we see that permutation emergence is capable of evolving a scale-free network into a network with more clustering than an equivalent small-world network! We have only to consult Table 7.4 to understand why. Parameters B and D are much higher for scale-free network emergence than for small-world emergence. This impressive fact is completely due to the much higher fraction of low-degreed nodes in a scale-free versus small-world network. In other words, emergence produces networks with both features—high-degreed hubs and high cluster coefficient value.

7.6   AN APPLICATION OF EMERGENCE

We can construct almost any kind of network using feedback emergence and properly selected microrules. This technology is useful for a number of routing and layout applications. As a concrete illustration, we show how to minimize the amount of wiring needed to connect a set of randomly placed components in two-dimensional space such as a printed circuit board, or houses in a neighborhood. The idea is simple: to establish a basic topology such as ensuring that all components are connected, and then applying permutation transformations until the desired minimum value of wiring is achieved. Instead of solving a set of equations, we let a computer do all the work!

In the first example, we scatter an anchored or ER random network over a two-dimensional area, and then perform permutations on link pairs. We accept permutations that shorten the total length of the network and reject all others. As it turns out, the minimum total length of links, $\sum e_i$, exponentially converges to a value proportional to $O(m/\sqrt{n})$.[12]

Next, we apply the same permutation method to the layout of components placed randomly on a surface, with restrictions on node degree. For the case where two links connect to all nodes, $degree(v) = 2$, the minimum-length connection is simply a 1-regular, or ring network connecting nearest adjacent nodes. For higher-degreed networks, emergence of minimum total length connects spatially nearest neighbors to one another.

7.6.1   Link Optimization by Random Permutation

Consider the following experiment. Create a random network with n nodes and m links using either the anchored random network or the ER generative procedure.[13] Scatter the nodes randomly over a surface. The method shown below uses random polar coordinates to scatter nodes, taking care to stay within the bounds of the screen. Any method that spreads n nodes over a sqrt(n) by sqrt(n) area will do.

```
public void NW_doRandomizeNodes() {
    for (int i = 0; i < nNodes ; i++) {
        int r = 2*(int)(CircleRadius * Math.random());
        double arc = Math.random() * (2.0*Math.PI)/nNodes;
        node[i].x = x0 + (int)(r*Math.cos(i*arc));
        if(node[ i] .x > xwide-40) node[ i] .x = xwide-40;
        if(node[ i] .x < 40) node[ i] .x = 40;
        node[i].y = y0 + (int)(r*Math.sin(i*arc));
        if(node[ i] .y > ytall-40) node[ i] .y = ytall-40;
        if(node[ i] .y < 40) node[ i] .y = 40;
    }//for
}//NW_doRandomizeNodes
```

---

[12]This is not a general result, but instead an artifact of the 2-D layout.

[13]Anchored random networks are required when the value of m is small because we want $G(0)$ to be a strongly connected network. This works most, but not all, of the time.

Generally, we repeatedly apply the permutation transformation. The permutation is discarded if the total length of links increases and is retained, otherwise. Over time we expect short links to replace long links, thus minimizing the total length over all links. The optimal solution emerges from repeated application of simple permutation.

Permutation transformation is not as straightforward as it appears. It must be constrained in a number of ways:

1. The randomly selected links must be distinct—no triangular subnetworks are allowed. If this is not possible, give up trying after m attempts.
2. Beware of existing links—we cannot duplicate existing links during a flip. Try to flip links vertically, and if that fails, try flipping them horizontally. If both fail, terminate the attempt.
3. Beware of components—terminate the emergent process if the network has more than one component. Avoid flipping links that lead to multiple components.
4. If steps 1–3 fail, revert to the previous topology and return the previous total length. Otherwise, retain the new topology and return the shorter total length.

The following Java method takes the current total length as an argument, and returns either a new total length or the original argument. Because it uses link permutations, the original network topology is preserved. Hence, this optimization is an applications of a fixed-point transformation. The total length decreases—when possible—by exchanging a longer link for a shorter link. Over time, total length reaches the minimum because all shorter links have been found.

Method isComponent(0) traverses the entire network commencing from node 0, to determine whether the network is strongly connected. It returns **true** if every node in $G(t)$ is reachable from node 0. If permutation causes the network to become disconnected, the permutation is abandoned. Once again, the microrule terminates if m attempts to flip a link pair fail. This method is repeated until reaching convergence. In the next section, we estimate how many iterations are needed to achieve convergence to the optimal solution.

```
public double NW_doShorter(double length) {
    String M = "+Shorten: Length = ";
    int link1 = (int)(nLinks * Math.random()); //Choose 2 links
    int link2 = (int)(nLinks * Math.random());
    int count = 0;                              //Avoid infinite loop
    while(count < nLinks
                        &&
        (Link[link2].head == Link[link1].head  //Distinct end nodes
                        ||
        Link[link2].head == Link[link1].tail
                        ||
        Link[link2].tail == Link[link1].head
                        ||
        Link[link2].tail == Link[link1].tail)){
```

```
        link2 = (int)(nLinks * Math.random());   //Distinct end nodes
        count++;
    }
    int saved_head1 = Link[ link1] .head;              //For revert...
    int saved_tail1 = Link[ link1] .tail;
    int saved_head2 = Link[ link2] .head;
    int saved_tail2 = Link[ link2] .tail;
    boolean flip = (count < nLinks);                   //Feasible to flip
    if(!flip) return length;                           //Otherwise give up
    if(Math.random() < 0.5){                           //Duplicate?
        flip = (!isConnected(Link[link1].tail, Link[link2].head))
                              &&
              (!isConnected(Link[link2].tail, Link[link1].head));
        if(flip){                              //Flip vertical
           Link[link1].head = Link[link2].head;
           Link[link2].head = saved_head1;
        }
    }                                              //Duplicate?
    else { flip = (!isConnected(Link[ link1] .head, Link[ link2] .head))
                              &&
               (!isConnected(Link[link1].tail, Link[link2].tail));
           if(flip){                              //Flip horizontal
              Link[link1].head = Link[link2].head;
              Link[link1].tail = saved_head1;
              Link[link2].tail = saved_tail1;
              Link[link2].head = saved_tail2;
           }
    }
    if(flip){                                          //No duplicates
           flip = isComponent(0);                 //Strongly connected?
           double new_length = NW_total_length(); //Has it shortened?
           if(new_length <= length && flip){
              Message = M+Double.toString(new_length)+" Flipped Links.";
              return new_length;
           }
    }
    Link[link1].head = saved_head1;                    //Revert
    Link[link1].tail = saved_tail1;
    Link[link2].head = saved_head2;
    Link[link2].tail = saved_tail2;
    Message = M+Double.toString(length)+" Warning: Cannot Permute Links.";
    return length;
}//NW_doShorter
```

7.6.2 Optimization by Deterministic Permutation

The foregoing emergent process seems wasteful of effort because of the unpredictability of random link pair selection. Is a deterministic algorithm for finding the minimum total length faster? Does it model natural processes? We next show that a deterministic algorithm takes approximately the same time, but does not represent natural processes, because it uses a purposeful or deterministic search heuristic.

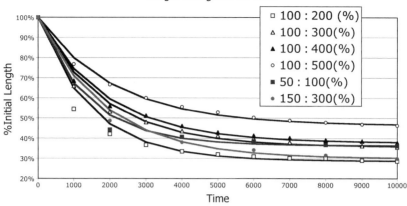

Figure 7.11   Emergence of shortest length/initial length for networks with $n : m$ nodes and links, and over $t = [0, 10,000]$ timesteps.

The minimum total length can be found in time proportional to $C_2^m = m((m - 1)/2)$ steps by simply enumerating all possible combinations of link pairs. Repeated passes over the link pairs reduces the length objective function and guarantees the minimum. Keep in mind that the emergent network must conform to the degree sequence of the original, so flipping of link pairs is still restricted as before. This combinatorially complex algorithm requires multiple passes, each of time complexity equal to $O(C_2^m)$.

A deterministic algorithm repeatedly forms pairs, starting from link 1, and link 2, link 3, to link n, then pairs from link 2 and links 3, 4, to link n, and so on until pair $(n - 1)$ and n are formed. Each pair is tested to see if the permutation retains the same degree sequence and does not create duplicates or disconnect the network. Each pass makes $m(m-1)/2$ comparisons. Multiple passes are required until length no longer declines. Typically, a dozen or so passes are required for the size of networks studied in Fig. 7.11.

The deterministic algorithm takes a multiple of $O(C_2^m)$ timesteps, which is very large for high m. For example, a network with $m = 1000$ links takes perhaps $10(C_2^{1000}) = 4,995,000$ timesteps to complete! Can we do better with the random emergent algorithm? As it turns out, the answer is "Mostly not." Both algorithms take approximately the same time because nodes are randomly spread over a 2D surface. Selection of links by deterministic order is "as random" as selection by random permutation. In fact, randomization intuitively takes longer to examine all link pairs. As we shall see below, there is little difference between the two approaches.

7.6.3   Model of Minimum-Length Emergence

Figure 7.11 shows the results of running method NW_doShorter() on a number of randomly generated and randomly scattered networks ranging in size from $n = 50$ to $n = 400$, and $m = 100$ to $m = 800$. Clearly, the minimum-length network emerges exponentially over time. Figure 7.11 plots the percentage of initial length versus time, from $t = 0$ to $t = 10,000$. While 10,000 timesteps do not guarantee convergence to the absolute minimum, it is clear that the emergence algorithm approaches minimum total length asymptotically within 10,000 timesteps, at least for the size of networks studied in Fig. 7.11.

Intuitively, total length increases proportional to m, because higher m means more links to sum. Total length should vary inversely proportional to sqrt(n), because sqrt(n) × sqrt(n) nodes are randomly scattered over a fixed area. As n increases, we must compress the space between nodes to fit all n nodes into the fixed-size area. Therefore, the separation distance between nodes decreases as sqrt(n).

Let α be a constant of proportionality and L the total length:

$$L \sim \alpha \frac{m}{\sqrt{n}} = \sum e_i$$

where e_i is the length of link i and summation is over all links.

Now consider the emergence of minimum total length as a function of time. Let $L(t)$ be the total length at timestep t, $L_0 = L(0)$, and let $L_\infty = L(\infty)$ be the minimum value guaranteed after infinite time. Initially, the randomly scattered nodes are connected by m links of total length $L_0 = \sum e_i$, but as time passes, the difference between current length $L(t)$, and minimum length L declines. We conjecture that the rate of change is proportional to this difference and the proportionality defined above:

$$\frac{\delta L}{\delta t} = \alpha \frac{m}{\sqrt{n}} [L_\infty - L(t)]$$

This first-order differential equation with boundary conditions specified by L_0 and L_∞ has the following solution:

$$L(t) = L_\infty + [L_\infty - L_0] \exp\left(-\alpha \frac{nt}{\sqrt{n}}\right)$$

After dividing by L_0 to convert $L(t)$ to a percentage $L'(t)$, and substitution of $A = (L_\infty/L_0)$, we obtain the model used to plot the solid lines in Fig. 7.11. This model is parameterized by A and α:

$$L'(t) = \frac{L(t)}{L_0} = A + [1 - A] \exp\left(-\alpha \frac{mt}{\sqrt{n}}\right)$$

In Fig. 7.11 we obtain estimates for $A = L'(10,000)$ and $\alpha = \alpha$-bar, by averaging over t:

$$\alpha - \text{bar} = \text{average}\left\{\frac{-\sqrt{n}}{mt} \sum \ln\left[\frac{L'(t) - A}{1 - A}\right]\right\}; \quad t = 0, 1, 2, \ldots, k$$

Parameter k is obtained by noting that we sample once every 1000 timesteps, which yields $k = 10$ in Fig. 7.11. Generally, the minimum, L_∞, is $O(m/\sqrt{n})$, but the exact

TABLE 7.5 Parameters Obtained from Fig. 7.11^a

n	m	$m\dfrac{m-1}{2}$	A	a	$a\dfrac{m-1}{\sqrt{n}}$
50	100	4,950	0.363	5.08E−05	7.19E−04
50	300	44,850	0.552	1.24E−05	5.28E−04
150	300	44,850	0.299	2.18E−05	5.34E−04
100	200	19,900	0.287	3.39E−05	6.78E−04
100	300	44,850	0.357	1.83E−05	5.50E−04
100	400	79,800	0.377	1.31E−05	5.26E−04
100	500	124,750	0.463	9.37E−06	4.68E−04

^{a}"Scientific" notation has been used here to conserve space (e.g., 5.08E−05 instead of 5.08×10^{-5}).

value is determined by parameter α. The larger α, the faster the minimum value L_∞ emerges.

Table 7.5 summarizes useful values and model parameters obtained by the experiments shown in Fig. 7.11. The reader can verify the correlation between the minimum L_∞ and $O(m\sqrt{n})$ by plotting the values in column A versus the values in the last column of Table 7.5. The reader can also verify that the optimal solution can be found within $10[m((m-1)/2)]$ timesteps.

7.6.4 Two-Dimensional Layouts

With the foregoing theory in place, we can apply the emergence method to practical layout problems such as wiring components on a printed circuit board. Suppose that we attach components on one side and wires connecting components point-to-point on the other side of the printed circuit board. This way, wires do not need to be routed around the components. We want to minimize the cost of wiring by minimizing the length of wire.

Further, components are connected by two wires—one input and one output. Therefore, the degree sequence distribution is that of a 1-regular network where all nodes have degree equal to 2. In fact, we construct the initial network, $G(0)$, by generating a 1-regular network, and then laying out the components (nodes) where we want them on the printed circuit board (see Fig. 7.12a). Once we have the nodes arranged on the board, we apply the emergence procedure and watch as the shortest-length configuration emerges (see Fig. 7.12b).

Figure 7.12 shows the initial network layout followed by the minimum-length result obtained by emergence. The total length of wiring before optimization is 1778 units, and after optimization it is 1329 units—a decrease of 25%. Also, note that the best layout forms a circular graph (*ring network*) by connecting nearest neighbors. Once we realize this, we can manually wire any 1-regular network by simply attaching wires to the nearest adjacent nodes.

The shortest-length wiring example illustrates a general idea: that complex optimization problems that are not easily described by equations or models with complex

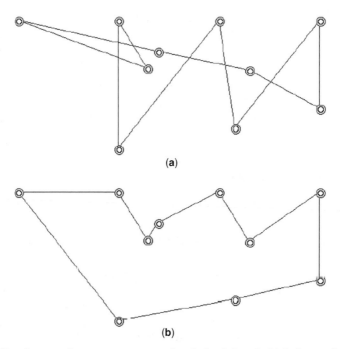

Figure 7.12 Layout of components on a printed circuit board: (a) before optimization—initial 1-regular network with $L_0 = 1778$; (b) after random emergence optimization—emerged 1-regular network with $L_\infty = 1329$.

boundary conditions can be solved by emergence. For example, complex flow models, restrictive degree sequence distributions, and nonlinear "cost models" might be impossible to solve analytically, but easily solved by emergence. However, time complexity may be very high, as illustrated by the costly minimum-length emergence.

7.7 EXERCISES

7.1. What is the approximate maximum hub degree of a "hub emerged network" containing $n = 100$ nodes and $m = 500$ links (Fig. 7.2), after 5000 timesteps? After 100,000 timesteps?

7.2. How many timesteps does it take to produce a hub with degree 100 by hub emergence, when $n = 100$ and $m = 1000$?

7.3. What is the entropy of a hub emerged network containing $n = 100$ nodes and $m = 500$ links (Fig. 7.3), after 5000 timesteps? After 100,000 timesteps?

7.4. Use program *Network.jar* to obtain estimates of parameters A, B, C, and D in the approximation for $I(G)$. What are the parameter's values for $n = 100$ and density 5%? For density 20%?

7.5. What is the approximate avg_path_length of the hub emergent network of density 10% shown in Fig. 7.3, after $t = 10,000$ iterations?

7.6. Collect results from *Network.jar* and construct a model of average path length versus time for the hub emergent networks of Fig. 7.3. What is the model of average path length versus maximum hub_degree?

7.7. Collect results from *Network.jar* and construct a model of cluster coefficient versus maximum hub_degree for the hub emergent network of Fig. 7.3. What is the relationship between cluster coefficient and elapsed time?

7.8. Approximately how many timesteps does it take to double the cluster coefficient of a random network, $n = 100$, $m = 500$, using the cluster coefficient emergent microrules? Assume that the initial cluster coefficient is 0.10.

7.9. Degree sequence emergence is guaranteed to converge only when duplicate links are permitted. Confirm this claim by modifying the NW_doAddLink() method in *Network.jar* and running the "per node" emergence algorithm on a number of examples.

7.10. Approximately how many timesteps does it take to reduce the total link length of a random network with $n = 50$ randomly scattered nodes, $m = 250$ links, to 75% of its initial length?

7.11. Consider a network model of the Koch string illustrated in Fig. 7.13. $G(0)$ initially consists of $n = 5$ nodes and $m = 4$ links of length 1, so the total length of $G(0)$ links is 4. We repeatedly apply the following rule at each time-step to all links in parallel: Replace each link of G with a replica of $G(0)$, but with links $\frac{1}{3}$ the length of the replaced link. Thus, $G(1)$ length is $\frac{16}{3}$. What is the

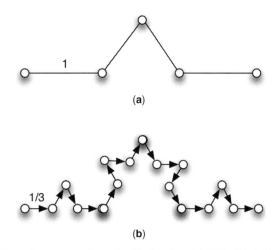

Figure 7.13 Network representations of a Koch string: (a) $G(0)$; (b) $G(1)$. At each time step the string replaces all of its links with a $\frac{1}{3}$ replica of $G(0)$.

expression for the total length of links of $G(t)$, and does this emergent process converge?

7.12. What does hub emergence do to the max_degree navigation path length after $t = 10,000$ iterations on a random network, $G(0)$, with $n = 50$ and $m = 200$?

7.13. Which of the following degree sequences are realizable by the Mihail et al. emergent process, for $n = 5$? Explain why the nonrealizable sequences are not realizable:

(a) {5,4,3,2,1}

(b) {2,3,1,1,1}

(c) {2,3,2,2,1}

(d) {1,3,2,2,1}

7.14. What is the shortest link length topology of a 1-regular network of n nodes arranged around a circular surface (disk) with diameter equal to 200? Assume that the degree of all nodes equals 2, and that the nodes are initially placed randomly on the circumference of the circular disk. What is the limiting value of the shortest total link length as n increases without bound?

8

EPIDEMICS

Mathematical models of epidemics have a long history reaching back to 1927, when Kermack and McKendrick fist postulated the mathematical model that still bears their name. The Kermack–McKendrick is a birth–death model—new actors in a population contract the infection with a certain rate, infected actors either die or recover with another rate, and everyone else in the population is susceptible. The model expresses the spread of an infection in terms of three rate equations, which can be solved analytically or numerically, depending on the complexity of assumptions.

For example, the SIR (susceptible–infected–removed) variant assumes that actors are in one of three states: susceptible, infected, or removed. Actors move from one state to the other, according to probabilities. A susceptible actor becomes infected with probability γ, the infection rate, and then moves into the recovered or removed state with probability Δ, the deathrate. The SIS (susceptible–infected–susceptible) variant assumes that actors recover from the infection and become eligible to contract the infection, again. The SIS model is of particular interest because it is possible, under certain conditions, for SIS contagions to persist, forever (indefinitely).

A variety of more complex models have been derived from the Kermack–McKendrick model. These models have been adapted to represent propagation of a contagion in human epidemiology as well as a variety of other fields. For example, epidemic models have been used to represent the spread of an idea, product, and faults in physical systems. Epidemic models are useful in other fields besides the study of human disease propagation.

Network Science: Theory and Practice. By Ted G. Lewis
Copyright © 2009 John Wiley & Sons, Inc.

Prior to the 1990s, most epidemic models assumed uniform of *homogeneous mixing*—the population of susceptible actors are spread uniformly throughout a geographic area, and the probability of contracting the infection is uniformly the same for all actors. Homogeneous mixing ignores pockets of highly congested actors, proximity, and frequency of contact. It also assumes that every actor eventually comes into contact with every other actor. Uniformity of contact simplifies the analysis, but is unrealistic for most applications of epidemic modeling.

This chapter is about network epidemics—epidemics that consider the nonhomogeneous structure of real populations. Links are used to model contact and nodes, to model actors. Actors may be in one state at a time: susceptible, infected, removed, or recovered. Network epidemiology is about the spread of a contagion throughout a network. Unlike the classical Kermack–McKendrick model, network epidemic models consider the topology of the network as well as infection rate, deathrate, and state transitions.

More generally, a *network epidemic* is a process of widespread and rapid propagation of a contagion through a network. Typically, the contagion is a condition of network nodes (working, failing, dormant, active, etc.) brought about by adjacent nodes through propagation along one or more links. Propagation by links means that node u is infected by node v through a connecting link: $u \sim v$. The *infection rate* $\gamma(v)$ is the probability that propagation of the contagion at node v successfully infects adjacent nodes via one or more of its links. Therefore, propagation is a function of the state of nodes, the network's topology, and the infection rate.

Network epidemics make excellent models for the study of many social and physical systems that support propagation of a signal:

1. Spread of a disease among living organisms, such as the common cold in human populations
2. Spread of malicious software (worms, viruses) throughout the Internet
3. Spread of interest in a product or fashion, such as music, movie, or clothing style
4. Spread of an idea, concept, news, or popular notion (e.g., that the earth is the center of the universe)
5. Propagation of a fault or failure in a material or system, such as the domino effect of a power grid outage

Network epidemics are a kind of dynamic process related to emergence and stability of networks—a topic that we discuss in the next chapter. Conceptually, the spread of an infection introduces instability into a system (infection) much like chaos in a nonlinear system. If the infection dies out, the system reaches a fixed point and remains there. If the infection recurs, the system oscillates, (indefinitely). In epidemiology, epidemics that die out are members of the class of SIR processes, and epidemics that do not, are members of SIS processes. An SIS process that oscillates between susceptible and infected, forever, is also called a *persistent process*.

This chapter initiates the study of SIR and SIS processes, as follows:

1. A *network epidemic* is a process whereby a node state or node condition is propagated through a network via links. Network epidemics are different from classical epidemics because the manner of propagation is determined by the topology of the network as well as classical parameters such as infection rate γ, recovery rate Δ, and time to recover t_r.

2. There are two general classifications of epidemics: SIR (susceptible–infected–removed) and SIS (susceptible–infected–susceptible). SIR network epidemics eventually die out (either every actor is removed or no actor remains infected), while SIS network epidemics may or may not die out, depending on the threshold, τ.

3. Epidemic threshold τ determines whether an SIS epidemic persists ($\tau > 1$) or dies out ($\tau < 1$). In the classical Kermack–McKendrick model of epidemics, which assumes large and homogeneous populations, τ is a function of γ and Δ, but for finite, nonhomogeneous networks, we show that τ is determined mostly by the network's spectral radius, ρ.

4. The peak infection density of an SIR network epidemic follows a power-law function of mean degree λ as follows: $i_{max} = A((1 - B)/\lambda^q)$, where parameters A, B, and q are determined by curve fitting. This approximation works for random, small-world, and scale-free networks, but with different parameter values, A, B, and q, for each class of network.

5. After sufficient time, an SIS epidemic on a *random* network either dies out with probability τ, or grows to fixed point, $i_\infty = (1 - \tau)$, with probability $(1 - \tau)$, where threshold, $\tau = \Delta/v$, and $v = \gamma\lambda$. Hence, threshold and fixed-point density of a finite, random network are determined by infection rate γ, recovery rate Δ, and the network's connectivity λ.[1]

6. The model of Z. Wang, Chakrabarti, C. Wang, and Faloutsos (*WCWF model*) defines the threshold $\tau = \rho(\mathbf{A})$, for any network with spectral radius $\rho(\mathbf{A})$.[2] We derive a modified quadratic WCWF model that improves the WCWF approximation for a larger range of probabilities: $\tau = \Delta/\gamma = \rho(\mathbf{A})(B - A\gamma)$, for parameters A and B, with

$$A = O\left(\lambda + \frac{\lambda}{\rho(A)}\right), \quad B = O\left(\frac{1}{\rho(A)}\right)$$

7. We show that fixed-point infection density i_∞ decreases linearly with spectral radius ρ in arbitrary networks according to $i_\infty = b - m\rho$, near the epidemic threshold. Parameters $b = 36\%$ and $m = 1\%$ for the experimental networks studied here (random, scale-free, small-world, and star networks of size $n = 100$ and 200 nodes).

8. An *antigen* is a *countermeasure* contagion that spreads like an epidemic but removes infection from infected nodes and inoculates susceptible nodes from

---

[1]Connectivity and mean degree are the same thing in a random network.
[2]WCWF define $\tau = \gamma/\Delta$, so their result is $\tau = 1/\rho(A)$.

future infection. We show that the most effective deployment of a countermeasure antigen starts at the hub or maximum-closeness node. The least effective countermeasure deploys the antigen at a randomly selected initial node.

9. We claim that the best way to "cure the Internet," and similar networks, is to strategically seed the Internet with antigens placed at network hubs or maximum-closeness routers and switches. The least effective way is to deploy antiviral software on desktop and laptop client computers, as we currently do.

This chapter uses program *Network.jar* to generate and analyze the epidemics described here. The Java methods given in this chapter are simplified versions of the code found in *Network.jar*, and are activated by the INFECT and ANTIGEN buttons on the front panel of *Network.jar*.

8.1 EPIDEMIC MODELS

Mathematical modeling of epidemics goes back to 1927 with the formulation of the classical Kermack–McKendrick equations. This pioneering model made many simplifying assumptions that have been relaxed over the past decades, but it still serves as a basic starting point. We describe it and then point out the assumptions that no longer apply to finite networks. Next, we adapt the classical model to networks, which establishes the fundamentals of network epidemiology.

The Kermack–McKendrick model assumes *homogeneous mixing*—the actors in the population are uniformly separated and uniformly likely to be exposed to one another. The model also assumes that the population is very large—large enough to ignore the finiteness of n. This may work in general, but limits the usefulness of the model when applied to finite networks. Finiteness of population increases the difficulty of accurately modeling an epidemic in a network, because the topology of the network can no longer be ignored. Furthermore, it is more realistic to assume that actors come into contact with a much smaller subset of the total population and, therefore, that networks more accurately represent real life.

We present the classical model and then proceed to adapt it to finite, structured networks. One of the major questions answered in this chapter is, "How does removal of the homogeneous mixing assumption affect the network model"? Another question addressed is that of structure: "What role does network topology play in determining the spread of a contagion in a network?" We show that topology largely determines infection spreading in a network as measured by the *spectral radius* of its *adjacency matrix*.

8.1.1 The Kermack–McKendrick Model

The first mathematical model of an epidemic was proposed by W. O. Kermack and A. G. McKendrick in 1927 and now bears their names (Kermack, 1927). The *Kermack–McKendrick model* assumes *homogeneous mixing* (where everyone has an equal chance of contracting the disease from anyone else) and a very large population (where n is unbounded).

In what follows, we use the terms *actor* and *node* interchangeably, in keeping with the social network analysis literature. The *connectivity* of an actor is exactly its degree, and the *adjacent nodes* are its neighbors. The connectivity of a network is characterized by the mean degree, λ.

The Kermack–McKendrick model classifies every actor according to one of four states: (1) an actor is *susceptible* if it can possibly become infected; (2) *infected*, if it has contracted the contagion; (3) *recovered*, if it has recovered from the infection and is now immune to future infection; and (4) *removed*, if it has died from the effects of the infection. We define γ as the rate of infection, Δ as the rate of removal or recovery, and t_r as the duration of a node's infected state before transition to a removed or recovered state.

Let $S(t)$ be the number of susceptible actors, $I(t)$ the number of infected actors, and $R(t)$ the number of actors removed from the population as a result of death or immunity after recovering from the illness, at time t. In a finite population, $n = S(t) + I(t) + R(t)$. The Kermack–McKendrick equations relate S, I, and R to one another through their time rate of change and initial conditions, as follows:

$$\frac{\delta S(t)}{\delta t} = -\gamma S(t)I(t); \quad S(0) = S_0 \tag{I}$$

$$\frac{\delta I(t)}{\delta t} = \gamma S(t)I(t) - \Delta I(t); \quad I(0) = I_0 \tag{II}$$

$$\frac{\delta R(t)}{\delta t} = \Delta I(t); \quad R(0) = R_0 \tag{III}$$

$$S(t) + I(t) + R(t) = n \tag{IV}$$

Equation I states that the rate of change in the number of susceptible actors declines proportional to the number of susceptible and infected actors. This claim is also tied to equation II because the number of susceptible actors increases or decreases in the opposite direction of the number of infected actors. Equation II says that the rate of change in the number of infected actors increases in proportion to the number of susceptible and infected actors, minus the number of infected actors that have been removed. The logic of equation II is that infection spreads from infected actors to susceptible actors. The more of each (susceptible and infected), the faster the contagion will spread. Equation III expresses a simple linear relationship between the number of infected and the rate at which they are removed. Equation IV says that the population remains constant regardless of the number of actors in each of the states.

It is often easier to work with normalized versions of S, I, and R, called *densities*,

$$s = \frac{S(t)}{n}, \quad i = \frac{I(t)}{n}, \quad r = \frac{R(t)}{n}$$

instead. In this case, we use lowercase notation without changing γ and Δ. The Kermack–McKendrick equations still hold, but solutions to s, i, and r fall into the interval $[0,1]$ instead of $[0,n]$. In terms of the normalized or density of actors in each state, we obtain

$$\frac{\delta s}{\delta t} = -\gamma si; \quad s(0) = s_0$$

$$\frac{\delta i}{\delta t} = \gamma si - \Delta i; \quad i(0) = i_0$$

$$\frac{\delta r}{\delta t} = \Delta i; \quad r(0) = r_0$$

$$s + i + r = 1$$

For example, assume $\Delta = 0$, $s + i = 1$, and solve for $i(t)$:

$$\frac{\delta i}{\delta t} = \gamma si = \gamma(1 - i)i; \quad i(0) = i_0$$

Rearrange terms in the differential equation, and integrate by parts:

$$\frac{\delta i}{i(1 - i)} = \gamma \, dt$$

$$\ln(i) - \ln(i_0) - \ln(1 - i) + \ln(1 - i_0) = \gamma \, t$$

where $\ln( )$ is the natural logarithm. Let $A = (1 - i_0)/i_0$, and solve for $i(t)$:

$$i(t) = \frac{1}{1 + A \exp(-\gamma t)}; \quad t \geq 0$$

This is the famous *logistic growth curve* found in many disciplines dealing with growth phenomena. It is shaped like an "S" and hence is known as an *S curve*. Solution to the simplified Kermack–McKendrick equations, under the assumption $\Delta = 0$, follows the logistic growth curve as the epidemic grows from some small value to 100% of the population, tracing out the S-shaped logistics growth curve (see Fig. 8.1).

Continuing with the example, suppose that $i_0 = 0.05$ (5%), and $\gamma = 0.75$ (75%), the density of infected actors at time $t = 10$ is 98.96%:

$$A = \frac{1 - 0.05}{0.05} = 19$$

$$i(10) = \frac{1}{1 + 19 \exp(-0.75(10))} = 0.9896 \ (98.96\%)$$

A plot of $i(t)$ versus t is shown in Fig. 8.1. If the population $n = 100$, then 99 actors will contract the infection by $t = 10$.

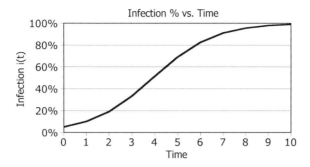

Figure 8.1 Logistics growth curve with $\gamma = 75\%$ and $i_0 = 5\%$.

8.1.2 Epidemic Thresholds

Nonlinear effects, such as the population reaching an epidemic threshold, and staying there, or oscillating between infected and susceptible states, complicate the behavior of an epidemic, especially in a finite population. In some epidemics, the contagion never dies out, while in others the number of infected actors reaches a peak and then subsides. *Epidemic threshold* τ is the infection rate that determines whether an infection recurs forever, or eventually dies out. Under certain conditions, an epidemic will die out if the infection rate $\gamma < \tau$, and persist, otherwise. When $\gamma \geq \tau$, we say that the epidemic *persists* and reaches a *fixed point*, $0 < i_\infty < 1$, and stays there forever. Epidemic threshold τ determines the balance between infection rate and recovery/removal rate that is barely sufficient to sustain a persistent epidemic, and i_∞ is the *fixed-point value* of a persistent epidemic. An epidemic is *endemic* if it persists and *pandemic* if it is widespread.

We are interested in discovering the conditions under which an epidemic becomes persistent and reaches a level of infectiousness without dying off. This leads to a quest for answers to the following questions:

1. What is the threshold τ that separates a persistent epidemic from one that dies out?
2. What conditions on λ and Δ lead to persistent epidemics?
3. What is the fixed point i_∞ for a persistent epidemic?
4. Are *network epidemics* any different from classical epidemics, and if so, why?
5. What countermeasures are most effective against epidemics?

The first two questions are addressed by careful modeling of the effects of infection rate and removal rate on threshold, and then modifying the classical Kermack–McKendrick equations to accurately model network epidemics. We show that network topology must be considered to obtain accurate results. The third question is answered by curve-fitting simulation data to a plot of fixed-point density versus *spectral radius* ρ. We show that the relationship—over the range of networks studied—is linear.

We also show why network epidemics differ from the classical model; epidemics in networks are shaped by the topology of the network. It does not matter whether a network is random, scale-free, or small-world as much as does connectivity—as measured by mean degree and spectral radius.

Finally, we show that the best countermeasure for eradication of a viral epidemic, such as the spread of a cyber virus via the Internet, is an antigen epidemic that started at the hub of the network. Hub seeding leads to faster eradication and a lower peak infection. This important result has immediate implications for combating the spread of malicious Internet software.

8.1.3   The Susceptible–Infected–Removed (SIR) Model

The susceptible–infected–removed (SIR) model is of particular interest in the study of animal populations because it models biological reality: each actor of a population goes through several states representing the contagion's progress: susceptible, infected, and recovered or removed. *Susceptible* means that an actor is susceptible to the infection, *infected* means that the actor has contracted the contagion, *recovered* means the actor has recovered from the contagion and is immune to subsequent infection, and *removed* means that the actor has died and is no longer susceptible or has recovered.

The SIR model is rigorously defined by is state diagram (see Fig. 8.2a). Initially, all nodes are susceptible, so this state applies to everyone in the population. Then a fraction of the population, i_0, contracts the infection and infects their neighbors, spreading the infection throughout the population.

In Fig. 8.2, "tr" is the recovery time t_r for actors in the SIR model; an infected actor remains infected for "tr" time units before it either dies (is removed) or recovers (becomes immune). An infected actor is removed with probability equal to "death-rate," or recovers and is immune to subsequent infection with probability equal to "1 − deathrate."

Initially, a small percentage of the population is infected. But, as we showed earlier, the percentage of infected actors increases according to an S-shaped curve until reaching a maximally infected peak. Subsequently, the density of infected actors declines as the number of infected, recovered, or removed actors reaches a maximum—there are simply fewer susceptible actors. The density of infected actors must decline because of an increase in the density of actors that have died or become immune. Thus, the profile of an SIR epidemic is wave-like (see Fig. 8.3).

Contrary to the SIR model, the SIS model allows for actors in the population to recover and become susceptible to the infection once again. Recurring or persistent SIS epidemics are observed in nature and on the Internet. We return to the SIS model in the next section.

The state diagrams of Fig. 8.2 annotate the probability of each state change with a label on each transition link, except for transition 3 of the SIR state diagram. For example, "2: infect" means that transition 2 occurs with probability γ. For the SIR state diagram, "3: tr > 0" means an infected actor remains infected as long as the duration of the infection is greater than zero. For each actor, t_r is set when the actor is infected, and decremented at each timestep, until reaching zero.

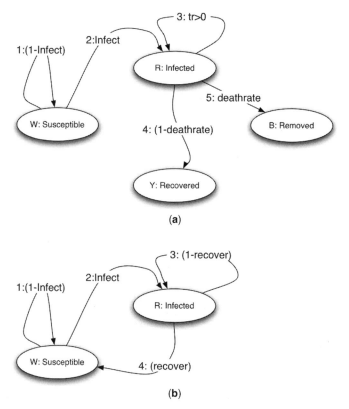

Figure 8.2 Models of epidemics: (a) SIR; (b) SIS (color code used by simulation program *Network.jar*: W—susceptible = white; R—infected = red; B—removed = black; Y—recovered = yellow).

Nodes are marked with a color—white indicates the susceptible state, red indicates the infected state, black indicates the removed state, and yellow indicates the recovered state.[3] Once an actor is removed (black) or recovered (yellow), it stays in the removed or recovered state.

The SIR model approximates what happens in nature—an infection strikes a single actor and then propagates the infection to neighboring individuals with probability γ. Each infection lasts for t_r time units. When the recovery/removal time elapses, the actor either succumbs to the infection with probability Δ, or recovers with probability $(1-\Delta)$.

The precise shape of the infection density curve is dictated by the values of γ, Δ, and t_r. Obviously, the higher the infection rate γ, the higher the infected population density at the peak of the wave (see Fig. 8.3a). However, the timespan of the wave stretches when the infection rate is lower because propagation is slower. Figure 8.3a shows how infection rate affects both the maximum density of infected

---

[3]These colors correspond to the color scheme of the nodes in *Network.jar*.

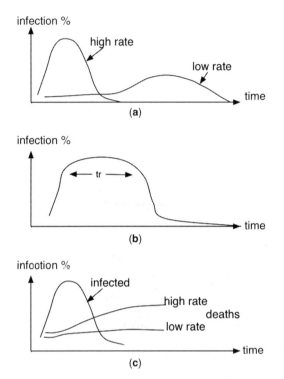

Figure 8.3 Infected actor density versus time for various epidemic parameter values: (a) infection rate variation; (b) long recovery time; (c) deathrate variation.

actors at the peak of the infection wave and the length of time that the contagion is active and spreading.

Increasing the removal rate Δ increases the percentage of the population that is removed or recovers, but has little effect on the percentage of infected. It merely changes the ratio of removed to recovered actors. Figure 8.3c shows a higher percentage of deaths when Δ is higher, and a lower deathrate when Δ is lower. This makes sense, because SIR removes actors only when they are infected, and the percentage of susceptible actors is the same regardless of the percentage of removed actors.

In general, increasing recovery time t_r also increases the percentage of infected actors, and broadens the wave-shaped curve (see Fig. 8.3b). For a given infection rate, greater recovery time flattens and raises the infection wave's peak. Intuitively, this is because infected actors remain infected for a longer period of time before recovering or being removed with probability Δ. The longer an actor is infected, the more opportunities it has to infect others.

The peak of the infection wave of a SIR epidemic in a random network also increases with the connectivity of the random network. Recall that *connectivity* is another way of expressing the density of a random network, because density increases when mean degree increases. If we hold γ, Δ, and t_r constant, then peak SIR infection in a random network must increase as a function of λ.

This is exactly what we observe in Fig. 8.4, for $\gamma = \Delta = 20\%$ and $t_r = 10$. For random networks, peak infection density obeys a power law:

$$i_{max} = A\frac{1-B}{\lambda^q}$$

where A, B, q are determined by curve fitting. The excellent fit shown in Fig. 8.4 was obtained from parameters $A = 1.03$, $B = 4.0$, and $q = 2.4$. In addition to the infection rate, recovery rate, and infection duration, Fig. 8.4 shows that peak infection is also related to the connectivity of a network. Moreover, we can estimate peak infection in a random network using a power-law function. This experiment is limited, but it shows that network epidemics differ from classical Kermack–McKendrick epidemics in an important way—network topology matters.

Does the power–law relationship between peak infection density and connectivity hold true for nonrandom networks? What are the peak infection rates of scale-free and small-world networks when an SIR epidemic breaks out?

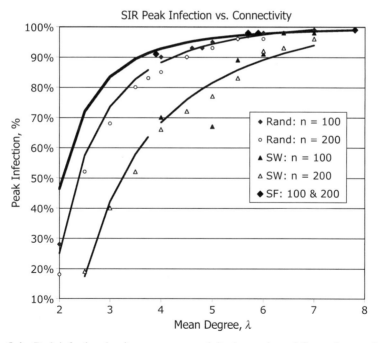

Figure 8.4 Peak infection density versus connectivity (mean degree) for random, scale-free, and small-world networks with $\gamma = \Delta = 20\%$, $t_r = 10$. Data were collected for Erdos–Renyi (ER) random, Watts–Strogatz (WS) small-world ($p = 10\%$), and Barabasi–Albert (BA) networks ($\Delta m = 2$) of size $n = 100$ and $n = 200$ nodes.

8.1.4 Peak Infection Density in Structured Networks

Figure 8.4 shows that peak infection density is a function of connectivity and therefore density in a random network. Does this relationship hold for structured networks such as a small-world or scale-free population? The answer is "Yes," but the power-law exponent differs in each class of network. The difference in peak infection densities for random, small-world, and scale-free networks is due to differences in the exponent of the power law (see Table 8.1). The higher the connectivity, the higher the peak infection density in each class of network. But the rate of increase is not as direct; small-world networks are located at one extreme of a spectrum of parameter values, and scale-free networks are at another extreme. We show that estimation of the rate and extent of infection spreading must incorporate density and a structural metric such as *spectral radius*.

Table 8.1 suggests that the power-law exponent is greatest for a scale-free network, second greatest for a random network, and much smaller for a small-world network. It is easy to understand why scale-free networks have such high peaks—hubs are *super-spreaders* of infection. Networks with very large hubs are very contagious. It is less obvious why random networks are nearly as contagious. Small-world networks are least contagious because they have clusters instead of hubs. Clusters tend to spread infection among close-knit neighborhoods more than do long-haul connections. This effect becomes more pronounced as density of links declines, as seen in Fig. 8.4. It is also reflected in the relatively low exponent, $q = 1.7$, in Table 8.1.

Figure 8.4 makes an important point: that infection density is more than a function of network density as measured by mean degree λ. Obviously, mean degree of a scale-free network is not very representative of the connectivity of its hub, nor does mean degree correlate with clustering of a small world. What metric incorporates both network density and topological structure? Recall that spectral radius ρ measures density and "amount of departure" from random network structure in an arbitrary network. What if we use the spectral radius to represent the connectivity of a network, instead of mean degree?

Figure 8.5 plots spectral radius of random, small-world, and scale-free networks versus connectivity λ. We know from Chapter 2 that spectral radius of a random network is identical to mean degree λ. Spectral radius of a star network is $\sqrt{(\text{hub})}$, and everything else falls in between. When topology is not random, but falls somewhere in between purely random and purely regular, spectral radius measures not only connectivity but also the nonuniformity of the topology as well. Spectral

TABLE 8.1   Curve-Fit Values for Fig. 8.4 Parameters

Parameter	Class of Network		
	Random	Small-World	Scale-Free
A	1.03	1.10	1.00
B	4.00	4.00	4.00
q	2.4	1.7	2.9

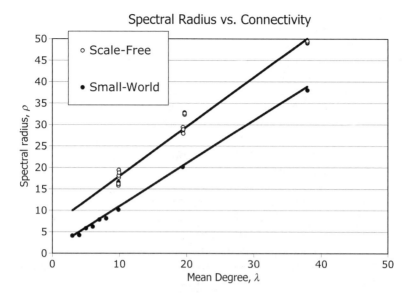

Figure 8.5 Linear relationship between spectral radius ρ and mean degree λ for scale-free and small-world networks with $n = 100, 200$.

radius is a better property for epidemic modeling than is mean degree or homogeneous mixing.

Figure 8.5 shows that spectral radius ρ varies linearly with λ, but at different rates for different classes of networks: $\rho(\lambda) = A\lambda + B$; where A, B are slope and intercept, respectively.

We find values of A and B by curve-fitting straight lines to the data provided in Fig. 8.5. For small-world networks, we assume a rewiring probability of 10%, and obtain the following parameter values:

$$
\begin{aligned}
\text{Random:} \quad & A = 1, \quad B = 0 \\
\text{Small-world:} \quad & A = 1, \quad B = 1 \\
\text{Scale-free:} \quad & A = 1.15, \quad B = 6.5
\end{aligned}
$$

The spectral radius of a scale-free network is higher than its mean degree, and increases more rapidly (than for random and small-world networks) as a function of mean degree. This supports the claim that spectral radius is a better measure of network structure and connectivity than is mean degree. In fact, we use this property to explain epidemic threshold in SIS epidemics.

Suppose that a small-world network and scale-free network each have mean degree $\lambda = 20$. The spectral radius of the small-world network is $\rho(\text{small-world}) = (1)(20) + 1 = 21$, using the approximation formula given above. The spectral radius of the scale-free network is $\rho(\text{scale-free}) = (1.15)(20) + 6.5 = 29.5$—a much higher spectral radius than for the small world. As it turns out, the higher the spectral radius of a network, the more likely it can sustain a persistent epidemic.

8.1.5 Susceptible–Infected–Susceptible (SIS) Epidemics

Figure 8.2b shows the state diagram for actors in an SIS epidemic. Actors are in one of two states—infected or susceptible. An actor starts in the susceptible state and transitions to the infected state with probability γ at each timestep. Then, it either returns to the susceptible state with probability Δ, or remains infected with probability $(1 - \Delta)$. Actors cycle from susceptible to infected and then back to susceptible, again; hence the designation SIS. Eventually, the population of actors will either completely recover, reach a steady state where the percentage of infected actors remains relatively constant, or oscillate in a wave-like fashion between upper and lower values of infected numbers.

SIS epidemics occur in many disciplines other than biology; they model the spread of ideas, fashion, and products and therefore are of interest to market researchers. They model the propagation of faults and the wave-like spread of congestion in physical systems such as the electrical power grid, Internet, and transportation systems. Therefore, it is important to understand when an epidemic might die out, oscillate, or never go away! The possibility of a never-ending epidemic leads us to ask three key questions:

1. Under what conditions might an epidemic be guaranteed to die out?
2. If an epidemic never dies out, what is the expected level of the infection?
3. Are SIS network epidemics any different from biological epidemics and if so, how and why?

To begin, suppose that we solve the Kermack–McKendrick equations for a very simple SIS epidemic that never dies out. We call such epidemics *persistent epidemics*, for obvious reasons. We show that for certain conditions on γ and Δ, a simple version of the Kermack–McKendrick model leads to a persistent epidemic. We use the following strategy:

1. Formulate a special version of the Kermack–McKendrick equations by mimicking a simple birth–death process, where births (infections) occur with probability γ, and deaths (recovery) occur with probability Δ.
2. Note that $\delta i / \delta t = 0$ at the fixed-point infection density i_∞. Solve for the fixed-point infection density by setting $\delta i / \delta t = 0$.
3. Note the condition under which the solution yields a fixed-point value. This condition is the epidemic threshold τ for the SIS epidemic.

Let the *fixed-point infection* percentage i_∞ be the steady-state value of $i(t)$ as t approaches infinity.[4] Because actors can be either infected or susceptible, $s(t) + i(t) = 1$. Further, let γ be the infection rate and Δ be the rate of recovery of infected actors, leading to the Kermack–McKendrick density equation for this

---

[4]This fixed point is also called the *endemic equilibrium* by some authors and designated i_0.

special case, as follows:

$$\frac{\delta i}{\delta t} = \gamma s i - \Delta i = \gamma(1-i)i - \Delta i = [\gamma(1-i) - \Delta]i$$

As time increases without bound, the rate of change of $i(t)$ levels off to zero, so that

$$\frac{\delta i}{\delta t} = 0 = [\gamma(1-i_\infty) - \Delta]i_\infty$$

Solving for i_∞ yields the persistent epidemic percentage:

$$i_\infty = 1 - \frac{\Delta}{\gamma}; \text{ assuming } \Delta \leq \gamma$$

$$i_\infty = 1 - \tau, \text{ where } \tau = \frac{\Delta}{\gamma}; \text{ so } \tau < 1 \text{ for the epidemic to spread}$$

For example, suppose that $\Delta = 15\%$ and $\gamma = 25\%$, so $\tau = \frac{15}{25} = 60\%$. The infected population starts at $i_0 < i_\infty$ and rises to $i_\infty = 1 - 60\% = 40\%$, where it stabilizes. Instead of rising to a peak value and then settling back down to zero, an SIS epidemic may steadily rise to a certain value, and stay there, forever!

Conversely, under the rather limiting restrictions of this model, the SIS epidemic will die out for values of $\gamma < \Delta$ because $i_\infty \leq 0$. The infection rate must be at least as great as the recovery rate in this model, to sustain a persistent epidemic. Otherwise, the SIS epidemic will eventually reach its steady-state upper limit, i_∞.

This simple model answers the first two questions stated above for an extremely simple SIS epidemic. However, this model does not incorporate the impact of network structure on spread rate, threshold, and steady state. Therefore, it is inadequate to describe how an SIS epidemic might spread through an arbitrary network.

8.2 PERSISTENT EPIDEMICS IN NETWORKS

Network epidemic models differ from the classical Kermack–McKendrick model in several important ways. First, we cannot assume uniformity of population—most networks of practical significance have nonuniform structure; for instance, they are small-world or scale-free. More significantly, we have already shown how the spread of an infection in a network is greatly impacted by mean degree λ, which varies according to a network's topology. Network connectivity counts, because each node is exposed to λ adjacent nodes, rather than the entire population, n.[5] Restriction of infection spreading to adjacent nodes places limits on the *total rate of infection* v, which tends to be near $v = \gamma/\lambda$, instead of γ.

Since the topology of a network governs the spread of a network epidemic, we cannot assume homogeneous mixing as in the Kermack–McKendrick model.

---

[5]The terms *mean degree* and *connectivity* are used interchangeably in this book.

Instead, network epidemics are governed by the degree sequence distribution of the particular network, and can be characterized by the *spectral radius* of the network.

Moreover, a network is finite, so we cannot use *mean-field theory* to approximate the behavior of a (small) network epidemic. Deterministic models like the Kermack–McKendrick model and mean-field theory models that "average out" the structure of nonhomogenous networks may not accurately describe epidemic behavior. Instead, we must resort to statistical or probabilistic models or models that accurately represent nonuniformity of topology.

In the following section, we answer the three fundamental questions posed at the beginning of this chapter:

Under what conditions does an SIS epidemic sustain itself?

What is the threshold value?

What is the steady-state fixed-point infection density?

How do network epidemic models differ from homogeneous, infinite population models?

We show that a combination of network connectivity λ and spectral radius ρ provide sufficient characterization of random, small-world, and scale-free networks so that we can accurately estimate threshold and fixed-point infection density of an arbitrary network from these two parameters.

8.2.1 Random Network Epidemic Threshold

Assume a random network with n nodes and connectivity given by mean degree λ. Further assume that the density of infected nodes is governed by infection rate γ and mean degree λ. Let $v = \gamma\lambda$ be the *effective spread rate*, and rewrite the Kermack–McKendrick equation as follows:

$$\frac{\delta i}{\delta t} = vi(1 - i) - \Delta i; \ \ i(0) = i_0; \ \ v = \gamma\lambda$$

This equation is identical to the standard Kermack–McKendrick equation except for the substitution of v in place of γ. We claim that v better represents epidemic spreading than does γ because each node directly interacts only with its λ adjacent neighbors rather than the remaining $(n - 1)$ nodes. This model, proposed by Kephart and White (KW) in 1991, approximates persistent SIS epidemics in random networks when threshold $\tau = \Delta/v < 1$, yielding a fixed point $i_\infty = (1 - \tau)$ (Kephart, 1991).

We follow Kephart and White's (KW) derivation of fixed point and threshold, and then add a new analysis to explain oscillations observed in simulated network epidemics. The oscillations are explained by numerically solving a discrete difference equation analog of the continuous variable KW solution. The analysis strategy is as follows:

1. Solve the KW equation by noting that it is a minor variation of the Kermack–McKendrick equation, which is satisfied by a logistic growth curve.

2. Solve the discrete difference equation analog to show where oscillations come from.

3. Find the epidemic threshold and fixed point by taking limits.

The solution to the KW modification of the Kermack–McKendrick equation for $i(t)$ leads to a logistic growth curve as before. The only difference is the substitution of v in place of γ:

$$\frac{\delta i}{\delta t} = vi(1 - i) - \Delta i = i[(v - \Delta) - vi]$$

Dividing both sides by $i[(v - \Delta) - vi]$, we obtain

$$\frac{\delta i}{i[(v - \Delta) - vi]} = \delta t$$

Now integrate the left side from i_0 to i, and the right side from 0 to t:

$$\ln\left(\frac{(v - \Delta) - vi}{i}\right) - \ln\left(\frac{(v - \Delta) - vi_0}{i_0}\right) = -(v - \Delta)t$$

Applying the exp( ) function to both sides, substituting the infection threshold $\tau = \Delta/v$ where appropriate, and rearranging terms lead to

$$i(t) = \frac{i_0(1 - \tau)}{i_0 + (1 - \tau - i_0)\exp(-v(1 - \tau)t)}$$

Note that exp( ) goes to zero as time increases without bound, and i_0 cancels from numerator and denominator, so the fixed-point solution i_∞ is easily obtained as a function of threshold τ:

$$i_\infty = 1 - \tau; \quad \tau = \frac{\Delta}{v} \quad \text{or} \quad \left(1 - \frac{1}{\tau}\right) \quad \text{if we define} \quad \tau = \frac{v^6}{\Delta}$$

The fixed-point solution exists below the threshold, or $\tau < 1$, so this condition guarantees a persistent infection. But this deterministic solution ignores statistical fluctuations in density that are observed in practice (see Fig. 8.7). The probability that the SIS epidemic dies out because it reaches zero increases as the severity of fluctuations increases.

What might be the source of these fluctuations? There might be two basic reasons: (1) the spread of an infection is stochastic—infection spreading is probabilistic (the deterministic model ignores statistical variations) or (2) the deterministic equation may be unstable for certain input parameters—the solution may turn chaotic for

---

[6]Some authors define $\tau = \gamma/\Delta$, so that persistent epidemics occur above the threshold.

certain values of infection rate and network connectivity λ. In most cases, chaotic oscillations are indistinguishable from stochastic variations.

We can gain a casual but intuitive understanding of the chaotic instability of the KW model by considering the discrete analog of the KW differential equation. The discrete analog is the finite-difference equation obtained by replacing the continuous derivative $\delta i / \delta t$ with the discrete difference $i(t) - i(t - 1)$:

$$i(t) - i(t - 1) = i(t - 1)[v (1 - i(t - 1)) - \Delta i(t - 1)]$$

Transposing $i(t - 1)$ to the right-hand side produces an iterative form:

$$i(t) = i(t - 1) + i(t - 1)[v (1 - i(t - 1)) - \Delta i(t - 1)]; \quad t = 1, 2, \dots$$
$$i(0) = i_0$$

Given the initial value $i(0)$, we can iterate through time to obtain a numerical solution to this finite-difference equation. A plot of finite $i(t)$ versus t, for $\gamma = \Delta = .2$, $\lambda = 4$, and $i_0 = 1/n$, appears as a smooth logistics curve in Fig. 8.6. A plot of the same discrete analog of $i(t)$ versus t, for $\gamma = \Delta = 0.2$, $\lambda = 12$, and $i_0 = 1/n$, appears as a chaotic sawtooth curve. The only difference between these two epidemics is connectivity, λ. The higher the connectivity, the more instability there is in the solution. The instability increases as the density increases in random networks because λ is a function of density: $\lambda = (n - 1)$ density.

Fluctuation may also be caused by wide variations in degree value from node to node, and the presence of locally varying infection rates. Node degree is uniform in a random network, but nonuniform in scale-free networks. Therefore, we would

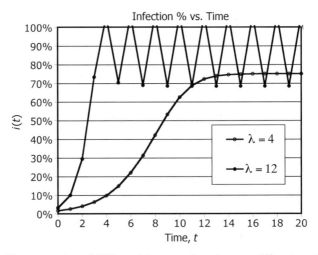

Figure 8.6 Discrete analog of KW model versus time for two different random network densities, $\lambda = 4$, and 12. The higher-degreed network leads to a chaotic solution.

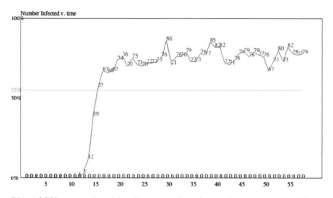

Figure 8.7   Plot of SIS network epidemic versus time for random network with $n = 100$, $\lambda = 4$, $\gamma = \Delta = 20\%$, and $i_0 = .01$ ($\tau = 25\%$).

expect to observe oscillations in nonuniform networks with high-degreed nodes as well.

Figure 8.7 illustrates oscillation of the deterministic fixed-point solution around $(1-25\%) = 75\%$, for $\tau = 25\%$ and connectivity $\lambda = 4$. The density of infected nodes rises according to a logistics growth curve, levels off, and then oscillates around the fixed-point density. The height of the fixed point is

$$\frac{1 - \Delta}{v} = \frac{1 - 0.2}{(0.2)(4)} = 0.75$$

as predicted by the KW model.

Figure 8.7 also illustrates a persistent SIS epidemic in a network with uniformly random connectivity. What happens when degree sequence distribution is nonuniform? For example, does the epidemic reach the same fixedpoint for a scale-free network with mean degree sequence $\lambda = 4$? The degree sequence distribution of a scale-free network is not uniform, so the answer is "No." To understand the answer, we need a more elaborate model that incorporates more information about the topology of the network.

Kephart and White showed that persistent epidemics do not occur unless the ratio of the rate at which an infected individual attempts to infect other individuals exceeds the rate at which individuals recover (Kephart, 1991). In terms of the solution provided above, this means that persistent epidemics occur in random networks when $\tau = (\Delta/v) < 1$. This result ignores fluctuations that lead to epidemic extinction with nonzero probability. An epidemic is not guaranteed to persist even when $\tau < 1$, because of probabilistic and chaotic side effects. But KW argued that persistence becomes increasingly probable as the infection rate is increased further above the threshold. Specifically, they showed the probability that an SIS epidemic dies out in a random network is $\rho(0, t) = \tau^{I(0)}$, where $I(0)$ is the number of initially infected actors. Typically, $I(0) = 1$, so the probability of the epidemic persisting in a random network is $(1 - \tau)$. Therefore, the probability of persistence and the value of the fixed point both increase with infection rate because $(1 - \tau)$ increases as γ increases. Infection rate can take on any value from threshold to 100% of the population: $\tau \leq \gamma \leq 1.0$.

8.2.2 Epidemic Threshold in General Networks

Few networks are random, and so the Kephard–White (KW) model has limited applicability to real networks. Is it possible to find a general solution to the problem of epidemic spreading in arbitrary networks? The answer is "Yes," and we provide it in this section. We follow the derivation of Z. Wang, Chakrabarti, C. Wang, and Faloutsos (*WCWF model*) (Wang, 2003a), who first proposed a general model of epidemic threshold and fixed-point density for any network. The WCWF model is quite impressive because it elegantly finds the epidemic threshold of any network, regardless of its structure, using the network's spectral radius. WCWF showed that network epidemic threshold $\tau = \rho$, where ρ is the spectral radius of the network, and $\tau = \Delta/\gamma$ as defined above.[7] This provides a general theory for network epidemics and soundly answers the final question regarding the difference between natural and network epidemics. SIS epidemics are governed by the spectral radius, which is a better measure of network topology than mean degree λ.

The WCWF model is a linear approximation to the nonlinear equations of Kermack–McKendrick. Linearization leads to inaccuracies for large infection rates, but gives very good results for relatively small infection rates.[8] The exact value of threshold involves solving nonlinear equations. Instead, we propose a quadratic approximation to the truly nonlinear model. The quadratic approximation slightly improves on the WCWF model, especially for large infection rate, γ.

The strategy for finding a general model of epidemics in an arbitrary network is

1. Formulate a state equation that relates the probability $p_i(t)$ that node i is infected at time t to its degree $(i) = k_i$ where adjacent nodes $j = 1, 2, \ldots, k_i$ may or may not infect node i.

2. Linearize the state equation by assuming small probabilities—call this the *WCWF approximation*—and then improve on the approximation by substituting a quadratic model for the nonlinear probability of infection to obtain an expression for threshold τ for large probabilities—call this the *modified WCWF model*.

3. We obtain the WCWF approximation by generalizing the single-node state equation to a system equation representing the infection probability for all nodes. This leads to system matrix $\mathbf{S}$, which is related to adjacency matrix $\mathbf{A}$ through the system equation. The spectral decomposition of system matrix $\mathbf{S}$ and adjacency matrix $\mathbf{A}$ leads to a scalar equation relating threshold to infection rates γ and Δ.

---

[7]WCWF defined $\tau = \gamma/\Delta = 1/\rho$, but we use the inverted definition to be consistent with Kephart and White.

[8]For the purposes of this chapter, $\gamma > 10\%$ is considered a "large" infection rate.

4. Use the fact that a network epidemic dies out when its largest system equation eigenvalue is less than one to find the epidemic threshold, $\tau = \Delta/\gamma = \rho$, where ρ is the spectral radius of adjacency matrix $\mathbf{A}$. Modify this relation to obtain the non-linear WCWF equation, $\tau = \rho[B - A\gamma]$, for parameters A and B.

Instead of modeling the *infection density* $i(t)$ as a function of time as Kermack–McKendrick did, WCWF modeled the probability $p_i(t)$ that node i is infected at time t, directly as the result of infection by its adjacent nodes at time $(t - 1)$. Suppose that $j = 1, 2, \ldots, k_i$ are the adjacent nodes of node i with degree k_i, and γ, Δ are infection and recovery rates as before. If node i is not already infected at time $(t - 1)$, then the probability of infection at time t is the sum of probabilities of being infected by the k_i adjacent nodes.

The probability that node i is not infected at $(t-1)$ is $\gamma[1 - p_i(t - 1)]$, and the probability of becoming infected by adjacent nodes is $\gamma \sum_j^{k_i} p_j(t - 1)$, so the joint probability is:

$$\text{Probability of infection from neighbors:} \gamma[1 - p_i(t - 1)] \sum_j^{k_i} p_j(t - 1)$$

If node i is already infected at time $(t - 1)$, then the probability that it will remain infected at time t is the joint probability that it was infected at time $(t - 1)$ and the probability that it does not recover, which is the product of $(1 - \Delta)$ times $p_i(t - 1)$:

$$\text{Probability of nonrecovery when already infected:} (1 - \Delta)p_i(t - 1)$$

Summing the two events yields the probability that node i is infected at time t:

$$p_i(t) = \gamma[1 - p_i(t - 1)] \sum_j^{k_i} p_j(t - 1) + (1 - \Delta)p_i(t - 1); \quad i = 1, 2, \ldots, n$$

Note that infection density is simply the sum of $p_i(t)$ at each timestep:

$$i(t) = \sum_i p_i(t)$$

We are more interested in the behavior of the node's probabilities than their states, so we advance to the second step of the strategy. The first term in the state equation for $p_i(t)$ is converted into matrix form by noting that the sum of adjacent node probabilities is exactly the same as multiplying column vector $\mathbf{P}(t)$ by the rows of adjacency matrix $\mathbf{A}$. Vector $\mathbf{P}(t)$ is the column vector $[p_1(t), p_2(t), \ldots, p_n(t)]^T$. Ones in row i of adjacency matrix $\mathbf{A}$ correlate exactly with the neighbors of node i. The adjacency matrix is symmetric, so $\mathbf{A}\mathbf{P}(t)$ is exactly the sum in the equation above.

Therefore, the matrix form of the state equation is

$$\mathbf{P}(t) = \gamma[1 - p_i(t - 1)]\mathbf{A}\mathbf{P}(t - 1) + (1 - \Delta)\mathbf{P}(t - 1)$$
$$= \{\gamma[1 - p_i(t - 1)]\mathbf{A} + (1 - \Delta)\mathbf{I}\}\mathbf{P}(t - 1)$$

where $\mathbf{I}$ is the identity matrix of dimension $n \times n$ and $\mathbf{A}$ is the network's adjacency matrix.

The state equation above is ideal except for the term $[1 - p_i(t - 1)]$, which does not fit nicely into the matrix formulation. WCWF assumed small probabilities, so this term could be replaced by 1 without great loss of accuracy. This greatly simplifies the solution because we now have everything needed to decompose the system matrix $\mathbf{S} = \{\gamma\mathbf{A} + (1 - \Delta)\mathbf{I}\}$, into its eigenvalues. Assuming the WCWF approximation is valid, the state equation becomes simply

$$\mathbf{P}(t) = \mathbf{S}\mathbf{P}(t - 1); \quad \mathbf{P}(0) \text{ given}$$

The solution to this first-order difference equation is $\mathbf{P}(t) = \mathbf{S}^t\mathbf{P}(0)$.

Spectral decomposition of system matrix $\mathbf{S}$ yields the relationship between network connectivity represented by adjacency matrix $\mathbf{A}$, and epidemic parameters γ and Δ. Let $\rho(\mathbf{S})$ be the largest nontrivial eigenvalue (spectral radius) of $\mathbf{S}$ and $\rho(\mathbf{A})$ the largest nontrivial eigenvalue (spectral radius) of $\mathbf{A}$. Then the diagonalized version of the system state equation is

$$\gamma\rho(\mathbf{A}) + (1 - \Delta) = \rho(\mathbf{S})$$

The system state equation solution, $\mathbf{P}(t) = \mathbf{S}^t\mathbf{P}(0)$, approaches zero if $\rho(\mathbf{S}) < 1$, and reaches some fixed point, otherwise. Therefore, the epidemic threshold is realized for $\rho(\mathbf{S}) = 1$:

$$\gamma\rho(\mathbf{A}) + (1 - \Delta) = 1$$

Solving for Δ and then dividing by γ to obtain τ yield

$$\Delta = \gamma\rho(\mathbf{A})$$

$$\tau = \frac{\Delta}{\gamma} = \rho(\mathbf{A})$$

The epidemic persists for $\tau = \Delta/\gamma \leq \rho(\mathbf{A})$, and dies out, otherwise. In terms of the semiinfinite plane defined by (ρ, Δ), $\rho > 0$, $\Delta > 0$, all epidemics falling into the region above the threshold line defined by τ die out, and all epidemics falling below the line persist. This result confirms the WCWF model, which simply states that epidemic threshold for any network is[9]

$$\tau = \frac{\Delta}{\gamma} = \rho(\mathbf{A})$$

or

$$\Delta = \gamma\rho(\mathbf{A})$$

---

[9]WCWF report the inverted version: $\tau = \gamma/\Delta = 1/(\rho(\mathbf{A}))$.

The relationship between Δ and γ holds along the *threshold line* dividing persistent and nonpersistent epidemics.

This elegant solution to the general problem of epidemic threshold in networks is accurate for small values of infection rate, but what happens in relatively small networks with high infection rate, γ?

Consider the following nonlinear WCWF model with $[1 - p_i(t - 1)] < 1$, or $p_i(t - 1) \gg 0$. From the Kermack–McKendrick and KW models we expect the probability of infection to follow an S-shaped logistics growth curve formed by the nonlinearity induced by $i(1 - i)$ or $\gamma(1 - \gamma)$. Suppose that we approximate this nonlinearity by substituting the quadratic, $\gamma(B - A\gamma)$, into the WCWF model, and see what happens. This leads to the following modified eigenvalue equation:

$$\gamma(B - A\gamma)\rho(\mathbf{A}) + (1 - \Delta) = 1$$

Solving for Δ and τ as before, we obtain

$$\Delta = \rho(\mathbf{A})\gamma(B - A\gamma) \quad \text{or} \quad \tau = \frac{\Delta}{\gamma} = \rho(\mathbf{A})(B - A\gamma)$$

Parameters A and B are found by fitting the modified expression for Δ to simulation data as shown in Fig. 8.8. Table 8.2 summarizes the results. Figure 8.8 plots the relationship between recovery rate Δ and infection rate γ along the threshold line $\tau = \rho(\mathbf{A})(B - A\gamma)$ for a number of different sizes and classes of networks. The epidemic dies out above the threshold line, and persists below it. Note that τ is a function of infection rate γ. Later we suggest an alternate formulation where τ is a function Δ.

In Fig. 8.8, we observe a near-linear relationship between Δ and γ for low values of γ. This confirms the WCWF approximation for small probability of infection. But the linearity decays as γ increases—diminishing at a quadratic rate determined by parameters A and B.

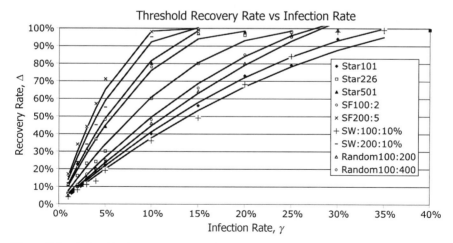

Figure 8.8 A (γ, Δ) plot: recovery rate Δ versus infection rate γ for random, scale-free, small-world, and star networks. The area below each curve is the *persistent epidemic region*, and the area above each curve represents the (γ, Δ) region where epidemics die out.

TABLE 8.2   Curve-Fit Parameters for Fig. 8.8

	ρ	λ	A	B
SW100:200	4.17	4.00	1.000	1.000
Star101:100	10.00	1.98	0.500	0.460
Rand100:200	4.94	4.00	1.000	1.000
SF100:2	7.37	3.94	1.000	0.770
Star226:225	15.00	1.99	0.950	0.500
Star501:500	22.36	1.99	1.200	0.460
Rand100:400	9.06	8.00	3.500	1.250
SW200:1000	10.13	10.00	5.000	1.410
SF200:5	15.85	9.85	4.000	1.020

The quadratic approximation improves on the WCWF model, but is much less satisfying because of its complexity. Threshold τ is no longer a simple function of spectral radius, but instead, depends on $\rho(\Lambda)$, γ, and λ. Indeed, the exact nonlinear functional relationship remains an unsolved problem.

We can rank the simulated networks listed in Table 8.2 and shown in Fig. 8.8 according to the threshold line dividing the Fig. 8.8 quadrant into persistent and non-persistent regions. Reading Fig. 8.8 from right (least persistent) to left (most persistent), the networks rank in order as listed in Table 8.2 (first number is n, second number is m for random and small-world, while second number is Δm for scale-free). For example, the least persistent network epidemics occur in SW100:200 (small-world network with $n = 100$, $m = 200$), and the most persistent network epidemics occur in SF200:5 (scale-free with $n = 200$, $\Delta m = 5$).

Generally, network epidemics become more persistent as the spectral radius of their network hosts increases, but connectivity also plays a role. This fact is evident in Table 8.2, where the rank ordering of networks is determined by the values of ρ and λ. Specifically, A and B may be (poorly) approximated as functions of spectral radius and connectivity—not just spectral radius, alone.[10]

For the networks simulated in Fig. 8.8 and summarized in Table 8.2, we observe that A and B increase with connectivity λ and decrease inversely with spectral radius ρ. For example, $A(\rho, \lambda)$ is directly proportional to λ, but inversely proportional to ρ, while $B(\rho, \lambda)$ is inversely proportional to ρ only. The following relationships were determined by curve fitting. Figure 8.9 plots the model equations for A and B versus empirically derived values given in Table 8.2.

$$A(\rho, \lambda) = \lambda\left(\frac{2}{\rho} + \frac{1}{4}\right) \sim O\left(\lambda + \frac{\lambda}{\rho}\right)$$

$$B(\rho, \lambda) = \frac{1}{\rho} + \frac{1}{4} \sim O\left(\frac{1}{\rho}\right)$$

[10]We assume the nonlinear case where γ is allowed to be "large." Otherwise, spectral radius is the dominant factor.

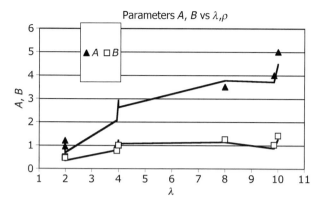

Figure 8.9 Parameters $A(\rho, \lambda) = \lambda((2/\rho) + (1/4))$ and $B(\rho, \lambda) = (1/\rho) + \frac{1}{4}$ versus λ for the simulated networks in Fig. 8.8.

For example, what is the threshold τ for a scale-free network with $n = 100$, $\Delta m = 2$, and $\gamma = 10\%$? From entry SF100:2 in Table 8.2, we obtain spectral radius of $\rho(\mathbf{A}) = 7.37$, connectivity of $\lambda = 3.94$, $A = 1.0$, and $B = 0.77$. Plug these parameters into the equations developed above to obtain threshold recovery rate Δ and threshold τ:

$$\Delta = \rho(\mathbf{A})\gamma(B - A\gamma) = (7.37)(0.10)((0.77 - 1.0)(0.10)) = 49.4\%$$

$$\tau = \frac{\Delta}{\gamma} = \frac{49.4\%}{10\%} = 4.94$$

Simulations yield approximately $\Delta = 48\%$ and $\tau = 4.8$ for equivalent scale-free networks, so the modified WCWF estimates are quite good. Any combination of (γ, Δ) resulting in $\tau < 4.94$ produces a persistent epidemic; otherwise, the epidemic dies out.[11]

The WCWF approximation appears to work very well for "small γ," while the modified WCWF approximation is appropriate for "large γ" epidemics. However, both approximations may fail to give accurate estimates for "extreme cases," such as very small networks, very structured or regular networks, or epidemics with very large infection rates. These extremes are explored by several exercises at the end of the chapter.

The modified WCWF formulation approximates Δ in terms of γ, but some applications may require the opposite: γ in terms of Δ. In such cases, solving the quadratic

---

[11]The reader should be aware that these approximations assume "middle of the road" networks, and are not likely to work for extreme cases such as a complete network, very small networks, or very large infection rates.

equation for γ yields an alternative formulation. This formulation is left as an exercise for the reader.

$$\gamma^2 - \left(\frac{B}{A}\right)\gamma + \frac{\Delta}{A\rho(\mathbf{A})} = 0$$

The nontrivial root of this quadratic equation, γ_1, is a function of Δ, so the threshold, in terms of Δ, is

$$\tau = \frac{\Delta}{\gamma_1}$$

Epidemic threshold is dominated by spectral radius, $t = \Delta/\gamma = O(\rho)$, and we know that spectral radius of a star network is $\rho(\text{star}) \sim \sqrt{(\text{hub degree})} \sim \sqrt{(n-1)}$. Therefore the threshold infection rate of a star network is

$$\gamma(\text{star}) \sim \frac{\Delta}{O\left(\sqrt{(n-1)}\right)}$$

As n increases without bound, $\Delta/[O(\sqrt{(n-1)})]$ goes to zero, so $\gamma_\infty(\text{star}) = 0$. An SIS epidemic will persist indefinitely in an infinite star network! More realistically, the infection rate decreases inversely proportional to the square root of network size, near the threshold line. In an unbounded star network, an epidemic with an infection rate greater than zero leads to a persistent epidemic, regardless of the recovery rate Δ of the nodes.

Pastor-Satorras and Vespignani (Pastor-Satorras, 2001) were the first to claim that epidemics persist indefinitely in unbounded scale-free networks. While we illustrate this using star networks, above, the conjecture appears to be true for any infinite network! Their claim is based on the argument that threshold declines as connectivity increases without bound. In a scale-free network, $\rho(\text{scale-free}) \sim O(\sqrt{(\text{degree}(\text{hub}))})$, and we know from our earlier study of scale-free networks that hub degree grows in proportion to network size. Therefore, unbounded scale-free networks also support persistent epidemics as infection rate becomes arbitrarily small:

$$\gamma(\text{star}) \sim \frac{\Delta}{O\left(\sqrt{(\text{degree}(\text{hub}))}\right)} \quad \text{which goes to zero in the limit.}$$

The Pastor-Satorras–Vespignani and star network results suggest never-ending epidemics in networks with hubs. Indeed, these hubs are called *superspreaders* in epidemiology—the larger the degree of the hub, the more impetus there is for persistence; and the larger the network, the larger the hub of a star or scale-free network. We show how superspreaders are used to counter epidemics in an effective manner, in the final section of this chapter.

8.2.3   Fixed-Point Infection Density in General Networks

Figure 8.10 plots steady-state fixed-point infection density as a function of spectral radius for the networks studied in Fig. 8.8. These networks ranged in value of spectral

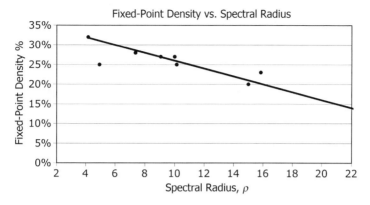

Figure 8.10 Linear approximation of fixed-point density versus spectral radius ρ for simulated networks in Fig. 8.8.

radius, from 2 to 22, and in size from 100 to 501 nodes. Network density was sparse—on the order of a few percentage points. The best-fitting straight line is, at best, a *rough* fit to the data obtained from these simulations.

Fixed-point infection declines with increase in spectral radius. Why? Intuition suggests the opposite, but remember that these data were obtained for epidemics *near their threshold*. As ρ(network) increases, so does Δ, and as Δ increases, the ratio of recovered actors to infected actors increases according to $\Delta/\gamma = \rho$ (network). Increasing Δ pushes the number of infected actors downward, hence the decline of fixed-point infection with increasing spectral radius.

The linear relationship near the threshold τ is $O(-\rho)$:

$$i_\infty = b - m\rho, \quad \text{with least-squares parameters: } b = 0.36, \quad m = 0.01$$

$$= 36\% - \left(\frac{\rho}{100}\right)\%$$

Generally, ρ increases with increase in connectivity λ (which is also directly proportional to network density), so the greater connectivity is, the lower the fixed-point density of infected nodes. In other words, a denser network is better able to sustain a low-level persistent infection than a sparser network is. This has important implications in human and animal populations—crowding is more likely to sustain a low-level persistent infection.

Perhaps the most interesting property of Fig. 8.10 is the conformance of all classes of networks to the $i_\infty(\rho)$ relationship. Spectral radius appears to be an excellent metric to use in the study of SIS network epidemics, but spectral radius is not the only factor that determines the threshold. As we have shown, threshold value τ becomes nonlinear as epidemic rate increases beyond double-digit percentages.

8.3 NETWORK EPIDEMIC SIMULATION SOFTWARE

The foregoing analysis relied heavily on simulation to obtain parameter values and study the behavior of epidemics over a wide range of networks. These simulations were performed by program *Network.jar*, which implements the spread of a contagion within a network by implementing the state machines of Fig. 8.2.

Method `NW_doEpidemic(boolean SIR)` implements the SIR state machine if `boolean` SIR is **true**, and the SIS state machine if parameter SIR is **false**. The algorithm has two parts: (1) a sweep over all links to propagate infection from one end of the link to the other and (2) a sweep over all nodes to determine if they have recovered or been removed.

Susceptible nodes are colored white, and infected nodes are colored red. Recovered nodes are white in SIS and yellow in SIR, and removed nodes are black (SIR). Some additional points of interest are

1. Method `NW_doEpidemic()` randomizes processing order by shuffling the links of the network, so there is no simulation bias due to link order. Randomization is carried out by `class Shuffler`, which simulates card shuffling.
2. The basic epidemic simulation algorithm is quite simple; for each link, examine the head and tail nodes and determine whether either are infected. If one end is infected but the other is not, infect the susceptible node with probability $\gamma = $ `InfectionRate`, and color it red. Also, set the timer of the newly infected node with the input value: $t_r = $ `RecoveryTime`. This timer is decremented for each timestep until it reaches zero. Infected (red) nodes either die with probability `DeathRate` or recover when their timers reach zero. Recovered nodes are colored yellow when SIR is **true**.
3. For SIS epidemics, the algorithm prevents a newly infected node from recovery in the same time interval as its infection, when `RecoveryTime` is greater than zero. This has an impact on the results. A user who wants to allow an infected node to recover immediately with probability `RecoveryRate` would set `RecoveryTime` to zero in the *preferences* panel of *Network.jar*.
4. For SIR epidemics, infected nodes cannot die (be removed) or recover (be recovered) until their timer has reached zero. When a timer reaches zero, the infected node is removed with probability `DeathRate`, or recovered with probability, `RecoveryRate`.

This code is invoked by pressing the INFECT button on the *Network.jar* control panel. A plot of infected density versus time will also appear, showing various parameters such as current, average, and peak infection densities:

```
public void NW_doEpidemic(boolean SIR){
    //Randomly Propagate the infection
    Shuffler random_list = new Shuffler(nLinks);
    for(int i = 0; i < nLinks; i++) random_list.card[ i] = i;
    random_list.SH_Shuffle(nLinks);              //Scramble link order
    //Part 1: Propagate infection via links
    for(int i = 0; i < nLinks; i++){
        Node n = null;              //Target of infection
```

```
            int j = random_list.card[ i] ;
            int tail = Link[ j] .tail;
            int head = Link[ j] .head;
            if(node[ tail] .color == Color.red           //From tail to head
                   &&
                node[head] .color == Color.white) n = node[head] ;
            else if(node[ head] .color == Color.red   //From head to tail
                      &&
                node[tail] .color == Color.white) n = node[tail] ;
            if(n != null && 100*Math.random() <= InfectionRate) {
                  n.color = Color.red;                  //Infect!
                  n.timer = RecoveryTime;               //SIR
            }
     }
     //Part 2: Handle SIR vs SIS Change in Red(infected) nodes
     for(int i = 0; i < nNodes; i++){
          Node n = node[i];
          if(n.color == Color.red){
             if(SIR) {                                  //SIR model
                 n.timer-;
                 if(n.timer <= 0){
                    if(100*Math.random() <= DeathRate) {
                       n.color = Color.black;         //SIR removed
                          }
                       else {
                          n.color = Color.yellow; //SIR recovered
                       }
                    }
                 }                                      //SIS model
             else if(100*Math.random() <= RecoveryRate) {
                 if(n.timer == 0)
                 n.color = Color.white;               //SIS recovered
                 else n.timer = 0;                     //1-shot
                }
             }
        }
     }
}//NW_doEpidemic
```

8.4 COUNTERMEASURES

The foregoing analysis explains how epidemics spread, but it does not explain how an epidemic might be stopped. In general, we want to know how to eradicate an epidemic in the quickest way possible, and to reduce the number of actors infected.

This important problem has applications to a variety of fields:

1. How do we limit the spread of a disease among living organisms (public health)?
2. How do we remove an undesirable virus from the Internet (computer science)?
3. How do we stop the propagation of a failure in an infrastructure system (cascade failure in an electrical power grid, telecommunications, etc.)?
4. How do we counter the spread of a competitor's idea, product, or fashion (marketing)?
5. How do we negate the spread of an undesirable idea, concept, news, or political notion (propaganda)?

These questions have many possible answers, which vary in strategy. We choose to study the use of *viral marketing* techniques as an intriguing approach to halting the spread of an epidemic in networks. The idea is simple—release a countermeasure contagion (let's call it an *antigen*) and let it spread like an epidemic to all nodes of the network.[12] Whenever the antigen encounters an infected node, it neutralizes the infection, and continues to spread. The antigen behaves just like the epidemic—spreading with the same rate and virulence. However, there is one important difference—the antigen is not subject to removal. It never dies out, but it may reach a fixed-point density just as any other epidemic.

The countermeasure antigen starts at a node (called the *seed node*) and spreads with the same rate γ of the epidemic. Simulations performed by program *Network.jar* paint infected nodes red, antigen nodes blue, and neutralized nodes yellow. Susceptible nodes are white, as before, but note that antigen (blue) nodes spread via white, red, and yellow nodes.

The question we pose is this: "Where is the best place to instigate the countermeasure?" We define "best" as "least time" and "lowest peak infection" and conjecture that the best strategy will depend on where the antigen is initially seeded. In this section, we compare four strategies or countermeasures applicable to an arbitrary network: (1) random seeding, (2) hub seeding, (3) central node seeding, and (4) maximum closeness node seeding. Further, we explore the behavior of each of these strategies and their effectiveness in halting epidemics in random, scale-free, and small-world networks.

8.4.1 Countermeasure Algorithms

Figure 8.11 shows the state diagrams for a red–blue antigen competition between the epidemic, represented by red, and the antigen, represented by blue. In Fig. 8.11a, the red epidemic converts white susceptible actors to red infected actors at infection rate γ. Red actors remain red until a blue antigen "cures" it—turning it yellow.

---

[12]We define an antigen as any contagion capable of eliciting an immune response, such as neutralizing infected nodes.

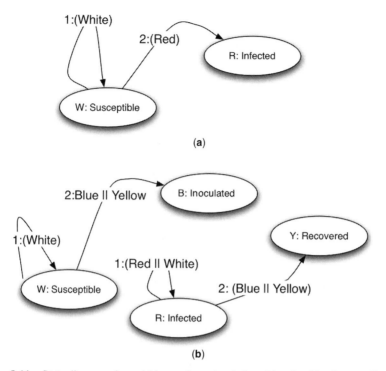

Figure 8.11 State diagrams for red-blue antigen simulation: (a) red epidemic spreading; (b) blue artigen spreading. Transitions are labeled with the adjacent-node color. All transitions occur with probability γ.

Without an antigen countermeasure, all nodes eventually become infected because there is no recovery process in this model. Conversely, if a blue antigen reaches a white susceptible actor before it is infected by a red actor, the white node is converted to an inoculated blue node with probability γ and remains blue, permanently.

The state diagram of Fig. 8.11b is more complex than Figure 8.11a because white nodes transition to blue nodes with probability γ, only if they are adjacent to either blue or yellow nodes. Similarly, red nodes transition to yellow (recovered and inoculated) nodes with probability γ only if they are also adjacent to blue or yellow nodes. Once a node reaches a blue or yellow state, it stays there. We assume that both red and blue contagions spread at the same rate, and ask, "What is the best node to seed with an initial blue antigen such that the red infection will be curtailed in the most effective way?"

In the following simulation, the two epidemic spreading processes alternate between infection spreading (Fig. 8.11a) and antigen spreading (Fig. 8.11b). A randomly chosen node is initially infected and its contagion spread to its adjacent neighbors followed by the countermeasure antigen starting from the seed node. The Java code avoids any processing biases by randomly selecting the links of the network. After each step, it examines each adjacent node and consults the state diagram to determine its next state.

8.4.2   Countermeasure Seeding Strategies

The idea of using an antigen to stop a virus is somewhat new. It is similar to setting up competition between two species—a red infection and a blue antigen species—and then letting the stronger species win. If successful, it offers an entirely novel way to combat Internet viruses as well as stop deadly human viruses. The idea is to fight fire with fire, but where is the best place to start?

We follow a strategy similar to that of Chen and Carley (Chen, 2004). However, our strategy looks at four much simpler seeding algorithms: (1) *random*—select a seed node at random, (2) *hub*—seed the node with the largest number of connections, (3) *center node*—seed the first node we find with the hortest distance from all other nodes, and (4) *closest node*—seed the intermediary node with the most paths running through it.

We conjecture that the hub-seeding algorithm gives the antigen an advantage because it has more adjacent nodes than does any other node, and the center node seed algorithm is fewer hops away from all other nodes and therefore should reach all other nodes before the epidemic does. As it turns out, hub seeding is much better than the other three, but surprisingly, the maximum-closeness algorithm is nearly equivalent to the hub-seeding algorithm.

A seeding algorithm is considered most effective if either it minimizes the time to eradicate the epidemic represented by the red infection, or minimizes peak infection density. A seeding algorithm that removes the epidemic as quickly as possible meets the time objective, and the objective of minimum peak infection is satisfied by an algorithm that infects the least number of nodes at its peak.

The results of numerous simulations using program *Network.jar* are shown in Fig. 8.12. Removal time in random, scale-free ($\Delta m = 4$), and small-world networks (5% rewiring probability) for networks with $n = 100$ nodes, $m = 400$ links, and an infection rate of 10% are compared in Fig. 8.12. Surprisingly, the maximum-closeness algorithm does as well, and in some cases slightly better, than the hub-seeding algorithm. Why? As it turns out, the closest node is also the hub in all classes except small-world networks.

From Fig. 8.12 we conclude that

1. The best (lowest) overall removal time was achieved by the hub-seeding algorithm—this confirms intuition. However, the hub-seeding algorithm is not as effective on a scale-free network as is the closeness-seeding algorithm. But, the difference is not significant.

2. The best (lowest) overall peak infection prior to removal is achieved by the hub-seeding algorithm—and is especially effective in a scale-free network, but far less effective in a small-world network. The closeness-seeding algorithm works slightly better than the hub-seeding algorithm for scale-free and small-world networks, but the difference is not large enough to be significant.

3. Removal speed does not differ significantly among the four algorithms when the network is random, but peak infection percentages do. Random and central seeding are the worst performing algorithms in all cases.

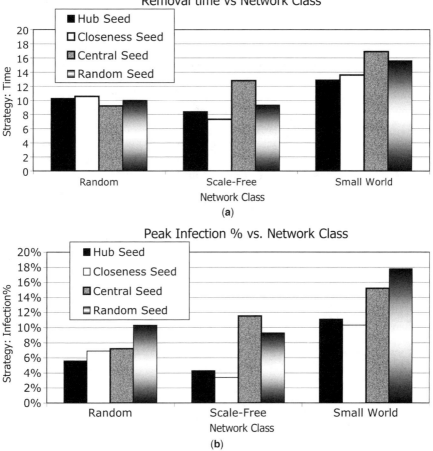

Figure 8.12 Results of the red-blue countermeasure simulation for (a) the minimum-time objective (time to eradicate infection) and (b) the minimum-peak-infection objective (for random, scale-free, and small-world networks). Network properties: $n = 100$, $m = 400$, $\Delta m = 4$, rewiring probability, $p = 5\%$, and infection rate 10%. Each data point was obtained by averaging over 10 runs.

These results are important in a number of disciplines, as mentioned earlier, but in particular, they have far-reaching implications for protecting the Internet. The current practice of protecting desktop and laptop computers by installing antivirus software at the local level is far less effective than hardening the hubs of the Internet. Hubs handle a large percentage of all traffic, so it makes much more sense to harden dozens of hub servers than millions of clients. Surprisingly, the closeness-seeding algorithm turns out to be a potent countermeasure, too. In terms of the Internet, maximum closeness means that more paths pass through the closest node than do any others. For example, the maximum-closeness router or switch handles more traffic than others do. So, it makes sense to launch a countermeasure from such a node.

These results lead to the conclusion that the most effective countermeasure for eradicating newly launched computer viruses from the Internet is to launch antigens from the dozen or so largest hubs or closest routers or switches, *rather than from individual client computers*! This strategy would be much more effective than protecting the millions of desktop and laptop clients. This radical conclusion is counter to the current cyber security practice, but it makes sense, because client computers are neither central, closest, nor network hubs.

Adoption of an antigen countermeasure approach to cyber security would be far more effective against a large number of Internet viruses—but not all. For example, it is not always easy to detect a malicious program or attachment. An unruly antigen that erases an important attachment is just as detrimental as a malicious virus! However, launching safe and simple antigens is inexpensive, easy, and apparently effective.

The results of this chapter show that hub and closeness seeding strategies are most effective against epidemics in large arbitrary networks, whether they are random, small-world, or scale-free. This conclusion supports similar work by Dezso and Barabasi (Dezso, 2002), who claim that the strategy of distributing "cures" randomly in a scale-free network is ineffective. Random cures are wasted on the least connected, and therefore least critical, nodes. Instead, they propose to cure the hubs—confirming the simulation results given here. We have shown that seeding the maximum-closeness node works as well, and in some cases better, than hub seeding, regardless of the network's topology.

8.4.3   Antigen Simulation in Java

The Java code that implements the red-blue antigen countermeasure simulation used to obtain the results of Fig. 8.12 is revealed in this section. Refer to the state diagrams of Fig. 8.11. Method `NW_doAntigen()` is called from program *Network.jar* by pressing the ANTIGEN button, after selecting a seeding strategy from the SETTINGS menu.

`NW_doAntigen(boolean RED)` is called twice in each time step: once with RED = **true**, and again with RED = **false**. The first instance spreads the infection (red) according to the state diagram of Fig. 8.11a, and the second instance spreads the antigen (blue) according to the state diagram of Fig. 8.11b. The code is straightforward except for the following.

Both infection and antigen are propagated by links, which are processed in random order. The randomization of links is handled by method `SH_Shuffle()` in class `Shuffler`. This method simulates the shuffling of a deck of cards, so method `random_list.card[i]` returns the *i*th randomized link index.

The reader should note that the contagion is spread through "next state" variable `int_color`—a component of every node element. This prevents unfair competition between red and blue contagions by forcing each to take its turn. For example, the use of a "next state" variable prevents the spread of contagion red from node A, to B, to C, . . . in one timestep. Instead, the red contagion may spread from node A to node B, but then it must wait until its next turn to continue with node C, and so forth. This inter-lacing of red and blue spreading is implemented in two phases—phase 1 establishes the "next state," while phase 2 advances the next state into the next timestep. Interlacing in this way avoids simulation biases that do not exist in the real world.

```
public void NW_doAntigen(boolean RED){
        //Randomly Propagate the infection
        Shuffler random_list = new Shuffler(nLinks);
        for(int i = 0; i < nLinks; i++) random_list.card[ i] = i;
        random_list.SH_Shuffle(nLinks);    //Scramble link order
        //Pass 1: calc next state
        int j;                              //Random link
        int tail, head;                     //End nodes
        if(RED){                            //Propagate red infection
          for(int i = 0; i < nLinks; i++){
          Node n = null;                    //Target of infection
          j = random_list.card[i];
          tail = Link[j].tail;
          head = Link[j].head;
          if(node[ tail] .color == Color.red //From tail to head
              &&
              node[head].color == Color.white) n = node[head];
          else if(node[ head] .color == Color.red  //From head to tail
              &&
              node[tail].color == Color.white) n = node[tail];
            if(n != null && 100*Math.random() <= InfectionRate) {
              n.int_color = 2;               //Infect! red
            }
          }
        }
        else for(int i = 0; i < nLinks; i++){ //Propagate blue
                                              countermeasure
          Node n = null;                      //Target of infection
          j = random_list.card[i];
          tail = Link[j].tail;
          head = Link[j].head;
          boolean tail_color = node[ tail] .color == Color.blue
                          ||
                  node[tail].color == Color.yellow;
          boolean head_color = node[ head] .color == Color.blue
                          ||
                  node[head].color == Color.yellow;
          //Spread blue
          if(tail_color                       //From tail to head
              &&
```

```
                  node[head].color == Color.white) n = node[head];
          else if(head_color           //From head to tail
                    &&
              node[tail].color == Color.white) n = node[tail];
          if(n != null && 100*Math.random() <= InfectionRate) {
                  n.int_color = 4;        //Inoculate! blue
            }
          //Recover yellow
          if(tail_color                //From red to yellow
                  &&
              node[head].color == Color.red) n = node[head];
          else if(head_color          //From head to tail
                    &&
              node[tail].color == Color.red) n = node[tail];
            if(n != null && 100*Math.random() <= InfectionRate) {
                  n.int_color = 3,        //Recover! yellow
            }
      }
      //Pass 2
      for(int i = 0; i < nNodes; i++) {
          switch (node[ i] .int_color) {
              case 1: { node[ i] .color = Color.white; break;}
              case 2: { node[ i] .color = Color.red; break;}
              case 3: { node[ i] .color = Color.yellow; break;}
              case 4: { node[ i] .color = Color.blue; break;}
          }
      }
}//NW_doAntigen
```

This code implements the state diagrams of Fig. 8.11, which in simple terms say to transition susceptible actors (white nodes) into either infected (red) or inoculated (blue) actors, and infected (red) actors into recovered (yellow) actors. Once an actor is inoculated, it remains inoculated (blue) permanently. Similarly, once an actor becomes recovered (yellow), it also remains recovered. Therefore, all nodes start as susceptible actors (white) and end up inoculated (blue or yellow).

Note that this method propagates the antigen through blue and yellow nodes; that is, whenever a red node appears adjacent to a blue or yellow node, the red node is converted to a yellow node with probability γ. The reverse never happens—a blue node is never converted to a red or yellow node. In fact, blue nodes occur only when a white node is converted to a blue node. Yellow nodes occur only when a red node is transformed into a yellow node by either a blue or yellow node!

8.5 EXERCISES

8.1. Assuming the Kermack–McKendrick model and $\Delta = 0$, how long does it take to infect 50% of the population, for $n = 100$, $i_0 = 0.01$ (1%), $\gamma = 0.005$?

8.2. Derive the time-varying solution to the Kermack–McKendrick equation when $\gamma > 0$, $\Delta > 0$. Consider two cases: $\gamma > \Delta$, and $\gamma < \Delta$:

(a) $\dfrac{\delta i}{\delta t} = \gamma si - \Delta i$

(b) $i(0) = i_0$

(c) $s + i = 1$

8.3. What is the approximate peak infection density for a random network with $n = 100$, $m = 200$, infection duration of 10 units, and infection rate equal to recovery rate equal to 20%?

8.4. What connectivity λ is required to achieve a peak infection density of no more than 50% in a small-world network with the parameter values given in Table 8.1?

8.5. Estimate the spectral radius of a small-world network with $n = 200$ and $m = 2000$. What is the estimated spectral radius of an equivalent scale-free network?

8.6. What is the approximate fixed-point (epidemic equilibrium) density of an epidemic in a random network with $n = 1000$, $m = 5000$, and epidemic parameters $\gamma = 33\%$ and $\Delta = 33\%$?

8.7. Consider a star network with $n = 4$ nodes and a hub at node 0. Furthermore, let column matrix $\mathbf{P}(t - 1) = [p_0, p_1, p_2, p_3]^T$ represent the probability that nodes of the star network are infected at time $(t - 1)$, and $\mathbf{A}$ the 4×4 adjacency matrix of the star network. Show that the probability that hub node 0 is infected by its neighbors, $p_0(t)$, at time t, is the product of matrix multiplication, $k[\mathbf{A} \times \mathbf{P}(t - 1)]$, where scalar $k = (1 - p_0)\gamma$. Also, given $\gamma = \frac{1}{3}$, what is the numerical value of $p_0(t)$, given $p_i(t - 1) = \frac{1}{2}$, for $i = 0,1,2,3$?

8.8. What is the minimum recovery rate Δ that allows an epidemic with $\gamma = 5\%$ to persist when infecting a star network of size $n = 65$?

8.9. What is the threshold infection rate γ for an epidemic with $\Delta = 15\%$ to persist when infecting a star network of size $n = 65$?

8.10. Consider a fully connected complete network, $n = 100$, and an epidemic with infection rate, $\gamma = 1\%$. What is the threshold recovery rate Δ? Compare the WCWF approximation and the quadratic approximation with simulation results.

8.11. In Exercise 8.10, what is the estimated fixed-point infection for the complete network with $\rho = 99$ and $\gamma = 1\%$?

8.12. What happens to the threshold infection rate

$$y_0 = \frac{\Delta}{\rho\,(\text{network})}$$

as the size of each of the following networks grows without bound?

(a) Toroidal network

(b) Hypercube network

(c) Binary tree network

(d) Random network

8.13. Which seeding strategy is most effective in reducing removal time in each of the following networks?

(a) Small-world

(b) Random

(c) Scale-free

8.14. Which seeding strategy is most effective in reducing peak infection density in each of the following networks?

(a) Small-world

(b) Random

(c) Scale-free

9

SYNCHRONY

Thus far, in this book we have studied networks from the perspective of their topological structure, and the state of their nodes (infected or not). This chapter expands on the dynamic nature of node states and asks the question, "What property of a network guarantees the synchronization of a network's nodes?" A network synchronizes when all of its nodes change or reach a certain state in unison. Otherwise, the network is *unstable* or *chaotic*.

1. A network is said to *synchronize* if the values of all of its nodes converge to some constant as the time rate of change of all of its node values approaches zero.

2. A dynamic network is considered to be *stable* if the value of its nodes synchronize, *transient* if its node values oscillate, *bistable* if its nodes oscillate between fixed values, and unstable or *chaotic*, otherwise.

3. We introduce *chaotic maps* to visualize the state of a node in a network: if a network eventually synchronizes, every node in the chaotic map will find a fixed point in its chaotic map called a *strange attractor*—and never leave it. A chaotic map is simply a plot of the state of a node at time $(t + 1)$ versus its state at time t.

4. We show how to synchronize most any network by *pinning* a node (holding constant at least one node value), attaching a *triangular cycle* (a complete subnetwork of three nodes), or augmenting a chaotic network with control links that form at least one triangular cycle.

Network Science: Theory and Practice. By Ted G. Lewis
Copyright © 2009 John Wiley & Sons, Inc.

5. A simple model of biological synchronization—that of chirping crickets—illustrates the impact of topology on network stability. The actors in a simulated cricket social network alternate between listening and chirping. The chirping crickets synchronize (chirp in unison and listen in unison) if there exists a cycle in the network whose length is an odd number, or at least one actor is pinned. Addition of a *triangular cycle* is sufficient to guarantee synchronization. One dominant cricket that unwaveringly alternates between chirping and listening is also sufficient. Otherwise, the chirping cricket network does not synchronize.

6. A more general algorithm by (Atay, 2006) assigns numerical values to each node and computes the change in state by averaging the difference between a node's state and its adjacent nodes' states. Like the cricket social network, an *Atay network* containing at least one cycle of odd length will synchronize. It will also synchronize if a triangular cycle is attached to an arbitrary node or by pinning at least one node.

7. Contrary to current literature on small-world networks and synchronization in biological systems such as heart pacemakers, small-world networks have no advantage over any other class of network as far as synchronization is concerned. However, because small-world networks naturally contain triangular cycles in the form of clusters, they are "natural synchronizers."

8. We define a *Kirchhoff network* as any fully connected network where the state of a node is the difference between the sum total of inflows and sum total of outflows. A Kirchhoff network synchronizes if the lengths of any pair of directed cycles are relatively prime numbers.

9. We apply the theory of synchronizing Kirchhoff networks to the electrical power grid of Pointville, and verify that the grid stabilizes itself whenever a damaged link or damaged node is removed, leaving a network containing relatively prime cycle lengths. Otherwise, the damaged grid reacts chaotically, and cannot synchronize. This property is a rather intriguing approximation to reality—actual electrical power grids have become unstable and entire regions have gone powerless following a fault in a single powerline.

Simple synchronization problems abound in nature, and more complex network synchronization phenomena typical of synthetic dynamical systems such as the Internet, electrical power grid, and various feedback control systems. Program *Network.jar* simulates each of the following networks, and provides insights into their behavior.

9.1 TO SYNC OR NOT TO SYNC

Many applications of network science deal with the state or values associated with nodes and links as well as the topology of the network. Node states might represent voltage in an electrical power grid; charge in a nervous system; or capacity of a parking lot, reservoir, or computer memory. These applications are modeled as dynamic networks containing nodes with dynamic values called *states*.

One critical question to ask is, "What is the nature of the behavior of a dynamic network?" Do the nodes increase or decrease in value until reaching infinity, or do they die off and eventually equal zero? Alternatively, do nodes oscillate back and forth between fixed values, or do they reach a certain level and stay there, indefinitely? These are stability questions, and the study of network synchrony is the study of network stability. We claim that a stable network eventually stabilizes when all node values synchronize. That is, a network stabilizes when all of its nodes either march together in lock-step synchrony or settle down to the same value.

Networks that march together in lock-step fashion are said to *oscillate*, and networks containing nodes that reach a common value are said to *stabilize*. A third possibility exists—networks that are so unstable that the states of some or all of its nodes "blow up" or rapidly increase or decrease without bound. Such erratic networks are unstable. Regardless of the eventual state of a network, the states of its nodes may behave erratically over a short period of time before stabilizing. We call such behavior *chaotic*, because states change erratically and unpredictably.

More formally, a dynamic network $G(t) = \{N(t), L(t), f(t)\}$ is a graph with annotated nodes and links defined as follows:

1. Each element of $N(t)$, v_i, is annotated with a state, $s_i(t)$, next state, $s_i(t + 1)$, which may be defined numerically or by some arbitrary property such as color.
2. Each element of $L(t)$, e_i, may also be annotated with a state and next state value, such as a flow or capacity of the link.
3. The mapping function $f(t)$ may or may not be dynamic—in the cases studied here, we assume $f(\ )$ to be static (e.g., the topology of the network does not change over time).

Dynamic networks with state are abstract entities—they may represent a physical apparatus such as a communications network, electrical power grid, or an abstraction such as a social network consisting of actors and relationships. For example, we illustrate the behavior of a cricket social network by modeling each animal as an actor (node) and the act of listening to an adjacent cricket chirp, as a link. Similarly, we model the social network of Pointville, Flatland as a collection of nodes with a product opinion—either positive or negative. This kind of network is useful to advertisers who want to promote a product by word-of-mouth marketing.

9.1.1 Chaotic Maps

A dynamic network is said to *sync* if, starting at some initial state $G(0)$, it evolves in finite time to another state, $G(t^*)$, and stays there, forever. We call $G(t^*)$ a *strange attractor*, and if the network remains at its strange attractor point indefinitely, it is also a *fixed point*. Networks that appear to bounce around from one state to another in no apparent pattern are considered *chaotic*. Networks that oscillate between two or more strange attractors are called *oscillators*. Oscillators—networks that alternate between or among several states, are also considered to be *pseudostable*. Such networks have both chaotic and stable behaviors. Pseudostable nodes often oscillate much like a bistable oscillator, or *flip-flop* circuit in a computer, so we also call them *bistable* networks.

For G to reach a fixed point, the state of every node (and link) in G must do the same—starting from an initial state $s_i(0)$, every node $i = 0,1,2,\ldots,n-1$, must reach a final state $s_i(t^*)$ and remain there, in order for the network to sync. A bistable node alternates between states, and an unstable node "blows up"—its state becomes unbounded, or takes on seemingly random values. We call these unstable states chaotic, even though they often repeat the same sequence of state values over and over again.

State transitions from $s_i(0)$, to $s_i(1),s_i(2),\ldots,s_i(t^*)$ form a *trajectory* in state space defined by plotting $s_i(t+1)$ along the vertical axis, and $s_i(t)$ along the horizontal axis of a chaotic map. A *chaotic map* is simply a plot of a node's trajectory in state space. Figure 9.1 illustrates the chaotic map of a stable node, a bistable node, and a chaotic node. A *stable node* is attracted to its fixed point regardless of its starting point.

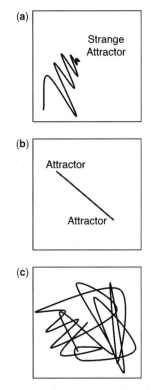

Figure 9.1 Chaotic maps: trajectories of (a) a stable node as it reaches its strange attractor, (b) a bistable node as it oscillates between two attractors, and (c) a chaotic node as it wanders around in state space.

The bistable node oscillates between two points, and the chaotic node traces out a random walk, or an apparently random walk. More generally, the trajectory of a chaotic node traces out the same erratic path, over and over again. It is not truly random, but rather, nonlinear.

9.1.2 Network Stability

While the term "chaotic" is perhaps too strong to describe a node or network—nodes may not be truly chaotic—it captures the erratic behavior of networks out of control. By this we mean that a disturbance in the form of a spike in a node's value or a disruption such as a damaged link, leads to abrupt changes in adjacent nodes. The node may not be able to return to its strange attractor value, for example. The issue is not whether the disruption alters the state of a node or network, but rather, whether the node or network recovers. A stable network will recover—perhaps very slowly—while an unstable network will not. *Stability* is the term we use to describe nodes and networks that recover from disruptions in their state.

If stability is the issue, then what conditions guarantee stability? We claim that stability is a state of synchronization, and chaos is a state of instability—that is, a network is stable if its nodes synchronize (all achieve their strange attractor values), and either bistable or chaotic, otherwise. The conditions that guarantee synchronization are the same as the conditions that guarantee stability.[1]

Two general techniques have been used for decades to analyze the stability of a coupled system: the Laplace or Z-transform (*Lyapunov*) method, and the Laplacian eigenvalue (spectral decomposition) method. We give a very brief overview of these two methods, but the reader is advised to study Lyapunov stability theory in more detail elsewhere in the literature, if interested (Kuramoto, 1984) (Lago-Fernandez, 1999). We will, however, describe the *Laplacian* eigenvalue method in some detail because it relates the largest eigenvalue of the network's state matrix to network stability.

9.1.2.1 Lyapunov Method

The general concept of Lyapunov stability in the context of a network is quite simple. Suppose that the state equations governing nodes v_i, $i = 1, 2, \ldots, n$ of G, form a system of first-order differential equations [where $s'(t)$ is the rate of change of $s(t)$ with respect to time, $f(\ )$ is a linear function, and $S(t)$ is the dynamic state vector of G]:

$$s_1'(t) = f_1(s_1(t))$$
$$s_2'(t) = f_2(s_2(t))$$

$$\vdots$$

$$s_n'(t) = f_n(s_n(t))$$

---

[1]Not generally, but this definition will do for this chapter.

Converting this into vector form, noting that $S(t) = [s_1(t), s_2(t), \ldots, s_n(t)]^T$, we obtain a compact representation of the change in state of network G at time t:

$$S'(t) = \mathbf{F}S(t),$$

where $\mathbf{F}$ is the matrix equivalent of $f_i(\ )$ applied to each $s_i(t)$. Given initial conditions, we can transform this system of time-domain differential equations into equivalent complex-domain algebraic equations using the Z-transform: $Z\{s(t)\} = s(z) = \sum_0^\infty \{f(t)z^{-t}\}$. For example, the Z-transform of a constant, $f(t) = 1$ is the infinite sum, $f(z) = \sum_0^\infty \{f(t)z^{-t}\} = \sum_0^\infty \{z^{-t}\}$:

$$f(z) = \sum_0^\infty \{z^{-t}\} = 1 + \sum_1^\infty \{z^{-t}\} = 1 + z^{-1} \sum_0^\infty \{z^{-t}\} = 1 + z^{-1}f(z)$$

Essentially, a constant in the time domain causes a shift in the complex domain. This shift is represented by the term z^{-1}. Solving for $f(z)$, we obtain

$$f(z) = 1 + z^{-1}f(z)$$
$$(1 - z^{-1})f(z) = 1$$
$$f(z) = \frac{1}{1 - z^{-1}}$$

Note that this solution is valid only for $|z| < 1$. If $|z| = 1$, the expression for $f(z)$ blows up. A singularity in the complex plane is called a *pole*. Thus, $|z| = 1$ is a pole for this particular transformation. In terms of Lyapunov stability theory, a system's state equation blows up at poles. Therefore, it is necessary that solutions to the z-plane equations avoid poles.

Z-Transform theory is applied to finite-difference equations rather than differential equations. Thus, we can apply Z-transform theory to the general state equation for networks by replacing $s'(t)$ with $\Delta s(t)$. The Z-transform of the first difference, $\Delta s(t) = s(t + 1) - s(t)$ is

$$Z\{s(t + 1) - s(t)\} = z^{-1}s(z) - s(0) - Z\{s(t)\} = (z^{-1} - 1)s(z) - s(0)$$

Consider the solution to a simple difference equation, $\Delta s(t) = h(t)$, where $h(t)$ is some linear function of t. We transform the time-domain difference equation into a simpler algebraic equation in the complex plane, and then solve for $s(z)$. We can convert $s(z)$ back into the time domain, or simply study its stability by noting where the poles lie. For the general equation, $\Delta s(t) = h(t)$, given here, we have

$$(z^{-1} - 1)s(z) - s(0) = Z\{h(t)\} = h(z)$$
$$s(z) = \frac{h(z) + s(0)}{z^{-1} - 1}$$

Since we are interested mainly in the stability of a network as opposed to its final state, we may choose to evaluate the behavior of $\Delta s(t)$ as t increases without bound, or $s(z)$ as z approaches *poles* in the complex plane.[2] For example, $s(z) = z/(z - 1)$ has a pole at $z = 1$, and

$$s(z) = \frac{z}{(z - 3)(z + 2j)}$$

where $2j$ is an imaginary number, has two poles—one at $z = 3$ and the other at $z = -2j$.

Lyapunov stability theory says that a linear system is stable, if and only if the poles of the complex-domain solution lie on or within the unit circle. In other words, if all poles in the solution lie within the unit circle defined by $|z| \leq 1$, we can be sure that the linear system won't blow up. In terms of network stability, we show that the complex-domain solution, $s(z)$, also follows the Lyapunov theorem. However, this does not imply that a network of oscillators will synchronize, as we shall see. However, it is a start!

9.1.2.2 *Spectral Decomposition*
Spectral decomposition is the process of transforming the network's system matrix into its eigenvalues, and then analyzing the largest eigenvalue to determine convergence to an attractor. In general, eigenvalues that are less than one in the time-domain solution, and eigenvalues that are less than zero in the first-order time-domain derivative lead to stability. However, we will illustrate several cases where these conditions are not sufficient to guarantee network stability. Well-behaved eigenvalues are a necessary, but not sufficient condition to guarantee network stability.

Convergence of the solution $S(t) = F^t S(0)$, in the time domain may mean that a strange attractor is reached so that $|S(t + 1) - S(t)| = 0$ as t increases without limit. Alternatively, convergence may mean that the derivative diminishes as t increases

$$|S'(t)| \text{ approaches zero as } t \text{ increases without bound}$$

In either case, the actual solution, $s(t)$, may or may not reach zero. Indeed, if the network syncs, it may occur because all nodes reach the same nonzero strange attractor. Therefore, we have two similar but not entirely identical criteria for sync: (1) the state of all of the network's nodes may go to zero and stay there, or (2) the state of all of the network's nodes may go to the same nonzero value and stay there.

Of course, a network may not sync, in which case the states of nodes may blow up or oscillate among two or more attractors. For example, the state equation of a simple barbell network consisting of two nodes connected by a single link, is given as follows:

$$s_1'(t) = -s_2(t); \quad s_1(0) = 1$$
$$s_2'(t) = -s_1(t); \quad s_2(0) = 0$$

---

[2]*Poles* are singularity points in the complex plane, for instance, points where the function $s(z)$ is unbounded.

In matrix form this is:

$$S'(t) = \begin{pmatrix} 0 & -1 \\ -1 & 0 \end{pmatrix} S(0)$$

Spectral decomposition of the matrix yields two eigenvalues, 1 and (-1). The largest eigenvalue is 1, so we suspect that the network cannot dampen out erratic state transitions. In fact, the barbell network is marginally unstable, oscillating between two attractors. More specifically, the barbell network is a *bistable oscillator* with a chaotic map as illustrated in Fig. 9.1b.

The problem with spectral decomposition, as we shall see later in this chapter, is that the eigenvalues may not be negative enough to thoroughly dampen out all chaotic trajectories in G (Wang, 2002a). The largest nontrivial eigenvalue of a network's *Laplacian matrix* is its *spectral gap*—$\sigma(G)$, which represents the least amount of dampening in a linear system represented by its adjacency matrix. In certain cases we can use the *spectral gap* to determine whether a network synchronizes, but the question of how negative the spectral gap must be in order to stabilize a specific network remains unanswered as of this writing.[3]

A general solution to the network sync problem is still an open research question. Instead, we follow a less ambitious approach that looks at each network through the lens of spectral decomposition and graph theory. We use spectral decomposition to obtain necessary, but not sufficient, criteria, and various graph theory techniques to obtain additional conditions necessary to guarantee synchronization:

1. First, we examine the extremely simple chirping crickets social network and note that chirping networks become bistable whenever the social network contains at least one odd-length cycle (e.g., a triangular subnetwork of size 3). Each node in the cricket network is in one of only two states: the value of each node is zero (white) if the actor is listening, and one (red) if the actor is chirping.

2. Next, we generalize the cricket network to model a network proposed by Atay et al., in which the state of each node takes on a numerical value, and the synchronizing algorithm is simply the average value of differences between a node and its adjacent neighbors. This network holds special interest because the system state equation is a function of the network's Laplacian matrix. Hence, we speculate that it can be analyzed using the spectral gap approach. However, we learn that this is not as successful as expected, because we do not know how negative a network's spectral gap must be to dampen all chaotic trajectories.

We next turn to a slightly more general and perhaps more useful class of networks proposed by the author. We model networks that attempt to stabilize on *Kirchhoff's first law*—that the sum total of a commodity flowing into a node must equal the sum total flowing out of the node. This model is useful because it represents many real-world systems such as electrical circuits, power grids, and so on. We discover that Kirchhoff networks sync when two conditions are met: (1) the Kirchhoff

---

[3]Wang's theory (Wang, 2002a) says $\sigma \leq (-T/c)$, for a network to sync, but leaves T undefined.

eigenvalue is less than one; and (2) the maximum element of its system matrix, B, raised to the nth power, is also less than one.

Finally, we study a social network in imaginary Pointville, Flatland used by hypothetical marketers to spread both positive and negative promotions (buzz) about a product. The *buzz network* of Pointville is a word-of-mouth communication network. Marketers plant a positive seed at one node and a negative seed at another node. Assuming that Pointville's social network is a closed word-of-mouth network, both positive and negative seeds spread through the network like an epidemic. Nodes are influenced by their innate stubbornness and the average opinion of their neighbors. We determine that maximum influence—whether positive or negative—is achieved by seeding the network's hub node. If a marketer wants to beat the competition, the best way to do so is to identify and seed the network's hub with the marketer's promotion.

Buzz networks always sync, but the question answered in the final section of this chapter is, "What influence does a promoter have over the entire network?" We show that the entire network syncs with a bias toward the promotion initiated by the network's hub. If the hub is positive, the entire network ends up with a positive bias. If it is negative, the entire network ends up with a negative bias. However, there is one exception to this rule when there are multiple hubs with equal degree.

9.2   A CRICKET SOCIAL NETWORK

Consider a simple social network consisting of crickets as actors (nodes) and links representing the proximity of neighboring crickets within earshot of one another.[4] Crickets either *listen* or *chirp* during each time interval. Therefore, each node of this network is in one of two states: listening—indicated by painting the node white—or chirping, which is indicated by painting the node red. After each chirp, a cricket listens for at least one time interval, but then it may either listen again, or chirp. Crickets chirp only if they hear a chirp from one or more neighbors (adjacent nodes). Initially, one cricket is selected to chirp.

The following Java code implements the simple listen–chirp model described above. Each node is painted either white (listen) or red (chirp), and assigned a `next_state` value, as chirping spreads like an infection from one neighbor to another. Initially, only one node is red. When the simulation starts, this node infects its immediate neighbors. An infected neighbor is scheduled to turn red in a future timestep but setting its `next_state` value to 2. The `next_state` value is decremented to 1, and possibly zero. When it reaches 1, the node is painted red; otherwise it is painted white. However, depending on the topology of the network, the timer may reach one or zero, or it may be reset to 2 before reaching zero. In this way, nodes alternate between red and white, while simultaneously trying to sync with chirping neighbors.

---

[4]We assume that crickets have ears!

The chirping algorithm is extremely simple to implement, but subtle. Method
NW_doChirp() makes two passes over the nodes. Pass 1 determines whether
each node has an adjacent node that is chirping during the current time period, and
pass 2 updates the states of each node.

Pass 1: For each node in the network, determine whether an adjacent node is
chirping (red), and if it is, schedule the node to chirp *one timestep* into the future
(alternate between red and white). This is done by setting the next_state
to 2, because next_state is decremented before testing to see if it is zero or
1, in pass 2.

Pass 2: Color each node in the network red if its next_state is one; otherwise,
color it white. Decrement the node's next_state, regardless, so crickets can
take a rest between chirps.

```
public void NW_doChirp(){
      Shuffler random_list = new Shuffler(nNodes);
      for(int i = 0; i < nNodes; i++) random_list.card[ i] = i;
      random_list.SH_Shuffle(nNodes);        //Scramble processing order
      for(int n = 0; n < nNodes; n++) {      //Pass 1: Find Red Neighbors
        int i = random_list.card[ n] ;        //Process nodes at random
        for(int j = 0; j < nLinks; j++){      //Find neighbors
          if(Link[ j] .head == i && node[ Link[ j] .tail] .color == Color.red
                 ||
          Link[j].tail == i && node[Link[j].head].color == Color.red){
            node[i].next_state = 2;           //Future Red
          }
        }
      }
      for(int i = 0; i < nNodes; i++){        //Pass 2: Listen or Chirp
        node[i].color = Color.white;          //Listen
        node[i].value = 0;                    //For chaotic map
        if(node[ i] .next_state == 1) {       //Alternate back-and-forth
        node[i].color = Color.red;            //Chirp
        node[i].value = 1;                    //For chaoticmap
      }
      node[i].next_state- -;                       //Flip-Flop state
      if(node[ i] .next_state < 0)
        node[i].next_state = 0;               //Bounded: 0: white, 1: red
      }
      }//NW_doChirp
```

This code uses method SH_Shuffle from class Shuffler, as we have done many
times before, to randomize the processing order of nodes, thus ensuring that there is

no bias introduced by the simulation. It also sets the value of each node to either 1 or 0, corresponding with red or white, so that the chaotic map function of program *Network.jar* can display state trajectories of any of the actors.

Simulation of this algorithm in a network produces either a bistable chaotic map as shown in Fig. 9.1b, or a chaotic map as shown in Fig. 9.1c. Thus, the network never syncs, but instead, reaches a bistable state (listen–chirp–listen) when certain conditions are guaranteed.

9.2.1 Sync Property of the Cricket Social Network

Crickets are staunch individuals with the freedom to commence chirping whenever they want, but once they begin, they incite adjacent crickets to chirp, also. This causes a feedback effect, whereby adjacent chirping neighbors chirp back—leading to recurrence of chirping. Unlike an epidemic, staunch individualism is sure to break down when a neighbor starts chirping. Subsequent crickets begin to chirp, and so forth, spreading the infectious chatter across the network.

We learned in the previous chapter that epidemics either die out or persist. When they persist, epidemics behave differently in networks with different topology, principally because of the *spectral radius* of the network. They often exhibit chaotic behavior as the infection density fluctuates over time. Does the cricket social network exhibit similar behavior for "chirping epidemics"? Does chirping spread through a network like an epidemic? Assuming one cricket randomly begins chirping, which leads to other chirping crickets and so forth, does this chain reaction ever stop?

We know from nature that certain species of crickets and fireflies synchronize their chirping and flashing—that is, starting from a single random chirp, a certain species of crickets will at some point commence to chirp in unison. After a period of cacophony, a rhythmic synchronized chirping emerges. We claim that this emergent behavior spontaneously occurs in some networks, but not others. The topological structure of a cricket's social network determines whether it syncs. However, contrary to early studies of synchronization in small-world networks, synchronization in the cricket network studied here is related not to small worlds, but instead, to the order of circuits in the small world (Watts, 1998, 1999a).

Under what conditions does a cricket social network synchronize? This simple control problem has a complex solution, as we shall see. Figure 9.2 illustrates the complexity of the chirping crickets control problem using a small and somewhat random social network of eight crickets. Figure 9.2a shows the initial network with $n = 8$ crickets and $m = 10$ relationships. Figures 9.1b and 9.1c show what happens after a short period of chaos—a repeating pattern emerges whereby chirping alternates between two halves of the network—one-half listens while the other half chirps, and alternatively, the other half listens while the first half chirps. Chirping repeats in a persistent rhythmic pattern—but no synchronization emerges.

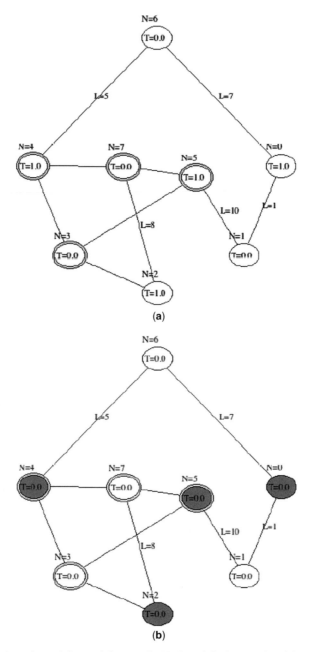

Figure 9.2 A random cricket social network: (a) the original network (with $n = 8$); (b) simultaneous chirping indicated by shaded (red) nodes; (c) alternating nodes that chirp while others listen; (d) synchronized chriping (one link has been added). In (b) and (c), chirping is not synchronized and alternates between one half and the other half of the network; in (d), chirping is synchronized by the addition of a single link—crickets chirp in unison and listen in unison.

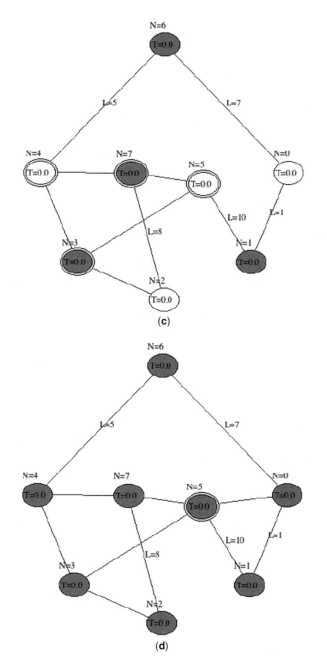

(c)

(d)

Figure 9.2. (*Continued*).

Figure 9.2d is identical to the initial network in Fig. 9.2a with one exception—a link has been inserted between nodes 0 and 5. Now, the network syncs regardless of which actor initiates the chirping. After a short period of spreading, the chirps reach all nodes, and the crickets begin to chirp together, alternating between chirping and listening in unison. The slightly modified network synchronizes! Why?

Consider the ring network of Fig. 9.3a, containing $n = 8$ (even-number) nodes. Selection of any initial node results in 50% of the nodes chirping in unison while the other 50% listen. Regardless of where chirping starts, an alternating pattern of 50% chirping while 50% are listening emerges. Now, add a link that bisects the ring network into two cyclic subgraphs as shown in Fig. 9.3b. The same 50%–50% alternating pattern emerges because the length of the two cycles formed by the bisection is an even number.

Next, add a link as shown in Fig. 9.3c such that the lengths of the two cycles is an odd number—in this case, one is 5 hops long and the other is 7 hops long. This network quickly synchronizes because of the odd-numbered cycle. Indeed, this phenomenon occurs (for the cricket chirping network) in all networks.

The chirping cricket social network is bistable—roughly 50% sync with one another in either a random or a ring network. The percentage of actors that sync depends on the topology of the network (see Table 9.1). Regardless, the chirping network does not sync 100%—that is the states of all nodes never reach a single strange attractor all at once. However, if the network contains a cycle of odd length, all nodes will oscillate between two attractors—one at $(1,0)$, and the other at $(0,1)$ in state space. Once this happens, the network oscillates indefinitely.

Table 9.1 summarizes the results of simulation of chirping crickets for the structured and unstructured networks studied in this book. In each case, the emergent pattern of listen–chirp–listen either alternates between subsets of nodes or eventually achieves bistable oscillation in lock-step fashion for all nodes in the network. Networks that contain odd-length *cyclic subgraphs* behave differently from networks with even numbers of nodes or even number of nodes in a cycle. Recall that a cycle is formed by a path connecting nodes $v_1, v_2, v_3, \ldots, v_n$, returning to v_1. The *length of a cycle* is equal to the number of nodes it contains.

Note that networks containing cycles of odd length generally become bistable oscillators (flip-flops) while all others do not. In other words, the entire chirping network oscillates if n is odd, or at least one cyclic subgraph contains an odd number of nodes. It is sufficient to add a single link to an even-numbered network to bistabilize the entire network! For example, chirping in all of the networks of Table 9.1 bistabilizes when n is odd, or at least when one cyclic subgraph contains an odd number of nodes, but fails to bistabilize, otherwise.

The reason the simple cricket colony bistabilizes when n is odd and does not when n is even is somewhat obvious. In an even-numbered network (or cycle), the pattern of red-white nodes alternates between red and white—RED, WHITE, RED, WHITE, RED,—and so forth all the way around the cycle. In an odd-numbered network (or cycle), this pattern is disrupted by two or more adjacent RED nodes—RED, WHITE, RED, RED, WHITE, and so on. The consecutive RED, RED nodes cause method NW_doChirp() to reset next_state of both nodes to 2, which disrupts their rhythm. It is as if someone in a marching band were to take two

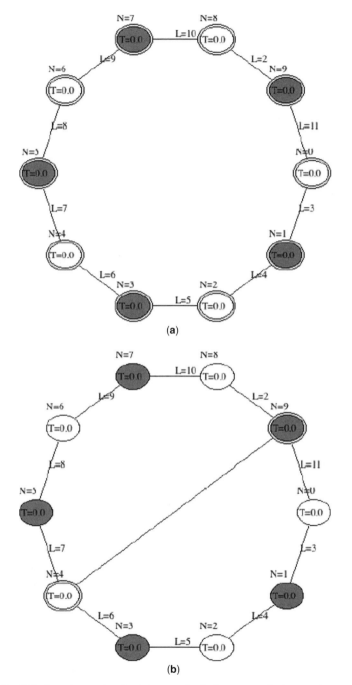

Figure 9.3 Chirping ring network: (a) even-sized ring network does not sync ($n = 8$); (b) even-sized ring network with two even-sized subgraphs of size $n = 6$; (c) even-sized ring network with two oddsized subgraphs, one of size $n = 5$ and the other of size $n = 7$. Only the network with an odd-length cycle realizes bistable chirping.

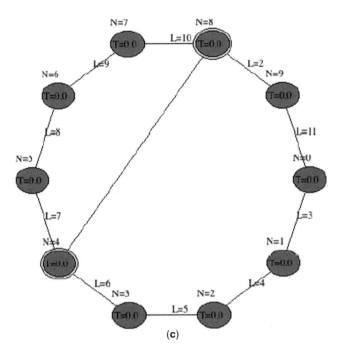

(c)

Figure 9.3. (*Continued*).

quick steps at once to bring him/herself into stride with the others. Hence, the algorithm aligns each node with the rhythm of the entire network. This eventually leads to global bistability.

As it turns out, the chirping network is a very special case of the more general Atay network studied next. Chirping networks will sync if they contain a three-node

TABLE 9.1   Sync Results for Regular and Nonregular Networks

Network	Bistable?	Comments
Barbell	No	Bistable oscillator
Line	No	50%–50% oscillations
2-Regular	Yes	Odd-sized cycles
Complete	Yes	Odd-sized cycles
Toroid	Yes	Odd-sized cycles
Binary tree	No	No cycles
Hypercube	No	Even-sized cycles
Random	Nearly always	Likely has odd-sized cycle
Small-world	Yes	Has clusters
Scale-free	Nearly always	Likely has odd-sized cycle
Star	No	No cycles
Ring	$N =$ odd number	Odd-sized cycle

cycle—a triangular cycle that is guaranteed to sync, or if at least one of the crickets dominates the chirping by unwaveringly chirping in a precise chirp–listen–chirp–listen–chirp . . . sequence. Thus, there are two explanations for synchronization in biological systems such as the chirping cricket nation: (1) a network topology that reinforces sync and (2) a dominant and incessantly rhythmic behavior of a lone actor.

This result contradicts pioneering research that stimulated renewed interest in synchronization of networks (Watts, 1998, 1999a; Hong, 2002; Barahona, 2002; Atay, 2006). The prevailing belief that small-world topology guarantees synchronization was shown to be wrong by Atay (Atay, 2006) and others, but the analysis provided here is the first study to show how pinning and augmentation with a stable control subnetwork can actually stabilize many networks—but not all! Chirping is only one of many behaviors that may lead to synchronization.

9.2.2 A More General Model: Atay Networks

Figure 9.3 and the cricket chirping algorithm illustrate two general principles of synchrony: (1) networks may or may not sync because of their topology, and (2) networks may or may not sync because of the nature of the state-changing algorithm. Topology determines the feedback signals that may or may not hinder synchronization, and the nature of the state-changing algorithm determines the magnitude of such feedback signals. The magnitude of a feedback may cause a network to "blow up," especially if it increases without bound as time passes. Therefore, we need to consider both algorithm and topology to establish necessary conditions on network synchronization.

First, we generalize the state-changing algorithm using a state equation proposed by Atay, Biyikoglu, et al. (Atay, 2006), and show that network topology plays a critical role in determining whether nodes sync (all node values tend to the same value) or do not sync (node values oscillate or "blow up"). Then, we establish some necessary conditions on network topology and node value that lead to stability. We obtain a result similar to that in the previous section, but with a more general state equation. Furthermore, we show that synchrony is possible in many non-small-world networks—contrary to early research into small-world networks.

The Atay algorithm studied next synchronizes in some networks and not others (see Table 9.2). For example, Atay synchronization fails in line, star, toroidal, binary tree, hypercube, and most other regular networks, but succeeds in 2-regular, complete, and scale-free networks. Under certain conditions, the algorithm succeeds in random, small-world, and ring networks. Furthermore, the ability to sync has little to do with the spectral gap of a network, as shown by Table 9.2. The question is, why does the Atay algorithm sync in some networks, and not in others?

Let the state of node i be given by s_i, so that column vector $S(t)$ is the system state of network G at time t. The time rate of change in $S(t)$ is denoted $S'(t)$, the transpose is $S^{T}(t)$, and $f(S(t))$ is some linear function operating on $S(t)$. Think of $f(\ )$ as the output function that turns state $S(t)$ into a numerical value at each timestep t. We define the

TABLE 9.2   Atay Synchronization in Networks ($n = 100$)

Network	Sync (Yes/No)	Typical Spectral Gap
Line	No	-0.001
Star	No	-1.000
2-Regular	Yes	-0.020
Complete	Yes	-100.0
Toroid	Yes	-0.382
Binary Tree	No	-0.018
Hypercube	No	-2.000
Random	Mostly	-0.287
Small world	Mostly	-0.080
Scale-free	Yes	-0.615
Ring	Sometimes	-0.004

system state of a *dynamical network system* as follows:

$$S(t) = [s_1, s_2, s_3, \ldots, s_n]^T = \text{state vector of } G; \quad S_j(t) = \text{row } j \text{ of } S(t)$$
$$f(s_j) = \text{linear function of state of node } j: \quad f(S) = \text{function applied to system}$$

Atay State Equation $S'(t) = f(S(t)) + \sum_{j \sim i}\{ f(S_j(t)) - f(S_i(t))\}$, where the summation $\sum_{j \sim i}$ is over the neighbors of node i, namely, $i \sim j$.

We want to know under what conditions the state equation leads to synchronization when applied to network G. In other words, does $S'(t)$ tend to zero as t increases without bound? In more formal terms, we say that system $H(t) = \{G(t), S(t)\}$, consisting of network G and state equation $S'(t)$, is

1. *Stable* if $S'(t)$ goes to zero, For example, if the states of all nodes go to zero or some constant value, and remain there.
2. *Transient* if $S(t)$ oscillates about some bounded values. A transient network is *bistable* if the values of its nodes oscillate between two attractors.
3. *Unstable*, or blows up, if any element of $S(t)$ becomes unbounded. For example, if one or more node values become increasingly positive or negative, eventually reaching infinity or negative infinity, we say that the network blows up.

Atay, et al. (Atay, 2006) proposed the following state equation, which we modify and explore in depth here. An *Atay network* is any connected network where each node's rate of change is determined by the average difference between each node and its adjacent nodes (where $d_i =$ degree of node i):

$$S'(t) = \sum_{j \sim i} \frac{f(S_j(t)) - f(S_i(t))}{d_i} = \sum_{j \sim i} \frac{S_j(t) - S_i(t)}{d_i}$$

Atay et al. selected the identity function $f(\ )$ to map state into an output value, and discretized the differential equation. In finite-difference form this is (where $j \sim i$ means the adjacent node of i)

$$s_i(t+1) = s_i(t) + \sum_{j\sim i} \frac{s_j(t) - s_i(t)}{d_i}$$

For each node i, this state equation computes the `next_state`, $s_i(t+1)$ by incrementing the current value $s_i(t)$ stored in each node by the sum of differences between the current value of each node and its adjacent neighbor nodes and normalizing by the degree of each node. Since each node has d_i neighbors, this is identical to averaging the differences over all neighbors.

Clearly, if the sum of differences decreases to zero, the difference at each node, $|s_i(t+1) - s_i(t)| = 0$, and the network stabilizes about some common value. More likely, the difference oscillates, which means that the network is transient. Or in some cases, a network may blow up because state values increase or decrease without bound. Which of these three possibilities fit the Atay formulation?

The following Java code implements the discrete Atay algorithm. Method `NW_doAtay()` assumes that initial values have been stored in `node[i].next_state` for all nodes in the network. Program *Network.jar* assigns a random number between 2 and 10 to each node, but this is rather arbitrary. Then it applies the Atay state equation to all nodes in two passes; pass 1 updates the value of each node to its next state, and pass 2 applies the next state equation—in discrete form—to each node. The resulting `next_state` updates the network during pass 1 in the next timestep. Thus, a trajectory in the corresponding chaotic map is the locus of `next_state` versus current `value`, for a particular node (see Fig. 9.4).

The Java method processes nodes in random order to avoid introduction of simulation bias. Initial values of `next_state` are assigned at random, and the algorithm runs indefinitely. In this case, synchronization means that all nodes ultimately

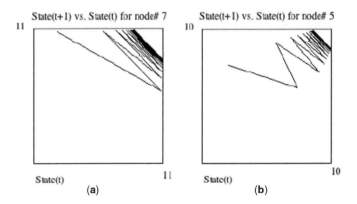

Figure 9.4 Chaotic map of Atay network trajectories: (a) stable node that reaches its strange attractor as the network syncs; (b) bistable node that oscillates about two attractors as the network does not sync.

reach the same value. This corresponds with an identical strange attractor point for all nodes.

```
public void NW_doAtay(){
        for(int i = 0; i < nNodes; i++){          //Pass 1: Update state
            node[i].value = node[i].next_state;
        }
        Shuffler random_list = new Shuffler(nNodes);
        for(int i = 0; i < nNodes; i++) random_list.card[ i] = i;
        random_list.SH_Shuffle(nNodes);           //Scramble node order
        for(int n = 0; n < nNodes; n++){          //Pass 2: Next State
            int i = random_list.card[ n];         //Random selection
            node[i].next_state = node[i].value;//Right-hand-side
            for(int j = 0; j < nLinks; j++){      //Neighbors
                int left = Link[ j].tail;
                int right = Link[ j].head;
                double d = node[ i].degree;       //Degree of node
                if(left == i) {                   //f(si)+sum[ f(sj)-f(si)]
                    node[i].next_state += (node[right].value -
                                            node[i].value)/d;
                }
                else if(right == i) {
                    node[i].next_state += (node[left].value -
                                            node[i].value)/d;
                }
            }
        }
    }//NW_doAtay
```

9.2.3 Stability of Atay Networks

In most cases, Atay networks either synchronize by reaching a strange attractor or oscillate between bistable values, forever. Because the degree term d_i, acts as a dampening factor, an Atay network never "blows up." But what determines whether an Atay network reaches a transient bistable state or a state of complete synchronization?

Table 9.2 was obtained by running NW_doAtay() for $n = 100$ on various networks and observing the convergence to a stable fixed point or oscillation of node values versus time. Clearly, some networks synchronize and others do not. More importantly, there is no correlation between spectral gap and the ability for an Atay network to synchronize.[5] There is, however, a very simple method that we can use to guarantee synchronization.

---

[5]Spectral decomposition is the preferred method of analysis, but in general it cannot tell us if the spectral gap is large enough to synchronize an arbitrary network.

We show that a network must contain at least one *pinned node* or at least one *triangular cycle* in order to synchronize. A node is said to be *pinned* if its value is fixed. A pinned node remains in its initial state (or some state established by outside control) for all time. A triangular cycle is a cycle of length 3 formed by connecting three nodes to one another. It is the simplest cluster possible, with cluster coefficient of 1.0.

Now we can correlate the ability for an Atay network to sync with its topology. All networks listed in Table 9.2 containing at least one triangular cycle synchronize, while all others oscillate; that is, the nodes in a stable Atay network reach a common value, while node values in a transient Atay network oscillate—typically between two alternating attractors.

The strategy for explaining why Atay networks sync when they contain a triangular cycle and do not otherwise proceeds as follows:

1. Show that an Atay barbell network ($n = 2$, $m = 1$) is a transient *bistable oscillator* (flip-flop).
2. Show that an Atay triangular network ($n = 3$, $m = 3$) is a stable network.
3. Show an Atay ring network is stable when n is odd, and transient when n is even.
4. Show that an Atay ring network with an added random link is stable if and only if the added link forms an odd-length cycle, otherwise it is transient.
5. Apply reduction algebra to ring networks to decide if an Atay ring satisfies the condition necessary for it to stabilize.
6. Generalize the results obtained in steps 1–5 to explain why small-world synchronization occurs more easily than does random or regular network synchronization. Specifically, note that not all small worlds synchronize!
7. Generalizing further, we claim, but do not prove, that Atay networks sync when at least one node is pinned. This follows from observing that a pinned node acts much like a stable triangular cycle.
8. Conclude that pinning (a property of the algorithm) and triangular cycles (a property of network topology) are sufficient to cause an Atay network to sync—contrary to earlier results.

First, we apply the Atay algorithm to the barbell network of Fig. 9.5a and do a more thorough analysis of its transient behavior:

$$s_1(t + 1) = s_1(t) + \{s_2(t) - s_1(t)\} = s_2(t)$$
$$s_2(t + 1) = s_2(t) + \{s_1(t) - s_2(t)\} = s_1(t)$$

Or, in matrix form, where A is the adjacency matrix of the barbell network:

$$S(t + 1) = \mathbf{A}S(t) \begin{pmatrix} 0 & 1 \\ 1 & 0 \end{pmatrix} = S(t)$$

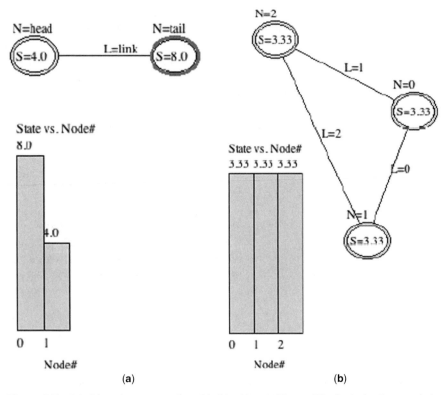

Figure 9.5 Primitive Atay networks: (a) bistable oscillator (flip-flop) implemented by a barbell network; (b) stable triangular cycle implemented by a complete network of size $n = 3$.

Solving in terms of initial state vector $S(0)$, we obtain

$$S(t) = \mathbf{A}^T S(0)$$

Matrix A is very simple, and A^t is even simpler: $A^t = \mathbf{I}$ when t is even (no change) and $(-\mathbf{I})$ when t is odd (flip-flop). Thus, the Atay barbell is a bistable oscillator: $S(t) = -\mathbf{I}S(0)$, when t is odd, $S(0)$, otherwise.

Now consider the triangular network of Fig. 9.5b, which is stable. Following the same approach, the solution to the state equation differs only by the fact that all nodes in the triangular network have degree 2. Therefore, we divide by 2:

$$S(t + 1) = 0.5\,\mathbf{A}S(t)$$
$$S(t) = (0.5\,\mathbf{A})^t S(0); \quad S(0) \text{ given}$$

$$\mathbf{A} = \begin{pmatrix} 0 & 1 & 1 \\ 1 & 0 & 1 \\ 1 & 1 & 0 \end{pmatrix}$$

TABLE 9.3   Reduction Algebra for Ring Synchronization

Rule	Structure	Reduction	Comment
1	Pinned node	Diamond	A pinned node is a stable node (diamond)
2	Odd-length cycle	Diamond	Replace cycle with stable node (diamond)
3	Even-length cycle	Node	Replace cycle with single oscillator node
4	Stable–stable pair	Diamond	Replace with single stable node (diamond)
5	Stable-node pair	Diamond	Replace with single stable node (diamond)

Note that A is the adjacency matrix of the triangular network. Therefore, spectral decomposition of A is identical to finding the spectral radius, $\rho = 2.0$, so the limit of $S(t)$ as t increases without bound is a constant:

$$S(t) \longrightarrow S(0) \quad \text{becasue} \quad ((0.5)(2.0))^t = 1.0$$

The Atay triangular network is stable. In fact, the value of each node in a stabilized triangular network equals the average of its initial values. Regardless of changes in any single node of a triangular cycle, an Atay triangular network is attracted to the average of its nodes' initial values. A node's trajectory in the chaotic map of this network looks like the map in Fig. 9.4a.

So now we have two building-block networks, one that oscillates about its initial values, and the other that reaches a stable strange attractor equal to the average of its initial node values. What happens if we combine these primitives? Combining an unstable cycle with a stable cycle causes the combination to sync.

In general, introducing a stable node or cycle into an unstable network causes it to stabilize. It appears that stability spreads like an epidemic through a network. Table 9.3 summarizes the combinations leading to stable nodes, designated by a diamond-shaped node, and oscillating nodes, designated by a circular node.

Consider the ring and small-world networks of Fig. 9.6. We use a simple graphical algebra as defined by the reduction rules of Table 9.3 to analyze each of these rings.[6] First, we replace all pinned nodes with a stable diamond-shaped node, if any exist. Next, we replace all odd-length cycles with a diamond, and all even-length cycles with a circular (oscillating) node. Node pairs are reduced as prescribed by Table 9.3. We repeat Table 9.3 reductions until the entire network has been reduced to an oscillator or stable diamond.

In Fig. 9.6, two networks are transient oscillators, and four are stable. The 4-ring in Fig. 9.6a reduces to an oscillator because it is one large even-length cycle. The 5-ring of Fig. 9.6b reduces to a stable diamond because it is one large odd-length cycle. On the contrary, the bisected 6-ring of Fig. 9.6c contains two even-sized cycles, which reduce to two oscillators; hence, the small world is transient.

Figure 9.6d illustrates the application of reduction on a small world that syncs because it contains at least one odd-length cycle. One cycle is reduced

---

[6]For best results, apply the rules in Table 0.3 in order, from top to bottom.

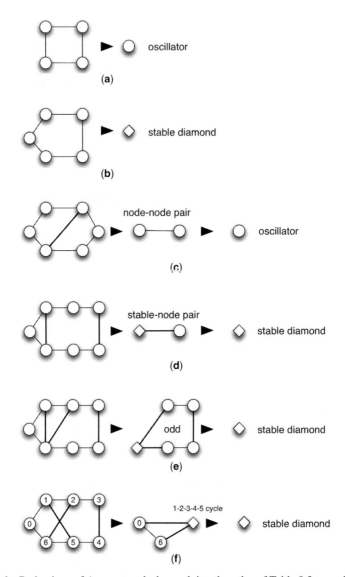

Figure 9.6 Reductions of Atay networks by applying the rules of Table 9.3 to cycles, nodes, and pinned nodes: (a) ring $n = 4$ is transient because n is an even number, (b) ring $n = 5$ is stable because n is an odd number, (c) bisected small world is transient because all of its cycles are even, (d) small world with an odd cycle is stable, (e) small world with nested cycle is stable because at least one cycle is odd, and (f) small world with nonnested cycles is stable because the odd-length cycle is reduced before the even-length cycle.

to a diamond and the other, to an oscillator node. Applying the "stable-node pair" reduction rule of Table 9.3 leads to a second reduction that ends with a stable node. This small world would sync even if it had an even number of nodes.

Figure 9.6e illustrates the application of reduction rules to a network with nested cycles. Innermost cycles are first reduced, followed by outer cycles—that is, apply the reduction to cycles contained within other cycles, first. In this case, the innermost cycle is odd, so it is replaced with a stable diamond. The outermost cycle remains, but it is odd, so the network is stable.

Figure 9.6f is even more instructive because it contains overlapping cycles. The rules of Table 9.3 must be strictly followed to correctly reduce the network. Rule 2 must be applied before rule 3. Therefore, odd-length cycles must be reduced before even-length cycles. Applying rule 2 in this case means reducing the cycle containing nodes 1, 2, 3, 4, and 5 to a single node. Because it is an odd cycle, we replace it with a diamond node. Note that duplicate links merge into single links, and the connection matrix of the reduced network conforms to the original connection matrix. This small-world network is stable, simply because it contained at least one odd-length cycle.

We obtain similar results for networks with a pinned node. Applying rule 1 immediately replaces the pinned node with a stable diamond. Therefore, a pinned node is equivalent to an odd-length cycle. Illustrating this feature of Table 9.3 is left as an exercise for the reader.

Generally, small worlds may not synchronize, but we know from earlier chapters that small-world networks contain a high number of clusters. Clusters are collections of triangular cycles, thus the likelihood of a small world not synchronizing is small. In most cases, small-world networks sync because most have triangular cycles. This is true to a lesser degree for random and scale-free networks.

Interestingly, we can synchronize any Atay network by adding a triangular cycle to an appropriate node. For example, a binary tree Atay network will not sync because its subtrees do not form a cycle. However, addition of two nodes plus three links to its root node will cause the entire network to sync! Amazingly, all nodes in the binary tree will converge to the same value. Table 9.4 summarizes this phenomenon, but we leave the proof as a research problem for the reader. Given an Atay network that does not sync, show that addition of a triangular cycle guarantees that it will sync.

We can go further, and claim, without proof, that every Atay network synchronizes if any single node is pinned—that is, holding the value of any node constant

TABLE 9.4 Networks that Sync by Adding a Triangular Cycle

Network	Attached Triangular Cycle
Barbell	Either end
Line	Any node
Binary tree	Root node
Hypercube	Any node
Random	Any node
Scale-free	Any node
Star	Any node
Ring	Any node

is sufficient to stabilize the entire network! Intuitively, this is because the stability of a single node spreads throughout the entire (connected) network much like an epidemic. Another interpretation is that a pinned node works just like a triangular cycle to sync neighboring nodes.

Every Atay network in Table 9.4 syncs if we pin a node instead of attaching a triangular cycle. This is true for 2-regular, complete, and small-world networks, too, but they typically sync without pinning or the addition of a triangular cycle. This is because they already contain a triangular cycle.

This conclusion has major implications in a variety of fields, including medicine, physics, computer science, and electrical engineering. Does a cricket social network sync because of one dominant cricket? Does the human heart beat in smooth rhythm because of a single dominant nerve impulse? The proof of the pinning conjecture is left as an exercise for the reader. Show that any Atay network will synchronize if at least one of its nodes is pinned.

9.3 KIRCHHOFF NETWORKS

We now study a class of networks that do not synchronize with the addition of a triangular cycle or pinning of a node. A *Kirchhoff network* is any directed network containing nodes and links that obey Kirchhoff's laws. Such networks model the flow of some commodity from source nodes to sink nodes, and are good approximations to many real-world systems. However, as we shall see, they are much more difficult to synchronize, if at all, than Atay networks.

Kirchhoff's first law states that the sum of flows into a node must equal the sum of flows out of the node. Kirchhoff's second law states that the sum of voltages around a circuit must equal zero. While these laws govern the behavior of electrical circuits found in microprocessors and electrical power grids, they also model many other phenomena, such as the flow of liquids in pipes and rivers, flow of messages in postal systems (ignoring lost letters), and the flow of commodities in many global distribution networks. A general answer to the question of stability is important because of its application to many fields.

What happens in a Kirchhoff network during a surge or immediately after a node is damaged, shut down, or taken off line? Does the network adapt to the new configuration and stabilize, or does it go into chaotic oscillation? This question is important to the well being of electrical power grids, logistical systems, and traffic networks. We want to know whether such systems are stable under stress, and even failure. To get an answer, we turn once again to simulation.

9.3.1 Kirchhoff Network Model

Let us define a *Kirchhoff network* as a directed network $K = \{N, L, f\}$, where the nodes of N and links of L are assigned a value, and links are directed. Each node has an *in-degree* (number of links pointing to the node) and an *out-degree* (number of links anchored to the node). A subset of nodes has no in-degree links, and so we call them *sources*; another subset has no out-degree links, and so we call them *sinks*. We assume that the values of all source nodes remain constant, while the values of all other nodes are determined by Kirchhoff's first law:

$$\text{node}[i].\text{next\_state} = \sum \text{node}[i].\text{in\_ flow} - \sum \text{node}[i].\text{out\_ flow}$$

where

$$\text{node}[i].\text{in\_ flow} = \sum \text{link}[j].\text{value, over in\_degree links}$$

$$\text{link}[k].\text{value} = \frac{\text{node}[i].\text{value}}{\text{node}[i].\text{out\_degree}} \quad \text{for the anchor node}$$

In other words, the value of each node is the difference between the sum of inputs via its incoming links and the sum of outputs via its outgoing links. We evenly divide outflow among out-degree links, so the value of a link is the value of its anchor node (at the tail) divided by the out-degree of the anchor node. This means that out_flow is equal to the current value of each node, a fact that we use later on to formally analyze the stability of Kirchhoff networks.

If everything goes as planned, the difference between inflows and outflows should be zero for every node in the network. If a single node value exceeds zero, it is in a transient state. If all nodes reach zero at the same time, the network will sync—all nodes will be attracted to the zero fixed point. We limit node values to values greater than or equal to zero because a negative value means that the flow has reversed. We consider only forward-flowing networks.

Method int NW_diKirchhoff(int done) computes the next state of nodes and returns an integer value equal to the number of nodes that changed value during one timestep. When this number reaches zero, the network has reached some stable state. Otherwise, it is in a transient or chaotic state.

The algorithm is implemented in two passes. Pass 1 updates the value of every node to its next state and paints sink nodes red, source nodes green, isolated or disconnected nodes black, and all other nodes white. In pass 2 the method sweeps over all links and updates the value of each link by equally dividing the value of its anchor node across all outgoing links and then computing the next state value of every node using Kirchhoff's first law. The values of all source nodes remain constant, and the sum total value of all sink nodes equals the total commodity flowing through the network.

Method NW_doKirchhoff() returns variable done, which is the cumulative number of times the method has returned zero changes to the network. Variable stable_time is zero only if none of the node values change in one time step. Variable done counts the number of times stable_time has returned zero. The idea is to stop the simulation after a sufficient number of iterations after the network reaches stability. Program *Network.jar* uses done to determine how many timesteps elapse before the network stabilizes. This assumes, of course, that every Kirchhoff network synchronizes—an assumption that is not valid for all networks.

As before, we eliminate artificially induced bias by randomizing the processing order, and we initially assign random values to nodes. A trajectory of a Kirchhoff network node in the chaotic map is a plot of Kirchhoff's first law at time $(t + 1)$ versus at time t; therefore, a node's stable attractor is at zero:

```
public int NW_doKirchhoff(int done){
        int stable_time = 0;                    //Pass 1: update nodes
        for(int i = 0; i < nNodes; i++){     //Color coding
            if(node[ i] .out_degree == 0) node[ i] .color = Color.red;
            if(node[ i] .in_degree == 0) node[ i] .color = Color.green;
            if(node[ i] .out_degree == 0
                    &&
                node[i].in_degree == 0) node[i].color = Color.black;
            if(node[ i] .value != node[ i] .next_state) stable_time++;
            node[i].value = node[i].next_state;    //Update state
        }
        if(stable_time == 0) done++;             //No state changes
        int tail_node, head_node;                //Tail and Head of Links
        for(int j = 0; j < nLinks; j++){     //Update link flow values
            tail_node = Link[j].tail;            //In case user deletes
                                                     during run
            Link[j].value = node[tail_node].value/node[tail_node].
                                                     out_degree;
        }

        Shuffler random_list=new Shuffler(nNodes);//Randomize nodes
        for(int i = 0; i < nNodes; i++) random_list.card[ i] = i;
        random_list.SH_Shuffle(nNodes);

        for(int n = 0; n < nNodes; n++){     //Pass 3: Next State
            int i = random_list.card[ n] ;       //Scrambled order
            node[i].next_state = 0;              //Next state of this node
            double inflow = 0.0;                 //Reset this in/out flow
            double outflow = 0.0;
            for(int j = 0; j < nLinks; j++){  //Across all links to this
                tail_node = Link[j].tail;
                head_node = Link[j].head;
                if(tail_node == i) {             //Flow out of this node
                    outflow += Link[j].value;
                }
                else if(head_node == i) {        //Flow into this node
                    inflow += Link[j].value;
                }
            }
```

```
        if(node[ i] .in_degree == 0) node[ i] .next_state =
                                        node[i].value;
        else node[ i] .next_state = inflow - outflow;
        if(node[ i] .next_state < 0.000001) node[ i] .next_state = 0;
    }
    return done;
}//NW_doKirchhoff
```

A Kirchhoff network synchronizes if and only if the states of all its nodes simultaneously reach zero—the strange attractor for Kirchhoff networks; that is, the sum of inputs equals the sum of outputs for every node in the network. Therefore, synchronization means that all nodes reach a value of zero at the same time, and stay there.

Method NW_doKirchhoff() clips the next_state value when it is close to zero to remove low-level (high-frequency) oscillations near the strange attractor. This accelerates convergence to synchronization—if the network synchronizes—without loss of generality. If a Kirchhoff network synchronizes, it will progressively drive all states to zero.

9.3.2 Kirchhoff Network Stability

Not all Kirchhoff networks sync, and the ones that do, behave rather oddly. Some networks will behave chaotically for hundreds of timesteps without ever synchronizing. Other networks will suddenly "snap" into sync after only a few iterations. Why? Analysis of Kirchhoff network stability shows that synchronization is completely defined by the network's topology. Specifically, networks containing directed cycles of lengths A and B, say, will sync if A and B are relatively prime. Networks containing directed cycles of length $A,B,C\ldots$ will never sync if the largest common factor of $A,B,C\ldots$ is greater than one; that is, at least two cycles must contain a relatively prime number of hops. We develop this theory in detail below.

Note the following strategy for deriving the condition necessary for Kirchhoff network synchronization:

1. Restrict the class of Kirchhoff networks analyzed to *closed systems*—networks with no source or sink nodes. Thus Kirchhoff networks are full of feedback links.
2. Derive the Kirchhoff network state equation in matrix form, where $S(t)$ is the state vector containing the value of each node, **B** is the out-degree network matrix, and (**B**-2**I**) is the system state matrix.
3. Show that the time rate of change of the state vector, $\Delta S(t)$, goes to zero (the strange attractor) as t increases without bound, but that this is not sufficient to guarantee synchronization. We call the largest nontrivial eigenvalue of (**B**-2**I**) the *Kirchhoff eigenvalue*, and designate it ε_k.
4. Show that convergence, $\Delta S(t) \to 0$, is necessary, but not sufficient to guarantee synchronization, because *signal strength* in cycles may or may not dampen the next_state value of nodes belonging to feedback cycles,

5. Show that, in addition to the first condition, $\Delta S(t) \rightarrow 0$, we must also guarantee that the signal strength from cycles in the network interfere with (rather than reinforce) one another in order for synchronization to happen, otherwise the network oscillates, indefinitely. We show why Kirchhoff networks containing relatively prime cycle lengths sync, while not all others do.

Networks with source nodes may not synchronize simply because the state of all source nodes remains constant. Similarly, networks with sink nodes may or may not sync, depending on the initial values of other nodes. For example, line, star, binary tree, and scale-free networks may not sync simply because they have at least one source or sink node.[7] Source or sink nodes lack any feedback links that might dampen oscillations. These networks are *open systems* because they have at least one source or sink node.

We restrict our study to *Closed systems*—networks that contain no source or sink nodes. Every node in a closed system has degree of at least 2—one in-degree and one out-degree link. In a closed system, signals flow through a node—they never get "trapped" in a node. For example, ring, k-regular, complete, toroidal, and hypercube networks are closed systems. We can convert a random, small-world, or scale-free network into a closed system by reversing the direction of certain links, and rewiring others. If we convert a scale-free network into a closed system, it may or may not sync, depending on the conditions necessary to synchronization of the network.

Now suppose that we proceed to the next step in the strategy for finding the two conditions for Kirchhoff network synchronization. Consider the ring networks in Fig. 9.7. These networks are closed systems, but two synchronize while the other two do not. We claim that the 1-regular ring network of Fig. 9.7a and the small-world network of Fig. 9.7d sync, while the other two do not sync. Why? As before, we begin the analysis by considering the network state equation, using Kirchhoff's first law.

Note that the sum of a node's outputs is exactly the state value of the node at time t, $s(t)$. Therefore, the state equation for a Kirchhoff network can be rewritten in matrix form as follows:

$$S(t+1) = \mathbf{B}S(t) - S(t) = [\mathbf{B} - \mathbf{I}]S(t); \quad S(0) \text{ given}$$

where $\mathbf{B}$ is the out-degree connection matrix and $\mathbf{I}$ is the identity matrix.

The out-degree connection matrix is obtained by ignoring all in-degree connections and setting element

$$b_{i,j} = \frac{1}{\text{out\_degree}(i)}$$

if $j \sim i$, where j is the tail node and i is the head node of the link connecting nodes j and i. Otherwise, $b_{i,j} = 0$. The rows of the out-degree matrix correspond to head

[7]This is partially an artifact of the way we generate networks—all links are directed toward the newly created nodes.

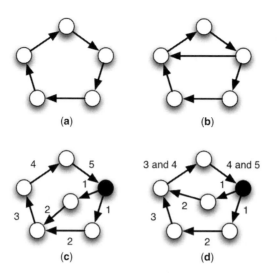

Figure 9.7 Kirchhoff networks: (a) chaotic 1-regular ring network; (b, d) stable and (c) chaotic small-world networks. Networks (a) and (c) do not sync because they violate one or both of the Kirchhoff stability conditions, but (b) and (d) sync because $\varepsilon_k \leq 1.0$ and they contain two cycles of lengths that are relatively prime numbers.

nodes and the columns, with the tail nodes. Therefore, the expression, $\mathbf{B}S(t)$ represents the inflows and $S(t)$ represents the total outflows from each node.

For example, the out-degree connection matrix of the ring network in Fig. 9.7a is

$$\mathbf{B} = \begin{pmatrix} 0 & 0 & 0 & 0 & 1 \\ 1 & 0 & 0 & 0 & 0 \\ 0 & 1 & 0 & 0 & 0 \\ 0 & 0 & 1 & 0 & 0 \\ 0 & 0 & 0 & 1 & 0 \end{pmatrix}$$

The out-degree matrix for the small world network of Fig. 9.7b is

$$\mathbf{B} = \begin{pmatrix} 0 & 0 & 0 & 0 & 1 \\ \frac{1}{2} & 0 & 0 & 0 & 0 \\ 0 & 1 & 0 & 0 & 0 \\ \frac{1}{2} & 0 & 1 & 0 & 0 \\ 0 & 0 & 0 & 1 & 0 \end{pmatrix}$$

A necessary, but not sufficient, condition for a Kirchhoff network to sync is convergence of $\Delta S(t)$ to zero. Subtracting $S(t)$ from both sides of the state equation and solving the equation in terms of the initial state $S(0)$, and out-degree matrix $\mathbf{B}$, we obtain

$$\Delta S(t + 1) = [\mathbf{B} - 2\,\mathbf{I}]S(t); \quad S(0) \text{ given}$$

Therefore

$$S(t) = [\mathbf{B} - 2\,\mathbf{I}]^t S(0); \quad t > 0$$

It is necessary for $[\mathbf{B} - 2\,\mathbf{I}]^t$ to go to zero, in order for $S(t)$ to go to zero. Spectral decomposition of $[\mathbf{B} - 2\,\mathbf{I}]$ yields the largest nontrivial eigenvalue of the state equation's solution. Suppose that we call this the *Kirchhoff eigenvalue* ε_k of the network. Then the Kirchhoff eigenvalue must be positive and less than one, for the next state to remain bounded. If ε_k is negative, the network will oscillate, and if it is greater than one, the solution will "blow up." Thus, a necessary (but not sufficient) condition for synchronization is $\varepsilon_k < 1.0$.

The Kirchhoff eigenvalue of the ring network in Fig. 9.7(a) is $\varepsilon_k = -1.0$, so the ring is bounded but oscillates. The Kirchhoff eigenvalue for the small world of Fig. 9.7b is also $\varepsilon_k = -1.0$, but this network syncs! Indeed, the Kirchhoff eigenvalue of all four networks in Fig. 9.7 is 1.0, and yet two synchronize and two do not! Why?

Suppose that we follow a signal around the two circuits formed by the network shown in Fig. 9.7c, starting with the shaded node in the upper right-hand corner. Network links are labeled with the number of hops from the shaded node, along paths in both cycles, ending back at the shaded node. Let us define the *strength* of the signal at each node as the value of the shaded node at each hop along each cycle. Let s_0 be the state of the shaded node at time $t = 0$. After each hop along the two cycles the strength of the signal at each successor node is $s_0/2$, $s_0/2$, $s_0/2 + s_0/2 = s_0, s_0$, returning as s_0 at the shaded node. The signal is reinforced (changed from $s_0/2$ to s_0) after 2 hops because Kirchhoff's law sums all inputs. Thus, the signal returns to the shaded node with the same strength s_0. There is no decrease in the strength of the signal on returning to the shaded node, so the network does not sync.

Now consider an almost identical version of the chaotic network, in Fig. 9.7d. This network syncs! Perform the same experiment—tracing a signal from the shaded node through the two cycles, back to the shaded node. After 1 hop along the paths of the two cycles, the strength of the signal at the immediate successor node is $s_0/2$. After a second hop the signal is still $s_0/2$. But notice what happens at the third successor. The two paths merge at the node with in-degree equal to 2, but the signal with strength $s_0/2$ reaches this node before the other signal (along the longer path), so the output from this node is $s_0/2$—not s_0. Thus, the shaded node receives $s_0/2$ as its next state. The shaded node receives a diminished, or dampened, input. Diminished signal strength is diminished even further each time it travels around the cycle, and returns back to the shaded node. This network syncs because its initial state is dampened. We say that the two cycles *interfere with* rather than *reinforce* one another.

We claim that Kirchhoff networks containing reinforcing cycles never sync, while networks containing interfering cycles may sync, depending on the pattern of interference. We take this idea one step further and claim that cycles interfere with one another if the lengths of two or more cycles (number of hops) are relatively prime; that is, the two cycle lengths contain no common factors, except one.

In general, we can model the strength of a signal around all cycles of an arbitrary network by repeated multiplication of its out-degree matrix, $\mathbf{B}$. Recall that $\mathbf{B}^k$ is the connection matrix for nodes separated by k hops. The maximum number of hops between any two nodes in a strongly connected network is n. Thus, after no more than n hops, the strength of a signal is $\mathbf{B}^n S(0)$.

If a network contains a cycle of length k, then at least one diagonal element of $\mathbf{B}^k$ will be nonzero, representing the strength of the cycle. Furthermore, k is the length of the cycle, so we simply check for a cycle of length 1 in B, of length 2 in $\mathbf{B}^2$, of length 3 in $\mathbf{B}^3$, and so on, until reaching n. Then we compare all pairs of cycles to determine whether they are relatively prime. If at least one pair are relatively prime, the network syncs.

For example, the Kirchhoff network of Fig. 9.7b contains two cycles—one of length 3 and another of length 5. The pair (3, 5) are relatively prime numbers; hence this network syncs. On the contrary, the network of Fig. 9.7c does not sync because its cycles are of lengths (5, 5), which evenly divide one another. The network of Fig. 9.7d syncs because (4, 5) is a relatively prime pair of numbers.

To guarantee that signal strength diminishes as a signal completes all feedback cycles we must add the condition: that the lengths of at least two cycles are relatively prime. This ensures that they interfere with one another, which dampens signal strength. Dampening causes the network to seek its strange attractor at zero.

Let $\mathbf{B}^k$ be the Kirchhoff out-degree matrix representing paths of length k hops. Let $b_{i,i}(k)$ be the diagonals of $\mathbf{B}^k$. A path of length k exists if $b_{i,i}(k) = 0$. Therefore, a Kirchhoff network synchronizes if it meets two conditions: (1) $\varepsilon_k < 1.0$ and (2) there exist cycles of length (k_1, k_2) such that k_1 and k_2 are relatively prime.

Program *Network.jar* contains a simple method for deciding whether two numbers are relatively prime using Euclid's greatest common factor algorithm. Recursive method GCF() is included here for convenience. Assuming $x \geq y$, if (x,y) are relatively prime, then GCF returns one, otherwise it returns zero. For example, given cycles of length (5,3), GCF returns 1, and given cycles of length (6, 3), GCF returns zero:

```
private int GCF(int x, int y){
    int quotient = x/y;
    int remainder = x - y*quotient;
    if(remainder < 1) remainder = GCF(y, remainder);
    return remainder;
}
```

9.4 POINTVILLE ELECTRIC POWER GRID

Now we apply the theory of synchronization developed in this chapter to a very practical problem—the stability (or lack of it) of an electrical power grid. This problem has great significance for almost any industrialized nation that depends on electrical power distribution through a grid such as the US Eastern Interconnect that failed in August 2003, leaving 50 million people in the dark. Amazingly, this massive blackout began with a rather insignificant fault in a powerline located in Ohio. The fault propagated from Ohio

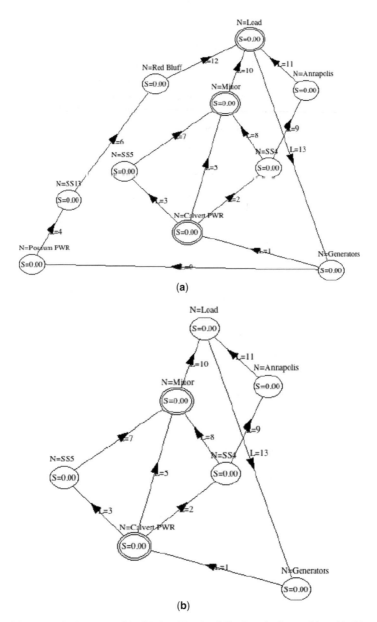

Figure 9.8 Electrical power grid of Pointville: (a) fully functioning stable grid; (b) partially functioning grid after the failure of one power station (viz., after Possum power generation failure); (c) fully inoperable grid after the failure of a single link.

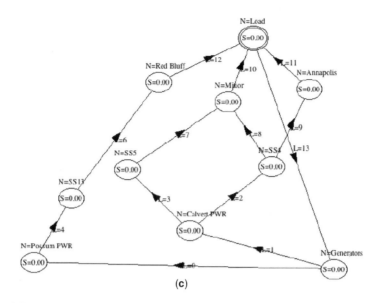

Figure 9.8. (*Continued*).

through eastern Canada and the United States, affecting people as far away as New York.

Pointville, Flatland is much smaller, but it still depends on the power grid shown in Fig. 9.8a. Like all electrical power grids, the system operator has a near-impossible task of maintaining Kirchhoff circuits as demand changes over time. In the morning, consumers consume large amounts of electrical power, but this consumption tapers off toward the evening, when consumers return home from work. Also, demand radically changes with the weather—cold weather means less power consumption than in hot weather because air conditioners consume a lot of power. Thus, operators must keep the *area control error* (ACE) near zero; that is, the sum of inflow must equal the sum of outflow at each node of the network. ACE is the term used by electrical power operators to describe Kirchhoff's first law.

What happens if ACE is less than zero? This condition means that not enough power is being generated to meet demand. Operators must either buy more electrons from standby generators or generate more electricity from existing generators. Similarly, operators must shed electrons, if ACE > 0. Demand from customers is constantly changing, so maintaining ACE = 0 is a difficult balancing act requiring computers and responsive human operators.

Accidents are even more unpredictable than consumer demand. If a power generator suddenly goes off line, ACE drops below zero, and operators must redirect power over the network to accommodate the abrupt change. Similarly, if ACE surges, operators must quickly reduce generation or redirect electrons to other cities along other powerlines. Redirection has its risks, as dramatically illustrated in 2003 when the Possum PWR generator of Fig. 9.8b failed. The failed generator took out the generator, substation SS13, and the consumers of neighboring Red Bluff—a city with a competing football team.

After failure of Possum, the Pointville power grid restabilizes and continues to operate—without supplying Red Bluff with power—after a short period of instability because the lengths of its remaining cycles are relatively prime. Removal of Possum, SS13, and Red Bluff leaves the network of Fig. 9.8b, which has two cycles of length 5 and one cycle of length 4. Since (5, 4) are relatively prime, the partially damaged grid stabilizes after approximately 100 timesteps.

The results are quite different with the removal of the link between Calvert PWR and a suburb named Minor (see Fig. 9.8c). If this powerline trips (fails), the network cannot synchronize because all remaining cycles are of length 5, and (5, 5) are not relatively prime numbers. Pointville's electrical power grid completely collapses, leaving all consumers without power!

The Pointville electrical power grid is made more resilient by adding a single link between two nodes—but which nodes? For example, construction of a powerline between SS5 and Red Bluff protects the grid against a Possum failure, but does not protect it against a link failure as shown in Fig. 9.8b. Construction of a longer powerline between Calvert PWR and Red Bluff prevents catastrophic failure if either Possum or the link between Calvert and Miner fails, but is more costly. The proof of this is left as an exercise for the reader.

In general, stability of networks increases with increasing density because the likelihood of relatively prime length cycles increases. Thus, random networks generally become better Kirchhoff networks as their density increases, but small-world

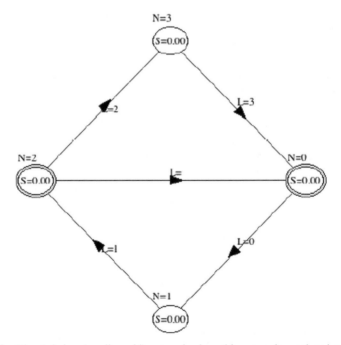

Figure 9.9 Bisected ring (small-world) network: does this network synchronize for chirp, Atay, and Kirchhoff network algorithms? See text for this exercise (Exercise 9.9).

networks may not improve their stability with the same vigor. This question is left as a research problem for the reader to contemplate.

9.5 EXERCISES

9.1. Using the Z-transform, show that the triangular cycle is a stable Atay network.

9.2. Show that an arbitrary Atay ring network syncs when a triangular cycle is appended to any of its nodes.

9.3. Show that an Atay network synchronizes if at least one node state is pinned, that is, held constant.

9.4. Show that an Atay binary tree network syncs if a triangular cycle is appended to its root node.

9.5. Does an Atay binary tree network sync if its root node is pinned?

9.6. Show that in general a closed-system Kirchhoff network cannot synchronize when one node is pinned.

9.7. What is the out-degree connection matrix for a Kirchhoff ring of size $n = 4$?

9.8. Why is it impossible for a Kirchhoff ring network to synchronize, regardless of its size, n?

9.9. Does the bisected ring network of Fig. 9.9 sync? Consider each algorithm studied in this chapter: chirping, Atay, and Kirchhoff networks.

9.10. Why does addition of a link between Calvert PWR and Red Bluff improve stability of the Pointville power grid in Fig. 9.8?

10

INFLUENCE NETWORKS

An *influence network* is a (directed or undirected) network, $G = \{N, L, f\}$, containing nodes N; directed, weighted links L; and mapping function $f: N \times N$ that defines the topology of the directed network. Because influence networks are excellent models of *social networks*, nodes are also called *actors*. Nodes and links have a value property that defines *influence* (for links) and *position* (for nodes) associated with a *proposition*. For example, the question of capital punishment is a proposition, the position of each node is either *pro* or *con*, and link $e: v \rightarrow u$ defines the *degree of influence* ϕ that actor v has on the position of actor u. Typically, the weight of a (directed) link e equals its *degree of influence*, $\phi =$ influence(s), and is a fraction between zero (no influence) and one (100% influence). In the theory developed here, influence will only be positive, $0 \leq \phi \leq 1$, ranging from none to total control.

Influence networks can model the consequences of certain social, economic, and political strategies and policies. For example, suppose that an influence network is used to model the national economy. One node may represent taxes, and others may represent consumers, employment, and government spending. Links (influences) represent the effects of a general tax increase or decrease on consumer spending, government spending, and so on. Each node in this network influences adjacent nodes through weighted links. For example, a tax cut might increase employment rate, which in turn increases consumer spending, which in turn increases tax revenues, which in turn might result in another tax cut. Given such an influence network, the degree of influences ϕ (link values) and initial positions of each actor, we might ask, "What are the consequences of raising taxes on consumer spending?" The

Network Science: Theory and Practice. By Ted G. Lewis
Copyright © 2009 John Wiley & Sons, Inc.

answer comes from study of the stable "output" from this influence network. For example, does the state of actors reach a stable value, or do they oscillate? The final state of such a network can be traced back to the influences that actors have over other actors, and the topology of the network.

Group decisionmaking and negotiation among competitors is a major concern in today's global economy. Is it possible, given accurate measurements of influence, to determine a priori, if a group of people can arrive at a consensus? We show that, under certain rather restrictive conditions, it is inevitable that a group consensus will emerge from an influence network. Consensus is equivalent to synchronization, and the strange attractor value of the synchronized network is equivalent to a group decision. This has significance in the practical field of negotiation and identification of the most powerful actor in the network.

The most influential actor in an influence network is the one that controls the eventual outcome or group consensus, assuming that a consensus can be reached. In other words, power is defined as the actor with the greatest influence on the network. Under certain conditions, we can assess why one actor is more powerful than another, and determine the source of that power. We show that a high degree of influence *on* others, coupled with a low degree of influence *from* others, equals *power* in an Atay type of influence network.

Influence network theory has a number of very important applications, which we explore in detail following the development of influence network theory. This theory is based on stability theory, studied in the previous chapter. In this chapter we study two basic influence networks and learn the following:

1. *Influence networks* (I-nets) are networks containing nodes called *actors* and links called *influences*. They model *social networks, n-party negotiations,* and interdependencies in complex systems such as the economy of a country or the interrelated steps of a manufacturing process. We develop a theory of *consensus* and *conflict* and apply it to the problem of identifying the most influential actor, actor with the highest degree of conflict, and the actor with the greatest *power* over the network.

2. Two major types of I-nets are studied: undirected networks such as the buzz network explored by Emanuel Rosen (Rosen, 2000) to study marketing, and directed networks such as the social networks formed by negotiating parties in a human group. We apply the techniques of synchronization learned in the previous chapter to determine whether these I-nets synchronize, and we develop a new theory of conflict, consensus, and power to explain behavior in social networks.

3. A "buzz network" is an *Atay network* where actor positions are represented by a node's state—a value in the interval $[-1, 1]$ representing positive or negative actor positions. A buzz network always syncs, but its strange attractor depends on the degree sequence of the network. If the nodes of a buzz network reach the same strange attractor value, we say that the network has reached a *consensus*. If the strange attractor always reaches zero, we say that

the I-net is *stalemated*. Typically, an I-net is unable to reach a nonstalemated state because of at least one conflict within the population of actors.

4. The consensus of a buzz network is completely determined by the position of the network's hub node. Therefore, the hub node has the greatest influence in a buzz network. This is a consequence of the fact that the state of each actor in a buzz network is the average value of adjacent actor nodes. Contrary to intuition, when it comes to determining the eventual consensus of a network, *hub degree* is more important than node *closeness*.

5. More generally, an *I-net* is a *directed* Atay network with generalized weights ϕ on directed links called *influences*. Actors take on states in $[-1, 1]$ representing contrarian and promoter positions, and gradations in between. I-nets reach a consensus (sync) if influences are in the range $|\phi| = [0, 1]$, the *spectral gap* of the *Laplacian* matrix is less than zero ($\sigma < 0$) and there are no conflicts among actors.

6. We define a new property of networks: *degree of influence* matrix Q, which is obtained from the network's Laplacian L and error-bound ε, as follows: $Q = [I + L]^{t^*}$, where t^* is determined by the inequality, $\mathrm{RMS}\{[I + L]^{t^*}\} < \varepsilon$. Function $\mathrm{RMS}[X]$ is the root-mean-square error obtained by differencing every column element of X with each column's diagonal element. The degree of influence of actor v_i equals the diagonal element, $q_{i,i}$, of Q: $q_{i,i} =$ degree_influence(v_i).

7. We define a new property of networks: the *degree of conflict* vector C, which is equal to the diagonal of system state matrix $[I + L]$, where I is the identity matrix and L is the Laplacian. The degree of conflict of actor v_i is equal to c_i. An actor is in conflict with its adjacent nodes only if degree_conflict(v_i) = $c_i < 0$. An I-net cannot reach a nonzero consensus if it contains at least one conflicted actor. Such an I-net is stalemated.

8. We show that I-nets with nonnegative degree of conflict C reach a nonzero consensus determined by the degree of influence matrix Q. When actors in an I-net differ in their initial positions, the final consensus is determined approximately by the sum of degree of influences over all positions initially held by the actors. Therefore, the final strange attractor value of an I-net is approximately equal to the sum of degree of influences of actors that agree, minus the sum of degree of influences of actors that disagree. Node closeness has little to do with final consensus.

9. We develop a theory of power in I-nets and show that the most powerful actors are (almost always) the actors with more outbound links than inbound links. While there are some notable exceptions to this rule, actor nodes increase their influence over the entire network by increasing the number of outbound links and/or the weights of outbound links. Additionally, decreasing the weight and number of inbound links increases power.

10. We illustrate the application of I-nets to social network analysis and show how to identify the most powerful actor, the conflicted actor (if one exists), and the conditions under which an I-net will arrive at a consensus.

This chapter uses the buzz network portion of program *Network.jar* and the influence, conflict, and closeness analysis functions of program *Influence.jar* to generate and analyze the networks described here. The Java methods for implementing various procedures given in this chapter are simplified versions of the code found on disk.

10.1 ANATOMY OF BUZZ

In his 2000 book on the spread of marketing information about a new product, Emanuel Rosen explains how product marketing—if done properly—can spread the word about a product much like a network infection (Rosen, 2000). Contagious information spreads by word of mouth faster than does dull or mundane information, and all word-of-mouth marketing hops from person to person through a social network. Rosen calls this "buzz" and lays down rules on whom to target in a social network to get the most buzz. He claims that small-world social networks spread the word faster than do random networks, for example, and describes various techniques for accelerating the propagation of buzz.

In this section we build a model of buzz—the spread of advertising hype (hyperbole) through social contact. In the advertising world consumers are confronted with a proposition—whether they like or dislike a certain product. Each consumer (actor) takes an initial position—pro or con—and over time may alter position because of influences from friends and neighbors. We model this process as a social network where nodes represent consumers (actors) and links represent persuasion or *influence*. We show that change in an actor's position depends on the actor's degree and stubbornness.

We challenge the notion that small-world networks are better spreaders of influence than are other classes of networks, and discover that the anatomy of buzz is mostly about the degree sequence of the social network—not the cluster coefficient, path length, or maximum betweenness/closeness. The model of buzz proposed here incorporates both positive and negative product critique, thus simulating competition between two products. In addition, we introduce the concept of *stubbornness*—resistance to change of personal opinion or belief.

Rosen claims that negative positions are stronger than positive positions. A "bad influence" might overpower "good influence" by as much as 200%. Therefore, it is important to stop a "bad influence" as soon as possible, and replace it by a "good influence." Regardless of the power of negative over positive positions, it is reasonable to assume that a negative opinion of product A is a vote in favor of product B, and the opposite—a negative opinion of product B is a vote in favor of product A. Therefore, we represent negative positions as a negative number in $[-1, 0)$, and a positive position as a positive number in $(0, +1]$. Zero represents a neutral position. We want to know which position flourishes in a social network—positive or negative. Indeed, if one position spreads to all actors, and settles on a strange attractor, we say that the network has reached a *consensus*. If not, we say that the network is stalemated. In other words, reaching network synchronization is equivalent to reaching group consensus.

We know that people vary in their susceptibility to persuasion. Some people are easily swayed, while others are not. Let $0 \leq \phi \leq 1$ be the *stubbornness factor* for the 129 citizens of Pointville, Flatland, who are the subject of a marketing campaign. When stubbornness factor $\phi = 0$ (weak-minded), a Flatlander is easily persuaded to change his or her mind. When $\phi = 1$ (close-minded), a Flatlander will never change his or her mind. Typically, we find the folks in Pointville to be somewhere in between.

Flatlanders tend to cluster in community groups to talk about their jobs, families, and consumer products. This appears to be a perfect place for consumer product companies to test new marketing ideas, prototype products, and solicit valuable marketing feedback. Therefore, it is important for market researchers to understand the dynamics of Pointville's influence network. Analysis of this influence network will answer the question, "Whom to target, and how to fend off negative comments?"

10.1.1 A Buzz Network

Let $0 \leq \phi \leq 1$ be a measure of stubbornness averaged over all citizens of Pointville, and let $(1 - \phi)$ be the weight attached to an average citizen's malleability. Further, let $S(t)$ be the state vector representing an actor's position: $S(t) = -1$ if the position is negative, $S(t) = 0$ if neutral, and $S(t) = +1$ if positive. The position of an actor regarding a product, idea, political belief, and so on is typically somewhere in between the two extremes:

$$-1 \leq S(t) \leq 1$$

$$S(t) = [s_1, s_2, s_3, \ldots, s_n]^{\mathrm{T}} = \text{state vector of } G; \quad S_j(t) = \text{row } j \text{ of } S(t)$$

Assume that buzz contagion is appropriately modeled by a modified *Atay equation* that holds at each timestep, commencing with initial condition, $S(0)$:

Buzz State Equation

$$S(t + 1) = \phi S(t) + (1 - \phi) \sum_{j \sim i} \frac{S_j(t)}{\text{degree}(i)}$$

where the summation $\sum_{j \sim i}$ is over the neighbors of node i, specifically, $j \sim i$ and $s_i = [-1, 1]$, $i = 1, 2, \ldots, n$.

Initially, the states of all actors in the social network equal zero, except for two seed nodes—one with a positive position $(+1)$, and the other with a negative position (-1). A value of $(+1)$ signifies that an actor is a promoter of the product, while a value of (-1) signifies that an actor is a detractor or contrarian. Intermediate values, such as 0.5 or -0.5, signify an undecided state, but with either a positive or negative bias.

Each seed actor spreads his or her product endorsement to adjacent neighbors, which in turn is spread to their neighbors, and so forth, much like the spread of an infection. The state of each actor depends on the strength of the individual's convictions ϕ and the positions of adjacent neighbors. Note that the aggregate neighborhood position is an average over the adjacent neighbor's positions.[1]

We simplify the state equation by noting that the summation is exactly the inner product of $S(t)$ with the connection matrix of the buzz network. However, we want each node averaged, so we define a *degree matrix* $\mathbf{B}$ as the adjacency matrix divided by each node's degree:

$$\mathbf{B} = \begin{pmatrix} 0 & \dfrac{1}{\text{degree}(1)} & \cdots & \dfrac{1}{\text{degree}(1)} \\ \dfrac{1}{\text{degree}(2)} & 0 & \cdots & \dfrac{1}{\text{degree}(2)} \\ \cdots & & 0 & \\ \dfrac{1}{\text{degree}(n)} & \cdots & \dfrac{1}{\text{degree}(n)} & 0 \end{pmatrix}$$

Then, $S(t+1) = \phi S(t) + (1 - \phi)\mathbf{B}S(t) = [\phi\mathbf{I} + (1 - \phi)\mathbf{B}]S(t)$; $S(0)$ given.

This state equation is explored later, but for now note that $\mathbf{B}$ is positive-definite, which means it has positive-valued eigenvalues. Therefore, this kind of buzz network always synchronizes—all nodes converge to the same value. The buzz network is stable, but its strange attractor value may or may not be zero. Depending on the placement of positive and negative seeds, the final state of the social network may reach zero or some value in the interval $[-1, 1]$. Specifically, the degree sequence of the social network completely determines whether the consumers of Pointville reach some kind of consensus. This important detail is the key to understanding what makes buzz work.

10.1.2 Buzz Network Simulator

Program *Network.jar* implements the virus-like buzz process described above. It can be set up to spread either positive or negative influences. Additionally, the user can either select a starting node, or let the program select a random or hub node. Whichever (positive or negtive) position the user selects, the program selects the opposite. As a consequence, the network will reach a consensus that depends on the initial states of nodes, and the topology of the network.

Method `NW_doBuzz(int done)` is very similar to `NW_doKirchhoff()` studied earlier. Pass 1 updates the current state to the next state of each node. If the relative difference between current and next state is small, variable `stable_time` is incremented, indicating that the emergent process has not stabilized. On the other hand, if `stable_time` remains zero, indicating that all nodes are nearly stable, the method

---

[1]The current values of adjacent nodes are totaled and divided by degree(i), which is the same as averaging over neighboring nodes.

increments return variable done. The calling method can then determine convergence to network stability by setting done to zero before calling NW_doBuzz, and interrogating the return value. A return value of one means that the network has stabilized.

Pass 2 is more complicated because it averages values of adjacent nodes—for every node of the network—and then increments each node by the average value. Nodes are processed in random order to remove simulation bias. Program *Network.jar* borrows variable InfectionRate, previously used in simulation of infections, to store the stubbornness value, ϕ. This parameter cannot exceed one, and since the state variable cannot exceed one, the next_state value of each node lies between (-1) and $(+1)$, as required. Also, since buzz networks are closed systems, the degree of every node must be greater than zero. Therefore, we do not have to worry about a divide-by-0 exception.

Finally, method NW_doBuzz() clips the next_state value to accelerate convergence to an attractor. Change in state becomes monotonically smaller and smaller (described in the next section), as the network approaches an attractor. Therefore, clipping does not change the inevitable state of the network. However, we show strange attractors need not be equal to zero. They can be equal to any value in the interval $[-1, +1]$:

```
public int NW_doBuzz(int done){
    int stable_time = 0;
    int tail_node, head_node;                    //Tail and Head of Links
    for(int i = 0; i < nNodes; i++) {    //Pass 1: Update to next_state
        double ns = node[i].next_state;    //Future state
        if(Math.abs((node[i].next_state - ns)/ns) > .00001)
            stable_time++;                        //Not stable yet
            node[i].value = ns;                //Update to future state
    }
    if(stable_time == 0) done++;         //No state changes
    //Randomize processing order
    Shuffler random_list = new Shuffler(nNodes);
    for(int i = 0; i < nNodes; i++) random_list.card[i] = i;
    random_list.SH_Shuffle(nNodes);
    for(int n = 0; n < nNodes; n++){   //Pass 2: Next State
        int i = random_list.card[n];      //Scrambled order
        double neighbor = 0.0;
        node[i].next_state = InfectionRate*node[i].value/100.0;//RHS
        for(int j = 0; j < nLinks; j++){ //Across all links to this node
            tail_node = Link[j].tail;
            head_node = Link[j].head;
            if(tail_node == i) {              //All neighbors
                neighbor += node[head_node].value;
            }
            else if(head_node == i) {
                neighbor += node[tail_node].value;
            }
```

```
    }
    node[i].next_state += (1.0-InfectionRate/100.0)*neighbor/
                          node[i].degree;
    //Clip next_state
    if(Math.abs(node[i].next_state) <.00001) node[i].next_state = 0;
  }
  return done;
}//NW_doBuzz
```

10.1.3 Buzz Network Stability

In the marketing world of Flatland both positive and negative product endorsements spread like an infection until they reach every actor in Pointville's buzz network. Whether the news is good or bad does not matter, but whether it reaches everyone, and influences a majority of the population, does matter to the advertiser. Assuming that the Pointville buzz network is a closed system, does it sync? If all nodes reach the same final state, we say that the network has reached a *consensus*. For what values does the Pointville network reach a consensus? These questions are important to marketing executives who spend millions to promote their products.

We show that the only property of a buzz network that matters is the *degree sequence*. Furthermore, we show that the only property of the degree sequence that matters to reaching a consensus is identification of the hub, or highest-degreed node. Contrary to some literature on marketing, it does not matter whether the social network is random, small-world, or scale-free. Also, the closeness property claimed by Rosen to be most important has little effect on persuasion because betweenness/closeness of a node does not correlate with its ability to spread word-of-mouth influence quickly. Instead, the hub node is the most important actor. Every network has at least one hub, and it is this hub that marketers should control in order to get the best result. We show that the hub determines the eventual position of all other actors. Therefore, the hub is the best place to seed an endorsement.

Suppose that the states of the 129 nodes of the Pointville network are initially set to zero, indicating neutrality of opinion regarding a certain product. Now suppose that a random node is selected to positively endorse the product—call this the *promoter*—and a second node is randomly selected to negatively endorse the product—call this the *contrarian*. In terms of program *Network.jar*, we set the state of the promoter to $(+1)$ and the state of the contrarian to (-1), initially. What is the final position of actors in Pointville after a sufficient time?

We repeatedly apply the state equation to the entire network—updating every node according to the state equation. First, does the network sync, and if so, what is the final value of all nodes? More to the point: Do the actors agree with one another, and if so, do they become promoters or contrarians? As marketers, we would like to seed one actor with a positive position $(+1)$, and have it spread to all others. However, as we show, this depends on the relative magnitude of the degrees of the

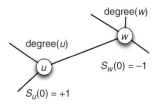

Figure 10.1 Illustration of the buzz network state equation: nodes with higher degree dominate nodes of lower degree.

initial promoter and contrarian nodes. The higher a seed's degree, the more powerful it is. Higher-degreed nodes trump lower-degreed nodes.

Figure 10.1 illustrates what happens when the promoter and contrarian are connected by a common link—as well as to other nodes. Assuming that the initial state of the other nodes is zero, we compute the next state of nodes u and w, using the state equation:

$$s_u(1) = \phi s_u(0) + (1 - \phi)\frac{s_w(0)}{\text{degree}(w)}; \quad s_u(0), \ s_w(0) \text{ given}$$

$$s_w(1) = \phi s_w(0) + (1 - \phi)\frac{s_u(0)}{\text{degree}(u)}$$

Now we average the two states by adding these two equations and dividing by 2. Let the average value of the combined state equations be designated by $s_{\text{avg}}(t)$:

$$s_{\text{avg}}(1) = \phi s_{\text{avg}}(0) + (1 - \phi)\frac{\dfrac{s_w(0)}{\text{degree}(w)} + \dfrac{s_u(0)}{\text{degree}(u)}}{2}$$

Or, more generally

$$s_{\text{avg}}(t + 1) = \phi s_{\text{avg}}(t) + (1 - \phi)\frac{\dfrac{s_w(t)}{\text{degree}(w)} + \dfrac{s_u(t)}{\text{degree}(u)}}{2}$$

The characteristic solution to this difference equation has an exponentially declining component given by ϕ^T, when $\phi < 1.0$. The particular solution has a monotonically decreasing, increasing, or constant term that depends on the sign of $F(t)$:

$$F(t) = s_u(t)\text{degree}(u) + s_u(t)\text{degree}(w)$$
$$\text{starting with } F(0) = s_u(0)\text{degree}(u) + s_u(0)\text{degree}(w)$$

In other words, the solution to the state equation contains a vanishing component and a component that tends toward zero, one, or minus one, depending on the initial conditions and the degree of u and w. Table 10.1 enumerates all possible combinations of the solution, ignoring the vanishing component.

TABLE 10.1   Possible Final States of a Buzz Network

Degree(w) vs. Degree(u)	$s_w(0) = +1$, $s_u(0) = -1$	$s_w(0) = -1$, $s_u(0) = +1$
$w > u$	+	−
$w < u$	−	+
$w = u$	0	0

The final state of nodes u and w in Fig. 10.1 are determined by the relative magnitude of each node's degree. Assuming one node to be a promoter ($+1$) and the other a contrarian (-1), the relative degrees of the seed nodes determine the final state of all nodes in the network! For example, a buzz network will tend toward a positive attractor ($+$) if degree(w) > degree(u) and $s_w(0) = +1$, $s_u(0) = -1$. However, the network will synchronize with states tending toward zero, if degree(w) = degree(u), regardless of the degree sequence of the network. If they have the same degree, initial promoter and contrarian positions cancel one another.

This result is verified by simulation. For example, all nodes in a ring or 2-regular network have the same degree. This means that the strange attractor should tend to zero, because all nodes are equal. The strange attractor of a 2-regular network is zero, while the consensus of a ring network is $1/n$. Thus, a ring buzz network syncs to zero in the limit as n increases without bound.

Complete, toroidal, hypercube, random, small-world, and scale-free networks tend toward zero (neutral consensus), if the degree of promoter and contrarian nodes are equal. Simulation studies also verify that hub nodes dominate in random, small-world, and scale-free networks when seeded with either positive or negative initial positions. If the hub node is seeded with (-1), the network's consensus will be negative. If it is seeded with ($+1$), the network's consensus will be positive. Therefore, buzz networks reach a consensus that is influenced by the dominant (hub) node. Contrary to intuition, a higher-degreed hub will win over a maximum-closeness node that has a lower degree. Intermediary nodes lack the power of highly connected nodes because higher connected nodes contribute to the small-world effect. Their position is propagated to other nodes faster than the position of others.

The consequences for marketing are obvious—the entire network is influenced by a single node, and the more connections the single node has, the greater its influence. The best marketing strategy is one that finds the hub and controls it in either positive or negative ways. As the hub goes, so goes the entire network.

There are a few exceptions to this rule that apply to *open systems*. For example, a line network is open because of its endnodes. Endnodes have a degree of 1, while intermediate nodes have degree of 2. Therefore, the intermediate nodes should have the greatest influence over the network. But, as it turns out, intermediate nodes have only a small influence on the consensus of the line network, even though they have higher degree than do endnodes. Why? Explaining this phenomenon will be left as an exercise for the reader.

10.2   POWER IN SOCIAL NETWORKS

Buzz networks are undirected, and the influence of one actor on another is rigidly determined by the network's degree sequence. This restriction limits the application of buzz networks to extremely simple social networks, and networks that model systems with interacting parts, such as the national economy and complex manufacturing processes. In this section we remove this restriction and propose a general theory of *I-nets* (*influence networks*) that combine the topology of a directed *Atay network* with the flexibility of directed weighted links called *influences*. I-nets are more general because each link is assigned a different weight:

> *Influence Network (I-net).* $G(t) = \{N(t), L(t), f\}$, where $N(t)$ is a set of actors (nodes) with time-varying state, $S(t)$ are states in $[-1, +1]$, $L(t)$ is a set of influences with weights ϕ in $[0, 1]$, and f is a static mapping of $N \times N$—the topology of G.
>
> *State Equation of I-Net.* Influence networks behave like directed Atay networks, but with differing influences. The rate of change in the state of an actor is dictated by the difference between the states of adjacent actors:

$$s_i(t+1) = s_i(t) + \sum_j [s_j(t) - s_i(t)]\phi^{\mathrm{T}}i, \ j; \ s_i(0) \text{ given}$$

> and ϕ^{T} is obtained from the network topology and influence weights assigned to links.

This expanded definition of I-net expands on the definition of the next-state equation. The *next state* is a function of differing weights and the difference in position between adjacent actors. Instead of averaging the value of neighbors, this next-state function computes the difference. Logically, an I-net reaches consensus when there are no differences of position among neighbors. Therefore, an I-net reaches consensus when all actor's differences shrink to zero!

In the following we show that an I-net exponentially reaches a consensus (strange attractor) if the spectral gap, $\sigma(L)$, is negative. Further, we show that the consensus (strange attractor) value is a fixed point determined by the transposed weight matrix ϕ^{T} and initial state vector $S(0)$. We are particularly interested in estimating an arbitrary I-net's strange attractor when consensus is reached, and the conditions that guarantee a nonzero consensus.

The applications of this theory to social network analysis are obvious—we can predict the probable outcome of negotiation among members of a social group, and the influence of one or more actors in a complex system. Conversely, we can estimate the conditions under which a complex system will never reach a nonzero consensus. In either case, we can also determine which actor has the most power, and which actor or actors are blocking progress toward consensus.

10.2.1   Two-Party Negotiation

A simple I-net consisting of two actors negotiating with one another is shown in Fig. 10.2. Two actors—the parties—are shown as nodes. A link from actor 0:Us to actor 1:Them is labeled 33%, meaning that actor 0 has a 33% influence on actor 1. Similarly, a 50% link from actor 1 to actor 0 indicates the amount of influence actor 1 exerts on actor 0. The influence of one actor on the other is calculated by multiplying the connecting link's weight by the source actor's state, and forwarding the product to the destination actor.

Influences might be determined by counting the percentage of times that actors agree with one another, or by collecting other historical data. For example, estimates of influence might be determined by casting votes and calculating the percentage of times that two actors agree with one another. An alternative strategy might involve observation of a negotiation to determine what percentage of the time one actor yields to another actor. In general, influence weights are measures of how often directly connected actors agree.

Negotiation is a process of interactive compromise over time. This process is simulated by iterating the next state function over many timesteps. At each step, the state of all actors is updated according to the next-state function (differences). Hopefully, the negotiation reaches a strange attractor or consensus. If so, each actor moves a bit closer to the other's position after each interaction. The amount of movement is determined by the value of the influence link and the difference between positions of the actors. This is precisely modeled by an *Atay state equation*.

Suppose that the two actors are diametrically opposed to one another at time $t = 0$. Let actor 0:Us initially take the positive position $(+1)$, and let 1:Them take the negative position, (-1). The initial state of actors is $Us(0) = 1$, and $Them(0) = -1$. Initially, the difference between their positions from the perspective of Us is $(-1 - 1) = (-2)$, and the difference between positions from the perspective of Them is simply $(+1 - (-1)) = (+2)$. Negotiation will either lead the divergent differences or iteratively diminish until reaching zero.

Two-party negotiation is a process of interactive compromise, step-by-step, so the two actors must narrow the difference in positions as perceived by each other if the network is to reach a consensus. That is, actor Us must move toward the position of Them by an amount determined by the influence link: 50%, and Them must move toward Us by 33% of their difference after each step. Repeated application of the next-state function does not guarantee reaching a state of zero, but it may lead to a difference of zero.

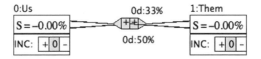

Figure 10.2   I-net representation of a two-party negotiation: actor Us versus actor Them, and influences of $\frac{1}{3}$ and $\frac{1}{2}$, respectively.

For example, after one timestep:

$$Us(1) = Us(0) + 50\%(Them(0) - Us(0)) = 1 + 50\%(-2) = 0$$
$$Them(1) = Them(0) + 33\%(Us(0) - Them(0)) = -1 + 33\%(2) = -33\%$$

Application of the next-state function is repeated for each timestep until the two reach a consensus, or they are stalemated. Naturally, we want to know the final positions of each, and more importantly, we want to know whether the two ever meet in the middle. By repeated application of the state equation

$$s_i(t + 1) = s_i(t) + \sum_j [s_j(t) - s_i(t)]\phi^T i, \; j;$$

we can determine where ϕ^T is the transpose of the influence matrix

$$Us(2) = Us(1) + 50\%(Them(1) - Us(1)) = 0 + 50\%(-0.33) = -0.167$$
$$Them(2) = Them(1) + 33\%(Us(1) - Them(1)) = -0.33 + 33\%(0.33) = -22\%$$

$$Us(3) = Us(2) + 50\%(Them(2) - Us(2)) = 0.167 + 50\%(-0.056) = -19\%$$
$$Them(3) = Them(2) + 33\%(Us(2) - Them(2)) = -22 + 33\%(0.056) = -20\%$$

The two actor's states converge, which means that they reach a consensus— additional application of the next-state function leaves the actor's in the same state. In this example, differences drop to zero and both actors reach a consensus state equal to negative 20%, which favors the initial position of Them. Therefore, 1:Them is more influential than actor 0:Us.

In general, consensus is determined by initial positions, and the influence matrix obtained by transposing the weighted connection matrix. In this simple example, the influence matrix ϕ^T is obtained as follows:

$$\phi = \begin{pmatrix} 0 & 0.33 \\ 0.50 & 0 \end{pmatrix}$$

$$\text{And the transpose } \phi^T = \begin{pmatrix} 0 & 0.50 \\ 0.33 & 0 \end{pmatrix}$$

10.2.2 I-Net State Equation

I-nets approximate the interactions internal to social networks; negotiators try to work toward a mutually satisfactory position—a consensus. But is it always possible to reach a consensus? Also, who has the most power in the negotiation? To answer these questions, we formally define *actor power* as the *degree of influence* an actor has over the eventual outcome of actor states.

Suppose that each actor in the social network takes an initial position, (-1), if against the proposition, and $(+1)$ if in favor of the proposition. We quantify disagreement between the actors as the difference in their positions, $(s_j - s_i)$. The degree of influence, $\phi(j, i)$, between actors v_i and v_j is a fraction in [0, 1] representing the ability of the two actors to "meet in the middle," or compromise during negotiation. In this model, actor v_i changes his or her position by an amount $\phi(j, i)(s_j - s_i)$ after each interaction:

$$\Delta s_i(t) = \phi(j, i)(s_j - s_i)$$

If actor v_i is influenced by multiple adjacent actors, change in future state is the sum over all influences on the actor

$$\Delta s_i(t) = \sum_j [\phi(j, i)(s_j - s_i)]$$

where j ranges over neighbors of v_i. It is easier to work with the transpose of $\phi(j, i)$, so we substitute $\phi^T(i, j)$ into the state equation

$$\Delta s_i(t) = \sum_j [\phi^T(j, i)(s_j - s_i)]$$

where j ranges over neighbors of v_i. The sum of differences is equal to the difference of sums, so we can replace the influence matrix by the *Laplacian* of the influence matrix. In matrix form, the state equation is $\Delta S(t) = LS(t)$, where L is the Laplacian of ϕ^T.

Figure 10.3a shows an I-net model of a simple social network consisting of three actors—hound, fox, and squirrel—and three influences—$\frac{1}{3}$, $\frac{1}{2}$, and $\frac{3}{4}$. The essential properties of this social network are summarized by the initial state vector $S(0)$ and the influence matrix ϕ, which we transpose and convert to its Laplacian by summing rows:

$$S(0) = [0, \ 0, \ 0]^T$$

$$\phi = \begin{pmatrix} 0 & 0.33 & 0 \\ 0 & 0 & 0.5 \\ 0.75 & 0 & 0 \end{pmatrix}$$

$$\phi^T = \begin{pmatrix} 0 & 0 & 0.75 \\ 0.33 & 0 & 0 \\ 0 & 0.5 & 0 \end{pmatrix}$$

Convert the transposed influence matrix into the Laplacian matrix by inserting row sums into diagonal elements:

$$L = \begin{pmatrix} -0.75 & 0 & 0.75 \\ 0.33 & -0.33 & 0 \\ 0 & 0.5 & -0.5 \end{pmatrix}$$

The I-net synchronizes if the state equation, $\Delta S(t) = LS(t)$, has negative eigenvalues—that is, a negative *spectral gap*, $\sigma(L) < 0$, is necessary, but not sufficient to guarantee stability of the I-net.

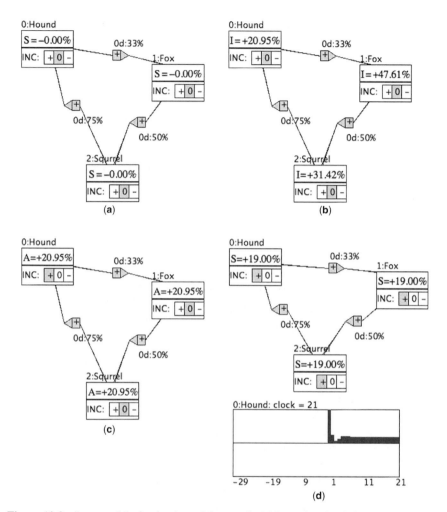

Figure 10.3 I-net model of a simple social network: (a) I-net showing influences; (b) degree of influence is shown in each actor; (c) strange attractor value for $S(0) = [1, 0, 0]^T$ is shown in each actor; (d) example display of evaluation results.

Note that solutions to the state equation, $S(t + 1) = S(t) + LS(t) = [I + L]S(t)$, are sums of exponentials: $E\{S(t)\} = [I + L]S(t)$, where E is the timeshift operator, $E\{S(t)\} = S(t + 1)$.
Simplifying, we obtain

$$[(E - I) - L]S(t) = 0$$

The characteristic solution to this operator equation is the weighted sum of the roots r_i, where $i = 1, 2, \ldots, n$, of the equation

$$[(r - 1)I - L] = 0$$

The set of roots form the *basis set* of the solution, $S(t) = \sum_{i,j} c_{i,j} r_i^t \,; t = 1,2,\ldots$. The roots are obtained by noting that they are related to the eigenvalues ε of the Laplacian **L**, by the following:

$$[\varepsilon \mathbf{I} - \mathbf{L}] = [(r-1)\mathbf{I} - \mathbf{L}], \quad \text{so} \quad r - 1 = \varepsilon, \quad \text{or} \quad r = 1 + \varepsilon$$

Therefore, each root is one greater than the corresponding eigenvalue of **L**. Also, because the solution is a linear combination of exponentials, the state of actors either increases or decreases exponentially, starting from initial values, $S(0)$. The final state of an actor depends on the eigenvalues of the state matrix $[\mathbf{I} + \mathbf{L}]$, and since **L** is determined by the topology of the I-net, and influence weights, we can estimate the outcome of a negotiation by analyzing $[\mathbf{I} + \mathbf{L}]$.

10.2.3   I-Net Stability

From the previous chapter we know that a network syncs when all of its nodes attain the same value. In social networks modeled as an I-net, synchronization is equivalent to reaching a consensus. We also know that synchronization in an *Atay network* is determined by the *spectral gap* of its Laplacian matrix. Therefore, a necessary (but not sufficient)—condition for reaching a consensus in a social network like the one illustrated in Fig. 10.3 is $\sigma(L) < 0$, where σ is the largest nontrivial eigenvalue of L.

The rate of convergence to a consensus is exponentially fast because the solution to its state equation is a linear combination of exponentials: that is, the roots are bounded by one because $r = 1 + \varepsilon$. If the largest root is exactly one, the solution contains exponentially decaying terms, and the solution cannot "blow up" because the term containing the root equals one. Thus, I-nets always converge to some strange attractor value, but not always to zero.

Consider the previous derivation, and the networks in Figs. 10.3c and 10.3d. The eigenvalues of L are $\varepsilon_0 = 0$, $\varepsilon_1 = -0.79 + 0.4i$, and $\varepsilon_2 = -0.79 - 0.4i$, respectively.[2] The nontrivial eigenvalues of L are all negative, and because they are complex numbers with imaginary parts, synchronization oscillates before settling in on a strange attractor. The spectral gap in this case is the real part of the largest nontrivial eigenvalue, $\sigma = \varepsilon_1 = -0.79$. The social network reaches consensus because $-0.79 < 0$.[3] Alternatively, if the spectral gap had been greater than zero, $\sigma > 0$, the I-net would "blow up" and not reach a consensus.[4]

Figure 10.3c shows the theoretical strange attractor value for initial condition $S(0) = [1, 0, 0]^T$. All actors reach consensus of 20.95%. A different consensus may be reached for a different initial condition, $S(0)$. The theoretical consensus of a group can easily be computed from its topology, influences, and initial state, $S(0)$. Program *Influence.jar* does this—using initial values set by the user. Although the

---

[2] Here i is the imaginary square root of (-1), and ε is the vector of eigenvalues of L.
[3] We will discuss exceptions to this conclusion in the next section.
[4] Program *Influence.jar* clips the state values, so states decay to zero instead of infinity.

theoretical consensus is an approximation, it is sufficiently accurate to gauge the power of individual actors. It is an upper bound on the consensus that can be reached in a non-conflicted network.

Figure 10.3d shows the results of evaluating the triangular or three-party I-net with initial condition $S(0)$. The actual consensus is 19% instead of 20.95%, as suggested by the theory. Generally, the theoretical estimate is slightly higher than the actual consensus. Keep in mind that the actual value is reached under several restrictions on the I-net. We discuss these restrictions in greater detail later.

Figure 10.3d also displays a plot of the state of actor "hound" versus time. Note how precipitously the initial value drops to the strange attractor value. This confirms the theoretical prediction that solutions converge exponentially. Also, if the solution to the state equation of an I-net contains imaginary roots, the solution will oscillate as it converges. This also confirms the theory developed by the foregoing analysis.

10.2.4 I-net Consensus

Social network analysis is the study of persuasive power in networks, but there are many different definitions of social power used in the literature. We choose to define *social power* as the aggregate influence an actor has over the final (strange attractor) value of the synchronized network. Social power may be approximated by the asymptotic solution to the state equation as time approaches infinity:

$$S(t + 1) = S(t) + \mathbf{L}S(t); \quad S(0) \text{ given}$$
$$= [\mathbf{I} + \mathbf{L}]S(t)$$

Therefore

$$S(t) = [\mathbf{I} + \mathbf{L}]^t S(0); \quad t = 1,2,\ldots$$

Let Q be the *power matrix* corresponding to each actor's influence on the final state (consensus) of the I-net. Q is the system state matrix, raised to some "large" power. As time increases without bound, and if $\sigma < 0$, then $S(t)$ converges to a strange attractor:

$$s(\infty) = [\mathbf{I} + \mathbf{L}]^\infty S(0)$$

But we cannot compute infinity, so we approximate it with t^* as follows:

$$\text{RMS}([\mathbf{I} + \mathbf{L}]^{t^*}) < \varepsilon$$
$$Q = [\mathbf{I} + \mathbf{L}]^{t^*}$$

where ε is typically 0.0001. Function RMS() is defined as the root-mean-square error obtained by subtracting each column's diagonal element of Q from every other column element, squaring the difference, summing, and then taking the square-root of the sum

$$RMS(X) = \text{sqrt}\left(\sum (x_{i,j} - x_{i,j})^2\right)$$

For example, t^* for the two-party negotiation network in Fig. 10.2b is 14, yielding the degree of influence vector [0.21, 0.48, 0.31]:

$$Q = [\mathbf{I} + \mathbf{L}]^{14} = \begin{pmatrix} 0.21 & 0.48 & 0.31 \\ 0.21 & 0.48 & 0.31 \\ 0.21 & 0.48 & 0.31 \end{pmatrix}$$

The actors of Fig. 10.2b are ranked according to the degree of influence vector, as follows (most powerful is first):

Actor 1: fox, 48%

Actor 2: squirrel, 31%

Actor 0: hound, 21%

In terms of social network analysis, this means that the fox's position will prevail over either of the other two, individually. But what happens if two actors vote against the third actor? In this case, the majority prevails (see Table 10.2). In effect, the degree of influence is additive—like votes—in determining the consensus of an I-net. However, the theoretical value obtained from Q is only an approximation to actual consensus, as Table 10.2 shows.

In Table 10.2 consensus is a function of initial states of the actors. In the top half of the table (no opposition), two actors are initially set to $(+1)$, while the third is set to 0. For example, actors "0&1" are set to $(+1)$, and their degree of influences are added together to get 69% = (21% + 48%). The actual consensus value was obtained by simulation using *Influence.jar*.

Similarly, the approximation of consensus for "0&1 vs. 2" is obtained by adding the influences of "0&1" and subtracting the influence of the opposition, "2." Thus,

TABLE 10.2   Consensus in Fig. 10.2

Actors	Approximation (%)	Actual (%)
No opposition		
0&1 vs. 2	69	66
0&2 vs. 1	52	50
1&2 vs. 0	79	76
Opposition		
0&1 vs. 2	37	34
0&2 vs. 1	8	3
1&2 vs. 0	58	55

the approximate consensus for this set of initial conditions is $37\% = (21\% + 48\% - 31\%)$. The actual consensus obtained by simulation, 34%, is much lower. In general, the approximation is higher than the actual consensus. More complex networks will have more complex additions and subtractions. Examples are left as an exercise for the reader.

10.2.5 Java Methods for Computing Influence

Computing the degree of influence of an actor is a straightforward application of matrix multiplication. All matrix calculations used in this book are performed by reusable classes provided by the JAMA, so we merely call standard matrix multiplication and eigenvalue methods from the JAMA package, when needed.[5]

First, we need a Java method for creating the connection matrix containing the influences in ϕ. Then method `Diagram_doInfluences()` calculates the theoretical degree of influence for each actor by repeated multiplication of $[I + L]$ to get $Q = [I + L]^{t^*}$. Power is calculated by repeated multiplication until $\text{RMS}[I + L]^{t^*} < \varepsilon$.

Method `ConnectionMatrix()` constructs matrix ϕ by copying the influence weights into Java matrix **M**. The method is more general than we need for the purposes of this chapter because it allows weights to be both positive and negative. We assume that all weights are positive and all links are unidirectional. The `Matrix` class provided by the JAMA package support access methods `M.get()` and `M.set()`—operations that get and set elements of matrix **M**:

```
//Directed Connection matrix with weights
private Matrix ConnectionMatrix() {
    Matrix M = new Matrix(nActors, nActors, 0.0);
    for(int i = 0; i < nInfluences; i++){
        int sign = 0;
        if(Influences[ i] .v > 0) sign = 1;
        else if(Influences[ i] .v < 0) sign = -1;
        double d = sign* Influences[ i] .weight/100.0;  //Tail-to-head
        M.set(Influences[i].from, Influences[i].to, d);  //Connection
    }
    return M;
}//ConnectionMatrix
```

Method `Diagram_doInfluences()` performs the matrix multiplications needed to calculate the theoretical degree of influences, and insert them into the I-net. The method has a direct side effect on the actors, returning degree of influence in `Actors[I].Actor_influence`, as well as returning the largest influence value and actor number. Finally, this method also calculates the strange attractor values corresponding to an initial condition $S(0)$, when parameter `use_initial_value` is **true**. These results are relayed back to the calling program through array, `Actors[row].next_v`. Program *Influence.jar* displays

---

[5]The *Journal of the American Mathematical Association* (JAMA) package for linear algebra.

influences or strange attractors, depending on which button in the control panel is pushed by the user:

```
//Calculate (I+L)^t*
public MatrixReply Diagram_doInfluences(boolean use_initial_value) {
    MatrixReply reply = new MatrixReply();
    //M = (I+L)
    Matrix M = ConnectionMatrix();
    M = M.transpose();                      //Influences
    for(int row = 0; row < nActors; row++){
        double sum = 0.0;
        for(int col = 0; col < nActors; col++)
            sum += M.get(row, col);
        M.set(row, row, 1.0-sum);       //I+Laplacian
    }
    double rms = 1.0;                       //root-mean-sq error bound
    Matrix I = M;
    int count = 10*nActors;                 //Avoid infinite loops
    while(rms > 0.0001 && count > 0){
        I = I.times(M);                     //Powers of (I+L)
        rms = ColumnRMS(I);                 //Over all columns
        count--;
    }
    //Store in I-network
    reply.max_value = I.get(0,0);
    for(int i = 0; i < nActors; i++){
        double influence = I.get(i,i);
        Actors[i].Actor_influence = influence;
        if(reply.max_value < influence){
            reply.max_value = influence;
            reply.row = i;
        }
    }
    reply.number = 10*nActors-count+1;//Overload as t*
    //Tacky but effective...way to estimate attractor from S(0)
    if(use_initial_value){
        for(int row = 0; row < nActors; row++){
            Actors[row].next_v = 0.0;
            for(int j = 0; j < nActors; j++){
                Actors[row].next_v += Actors[j].current_v * I.get(row, j);
            }
        }
    }
        return reply;
}//Diagram_doInfluences
```

10.3   CONFLICT IN I-NETS

The foregoing analysis assumes that actors are cooperative and that they combine their influences to reach consensus, together. But in real life, social networks are full of "contentious" relationships. Positive and negative feedback influences lead to conflict, and conflict prevents the I-net from reaching a nonzero consensus. Regardless of the theoretical approximation given by Q, the actual consensus may be a stalemate. In this section we investigate conflict and discover that it prevents an I-net from reaching consensus.

Conflict is a direct result of feedback cycles in an I-net. Feedback loops in the I-net may either reinforce or dampen the state of actors, because influence links may create network cycles that either enhance or retard convergence to a nonzero strange attractor. These cycles may diminish the effectiveness of influence to the point where the network reaches a *stalemate*—a zero-valued strange attractor. When this happens, we say that the I-net is *conflicted*, because one or more actors are in *conflict*.

10.3.1   Degree of Conflict

The *degree of conflict* is a property of an actor that prevents the I-net from reaching a consensus, by working against synchronization. A positive degree of conflict leads to a positive consensus while a negative degree of consensus leads to stalemate. An actor is *conflicted* if its degree of conflict is negative. When the I-net contains a conflicted actor, the states of all actors oscillate downward until reaching zero. This represents a "no position" state for the actors. Thus, a single actor with a negative degree of conflict will override the effects of all other influences, and make it impossible for actors to agree on a non-zero position.

Consider the conflicted I-net in Fig. 10.4. According to the theory, the sum total of influences among the actors of Fig. 10.4 should equal 100%: actor 0:24.4%, actor 1:55.2%, and actor 2:20.3%. If a consensus is possible, it will emerge as actors

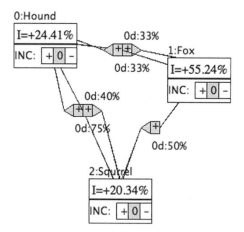

Figure 10.4   Conflict in an I-net arises due to dampening feedback in a countercycle.

reach values of approximately 24.4%, 55.2%, 20.3%, or combinations of these values, depending on the initial conditions of the actors. Think of the degree of influence as approximately equal to the number of votes each actor controls in arriving at a decision. If actors 0, 1, and 2 are initially set to [1, 1, −1] the I-net should reach a consensus of approximately $(24 + 55 - 20) = 59\%$.

Unfortunately, the I-net of Fig. 10.4 does *not* reach the consensus value predicted by the foregoing analysis! In fact, its strange attractor is zero for all initial states except for [1, 1, 1]. Why? The answer lies in understanding feedback cycles in I-nets. In particular, we have to examine the topology of the I-net in terms of feedback and feedforward links. As it turns out, this problem is similar to the problem of inhibiting feedback loops in Kirchhoff networks studied in the previous chapter.

The conflicted I-net of Fig. 10.4 contains three cycles: two small cycles of length 2 hops between actors 0&1, and 0&2, and one larger cycle enclosing all three actors. The cumulative influence in the 3-hop cycle from actor 0 to 1, 2, and back to 0 is the product of influences along the cycle: $\left(\frac{1}{3}\right)\left(\frac{1}{2}\right)\left(\frac{3}{4}\right) = \frac{1}{8}$. We designate this as the feedforward cycle. Similarly, the countercycles from actor 1 to 0 and actor 2 to 0 produce a feedbackward cycle of influence $-\left(\frac{1}{3}\right)\left(\frac{4}{10}\right) = -\frac{4}{30}$. Adding these together yields a net feedbackward influence of $\left(\frac{1}{8}\right) - \left(\frac{4}{30}\right) = -\left(\frac{1}{120}\right)$. The feedbackward cycle causes an exponential decrease in "gain" throughout the I-net, which dampens the consensus, eventually driving it to zero.

Conflict is negative influence, and it is exerted through feedbackward influence in an I-net. As it turns out, the negative effect of negative conflict shows up immediately in the topology of the network. This effect is captured in the system matrix C. Let the degree of conflict equal the diagonal of $C = [I + L]$. The diagonal elements of C, $c_i = 1, 2, \ldots, n$, are measures of the degree of conflict introduced into the network by actor v_i. When $c_i < 0$, we observe negative conflict, which has a dampening effect on consensus.

We readily see that the rate of change of state vector $S(t)$ diminishes if $c_i < 0$:

$$|\Delta S(t)| < 0 \quad \text{if there exists an actor } v_i \text{ such that} \quad c_i < 0$$

Therefore, the strange attractor of an I-net containing at least one negative degree of conflict is driven to zero. We call actor v_i corresponding to $c_i < 0$ *conflicted*, and declare the I-net *stalemated*. All conflicted actors must be removed before the I-net can reach consensus.

Continuing with the example in Fig. 10.4, identify the conflict by computing vector C from system matrix $[I + L]$, as follows:

$$\phi = \begin{pmatrix} 0 & 0.33 & 0.40 \\ 0.33 & 0 & 0.50 \\ 0.75 & 0 & 0 \end{pmatrix}$$

$$\phi^T = \begin{pmatrix} 0 & 0.33 & 0.75 \\ 0.33 & 0 & 0 \\ 0.40 & 0.50 & 0 \end{pmatrix}$$

$$\mathbf{L} = \begin{pmatrix} -1.08 & 0.33 & 0.75 \\ 0.33 & -0.33 & 0 \\ 0.40 & 0.50 & -0.90 \end{pmatrix}$$

$$[\mathbf{I} + \mathbf{L}] = \begin{pmatrix} -0.08 & 0.33 & 0.75 \\ 0.33 & 0.67 & 0 \\ 0.40 & 0.50 & 0.10 \end{pmatrix}$$

$$C = [-0.08, \ 0.67, \ 0.10]^T$$

Only one element of C is negative, but this is enough to force the consensus to zero. The negative degree of conflict on actor 0, degree_conflict$(v_0) = -0.08$, can be removed by changing the weights of influences connecting it to adjacent actors. For example, in Fig. 10.4 changing the weight of the link between actors 1 and 0 from 33% to 25% yields a new degree of conflict vector without a negative element:

$$C = [0, \ 0.67, \ 0.25]^T$$

This modification removes the conflict. The revised I-net will reach a consensus of 23%, 53%, 23%, or combinations of these three fixed-point values, depending on the initial state of the actors. The reader may verify this by running program *Influence.jar* and selecting this network from the "Examples" menu.

10.3.2   Java Method for Computing Degree of Conflict

Method `Diagram_doConflict()` is similar to—but less complex than—the method for approximating degree of influence. It simply composes system matrix $[I + L]$ and then transfers its diagonal elements to network array `Actors[i].Actor_conflict`. In addition, conflicted actors are painted red, indicating that they are conflicted. The method returns **true** if it finds a conflicted actor and **false** if it does not:

```
//Find conflicting actors
public boolean Diagram_doConflict() {
        boolean reply = false;               //Assume no conflict
        Matrix M = ConnectionMatrix();
        M = M.transpose();                   //Influences
        //Convert to Laplacian+I
        for(int row = 0; row < nActors; row++){
                double sum = 0.0;
```

```
for(int col = 0; col < nActors; col++) sum += M.get(row, col);

double diagonal = 1.0-sum;

M.set(row, row, diagonal);

Actors[row].Actor_conflict = diagonal;

if(Actors[ row].c == 1) Actors[ row].c = 0; //Non-conflicted white

if(diagonal < 0) {

        reply = true;

        Actors[row].c = 1;                          //Conflicted red

    }

}

return reply;

}//doConflict
```

Now we have a complete theory of I-nets and the social networks that they model. An I-net will reach a nonzero consensus if its spectral gap is less than zero and none of its actors have a negative degree of conflict. Furthermore, the stability of the I-net and emergence of a nonzero consensus is completely a function of its Laplacian matrix:

Summary of Calculations and Necessary Conditions

$\phi =$ influence matrix; $\phi^T =$ transposed influence matrix

$L = \phi^T -$ diagonal; where diagonal $=$ sum of rows of ϕ^T

Synchronization condition: $\sigma(L) < 0$

Degree of influence (power) $Q = [\mathbf{I} + \mathbf{L}]^{t^*}$

Degree of conflict $C =$ diagonal $[\mathbf{I} + \mathbf{L}]$

Notice that the popular notion of middle-person or maximum-closeness node is completely absent in this analysis. The most powerful actor is the one with the most influence, regardless of its closeness property. Static network topology is more important than number of paths running through a node.

10.4   COMMAND HIERARCHIES

The tree-structured social network or *command hierarchy* is one of the oldest and most widely adopted social structures. It is the model used by military commanders, corporation managers, and many governmental bureaucracies. But recent advances in global communications and an enlightened management class have caused a re-thinking of the value of command hierarchies, especially as they apply to virtual and expertise-based organizations. The knowledge worker, for example, is often ineffective in tightly controlled command hierarchies, raising the question of whether command hierarchies are valid on the modern age of the Internet.

In this section we raise the question, "Is the tree-structured command hierarchy still valid as a management tool?" More to the point, "Where does power lie in a tree-structured organization, and when is a command hierarchy able to reach

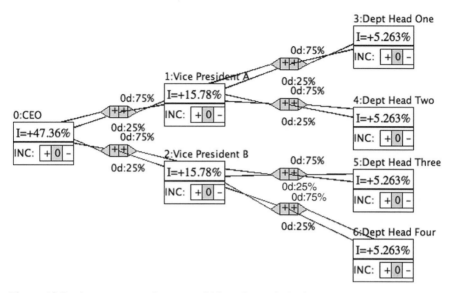

Figure 10.5   A tree-structured command hierarchy typical of corporate management. This I-net is conflicted because of overly strong control from managers.

consensus and avoid stalemate?" We show that command hierarchies are efficient, but also prone to stalemate when too much top-down influence is imposed on workers. This result is a direct consequence of the topology of command structures and the magnitude of the weights associated with influence links.

Figure 10.5 illustrates a very simple command hierarchy consisting of a chief executive officer (CEO), two subordinate vice presidents, and four department heads reporting to each vice president. This is a simple binary tree with three levels of command. Suppose we assume supervisors exercise a high degree of influence over subordinates (75% influence), and subordinates exercise a small degree of influence over their supervisors (25%)., as shown in Fig. 10.5.

The question naturally arises, "what power does the executive manager have over his or her subordinates?" Figure 10.5 and Table 10.3 summarize the degree of influence each actor has within the hierarchy. The effectiveness of influence becomes additive as long as there are no conflicts in the I-net. However, analysis of matrix $C =$ diagonal $[I + L]$ reveals two inherent conflicts—one each with the vice presidents. Instead of arriving at a consensus per the degree of influences of Table 10.3, this command hierarchy is stalemated. Regardless of the initial state of actors in Fig. 10.5, the network's strange attractor is zero. The influence weights are too large, leading to two negative influences.

The command hierarchy of Fig. 10.5 is overly controlled; that is, the managers do not give enough power to their subordinates. Conflicts can be removed by lowering forward influences from 75% to 50%. Essentially, the managers must reduce their influence on subordinates if they want to lower consensus-blocking conflict. This sharing of power allows a consensus to develop. Now the CEO (chief executive

TABLE 10.3   Properties of Command Hierarchy in Fig. 10.4

Actor	Link Influence (%)	Adjacent Actor	Degree of Influence (%)	Degree of Conflict (%)
0: CEO	75	1: VP A	47.36	50
1: VP A	25	0: CEO	15.78	−25
2: VP B	25	0: CEO	25	−25
1: VP A	75	3: Dept. 1	15.78	−25
1: VP A	75	4: Dept. 2	15.78	−25
2: VP B	75	5: Dept. 3	15.78	−25
2: VP B	75	6: Dept. 4	15.78	−25
3: Dept. 1	25	1: VP A	5.26	25
4: Dept. 2	25	1: VP A	5.26	25
5: Dept. 3	25	2: VP B	5.26	25
6: Dept. 4	25	2: VP B	5.26	25

officer) and two vice presidents rule by majority instead of dictate, because their degrees of influence equal 33.33% (CEO), and 16.67% for each of the vice presidents, respectively.

What happens when one vice president disagrees with the CEO and the other vice president? According to the theory developed here, the sum of influences of CEO and vice president is 50%, which is not enough to form a majority. Does management reach a nonzero consensus, or does the network stalemate? This is left as an exercise for the reader.

The simple command hierarchy of Fig. 10.5 suggests that tightly controlled command hierarchies are prone to conflict. Indeed, if top–down pressure is too heavy, the social network will not operate efficiently because of autocratic control. It is much more effective to share power by reducing the requirement that managers have much more control than do subordinates. However, managers may not always get their way because they risk losing their majority position, when degree of influence slips below 50%.

Too much autocratic control leads to inefficient governance of an organization, but flattened network organizations can also be overly controlled as we demonstrated in the previous section. Any influence network, whether it is random, scale-free, or small-world, can stalemate owing to the amount of influence and nature of feedback-ward links in the network. It would be unwise to assume that an arbitrary network organization is more efficient than a tree-structured command hierarchy (see Table 10.3) simply because of its topology. We must incorporate the influence matrix as well in the analysis.

10.5   EMERGENT POWER IN I-NETS

The foregoing provides a fundamental theory for social networks and dependence analysis in complex adaptive systems such as groups of human negotiators, factors affecting a complex economic system, critical infrastructure risk assessment, and so forth. But the theory does not explain how actor power arises in such systems, or what it takes for an individual actor to become "powerful." The next step is to explore how power—in the form or influence over the entire network—is acquired. We approach this problem experimentally, using an emergent algorithm that increases individual actor's degree of influence by altering influence weights on inbound and outbound links.

Suppose that we define *power* as the degree of influence an actor has over all other actors in the I-net. The degree of influence—and therefore power of an individual actor—is equal to its corresponding diagonal element in matrix Q. But how does individual degree of influence impact the degree of influence of other actors? To more fully understand how power is acquired in an I-net, we perform two experiments in the next two sections: (1) acquisition of *weight influence*—the *emergence of power* through the manipulation of the weights (degree of influence) on links and (2) acquisition of *link influence*—emergence of power through rewiring links. Weight influence simulates the acquisition of power through skillful persuasion, while link influence is related to the familiar "human networking" that is thought to benefit workers by "whom you know, not what you know."

We discover that acquisition of power by changing the weights of inbound and outbound links leads to domination by a small number of actors over all others. Specifically, the best strategy for an actor seeking to gain power in an I-net is to reduce the weights of inbound links, and increase the weights of outbound links. In terms of social network analysis, this recommends that individual actors ignore advice from adjacent actors, and focus on increasing their influence on other actors. In human terms, a persuasive extrovert is generally able to gain more power than a convincing introvert! Indeed, we show that this strategy leads to domination of the I-net—*most of the time*.

We discover the opposite result in link influence emergence—rewiring of links to gain power in an I-net has very little effect. In fact, we show that link influence emergence leads to chaos, and has no utility as far as acquisition of power is concerned. This negative result is important to know because it is often assumed that power can be gained by associating with other powerful actors. However, we show this to be false—at least for the model developed here.

10.5.1 Weight Emergence

The general idea of weight emergence is to increase the outbound link weights to increase an actor's influence on its outbound neighbors, and decrease the inbound link weights to minimize the influence other actors have on the (ambitious) actor. This approach makes sense when viewed from the influence matrix ϕ. Row i of ϕ represents the influence of actor i over other actors, and column j represents the influence that other actors impose on actor j. Clearly, increasing the total of row i and decreasing the total of column i has two advantages for actor i: (1) it increases the total influence that actor i imposes on its neighbors, and (2) it decreases the total influence imposed on actor i by other actors. Both actions increase the degree of influence of actor i.

The problem with increasing the row totals and simultaneously decreasing the column totals of matrix ϕ is quite clear—these are opposing actions. Decreasing column totals also decreases row totals, and conversely, increasing row totals also increases column totals. We cannot do both simultaneously. The proposed strategy is mathematically meaningless.

Instead of mathematically addressing this paradox, let the I-net find a solution for us by the process of emergence. Instead of writing an equation, we propose to write simple microrules for each actor to independently follow, and then observe the resulting macroproperty emerging from hundreds of applications of the microrules. The I-net will either converge or diverge. If it converges, the degrees of influence of the (partially) stable actors answers the question, "Who is the most powerful actor in the I-net?"

The weight emergence algorithm is simple: select two (row, column) pairs from the influence matrix ϕ corresponding to an inbound link and outbound link of actor #row. Then subtract one point of weight from the inbound link and add one point to the outbound link. If conditions are right, incrementally altering weights of the In and out links leads to an increase in the randomly selected actor's degree of influence, but if not, we revert to the previous weights. This process is repeated until the degrees of influence of all actors remain (relatively) stable—but perhaps different from one another.

What are the right conditions for this emergence to work? There are three conditions to consider: (1) the column and row totals of matrix ϕ must not exceed 100%, nor may they drop below 0%; (2) the 1% change in influence (weights on links) must not create a conflicted node in the I-net; and (3) the degree of influence of the selected actor must not decrease. The following heuristic accommodates all three conditions.

Weight Emergence

1. Randomly select a link connecting actor #row_1 to an incoming actor, and a second link to an outbound actor:

$$\text{Outbound link: } row_1 \rightarrow col_1$$
$$\text{Inbound link: } row_2 \rightarrow col_2$$

2. Calculate inbound and outbound totals from summing rows and columns of influence matrix ϕ:

$$\text{Inbound total} = \sum_r \phi(r, \ col_2)$$
$$\text{Outbound total} = \sum_c \phi(row_1, \ c)$$

3. Save copies of inbound and outbound link weights in case conditions are not right to change them.
4. If outbound total $\leq 99\%$ and outbound link weight $\leq 99\%$, increase outbound link weight by 1%.

5. If inbound-total $\geq 1\%$ and inbound link weight $\geq 1\%$, decrease inbound link weight by 1%.
6. Recalculate influences, $Q = [I + L]^{t^*}$, and check for conflicts.
7. If influence of actor #row_1 decreases or a conflict is found, revert to saved weights.

Weights on outbound links can only increase, and weights on in-bound links can only decrease. Therefore, outbound links gain more and more influence, and inbound links lose influence. But an inbound link of one actor is an outbound link of another. Raising and lowering inbound and outbound links appears to create a paradox. This paradox raises a question, "Does this emergence process lead to a stable pattern, or does it lead to uncontrolled oscillations?" If actors had exactly the same in-bound and out-bound link degrees, we would expect uncontrolled oscillations, but in general, I-nets are asymmetric; that is, the degree sequence is not uniform. This suggests that actors with more outbound links than inbound links are inherently stronger than actors with fewer outbound links than inbound links. If conditions are right, the stronger actor should gain in power, because its outbound links gain more influence than its inbound links lose. This is exactly what emerges from the weight emergence process. However, the underlying assumption is that the degree sequence of a convergent I-network is asymmetric—or at least nonuniform.

10.5.2 Java Method for Weight Emergence

Link weights are changed by method `Diagram_doWeightEmergence()`, which is repeated over hundreds of timesteps, by program *Influence.jar*. The algorithm is simple in concept, but messy in implementation, because it must manipulate the influence matrix, check three conditions necessary to keep the network stable, and map row–column coordinates into link indices.

Influence matrix ϕ is central to the operation of emergence. It is stored in matrix W of the method. Most microrules are performed by manipulation of W, which makes it necessary to convert [row, column (r,c)] coordinates of W into the link index of the Influence array. Conversion is performed by method `connection(r, c)`, which translates matrix coordinates (r, c) into link index:

```
private int connection(int from, int to){      //Map (from, to) -> link#
    int reply = -1;                             //Return link index or (-1)
    for(int i = 0; i < nInfluences; i++){
        if(Influences[ i] .from == from && Influences[ i] .to == to) {
           reply = i;
           break;                               //Found
           }
        }
       return reply;
    }//connection
```

Method `Diagram_doWeightEmergence()` must also guarantee that the randomly selected inbound and outbound links are unique, and do not correspond to the same element in matrix *W*. If by serendipity the two randomly selected links are the same, another random link is selected. A `count` variable is used to guarantee that the **while** loops used to find unique links terminates. Failure to meet this condition leads to immediate exit from the method.

The next major step is to guarantee that the first of the three conditions necessary for convergence—if possible—of the emergent process: column and row totals do not exceed 100%. The inbound and outbound influences are totaled by summing the appropriate rows and columns of *W*. These sums are checked against bounds of 1% and 99%. Note the use of *W*.get and *W*.put to manipulate the elements of *W*. These access methods are defined by the JAMA package used to perform matrix class operations.

The second condition—that there be no conflicted node—is satisfied by calling `Boolean` method `Diagram_doConflict()` to evaluate the I-net for conflicts. If there is a conflict, the altered influences are changed back to their previous weights. Recall that it takes only one conflicted actor to render the I-network unstable.

The third condition is satisfied by calling method `Diagram_doInfluences(false)` to calculate the change in actor degree of influence as a result of changing inbound and outbound links. If influence of the randomly selected actor has declined, the changed influences are reset to their previous weights. This method is repeated for as long as the user allows. Typically, the process is halted when the emergence process begins to encounter conflicts. But this is not always the case, as experimentation will show.

```
public void Diagram_doWeightEmergence(){
    Matrix W = ConnectionMatrix();
    int row1 = (int)(nActors*Math.random());   //Random actor #row1
    int col1 = (int)(nActors*Math.random());
    int out_link = connection(row1, col1);
    int count = 100;
    while(count > 0 && (row1 == col1              //Distinct, actual out-link
         ||
      out_link < 0)){
      row1 = (int)(nActors*Math.random());
      out_link = connection(row1, col1);         //Map to link #
      count--;                                    //Avoid infinite loop
    }
    if(count == 0) return;                        //Out-link doesn't exist
    int col2 = (int)(nActors*Math.random());
    int in_link = connection(col2, row1);
    count = 100;
    while(count > 0 && (row1 == col2              //Distinct, actual in_link
       ||
      in_link < 0)){
```

```
    col2 = (int)(nActors*Math.random());
    in_link = connection(col2, row1);                //Map to link #
    count--;
}
if(count == 0) return;                               //In-link doesn't exist

//Sum in-link, out-link influences
double in_sum = 0.0;
for(int row = 0; row < nActors; row++)
    in_sum += W.get(row, col2);

double out_sum = 0.0;
for(int col = 0; col < nActors; col++)
    out_sum += W.get(row1, col);

//Save for reverting, if necessary
double save_out_link_weight = Influences[ out_link] .weight;
double save_in_link_weight = Influences[ in_link] .weight;

if(out_sum <= 0.99 && Influences[ out_link] .weight < 99)
    Influences[out_link].weight += 1;
if(in_sum >= 0.01 && Influences[ in_link] .weight > 1)
    Influences[in_link].weight -= 1;

//Revert if conflicted or decrease in influence
global.Message = "Weight Emergence: ";
boolean conflicted = Diagram_doConflict();
if(conflicted)
    global.Message += "Conflicted at Actor #"+Long.toString(row1);

double before = Actors[ row1] .Actor_influence;    //Save current influence
Diagram_doInfluences(false);                        //Has influence improved?

if(before < Actors[ row1] .Actor_influence || conflicted){
    Influences[out_link].weight = save_out_link_weight;
    Influences[in_link].weight = save_in_link_weight;
    global.Message += " Reverting.";
}
else
    global.Message += " Increasing Actor #"+Long.toString(row1)+
    ",Influence = "+s0.toString(100*Actors[row1].Actor_influence)+"%";
}//Diagram_doWeightEmergence
```

Note how this algorithm permits a change in the weight of one or both randomly selected links. Specifically, an inbound influence can be decreased by 1% regardless of whether the outbound influence is increased by 1%. Therefore, the emergent process is a series not really of small exchanges, but of small *decreases* in inbound influences and small *increases* in outbound influences. Intuitively, it seems that this process would always lead to inbound influences with zero weight and outbound influences with 100% weight, but the story is more complicated.

10.5.3 Stability of Weight Emergence

We use program *Influence.jar* to study the stability of weight emergence, and answer a number of questions raised in the previous sections. The following experiments test the hypothesis that convergence is (partially) guaranteed, and the most powerful actors end up with the greatest degree of influence. We claim that power is directly related to the number and amount of influence assigned to outbound links. Inbound links diminish an actor's power, and hence they should be minimized. Actors with more outbound than inbound links are the "most powerful," and actors with more inbound inks are the "weakest." We test this hypothesis by simulation.

During simulation of weight emergence actors are painted red if they are conflicted and blue if they have more outbound links than inbound links. We expect the process to converge when actors reach a conflicted state as indicated by their red color, and we expect blue actors to end up with the highest degree of influence. If they do, then we have empirical evidence that the hypothesis is correct. However, we caution the reader that such empiricism is no match for a mathematical proof! We leave the formal proof as an exercise for the reader.

The "spoke and hub" network of Fig. 10.6 is used to perform the experiment and collect results. Initially all links are assigned a small weight, say, 10%. Then method

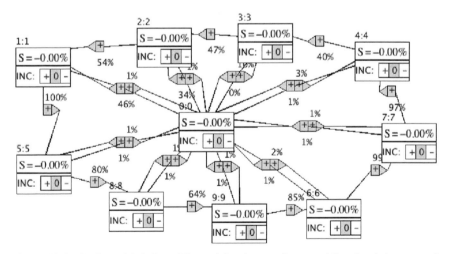

Figure 10.6 Spoke-and-hub I-net. The peripheral actors form a unidirectional ring network around node 0, and node 0 is linked to each actor through bidirectional links.

`Diagram_doWeightEmergence()` is repeatedly called until the level of conflict reaches a point where few, if any, increases in individual actor influences are allowed by the method. This signals the approximation of convergence to some steady state. However, the observant reader will notice that the influence network never reaches a strange attractor and therefore never completely syncs. The emergence alters weights in an erratic pattern. Typically, a pattern emerges in the form of one or more dominant actors that gain most, if not all, of the influence.[6]

Weight emergence exhibits *partial stability most of the time*—nodes with fewer inbound links dominate nodes with greater inbound links.[7] We call actors with more outbound than inbound links *dominant actors*, and hypothesize that they eventually gain the most power over the entire network. Program *Influence.jar* paints these nodes blue to indicate that they are likely to be among the dominant actors in the network. In practice, which actor eventually achieves the most influence is partially the result of chance—the random selection process arbitrarily favors actors that were chosen early in the emergence process.

Figure 10.7 illustrates the effect of number of inbound and outbound links on the degree of influence, and therefore, power of an actor to dominate an I-net consisting of 10 actors. Two topologies were used to obtain the data for Fig. 10.7: (1) the pure "spoke and hub" topology shown in Fig. 10.6 and (2) a pure ring topology similar to that in Fig. 10.6, but with one of the peripheral nodes serving as hub. The ring

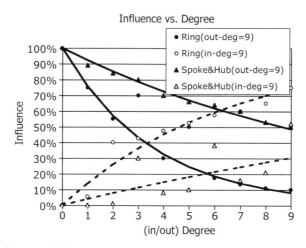

Figure 10.7 Exponential increase in degree of influence of the most dominant actor of Fig. 10.6 as a function of increasing its number of outbound "spokes" and exponential decrease in degree of influence as a function of increasing its number of inbound "spokes."

---

[6]Dominance is defined as "high degree of influence" and is most often associated with nodes that have more outbound links than inbound links.

[7]The phrase "most likely" has to be taken seriously here because weight emergence does not guarantee convergence to a dominant actor.

topology is obtained by removing the link between nodes 1 and 5 of Fig. 10.6. This has the effect of creating an additional dominant actor for the hub to compete with. As expected, this competitor will take some influence away from the hub.

Two experiments were performed—one with the number of outbound links fixed at 9 while the number of inbound links varied from 0 to 9, and the other with the number of inbound links fixed at 9 while the number of outbound links varied from 0 to 9. The two experiments produced two sets of data corresponding with two pairs of curves in Fig. 10.7.

The pure ring topology results (corresponding to the "ring" designation or solid line) show an exponential decline in degree of influence as the number of inbound links increases from 0 to 9, while holding the number of outbound links constant. The dashed lines in Fig. 10.7 show an asymptotic exponential rise in influence as the number of outbound links increase, while holding the number of inbound links constant. A similar, but less pronounced, exponential relationship was found for the spoke-and-hub topology.

This experiment provides empirical evidence in support of the hypothesis. At least for this pair of I-nets, increasing the number of outbound influence links increases an actor's power, while increasing the number of inbound influence links decreases power. Specifically, the data of Fig. 10.7 fit exponential relationships—the solid lines fitting better than the dashed lines:

Outbound degree $= 9$

    Actor_power(in_degree, 9) $= \exp(-0.28(\text{in\_degree}))$, for ring

    Actor_power(in_degree, 9) $= \exp(-0.08(\text{in\_degree}))$, for spoke and hub

Inbound degree $= 9$

    Actor_power(9, out_degree) $= 1 - \exp(-0.15(\text{in\_degree}))$, for ring

    Actor_power(9, out_degree) $= 1 - \exp(-0.04(\text{in\_degree}))$, for spoke and hub

The curve-fits of Fig. 10.7 are much more accurate for variation of the number of outbound links than for that of inbound links, which leads us to conjecture that power in I-nets is strongly related to the number of outbound links and weakly related to the number of inbound links. Addition of outbound links can increase power, while addition of inbound links can inhibit power. In social networks, it is better to persuade others to your way of thinking than to be persuaded by others!

What happens when two or more actors have the same number of outbound links? If the two are connected by a single directed link, then the "to actor" is influenced by the "from actor," but not the reverse. The outbound link prevails, which means that the "from actor" is the more powerful.

If the two are connected by both inbound and outbound influences of equal weight, they nullify each other; that is, the two are tightly coupled as shown in Fig. 10.2. Furthermore, if two dominant actors nullify each other, a third actor may dominate them and the network even if it has more inbound links than outbound links! Mutual blocking of powerful actors leaves a power vacuum that other actors may fill. Why? This problem is left as an exercise for the reader.

10.5.4 Link Emergence

Actors gain power in an I-net by ignoring inbound influences and increasing the weights on outbound influences, but can they gain power by switching links to point to more powerful adjacent actors? The idea of link emergence is simply to randomly rewire links in a process similar to preferential attachment used to create a scale-free network. Instead of preferring nodes with high degree, link emergence prefers nodes with high degree of influence. Intuitively, the influence of an actor should grow as it influences more powerful neighbors. But we discover that this is not the case!

Program *Influence.jar* implements link influence emergence as follows. Randomly select an actor and one of its outbound links. If rewiring the outbound link so that it points to a neighboring actor with greater degree of influence increases the degree of influence of the actor, keep the new link. Otherwise, revert to the previous connection. The weights on links do not change—only their connections.

We hypothesize that link preference for actors with high degree of influence causes the I-net to evolve into a network with a few highly connected, highly influential actors and a large number of lonely, weak actors. But we know from the previous section that inbound links diminishes influence, rather than enhancing it. In fact, powerful actors are "dragged down" by too many inbound links. Once again, we face a paradox—weaker actors associating with powerful actors decreases the power of the powerful. As their power diminishes, link emergence rewires links away from the weakening actors, leading to subsequent increases in their power! Link emergence leads to chaos!

10.6 EXERCISES

10.1. What are the possible attractor values of a binary tree buzz network?

10.2. Develop a theory and explanation for the behavior of line buzz networks: What are the possible attractor values of a line network?

10.3. What, if any, is the mathematical relationship between the attractor value of a buzz network and the degrees of promoter and contrarian?

10.4. What are the degrees of influence of actors 0, 1, and 2, in Fig. 10.3 if the weights on links are changed from 33% to 20%, from 50% to 40%, and from 75% to 60%? What is the consensus of the I-net if $S(0) = \{+1, 0, -1\}$?

10.5. The I-net of Fig. 10.4 is conflicted. Is it still conflicted if the influence from 1: fox to 0: hound is reduced from 33% to 25%? to 26%?

10.6. Let the forward influence links of Fig. 10.5 be reduced to 50% instead of 75%, as suggested in the text. The feedbackward links remain at 25%, as in the figure. What is the consensus of the binary tree when the CEO and vice president A agree $(+1)$, and vice president B disagrees (-1)? What is the value of the consensus if vice president B is neutral (0)?

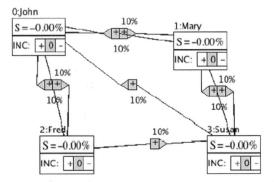

Figure 10.8 Counterexample: an exception to the rule that dominant actors have more outbound links than others.

10.7. The I-net of Fig. 10.8 proves an exception to the rule that actors with more outbound than in-bound links are dominant. Which node is the most powerful actor after weight emergence? Explain why the actor with more outbound than inbound links is *not* the most powerful actor.

10.8. Consider the I-net model of macro-economics shown in Fig. 10.9. Which actor has the highest degree of influence when all influences are 20%? Which actor rises to the position of most powerful after weight emergence?

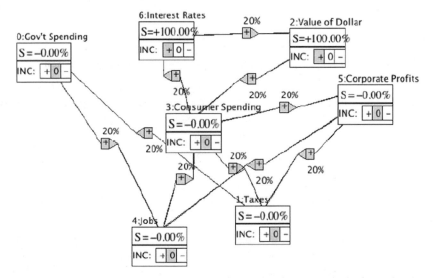

Figure 10.9 A simple macroeconomic model of the national economy in the form of an I-net.

10.9. [Research.] Explain the result of weight emergence when applied to a simple line network. Does your line I-net defy the rule that the most powerful nodes have more outbound links than inbound links? Why?

10.10. [Research.] Develop a complete theory and state the necessary and sufficient conditions for an actor in an I-net to become the most powerful actor, regardless of the number of inbound and outbound links.

11

VULNERABILITY

There are many ways to define vulnerability, risk, and consequence, but few definitions of *network vulnerability*, risk, and failure consequences have been provided in the literature. This is because network science is a new field and it is not clear how networks fail. For example, does a network fail when one link is destroyed? Are nodes more critical than links? We go out on a limb and classify network vulnerability along three dimensions: vulnerability due to (1) failure of one or more nodes, (2) failure of one or more links, and (3) instability of a (Kirchhoff) network due to removal of a stabilizing link. Thus, nodes and links are targets that result in different kinds of failure. First, we study the effects of damage to nodes, then the effects of damage to links.

Furthermore, the consequences of node or link failures in a network are not well understood. Is it necessary for a network to separate into isolated components in order to classify it as failed? Alternatively, in a dynamic network that supports flow, such as in a Kirchhoff network, is failure defined as the cessation of flow? Finally, is failure defined as a synchronized network that is no longer synchronized because of the removal of a link?

The concept of *resilience* adds to the confusion because there is no standard definition of resilience of a network. How do we compare the resilience of one network with the resilience of another? Intuitively, resilience is proportional to the amount of functionality remaining in the network as nodes and links are removed. One concrete idea pursued here is the application of a different resilience metric to node removal and link removal. For example, we explore the tolerance of networks to node and

Network Science: Theory and Practice. By Ted G. Lewis
Copyright © 2009 John Wiley & Sons, Inc.

link removal, and in the case of a Kirchhoff network, the maximization of flow through a directed network. In this restricted case, resilience is simply the fraction of maximum flow of a commodity through the network, as a function of the reliability of its nodes and links.

There is common agreement within the financial and engineering community on what constitutes vulnerability, risk, and consequence in nonnetwork systems. We call these *standard definitions*. *Vulnerability V* is the probability that a component or asset will fail when attacked. *Risk R* is the expected loss due to failure, and *threat T* is the probability that an attack will be attempted. Successful attacks have a *consequence C*, which is the damage caused by an attack. Therefore, standard risk is succinctly defined as the product: $R = TVC$.

Standard Threat, Vulnerability, and Risk

T = probability an attack will be attempted

V = probability an attempted attack will succeed

C = consequence or damage caused by a successful attack

R = standard risk, defined as product TVC

In this chapter we extend these standard definitions to networks containing many components or assets (nodes and links). Network threat, vulnerability, consequence, and risk will be an aggregation of individual component or asset threat, vulnerability, and consequences. Assuming that a component is either a node or a link, we define network risk as the sum over all nodes and links, of individual components.

Network Threat, Vulnerability, and Risk

t_i = probability of an attack on component i—we assume $t_i = 1$ without loss of generality because wherever v_i appears, we can substitute $t_i v_i$, if $t_i \neq 1$

v_i = probability that an attack on component i succeeds

c_i = damage or consequence of a successful attack on node/link i

$r_i = t_i v_i c_i$: individual component risk

$R = \sum_{i=1}^{n+m} r_i = \sum_{i=1}^{n+m} t_i v_i c_i = \sum_{i=1}^{n+m} v_i c_i$ because we assume $t_i = 1$

We will find it convenient to normalize risk by scaling it to the [0, 1] interval. In this case, normalized risk is the ratio of risk to its worst-case scenario ($v_i = 1$):

$$R_{\text{norm}} = \frac{R}{R(1)} = \frac{\sum\limits_{i=1}^{n+m} v_i c_i}{\sum\limits_{i=1}^{n+m} c_i}$$

These are the most basic definitions possible, and they are easy to apply. Collectively, they form the probabilistic risk analysis (PRA) equations for risk in any system where a priori approximations of the probability of failure v_i can be reasonably estimated. However, we extend the PRA definitions to accommodate the topology of networks under attack. In fact, we ask two basic questions, "What is the nature of risk in a network, and how might a defender apply limited resources to reduce network risk?" Specifically, we examine risk in terms of attacks on network nodes and links. We show that there are optimal strategies for protecting networks against attacks on links and attacks on nodes.

In this chapter we learn that

1. Networks are damaged by accidental or natural acts (random node/link removal) or targeted attacks (criminal and terrorist acts) on nodes and links. We show that there are optimal attack strategies that have consequences directly related to the topology of the network. For example, removal of high-degreed hubs has a greater impact on network damage than does removal of low-degreed nodes.

2. Network risk is defined as $R = \sum_{i=1}^{n+m} t_i v_i c_i$, where threat t = probability of an attack, vulnerability v = probability of success if an attack is attempted, and consequence c = consequence or damage if a successful attack occurs. But function $\Phi = \sum_{i=1}^{n+m} g_i v_i c_i$ is found to be more useful as an optimization objective function because it incorporates the degree sequence distribution of the network. This makes it possible to correlate the topology of a network with its risk properties.

3. Network risk strategies are equivalent to resource allocation strategies that "buy down" risk through optimal resource allocation; the risk of nodes/ links is reduced through various protection means that reduce vulnerability. We solve the optimal resource allocation problem for networks for two important cases: linear cost and exponential cost models.

4. Critical nodes/links are assets with the highest value of $gC/\max DA$, where $g = 1$ for links and $g = \text{degree}(v)$ for nodes; C = consequence, and vulnerability reduction cost ($\max DA$) equals the resource needed to remove most or all of a vulnerability. We show that optimal allocation strategies obey the rank-order property established by $gC/\max DA$, regardless of the relationship between vulnerability and resource allocation, DA.

5. *Critical nodes* and links are defined as the nodes/links with highest $gC/\max DA$ value. The best resource allocation strategies allocate more to critical nodes/links than to other nodes and links.

6. We study the attacker–defender model of Al-Mannai and Lewis and show that the best strategy of the attacker is asymmetric—the attacker should allocate its resources diametrically opposed to the defender—allocating more to nodes and links that are less critical than more critical. The defender should allocate most of its resources to the critical nodes/links, rather than the less critical nodes and links. This result assumes that attacker and defender know each other's strategies and allocations.

7. We show that the linear allocation strategy is best for a network defender that has no knowledge of the attacker's allocation strategy, and that the exponential allocation strategy is best for the attacker. The linear strategy minimizes the defender's risk, and the exponential strategy maximizes the attacker's risk.

8. *Link resilience* is defined as the fraction of links that must be removed to separate a network into components. We show that small worlds are the most link-resilient, random networks are next, and scale-free networks are the least resilient. In other words, a scale-free network separates into components when fewer links are removed, while the random or small–world class of networks does not.

9. *Flow resilience* is defined as the fraction of maximum flow that a directed network supports as links are blocked or removed. We study an optimal allocation heuristic that allocates resources to protect a flow network from failure due to link removal along the network's most critical paths, first, in rank order according to the efficiency metric $\min C_i / \max DA_i$.

10. Removing one or more critical links destabilizes a Kirchhoff network. The class of Kirchhoff networks is unable to stabilize unless the lengths of its feedback circuits are relatively prime numbers. *Critical links* are links that lead to instability in a Kirchhoff network if removed. This occurs because removal of a critical link alters the length of feedback circuits—removing a cycle that is relatively prime in length with another cycle. *Stability resilience* is defined as the fraction of links that are *not* critical to stability.

11.1 NETWORK RISK

The concept of attacking a network as opposed to a single asset is nothing new. It is essentially a strategy designed to disrupt or destroy an entire system by removing only one component. For example, during World War II allied bombers destroyed Germany's only factory for manufacturing ball bearings, knowing that the production of numerous war machines such as airplanes, tanks, troop carriers, and ships would come to a halt, because ball bearings were used in nearly every kind of machinery. The allied armies understood systems and their dependence on critical components. In this case, the German ball-bearing factory just happened to be an essential component of a larger system that everything else depended on.

Network science is an excellent vehicle for modeling complex interdependent systems such as critical infrastructure, manufacturing logistics chains, and manufacturing processes. Lewis has analyzed a number of power grids, water systems, telecommunication systems, energy distribution networks, and transportation systems using the techniques described here (Lewis, 2006). He concluded that infrastructure networks are indeed structured and the topological structure of power grids, telecommunication networks, and the Internet can be protected efficiently by protecting only a very small handful of nodes and links—the so-called *critical nodes* and links. A number of other investigators have explored this theme by examining the effects of node and link removal on the survival of the network. However, there is no general agreement on the definition of survivability, vulnerability, reliability, or resilience of a network. We take up this topic in the following exposition.

Because of their abstract nature, networks can model most any system that can be broken down into components—nodes—and their relationships—links. For example, the German war machinery system could have been represented as a system of factories—nodes—and supply routes—links. Obviously, nodes depend on supplies from other nodes, and other nodes depend on additional nodes further upstream, and so on, until the nodes representing the source of raw materials are reached. Supply chain links represent the movement of materials and partially manufactured parts from raw material to finished product. In this sense, a supply chain is a network that models the flow of a commodity or commodities from source to sink nodes.

A network might represent the flow of materials, dependences along a chain of manufacturing steps, or the flow of control (both human and automation) leading to the production of some commodity or decision. The question we ask is, "How might such a system be disrupted or halted?" Furthermore, what measures of disruption should be considered? In general, destroying or disabling one or more of its nodes or links disrupts a network. Conversely, we can protect a network by protecting or *hardening* its nodes or links, or both. Assuming that it is too expensive to protect or harden every node and link, what is the best strategy for minimizing damage under budgetary constraints? This question is answered by formulating and solving a family of resource optimization equations that find the optimal allocation of a fixed budget to harden nodes and links as best we can, under existing budgetary constraints.

First, we explore the problem of protecting a network by protecting its nodes— which leads to *critical node analysis*. Then, we explore the problem of protecting a network by protecting its links—which leads to *critical link analysis*. Finally, we introduce a new concept of network vulnerability—instability caused by link removal in a Kirchhoff network.

Networks are susceptible to threats to nodes and links, but what is a threat, and what does it mean for a network to be vulnerable to a threat? What is the difference between vulnerability of a single asset such as a factory (node) and vulnerability of a system, such as a logistics supply chain (network)? We define a *threat* as a specific form of attack such as a cyber worm used to disable computers on the Internet, or a bomb used to destroy a building. We further define *vulnerability* as a measure of weakness in a system. For example, a computer in a communication network may be vulnerable to an attack by a computer virus or cyber worm because of a weakness in its firewall. Finally, let *consequence* be defined as the loss—in terms of time, money, or lives—that result from a successful attack. *Risk* is the expected loss due to successful attacks on a system.

Let vulnerability and threat be probabilities, and risk be the expected loss due to a threat and vulnerability. The following axiomatic definitions are used throughout this chapter:

T = threat: the probability of an attack, typically via a specific weapon
V = vulnerability: the probability of a successful attack

C = consequence: the loss incurred as a consequence of a successful attack

R = risk: the expected loss, $R = TVC$

These are well-known engineering and financial analysis definitions employed in *probabilistic risk analysis* (PRA). PRA defines risk as an expected value, *TVC*, where T depends on the nature of the attack—bomb, cyber worm, or biological contagion; V is the probability that a component or asset will fail if attacked or stressed—also dependent on the nature of the attack; and C is the (financial or fatality) consequence if a failure occurs. Threat and vulnerability are a priori estimates of the probability of failure. Consequence C is typically measured in dollars or lives.

The simple PRA definitions must be expanded to calculate risk in a system because system failure is also a function of the interdependences of nodes. In other words, network connectivity matters when computing risk. The failure of the only ball-bearing factory in Germany during WWII had great consequences because of its connectivity to many other factories. Accordingly, we need an extended definition that represents risk in a system of components; that is, we need a definition of risk that works for a network. In the following analysis, individual node/link risks are summed over the network to arrive at a total network risk.

11.1.1 Nodes as Targets

First, consider the risk associated with damaging a node. The loss to the system is compounded by the loss of network connectivity as well as the value of the single node, itself. Intuitively, the target value of a node should include its intrinsic value and its value to the overall network. A simple and logical extension of the PRA definition of risk defines the target value of a node as $g_i C_i$, where g_i is the degree of the node and C_i is the consequence associated with the node's intrinsic value. A node is considered twice as valuable if it has twice as many links because its removal causes twice the damage to the network.

Lewis and Al-Mannai used the degree-weighted model of network risk to determine which nodes in a network are most critical to the overall security of the network (Al-Mannai, 2007). Because the node with the highest risk contribution, $r_i = g_i C_i$, is most vital to the security of the entire network, the Al-Mannai–Lewis method is called *critical node analysis*. Lewis applied critical node analysis to a variety of critical infrastructures such as water, power, energy, transportation, and telecommunication systems and showed where to find their most vital points of failure (Lewis, 2006). Critical node analysis is explored in greater detail later in this chapter.

Lai, Motter, and Nishikawa studied the effect of node failure on cascades in networks (Lai, 2004). A *network cascade* is a sequence of failures that start with the failure of a single node/link and propagate, like an epidemic, to connected nodes. Lai et al. modeled the target value of node w_i in terms of its load L_i and tolerance parameter $\alpha \geq 0$. Parameter α may be regarded as a *redundancy* factor, providing redundant capacity if and when the primary node fails. The consequence of a failure in node w_i is related to its load and redundancy parameter as follows:

$$C_i = (1 + \alpha)L_i, \quad i = 1,2,\ldots,n$$

Lai et al. showed that the most critical nodes are the ones with the highest loads, For example, the highest consequence. Also, the network is more vulnerable to failure as the distribution of loads becomes more heterogeneous—greater differences in loads, from node to node. They explain this effect by noting that it is more difficult for a network to spread the increase in load resulting from a high-load node failure to other (adjacent) nodes. The difficulty increases as heterogeneity increases.

The load on a node is increased with an increase in number of links. Therefore, the Lai et al. model becomes more like the Al-Mannai–Lewis model as a network becomes scale-free. In fact, hubs contribute more to the overall network risk because removal of a hub also disables the most links. In fact, Albert and Barabasi called network hubs the *Achilles heels* of networks, because they are the most important nodes in terms of network destruction (Albert, 2000). Lewis showed, by simulation, that the probability of complete failure of an entire network due to cascading significantly increases with an increase in degree of the target node (Lewis, 2006). If the defender has limited resources, the best strategy is to protect the highest-degreed nodes. This conclusion assumes that all nodes and links are of equal value—the network is homogeneous. When consequences vary among nodes and links, this result does not hold—defense of heterogeneous networks depends on the consequence and cost of hardening nodes, as well as degree sequence.

We conclude that homogeneous scale-free networks are more tolerant than are random networks if nodes are randomly targeted, but the opposite is true if hubs are targeted. Because of their high connectivity, hubs are the most critical of all nodes, while low-degreed nodes are less critical. But this conclusion assumes that all nodes are of equal value. When the target value of any node is high, we must consider both connectivity and consequence value of the node. This will lead to a more formal analysis—critical node analysis—to follow.

11.1.2 Links as Targets

Links are also important to the operation of networks, especially if the network represents a system containing flows of some commodity. Albert and Barabasi studied the effects of randomly deleting links from networks until the giant connected component split into two. But random removal of links with equal target value is meaningless in the real world. Accordingly, Lai et al. have studied the effects of removal of links on the integrity of small-world and scale-free networks containing links with heterogeneous loads. Once again, the most heavily loaded links are more critical than lightly loaded links. Lai et al. also discovered a counterintuitive result in networks with the small-world effect—scale-free networks are more vulnerable to attacks on short-range links than attacks on long-range links. Recall that long-range links are the network bisecting shortcuts that contribute to the small-world effect. Why are local links more critical than shortcut links?

Lai's counterintuitive result is not general, however, because it is a consequence of the fact that short-range (local) links carried the greatest loads, in the simulations performed by Lai et al. This result simply confirms the correct intuition suggesting that links with higher target value are more critical than links of lower value. Therefore, it is important to consider the consequence of both nodes and links when calculating network risk.

In Chapter 9 we showed that network topology is vital to the stability of a network. Topology is determined by the pattern of connections between nodes, which is a property of mapping function f. A stable network may be rendered unstable by removal of a link, because link deletion changes the network's topology. This raises a research question, "Is it possible to attack a single link and render a stable network unstable as a consequence?" We will explore this question in detail for flow networks.

11.2 CRITICAL NODE ANALYSIS

Critical node analysis identifies which nodes of a network are the most critical to the overall operation of the network. We know that the most vital nodes are those that have either many connections or have large target values—leading to major consequences. We also know that removal of nodes with many connections contributes to more damage than removing nodes with few connections, unless the values of the nodes are vastly different as in a heterogeneous network. What we don't know is how best to manage the protection of nodes given a limited budget (resources) and a heterogeneous network with varying target values and costs for protecting each node and link.

Critical node analysis is a static technique that considers both node/link target values and network topology. The idea of hardening the most critical nodes is simple and straightforward, and hence a compelling place to start. Let network risk be defined in terms of topology, node/link consequence, and cost to harden each node/link. Given limited resources in the form of a budget, what is the best allocation of resources to each individual node/link such that network risk is minimized? This is the *critical node resource allocation problem*:

B: fixed budget

DA_i: amount of investment in node/link $i = 1, 2, \ldots, (n + m)$

$v_i(DA)$: vulnerability of component i as a function of investment

max DA_i: amount of investment to reduce $v_i(DA)$ to its minimum

c_i: damage or consequence of a successful attack on node/link i

$R = \sum_{i=1}^{n+m} r_i = \sum_{i=1}^{n+m} v_i(DA)c_i$

Constraint: $\sum_{i=1}^{n+m} DA_i \leq B$

The following strategy for deriving optimal resource allocation for a network defender focuses on identifying the most critical nodes and allocating the greatest portion of the budget to the critical nodes in rank order, until the budget is depleted:

1. Define an objective function Φ that accounts for heterogeneous nodes and links (as they have different target values and different costs associated with hardening), and network connectivity in the form of the network's degree sequence distribution. Minimization of this objective function also minimizes network risk.

2. Define a reasonable relationship between vulnerability and cost; the more resources we allocate to an asset (node or link), the lower its vulnerability. Therefore, risk is reduced by "buying down" vulnerability. Recall that vulnerability is equal to the probability of a successful attack, and risk is the product TVC. Buying down V also reduces risk.

3. Solve for node/link allocations DA_i within the constraints, by minimizing the objective function. Thus, the allocation we seek is a byproduct of optimization.

As it turns out, the objective function may be defined in a number of ways. Perhaps the simplest objective function that is also related to network risk defines objective function Φ as the sum of risks contributed by each node–link–node subgraph in the network, as shown in Fig. 11.1. Thus, every network can be regarded as a system of *barbell* subgraphs, with each barbell contributing a portion of risk to the overall network. This definition has an easily understood meaning, and the barbell model preserves the degree sequence property that we seek.

The simple barbell model also makes it easy to incorporate heterogeneous target values for both links and nodes. Each barbell contains two nodes and one link. Each of the two nodes and connecting link has an associated consequence c_i, vulnerability elimination or reduction cost max DA_i, and probability of failure $v_i(DA_i)$. Given an equation $v_i(DA_i)$ that relates investment DA_i to vulnerability, and an objective function Φ, the optimal allocation vector DA can be found.

11.2.1 The Barbell Model

Figure 11.1a shows how an arbitrary network is decomposed into node–link–node barbells. There are m barbells in a network with m links, with each barbell corresponding to a link. The overlap in barbells is purposeful—we want to define objective function Φ in terms of the individual risks of nodes and links, and in terms of the connectivity of the network. Overlapping barbells does this because a node of degree g is counted g times—once for each overlapping barbell.

Objective function Φ is defined in terms of the sum of all barbell risks, and budgetary constraint $\sum_{i=1}^{n+m} DA_i \leq B$. Letting r_j be the risk associated with barbell j, the unconstrained objective function is $\Phi = \sum_{j=1}^{m} r_j$, where $m =$ number of links.

Barbell risks r_i are obtained from the fault tree of Fig. 11.1b. A barbell is vulnerable to attack by removal of a node, link, or combination of nodes and link. All

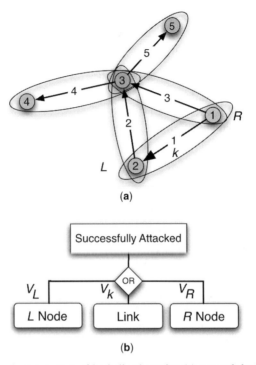

Figure 11.1 Network as a system of barbell subgraphs: (a) network barbells—each node–link–node barbell overlaps other barbells according to the connectivity of the network; (b) fault tree model of barbell failure modes.

possible combinations are found in a fault tree that uses OR logic to model the probability that one, two, or all three components may fail with associated probabilities, V_L, V_k, and V_R. Expanding the fault tree into an event tree shows all possible combinations of failures and the risks associated with each combination (see Fig. 11.2). The unconstrained objective function is simply the sum of the individual event risks to obtain the barbell risk r_j.

Fault trees represent all possible ways in which a system can fail. They can be many levels deep and contain logic gates such as AND, OR, and NOT. An OR logic gate means that a fault propagates up the tree if component A or B or both fail. An AND logic gate means that the fault propagates only if A and B fail. Components— shown as leaves in the fault tree—either fail or not, depending on their vulnerability. We label the potential faults with the probability of failure V, and use Boolean logic and probability theory to calculate the likelihood that one or more component failures will propagate to the top of the tree, thus causing the system to fail.

Consider the fault tree of the kth barbell of Fig. 11.1a as shown in Fig. 11.1b. At the top of the tree is the attacker's goal—to cause the system to fail. The OR logic diamond below the goal box says to consider all possible combinations of failures. The barbell is successfully attacked if the L node is successfully attacked with

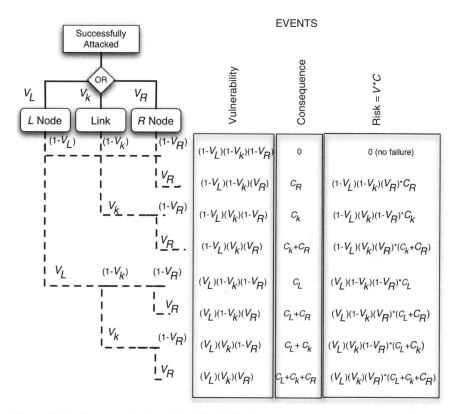

Figure 11.2 Event tree for barbell k of Fig. 11.1. For a fault tree with p components, 2^p events and combinations of events must be considered. In this case, $p = 3$, so eight events must be considered.

probability V_L, link k is successfully attacked with probability V_k, node R is successfully attacked with probability V_R, or any combination of nodes and link are successfully attacked. In this case there are three components that might fail, and so there are $2^3 = 8$ possible events to consider.

Furthermore, let C_L, C_k, and C_R be the consequences of a successful attack on node L, link k, and node R, respectively. We apply the fundamental PRA risk equation to the fault tree by expanding it into its corresponding event tree (see Fig. 11.2). An *event tree* simply enumerates all possible events produced by the OR logic of the fault tree. There are eight possible events because the fault tree has three components that can fail. Each combination may occur with a probability calculated by multiplying probabilities along a path from the fault tree to the combination event, as shown by the dashed lines in Fig. 11.2. For example, consider the combination

L node: fails with probability V_L

Link k: does not fail with probability $(1 - V_k)$

R node: fails with probability V_R

The probability of this combination of events is simply the product of probabilities along the dashed line leading to the corresponding event:

$$\text{Prob}(L \text{ fails}, k \text{ succeeds}, R \text{ fails}) = V_L(1 - V_k)V_R$$

This probability corresponds to the vulnerability of the fault tree to this combination event, as shown in the vulnerability column in Fig. 11.2.

Similarly, the consequence of two node failures, L node and R node, is the sum of the consequences: $C_L + C_R$. This is shown in the column labeled "Consequence" in Fig. 11.2. Finally, we can apply the fundamental PRA risk equation to this combination event to obtain the risk contribution:

$$\text{Risk}(L \text{ fails}, k \text{ succeeds}, R \text{ fails}) = V_L(1 - V_k)V_R(C_L + C_R)$$

The total of all risk contributions due to all possible combinations of failures equals the risk contribution r_k of this barbell to the overall network risk:

$$\begin{aligned}
r_k = {} & (1 - V_L)(1 - V_k)(V_R)C_R + (1 - V_L)(V_k)(1 - V_R)C_k + (1 - V_L)(V_k) \\
& \times (V_R)(C_k + C_R) + (V_L)(1 - V_k)(1 - V_R)C_L + (V_L)(1 - V_k)(V_R) \\
& \times (C_L + C_R) + (V_L)(V_k)(1 - V_R)(C_L + C_k) + (V_L)(V_k)(V_R)(C_L + C_k + C_R)
\end{aligned}$$

Factoring around consequences and grouping terms, we obtain

$$r_k = V_R C_R + V_k C_k + V_L C_L$$

More generally, $r_k = \sum_{j \in k} V_j C_j$, where j ranges over the two nodes and one link of barbell k.

Now, for the second step in the derivation of extended risk, let objective function Φ be defined as the sum of all barbell risks, which means that we count each node g_i times, because each node is a member of g_i barbells: $\Phi = \sum_{k=1}^{m} r_k = \sum_{k=1}^{m} \sum_{j \in k} V_j C_j = \sum_{k=1}^{n+m} g_k V_k C_k$, where $g_i = 1$ for $k > n$. In other words $g = 1$ for links; $g =$ degree, for nodes. The meaning of this equation is quite obvious—Φ is the sum of *weighted risks* of its nodes plus the risks of its links. Nodes contribute more to Φ than do links because the removal of a node affects not only the node but also all links connected to it. Thus, we have preserved the meaning of PRA risk for networks while incorporated arbitrary network topology as well. This objective function relates risk to network topology.

For example, consider the network in Fig. 11.1a with properties given in Table 11.1. Assuming that nothing is protected, each node and link is 100% vulnerable to removal. Therefore, $V_k = 1$. Node 1 has two links, so $g_1 = 2$, and the consequence of its removal is 10 units. Therefore, its contribution is the product $2(1)(10) = 20$. There are five links, all with the same risk, so links contribute

TABLE 11.1 Properties of the Network of Fig. 11.1a

Node/Link	g	C	max DA	$r: gC$
Node 1	2	10	15	20
Node 2	2	20	5	40
Node 3	4	10	10	40
Node 4	1	5	5	5
Node 5	1	15	1	15
Link 1	1	10	1	10
Link 2	1	10	1	10
Link 3	1	10	1	10
Link 4	1	10	1	10
Link 5	1	10	1	10
Totals	—	110	41	170

$5(1)(1)(10) = 50$ units of risk. Summing all contributions yields an objective function value of 170 units. PRA risk for the same network is 110 units—smaller because PRA risk ignores node degree.

11.2.2 Minimizing Network Risk

From Table 11.1 we can determine where the greatest contribution to objective function Φ lies in the example network of Fig. 11.1a by looking under the column labeled r. Nodes 2 and 3 each contribute $40/170 = 23.5\%$ of the total, by far the largest portion. The contribution of node 2 is due to its high consequence, 20, and the contribution of node 3 is due mainly to its high connectivity. Intuitively, these high-valued nodes should receive the most investment because they contribute the most to Φ. However, a third factor must be considered: the cost of vulnerability reduction, max DA. The most critical nodes may be high-valued targets, but the cost of hardening them may also be high. Therefore, resource utilization is low for these high-valued nodes—perhaps too low. The key to optimal allocation of defenses is to balance resource utilization against consequences.

Risk reduction is the process of reducing consequence, vulnerability, or both, to lower risk. *Resource optimization* is the process of getting the most from limited resources. In this case it is better to apply more of the limited budget to node 2 than node 3 because it is less expensive (max $DA_2 = 5$) to reduce node 2 vulnerability than node 3 vulnerability (max $DA_3 = 10$). This is the concept underlying critical node analysis—an approach that attempts to minimize risk as well as maximize resource utilization.

11.2.2.1 The Linear Cost Model Obviously, the simplest strategy for risk reduction is to allocate resources randomly or uniformly across all nodes and links;

that is, given a budget B, evenly divide B across $(n + m)$ assets. Therefore, $DA_i = B/(n + m)$, and risk is reduced accordingly:

$$R = \sum_{k=1}^{n+m} V_k C_k = \sum_{k=1}^{n+m} \left(1 - \frac{B}{(n+m)}\right) C_k$$

$$R_{\text{norm}} = \frac{\sum_{k=1}^{n+m} \left(1 - \frac{B}{(n+m)}\right) C_k}{\sum_{k=1}^{n+m} C_k}$$

It does not make sense to allocate more than max DA_i to an asset, so vulnerability cannot be reduced below zero. For example, random/uniform allocation of $B = 20$ to the network of Fig. 11.1, with the properties given in Table 11.1, reduces PRA risk from 110 units to 31.67 units as follows:

$$DA_i = \frac{B}{(n + m)} = \frac{20}{10} = 2$$

$$v_i = \max\left\{\left(1 - \frac{2}{\max DA_i}\right), 0\right\}$$

$$R_{\text{norm}} = \frac{\sum_{i=1}^{n+m} v_i c_i}{\sum_{i=1}^{n+m} c_i} = \frac{\sum_{i=1}^{n+m} \max\left\{\left(1 - \frac{2}{\max DA_i}\right), 0\right\} c_i}{110} = \frac{31.67}{110} = 28.8\%$$

In this case we assumed a linear decline in vulnerability with increase in allocation. We also assumed that uniform allocation across all nodes and links yields the best return on investment, B—and a significant reduction in risk was the result. But can the defender do better? Assuming a linear relationship between node/link security and size of investment in node/link protection, is it possible to allocate more resources to *critical nodes/links* and less resources to less critical nodes/links and reduce risk even further?

Suppose that the following linear relationship between vulnerability and resource allocation is assumed. Let vulnerability decline in proportion to investment in protecting each node and link. Furthermore, allocate a disproportionate amount of budget B to critical nodes/links and a smaller amount to less critical nodes/links. In fact, we may allocate zero resources to some nodes/links and significant amounts to other nodes/links. We call this the *linear cost model* of risk reduction.

The more funds allocated DA_k to protect asset k, the less vulnerable is the asset—up to a maximum investment, max DA_k, as follows:

$$V_k(DA_k) = 1 - \alpha_k DA_k; \quad 0 \leq DA_k \leq \max DA_k$$

where DA_k = allocation of resource to harden node/link k
  max DA_k = amount of resource allocation to entirely eliminate vulnerability
  α_k = slope of straight line such that $0 = 1 - \alpha_k \max DA_k$

The slope is determined by the cost of 100% hardening, which is $\max DA_k$. Vulnerability is driven to zero when $DA_k = \max DA_k$, so $\alpha_k = 1/\max DA_k$. This leads to the simple linear cost model of risk reduction:

$$\Phi = \sum_{k=1}^{n+m} g_k V_k C_k = \sum_{k=1}^{n+m} g_k C_k \max\left\{\left(1 - \frac{DA_k}{\max DA_k}\right), 0\right\}$$

Resources are limited by the defender's budget, B_D: $\sum_{k=1}^{n+m} DA_k \leq B_\mathrm{D}$; $DA_k \geq 0$.

What pattern of resource allocation to nodes and links minimizes risk, under the linear model assumption? Specifically, find DA_k, $k = 1, 2, \ldots, n, (n+1), \ldots, (n+m)$ such that Φ is minimized, subject to the budget constraint:

$$\min\{\Phi(DA)\} = \min \sum_{k=1}^{n+m} g_k C_k \max\left\{\left(1 - \frac{DA_k}{\max DA_k}\right), 0\right\}$$

$$\text{subject to} \quad \sum_{k=1}^{n+m} DA_k \leq B_\mathrm{D}; DA_k \geq 0$$

where DA = vector of allocations—the result we seek

g = degree sequence of nodes; 1 for links

C = vector of consequences

$\max DA$ = vector of elimination costs to reduce vulnerability to zero

B_D = defender's budget

Lewis and Al-Mannai showed that the best pattern of allocation of resources to nodes and links uses simple ranking. Allocation is performed by ranking nodes and links, from highest to lowest values according to the product $g_k C_k/\max DA_k$, and then eliminating vulnerability entirely by assigning $\max DA_k$ units to the highest-ranking assets, until budget B_D is depleted. All remaining assets receive zero allocation.

Intuitively, this allocation maximizes the cost–benefit ratio by allocating more to the most efficient asset, in terms of resource utilization, and allocating less to less efficient assets. Specifically, high-consequence, low-cost assets get the most protection, while high-cost and low-consequence assets receive the least.

To calculate the actual allocation to each node and link, sort the list of nodes and links according to their weighted consequence values, where j enumerates assets in ascending order by the product, $g_k C_k/\max DA_k$:

$$g_{j_1} C_{j_1} \max DA_{j_1} \geq g_{j_2} C_{j_2} \max DA_{j_2} \geq \cdots \geq g_{j_{n+m}} C_{j_{n+m}} \max DA_{j_{n+m}}$$

Next, allocate $\max DA_{j_1}$ to the highest, $\max DA_{j_2}$ to the next highest, and so on, until the remaining budget is less than $\max DA_k$. The remaining budget, $\sigma < \max DA_k$, is allocated to the kth ranked asset, and zero is allocated to all remaining assets. In this way, the links/nodes that use resources in the most efficient manner are given highest priority and the highest amount possible.

The ranked-order allocation strategy is optimal because it efficiently reduces the risk contribution of the highest-risk/reward nodes/links, first, until the budget is depleted. Thus, the ranked-order allocation maintains the rank-order property established by weighted consequences:

$$g_{j_1} C_{j_1} \frac{\text{max}DA_{j_1}}{\text{max}DA_{j_1}} \geq g_{j_2} C_{j_2} \frac{\text{max}DA_{j_2}}{\text{max}DA_{j_2}} \geq \cdots \geq g_k C_k \frac{\sigma}{\text{max}DA_k} \geq 0 \geq 0 \geq \cdots \geq 0$$

$$g_{j_1} C_{j_1} \geq g_{j_2} C_{j_2} \geq \cdots \geq g_k C_k \frac{\sigma}{\text{max}DA_k} \geq 0 \geq 0 \geq \cdots \geq 0; \quad \frac{\sigma}{\text{max}DA_k} < 1$$

Therefore, the *optimal linear defender allocation* is

$$DA_{j_1} = \text{max}DA_{j_1}$$
$$DA_{j_2} = \text{max}DA_{j_2}$$

$$\vdots$$

$$DA_k = \sigma = \frac{\text{remaining } B}{\text{max}DA_k}$$

$$DA_i = 0; k < i \leq n + m$$

This allocation reduces vulnerability according to the linear relationship between allocation and vulnerability elimination cost, $\text{max}DA_k$:

$$V_k(DA_k) = 1 - \alpha_k DA_k = \left(1 - \frac{DA_k}{\text{max}DA_k}\right)$$

For example, given a budget of 20 units and the simple network shown in Fig. 11.1a and Table 11.1, PRA risk is reduced from 110 to 16.0 units (14.5%), and network risk Φ is reduced from 170 to 29 (17.1%) by linear allocation—a 50% better result than random/uniform allocation. The spreadsheet shown in Table 11.2 summarizes this calculation. More importantly, linear allocation obeys the rank-order property established by the product of $g_i C_i / \text{max}DA_i$—see the column labeled gC/maxDA and Fig. 11.3. This property determines allocation priority—from highest to lowest: node 5, links 1 through 5, node 2, node 3, node 1, and node 4. In fact, this property is observed in allocation strategies regardless of whether the relationship between allocation and vulnerability reduction is linear, exponential, or a power law! This establishes a hierarchy among nodes and links; the most critical nodes/links of a network are those with the highest gC/maxDA value.

TABLE 11.2   Linear Cost Model Results for $B_D = 20$

Node/Link	g	C	gC	maxDA	$gC/$ maxDA	DA	V (%)	Φ
Node 1	2	10	20	15	1.33	0.0	100	20.0
Node 2	2	20	40	5	8.00	5.0	0	0.0
Node 3	4	10	40	10	4.00	9.0	10	4.0
Node 4	1	5	5	5	1.00	0.0	100	5.0
Node 5	1	15	15	1	15.00	1.0	0	0.0
Link 1	1	10	10	1	10.00	1.0	0	0.0
Link 2	1	10	10	1	10.00	1.0	0	0.0
Link 3	1	10	10	1	10.00	1.0	0	0.0
Link 4	1	10	10	1	10.00	1.0	0	0.0
Link 5	1	10	10	1	10.00	1.0	0	0.0
Budget = 20	—	110	170	41	—	20	Total $R =$	29.0

Note that optimal pattern of allocation may not be unique. When there is a tie in rank order among nodes and links, arbitrary assignment among peers can produce the same minimum risk. This is especially true when there is insufficient budget to allocate maxDA to all assets of equal rank. In this case, the optimal solution may produce multiple answers.

Further, optimal allocations are indeed the best possible allocations given the assumption that protection increases linearly with investment. Any other allocation that does not violate the linear assumption and its constraints results in an equal or higher network risk—but not necessarily PRA risk, because Φ is the objective function. For example, exchanging the allocation of one unit of resource between nodes 4 and 5 increases network risk from 29 to 48 units! Proof of this is left as an exercise for the reader.

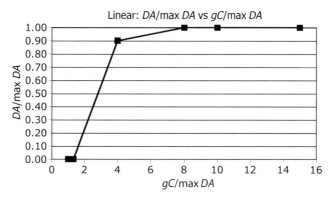

Figure 11.3 Linear allocation strategy is equivalent to rank-ordering nodes and links according to $gC/$maxDA. The most critical asset in this example is node 5 because $gC/$max$DA = 15$, which is the largest value for all nodes and links.

11.2.3 The Exponential Cost Model

It can be convincingly argued that the linear cost model is unrealistic. In practice, a node's security may be increased by 50% for 10% of the budget, but only another 20% by allocating twice as much. For example, a building's security might be increased by 50% by adding more lighting at a cost of $10,000, but constructing a fence for another $20,000 may improve the building's security by only an additional 10%. In other words, vulnerability reduction may suffer from *diminishing returns*. For this reason, the *exponential cost model* may be preferred.

The exponential model is exactly the same as the linear model except for the relationship between allocation and vulnerability reduction. Furthermore, the allocation strategy is the same; the nodes/links with the highest rank, according to the rank-order property, $gC/maxDA$, receive more resources than do lower-ranked assets. Indeed, allocation follows the familiar S-shaped curve we have seen before, whenever a dwindling resource suffers from diminishing returns.

The exponential cost model differs from the linear model in two important ways: (1) the actual allocations DA are different, and (2) network risk is typically higher because an infinite investment is required to eliminate vulnerability entirely. A simple exponential function for vulnerability reduction is

$$v_i(DA_i) = e^{-\alpha_i DA_i}; \quad 0 \le v_i(DA_i) \le 1$$

Clearly, this function asymptotically declines to zero, but reaches zero only when an infinite allocation is assigned to this asset. Unlike the linear strategy that entirely eliminates vulnerability from the most critical nodes and links, the exponential cost allocation never completely removes vulnerability.

Allocation of budget B to nodes and links is optimal when objective function Φ is minimized, with the following budgetary constraint:

$$\Phi = \sum_{i=1}^{n+m} g_i v_i c_i = \sum_{i=1}^{n+m} g_i e^{-\alpha_i DA_i} c_i - \lambda_1 \left[\sum_{i=1}^{n+m} DA_i - B \right]$$

The reader can show that optimal allocation vector DA is obtained by the following formula:

$$DA_i = \frac{\log(\alpha_i g_i C_i) - \log(\lambda_i)}{\alpha_i}$$

$$\log(\lambda_i) = \frac{\sum_{i=1}^{n+m} \dfrac{\log(\alpha_i g_i C_i)}{\alpha_i} - B}{\sum_{i=1}^{n+m} \dfrac{1}{\alpha_i}}$$

Applying this model to the simple network of Fig. 11.1 and Table 11.1 with budget of 20 units yields a reduced network risk of $\Phi = 37.9$ units ($37.9/170 = 22.3\%$), which is higher than the linear allocation, because the exponential model never reduces vulnerability to zero. However, the allocation yields lower risk than the random/uniform allocation does because exponential allocation follows the $gC/\text{max}DA$ rank order. The elements of solution vector DA are found by plugging into the equations above, but this is left as an exercise for the reader.

11.2.4 The Attacker–Defender Model

Al-Mannai and Lewis extended the linear cost model in two directions (Al-Mannai, 2007): (1) an exponential cost model replaced the linear cost model, and (2) Al-Mannai and Lewis added an adversary in the form of an *attacker*. This configuration creates a two-party competitive game in which the defender attempts to reduce risk, and the attacker attempts to increase risk.[1] In mathematical terminology, this is a two-person game with an objective function that is maximized by the attacker and minimized by the defender.

The exponential cost model described in the previous section is adequate as a defender allocation model. Similarly, the attacker's allocation strategy is modeled as a diminishing returns exponential function. Because the attacker vulnerability model mirrors the exponential model of the defender, we say that the attacker–defender problem is *symmetric*. In military terms, symmetric conflict is equivalent to force-on-force combat, where each competitor has the same advantages and disadvantages as the other. Symmetric force-on-force battles are typically won by cunning and the application of superior assets. The attacker–defender network problem is no different.

The attacker must also live within a budget B_A just as the defender is constrained by its budget B_D. The objective of the attacker is to allocate AA_k dollars to node/link k in order to increase the probability of a successful attack, while the defender allocates DA_k dollars to lower vulnerability. Both parties must allocate resources within the constraints of their budgets. We consider two cases: (1) the opponents know of each other's allocation strategies, and (2) the allocation strategies of each opponent are unknown to the other opponent. As it turns out, the allocation strategy of the attacker in the first case will be radically different from that in the second case.

Figure 11.4 illustrates the exponential cost models for attacker and defender. From the attacker's perspective, vulnerability rapidly increases for a small investment and then tapers off as more investment is made. Theoretically, an infinite investment is necessary to drive vulnerability to 100%. Instead, vulnerability rises to $\text{max}\,AV\%$ with an investment of $\$\text{max}\,AA$ as shown by the dotted lines. These two numbers determine the shape of the attacker vulnerability curve g:

$$\gamma_i = \frac{-\ln(1 - \text{max}\,AV_i)}{\text{max}\,AA_i}; \, 0 \le \text{max}\,AV_i < 1$$

---

[1]This is similar to a Stackelberg leadership game in economics.

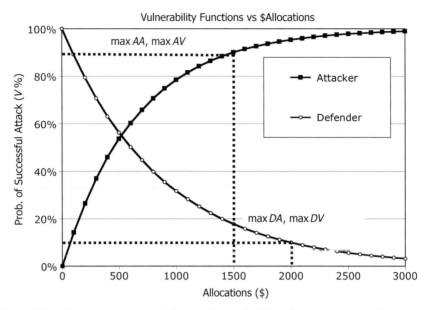

Figure 11.4 Exponential cost models. Attacker probability of success grows with increased investment, and defender vulnerability decreases with increased investment.

From the defender's perspective, vulnerability rapidly decreases for a small investment and then tapers off as more investment is made. While vulnerability is asymptotic to zero, it takes an infinite investment to drive it to zero. Instead, the defender can drive vulnerability to max $DV\%$ with an investment of \$max DA. These two numbers determine the shape of the defender's vulnerability curve α:

$$\alpha_i = \frac{-\ln(\max DV_i)}{\max DA_i}; \quad 0 \le \max DV_i \le 1$$

Both attacker and defender must live by the rules of diminishing returns. Both exponentials represent vulnerability from the competing player's perspective. The attacker tries to raise vulnerability, and the defender tries to lower it. In each case, vulnerability rises or diminishes as competitors spend their limited budgets. Therefore, these exponentials relate investment to probability of successful attack, on each node and link. In effect, the attacker's vulnerability $v(AA)$ is exponentially equivalent to the attacker's allocations AA and the defender's vulnerability $v(DA)$ is exponentially equivalent to the defender's allocations DA. The conflict is centered on the amount of each competitor's budget, and the ability of each to strategically allocate resources.

More formally, let the exponential cost model for the defender be a simple declining exponential, with a rate constant determined by parameters max DA and max DV, designated by dotted lines in Fig. 11.4:

$$v_i(DA_i) = e^{-\alpha_i DA_i}; \quad 0 \le v_i(DA_i) \le 1$$

where

$$\alpha_i = \frac{-\ln(\text{max}DV_i)}{\text{max}DA_i}; \quad 0 \le \text{max}DV_i \le 1$$

where $\text{max}DV_i$ is the reduced vulnerability when $\text{max}DA_i$ is invested in node/link i and DA_i is the allocation by the defender to protect node/link i.

Note that vulnerability is 100% when there is no allocation, $DA_i = 0$. On the other hand, it takes an infinite allocation to entirely eliminate vulnerability. Parameter α_i is chosen so that vulnerability decreases to $\text{max}DV_i$ when $DA_i = \text{max}DA_i$. Typically, $\text{max}DV_i = 10\%$, as in Fig. 11.4.

The same argument is made for the attacker, except vulnerability *increases* with the amount of funding AA_i applied by the attacker. Therefore, the exponential function is inverted:

$$v_i(AA_i) = 1 - e^{-\gamma_i AA_i}; \quad 0 \le v_i(AA_i) \le 1$$

where

$$\gamma_i = \frac{-\ln(1 - \text{max}AV_i)}{\text{max}AA_i}; \quad 0 \le \text{max}AV_i < 1$$

where $\text{max}AV_i$ is the vulnerability corresponding to an investment of $\text{max}AA_i$ and AA_i is the allocation to node/link i.

Once again, rate parameter γ_i is chosen to calibrate the exponential curve per inputs $\text{max}AV$ and $\text{max}AA$. Typically, $\text{max}AV_i = 90\%$, as in Fig. 11.4. For example, given $\text{max}AV_i = 90\%$, $\text{max}AA_i = \$1500$, $\text{min}DV_i = 10\%$, and $\text{max}DA_i = \$2000$, the rate parameters α_i and γ_i are

$$\alpha_i = \frac{-\ln(0.10)}{2000} = 0.00115$$

$$\gamma_i = \frac{-\ln(1 - 0.90)}{1500} = 0.00154$$

The two separate exponential cost models are now combined into a single model by noting that attacker and defender vulnerabilities are probabilities of events in a system modeled as an AND gate fault tree. The fault tree of Fig. 11.5 contains two threats facing a node/link: an attacker attempting to succeed with probability $V(AA)$, and a defender that may fail to prevent an attack with probability $V(DA)$. Note that the attacker's chances increase with increased attacker allocation, and the chances of the defender failing decreases with an increase in defender

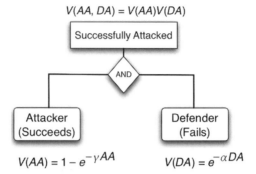

Figure 11.5 Fault tree for combined attacker–defender model. The probability that an attack is successful equals the product of the probability of a successful attack and an unsuccessful defense.

allocation. Therefore, the joint probability of a successful attack is the product of the two probabilities:

$$v_i(AA_i, DA_i) = v_i(AA_i)v_i(DA_i)$$

$$= [1 - e^{-\gamma_i AA_i}]e^{-\alpha_i DA_i}$$

This equation is important because it defines risk in terms of combined attacker and defender resource allocation. For example, if both players allocate nothing, $AA_i = DA_i = 0$, the combined vulnerability is 100%. If the defender allocates nothing and $AA_i \geq 0$, vulnerability depends on the attacker's allocation and therefore the attacker's probability of success, $V(AA)$. Conversely, if the attacker allocates nothing, then it does not make sense for the defender to allocate anything because $V(AA) = 0$. The combined vulnerability is equal to the defender-only vulnerability, $V(DA) = \exp(-\alpha DA)$. In this case, the defender's best strategy is to allocate resources elsewhere.

There are two major cases to be considered by this analysis: (1) the attacker and defender know each other's allocations and adjust their allocations accordingly, and (2) the attacker and defender are ignorant of each other's strategies, and make allocations according to certain assumptions about the opposition. We examine each of these in turn.

Assume that the exponential vulnerability reduction cost equation and assume attacker and defender know each other's strategies. The attacker tries to maximize risk and the defender tries to minimize risk. Furthermore, we use objective function Φ for network risk as defined earlier because we want to protect higher-degreed nodes more than lower-degreed nodes. Recall that Φ considers the degree sequence of the network as well as consequence and vulnerability reduction costs. Therefore, the objective of the attacker is to increase Φ, and the objective of the defender is to decrease Φ.

This is a two-party game, which is mathematically expressed in terms of an *attacker–defender optimization problem*:

$$\max_{AA} \min_{DA} \{\Phi(AA, DA)\}$$

where AA = vector of attacker allocations and DA = vector of defender allocations and

$$\Phi(AA, DA) = \sum_{k=1}^{n+m} g_k v_k(AA_k, DA_k)C_k = \sum_{k=1}^{n+m} g_k[1 - e^{-\gamma_i AA_i}]e^{-\alpha_i DA_i}C_k$$

$$\sum_{i=1}^{n+m} AA_i \le B_A; \, AA_i \ge 0$$

$$\sum_{i=1}^{n+m} DA_i \le B_D; \, DA_i \ge 0$$

where C_k represents consequences, target value, or damages and B_A = attacker's budget and B_D = defender's budget.

This constrained optimization problem can be converted into an unconstrained optimization problem using Lagrange multipliers λ_1 and λ_2:

$$\max_{AA} \{\min_{DA} \{\Phi\}\}$$

$$\Phi = \left\{ \begin{array}{l} \sum_{k=1}^{n+m} g_k[1 - e^{-\gamma_k AA_k}]e^{-\alpha_k DA_k}C_k \\[2mm] -\lambda_1 \left[\sum_{i=1}^{n+m} DA_i - B_D\right] \\[2mm] -\lambda_2 \left[\sum_{i=1}^{n+m} AA_i - B_A\right] \end{array} \right\} \quad \text{subject to} \quad AA_i \ge 0; \, DA_i \ge 0$$

Now the problem is to find allocation vectors AA and DA that satisfy the objective function with its budget constraints. The solution vectors AA and DA are obtained by setting derivatives to zero relative to AA, DA, λ_1, and λ_2, and solving the resulting simultaneous equations. The mathematics appears formidable, but this problem is easily solved through a combination of mathematical optimization and algorithmic iteration. We follow the approach of Al-Mannai and Lewis, who proposed a mixture of analytic and computational methods leading to an optimal allocation strategy for both attacker and defender.

Al-Mannai and Lewis proposed an *arms race algorithm* to derive vectors AA and DA, such that the defender minimizes risk and the attacker maximizes risk. The algorithm is straightforward, except for a singularity that occurs when the attacker allocation is zero. In this case, the defender also allocates zero because a wise defender will not waste resources on an asset that is not threatened by an attacker.

Arms Race Algorithm

1. Set the initial defender allocation vector DA to zero. Divide the attacker budget evenly among all nodes and links: $AA_i = B_A/(n + m)$. Calculate α_i and γ_i for all nodes and links. Mark all nodes/links as available for allocation: `negativeAlloc = `**`false`**. Compute an initial risk, assuming that probability of failure is one: $R = \Sigma c_i$.

2. Repeat the following optimization calculations until there is very little change in combined risk:

   a. Hold attacker allocation vector AA constant and use the Lagrange multiplier method of finding the minimum defender allocation vector DA in terms of vector AA. If any allocations are negative, set the allocation to zero, and mark the node/link: `negativeAlloc = `**`true`**. Remove these nodes/links from further consideration during subsequent iterations.

   b. Using the defender allocation vector DA obtained as above, and a second Lagrange multiplier for maximization, find the optimal allocation of attacker resources AA in terms of the previously calculated DA. If any allocations are negative, set the allocation to zero, and mark the node/link: `negativeAlloc = `**`true`**. Remove these nodes/links from further consideration during subsequent iterations.

   c. Compute a new risk using the joint probability of failure equation obtained from the AND logic fault tree, and compare with the risk calculation of the previous iteration. Stop when the change is negligible.

As it turns out, this algorithm converges very quickly to a fixed point where further changes in DA and AA have little effect on the combined risk. Like the arms race of the Cold War, players eventually reach stalemate—further refinement of their allocation strategy is not possible without suboptimization. Deviation from this fixedpoint produces a suboptimal strategy for both attacker and defender. At this fixed point, the best resource allocations are stored in vectors AA and DA.

Step 1 of the arms race algorithm assumes an initial vector AA equal to $B_A/(n + m)$ and allows the defender to make an initial allocation that minimizes risk, using the attacker allocation vector. The defender tries to minimize risk, so we find a temporary solution to the defender's minimization problem by solving for vector DA in terms of the initial AA values. Differentiating with respect to DA_i and λ_1 yields a set of solvable equations:

$$\frac{\partial \Phi}{\partial DA_i} = 0 = -\alpha_i g_i C_i (1 - e^{-\lambda_i AA_i}) e^{-\alpha_i DA_i} - \lambda_1$$

$$\frac{\partial \Phi}{\partial \lambda_1} = 0 = -\sum_{i=1}^{n+m} DA_i + B_D$$

Solving for DA_i in terms of $\ln(\lambda_1)$ in the first equation, and then plugging into the second equation to solve for $\ln(\lambda_1)$ yields vector DA in terms of vector AA:

$$DA_i(AA_i) = \frac{\ln(\alpha_i g_i C_i) - \ln(\lambda_1) + \ln(1 - e^{-\gamma_i AA_i})}{\alpha_i}$$

$$\ln(\lambda_1) = \frac{\displaystyle\sum_{i=1}^{n+m} \left[\frac{\ln(\alpha_i g_i C_i) + \ln(1 - e^{-\gamma_i AA_i})}{\alpha_i} \right] - B_D}{\displaystyle\sum_{i=1}^{n+m} \frac{1}{\alpha_i}} ; AA_i > 0$$

Numerically solving for $\ln(\lambda_1)$ is straightforward because all of the variables on the right-hand side are known. Plugging $\ln(\lambda_1)$ into the right-hand side of the equation for DA_i is also numerically trivial because vector AA is assumed from the start. Thus, vector DA is given in terms of vector AA, but AA was an initial estimate of the fixed-point solution—not the final solution. The next step in the arms race algorithm uses vector DA to solve for "a better AA." We iterate both solutions until further change in combined risk is impossible.[2] Vector AA is obtained in a similar fashion, using previously calculated vector DA and another Lagrange multiplier, λ_2:

$$AA_i(DA_i) = \frac{\ln(\gamma_i g_i C_i) - \ln(\lambda_2) - \alpha_i DA_i}{\gamma_i}$$

$$\ln(\lambda_2) = \frac{\displaystyle\sum_{i=1}^{n+m} \left[\frac{\ln(\gamma_i g_i C_i) - \alpha_i DA_i}{\gamma_i} \right] - B_A}{\displaystyle\sum_{i=1}^{n+m} \frac{1}{\gamma_i}} ; AA_i > 0$$

Once again, $\ln(\lambda_2)$ is calculated by plugging known values into the right-hand-side. Then, vector AA is numerically calculated by plugging $\ln(\lambda_2)$ and vector DA into the right-hand-side of the equation for $AA_i(DA_i)$. For a large network, the calculations are tedious, so a computer program is recommended; see program *NetworkAnalysis.jar*.

Careful study of the allocation equations reveals a singularity when $AA_i = 0$ because $\ln(1-\exp(-\gamma_i AA_i))$ is undefined—logarithms go to minus infinity as they approach zero. This singularity causes the calculation of defender allocation to blow up. Logically, we can set the defender allocation to any value we want when the attacker allocation is zero. But if there is no threat from the attacker, it makes sense for the defender to also allocate zero to the asset, and use the resource somewhere else. This singularity is handled by the Java implementation discussed later.

Iteration of $DA(AA)$ and $AA(DA)$ until there is little change in risk yields the fixed-point solution representing the best that attacker and defender can do with their

---

[2] Program *NetworkAnalysis.jar* uses `Math.abs(SL-newSL)/newSL` $<=$ `0.000001` as the stopping criterion, where `SL` and `newSL` are subsequent network risks.

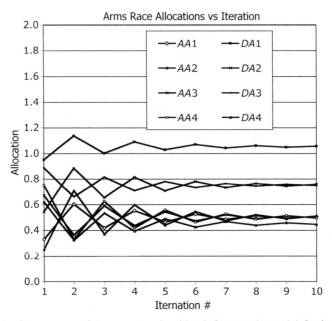

Figure 11.6   Convergence of the arms race algorithm is fast: attacker and defender allocations AA and DA versus iteration of the arms race algorithm.

budget constraints. Convergence is typically fast, as shown in Fig. 11.6, for the simple four-node/link network of Fig. 11.1a. The sawtooth shape of the converging solution is due to the attacker attempting to maximize risk, while the defender attempts to minimize risk. At each step, the attacker increases risk, followed by the defender decreasing risk. Sooner or later, the two converge to a fixed-point or stalemated configuration.

Figure 11.7 compares results obtained for the simple network of Fig. 11.1a, using the data of Table 11.2. Allocations are rank ordered by $gC/$max Alloc, as before, and normalized to Allocation/max Allocation. Curves are drawn for defender-only linear and exponential algorithms versus the arms race algorithm on the same data. Identical budgets, consequences, and vulnerability removal costs were used to make the comparison equitable.

This example shows that defender allocations are correlated with the same benefit ratio, $gC/$max Alloc, as before with the linear algorithm. Thus, the linear and exponential defender-only strategies distribute resources to assets with highest-weighted benefit/cost ratio, $gC/$max Alloc, in rank order. In fact, the curves for linear and exponential strategies are similar to one another. Regardless of the vulnerability reduction cost equation used, efficient allocation follows the same rank order rule.

Then, the behavior of attacker and defender are shown as dashed lines in Fig. 11.7. The defender closely follows the exponential allocation curve, nearly approximating it. However, the attacker does the opposite! The attacker tends to allocate resources *asymmetrically*—contrary to the defender. In other words, a low allocation by the

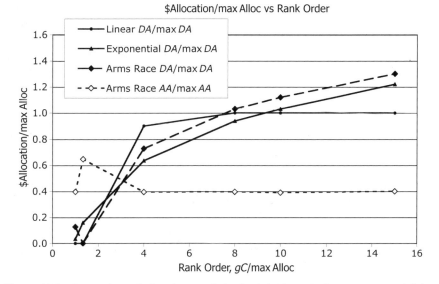

Figure 11.7 Comparison of allocations made by the defender-only linear strategy and defender-only exponential strategy versus attacker and defender allocations made by the arms race algorithm. Data are arranged in rank order by ascending $g_i C_i / \max \text{Alloc}_i$. Attacker and defender parameters are identical, including budgets: defender budget = attacker budget = 20 units.

defender is an opportunity for the attacker because low defender allocations leave the node/link vulnerable. Hence, the attacker allocates more to these less protected assets at the expense of reduced allocations at other targets. We conclude that the optimal strategy of an attacker is *asymmetric*—attacking weaker nodes/links while ignoring the well-protected nodes/links.

A final note is needed to explain the curves of Fig. 11.7. It appears that risk is higher when using the exponential vulnerability reduction cost function than the linear function. This is true because the exponential functions span the real line from zero to infinity. An infinite budget is needed to remove all vulnerability from a node/link according to the exponential models. On the contrary, the linear model intersects with zero vulnerability at max DA allocation; that is, all vulnerability (and hence risk) may be removed by a sufficient and finite budget if the linear model is assumed. Therefore, risk is always higher when using the exponential model than when using the linear model. But, this is an artifact of the models, themselves, and not of the network.

11.2.5 Java Arms Race Methods

The attacker–defender allocation algorithm is implemented by five Java methods: one root method for carrying out the steps described above in the arms race algorithm, two methods for computing λ_1 and λ_2, and one method each for defender and attacker allocation calculations. The methods are written to handle attacker-defender competition as well as the independent exponential cases. When flag `competition` is **true**, attacker and defender use each other's allocations to compute their own. When **false**, the two parties ignore each other's allocations. In this case, the allocation is identical to the allocations obtained from exponential vulnerability reduction equations. A second flag, `network`, is used to indicate the use of node degree in the allocations. When `network` is **true**, degree sequence *g* is used; otherwise *g* is set to one for all nodes and links.

The root method, `NW_doExponentialArmsRace()`, paraphrases the arms race algorithm without exception. Initially, the attacker budget is evenly distributed over all nodes/links, and the exponential parameters α and γ are calculated. Negative allocation flags are set to false, indicating that initially, all allocations are nonnegative. Then the arms race algorithm iterates between defender and attacker allocations. If either budget is zero, the allocations follow the one-sided exponential strategy:

```
public void NW_doExponentialArmsRace(boolean network, boolean competition){
    NW_Zero_Allocation();    //Reset Budget and Point allocation to zero
    for(int i = 0; i < nnodes; i++){
        nodes[i].AttackerAlloc = aBudget/(nnodes+nedges);
        nodes[i].alpha = -Math.log(nodes[i].DefenderFrac)/nodes[i].maxDA;
        nodes[i].gamma = -Math.log(1-nodes[i].AttackerFrac)/nodes[i].maxAA;
        nodes[i].negativeDefenderAlloc = false;
        nodes[i].negativeAttackerAlloc = false;
    }
    for(int i = 0; i < nedges; i++){
        edges[i].AttackerAlloc = aBudget/(nnodes+nedges);
        edges[i].alpha = -Math.log(edges[i].DefenderFrac)/edges[i].maxDA;
        edges[i].gamma = -Math.log(1-edges[i].AttackerFrac)/edges[i].maxAA;
        edges[i].negativeDefenderAlloc = false;
        edges[i].negativeAttackerAlloc = false;
    }
    SL = 0;
    newSL = 100;
    while(Math.abs((SL-newSL)/newSL) > .000001){
        if(aBudget > 0) doNetworkDefenderAllocation(network, competition);
            else doNetworkDefenderAllocation(network, false);
        if(dBudget > 0) doNetworkAttackerAllocation(network, competition);
            else doNetworkAttackerAllocation(network, false);
        SL = newSL;
        doExponentialV();    //Calculate combined vulnerability
            newSL = NW_calculateNetworkRisk();
        }
        doExponentialV();
        NW_calculateNetworkRisk();
}//NW_doExponentialArmsRace
```

```
private void doExponentialV(){
    double probA, probD;
    for(int i = 0; i < nnodes; i++){
        probA = 1-Math.exp(-nodes[i].gamma*nodes[i].AttackerAlloc);
        probD = Math.exp(-nodes[i].alpha*nodes[i].DefenderAlloc);
        nodes[i].ProbOfFailure = FaultTree(probA, probD);
    }
    for(int i = 0; i < nedges; i++){
        probA = 1-Math.exp(-edges[i].gamma*edges[i].AttackerAlloc);
        probD = Math.exp(-edges[i].alpha*edges[i].DefenderAlloc);
        edges[i].ProbOfFailure = FaultTree(probA, probD);
    }
}
private double FaultTree(double probA, double probD){
    if(probA < 0) probA = 0;
    if(probD < 0) probD = 0;
    if(probA > 1) probA = 1;
    if(probD > 1) probD = 1;
    if(dBudget == 0) return probA;
    if(aBudget == 0) return probD;
    return probA*probD;
}
```

The defender and attacker allocation methods repeatedly calculate and recalculate the optimal allocations, given previous allocations, until all negative allocations are removed. This enforces the constraints on $AA > 0$, and $DA > 0$ required by the problem formulation. Each time a negative allocation is found, it is removed and the allocation is repeated on fewer assets. Once removed, an allocation is set to zero and never changes. Additionally, the defender method avoids the singularity caused by a zero attacker allocation. If the attacker allocates zero to a node/link, the defender does the same, and removes the node/link from further consideration. Thus, the defender strategy is identical to the strategy for dealing with negative allocation. While this is not a direct result of applying the equations for defender allocation, it makes sense in real-world terms—if there is no threat, then why allocate a protective resource?

```
private void doNetworkDefenderAllocation(boolean network, boolean competition){
    boolean no_negatives = false;
    int degree;
    while(!no_negatives){
        no_negatives = true;
        double logLambda1 = NW_doNetworkLambda1(network, competition);
        for(int j = 0; j < nnodes; j++){
            if(!nodes[j].negativeDefenderAlloc){
```

```
      if(network) degree = nodes [ j] .g; else degree = 1;
      if(competition && aBudget > 0 && nodes [ j] .AttackerAlloc <= 0)
            nodes[j].DefenderAlloc = -1; //Remove it
      else {
            double VA = nodes [ j] .gamma*nodes [ j] .AttackerAlloc;
            if(!competition) VA = 0;
                else VA = Math.log(1-Math.exp(-VA));
            nodes[j].DefenderAlloc = (Math.log(nodes[j].alpha*degree*nodes[j].C)-
logLambda1+VA)/nodes[j].alpha;
        }
      }
      if(nodes [ j] .DefenderAlloc < 0){ //Remove negatives
            nodes[j].DefenderAlloc = 0;
            nodes[j].negativeDefenderAlloc = true;
            no_negatives = false;
      }
   }//nnodes
   for (int j = 0; j < nedges; j++){
      if(!edges [ j] .negativeDefenderAlloc) {
         if(competition && aBudget > 0 && edges [ j] .AttackerAlloc <= 0)
               edges[j].DefenderAlloc = -1;
         else {
            double VA = edges [ j] .gamma*edges [ j] .AttackerAlloc;
            if(!competition) VA = 0;
            else VA = Math.log(1-Math.exp(-VA));
            edges[j].DefenderAlloc = (Math.log(edges[j].alpha*edges[j].C)-
logLambda1+VA)/edges[j].alpha;
         }
      }
      if(edges [ j] .DefenderAlloc < 0){
            edges[j].DefenderAlloc = 0;
            edges[j].negativeDefenderAlloc = true;
            no_negatives = false;
      }
   }//nedges
 }
}//doNetworkDefenderAllocation

private void doNetworkAttackerAllocation(boolean network, boolean competition){
      boolean no_negatives = false;
      int degree;
      while(!no_negatives){
            no_negatives = true;
            double logLambda2 = NW_doNetworkLambda2(network, competition);
            for(int j = 0; j < nnodes; j++){
            if(!nodes [ j] .negativeAttackerAlloc) {
```

```
         double VD = nodes[ j] .alpha*nodes[ j] .DefenderAlloc;
         if(!competition) VD = 0;
         if(network) degree = nodes[ j] .g; else degree = 1;
         nodes[j].AttackerAlloc = (Math.log(nodes[j].gamma*nodes[j].C*degree)-
logLambda2-VD)/nodes[j].gamma
         if(nodes [ j] .AttackerAlloc < 0){
             nodes[j].AttackerAlloc = 0;
             nodes[j].negativeAttackerAlloc = true;
             no_negatives = false;
         }
      }
   }//nnodes
   for(int j = 0; j < nedges; j++){
      if(!edges[ j] .negativeAttackerAlloc) {
         double VD = edges[ j] .alpha*edges[ j] .DefenderAlloc;
         if(!competition) VD = 0;
         edges[j].AttackerAlloc = (Math.log(edges[j].gamma*edges[j].C)-
logLambda2-VD)/edges[j].gamma
         if (edges[ j] .AttackerAlloc < 0){
             edges[j].AttackerAlloc = 0;
             edges[j].negativeAttackerAlloc = true;
             no_negatives = false;
         }
      }
   }//nedges
 }
}//doNetworkAttackerAllocation
```

Parameters $\ln(\lambda_1)$ and $\ln(\lambda_2)$ are computed in a similar manner, except it is not necessary to iterate until negative allocations have been removed, since they have already been removed by the corresponding allocation method. The two methods for computing lambdas (λs) check the appropriate negativeAlloc flag, and ignore the nodes/ links marked as negative. The methods must also avoid blowing up because of a zero attacker allocation. Is this possible? This is left as an exercise for the reader.

```
public double NW_doNetworkLambda1(boolean network, boolean competition){
   double Lambda1 =0.0;
   double sumAlpha = 0.0;
   int degree;
   for(int i = 0; i < nnodes; i++) {
      if(!nodes[ i] .negativeDefenderAlloc)
      {
         if(network) degree = nodes[ i] .g; else degree = 1;
         double VA = nodes[ i] .gamma*nodes[ i] .AttackerAlloc;
         if(!competition || VA <= 0) VA = 0;
             else VA = Math.log(1-Math.exp(-VA));
```

```
        Lambda1 +=(Math.log(nodes[i].alpha*degree*nodes[i].C)+VA)/nodes[i].alpha;
        sumAlpha += (1/nodes[i].alpha);
  }
}

    for (int i = 0; i < nedges; i++){
      if(!edges[ i] .negativeDefenderAlloc)
      {
        double VA = edges[ i] .gamma*edges[ i] .AttackerAlloc;
        if(!competition || VA <= 0) VA = 0;
          else VA = Math.log(1-Math.exp(-VA));
        Lambda1 += (Math.log(edges[i].alpha*edges[i].C)+VA)/edges[i].alpha;
        sumAlpha += (1/edges[i].alpha);
       }
      }// for nedges
      if(sumAlpha == 0) return 0;
      else Lambda1 = (Lambda1-dBudget)/sumAlpha;
      return Lambda1;
  }// NW_doNetworkLambda1


public double NW_doNetworkLambda2(boolean network, boolean competition){
      double Lambda2 =0.0;
      double sumGamma = 0.0;
      int degree;
      for(int i = 0; i < nnodes; i++) {
          if(!nodes[ i] .negativeAttackerAlloc) {
              double VD = nodes[ i] .alpha*nodes[ i] .DefenderAlloc;
              if(!competition) VD = 0;
              if(network) degree = nodes[ i] .g; else degree = 1;
              Lambda2 += (Math.log(nodes[i].gamma*degree*nodes[i].C)-
                          VD)/nodes[i].gamma
              sumGamma += (1/nodes[i].gamma);
          }
      }
      for (int i = 0; i < nedges; i++) {
        if(!edges[ i] .negativeAttackerAlloc) {
            double VD = edges[ i] .alpha*edges[ i] .DefenderAlloc;
            if(!competition) VD = 0;
             Lambda2 += (Math.log(edges[i].gamma*edges[i].C)-VD)/
                        edges[i].gamma
            sumGamma += (1/edges[i].gamma);
          }
        }// for nedges
      if( sumGamma == 0 ) return 0;
      else Lambda2 = (Lambda2-aBudget)/sumGamma;
      return Lambda2;
  }// NW_doNetworkLambda2
```

11.3 GAME THEORY CONSIDERATIONS

The attacker–defender arms race model assumes both network opponents use the same strategy—and apply the same exponential cost model. In addition, it assumes that each player knows the other player's allocation after each round of reallocations. These assumptions are perhaps valid in many situations, but what happens if attacker and defender know nothing of each other's allocation strategy? Specifically, what is the best allocation strategy when neither party knows the strategy of the other party?

We turn to game theory to analyze this question. In a simple two-party game, the defender adopts one of many strategies by assuming that it knows something about the opponent's allocation strategy, and conversely, the attacker adopts one of many strategies by assuming that it knows something about the defender's strategy. In reality, the assumption about the opponent may be wrong. Nonetheless, once a strategy is adopted, it remains in place for at least one round of the game.

A payoff matrix consists of the payoff (benefit) to each party resulting from each player's allocation strategy. Each element in the $n \times n$ payoff matrix contains the normalized network risk obtained by applying each strategy to a given network and calculating the resulting network risk. We use the normalized network risk defined by

$$\Phi(AA, DA) = \sum_{k=1}^{n+m} g_k v_k(AA_k, DA_k) C_k$$

$$\Phi(AA, DA)_{\text{normalized}} = \frac{\Phi(AA, DA)}{\Phi(0, 0)}; \quad \Phi(0, 0) = \sum_{k=1}^{n+m} g_k C_k$$

For example, Table 11.3 contains the payoff matrix for the two-party game played by each player selecting one strategy from among the choices described in this chapter. This payoff matrix is for the simple network of Fig. 11.1a, and uses the parameters given in Tables 11.1 and 11.2. It includes the results of running the arms race algorithm both with and without degree sequence objective functions, for comparison purposes.

Surprisingly, the best strategy for both players is the linear allocation that places resources on the most critical nodes/links according to the rank-order property. Why? One explanation is that it takes an infinite allocation to completely remove vulnerability when using the exponential function, but linear allocation can reduce risk to zero by allocating a finite amount, max Alloc. The difference between linear and exponential functions leads to higher estimates of risk when using the exponential functions. As shown in Table 11.3, the difference is rather significant for the exponential-to-exponential entry versus the linear-to-linear allocations.

The game theory model is different than the attacker–defender model explored previously because it assumes that the players know nothing of each other's allocations. The attacker–defender model combined vulnerabilities into one combination vulnerability function, but in this game theory formulation, we assume independent probabilities of success. Therefore, attacker and defender allocate resources as if the other opponent did not exist. When the attacker and defender know each other's allocations, the attacker is able to take advantage of this information and drive risk higher than if the knowledge is unknown.

TABLE 11.3 Payoff Matrix for Simple Example

Defender (Budget = 20)	Attacker (Budget = 20)					
	No Allocation (%)	Random (%)	Linear (%)	Exponential (%)	Arms Race $(g \geq 1)$ (%)	Arms Race $(g = 1)$ (%)
No allocation	100.0	55.10	82.90	77.70	77.70	74.80
Random	44.9	11.50	31.10	30.23	—	—
Linear	17.5	3.21	2.11	4.06	—	—
Exponential	22.3	7.60	9.65	12.26	—	—
Arms race $(g \geq 1)$	22.30	—	—	—	15.95	—
Arms race $(g = 1)$	25.10	—	—	—	—	17.35

Disregarding payoff entries corresponding to when budgets are set to zero, what is the optimal strategy for each player? Attacker and defender may chose random, linear, or exponential allocations, but neither party knows what the other will choose. For example, if the defender chooses the linear allocation strategy because it contains the smallest risks, the attacker might choose the exponential allocation strategy because it contains the largest risks. In this case, the payoff is 4.06%—the payoff cell at the intersection of defender—linear and attacker—exponential row and column.

In this example, the defender can do no better than adopt the linear allocation strategy because regardless of the strategy adopted by the attacker, risk will increase only from the perspective of the defender. Similarly, the attacker can do no better than to adopt the linear allocation strategy because risk will decrease only from the perspective of the attacker, if either random or exponential defender strategies are adopted. Without knowledge of the opponent's allocation strategy, each player must select the strategy that looks best from its perspective. Is this true for the simple example, regardless of budgets? This is left as an exercise for the reader.

11.4 THE GENERAL ATTACKER–DEFENDER NETWORK RISK PROBLEM

The network attacker–defender problem is *asymmetric*, meaning that the attacker has an (unfair) advantage over the defender because the attacker has fewer constraints. Generally, an attacker can select the location, time, and threat, while the defender has few options but to defend everything, all the time, against all threats. The asymmetry in attacker strategy comes from this imbalance between options.

Attacker Problem. The attacker is unconstrained by what, when, and how it attacks—that is, the attacker may attack any part of the network, at any time, and with any weapon. However, like the defender, the attacker is constrained by cost. Attacks are not free.

Defender Problem.   The defender is constrained by what, when, and how it defends the network—that is, the defender cannot protect everything in the network, all of the time, and with an unlimited defense. The defender is constrained by the cost to defend nodes and links. Security is not free.

The solution to the attacker–defender problem is nontrivial because of this asymmetry. Generally, the defender is unable to defend everything against all threats, while the attacker is resource-limited and cannot afford to attack everything with any force. This leads to a game-theoretic approach, whereby the defender protects only the most vital components while the attacker attempts to maximize damage. In game-theoretic terms, the defender tries to minimize risk, while the attacker tries to maximize risk. More formally, we define the general attacker–defender problem as follows:

$$\Phi = \left\{ \begin{array}{c} \sum\limits_{k=1}^{n+m} g_k V_k(AA_k, DA_k)C_k \\[2mm] -\lambda_D \left[\sum\limits_{i=1}^{n+m} DA_i - B_D \right] \\[2mm] -\lambda_A \left[\sum\limits_{i=1}^{n+m} AA_i - B_A \right] \end{array} \right\}; \ AA_k \geq 0; \ DA_k \geq 0$$

Solve

$$\frac{\partial \Phi}{\partial DA_i} = 0; \ \frac{\partial \Phi}{\partial \lambda_D} = 0$$

$$\frac{\partial \Phi}{\partial AA_i} = 0; \ \frac{\partial \Phi}{\partial \lambda_A} = 0$$

This risk problem has been analyzed by a number of people, using a number of assumptions. Major formulated this problem as a nonnetwork resource allocation problem with n assets (Major, 2002). His formulation tied together attacker and defender vulnerability as a function of both attacker and defender resources, AA, and DA, and the consequence of a loss due to destruction of each asset, C:

$$V(AA_i, DA_i) = \{e^{(-AA_i DA_i)/\sqrt{C_i}}\} \left\{ \frac{AA_i^2}{AA_i^2 + C_i} \right\}$$

Unfortunately, this function is undefined for $C_i = 0$ and $AA_i = C_i = 0$. Furthermore, it is not based on the a priori probability of success, should an attack take place. However, it was the first model to combine the effects of both attacker and defender resource allocation on vulnerability in a nonnetwork world.

Powers and Powell extended Major's risk model for nonnetworked assets by allowing simultaneous attacks on multiple assets and formulated the max−min objective function given above (Powers, 2005; Powell, 2006). In principle, this approach leads to a spiraling *arms race*, where each player counters by increasing its budget in response to the other player. We showed that the arms race converges, under certain conditions, leading to an optimal allocation for both attacker and defender.

These models are appropriate for nonnetworked assets such as single buildings, bridges, tunnels, and other structures, but they do not model the impact of an asset failure on an entire system. Networked systems must consider the networkwide effect of one or more attacks on a node or link. The network science approach required a new definition of risk and a vulnerability model that works for networked assets. This extension leads to the Al-Mannai–Lewis model previously presented in some detail. However, the Al-Mannai–Lewis model does not tell the whole story because it focuses largely on the degree sequence distribution. The Al Mannai–Lewis attacker–defender risk problem gives too much weight to nodes. Unless links are highly valued, the Al Mannai–Lewis arms race algorithm rarely selects links as critical. For this reason, we perform a critical link analysis, instead.

11.5 CRITICAL LINK ANALYSIS

Now we turn attention to the problem of protecting a network from destruction or inoperability when its links are attacked. For purposes of this discussion, suppose that a network becomes *inoperable* when it separates into components, leaving one or more nodes unreachable from other nodes. This might represent a power grid outage, for example, when one or more power lines *trip*—failing to transmit electricity. It also represents the cessation of a route in an airline, commuter line, or shipping route in a transportation network. Removal of a link disrupts a network because of loss of continuity, or because separation into disjoint components halts the network's operation.

Let *link resilience* be defined as the percentage of links that must be removed in order to separate the network into components:

$$\text{Link\_resilience} = \frac{t}{m}$$

where t = number of damaged or removed links and m = original number of links.

Obviously, the higher the value of link resilience, the more difficult it is to separate a network, and therefore, the more resistant it is to attacks on its links. A link resilience of 50% means that one-half of the links must be removed. In this section we explore the resilience of random, small-world, and scale-free networks to random attacks on their links, and find that small worlds are the most resilient, random networks are next, and scale-free networks are the least resilient.

A logistics network containing commodities that flow from source to sink nodes is also vulnerable to link attacks, especially when removal of a link shuts off the flow of the commodity. In this case, the network may cease to provide an adequate flow of a commodity even though it does not separate into components. We define resilience in this case as the fraction of maximum flow sustained by the network as links are blocked or removed:

$$\text{Flow\_resilience} = \frac{c}{\text{max}\_c}$$

where c = flow from source to sinks and c_max = maximum possible flow from source to sinks.

Once again, this measure of resilience ranges from 0 to 100%—increasing with increase in actual flow of the commodity. In this section we show that the optimal allocation of resources to protect links occurs when the maximum-capacity critical paths are protected, first, followed by lower-capacity paths, second. We provide a heuristic for allocating resources to links such that flow is maximized along these most critical paths.

Another form of resilience is also important to the security of a network—*stability*. Recall that a dynamic network may fail to stabilize, depending on its next-state function and topology. Is it possible to destabilize a network by removing certain links? This problem is of great importance to the proper design of resilient electrical power grids, transportation systems, and electronic components. Without stability resilience, we cannot prevent massive destabilization of a network by malicious destruction of a small number of its links.

Let *stability resilience* be defined as the fraction of links that leave a network stable when removed:

$$\text{Stability\_resilience} = 1 - \frac{s}{m}$$

where s = number of links that destabilize the network if removed and m = number of links.

We study the stability resilience of Kirchhoff networks, which were defined and studied earlier (see Chapter 9). Recall that Kirchhoff networks are directed networks that stabilize when the sum of incoming flows equals the sum of outgoing flows at each node. The issue is how removal of a link affect's the ability of the resulting network to stabilize itself and resume operation. Identification of the removed links that lead to an unstable network also leads to a solution—either harden these critical links or add redundant substitutes.

11.5.1 Link Resilience

Let G be a strongly connected network with n nodes, m links, and arbitrary topology. Suppose we delete links at random until the network separates into two or more components. Removing a link to a node with a single link easily divides a network into two components. The network is now divided into two components—one with $(n-1)$ nodes and the other with one node. But what if there are no such nodes? Furthermore, what if links are deleted at random? How many links must be removed, on average, to separate such an arbitrary network?

Percolation is the process of adding links until a giant connected component forms. *Depercolation* is the opposite—removal of links until the giant connected component separates into smaller components. Typically, separation occurs when a single node is isolated by removal of its only link. The fraction of links removed at the point of separation into components due to depercolation yields an estimate of its link_resilience.

The following Java method implements this simple process. The algorithm is very simple—randomly select a link, and if the network is connected, remove the link. If the network is already separated, reply1.bit will be **true**, and the largest component will be found by counting nodes twice—starting from the node at each end of the link. Method isComponent traverses the spanning trees with roots at edges[e].to and edges[e].from—searching for a complete spanning tree in both directions. If the search finds all nodes, the method returns **true**. Otherwise, it returns **false**. In either case, method NW_doDepercolate() returns the size of the largest component found. This code can be found in program *NetworkAnalysis.jar*, and uses edges[] instead of links[] to store network links:

```java
class isComp {      //Return plex
    boolean bit = false;                    //Not a component
    int size = 0;                           //Number nodes visited
}
public boolean NW_doDepercolate(){
    int e = (int)(Math.random()*nedges);       //pick any link at random
    isComp reply1 = isComponent(edges[e].to); //Count nodes twice
    isComp reply2;
    if(reply1.bit){
      NW_doCutEdge(e);
    }
      else {
         reply2 = isComponent(edges[e].from);    //Check both ends of link
         if(reply1.size < reply2.size) reply1 = reply2;
      }
      return reply1.bit; //Return size of largest
    }//NW_doDepercolate
```

Method isComponent() resets all flags and starts the recursive descent process of visiting all nodes connected to the start node. A depth-first search is used, but a breadth-first search would work just as well. Why? Next, method isComponent() tallies the number of nodes visited and compares the tally with the size of the network:

```
private isComp isComponent(int start_node){
      isComp reply = new isComp();
      reply.size = 0;                    //Number nodes visited on each trip
      for(int j = 0; j < nnodes; j++){ //Reset flags
        nodes[j].visited = false;
      }
        visit_next(start_node);
        for(int j = 0; j < nnodes; j++){ //Reset flags
          if(nodes[ j] .visited) {
          reply.size++;
          nodes[j].visited = false;
          nodes[j].color = Color.red; //Visited nodes are red
        }
      }
      reply.bit = (reply.size == nnodes);
      return reply;
   }//isComponent
      //Recursive method
      private void visit_next(int j) {
        if(!nodes[ j] .visited){
          nodes[j].visited = true;
          for(int e = 0; e < nedges; e++){        //Push successors
          if(edges[ e] .to == j
                  &&
            !nodes[edges[e] .from].visited)
                visit_next(edges[e].from);
          else if(edges[ e] .from == j
                  &&
          !nodes[edges[e] .to] .visited)
           visit_next(edges[e].to);
             }//for
          }//if
      }//visit_next
```

Figure 11.8 illustrates the application of method NW_doDepercolate() to random, small-world, and scale-free networks of modest size, $n = 200$, $m = 1000$. Using program *NetworkAnalysis.jar*, depercolate hundreds of networks and count the number of removed links that led to separation. These counts were placed in bins representing 0–50 removed links, 51–100, 101–150, ..., 951–1000. The ratio of removed links to number of trials provides an estimate of the probability of separation as a function of removed links. The empirical data obtained from simulation are marked with open geometric symbols in Fig. 11.8, and estimates based on curve fitting are

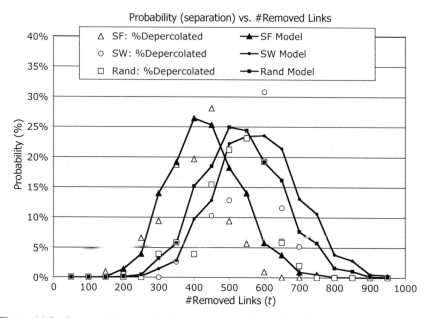

Figure 11.8 Depercolation results for random, small-world, and scale-free networks with $n = 200$, $m = 1000$, rewiring probability $p = 5\%$, $\Delta m = 5$, and $\lambda = 10$. Solid lines are models based on the derivation in the text. Parameter $\alpha = 0.42$ for small-world networks, 0.50 for random networks, and 0.75 for scale-free networks.

marked with closed geometric symbols. An approximation equation is derived in the next section, but clearly, link resilience depends on network topology.

What are the results of the simulations? There are significant differences between random, small-world, and scale-free networks of similar density. In terms of link_resilience, the small-world network is *most* resilience with separation taking place when approximately 60% of the 1000 links are removed. The scale-free network is the *least* resilient, requiring removal of only 45% of its links to separate it into components. The random network is positioned nearly in the middle, requiring 55% of its links to be removed before separating. In terms of link resilience, the three classes of networks rank as follows:

Small-world—highest link resilience

Random—next

Scale-free—least link resilience

This nonintuitive result is contrary to intuition, which might suggest that random networks are more resilient than small-world networks, but this is not the case. Why?

1. It is obvious why a scale-free network is the least tolerant—it contains many nodes with low degree. Hence, it takes fewer link removals to disconnect them.

The probability of selecting a link connected to a hub is higher, but the probability that the node at the opposite end of the link has few links is also higher. This imbalance between number of low-degreed nodes and number of hubs leads to lower link resilience. Quite simply, scale-free networks have too many low-degreed nodes.

2. The probability of removing a link from a low-degreed node is lower in a small-world network than in a random network because its degree sequence distribution is narrower—meaning that most nodes have an average number of links. Few nodes have a low degree. The distribution of degree—and therefore links—is broader in a random network, meaning that it is more likely that one node of the randomly selected link will connect to a lower-degreed node. In other words, we double our chances of separating a node from the network because every link has two endnodes. This double jeopardy leads to an increase in chances of separation. The increase is even greater for a network with a broad degree sequence distribution, which leads to earlier separation in a random network. Thus, small-world networks are more resilient than random networks. This difference diminishes, however, as a small world's entropy increases due to an increase in rewiring probability.

3. The results of Fig. 11.8 suggest that the probability of separation as a function of number of removed links—and hence link resilience—follows a binomial or Poisson distribution. If true, this would not be a surprise for the class of random networks, somewhat unexpected for the class of small-world networks, but completely counterintuitive for the class of scale-free networks. Generally, random removal of links is like the Erdos–Renyi generative process in reverse. Randomization is the result of random link removal because it tends to restructure any network by introducing entropy. The more random links that are removed, the more entropy, and this leads to a somewhat random-like degree sequence distribution. In other words, random link removal restructures the degree sequence distribution into a binomial-like distribution. But, it is not a pure binomial distribution, as we shall see.

We derive an approximation for link resilience in the next section, and show that depercolation restructuring is similar, but not equal, to pure randomization of the degree sequence distribution. The two are similar because depercolation injects entropy into the network. They are different because, as it turns out, link removal changes the degree of two nodes at a time—one at each end of the link. Changing two nodes at a time is not a pure Poisson process. In fact, the solid-line curves shown in Fig. 11.8 are not Poisson.

11.5.2 Model of Link Resilience

Assuming a Poisson process is a reasonable place to start the development of an approximation to the probability of separation distribution of Fig. 11.8, because depercolation is similar to the Gilbert generative procedure used to produce random networks. We model the departure from purely Poisson processes in two ways:

1. Let α be a constant that characterizes the departure from uniformity of degree sequence in the depercolating network: $0 \leq \alpha \leq 1$.

2. Let the probability of separation be the result of deletion of a stub at each end of a link, altering the degree sequence distribution by altering the degree of both end nodes of a deleted link. This probability is affected by the chance that a deletion at either end of a link may cause the network to separate into components.

After t links have been removed, let the mean degree and probability of selecting a node belonging to a deleted link be

$$\lambda = \frac{2(m - t)}{n}$$

$$p = \frac{2\alpha\lambda}{(m - t)} = \frac{4\alpha}{n}$$

where m = number of original links

n = number of nodes

t = number of removed links

α = degree-sequence-dependent constant to be determined

p = probability of selecting a node with mean degree λ

The probability of selecting a node with mean degree λ is obtained by noting that $(m - t)$ links remain after t links have been removed, and the probability of one end node being part of the selected link is $\lambda/(m - t)$. Therefore, the probability of both end nodes belonging to the link is $2\lambda/(m - t)$. Parameter α will be determined later through curve fitting.

The process of selecting a random link in t trials is a Poisson process with parameters t, λ, and p. Therefore, we use a binomial distribution to model the probability of selecting λ links connecting nodes with degree λ in t trials. A node becomes isolated after all λ of its links have been removed. Random link selection deletes t links, but affects $2t$ nodes. A typical node is separated from the others after deleting λ links, but link removal has an impact on both ends of the link. Therefore, the binomial distribution represents the probability of deleting a link from two typical nodes each time a link is removed. This is why we set $p = 2\lambda/(m - t)$ instead of $\lambda/(m - t)$.

Using the combinatorial function and rounding up; we obtain

$$B(t, \lambda; p) = C_\lambda^t p^\lambda (1 - p)^{t - \lambda}$$

$$C_\lambda^t = \frac{t!}{(t - \lambda)\lambda!}$$

where

$$\lambda = \text{roundup}\left(\frac{2(m - t)}{n}\right)$$

Although B is the probability of selecting either end node, it is not the probability of separating the network. We obtain the probability of separation by considering all possible events—separation at one end of the link, separation at the other end, or separation at both ends. Using DeMorgan's law as we did in Fig. 11.1b, but for two faults instead of three, and including the curve fitting parameter α, we obtain

$$\text{Prob(separation)} = 1 - [(1 - B)(1 - \alpha B)] = B(1 + \alpha - \alpha B)$$

where α = class of network parameter
$\quad\quad B$ = modified binomial distribution function

This result was obtained by considering two faults: one occurring with probability B, and the other occurring with probability αB. For example, if $\alpha = 1$, probability of separation at one or both ends of the link is $B(2 - B)$. If $\alpha = 0$, the probability is simply B. Parameter α represents the fact that a typical node is not very typical— its degree differs from mean degree λ. In fact, parameter α should be low for a small-world network because the variation in node degree is slight, whereas α should be large for a scale-free network because the variation in node degree is high. Experimentation supports this claim.

Now we have a complete model of the probability of separation after t links have been removed:

$$\text{Prob(separation; } n, m, t, \alpha) = B(1 + \alpha - \alpha B)$$

$$\lambda = \frac{2(m - t)}{n}$$

$$p = \frac{4\alpha}{n}$$

$$B(t, \lambda; p) = C_\lambda^t p^\lambda (1 - p)^{t - \lambda}$$

$$C_\lambda^t = \frac{t!}{(t - \lambda)\lambda!}$$

where

$$\lambda = \text{roundup}\left(\frac{2(m - t)}{n}\right)$$

$$\alpha = \text{class of network parameter}$$

Parameter α for the empirical data used in Fig. 11.8 varies as follows:

Small-world $\alpha = 0.42$
Random $\alpha = 0.50$
Scale-free $\alpha = 0.75$

These results support the claim that α represents the variance in degree sequence distribution of the classes of network studied here. The effect of α on the shape of the curves in Fig. 11.8 is to shift the distribution left or right, corresponding to a change in the mean degree of a typical node. But mean degree λ is the same for all networks with $n = 200$, $m = 1,000$, so why the shift? As links are removed, the mean degree decreases. As it decreases, the probability of separation shifts left—toward the origin of the graph. The scale-free class of networks suffers more than the others, so its separation distribution is shifted left more than are the other two classes. Thus, scale-free α is largest among the three classes—representing the largest shift in mean degree.

Parameter α decreases with increase in link resilience, so it is correlated with resilience, too. We might be temped to use $(1 - \alpha)$ as a measure of resilience, but it does not behave in a linear fashion. Doubling resilience does not correspond with cutting $(1 - \alpha)$ in half. Additionally, parameter α is not clearly related to the number of removed links. For these reasons, we ignore the temptation to use it as a measure of resilience.

The approximation derived here is very rough. We leave the task of finding a better approximation to the reader. In summary, link removal tends to randomize a network, increasing its entropy and lowering its density. The network eventually separates into components at some density threshold determined by the network's topology. We discovered that small-world networks remain intact at a much lower density than do random and scale-free networks. This is perhaps due to the high degree of clustering inherent in the underlying k-regular network. Scale-free networks, on the other hand, become separated at much higher densities, perhaps because they start with too many low-degreed nodes.

11.5.3 Flow Resilience

Up to this point we have assumed that the network represents a static system. In many real-world applications, networks represent the flow of a commodity through a system. For example, a network model of a water supply system has directional flow; a telecommunication network has bidirectional flow, and an electrical power grid might support flow in one direction, for a period of time, and then reverse flow to the opposite direction. This naturally raises the question of vulnerability in systems with directional flow.

If the network represents flow from *source* to *sink* nodes, then obviously the source nodes are extremely critical, because without them, nothing flows! Clearly, we should protect the source nodes, regardless of their degree or expense. Additionally, if a link is broken in the network, an entire subgraph of links and nodes can be deprived of the commodity. Intuitively, we would expect "upstream" nodes and links to be more important than "downstream" nodes and links, but whether they are of the highest priority depends on the cost of protecting each one. In the following we propose a heuristic emergence process for finding the optimal allocation of limited resources to nodes and links such that the total amount of commodity flowing to the sink nodes is maximized.

Flow optimization is an old problem in operations research, so this problem should be an easy one to solve. However, the following problem has no known closed-form solution because it asks, "What is the optimal allocation of resources to links and nodes, such that the *expected value of flow* to sink nodes is maximized?" This formulation poses some analytical challenges, as we show. Once again, the simple network of Fig. 11.1a is used to illustrate the technique.

Consider additional properties of a directed-flow network for the example in Fig. 11.1a, as follows. Let node/link capacity be equated with consequence, C_i; let max DA_i be equal to the cost of vulnerability removal; v_i, equal to vulnerability; and g, equal to degree, as before. To simplify the notation, define availability a_i as the probability that each node/link will *not* fail:

C_i	Consequence or loss due to failure in node/link i
max DA_i	Resource needed to completely remove vulnerability
a_i	$(1-v_i)$: probability that node/link i will not fail (availability)
f_i	Amount of flow of a commodity, $0 \le f_i \le C_i$, through a node
h_i	Amount of flow of a commodity, $0 \le h_i \le C_i$, through a link
$w_j \xrightarrow{\text{flow}} h_i$	Commodity flows from node w_j to link h_i
$w_j \xleftarrow{\text{flow}} h_i$	Commodity flows from link h_i to node w_j.
n	Number of nodes; m number of links.

Now, define the flow at each node/link as the weighted minimum of its capacity or sum of inputs from incoming links/nodes:

$$\text{Links:} \quad h_i = a_i[\min\{C_i, f_j\}]; \; w_j \xrightarrow{\text{flow}} h_i$$

$$\text{Nodes:} \quad f_i = a_i\left[\min\left\{C_i, \sum_{w_j \xrightarrow{\text{flow}} h_i} h_j\right\}\right]$$

In other words, the amount of commodity flowing through a node/link is limited by its capacity, and by the product of availability a_i times incoming flows. *Expected flow* is availability times actual flow. In a sense, expected flow is the likelihood of a certain level of commodity flowing through a node/link. For links, this means that the expected amount of commodity is equal to its expected source node flow or expected maximum consequence. For nodes, this means that expected flow is the expected sum of incoming link flows, or its expected maximum consequence.

Sink node flow is simply the sum of inputs or maximum capacity, times availability. Source nodes have no incoming links, so their flow is determined by the availability and maximum capacity of the node:

$$\text{Sink node:} \quad f_i = a_i\left[\min\left\{C_i, \sum_{w_j \xrightarrow{\text{flow}} h_i} h_j\right\}\right]$$

$$\text{Source node:} \quad f_i = a_i C_i$$

The total output of a network is equal to the total of flows to all sink nodes F. The expected total output is the sum of expected flow over all sink nodes. This total is not limited by the capacity or availability of sink nodes because we do not want sink nodes to have such an overarching limiting effect on maximum flow. Furthermore, note that the sum total of output flow from each interior node may exceed the interior node's capacity—thus violating *Kirchhoff's law*. This overage may occur when a node has more than one outgoing link, each carrying an amount equal to the capacity of the node. For example, node w with consequence 100 and two outgoing links, transmits 100 units to each of the two outgoing links. Hence, it transmits a total of 200 units. This means that the total output may exceed the total supply provided by summing over all source node flows. We return to this problem later, but for the analysis of maximum flow, let F be equal to the summation of all flows reaching all sink nodes. F is the objective function that we want to maximize subject to budget B:

$$ F = \sum_{s=1}^{k} w_j - \sum_{s=1}^{k} a_s \left[\min \left\{ C_s, \sum_{w_s \xrightarrow{\text{flow}} h_i} h_j \right\} \right] \quad \text{subject to:} \quad 0 \le a_i \le 1 $$

Assuming a linear relationship between availability and resource expenditure, we equate availability with resource allocation as follows:

$$ a_i = \frac{DA_i}{\max DA_i} $$

Finally, resources are limited, so we add one more constraint:

$$ \sum_{i=1}^{n+m} a_i = \sum_{i=1}^{n+m} \frac{DA_i}{\max DA_i} \le B $$

Given a budget B, the objective is to find a_i such that total flow F is maximized:

$$ \max_{a_i} \left[F = \sum_{s=1}^{k} a_s \left[\min \left\{ C_s, \sum_{w_s \xrightarrow{\text{flow}} h_i} h_j \right\} \right] \right] $$

$$ \sum_{i=1}^{n+m} a_i \le B $$

This optimization problem seems simple at first glance. Using the Lagrange multiplier approach as we did earlier for the linear allocation algorithm leads to a system of non-linear equations of the form $xyz - \lambda = 0$. There is no unique solution (x, y, z) of such a nonlinear system, without more constrains than provided by the flow model, above. The mathematical system of simultaneous equations is underdetermined, so a unique solution is unobtainable. In fact, there is no guarantee that there is a unique solution—the reader may be able to find more than one maximum flow network identical to

Fig. 11.1a, but with different allocations of resource to individual nodes and links. This leads to a heuristic approach that computes the optimal solution by an emergent process.

11.5.4 Java Methods for Flow Heuristic

Calculation of network flow begins by identifying the sink nodes and then backtracking through the network to the source nodes, recursively, until all nodes and links have been traversed. This is carried out by one root method and two recursive submethods—one for nodes and the other for links. Method NW_doFlow() assumes that nodes have been previously painted red (sinks), green (sources), yellow (visited), or white, indicating their status as sinks, sources, visited, or internal nodes. It finds the red (sink) nodes and backtracks along a path from sink to source(s), calculating the flow at each node/link along its backtracking path. Cycles are avoided by coloring a node yellow as soon as it is visited. NW_doFlow() returns the total flow over all sink nodes.

```
public double NW_doFlow(){
    double totalFlow = 0;
    NW_RestoreNodeDegree();         //Restore color (White) and node degree
    for(int i = 0; i < nnodes; i++){    //Backtrack from sink (red) nodes
        if(nodes[i].color == Color.red) {
            totalFlow += nodeFlow(i);           //Objective function
        }
    }
        return totalFlow;
}//NW_doFlow
```

Methods nodeFlow and linkFlow do exactly what their names imply—they return the amount of commodity flow in units of consequence C_i for each node/link. Note that each node/link has an associated flow, probability of failure, and consequence c. These program variables match the mathematical formulation as follows:

nodes/edges.flow:	f_i
nodes/edges.ProbOfFailure:	v_i, where v_i is vulnerability
nodes/edges.maxDA:	max DA_i
nodes/edges.C:	C_i

Method nodeFlow calls method linkFlow, then linkFlow calls nodeFlow, and so on. So, the two methods recursively backtrack from sink to source, alternating between nodes and links until a source node is found. In terms of graph theory, NW_doFlow() constructs a *spanning tree* that reaches from source to sink node(s). For example, the spanning tree of the network in Fig. 11.1a contains all nodes and links, except for link 2, between nodes 1 and 3. The network is connected, so every node is reachable from every sink node, but it is not necessary to include every link in the spanning tree.

```
//Recursively calculate flow
private double nodeFlow(int node){
    double flow = 0;
    if(nodes[ node] .color == Color.yellow)        //Already visited node
      return nodes[ node] .flow;
    if(nodes[ node] .color == Color.green){         //Source node
        flow = nodes[node].C*(1.0-nodes[node].ProbOfFailure);
        nodes[node].flow = flow;
        return flow;
    }
    if(nodes[ node] .color == Color.white)
    nodes[node].color = Color.yellow;              //Mark it as visited
    for(int j = 0; j < nedges; j++){              //Process all incoming links
      if(edges[ j] .to == node){
        flow += Math.min(nodes[node].C, linkFlow(j))*(1.0-
nodes[node].ProbOfFailure);
          }
    }
    nodes[node].flow = flow;
    return flow;
    }//nodeFlow

    //Recursively calculate flow
    public double linkFlow(int link){
      Edge e = edges[link];
      double flow = Math.min(e.C, nodeFlow(e.from))*(1.0-e.ProbOfFailure);
      e.flow = flow;
      return flow;
    }
```

11.5.5   Network Flow Resource Allocation

Lacking a closed-form solution to optimal resource allocation in flow networks forces us to turn to empirical methods. We study the properties of a heuristic that can find an optimal solution by emergence but does not guarantee optimality every time. Instead, the *emergent flow optimization heuristic* finds an optimal solution most of the time. If we run the emergent process many times, and select the best solution from the sample, we can obtain what we think is the best allocation. However, we cannot guarantee that it is best!

Like all of the emergent processes proposed in this book, the optimal flow emergent process is extremely simple. Initially, the budget is distributed along the maximum flow paths as determined by the efficiency metric: $\min C_k / \max DA_i$, where $minC_k$ is the smallest consequence found along all paths from sink k to all source nodes. We obtain $minC_k$ by setting availability to 100%, computing maximum flow, and then rank-ordering sink nodes. The flow from sink node k is exactly $minC_k$.

Starting from the highest-flow sink, backtrack along a path defined by maximizing $minC_k/maxDA_i$ until reaching a source node. Then, reverse the process, stepping from source to sink, allocating as much of the budget as possible, to nodes and links along the maximum $minC_k/maxDA_i$ path. The logic of this initialization phase is that maximum $minC_k/maxDA_i$ paths better utilize resources. But, as the simple example shows, this is not always the case. Hence, the heuristic must guard against this counter-intuitive scheme using a second phase.

The initial phase is followed by an extensive emergence phase, whereby a small amount of availability is exchanged between node/link pairs, the output flow is recalculated and compared with the previous output, and so forth, until the sum total of all flows into sink nodes reaches a maximum. This process continues indefinitely, or until it appears that further increase in flow is unobtainable. The logic of this phase is that maximum flow will emerge from small changes—over a large amount of time—because successful exchanges are kept and unsuccessful exchanges are rejected.

Emergent Optimal Flow

1. Initially, set $a_i = 1$ for all nodes/links, and compute the maximum possible flow, F_{max}. This establishes a ranking among sink nodes, from highest flow, to lowest flow: $f_{j_1} \geq f_{j_2} \geq \cdots f_{j_z}$. It also determines $minC_k$: $minC_{j_1} = f_{j_1}$, $minC_{j_2} = f_{j_2}, \ldots, minC_{j_z} = f_{j_z}$.

2. Paint sink nodes red, source nodes green. Reset the availability of all nodes/links to zero: $a_i = 0$. Set the *available budget* $b' = B$.

3. Phase 1: Repeat until all sink nodes $s = 1, 2, \ldots, k$, have been processed, or the available budget has reached zero ($b' \leq 0$):

   a. Find a maximal path from sink node s to source node z by selecting each node/link i according to the highest efficiency ratio: $minC_s/maxDA_i$; that is, follow the maximum $minC_s/maxDA_i$ path from sink to source node.

   b. Starting from source node z identified in step 3a, backtrack to sink node s along the maximal path, allocating $DA_i = \min(b', maxDA_i)$ to each node/link along the path.

   c. Deduct each allocation from the available budget: $b' = b' - DA_i$.

4. Phase 2: If any budget b' remains, spread it evenly across all nodes/links with less than $max\ DA_i$ allocation.

5. Repeat ad infinitum:

   a. Randomly select a DONOR node/link and RECIPIENT node/link. Exchange one unit of resource: take one unit of DA_{DONOR} from DONOR and give it to RECIPIENT.

TABLE 11.4   Allocation of Resources via Flow Analysis

Node/Link	C	maxDA	DA	Vulnerability (%)	Flow	Risk
Node 1	10	15	8.5	43	5.7	4.3
Node 2	20	5	0.0	100	0.0	20.0
Node 3	10	10	8.5	15	4.8	1.5
Node 4	5	5	0.0	100	0.0	5.0
Node 5	15	1	1.0	0	4.8	0.0
Link 1	10	1	0.0	100	0.0	10.0
Link 2	10	1	0.0	100	0.0	10.0
Link 3	10	1	1.0	0	5.7	0.0
Link 4	10	1	0.0	100	0.0	10.0
Link 5	10	1	1.0	0	4.8	0.0
Totals	110	41	20.0	—	4.81	60.8

b. Calculate total flow.

c. If total flow decreases, reverse the DONOR/RECIPIENT allocations: put back one unit to DONOR and reinstate RECIPIENT. Otherwise, do nothing.

This algorithm is implemented in program *NetworkAnalysis.jar* as "Max Flow," which produces the allocation shown in Table 11.4 for the simple network of Fig. 11.1a with a budget of 20 units. Phase 1, for example, identifies the first maximal path from node 5, through link 5 to node 3, then link 2 to node 2, and finally, link 1 to node 1. As it turns out, this is not the path that yields optimal flow, but only an initial allocation. In phase 1, $minC$ for sink nodes 4 and 5 are 10 and 5, respectively. Node 5 is selected as the starting point because $minC_5/maxDA_5$ is greatest for node 5: $\frac{10}{1}$, versus $\frac{5}{5} = 1$ for node 4.

Following link 5 to node 3, and then link 2 to node 2 yields the maximal path, because $minC/maxDA$ for link 2 is 10, and $minC/maxDA$ for node 2 is 4. Continuing with link 1, phase 1 reaches source node 1, where it stops. Backtracking along this path, allocate 15 units of budget to node 1, one unit to link 1, five units to node 2, one unit to link 2, and so forth, until the budget decrements to zero, or sink node 5 is reached. If there is sufficient budget, do the same for the maximal path from sink node 4 to source node 1.

As it turns out, the optimal allocation excludes links 2 and 1, and node 2, for a budget of 20 units (see Table 11.4). Phase 2 of the algorithm takes over and gradually shifts resources from these two links and node, because flow is increased by allocation to the shorter (direct) path from node 1, through link 3 to node 3, and through link 5 to node 5. Thus, nodes 1, 3, 5, and links 3 and 5 receive nonzero allocations, thus establishing a maximal flow path from source to sink.

Method NW_doFlow() returns a flow of 4.81 units using the allocation vector *DA* of Table 11.4. This is the best flow possible with a budget of 20 units. Because links are very cost-efficient, they are allocated the full amount, reducing their vulnerability to zero. Next, the source and sink nodes are protected as much as the budget will allow, while securing intermediate node 3.

First, note that this resource allocation vector is very different from the allocation vector obtained by the linear and attacker–defender algorithms. Maximum flow reduces risk to 60.8 units versus 16 units for the linear allocation strategy. Flow optimization tends to spread resources along a path, rather than concentrate them on critical nodes. In fact, flow optimization distributes most of the limited resources along a *critical path*, defined by the ratio of minimum consequence to maximum vulnerability elimination cost max*DA*. The emergent heuristic selects a path containing highest efficiency ratios—not lowest risk.

Flow optimization defines vulnerability in terms of maximum flow, rather than minimum risk. This is a departure from the objective of reducing risk. In other words, flow maximization may lead to high network risk because the two objective functions are different. Maximization of flow dilutes resources because it spreads them along a path, which leads to a much higher network risk.[3]

Finally, the emergent heuristic does not define the magnitude of the unit of resource exchanged between DONOR and RECIPIENT. This is problematic because a small setting such as 0.01 is prone to entrapment in a false maximum. If steps are too small, the emergent process can never escape a pothole in the road to maximization. On the other hand, a large unit of exchange is prone to stop short of the maximum due to low resolution—the pothole is simply too small to fall into! Running *NetworkAnalysis.jar* with step size of 0.1, initially, and then lowering it to 0.01 after 5,000 iterations produced the maximum flow of 4.81, shown in Table 11.4. A total of over 20,000 iterations were required to find the maximum flow!

The unit of exchange—called `Dollar_Step` in program *NetworkAnalysis.jar*—should initially be set high. A good approximation is to set it equal to approximately 1% of the largest max*DA* value. As the emergence gets closer to the maximum fixed point, the unit of exchange should be decreased. This makes it possible for the process to resolve small changes in the objective function (flow), and seek out the pinnacle of maximum flow. The smallest unit of exchange allowed in program *NetworkAnalysis.jar* is 0.01.

In summary, the emergent process described here is based on two major claims that have yet to be proved:

1. Resources are best allocated along a path that is most efficient in terms of resource utilization, min*C*/max*DA*. Phase 1 is used to get "close" to the optimal solution, thereby avoiding false maxima that may stop further gains before reaching the true maximum flow.
2. A randomized exchange of small amounts of resource eventually leads to a maximum fixed point. This claim has not been proved, but in practice, randomization reaches the maximum fixed point if the unit of exchange is properly

---

[3]This is an artifact of how we define network risk as much as the fact that resources are spread along paths.

chosen—most of the time. However, there is little guidance on how to select a unit of exchange. This remains an open research problem.

Regardless of these weaknesses, the emergent process finds maximum flow allocations that utilize limited resources in the most efficient and effective manner. In practice, it may take many trials to find the maximum fixed point on modest networks of a few hundred nodes. Each trial may consume copious amounts of computer time, but if the answer is important, expending computer time is worthwhile.

11.5.6 Maximum Flow in Structured Networks

Does maximum flow depend on the topology of a network? Suppose that we hold all variables constant, such as network size n, number of links m, and node/link properties C and maxDA, and vary the topology of the network. Let the network's topology be either random, scale-free, or small-world. Further, let the budget vary, so that we can observe how each class of network utilizes resources.

Figure 11.9 shows results of optimal allocation to maximize flow through one random and two scale-free networks, versus budget. As budget increases, we expect the level of flow to also increase. But the shape of the increase is surprising. The relationship is linear for a random network, and linear for a scale-free network containing one source (hub) and many sinks (reversed scale-free). Surprisingly, the relationship is nonlinear for a scale-free network containing one sink and many sources!

The ER (Erdos–Renyi) generative procedure produces random networks with a uniform distribution of source and sink nodes. It is also expected that paths are roughly of the same length and cost-effective in terms of C/maxDA. Therefore,

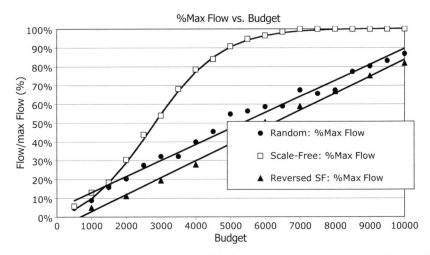

Figure 11.9 Percentage of maximum possible flow versus resource budget, with $n = 50$, $m = 100$ ($\Delta m = 2$), $C = 100$, maxDA $= 100$ for all nodes and links.

the proportion of flow reaching sink nodes follows a straight line. The more budget made available, the more commodity flows. This satisfies intuition.

The plot of flow versus budget for the two scale-free networks is nonintuitive, and its shape is unexpected. The BA (Barabasi–Albert) generative procedure for produc-ing scale-free networks is set up to direct all links toward the network, as they are added. This produces a directed network with many sources and only one sink, typi-cally the network's hub node. If we reverse the direction of all links, a scale-free network with many sinks and only one source is produced.

Figure 11.9 shows results for both: scale-free and reversed scale-free. The scale-free network with many sources but only one sink allocates resources so that flow follows a logistics curve, while the reversed link scale-free network (one source, many sinks) produces a linear relationship similar to that of a random network. In other words, optimal allocation of resources to maximize flow produces a linear increase in output when there are many output nodes, but a logistics curve when there is only one output node.

Why does the single-sink scale-free network obey a logistics curve? This is a classic example of typical behavior of a system under heavy demand but with limited supply. In other words, there is a scarcity of nodes to allocate resources to, when only one output node is present. Initially, the percentage of commodity allowed to flow rises rapidly, but as fewer and fewer nodes are able to deliver an increase in flow, the returns diminish along the flattening S curve. The curve fit is textbook-perfect for the following equation:

$$\frac{F}{\max F} = \frac{1.07}{(1 + 15e^{-B/1000})} - \frac{1.07}{1 + 15}; B = 1000, 2000, \ldots$$

For example, the percentage of maximum flow obtained from a scale-free network with parameters defined in Fig. 11.9 and a budget $B = 5000$ is 90.5%:

$$\frac{F}{\max F} = \frac{1.07}{(1 + 15e^{-5000/1000})} - \frac{1.07}{1 + 15} = 0.972 - 0.067 = 0.905$$

Random networks linearly utilize resources to produce maximum flow; structured networks such as the scale-free network studied here nonlinearly utilize resources. A shortage of sink nodes creates a bottleneck that cuts off further increases in flow, regardless of how many resources are allocated. The logistics curve of flow versus resource budget obeys the *law of diminishing returns* almost perfectly.

Small-world networks have no source or sink nodes, but if we insert a source and sink node into a small-world network, it will also behave nonlinearly. Flow in a small world depends principally on how close a source/sink node is to a shortcut link. Furthermore, addition of one source and one sink node creates a supply shortage/bot-tleneck similar to that of the single sink scale-free network, which means that the relationship between budget and maximum flow will be nonlinear. Exploration of maximum flow allocation in a small-world network is left as an exercise for the reader.

11.6   STABILITY RESILIENCE IN KIRCHHOFF NETWORKS

In many applications of network science to real-world systems, it is important to protect the stability of the network as well as its nodes and links. For example, electrical circuits, power grids, and mechanical control systems with feedback links may not become disconnected by removal of one or more links, but they may become unstable with the removal of a single link. Potential instability lurks beneath the surface of almost any network containing the flow of some commodity such as water, electrons, Internet packets, and signals in biological systems. Hence, this form of resilience cannot be ignored.

We introduced closed-system Kirchhoff networks in Chapter 9. These networks model directional flow in a system without sources and sinks. Obviously, flow in a directional network is seriously disrupted if a source or sink node becomes disconnected from the network. But the potentially destabilizing effect caused by removal of certain internal links has yet to be fully explored in the literature. We show that removal of a single link can lead to destruction of the entire network by destabilizing Kirchhoff flow. Once destabilized, a Kirchhoff network cannot regain stability unless necessary and sufficient conditions for sync are not met by the remaining nodes/links of the network.

Recall from Chapter 9 that a Kirchhoff network synchronizes if two conditions are met: (1) its *Kirchhoff eigenvalue* is less than one, and (2) it contains relatively prime length cycles. A simple example of an unstable Kirchhoff network is any ring network of size greater than 2. A Kirchhoff network cannot regain stability if it has a pinned source node, but it may restabilize if link removal leads to a sink (but not source) node. If a source node is created by the removal of a link, we are not concerned in this analysis. This special case is left as an exercise for the reader.

Reconsider the Pointville power grid of Fig. 9.8 in Chapter 9. Removal of the link from Calvert PWR to Minor (link 5) does not block flow in the system because of redundant paths provided by Calvert PWR $\rightarrow$ SS5 $\rightarrow$ Minor, and Calvert PWR $>$ SS4 $\rightarrow$ Minor. In fact, if we consider feedback link 13 (from load to generators) as a control link rather than an electron-carrying power line, then flow optimization with a budget of 1000 units provides 99% of maximum power flow for consequence $= 100$, max$DA = 50$, for all nodes and links. Removal of link 5 has very little effect on flow—a budget of 1000 units still protects the flow of 99% of maximum power under the same conditions. The electrons simply flow through the redundant path. However, removal of link 5 destabilizes the network, and renders it unable to sync! This means that the Kirchhoff network destabilizes and causes the power grid to fail.

Removing any of the following single links destabilizes the Pointville power grid: link 1 (between generators and Calvert PWR), link 5 (between Calvert PWR and minor), or link 10 (between minor and load). Removal of these links has little or no effect on the flow capacity of the network, but they are essential to the stability of the network. In other words, loss of capacity due to removal of a single link is not as critical as loss of stability. Link resilience is high, but stability resilience is low.

The Pointville power grid illustrates yet another definition of *critical link*. Such links are identified by calculating the network's Kirchhoff eigenvalue, and the lengths of all cycles remaining in the network after removal of each link. If link removal increases the Kirchhoff eigenvalue to greater than one, or any two cycles fail to have relatively prime lengths, the link is critical to stability. This is a prescription for determining link stability of any network.

The following critical link analysis algorithm "removes" each link, one at a time, and computes the Kirchhoff eigenvalue and cycle lengths of the remaining cycles in the network. The network becomes unstable if the eigenvalue is greater than one or the lengths of cycles are *not* relatively prime numbers. If one or both of these conditions exist, the link is marked as "critical." Each link is tested, and if one is found to be critical, then the entire network is vulnerable to removal of that link.

Program *NetworkAnalysis.jar* paints critical links red, indicating that removal of the link destabilizes the network. For the Pointville power grid example, *NetworkAnalysis.jar* finds three critical links: link 1 (generators → Calvert PWR), link 5 (Calvert PWR → Minor), and link 10 (minor → load), and paints them red. Therefore, $\frac{3}{14} = 21.4\%$ of the links are marked as critical. The stability resilience of Pointville power grid is $\frac{11}{14} = 78.6\%$.

Critical Link Analysis

1. Repeat for each link L in the network:
    a. Mark the link as "removed." Let q be 1 if there are no cycles or if there are cycles with relatively prime lengths.
    b. Compute Kirchhoff eigenvalue ε_k, and cycle lengths for the network without marked link L.
    c. If there are no cycles, set $q = 1$; otherwise set $q = 0$. If there are cycles and any two are relatively prime in length, set $q = 1$.
    d. If $\varepsilon_k > 1.0$ or $q \neq 1$, paint L red and mark it as critical.

This algorithm may be time-consuming, because it computes an eigenvalue and cycle lengths of cycles up to length n by raising system matrix B to a power B^n for each link. Matrix multiplication requires $O(n^2)$ calculations; B^n and eigenvalue calculations require $O(n^3)$ calculations. Therefore, a network with n nodes and m links requires $O(mn^3)$ floating-point calculations!

Curiously, random networks contain many cycles, so the likelihood that the lengths of any two cycles are relatively prime numbers is high. Therefore, random networks are inherently stable! For example, a random network with $n = 50$, $m = 150$ is likely to contain 50–100 cycles. It is necessary to contain a cycle of only lengths 2 and 3 to achieve the relatively prime condition, because 2 and 3 are relatively prime numbers.

Scale-free networks typically have few cycles, but they contain many sources and sinks. Therefore, scale-free networks are inherently unstable. Rewiring the network to eliminate sources and sinks introduces cycles, and the likelihood that two or more cycles are relatively prime numbers in length means that a closed system scale-free network is likely to sync. Therefore, a cyclic scale-free network has a small number of critical links.

Finally, small-world networks have no sources or sinks, but they have many cycles; hence they are likely to sync, and are therefore stable. Addition of only a few random links is likely to introduce cycles with relatively prime lengths. Therefore, small-world networks, like random networks, are prone to stability—none of their links are critical.

Critical links exist in structured flow networks such as an electrical power grid. This is not just a theory—the 2003 power grid blackout affected 50 million people in the United States and Canada, and was perhaps due to a single link tripping in Ohio. The 11 western states of the United States and parts of western Canada were without power for many hours following the failure of a single tieline near the border between Oregon and California in 1997. These failures occur even though the electrical utility companies run sophisticated modeling and simulation software to predict and control power surges throughout the grid. Could it be that network science holds the key to understanding such complex systems? This is left as an exercise for the reader.

11.7 EXERCISES

11.1. Suppose that the simple network of Fig. 11.1a contains nodes and links with identical consequences equal to 2, and identical vulnerability reduction costs equal to 1. What is the optimal defender's allocation pattern and normalized network risk for a budget of 5:

(a) Using the random allocation strategy?

(b) Using the linear vulnerability reduction allocation?

(c) Using the exponential vulnerability reduction allocation?

(d) Using the maximum flow optimization heuristic?

11.2. Using the same network as in Exercise 11.1, and an attacker budget of 5 units and defender budget of 6 units, what is the optimal allocation of resources, and normalized network risk for:

(a) Random defender, random attacker?

(b) Linear defender, linear attacker?

(c) Exponential defender, exponential attacker?

(d) Exponential arms race?

11.3. In Exercises 11.1 and 11.2, consider all possible combinations of random, linear, and exponential strategies for both attacker and defender. What is the worst-case pair of strategies from the perspective of the defender?

11.4. Show that $r_k = V_R C_R + V_k C_k + V_L C_L$ for the barbell fault tree of Fig. 11.1b.

11.5. What is the value of network risk function Φ for the simple network defined by Fig. 11.1 and Table 11.1, and the linear allocation of $B = 10$, summarized in Table 11.2?

11.6. Show that network risk in the simple network of Table 11.2 rises from 29 to 43 units if the allocations to nodes 4 and 5 are exchanged.

11.7. Add two links to the simple network of Fig. 11.1a: one from node 4 to node 2, and a second link from node 5 to node 2. How many critical links does the revised network contain, and what are they?

11.8. Construct a plot of percentage of maximum flow versus budget, as in Fig. 11.9, for a 2-regular small-world network with $n = 200$, $p = 4\%$, and budget ranging from 10% to 50% of initial risk. Create a single source and sink node at some random location in the network, and assume that consequences C and vulnerability reduction costs maxDA are 100 each, as in Fig. 11.9.

11.9. What is the normalized network risk of the Pointville power grid example for attacker and defender budgets equal to 300, using the arms race algorithm? What is it for the exponential attacker allocation versus exponential defender allocation strategies? What does this say about the difference between secret and public strategies?

11.10. What is the approximate number of links—as a percentage of the initial number—that must be removed by depercolation to cause the networks of Fig. 11.8 to separate with probability of 20%:

(a) For the random network?

(b) For the scale-free network?

(c) For the small-world network?

11.11. Is it necessary to check for a zero attacker allocation in the Java methods for computing $\ln(\lambda_1)$ and $\ln(\lambda_2)$? Why or why not?

11.12. What is the optimal defender's allocation for the simple network of Fig. 11.1a and Table 11.1, when using a defender's budget of 20 units, attacker's budget of zero units, and the exponential vulnerability reduction equation?

12

NetGain

Netgain is a property of networks containing competitive nodes that leverage the structure of a network to their advantage, typically through *preferential attachment* or some other *value proposition* associated with nodes and links. *Netgain networks* are appropriate models of networked societies whereby individual actors (nodes) adopt a product, idea, or service on the basis of a competitor node's value proposition, popularity, or fashion. Thus, a competition between one category of nodes, called *competitors*, for the attention of another category of nodes called *consumers* drives an emergent process that eventually leads to some stable fixed point for the network. In this chapter we explore the various methods of evolving a netgain network from a random initial state to a nonrandom or synchronized fixed point.

Since the late 1950s, netgain has appeared in the literature under a number of names such as *increasing returns*, *Metcalf's law*,[1] *network economy*, *friction-free economy*, and *network effect*. All of these terms have been used to describe any networked system that is more than the sum of its parts. Netgain is a form of emergence that shapes the network's topology according to some internal or external property such as product price, operational efficiency, or consumer preference. For example, a random social network (fans of a musician) may evolve into a scale-free network (most famous musician) because nodes prefer the "popularity" of a certain node (a "star"), which becomes the hub.

---

[1]The power of a network is proportional to the square of its size, n.

Network Science: Theory and Practice. By Ted G. Lewis
Copyright © 2009 John Wiley & Sons, Inc.

We claim that the cause of emergence of a certain state of a netgain network can be traced to some property of the network or some microrule operating at the microscopic level. If we can identify such a driving property or microrule, then perhaps we can explain how netgain systems work, and moreover, how they might be steered. In this chapter we are particularly interested in economic markets, and ask, how does a business, operating within a network economy, survive and prosper?

We assume that netgain networks accurately model consumers and competitors as nodes, links as product demand, and competition among competitors as an emergent process. We study what happens when a small number of competitors vie for consumer's attention and buying power. This allows us to investigate the behavior of markets as the number of competitors and products increase. The number of links that point from consumer nodes to competitor nodes is a measure of demand. Competitors are ranked according to their degree (demand for their product), and consumers indicate their loyalty to a competitor or its products by attaching a link to the preferred competitor node(s).

The formal study of netgain has its roots in epidemiology. Early models of the spread of an innovation through a market—called *diffusion*—treated innovation as an epidemic. The early diffusion models work well when we assume that the population is homogeneous and static. But, as we shall see in this chapter, purely epidemic models are inadequate to describe netgain networks, and especially dynamic networks that undergo topological change as a consequence of competition.

Netgain is more than the application of epidemic theory to the spread of an innovation through a static population. Netgain networks contain two different types of nodes—*consumers* and competitive *producers*. In addition, netgain networks undergo a transformation in their degree sequence distribution, node and link values, or both, as competition progresses through time. Netgain emergence reshapes the network, and hence is modeled by a dynamic and bipartite network, $G(t) = \{P(t), C(t), E(t), f(t)\}$, where $P(t)$ is the set of producers (competitors), $C(t)$ is the set of consumers, $E(t)$ is the set of links connecting consumers to competitors, and $f(t)$ is the mapping function $f: C \rightarrow P$. Network G is directed, such that a link from consumer node c_i to producer node p_j; $e: c_i \rightarrow p_j$, means that c_i has *adopted* a product, idea, or service produced by p_j.

A netgain network undergoes a transformation through *diffusion*, defined as the process of product, idea, or service adoption in a social network. Actors are exposed to information regarding a product, for example, and decide whether to buy (adopt) or reject the product depending on the information they receive via *influence links*. However, unlike the actors in influence networks studied earlier, netgain actors alter the network's topology when they adopt or drop a product—by adding or deleting a link to a producer node. In simple terms, diffusion is the process of adding or dropping links in netgain networks.

Diffusion research is concerned with modeling the diffusion process. Many mathematical models have been developed to describe diffusion processes. This chapter is much less ambitious—we introduce the rudimentary elements of diffusion as it pertains to social network analysis. For more general discussions, we recommend the texts by Stoneman and Forman (Stoneman, 2002; Forman, 2005). In this chapter

1. We study several classes of netgain networks (simple monopoly, multiproduct, nascent market, creative destruction, and mergers–acquisitions) that synchronize and reach a fixed-point market share defined as: market_share$(v) =$ degree$(v)/m$, for all competitor nodes, $v = 1,2,3,\ldots,n_p$.

2. Competition in a simple *monopoly network* results in the rise of a single monopoly competitor, assuming a random netgain network, initially the number of links m equal to the number of consumers n_c, and a market defined by competitors offering a single product of equal value.

3. The fixed-point market share achieved by competitors in a *multiproduct* netgain network is approximated by a series of power laws that define market positions of an oligopoly of competitors when $m \gg n_c$, and products have equal consumer value. Thus, multiproduct markets are inherently oligopolies.

4. An *innovator* is a competitor that first introduces a new product, service, or idea into a market. Innovators are *first movers*. An *imitator* is a competitor that copies or mimics the innovator. Imitators may also be *fast followers*, especially if they are quick to copy the innovator. All things being equal, an innovator rises to a monopoly position simply by being first to market.

5. Fixed-point market share in a nascent market network is governed mainly by the probability that a consumer (randomly) subscribes to multiple competitors through a Poisson process of selection. This places a lower bound on the fixed-point market share distribution of {63%, 26%, 8%, 2%] for $n_p \geq 3$ competitors. The number 3 is significant, suggesting that nascent markets are capable of supporting only two to three leading competitors, regardless of the number of competitors that enter the market.

6. The speed of a market is defined as *market speed* $=$ (new link arrival rate/new competitor arrival rate). As market speed increases, the innovator (first mover) has an advantage over imitators (fast followers). Conversely, the slower the market, the better chance an imitator has of surpassing the innovator. This may explain why first movers have an advantage in high-technology (hi-tech) industries.

7. Schumpeter's *creative destruction* is an emergent process modeled by creative destruction networks that represent a consumer's value proposition as a competitor node's value (Schumpeter, 1942); weak competitors increase their node value while strong competitors increase their profit margins (lower node value). This leads to the downfall of the monopoly competitor and the rise of subsequent leaders—a process called *creative destruction*. We show that creative destruction leads to industry cycles—and the rise and fall of market leaders.

8. Simulation of the *square-root law* of switching in a random creative destruction network shows that a stable fixed point emerges regardless of now many

competitors, $n_p \geq 3$, set out to dominate. In addition, one competitor will emerge and remain dominant. If the minimum player threshold is small enough, a fast follower will also emerge with much less share, and remain second, forever. The lower the minimum player threshold, the higher the number of fast followers that emerge. We show that the fixed-point market share of the leader, in a creative destruction network with monopoly threshold $m = 60\%$, is approximately: market_share_leader$(m,p) = m + 5*p*(1-p-m)$, where m is the market share that defines a monopoly, and $0 \leq p \leq (1-m)$.

9. A merger of competitors in a mergers–acquisitions network is defined as the merger of two competitor nodes such that the links of the smaller market share node are assigned to the larger market share node. We show that mergers and acquisitions speed up the inevitable formation of a monopoly or duopoly when combined with creative destruction. We further show that the fixed-point market share of the leader, in a creative destruction network plus merging (monopoly threshold $m = 72\%$) is: market share leader$(m,p) = m + 6.5*p*(1-p-m)$, where m is the market share that defines a monopoly, and $0 \leq p \leq (1-m)$.

12.1 CLASSICAL DIFFUSION EQUATIONS

A social network provides a vector for the spread of products, ideas, or services through a society. Products, ideas, and services are generally divided into innovations and imitations. An *innovation* is any product, service, or idea that is first in its category, while an *imitation* is a variation on the innovation. We call the process of widespread adoption of either an innovation or imitation *diffusion*.

In a business sense, *diffusion* is the process of product adoption, which is modeled in a netgain network as the insertion of a link between a consumer node and a producer node. *Adoption* is an actor's decision to use a new product, idea, or service, on the basis of information provided to the consumer through separate mechanisms described in previous chapters. For example, word-of-mouth diffusion occurs when people talk to one another about a product, and media diffusion occurs when an advertisement appears on a television screen.

To understand the mechanisms of diffusion, we model adoption processes as microrules in an emergent network, and then classify the resulting macroscale patterns in terms of network topologies. For example, we show that diffusion of innovation based on simple measures of product acceptance such as *popularity* result in scale-free network topology. Additionally, we observe the formation of macroscale patterns in social networks as a consequence of competitor node's state or *value proposition*. Convergence due to the value of nodes synchronizes the social network around a stable fixed point. For example, a netgain network always converges to a fixed point in terms of market share, when a square-root microrule is repeatedly applied to its nodes and links.

Emergence of a ruling *duopoly* of competitor nodes is a consequence of competition among many nodes in an initially random network. The persistence of monopoly and duopoly patterns emerging from simulations in this chapter raise intriguing questions about the inevitability of dominant competitors. Is it inevitable, in any openly competitive market, that one, two, or three firms will dominate? Is it inevitable that smaller firms always die out?

12.1.1 Market Diffusion Equations

Of course it is not necessary to use network science to model diffusion. In fact, the earliest models of diffusion were based on mathematical epidemic equations.[2] These equations assume that diffusion of an innovation or imitation is equivalent to the spread of an infectious disease. The more infectious the product is, the faster the diffusion of the innovation. In terms of product marketing, the number of infected actors is called *market penetration* or *market share*, instead of *infection density*. *Adoption rate* is used instead of *infection rate* to describe the speed with which an innovation spreads.

High market share—the high percentage of the population that has adopted the new product in previous timesteps—increases the adoption rate, which in turn elevates market penetration, and so forth. This kind of feedback mechanism is yet another interpretation of *preferential attachment*. In an idealized world, preferential attachment leads to a logistics growth curve similar to the growth curve obtained in Chapter 8 (Ryan, 1943).

In a netgain network, the function describing adoption rate versus time may be different, because the network's topology may inhibit or accelerate the rate of adoption. This is one of the questions we pose, "Is diffusion affected by network topology?" If the answer is "No," then the tried-and-true equations from epidemiology will suffice.

Market share at time t, $0 \leq s(t) \leq 1$, like *infection density* in a social network, is a basic measure of effectiveness in product diffusion. It is the fraction of the population that has adopted a product. Obviously, market penetration varies with time—starting near zero and increasing to some maximum, and then remaining there, or declining after some period of time. *Adoption rate* is the first derivative of market share versus time: $\delta s / \delta t$. Plotting market share versus time, $s(t)$ versus t, gives the *adoption curve* of a product.

Figure 12.1 illustrates some well-known adoption curves for common products, and suggests that $s(t)$ is simply a logistics function. We learned in Chapter 8 that the most elementary solution to the *Kermack–McKendrick* equations is a logistics curve. This seems to confirm the equivalence of diffusion and the spread of an

---

[2]Even today, the term "viral marketing" is used to refer to the use of epidemic modeling to describe the diffusion of an innovation.

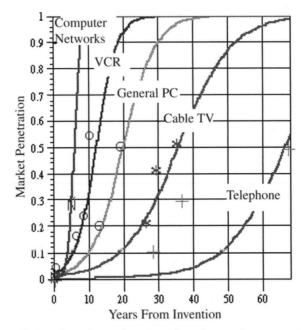

Figure 12.1 Diffusion of new innovations through society: market penetration as fraction of total population that adopted the product since its invention.

infection. Indeed, Bass was the first to apply an epidemic model to explain product adoption (Bass, 1969). Figure 12.1 substantiates the Bass model:

Bass Equation

$$s(t) = \frac{1 - e^{-bt}}{1 + ae^{-bt}}$$

$$s(0) = 0$$

$$t > 0$$

(where a and b are constant parameters). The Bass functions for the adoptions in Fig. 12.1 may be obtained by suitable least-squares approximations to estimate parameters a and b. Clearly, the adoption rates shown for telephone, cable TV, personal computer, and Internet market penetration have steadily increased as technology advances. The length of time to achieve 50% penetration has declined by a factor of ≥ 10 over the past 100 years. Thus, parameters a and b differ from one innovation to another, and change over time.

The S-shaped adoption curves produced by various values of a and b in the Bass equation rise exponentially from zero to an *inflection point* $t^* = \ln(a)/b$. Then, the curve gradually flattens out until reaching its *saturation point* s^*, which in Fig. 12.1 is 100%. We might think of the exponentially rising part as representing a period of *increasing returns*, and the latter part as representing *diminishing returns*. The inflection point t^* represents a turning point from an *early adopter* to a *mature market*.

Fisher and Pry (Bass, 2001; Norton, 1987) proposed a simplified but closely related model of diffusion. In their model, the time derivative of market share $\delta s/\delta t$ is proportional to the share already taken, $s(t)$, and the share that remains, $[1 - s(t)]$:

Fisher–Pry Equation

$$\frac{\partial s(t)}{\partial t} = rs(t)[1 - s(t)]$$

$$s(0) = 0$$

$$t > 0$$

(where r is a rate parameter). Assuming $s(0) = \frac{1}{2}$, this logistics equation can be solved as before:

$$s(t) = \frac{1}{1 + e^{-rt}}$$

$$t > 0$$

where r is the slope of the line:

$$\ln\left(\frac{s}{1 - s}\right)$$

The Fisher–Pry model is related to—but different from—the Bass model. Not only does it have different initial conditions; the Fisher–Pry formulation produces logistics curves with different slopes.[3] We can compare the two models by transforming the Fisher–Pry timescale to account for the difference in initial conditions, $s(0) = \frac{1}{2}$, instead of $s(0) = 0$. Substitution of $(t - t^*)$ for t, and insertion of an offset y yields an approximation to the Bass equation. In terms of Bass parameters, a, b, and t^*, the Fisher–Pry diffusion equation is as follows:

Modified Fisher–Pry Equation

$$s(t) = \frac{1}{1 + e^{-r(t-t^*)}} + y$$

$$s(0) \sim 0$$

$$t^* = \frac{\ln(a)}{b}$$

$$y = \frac{1}{1 + e^{bt^*}}$$

[3]The Fisher–Pry logistics curve will be slightly below an equivalent Bass logistics curve.

The foregoing pioneering work assumes homogeneous mixing of the market population and ignores the topology of social networks. It is inadequate to explain how some forms of network diffusion work. Specifically, it cannot predict what network topology will emerge from a market involving many competitors. We address this issue in a netgain network model that shows how simple preferential attachment leads to a scale-free-like topology. This confirms the Bass and Fisher–Pry models of diffusion for simple, single product markets, but it leaves open the question of multicompetitor, multiproduct markets. Additionally, netgain models may hold the key to explaining how unexpected disruptive technologies are able to displace market leaders in accordance with Schumpeter's *creative destruction* theory (Schumpeter, 1942).[4]

We extend the theory of diffusion in netgain networks by adding an emergence component: that competitor nodes vie for customer links through repeated application of microrules. One set of microrules simulates the application of a value proposition applied by customers when they compare products. Competitors are allowed to increase or decrease the value of their products to attract customers or optimize profit.

We show that a variable value proposition leads to a stable state of the network with one dominant competitor, and one (or two) much less successful followers. This theory suggests that a network containing a single monopoly and a single subordinate competitor is the most stable state for certain kinds of networks. This claim is confirmed by the simulation experiments described below.

12.1.2 Simple Netgain Networks

Does market share expansion in a finite-dimensional, random network behave according to the diffusion theories of Bass, Fisher, and Pry? We perform an experiment to find out. Consider the following netgain network. A randomly wired directed network of n_c consumer nodes, n_p competitor nodes, and m directed links is initially organized such that a link from consumer v_c to competitor v_p means that consumer v_c is a customer of competitor v_p. The network is random, initially, because each link connects to a randomly chosen competitor node. We allow more links than consumers so that we may model multiproduct companies.

Figure 12.2 illustrates such a network with three competitors and 40 consumers. Program *NetGain.jar* color-codes netgain nodes according to their function: consumers are solid black dots, and competitors are rectangular boxes with node index and node market share or product value inscribed within the rectangle. Market share cannot exceed 100%, and is computed very simply:

$$\text{Market\_share}(v_p) = \text{degree}(v_p)/m; \text{ where } m = \text{number of links}$$

---

[4]An Austrian economist and political scientist, Joseph Schumpeter (1883–1950) argued that capitalism leads to "creative destruction," in which incumbents are destroyed and replaced by new market leaders.

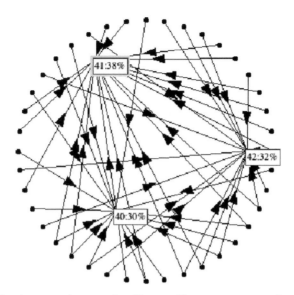

Figure 12.2 Random netgain network with $n_c = 40$ consumers, $n_p = 3$ competitors, and $m = 50$ random links. Competitor nodes are numbered and labeled with their market share percentages (shown here) or value propositions.

In fact, we do not allow duplicate links between consumer and competitor nodes, so market share will be less than degree$(v_p)/m$ when $m > n_c$. In this case

$$\text{Market\_share}(v_p) \leq \frac{n_c}{m};$$

Competitor nodes contain a value, which may be interpreted as the value of a product, service, or idea, from the perspective of the market. For example, the value of a commodity may be due to its relatively low price, high quality, or fashion statement. Product value is judged from the perspective of buyers as they compare products among competitors. This is the so-called *value proposition* that every competitor communicates to customers. For the time being, we assume value to be identical for all products and competitors.

Links are directed from consumer to competitor nodes, indicating that the consumer subscribes to a product offered by the competitor. Multiple (but not duplicate) links attached to a consumer node may be interpreted as split loyalty, or represent different products from different companies. If there are more links than consumers, $m > n_c$, we assume that the netgain network represents a multiproduct marketplace.

What happens in a random netgain network, over time, as customers change preferences and loyalties? What determines customer preference in a market such as the one depicted in Fig. 12.2? We address these questions by performing the following "popularity contest" emergent process. At each timestep, select a competitor node, $V_{\text{challenger}}$, at random, and a random link that points to node $V_{\text{challenger}}$. Rewire the link by connecting it to the node with the highest degree (market share). This simulates human *flocking behavior*—people want to own what other people own. It is also a simple variant of the scale-free network generation procedure described in Chapter 6.

Multiproduct Emergence

1. Initially generate a random netgain network with n_c consumer nodes, n_p competitor nodes, and m randomly placed directed links connecting consumer nodes to competitor nodes.
2. Repeat indefinitely or until halted by the user:
   a. Select link `any_link` at random; `any_link` connects `consumer_node` to `incumbent_node`, by definition.
   b. Select competitor node `challenger_node` at random.
   c. Switch the head of `any_link` from `incumbent_node` to `challenger_node` if the degree of `challenger_node` exceeds the degree of `incumbent_node`. Otherwise, do nothing.

What emergent network results from this simple process? Intuitively, the random network transforms into a *star network*—that is, the competitor with the largest initial market share will increase its market share because links are attracted to the node with the largest degree. In fact, this intuition applies only for the case where $m \leq n_c$. When there is a scarcity of consumer demand (limited number of links), the largest market share competitor gets even more market share until it becomes a monopoly with 100% of all links pointing to it.

Competitors drop out because their degree drops to zero—they are victims of a market *shakeout*. In every market there are a number of *laggards*, possibly a few *players* (competitors that are neither dominant, nor laggards), and possibly a *monopoly* competitor. In this case, all but one competitor drops out, leaving one monopoly competitor.

The multiproduct emergence process transforms a netgain network into a synchronized stable state defined by market share percentages that never change once they reach their fixed points. We call such a stable converged network, and the distribution of unchanging market share percentages, a *fixed point* of the converged network. All of the netgain networks studied in this chapter synchronize and reach their fixed-point market share distributions in finite time.

The simple single-product network confirms and supports the product diffusion model of Bass and Fisher–Pry. Regardless of its initial state, the single-product network reaches a monopoly fixed point. The leading competitor reaches its fixed-point market share according to the Bass and Fisher–Pry models (see Fig. 12.3). This can be observed by running program *NetGain.jar*, which fits a logistics equation to the market share data as the network evolves through time. Clearly, when $m \leq n_c$, the competitor with slightly more connections rises to the top in accordance with the Bass equation. It becomes a monopoly.

Because the initial state of the netgain network is random, competitors are allocated nearly the same number of links, initially. But one lucky competitor

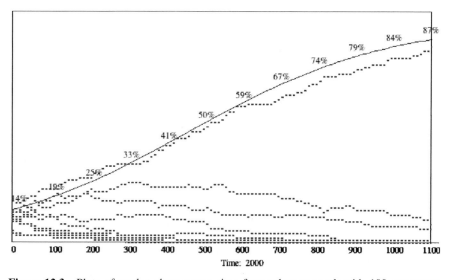

Figure 12.3 Plots of market share versus time for random network with 100 consumers, 5 competitors, initially, and 100 links, confirming the Bass equation.

serendipitously obtains more links than the others, which sends it on its way to a monopoly. Its market share rises according to the Bass equation:

$$s(t) = \frac{1 - e^{-bt}}{1 + ae^{-bt}}; \quad 0 \le t \le 1000$$

(where $a = 5.86$ and $b = 0.0039$). This equation matches the market share data of Fig. 12.3 almost perfectly! The other four competitors also rise in market share during the early stages, reach a peak, and then decline as the market leader accelerates because of the increasing returns effect of preferential attachment. The more market share a competitor has, the more it gets.

12.2 MULTIPRODUCT NETWORKS

A more interesting and realistic network contains multiple competitors offering multiple products so that $m \gg n_c$. Each consumer has multiproduct *preferences*, which may be spread across multiple competitors. In fact, consumers will have allegiances to more than one competitor simply because there are more links than consumers. Because of the abundance of links, the multiproduct network will evolve into an oligopoly of market leaders.

We model such a market the same way, starting with a random topology, followed by repeated application of preferential attachment. Once again, a dominant competitor emerges, but also a number of players and laggards emerge. In particular, the multiproduct netgain simulation shows that a number of competitors coexist with a dominant—even a monopolistic—competitor. In contrast to the simple emergence of a single monopoly examined above, multiproduct markets support multiple competitors. The fixed-point market share distribution supports a mixture of players, laggards, and one dominant competitor.

Figure 12.4 plots the simulated results of five competitors in a netgain network of $n_c = 100$ consumers, and $m \geq n_c$ links (demand). Competitors are ranked according to market share, with $s_1 \geq s_2 \geq s_3 \geq s_4 \geq s_5$. Intuitively, we expect the first 100 links to go to s_1, the next 100 links to s_2, and so forth, until all links have been assigned a competitor. But this does not happen. Instead, some links, once assigned to a competitor, never leave. Over time, the netgain network reaches a fixed point that defies the obvious. Instead of a single dominant competitor emerging, an oligarchy of competitors emerges! Why?

The market share curve for leading competitor s_1 in Fig. 12.4 is easily determined because the dominant competitor iteratively gets more market share up to the limit dictated by number of consumers. But why does its share of the market decline versus the ratio of links to customers? The adoption curve is clearly not a Bass or Fisher–Pry logistics curve.

As the total number of links increases beyond n_c, and the leader achieves its maximum of 100 links, the proportion of $100/m$ declines according to the relationship:

$$\text{Market\_share}(s_1) = \frac{n_c}{m} ; \, n_c \leq 100$$

$$= \frac{100}{m} ; \, n_c > 100$$

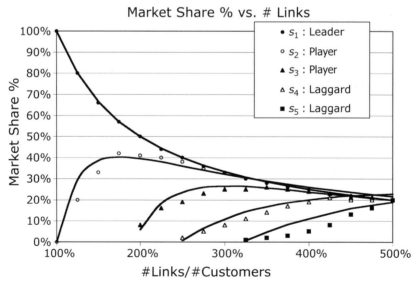

Market Share % vs. # Links

- s_1 : Leader
- s_2 : Player
- s_3 : Player
- s_4 : Laggard
- s_5 : Laggard

Figure 12.4 Emergence results for $n_c = 100$ consumers, $100 \leq m \leq 500$ links, and $n_p = 5$ competitors, initially. For low values of m/n_c, laggards drop out. For high values, several competitor nodes become players.

Therefore, market share of the dominant competitor decreases inversely with increase in number of links. The curve in Fig. 12.4 is clearly $O(1/m)$, which is a kind of *power law*.

In general, multiproduct emergence is so closely related to scale-free network emergence, that all data in Fig. 12.4 should fit a *power law*. The power law $1/[n_c/m]$ is an excellent fit to market_share(s_1), but is it suitable for estimating the fixed-point market share of the other competitors? The answer is "Yes," and the resulting modified power laws replace the single-product Bass and Fisher–Pry diffusion models.

Let $A_i = \sum_{j=1}^{i}$ market_share(s_j) be the *partially consumed market share* when competitors $s_1, s_2, \ldots, s_i$ have reached their ultimate market share values, and let B_i and C_i represent the *stickiness* resulting from reluctance to switch links as emergence of an oligarchy occurs. We obtain B_i and C_i by curve-fitting the following power laws to the data shown in Fig. 12.4. Then, the approximate market share of competitor s_{i+1}, $i \geq 1$ is

$$s_{i+1} = \frac{m/n_c - B_i - A_i}{(m/n_c - C_i)^{q_i}}; \quad i \geq 1$$

$$A_i = \sum_{j=1}^{i} \text{market\_share}(s_i)$$

where B_i, C_i, and q_i are obtained by curve fitting to the data of Fig. 12.4.

Table 12.1 summarizes parameter approximations obtained by curve fitting for each competitor in Fig. 12.4. As the number of links (demand) increases, A_i and B_i, also increase because of stickiness of links. As the number of links grows, all competitors reach an equal fixed point (20% each in Fig. 12.4) because there are enough links for all competitors to achieve their maximum of 100 links.

Intuitively, the dominant competitor should acquire 100 links, then the next dominant competitor should acquire the next 100 links, and so on until all links have been attached. For example, if $m = 300$, we would expect $s_1 = 33\%$, $s_2 = 33\%$, $s_3 = 33\%$, and all other competitor shares to decline to zero. Instead, repeated simulation of the network in Fig. 12.4 yields $s_1 = 33\%$, $s_2 = 33\%$, $s_3 = 25\%$, $s_4 = 8\%$, and $s_5 = 0\%$. Three laggards share the last 33%! Why?

TABLE 12.1   Stickiness Parameters for Fig. 12.4

Competitor i	B_i	C_i	q_i	Range of m/n_c
1	0	0	1	$m \geq n_c$
2	0	0	1.95	$m \geq n_c$
3	1.0	0.75	2.0	$m \geq 2n_c$
4	1.5	0.10	1.6	$m \geq 2.5n_c$
5	2.25	0	1.45	$m \geq 3n_c$

The multiproduct network convergence to an oligopoly and fixed-point market shares defy intuition, because some consumers are linked to all competitors. When this happens to consumer nodes v_1 and v_2, they cannot swap links to a stronger competitor because they are already connected. Duplicate links are not permitted, and so preferential attachment is no longer operative.

As the number of links goes up, the probability that a consumer node is already attached to a stronger competitor also rises. Stickiness is not simply a consumer's loyalty to a competitor—it is also a statistical fact that randomly chosen consumers can have n_p links. In fact, linking a consumer to k competitors is a Poisson process governed by the binomial distribution. Finding the expected fixed-point market share of any competitor in a multiproduct network is left as an exercise for the reader.

Application of the fixed-point approximation equations for a multiproduct market is straightforward. Simply get parameter values from Table 12.1 and plug them into the equations. For example, what is the approximate market share for each of five competitors when $m = 250$, $n_c = 100$? Applying the power-law equation just derived; we obtain

$$m/n_c = \frac{250}{100} = 2.5 \quad \text{so} \quad \frac{1}{[m/n_c]} = \frac{100}{250} = 0.40$$

$$s_1 = 100/250 = 40\%$$

$$A_2 = 40\%$$

$$s_2 = \frac{[12.5 - 0 - 0.4]}{[(2.5 - 0)^{1.95}]} = \frac{2.1}{5.97} = 35\%$$

$$A_3 = 40\% + 35\% = 75\%$$

$$s_3 = \frac{[2.5 - 1.0 - .75]}{[2.5 - 0.75)^{2.0}]} = \frac{0.5}{3.063} = 16\%$$

$$A_4 = 91\%$$

$$s_4 = \frac{[2.5 - 1.5 - 0.91]}{[(2.5 - 0.1)^{1.6}]} = \frac{0.09}{4.06} = 2\%$$

$$A_5 = 93\%$$

$$s_5 = 0 \quad \text{because} \quad m < 3n_c$$

The approximation $s = [40\%, 35\%, 16\%, 2\%, 0\%]$ compares favorably with the data in Fig. 12.4, yielding $[40\%, 38\%, 19\%, 2\%, 0\%]$ by simulation. Estimating the fixed-point market share without concern for stickiness yields $[40\%, 40\%, 20\%, 0\%, 0\%]$.

Multiproduct netgain networks evolve into scale-free networks. The exact distribution of links to nodes depends on the overall demand (m links), but generally the fixed-point distribution is a sharply declining power law. Multiproduct emergence leads to an oligopoly rather than a monopoly, characterized by a handful of leaders, some players, and possibly a laggard.

We have shown that a market leader emerges through preferential attachment in a simple single-product network, and follows the Bass diffusion equation. In this respect, finite, nonhomogeneous netgain networks behave as predicted by previous diffusion theory. But several assumptions were made in the process: (1) all products are considered of equal value as perceived by consumers; (2) the network starts out as a fully developed, but randomly connected, netgain network; and (3) there are not enough links to go around, so only one competitor survives.

In a multiproduct network there are many more links than consumers, so an oligopoly rises instead of a monopoly. Products are still considered of equal value as perceived by customers, and the network starts out random, but there is a "surplus" of links. This allows many competitors to survive, leading to an oligopoly. But competitors are limited by 100 links, and stickiness of links leads to fixed-point shares that obey a power law. Stickiness is a statistical fact of life—links are allocated to nodes according to a Poisson process that allows for some consumer nodes to be attached to all competitors. This nullifies the effects of preferential attachment.

One conclusion from this experiment is that monopolies emerge and thrive in economically poor social networks; that is, sparse netgain networks evolve into scale-free monopolistic networks. On the contrary, rich social networks—dense networks—evolve oligopolies. These are scale-free-like networks, and not purely scale-free. Affluent societies are able to support many producers, while poor societies cannot.

12.3 JAVA METHOD FOR NETGAIN EMERGENCE

Method `NW_doCompete()` implements the multiproduct emergence process for a network of n_c = nConsumers consumer nodes, n_p = nCompetitors competitor nodes, and m = nInputLinks links. The Java implementation paraphrases the *multiproduct emergence* algorithm described earlier almost perfectly.

First, `any_link: consumer -> incumbent` is randomly selected as a candidate link to be rewired. Next, a candidate challenger node is selected and its degree is compared with the degree of the incumbent node. Link `any_link` may be switched to `consumer -> challenger` if the degree of challenger is greater than the degree of the incumbent.

The Java method is very conservative. It checks for possible divide-by-0 arithmetic, and it uses method `NW_doAddLink()` to check for potential duplicate links. The rewired link is inserted before the old link is removed by method `NW_doCutLink()`. Global string **Message** communicates the status of the competition to the user through a display method that is not shown here. Other global parameters used by `NW_doCompete()` are nInputConsumers, nInputCompetitors, nInputLinks, nConsumers, and nCompetitors. These parameters are self-explanatory and can be changed through the preferences dialog of program *NetGain.jar*:

```
public void NW_doCompete(int t) {
    if(nInputConsumers <= 0 || nInputCompetitors <= 0 || nInputLinks <= 0) return;
    int any_link = (int)(nLinks*Math.random());           //Random link
    Link e = Links[any_link];
    int consumer_node = e.from;              //consumer node -> competitor node
    Node incumbent = nodes[e.to];        //links always point to competitor
    int challenger_node = nConsumers+(int)(nCompetitors*Math.random());
    Node challenger = nodes[challenger_node];
    double denominator = challenger.degree;
    if(incumbent.degree <= 0                        //Eliminate competitors with no share
        ||
        denominator <= 0) return;                   //Eliminate divide-by-zero error
    if(challenger.degree > incumbent.degree) { //Switch
        if(NW_doAddLink(consumer_node, challenger_node)) {//Avoid duplicate link
            NW_doCutLink(any_link);
            Message = "Switching to challenger: "+
                  [degree(challenger)="+Long.toString(challenger.degree)+
                  ">"+Long.toString(incumbent.degree)+" = degree(incumbent)]";
        }
    }
}//NW_doCompete
```

12.4 NASCENT MARKET NETWORKS

A *nascent market* is a market in development—the number of customer links starts at zero and steadily increases over time. As the number of links increases, new competitor nodes appear to address the growing demand represented by growth in links. Typically, a single innovator introduces a new product and enjoys a monopoly for a period of time. This innovator is also known as the *first mover*. Soon other competitors join in, especially if the first mover is making a profit. These imitators are known as *fast followers* for obvious reasons.

As demand increases because of stimulation of the market by the first-mover and fast-follower competitors, more competitors jump in, and so forth, until the market is fully populated by competitors. But then demand peaks and the number of links remains constant. The nascent market becomes a *mature market* at this point, and the number of competitors begins to decline because of competition. This is known as the *shakeout phase*, because less successful competitors lose market share and go out of business. Eventually, only a handful of competitors remain.

Entirely new categories of products create nascent markets in their early years of adoption. The VCR (videocassetterecorder) is a classical example—prior to the introduction of the first VCR (by RCA) there was no market for a VCR. It took 12 years for 50% of American homes to own a VCR (see Fig. 12.1). Eventually, the VCR market reached a peak and a shakeout period ensued, leaving only a handful of competitors. In the case of the VCR, a new innovation—the DVR (digital video-recorder)—replaced it, and the process started over again.

We want to understand the dynamics of nascent markets. Do they obey the Bass and Fisher–Pry adoption models? Do they always result in a monopoly, duopoly, or oligopoly? What is the nature of nascent markets, and what is the best strategy for a competitor that wants to become the dominant player? We use simulation of emergent netgain networks to find out.

12.4.1 Nascent Market Emergence

Consider a nascent market initially monopolized by a single competitor—the innovator. Demand, in the form of additional links, is assumed to steadily increase at a constant rate. For example, let a new customer link be added once every fifth timestep. Similarly, imitators are attracted to the nascent market because of increasing demand. We simulate entry of competitors by adding a new competitor node once every twentieth timestep, until n_p competitors have been added. The ratio $\frac{20}{5} = 4$ is a measure of the *speed* of the nascent market because four links (demand) are added each time a competitor is added, up to the limit of n_p competitors. Demand continues to grow up to the limit $m = \text{nInputLinks}$.

Existing links are being rewired according to preferential attachment while new links and nodes are being added to the network. Market share is defined as node degree divided by total number of links, so as the total rises, it is conceivable that a competitor loses market share over time, unless it takes more than its share away from weaker competitors. Thus, two factors determine the ultimate fixed-point share of competitors: (1) addition of new links and (2) preferential attachment.

Suppose that a new link is regularly added after nNewLinkInterval timesteps and a new competitor node is added after every nNewNodeInterval. Further, assume that growth of market share subsequently occurs through preferential attachment. The following code fragment from program *NetGain.jar* succinctly captures the growth of a nascent netgain network, while method NW_doCompete() described earlier simulates preferential attachment:

```
int consumer_node = (int)(nConsumers*Math.random());
int challenger_node = nConsumers+(int)(nCompetitors*Math.random());
//Add competitor
if(doNascent && nCompetitors < nInputCompetitors
            &&
    t == nNewNodeInterval*(t/nNewNodeInterval)){
            NW_doAddNode(Long.toString(nNodes));
            nodes[nNodes-1].color = Color.blue;
            nCompetitors++;
            NW_doAddLink(consumer_node, nNodes-1);
            Message = "New Competitor:";
    }
//Add new link
if(doNascent && nLinks < nInputLinks && challenger_node >= nConsumers
            &&
        t == nNewLinkInterval*(t/nNewLinkInterval)){
                if(NW_doAddLink(consumer_node, challenger_node))
                    Message = "New Customer:";
    }
```

Note that a new competitor also has a new link attached to it—thus every new competitor has at least one customer, initially. Competitor nodes are painted blue in program *NetGain.jar* to distinguish them from customers. As soon as n_p competitors have been added at regular intervals, no more are added.

New links are added at regular intervals, too, but method NW_doAddLink()
checks for duplicates and returns false if it is unable to insert a link. Duplicate
links are avoided, which means n_p is the maximum degree possible for any consumer
node. All competitor nodes are numbered above nConsumers-1, which is why
this code fragment checks for challenger_node >= nConsumers.

12.4.2 The Nascent Market Fixed Point

We model the attachment of new links to existing and new competitors as a *Poisson
process* identical to the generative procedure given for creation of a random network.
However, instead of connecting consumer nodes to other consumer nodes, we
connect randomly selected consumer nodes to competitor nodes. The probability of
connecting a link to one of n_c consumer nodes is $1/n_c$, and the probability of connecting k links to a consumer node in m trials, is simply the binomial distribution:

$$B(m, k) = C(m, k)\left(\frac{1}{n_c}\right)^k \left(1 - \frac{1}{n_c}\right)^{m-k}$$

Intuitively, we would expect market share to be evenly split among all n_p competitors,
but this does not happen because of the binomial distribution, which allows consumers to connect to more than one competitor with probability Prob(degree $\geq k$):

$$\text{Prob(degree} \geq k) = \sum_{j=k}^{m} B(m, j)$$

The probability that a consumer node has at least k links, and hence its degree is k or
greater, is shown in Fig. 12.5 for $m = 100$ links and $n_c = 100$ competitors. The significance of this statistical fact is critical to the fixed point of the nascent market
because it prevents rewiring of links due to preferential attachment when a consumer
node is connected to all competitors. Regardless of the degree of a competitor, no

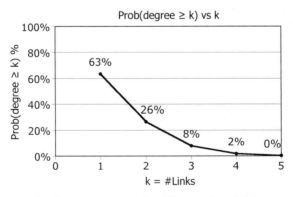

Figure 12.5 Probability that a consumer node will have at least k links versus k for $m = 100$,
$k = 1,2,3,4,5 = n_p$, and $n_c = 100$ consumers.

rewiring is possible when a consumer is already wired to a competitor. Consumers that are connected to all competitors cannot be rewired.

The stickiness of the binomial distribution means that the nascent market will be divided among competitors in roughly the following proportions (see Fig. 12.5):

Fixed-Point Market Share for Nascent Market: $n_p = 5$

Market leader: 63%
Fast follower: 26%
Laggards: 8%, 2%

This is a consequence of probability theory, not of competition or preferential attachment. However, when $n_p \leq 3$, preferential attachment takes over and more dominant competitors "roll up" links not consumed by the laggards.

Fixed-Point Market Share for Nascent Market: $n_p = 4$

Market leader: 65%
Fast follower: 27%
Laggards: 8%

Fixed-Point Market Share for Nascent Market: $n_p = 3$

Market leader: 73%
Fast follower: 27%
Laggards: 0%

The speed of the market is the ratio of a number of new links being added to the number of new competitor nodes being added. Program *NetGain.jar* allows the user to enter these rates as time intervals. So, for example, if a new link is added at intervals of 10 ticks, and new competitors are added at intervals of 25 ticks, the speed of the market is $\frac{25}{10} = 2.5$ because 2.5 links are added for each additional competitor. In terms of the nNewLinkInterval and nNewNodeInterval input parameters of program *NetGain.jar*, market speed is

$$\text{Market speed} = \text{nNewNodeInterval/nNewLinkInterval}$$

Figure 12.6 summarizes results obtained by simulation using program *NetGain.jar*. Fixed-point values of market share were plotted versus $\log_2$(market speed) for $m = 100$ links; 100 consumers; and 3,5, and 10 initial competitors. The emergence process regularly attaches links to randomly selected competitors at one rate, and regularly creates a new competitor at another rate. Market share is plotted against the logarithm of the ratio of these rates.

The graph of Fig. 12.6 is divided into two halves: the left half (negative x axis) represents a *slow market*, while the right half (positive x axis) represents a *fast market*. A fast market adds links faster than competitors:

$$\text{Fast market: } \log_2(\text{market speed}) > 0$$

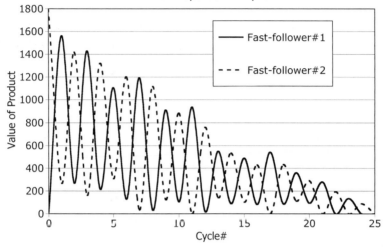

Figure 12.6 Fixed-point market share for top three competitors in a nascent market. Market share versus logarithm of market speed confirms binomial distribution fixed-point market share values for $3 \le n_p \le 10$.

The number of surviving competitors in a nascent market rapidly falls off as n_p increases. The binomial distribution's impact is evident as an initially large field of competitors tends to spread links over more competitors. The probability that a consumer will be linked to all competitor nodes is lower. This lowers the fixed-point market share of the leader. It is more difficult to become a monopoly in a large field of competitors than in a small field.

In addition, note that it is more likely for the first mover to be replaced by a fast follower in a slow market, because a slow market gives the imitator plenty of time to gain on the innovator. In the very early stages of the nascent market, a change in one or two links can alter the leadership position on the basis of node degree. Links are selected at random for rewiring, so it is possible for an imitator to surpass the innovator in the number of links "by accident." In a slow market, there are many rewiring steps in between the introduction of new links. This means that there can be many changes of leadership position in the early stages of emergence.

Nonetheless, it is interesting that the nascent market network tends to become a three-way oligopoly with the leader achieving a near-monopoly simply by being early to market. This conclusion is not surprising to the practitioner of the two-person Lanchester strategy. *Lanchester strategy* was used in World War II and during the Cold War to allocate troop strength.[5] Japanese business strategists subsequently adapted it in the 1980s, which led to the formation of the *new Lanchester strategy* (Yano, 1990).

---

[5]Frederick William Lanchester, 1868–1946, created the first mathematical model of warfare as described in, *Aircraft in Warfare, the Dawn of the Fourth Arm*, in 1916.

According to the new Lanchester strategy, a competitor is balanced on a tipping point when it has 41.7% market share. Future share can go either way once a competitor reaches 41.7%—rising to a monopoly or declining to a laggard. In a two-party competition, the leading competitor can achieve a monopoly share of 73.88%, or fall to a laggard status of 26.12%. The new Lanchester strategy warns against attempting to gain more than 73% market share because a monopoly invites more competition and reduces effectiveness of the organization. It also admonishes against falling below 26%, because this means that you are about to become a victim of shakeout.

These new Lanchester strategy explains two-competitor market dynamics, but it does not generalize to $n_p \geq 3$. The model proposed here matches the new Lanchester strategy very well, and suggests that three dominant competitors always emerge from a field of $n_p \geq 3$ competitors. The simulation result of Fig. 12.6 conforms to the new Lanchester strategy and shows that no more than two leaders can survive a nascent market.

In general, a nascent netgain network converges to a stable fixed-point market share as follows:

1. When $n_p = 2$, the leader will emerge with approximately 73% of the market and the other competitor will emerge with only 27%.
2. Regardless of the number of innovators and imitators, $n_p \geq 3$, after sufficient time, only three dominant competitors emerge, and the top two will achieve at least 63% and 26% of the market, respectively. Also, increasing n_p decreases the leader's market share and increases the probability that more competitors will survive.
3. As the speed of the market decreases, the first-mover advantage decreases— slow markets may be monopolized by fast followers. The slower the market (rate of adding new links is lower), the better chance an imitator has to become the market leader. Slow markets favor incumbents.

12.5 CREATIVE DESTRUCTION NETWORKS

Up to this point we have assumed that all products, services, and ideas have the same perceived value. In fact, consumers base their buying decisions on comparisons of many properties of a product, service, or idea, which we lump together and simply designate as *product value*. Product value can be tied to price, quality, fashion, or psychological value, and may have little to do with the intrinsic value of the product. Regardless of how consumers rank competitive products, their decision to buy one product over another inevitably comes down to a *value proposition* that is based on the perceived value of the product.

Competitors gain or lose market share in relation to changes over time in product value. A certain company may gain market share by lowering the price of its television, increasing its performance, or increasing advertising to make its television more appealing. In a capitalistic system, competitors compete by constantly improving their value proposition. Failure to keep pace with constant improvement leads to loss of market share and eventually to the competitor's demise.

Apparently, the ability to improve on a product's value proposition may decline as a competitor becomes a market leader. One can argue that success leads to a market leader's increase in size and corresponding decrease in agility. As an organization grows, it takes more time to make decisions. As an organization becomes more successful, it becomes risk-averse and opts for more conservative improvements. This burden can lead to reduction in the value proposition of the leader's products.

We argued that a market leader will increase its profit margin merely because it can —after all, it is the market leader. As the incumbent, the leader leverages its brand name to lock in customers regardless of price increases or decline in quality, price, or performance. Profits may be increased even as the competitor is losing market share because profits rise on fewer sales. This strategy may go too far, leading to the point of no return and the demise of the market leader.

For whatever reasons we can imagine, it is an observable fact that a competitor's rate of innovation tends to slow down as market share increases. Clayton Christensen, for example, attributes this slowdown to the *innovator's dilemma*, which states that large established market leaders ride a sustaining technology path of incremental improvement, which makes them vulnerable to technological surprise by an upstart innovator (Christensen 2003).

In contrast to a safe and secure sustaining technology path, an innovator rides the *disruptive technology* path characterized by lower performance, lower price, and an intense focus on an underserved segment of the market. The innovator's ability to move fast and make rapid improvements in its technology's performance means that the innovator's product soon exceeds the value proposition of the incumbent's offering. Before the market leader knows it, its market is gone—and the innovator starts the process over again.

What value proposition drives consumers to a new product, service, or idea, leaving behind their old product, service, or idea? We learned that a certain loyalty in the form of "stickiness" exists in random and nascent markets. Stickiness is often due to high *switching costs* that make consumers reluctant to change. For example, a consumer may not want to use a new computer or software application because of its steep learning curve, or may resist purchasing a new car because of a preference for the styling of the old car. It may be easier for a consumer to continue to use an existing product, simply to avoid paying tangible or intangible switching costs. Thus, the incumbent may hold onto a portion of the market even while being disrupted by a disruptive technology.

History has shown, however, that switching costs are eventually overcome, and entire industries capitulate to the disruptive technology. The switch from chemical photography to digital photography, from mainframes to personal computers, from proprietary network protocols to TCP/IP (Transmission Control Protocol/Internet Protocol) protocols, and from vinyl records to digital MP-3 music players are well-known examples of disruptions to entire industries. In each case, the challenger started out with a lower-quality, lower-performance niche product that quickly improved until it exceeded the minimum value proposition of the consumer.

For whatever reason, market leaders and monopolies are destined to decline and are replaced by new innovators. The rise and fall of market leaders is a natural consequence of capitalism—not the exception. Joseph Schumpeter called this *creative destruction*. It explains how capitalism perpetuates itself through competition and serial innovation. We can understand and appreciate how creative destruction works in a netgain network by considering another simple emergence model—the creative destruction model. We show that creative destruction in networks leads to a stable fixed point just as before, but the value of the leader's fixed-point market share is a quadratic function of the minimum market share threshold that signals an increase in value proposition. For the square-root law described here, the optimal value of switching threshold is approximately $27\%/2 = 13.5\%$.

12.5.1 Creative Destruction Emergence

Schumpeter was perhaps the first to observe the cycle of innovation–leadership–decline in a capitalist system. His *creative destruction* theory describes a cyclic process of early-stage innovation followed by a rise to the top, followed by an eventual decline and downfall as the market leader meets a challenger with a new innovation. In Schumpeter's worldview, creative destruction "incessantly revolutionizes from within, incessantly destroying the old one, incessantly creating a new one" (Schumpeter, 1942). Creative destruction is an essential fact of life in a capitalistic system.

In the following paragraphs we develop a netgain network model of creative destruction based on a value proposition that attracts customers to high-valued products at the expense of lower-valued products. Switching is still influenced by preferential attachment, but in addition, customers weigh the value proposition of each competitor's products as well. If the combination of value proposition and market share position of the competitor falls below that of a challenger, the consumer switches to the better choice.

Competitors are aware of this, so they adjust their value proposition upward to compete. This is done in a number of ways, such as cutting prices, increasing quality, and so on. But competitors are also greedy—they seek to maximize profits, which compels them to adjust their value proposition downward when they can. As long as a monopoly is able to maintain a commanding lead in market share, why sacrifice profits? The leader is tempted to reduce the value of its product and risk loss of share to an upstart while profiting. If market share begins to slip, however, the leader must resort to increasing value by improving its product's quality, price, or advertising budget—all at the expense of profits.

Innovators, on the other hand, attack the leader with a compelling value proposition designed to destroy the market leader. Having nothing to lose and possibly some market share to gain, the innovative challenger sacrifices profits, in the short term, for market share. It does this by giving the consumer a better deal—higher quality, lower price, more advertising. In the extreme, a challenger may "buy market share" by selling at a loss—a short-term strategy that can reverse the leadership position.

In this game of netgain competition, let the market share of challenger and leader nodes be a measure of their success, and the value of each competitor node—a positive number—represent the perceived value proposition of the competitor's product. On one hand, each competitor wants to increase its market share, while on the other hand, it wants to also increase its profit. Generally, sacrificing value proposition can increase profit, and sacrificing profit can increase value. Thus, a tug-of-war exists between two objectives—gain market share versus maximize profit.

Suppose that the change in a competitor's node degree (market share) is proportional to the ratio of incumbent to challenger's value times the degree of the incumbent:

$$\Delta\text{degree(challenger)} = \frac{V_{\text{incumbent}}\ \text{degree(incumbent)}}{V_{\text{challenger}}}$$

Similarly, the degree of the incumbent decreases when the degree of the challenger increases, proportional to the ratio of values:

$$\Delta\text{degree(incumbent)} = \frac{-V_{\text{challenger}}\ \text{degree(challenger)}}{V_{\text{incumbent}}}$$

Dividing the second equation into the first yields the ratio

$$\frac{\Delta\text{degree(challenger)}}{\Delta\text{degree(incumbent)}} = \frac{-k\ \text{degree(incumbent)}}{\text{degree(challenger)}}$$

where $k = [V_{\text{incumbent}}/V_{\text{challenger}}]^2$. In other words, change in degree is proportional to the square of difference in value proposition. Alternatively, change in value proposition is proportional to the square root of degree. This is the *square-root law* of creative destruction.

We are interested only in the switching threshold necessary to cause one link to switch from the incumbent to the challenger. When this happens, the degree of the challenger is incremented by one link and the degree of the incumbent is decremented by one link:

$$\Delta\text{degree(challenger)} = +1$$
$$\Delta\text{degree(incumbent)} = -1$$

Substitution into the ratio equation yields

$$-1 = \frac{-k\ \text{degree(incumbent)}}{\text{degree(challenger)}}$$

Substituting for k and solving for $\eta = V_{\text{challenger}}/V_{\text{incumbent}}$ gives the *switching threshold*:

$$\eta = \frac{V_{\text{challenger}}}{V_{\text{incumbent}}} = \sqrt{\frac{\text{degree(incumbent)}}{\text{degree(challenger)}}}$$

Consumers *switch* from incumbent to challenger when the following value proposition holds: If $V_{\text{challenger}} > \eta^* V_{\text{incumbent}}$, then

$$\eta = \sqrt{\frac{\text{degree(incumbent)}}{\text{degree(challenger)}}}$$

Suppose, for example, that challenger and incumbent have the same market share: degree(challenger) = degree(incumbent). The customer will decide to switch on the basis of product value, $V_{\text{challenger}} > V_{\text{incumbent}}$. Otherwise, no switching occurs. This makes sense, because all other factors are assumed to be equal, so the consumer's decision is based on product value.

Now suppose the opposite: that the product values are identical, $V_{\text{challenger}} = V_{\text{incumbent}}$, so switching takes place only when the challenger has more links than the incumbent—that is, when degree(challenger) > degree(incumbent). In this case, the model reverts to the preferential attachment microrule of the random and nascent market models studied earlier.

Creative destruction is an emergent process whereby a nascent market grows from a niche into the mainstream market with an established oligopoly as studied earlier. The leader has a monopoly position, say, 67–72% market share, and the leading imitator has a player position, say, 26–28% market share. Once this fixed point is reached, the only strategy that will displace the incumbent is a change in value proposition. This may be accomplished by the rules of disruptive technology, or some other means. Without a disruption, the challenger must buy market share in the form of decreased profits, higher research and development costs, or greater advertising costs.

The incumbent may afford to give up some share in order to maximize profit. For example, a monopoly competitor with 67–72% share can afford to decrease the value proposition of its product to increase its profit. Feeling safe in its position, profit taking takes its toll on the value of its product; hence the product value of the incumbent begins to fall. At some point, profit taking may lead to erosion in position, which may overcome the incumbent. The challenger may become the market leader, or the market leader may regain its leadership role by sacrificing profit in order to buy back its lost market share.

If a market leader faces a disruptive technology, it may never be able to regain its leadership role because of a number of associated difficulties. Prevalent among these challenges is the lack of technology (patents, processes, employee capability). In some cases, such as the rapid transition from mainframe to personal computers, the incumbent's business model may be rendered obsolete to such an extent that the incumbent succumbs to Schumpeter's creative destruction regardless of efforts to reverse the inevitable.

The creative destruction model is a superset of the previous models that were based solely on market share. It implements preferential attachment and the square-root switching law with the addition of the following:

Creative Destruction Emergence

1. Initially assign identical values to competitor nodes, say, 1.0.
2. Let `nPlayer` be the smallest market share needed to begin creative destruction, and let `nMonopoly` be the largest market share allowed before the market leader begins to decline because of creative destruction.
3. Repeat indefinitely or until halted by the user:
   a. Find the value of the largest market share competitor, `max_share`.

b. If `max_share` > `nPlayer`, invoke creative destruction; otherwise skip.
  i. Creative destruction: for all competitors:
    (1) If `market share` < `nPlayer`, increment value.
    (2) If `market share` > `nMonopoly`, decrement value.

This method does not do the actual rewiring of links—this is done elsewhere. Instead, it revalues all competitors' value propositions according to the conditions of the market. Laggards with less than the minimum market share do nothing, but players with at least the minimum player threshold increase their values to gain even more links, and leaders with more than the maximum market share decrease their values to maximize profit.

Creative destruction occurs because competitors vie for a limited number of customers, and these customers—represented by links—gravitate toward the competitor with the best value proposition. We simulate this in method `NW_doCreativeDestruction()`, which is invoked with each timestep to determine whether the incumbent should lower its value and the challenger should increase its value. A competitor increases its value to gain market share, while a monopoly decreases its value to maximize profits.

Input parameters `nPlay` and `nMonopoly` establish thresholds for when to increase value or maximize profit: `nPlayer` represents the lower end of market share, typically 26%, and `nMonopoly` represents the higher end of market share, typically 72%. The incumbent lowers its product's value when its market share exceeds `nMonopoly`, and the challenger increases its product's value when its market share is below `nPlayer`.

Market share of a competitor node is equal to the node's degree divided by the total number of links in the netgain network. A *mature market* is defined as a netgain network containing at least one competitor node with a market share in excess of `nPlayer`. Thus, the method must first identify the high-valued competitor node to determine whether any adjustments in value are needed. If not, the method does nothing.

```
public void NW_doCreativeDestruction(){
    double max_marketshare = 0.0;
    double market_share;
    for(int i = nConsumers; i < nNodes; i++){        //Find largest %
      market_share = (float)nodes[ i] .degree/nLinks;
      if(market_share > max_marketshare) max_marketshare = market_share;
    }
    if(max_marketshare >= nPlayer/nLinks)            //Mature market
      for(int i = nConsumers; i < nNodes; i++){
        market_share = (float)nodes[ i] .degree/nLinks;
        if(market_share <= nPlayer/nLinks && market_share > 0){
            nodes[i].value++;                        //Buy market share
        }
        if(market_share >= nMonopoly/nLinks && nodes[ i] .value >= 1){
            nodes[i].value- -;                       //Increase profits
        }
    }
}//NW_doCreativeDestruction
```

At the same time that competitors are revaluing their products to attract customers or maximize profit, links are being rewired according to the value propositions offered by each competitor and the switching threshold described earlier. This process is simulated by Java method NW_doCompete(), which has two modes: nascent and nonnascent. This method is an extension of the random emergence process and implements two additional functions: (1) it adds a new competitor at nNewNodeInterval time intervals, until all n_p = nInputCompetitors have been added; and (2) it adds a new link at nNewLinkInterval time intervals, until all m = nLinks links have been added. Thus, the speed of the market is nNewNodeInterval/nNewLinkInterval. For example, if a new link is added at 10,20,30,...ticks of the clock, and a new competitor node is added at 25,50, 75,...ticks, the market speed is $\frac{25}{10}$ = 2.5. This relatively fast market adds 2.5 links for every new competitor.

This method implements the switching threshold derived for creative destruction on the basis of value propositions: namely, rewire the link when challenger.value > (threshold)incumbent.value. *Threshold* is the square root of the ratio of incumbent to challenger node degree. Switching occurs either because the challenger has a large market share or because its value proposition is large relative to the incumbent's.

```
public void NW_doCompete(int t, boolean doNascent) {
  if(nInputConsumers <= 0 || nInputCompetitors <= 0) return;
  int consumer_node = (int)(nConsumers*Math.random());
  int challenger_node = nConsumers+(int)(nCompetitors*Math.random());
  //Add competitor with one link
  if(doNascent && nCompetitors < nInputCompetitors
       &&
    t == nNewNodeInterval*(t/nNewNodeInterval)){
      NW_doAddNode(Long.toString(nNodes));
      nCompetitors++;
      NW_doAddLink(nodes[consumer_node].tag, nodes[nNodes-1].tag);
      Message = "New Competitor:";
  }
  //Add link
  if(nLinks < nInputLinks && challenger_node >= nConsumers
       &&
    t == nNewLinkInterval*(t/nNewLinkInterval)){
   if(NW_doAddLink(consumer_node, challenger_node))
      Message = "New Customer:";
  }
  if(nLinks <= 0) return;
  //Switching threshold
  int any_link = (int)(nLinks*Math.random());
  Link e = Links[any_link];
  Node consumer = nodes[e.from];    //consumer node -> competitor node
  Node incumbent = nodes[e.to];     //links always point to competitor
  //pick a challenger at random
  challenger_node = nConsumers+(int)(nCompetitors*Math.random());
  Node challenger = nodes[challenger_node];
  double denominator = challenger.degree;
  if(incumbent.degree <= 0              //Eliminate competitors with no share
       ||
     denominator <= 0) return;       //Eliminate divide-by-zero error
```

```
    double threshold = Math.sqrt((incumbent.degree)/denominator);
    if(challenger.value > threshold* incumbent.value
            &&
        challenger.degree < nMaximumDegree) {           //Switch
        if(NW_doAddLink(consumer.tag, challenger.tag)) { //Avoid duplicate
            NW_doCutLink(any_link);
            Message = "Switching to challenger:"+
                "[degree(challenger) ="+Long.toString(challenger.degree)+
                ">"+Long.toString(incumbent.degree)+" = degree(incumbent)]";
    }
    }
}//NW_doCompete
```

12.5.2   The Square-Root Law Fixed Point

What happens when competitors change their value propositions to attract greater market share? Intuitively, market share should oscillate between competitors—first the challenger increases value proposition until it achieves a leadership role, while the leader takes profit. When positions are reversed, the incumbent leader must do the same. Thus, we expect the exchange of leadership position to repeat indefinitely. But this is not the case.

If we start with a random network and employ the creative destruction square-root algorithm described above, a stable nonrandom network will emerge from the random network. Emergence takes the random network through two phases. First, the random network will identify leaders, players, and laggards as before. Typically, a field of $n_p \geq 3$ competitors will shrink to three or four nodes according to the shakeout model derived in the previous section. Then, the remaining competitors will exchange leadership positions for a number of cycles, eventually reaching a stable state.

Oscillation of the values of the top two competitors is shown in Fig. 12.7. Note that the amplitude of each wave steadily declines until reaching zero. When this occurs, the network has reached its fixed point. Convergence can be slow—program *NetGain.jar* may require as many as 200,000 timesteps to come to a stable fixed point—especially if the minimum threshold nPlay and monopoly threshold nMonopoly sum to 100%.

In a competition between competitors in a random network using the square-root algorithm, two or three competitors quickly become dominant because of the increasing returns property of preferential attachment. As soon as a competitor surpasses the minimum threshold to become a player, say, 27%, it begins to increase its value proposition to gain even more market share. When the fast follower reaches the monopoly threshold nMonopoly, it does the opposite—decreases its product's value to increase profit. When this happens, the new leader is challenged by the second fast follower, and the process repeats. But it does not repeat, indefinitely!

In the second phase of creative destruction emergence, one of the top competitors slowly begins to gain on the other one. The amplitude of each value proposition cycle is slightly lower than the previous one—but takes longer to reach. Sooner or later, the value of a competitor will reach zero. All other competitor nodes with a value proposition greater than zero will continue to compete, but eventually another node will

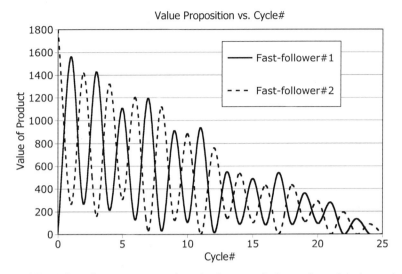

Figure 12.7 Value of top two competitors in the second phase of creative destruction—shakeout. Initially, the random network has 100 customers, 10 competitors, and 100 links, and the value proposition is 1.0 for all competitors.

reach a value of zero. When all surviving competitor nodes reach zero, the fixed point has been reached.

What is the market share value of surviving competitors when the fixed point emerges? An analytic answer to this question is currently an unsolved research problem, so we address it empirically. Consider a random network with 100 links, 100 consumers, and 10 competitors, initially. Run program *NetGain.jar* for long periods of time to produce fixed-point market share results for "typical runs"—say, monopoly thresholds of 72% and 60%. Let the minimum player threshold vary from zero to 50%, and plot the average of the network's stable fixed-point market share for each surviving competitor as in Fig. 12.8. These averages are plotted against the minimum player threshold, which is varied. Then develop an approximation model as shown by the solid lines in Fig. 12.8, and compare the two.

The "fish-like" curves of Fig. 12.8 were obtained by approximating the fixed-point market share as a function of minimum player threshold. When the minimum player threshold plus the monopoly threshold exceeds 99%, the fixed-point market share of all except one competitor is zero. The leading competitor ends up with 100% share. This appears as the "tail of the fish" seen in Fig. 12.8. A high minimum player threshold isn't very interesting because it always leads to a monopoly. In general, the monopoly threshold used by the creative destruction algorithm sets an upper bound on how many competitors survive the competition:

$$\text{Minimum player threshold} < (1 - \text{monopoly threshold})$$

Now consider the range of minimum player threshold values below $(1 - \text{monopoly threshold})$. Empirical results suggest that the top two competitor's fixed-point

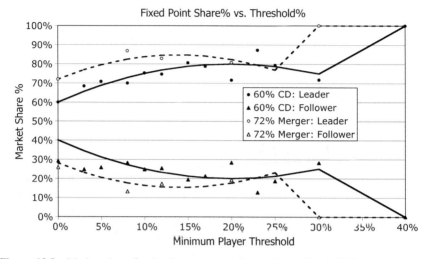

Figure 12.8 Market share fixed-point versus minimum-player threshold for two emergent creative destruction networks—one creative-destruction-only network with monopoly threshold of 60%, and another network with creative destruction plus mergers and acquisitions and monopoly threshold of 72%. All networks contain 100 links and 100 consumer nodes, and start with $n_p = 5$ competitors.

market share follow a quadratic relationship that forms the "body of the fish." Indeed, we approximate this relationship by noting that the market share of the top two contenders roughly follows the first derivative of the Bass and Fisher–Pry equations studied earlier. Recall that the right-hand-side of the Bass and Fisher–Pry state equation is a quadratic function of market share. Borrowing from Bass and Fisher–Pry, we claim that the fixed point of the leading competitor also follows this rule.

We approximate the fixed-point market share of the leader as a function of minimum player threshold as follows:

$$\text{Market\_share\_leader}(m,p) = m + rp(a - p)$$
$$\text{Market\_share\_follower}(m,p) \leq 1 - \text{market\_share\_leader}(m,p)$$

where

$$m = \text{monopoly threshold,}; \; \texttt{nMonopoly}$$
$$0 \leq p \leq (1 - m) = \text{minimum player threshold, } \texttt{nPlayer}$$
$$r = \text{rate of link rewiring parameter}$$
$$a = 1 - m$$

Substituting constants obtained by curve fitting, and noting that $a = (1 - m)$, we obtain an approximation in terms of player and monopoly thresholds, only (elimination of parameter a, and setting $r = 5$ for this case):

Fixed-Point Market Share of Leader

$$\text{Market\_share\_leader}(m,p) = m + 5p\,(1 - p - m)$$

where m = monopoly threshold and p = minimum player threshold.

For example, letting $m = 72\%$, $p = 10\%$, we obtain

$$\text{Market\_share\_leader}(0.72, 0.1) = 0.72 + 5 * 0.1 * 0.18 = 81\%$$
$$\text{Market\_share\_follower} = 100\% - 81\% = 19\%$$

The average fixed point over five simulated runs is 83%–17% for monopoly and player, respectively.[6] The approximation equation is rather good, considering that variance is high in the simulation data and only five samples were obtained for each data point.

Creative destruction, using the square-root algorithm, leads to a duopoly if the minimum-player threshold is kept small.[7] For the simulations performed here, the player threshold must be less than 27% (assuming a monopoly threshold of 72%). The more interesting conclusion is that a duopoly emerges even though we started with five competitors. This conclusion holds regardless of the number of initial competitors and $n_p > 3$. A decrease in the minimum player threshold increases the probability of survival of an underdog, because it means that the underdog begins increasing its value proposition earlier in the process. The higher the threshold, the later an underdog begins to adapt its value to the reality of the market.

The relationship between minimum threshold and fixed point is not linear. Figure 12.8 shows a U-shaped market share curve for the follower, and an inverted U-shaped curve for the market leader. For the parameters used in Fig. 12.8, the optimal minimum player threshold is approximately midway between zero and the minimum player threshold set by the user of program *NetGain.jar*. What is the optimal player threshold when $m = 72\%$? This is left as an exercise for the reader.

It may be dangerous to generalize too much on these limited data. The experimental results shown in Fig. 12.8 depend on the initial parameters of the netgain network. We assumed a random initial network, 100 consumer nodes,100 links, and $n_p = 5$. Initially, competitors start with a value of 1.0. The reader is invited to try other combinations of initial values. These results leave fertile ground for further research into the behaviors of creative destruction emergence.

12.6 MERGER AND ACQUISITION NETWORKS

According to Schumpeter, creative destruction is an inevitable result of competition. Human ingenuity and network effects make it not only possible but also inevitable.

---

[6]The raw data of Fig. 12.8 is averaged over 5 runs for each data point.
[7]A monopoly may emerge with non-zero probability as well as three survivors, but the probabilities of these events are low.

Mergers and acquisitions, on the other hand, provide a more direct means of controlling market share among competitors. When two competitors merge into one, hopefully the value proposition of the combined entity increases and makes the new business more competitive. While this may or may not be true in all cases, a merger does increase market share simply because the merged entity's share equals the sum of both competitor's market shares—at least for a while. Thus, acquisition of a competitor is one way to increase a competitor's standing in the market.

Is it possible to rise from a laggard to a leader by employing a strategy of merging with other laggards? In this section we test this hypothesis and learn that merging is helpful, but does not guarantee a rise to the top of the capitalist food chain.

Consider the following microrule for a netgain algorithm that merges two nodes together when the sum of their market share percentages is less than the minimum player threshold. This idea is simple—if two laggards merge, they can leapfrog from laggard to player by combining their customers. Does this leap propel the merged competitor into a player position? Hopefully, the newly merged competitor can parley its sudden increase in market share into an even greater percentage by increasing returns. If so, then mergers and acquisitions could be an effective strategy of the weak.

Merger–Acquisition Microrule

1. Select two competitors, X and Y, at random. Let X.share, Y.share be the market share of competitors X and Y, respectively.
2. If X.share + Y.share < minimum player threshold; then
   a. Merge the node with less market share, say, X, into the node with more market share, say, Y:
      i. Copy all of X's links to Y
      ii. Erase node X

Note that the value proposition of the merged competitor is still the same—only the degree, and hence the market share, of the merged node changes. The newly created node should increase its market share at a greater rate, and if its newly acquired market share propels it beyond the monopoly threshold, it becomes the new incumbent leader. This claim is examined in great detail in the next section.

12.6.1   Java Method for Merging Nodes

The following Java methods implement the merger–acquisitions microrule. Method NW_doMerge() paraphrases the microrule specified above. It guarantees that two distinct competitor nodes are selected at random, and decides whether the sum of their market shares is small enough for the two to be merged.

Method NW_doMergeNodes(**int** left, **int** right) does the dirty work of rewiring links from one node to the other, and then erasing the smaller node. It assumes that right is the smaller market share node, so all links are moved to the `left` node. Every link is examined, and if it points to node `right`, it is rewired to point to node `left`. The corresponding degree of each node is adjusted. However, the value of the merged node is left unchanged.

```
public void NW_doMerge() {
        if(nCompetitors <= 1) return;
        int j = nConsumers+(int)(nCompetitors*Math.random());   //Pick one
        int k = nConsumers+(int)(nCompetitors*Math.random());   //Pick another
        while(j == k) k = nConsumers+(int)(nCompetitors*Math.random());
        double ms_left = (float)nodes[ j].degree/nLinks;
        double ms_right = (float)nodes[k].degree/nLinks;
        double threshold = (float)nPlayer/100.0;                //Laggard share
        //Does Merger make sense?
        if(ms_left+ms_right < threshold){
            if(ms_left > ms_right)
                NW_doMergeNodes(j, k);
            else
                NW_doMergeNodes(k, j);
        }
    }//NW_doMerge

 public void NW_doMergeNodes(int left, int right){
    for(int j = 0; j < nLinks; j++){
        if(Links[j].to == right) {
            Links[j].to = left;
            nodes[left].degree++;
            nodes[right].degree- -;
        }
    }
    NW_doEraseNode(right);
 }//NW_doMergeNodes
```

12.6.2 Merging Speeds Up Creative Destruction

Figure 12.8 shows the results of combining the creative destruction and merging algorithms. The dotted line and open data points correspond to a monopoly threshold of 72%, creative destruction, and mergers and acquisitions all running simultaneously. In each case, the emergent network reaches a fixed-point market share value for surviving competitors. These fixed points were averaged over five simulation runs, and plotted along with the pure creative destruction data so that the two can be compared.

We obtain a "fish diagram" as before, but with two major differences: (1) the fish diagram of the combined creative destruction and merging processes is shifted to the left relative to pure creative destruction, and (2) the amplitude of the combined process is slightly higher. The first difference is due mainly to merging, while the second is due mainly to the higher monopoly threshold (72% vs. 60%).

Merging has the effect of increasing the speed with which the inevitable shakeout occurs. This means that the dashed lines of Fig. 12.8 rise faster and fall faster as the minimum player threshold increases. The simulation also converges to the network's fixed point sooner—from 5 to 10 times faster. This means that the process of merging accelerates the shakeout of weaker competitors—the lower the minimum player threshold, the faster the shakeout. In effect, merging speeds up the inevitable.

The second difference is perhaps a consequence of the first difference between creative destruction with and without merging. But it is also a consequence of a higher monopoly threshold. The model for the market leader fixed-point share is slightly more accentuated because $r = 6.5$, instead of 5:

$$\text{Market\_share\_leader}(m,p) = m + 6.5\,p\,(1 - p - m)$$

For example, let $m = 72\%$, $p = 12\%$:

$$\text{Market\_share\_leader}(0.72,0.12) = 0.72 + 6.5 * 0.12 * 0.16 = 84\%$$
$$\text{Market\_share\_folllower} = 100\% - 84\% = 16\%$$

The average fixed point over five simulated runs is 83% and 17% for monopoly and player, respectively. Once again, the approximation equation is rather good, considering that variance is high in the simulation data and only five samples were obtained for each data point.

Mergers and acquisitions speed up the process of creative destruction by eliminating weaker competitors sooner, rather than later. While merging is commonly used to bump up market share and gain economies of scale in the real world of business, mergers generally do not change the inevitable fixed point. However, the simulations done here to support a numerical conclusion do not tell us which competitor eventually becomes the leader. This analysis only tells us that one will emerge. In the real world of business, we are also interested in predicting which competitor will win. Mergers and acquisitions can change the leadership position of a competitor. The problem of predicting which laggard ends up a winner because of a merger is left for the reader to solve.

12.7 EXERCISES

12.1. How many time periods does it take for the monopoly competitor of the single-product network of Fig. 12.3 to rise to 50% share?

12.2. What is the market share estimate obtained by applying the Bass equation to the network of Fig. 12.3, using the results of Exercise 12.1?

12.3. What is the approximate distribution of fixed-point market share among $n_p = 5$ competitors in a multiproduct network for $n_c = 100$, $m = 350$, and the parameters given in Table 12.1?

12.4. Perform an experiment similar to the experiment performed to obtain the data in Fig. 12.4 and Table 12.1. Let $n_p = 3$, and let m range from 100 to 200 links.
    (a) Does market share follow a power law?
    (b) How many competitors remain after the emergence reaches its fixed point?
    (c) What is the fixed-point market share for the three competitors when $m = 200$?

12.5. What is the probability, in a random netgain network with $m = 100$ links, $n_p = 4$ competitors, and $n_c = 50$ consumers, that a consumer node will have four links? What is the probability it will have at least three links?

12.6. What is the speed of a nascent netgain network market when the interval between new links is 100 and the interval between new competitors is 20?

12.7. Does a nascent netgain network always produce an oligopoly of two or three competitors? If so, why?

12.8. What is the optimal value of minimum player threshold such that the leader in a creative destruction emergence ends up with the most market share? Assume monopoly threshold, $m = 60\%$, and $r = 5$.

12.9. In creative destruction emergence, a consumer switches to a challenger when the square-root law favors the challenger. Assuming that the value of the incumbent's product is $100, what must be the value of the challenger to cause the consumer to switch, if the incumbent has 72% market share and the challenger has 27%?

12.10. How many competitors survive a lengthy creative destruction emergence with merging when $n_c = 50$, $m = 100$, $n_p = 10$, monopoly threshold $= 72\%$, and the minimum player threshold $= 10\%$?

13

BIOLOGY

Network science has recently been applied to the study of biological systems at many levels (Albert, 2007; Jeong, 2000). For example, food webs are high-level network models of the ecology of interdependent living systems. Nodes are species and links correspond to predator–prey relationships among the competing organisms. At the other extreme of biology, biochemical processes among proteins, DNA, and mRNA (messenger RNA) at the cellular level also form networks. These networks are analogous to electronic circuits in a microelectronic chip, but instead of regulating the flow of electrons, *protein expression networks* describe the regulation of protein, amino acids, and other metabolites involved in protein–protein interactions. In this case, nodes are DNA, mRNA, and proteins, and links represent mass flow of regulatory chemicals.

The field is young and undeveloped. So far, the emergence of network science in biology follows two basic approaches: *static analysis*, in which the topological structure of the biological network is related to function—that is, function follows form; and *dynamic analysis* in which the biochemical processes in some living system are equated with flows or signals running through the network. In dynamic analysis, the functioning of the biological network is modeled by a state equation or state matrix, similar to the analysis introduced in Chapter 9.

Static analysis tries to relate *degree sequence distribution*, *average path length*, *closeness* (*betweenness*), and *cluster coefficient* to the behavior of an organism. For example, it is claimed that biological networks tend to form scale-free networks because scale-free networks are less susceptible to failure due to random attacks or

Network Science: Theory and Practice. By Ted G. Lewis
Copyright © 2009 John Wiley & Sons, Inc.

accidents. We showed in Chapter 11 how networks might be attacked, and indeed, high-degreed nodes are critical to the functioning of a scale-free network.

Dynamic analysis is much more difficult and remains a leading-edge research topic at the time when this book was written. In simple terms, dynamic analysis attempts to do for microbiology what circuit design principles have done for microelectronics. Is it possible to discover rules governing biological networks that explain the dynamic behavior of an organism? For example, do biological networks obey an equivalent to Kirchhoff's law? Dynamic analysis is perhaps the most fascinating application of network science. Therefore, this chapter focuses on dynamic models at the risk of leaving many questions unanswered in its wake.

In this chapter we raise the following issues and speculate on a number of pending research questions:

1. Biological networks are diverse, ranging from macrolevel food webs to microbiology-level protein interaction networks within individual cells. Furthermore, there is currently no standard definition of a biological network. Proposals range from electronic circuit-like Boolean networks, Bayesian networks, and influence networks, to linear and nonlinear continuous system networks.

2. Biological network models can be roughly categorized as *static* versus *dynamic*, *Boolean* versus *continuous*, and *linear* versus *nonlinear*. In this chapter we focus mainly on microbiological continuous linear models at the subcellular level, but we also consider Boolean approximations of continuous networks and the effects of nonlinearity on some behaviors.

3. Many biological networks exhibit properties of scale-free networks with small-world effects. It is argued that function follows form—*scale-free networks* are more tolerant of random failures, and *small-world* effects enable an organism to respond more quickly to perturbations. We investigate this claim from a slightly nontraditional approach—by comparing the spectral radius of random and scale-free networks. We find that weights on links—representing transduction scalars—are at least as important to the size of a mass kinetic network's spectral radius as its degree sequence distribution.

4. Certain prewired subnetworks have been found in abundance in *protein expression networks* called *motifs*: *bifan*, *biparallel*, *feedforward loop* (FFL), and *bifeedforward loop* (bi-FFL). These motifs are thought to regulate the acceleration or delay of signals within a biological network and start and stop chains of biochemical reactions at the subcellular level.

5. We examine two biological network models in detail: linear continuous protein expression networks, and linear continuous *mass kinetics networks*. The state equations for linear continuous networks is $\partial S/\partial t = W^T S$; $S(0) = S_0$, and the state equation for mass kinetics networks is $\partial S/\partial t = \sum_{j \in \text{inlinks}} \text{inFlow}_j - \sum_{k \in \text{outlinks}} \text{outFlow}_k$, where W^T is the transposed adjacency matrix corresponding to the directed weighted network, and inflow/outflow matrices are obtained from W^T.

6. The *Boolean network* equivalent of a continuous network is an approximation of a nonlinear network. Boolean networks contain nodes that take on Boolean values—0 or 1, and perform Boolean operations—AND, OR. Links provide gating functions—a link weight of $+1$ means that a signal is transported from one node to another without alteration. A link weight of -1 means that the signal is logically inverted: $1 \rightarrow 0, 0 \rightarrow 1$.

7. We show by simulation that an emergent process that increases *entropy* by randomly rewiring links also increases the degree of the network's hub, leading to a scale-free-like network. This may be one reason why scale-free networks are found in nature. However, randomly rewiring links to decrease *spectral radius* (and therefore increase dynamic stability) fails to reduce the spectral radius of a random network to that of a stable network.

8. We show by simulation that mass kinetic networks are more stable when the sum of their output link weights equals one. Scale-free networks tend to be more stable than random networks, but the simulation results also show that random networks are stable when the sum of their output link weights equals one.

Simulations of the dynamic behavior of protein expression networks described in this chapter are performed by program *BioNet.jar*, which is related to *Influence.jar*. *BioNet.jar* supports both *continuous* and *Boolean network* models, and automates the calculation of spectral radius, fixed-point attractors (approximation), and several emergence processes studied in the following sections.

13.1 STATIC MODELS

Static analysis attempts to correlate function with form—or in network science terminology, the topology of a network is correlated with its function and behavior. Table 13.1 summarizes the evidence collected to date (2008) in support of static analysis (Albert, 2007). While the evidence is somewhat speculative at this point,

TABLE 13.1 Network Property versus Biological Function

Network Property	Biological Function	Comment
Scale-free	Fault tolerance	Unlikely to fail because of random node removal
Small-world effect	Rapid response	Short paths mean shorter time to respond to changes in environment or "shocks"
Clustering	Modularity	Efficient hierarchical designs lead to efficient functioning
Closeness (betweenness centrality)	Fault tolerance, rapid response, efficient	Probably a consequence of scale-free topology since most-central nodes are also the hubs

it makes sense in terms of previous analysis given in this book and elsewhere. However, the reader should be cautioned that this is leading-edge research and many questions remain unanswered.

13.1.1 Scale-Free Property

Reka Albert provides a good survey of the relationship between scale-free topology and functionality of protein expression networks (Albert, 2005). A *protein expression network* represents proteins, DNA, RNA, and other small molecules inside the cell as nodes, and signaling pathways and other regulatory mechanisms as links. Signaling and regulation is essentially a process that alters the level of chemicals in the cell as it manufactures DNA, RNA, and other products of metabolism. *Expression level* corresponds to concentration of a certain chemical in the process, and *behavior* corresponds to network assembly and evolution. We study protein expression networks in more detail, later.

Most studies are based on very simple organisms such as *Escherichia coli* and *Saccharomyces cerevisiae* (also known as "brewer's" or "baker's yeast." (For example, Albert reports that the yeast protein network is scale-free with an exponent of 2.5 and cluster coefficient $O(1/\lambda^2)$. Other researchers also report small-world effects with small average path length and dense local neighborhoods in the yeast protein network. What is the function of this structure?

Giaever et al. observed that up to 73% of *S. cerevisiae* genes are nonessential, claiming that removal of these nonessential genes has little effect on the cell (Giaever, 2002). This confirms the genetic robustness of yeast under random gene removal attack—where it is most likely that an unimportant gene will be removed. However, the yeast cell is vulnerable to the loss of highly connected hubs or nodes with high *closeness centrality*. In scale-free networks the hub is highly likely to be the one with maximum closeness. So, this confirms the general view of scale-free network robustness. However, it is not clear what came first—highly connected hub structure or evolutionary factors leading to scale-free structure.

Zhu, Gerstein, and Snyder (Zhu, 2007) argue that the scale-free topology of biological networks stems from "link dynamics" rather than preferential attachment as in the BA (Barabasi–Albert) *generative procedure*. *Link dynamics* is vaguely described as interaction loss and preferential interaction gain that leads to scale-free hubs. Perhaps link dynamics is just another name for the *Mihail generative procedure* described in Chapter 7. Recall that Mihail et al. proposed an emergent process that produces a *designer network* with topology predefined by degree sequence distribution. Networks are designed to emerge with a certain degree sequence distribution simply because they have prewired *stubs* at each node.

This is speculation, but perhaps the biochemical structure of each protein dictates how many expression processes the protein is able to support. A high-degreed protein may have more receptor sites (for binding) than a low-degreed protein—hence its ability to be more highly connected. If so, the abstract concept of a prewired set of stubs at each node corresponds to real-world biochemistry.

13.1.2 Small-World Effects

Small-world effects such as clustering and short average path length are thought to be a consequence of a biological network's ability to quickly respond to a perturbation. Fast and efficient reaction to metabolic and protein interactions have been observed in protein networks with short and redundant paths, as well as highly clustered local neighborhoods—both properties of small-world networks. It is as if biological networks organize themselves to be as responsive as possible by guaranteeing short average path length.

Clustering may be a consequence of modularity of cellular networks; that is, the architecture of a cellular network follows commonsense design rules found in optimal electronic circuit design. Electronic circuits are designed in highly modular structures to reduce overall complexity. A system with many simple components is less complex than a system with one large complex component. The same idea permeates software design—complexity is replaced with modules, and modules are expected to be self-contained with minimal linkages to other modules. This often leads to hierarchical designs.

Modules called *motifs* have been observed in abundance in biological networks, suggesting that nature repeatedly applies the same tried-and-true design principle over and over. A *motif* is a small subgraph with a well-defined topology that is used by the organism in various ways (see Fig. 13.1). Think of a motif as a simple component in a complex biological system that diminishes the overall complexity of the network in the same way that electronic circuits and computer software reduce complexity.

The *bifan motif* of Fig. 13.1a represents a cluster found in higher abundance than expected from randomly connected regulatory networks. Nodes represent proteins, DNA, or other metabolites involved in a biochemical reaction inside a cell. A link marked with a plus sign represents an *activation* reaction—essentially a *feedforward* mechanism for increasing the concentration of a certain metabolic chemical. A link marked with a minus sign represents the opposite—*inhibitory* reaction that is essentially a negative feedback mechanism. The bifan's feedforward signal or expression level accelerates the concentration of a metabolic inside a cell.

Similarly, the *biparallel motif* shown in Fig. 13.1b represents a chain reaction; protein A activates DNA B and C, which in turn activate protein D. The single input and feedforward loop (FFL) motifs represent simple feedforward mechanisms, while the bi-FFL is more complex—representing the activation of metabolites B, C, and D by A, and the further acceleration of reactions by metabolite B.

These feedforward motifs are thought to regulate the acceleration or delay of signals within the network. The feedforward loop (FFL), for example, may be the source of pulse generation, which signals the production of certain metabolites in cells. Alternatively, the feedback loop is thought to control state locking—achieving and holding a certain state of the network. The analogy with electronic circuit design is unavoidable, but the exact rules governing the dynamic behavior of these "chemical circuits" is not yet fully understood.

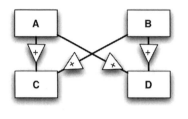

(a)

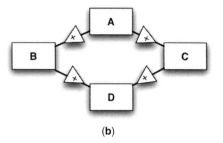

(b)

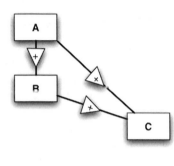

(c)

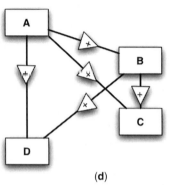

(d)

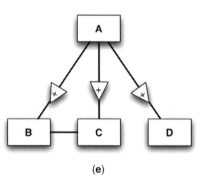

(e)

Figure 13.1 Common motifs found in cellular networks: (a) bifan; (b) biparallel; (c) feedforward loop (FFL); (d) bifeedforward loop (bi-FFL); (e) single input.

Apparently, cellular processes are made up of hierarchically structured modules, which are decomposable into submodules, and so on, much like a well-designed electronic circuit or computer program. There is a high degree of *crosstalk* and overlap between modules (Albert, 2005). Furthermore, triangles (clusters) are found in abundance in protein networks, with both positive and negative feedback mechanisms. We know from previous chapters that triangles are largely responsible for synchronization and dynamic stability in dynamic networks. Do triangular subgraphs play a similar role in biological networks?

13.2 DYNAMIC ANALYSIS

Evidence is mounting in support of the idea that regulatory networks behave the way they do because of their structure—that is, function follows form. This is most apparent in microbiological systems modeled as *expression networks*. The goal of this approach is to accurately predict the behavior of a biological process much as we would predict the behavior of an electronic circuit. The following analysis applies mainly to gene expression or *protein expression* networks because these networks have been explored in more detail than related biological networks. However, the concepts may be applied to other biological systems.

A gene–protein expression network is a kind of *influence network*, but with some notable exceptions: (1) the next-state functions are quite different and often nonlinear in a biological network and (2) biological networks are full of inhibitory feedback loops. Such enhancement of the basic influence or I-net model of Chapter 10 significantly increases the complexity of influence networks. We examine the simple linear continuous dynamic model first and return to the more complex non-linear dynamic model later.

13.2.1 Linear Continuous Networks

Figure 13.2 illustrates some basic building blocks of linear continuous expression networks. Such expression networks are special forms of *influence networks* studied in Chapter 10. Therefore, we apply the same theory to these linear biological networks. Unfortunately, our theory is incapable of expressing the behavior of nonlinear biological networks. Recall that a network is linear when its next-state function is linear and continuous when we use smooth continuous functions to describe state transitions.

The simple protein expression barbell of Fig. 13.2a models the most basic interactions of linear protein expression networks. Protein A binds with an amino acid

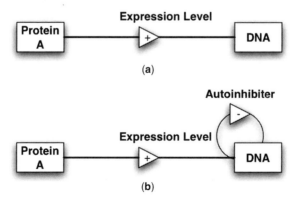

Figure 13.2 Basic protein expression network components: (a) simple expression; (b) inhibited expression.

of DNA, leading to some byproduct. The *expression level*—concentration of mRNA in this case—may vary from negative (negative feedback) to some positive level.

Expression may occur because of *transcription*—the process of transferring genetic information from DNA to RNA, or *translation*—the process that takes information passed from DNA as mRNA (messenger RNA) and turns it into a series of amino acids bound together with peptide bonds. This process occurs in the cell's *ribosome*. To simplify, we treat transcription and translation the same—as weighted and directed links in a generalized biological network.

Simple expression is an integrating function, as shown in Fig. 13.2a. Without some form of negative feedback, the level of concentration at the DNA node of Fig. 13.2a is unbounded. The influence of protein A expression on DNA in Fig. 13.2a is mathematically modeled by the differential equation $(\partial/\partial t)\text{DNA} = w(A)$, where DNA is the concentration of byproduct DNA, w is a weighting factor representing the expression level, and A is the concentration of protein A. The final state of each node is obtained by integrating differential equations. Given a constant level of protein A, the level of DNA will grow without bound.

Autoinhibition is the process of dampening expression levels using negative feedback. The network shown in Fig. 13.2b is autoinhibited because existing levels govern concentration levels. In terms of mathematical modeling, the rate of change of DNA concentration is governed by two inputs: the weighted (constant) level of protein A and the negatively weighted level of DNA:

$$\frac{\partial}{\partial t}\text{DNA} = w_A A - w_{\text{DNA}}\text{DNA}$$

$$\text{DNA}(0) = \text{DNA}_0$$

$$\frac{\partial}{\partial t}A = 0$$

$$A(0) = A_0$$

For example, assume unit levels of protein A, unit weights, and initial conditions as follows:

$$\frac{\partial}{\partial t}\text{DNA} = A - \text{DNA}$$

$$\text{DNA}(0) = 0$$

$$\frac{\partial}{\partial t}A = 0$$

$$A(0) = 1$$

This set of simultaneous equations has the following solution:

$$\text{DNA}(t) = 1 - e^{-t}$$

$$A(t) = 1$$

The level of concentration of DNA rises from zero to 1.0, as time passes, and remains there. The feedback loop inhibits expression beyond a vanishing point called the *fixed point* or *strange attractor*, rather than allowing the node's state to grow without bound. This simple network has a fixed-point attractor at $(1,1)$:

$$\lim_{t=\infty} A(t) = 1$$

$$\lim_{t=\infty} DNA(t) = 1$$

More generally, linear expression networks are influence networks where matrix W is the adjacency matrix obtained from the weights of outgoing links and vector $S(t)$ is the state vector corresponding to node values. The rate of change due to weighted expression links is given by the state equation

$$\frac{\partial S}{\partial t} = W^T S; S(0) = S_0$$

$$W = \begin{bmatrix} w_{1,1} & w_{1,2} & \cdots & w_{1,n} \\ w_{2,1} & w_{2,2} & \cdots & w_{2,n} \\ \cdots & \cdots & \cdots & \cdots \\ w_{n,1} & w_{n,2} & \cdots & w_{n,n} \end{bmatrix}$$

Elements of connection matrix W are positive for feedforward *activation* expressions and negative for feedbackward or *inhibitor* expressions. Vector $S(0)$ is the initial state of nodes in the expression network.

We are particularly interested in the fixed-point solution to the network's state equation—if one exists. Recall that in a linear system, fixed points are possible only when the *spectral radius* of W^T is bounded by zero:

$$\rho(W^T) < 0$$

Also, in a linear influence network, the strange attractor values equal the state of each node at the vanishing point:

$$\lim_{t=\infty} S(t) = [W^T + I]^t$$

Program *BioNet.jar* approximates attractors by iterating matrix multiplication t^* times, until there is little change in $abs[(S(t+1) - S(t))/S(t)]$. But there is no guarantee that an arbitrary protein expression network will converge to some finite-valued fixed point. In fact, the most likely result is nonconvergence! Therefore, we must check for stability.

The stability of a linear biological network depends on the spectral radius, but this theory is valid only for linear systems. So far, we have assumed that expression networks are linear systems, but this assumption may not hold in nature. In fact, there are very few mathematical tools for evaluating a nonlinear network for stability.

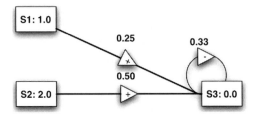

Figure 13.3 Simple expression network with an autoinhibited node and expression weights of $\frac{1}{4}$, $\frac{1}{2}$, and $-\frac{1}{3}$, respectively.

Nonetheless, we can study linear systems stability and learn some things about biological networks.

Consider the simple linear expression network of Fig. 13.3. Two protein nodes, S_1 and S_2, regulate an autoinhibited DNA node, S_3. We ask, "Is this network stable, and if so, does it reach a fixed point?" What is the fixed point? Initially, $S_1(0) = 1.0$, $S_2(0) = 2.0$, and $S_3(0) = 0$, and weights $w_{1,3} = 0.25$, $w_{2,3} = 0.50$, and $w_{3,3} = -0.33$. All other expression weights are zero.

Mathematically, this network is governed by its state equation:

$$\frac{\partial S}{\partial t} = W^T S; S(0) = \begin{bmatrix} 1.0 \\ 2.0 \\ 0.0 \end{bmatrix}$$

$$W = \begin{bmatrix} 0 & 0 & 0.25 \\ 0 & 0 & 0.50 \\ 0 & 0 & -0.33 \end{bmatrix}$$

$$\rho(W^T) = -0.33$$

Note that this network is stable and has a fixed-point attractor because its spectral radius is less than zero. In fact, there is no oscillation (imaginary) part, so the fixed point is reached without chaotic oscillations. This assures us that an attractor exists for each node. For the initial condition S_0, we obtain an approximation to the attractor values after $t^* = 20$ matrix multiplications:

$$[W^T + I] = \begin{bmatrix} 1 & 0 & 0 \\ 0 & 1 & 0 \\ 0.25 & 0.50 & 0.66 \end{bmatrix}^{20} \begin{bmatrix} 1.0 \\ 2.0 \\ 0.0 \end{bmatrix} = \begin{bmatrix} 1 & 0 & 0 \\ 0 & 1 & 0 \\ 0.75 & 1.50 & 0 \end{bmatrix} \bullet \begin{bmatrix} 1.0 \\ 2.0 \\ 0.0 \end{bmatrix}$$

$$= \begin{bmatrix} 1.0 \\ 2.0 \\ 3.75 \end{bmatrix}$$

The attractors are 1, 2, and 3.75, respectively. Program *BioNet.jar* finds the approximate solution by iteration: 1, 2, and 3.79, because 0.33 is only an approximation of $\frac{1}{3}$. What is the attractor value of node S_3 when the initial state is $[2, 5, 0]^T$? This is left as an exercise for the reader.

13.2.2 Boolean Networks

The linear continuous model has its limitations, especially when it comes to modeling nonlinear next-state functions. For example, instead of expression levels being summed at each node, suppose that levels are multiplied. Such networks are no longer linear, and so they can no longer be analyzed using the linear system tools developed for influence networks. In fact, nonlinear continuous models are difficult to solve for fixed points without numerical techniques. Numerical integration of nonlinear differential equations is subject to instabilities and computational limits, so many investigators have resorted to an approximation by simplification. We substitute the continuous network with an equivalent Boolean network.

A *Boolean network* is a biological network containing logical operations, AND (*) and OR (+), and Boolean states. Links transmit Boolean signals: "+" means that the signal is logically unaltered, while "−" means that the signal is inverted such that a Boolean 1 arrives as zero, and a Boolean zero arrives as a 1. For example, a negative Boolean feedback link inverts the state of a node.

In terms of biology, an expression level is subject to threshold digitization; a level that exceeds 0.5 is rounded up to a Boolean 1, and a level less than 0.5 is rounded down to a Boolean zero. Similarly, the state of a node is either zero or one, depending on the threshold 0.5. There are no negative values in a Boolean network—only zero and ones. Subtraction is equivalent to inverting a bit: $1 \rightarrow 0$ or $0 \rightarrow 1$.

Boolean expression networks are essentially digital circuits. Therefore, our model of an organism approximates the model of a machine governed by digital logic. The organism's behavior is approximated as a logical circuit such as the *half-adder* with the carry network shown in Fig. 13.4. This "motif" is found in arithmetic units of all digital computers. It implements binary addition, with carry bit—the most basic operation of all for computers that add two numbers together. For example, three half-adders with carry bits are used (in parallel) to sum the two binary numbers, $101 + 110$:

$$+101$$
$$+110$$
$$+011 = \text{half-adder}$$
$$100 = \text{carry}$$
$$1011 = 11 \text{ (the number ``eleven'')}$$

In Fig. 13.4, let $A = 1$ and $B = 0$ represent the least-significant bits of the two numbers (101 and 110). The carry bit is easily calculated by multiplication

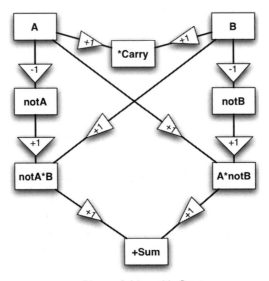

Binary Adder with Carry

Figure 13.4 Half-adder with carry network containing OR and AND nodes. This network adds binary numbers, one pair of bits at a time.

(AND): $1*0 = 0$. The half-adder sum is more complicated to calculate. First, each bit is inverted by the link connecting node A to node notA, and node B to node notB. A is inverted to 0, and B inverted to 1 and stored in the notA and notB nodes, respectively. At the same time, A and B bits are transmitted to multiplier nodes, notA*B and A*notB. At node notA*B multiply $0*0 = 0$, and at node A*notB multiply $1*1 = 1$. Finally, the OR node Sum adds its two inputs: $0 + 1 = 1$. The least significant half-adder bit is 1. Similarly, the next-significant bit is 1, and the most-significant bit is 0, with a carry bit of 1. The sum, in decimal, is 11.

Binary addition simulates digital addition in a computer, but in an organism, AND and OR logic approximates expression levels. For example, an expression level may be "turned on" only by the presence of sufficient concentrations of two metabolites—corresponding to a logical AND node. Conversely, if only one or more metabolites are needed to activate a reaction, the OR node is used.

Boolean networks are only approximations to linear continuous networks. For example, the linear continuous network of Fig. 13.3 reaches a fixed point of $S_3 = 1$, with initial state $S_0 = [1, 1, 0]^T$, when treated like a Boolean network. It is easy to see why. In the first iteration of the network, the auto inhibitor link reverses the logic of $S_3 = 0$ to $S_3 = 1$. Boolean addition of 1 from S_2 sums to one, and addition of $\frac{1}{4} = 0$ from S_1 does not change the sum. Hence, S_3 reaches its Boolean attractor in one step.

In general, the next-state function of a Boolean network is the logic table corresponding to its *Boolean algebra*. At each timestep, the next state of a node is equal to the logical combination of its inputs. Therefore, for Fig. 13.3, the set of Boolean algebra equations are

$$S_1(t+1) = S_1(t); S_1(0)\text{given}$$
$$S_2(t+1) = S_2(t); S_2(0)\text{given}$$
$$S_3(t+1) = \lceil [0.5S_2(t)] \text{ or } [0.25S_1(t)] \text{ or } \{ \text{NOT} [0.33S_3(t)] \} \rceil; S_3(0)\text{given}$$

Given the initial state $[1, 2, 0]^T$, the final state of this network is

$$S_1(t) = 1$$
$$S_2(t) = 2 = 1$$
$$S_3(t+1) = \lceil (1) \text{ or } (0) \text{ or } \{ \text{NOT}(0) \} \rceil = (1) \text{ or } (0) \text{ or } (1) = 1$$

Suppose the initial state is $[1, 0, 0]^T$. What is the final state of the network of Fig. 13.3? Direct substitution into the logic equation above gives a misleading answer, unless time is taken into consideration. Finding the correct answer is left as an exercise for the reader.

We can approximate the behavior of a nonlinear expression network by simplifying it and treating it as a Boolean network. This allows us to obtain a solution by direct application of Boolean algebra, but it is still an approximation. This approach also has analysis limitations—we cannot determine its stability or fixed-point attractor values directly from its Boolean algebra state equation.

13.3 PROTEIN EXPRESSION NETWORKS

A protein expression network is a directed influence network containing *metabolites*—genes, mRNA, DNA, proteins, or other molecules—as nodes, and chemical transformations, translational or transcriptional expressions, and other regulatory relationships as links. The state of each node is typically a dynamically varying concentration level of some chemical. The weight associated with a link is typically an approximation of the level of expression or effect one concentration has on another (degree of influence that one node has on another). Positive links represent *activation* of an expression and negative links represent *inhibition* of an expression.

A *Boolean network* model can determine the presence (absence) of link activation and presence (absence) of a metabolite at a node. A continuous model attempts to predict the response of an organism to a perturbation. For example, what happens when the level of concentration of a certain metabolite increases? The increase spreads through the network much like a contagion—except that the rules for spreading are different.

The general system state equation of a Boolean network is a logic equation describing the next state of each node from the previous state and the network's connection topology. Arbitrary function $f(x)$ may be linear or nonlinear:

$$S(t+1) = f(S(t)); S(0) = S_0$$

The general system state of a continuous network is defined by a system of differential equations representing changes in concentration levels or changes in mass. Again, arbitrary function $f(x)$ may be linear or nonlinear:

$$\frac{\partial}{\partial t} S(t) = f(S(t)); S(0) = S_0$$

We have shown in the previous sections that such networks are inherently unstable and tend to "blow up" because of feedforward connections in the network. Even linear network models are highly likely to be unstable and unable to converge to a fixed-point solution. Often the attractor values grow without bound. This is partially due to the presence of source and sink nodes that lack feedback loops to control concentration levels. It is also partially due to the topology or wiring diagram of the networks. We investigate this problem in more detail using spectral decomposition.

In linear networks we know that stability depends on the network's spectral radius. If the spectral radius is less than zero, the network achieves its finite fixed point and the attractors are bounded. Typically, attractors are equal to zero, and the state of nodes reaches zero after some oscillation or dampening. However, if the spectral radius exceeds zero, there are no guarantees of boundedness. This raises a question regarding biological networks and evolution. Could biological networks possibly have evolved from random networks through an emergent process that minimizes the spectral radius? We test this hypothesis in the next section.

13.3.1   Emergence of Biological Networks

The *protein expression network* is inherently unstable as formulated because its spectral radius tends to be greater than zero—unless a significant number of links are inhibitors, or there is sufficient restriction on link weights. This is largely due to the positive definite adjacency matrix resulting from feedforward motifs. In addition, the research literature confirms that biological networks tend to be scale-free. This evidence raises a question that we address by simulation—how does a biological network emerge as a scale-free network with low spectral radius?

We test two hypotheses by simulation:

Hypothesis 1. Emergence of a scale-free network with a high-degreed hub from a random network lowers the spectral radius of a biological network and promotes stability, and therefore "evolves" biological networks that reach a fixed point.

Hypothesis 2. Emergence of a biological network with high entropy from a random network lowers its spectral radius and promotes stability. Such emergent networks dynamically converge to stable attractors.

We know from previous chapters that the spectral radius of a scale-free network is approximately 75% higher than that of an equivalent random network. For example, a random network with $n = 100$ nodes and $m = 200$ links has a spectral radius of approximately 4.8, whereas a network generated by the *BA generative procedure* produces a scale-free network with a spectral radius of approximately

7.25. In Chapter 7 ("Emergence"), we transformed equivalent random networks into scale-free-like networks with very large hubs and spectral radii of approximately 12.0 for $n = 100$ and $m = 200$. Thus, we have an intuitive sense that the spectral radius of a scale-free network is somewhere between 2 and 3 times that of an equivalent random network.

But what happens if the goal of the transformation is to evolve a random network into a biological network with a smaller spectral radius? For example, suppose that an emergent process is applied to a random network as follows. Starting with a random biological network as defined in this chapter, exchange the endpoints of links at random, and reject the exchange, unless the network's spectral radius lowers. Repeat this process indefinitely, or until stopped by the user. What is the effect on spectral radius, hub degree, and entropy?

To test hypothesis 1, we apply the following emergent process to a random biological network consisting of $n = 50$ nodes and $m = 100$ activation links (weights are equal to 1.0). The emergent process is allowed to run for at least 3000 iterations, which is typically sufficient to reach a final state.

Minimize Spectral Radius

1. Repeat indefinitely:
   a. Randomly select a link L and randomly select either its head H or tail node T. Ignore inhibitory loops.
   b. Randomly select a distinct node V.
   c. Randomly rewire the H or T to connect to V, taking care to avoid duplicate links and loops.
   d. Calculate the spectral radius ρ. If $\rho >$ previous spectral radius, restore L to its previous connection. Otherwise, set the network's spectral radius to ρ.

This emergent process—implemented in program *BioNet.jar*—was used to average the resulting spectral radius over 10 runs each on random networks. In addition to measuring the effect of the emergent process on spectral radius, we also measured the effect on hub degree and entropy (see Fig. 13.5).

Spectral radius decreases to approximately zero, from an average value of 1.67, but this had little effect on hub degree and entropy. In fact, entropy and hub degree changed by only 4% each, while spectral radius plunged by 100%. Thus, hypothesis 1 is rejected.

To test hypothesis 2, increase entropy by randomly rewiring links—from either head or tail—keeping only the rewired links that increase entropy. So, rewiring is biased. But which way is the bias? From Fig. 13.5 we see that entropy and spectral radius change by approximately 29% and hub degree changes by 35%; that is, hub degree increases nearly proportionally (on a percentage scale) to entropy. This rejects hypothesis 2.

At first, the results seem contrary to the definition of a random network. How is it possible to increase the randomness of a random network? The anchored random network generative procedure was used to produce these simulation results, but

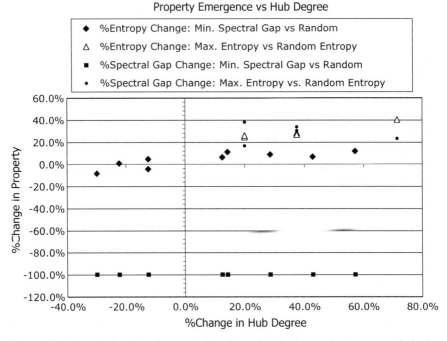

Figure 13.5 Simulation data for spectral radius minimization and entropy maximization emergence.

this does not explain the paradox. Remember that a random network is one instance of a network from a very large set of possible networks. Therefore, each time a random network is generated, it is possible—with nonzero probability—that it is not the maximum entropy network, but rather a sample from the distribution of all possible networks generated by considering all possible combinations of nodepairs. The maximum entropy emergence process used to discount hypothesis 2 simply increases entropy where possible.

Hypothesis 2 was rejected because spectral radius is increased instead of decreased by entropy maximization. Therefore, we must reject the idea that emergence of stable and convergent biological networks is a result of entropy maximization or spectral radius minimization. However, hub degree increases, which suggests that it is possible for rewiring to turn a random network into a scale-free-like network. This is an unproven conjecture left as an exercise for the reader. Most likely, some other force of nature causes biological networks to evolve into stable, convergent networks.

13.4   MASS KINETICS MODELING

The foregoing "failed experiments" suggest that simple emergence of stable biological networks is insufficient to explain how biological networks are able to "compute an end state" from some arbitrary initial state. This leads us to speculate on the validity of the model developed so far. In this section, we explore extensions to the known literature on the dynamics of biological networks. The extension is based on a reasonable premise—biological networks such as the protein expression network described above are essentially mass kinetics networks. *Mass kinetics* is a branch of chemistry that models rates of change in the concentration of reactants in a chemical reaction. It is largely concerned with the flow of liquids through a system. For example, mass kinetics can be used to model the concentration of metabolites at the cellular level—providing a state equation for the metabolic network. This requires that we obey the *conservation of matter* law of physics at each node of the network. Rate of change in the state of a node is as follows:

$$\frac{\partial S}{\partial t} = \sum_{j \in \text{inlinks}} \text{inFlow}_j - \sum_{k \in \text{outlinks}} \text{outFlow}_k$$

where $S = (\text{flow in}) - (\text{flow out})$ This relationship is similar to *Kirchhoff's law*, except that it does not require inflow to equal outflow because nodes are allowed to accumulate mass, whereas a Kirchhoff node must balance inputs and outputs. This is an important difference as it changes the behavior of mass kinetics networks.

   In addition, the state of a node can never go negative:

$$0 \le S(t)$$

This model is valid only for a linear system. Nonetheless, if we assume linearity, the linear systems theory developed earlier still applies, and basic conditions on network convergence—as well as the fixed-point or attractor values—can be approximated.

13.4.1   Mass Kinetic State Equations

Consider the simple expression network of Fig. 13.6a. Two source nodes, S_1 and S_2, supply inputs to one sink node, S_3, but with different levels, 25% and 50%, respectively. Node S_3 undergoes a change in state at a rate determined by inputs from S_1, S_2, and inhibitor feedback from S_3, itself. The mass kinetics equations for these three nodes establish the network's state equations:

$$\frac{\partial S_1}{\partial t} = -0.25 S_1; S_1(0) = 1$$

$$\frac{\partial S_2}{\partial t} = -0.50 S_2; S_2(0) = 2$$

$$\frac{\partial S_3}{\partial t} = 0.25 S_1 + 0.50 S_2 - 0.33 S_3; S_3(0) = 0$$

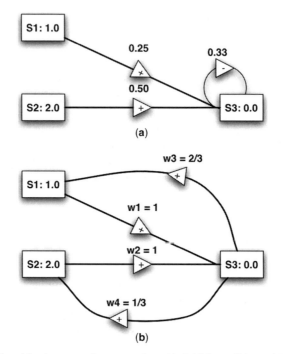

Figure 13.6 Mass kinetic expression networks with initial conditions: (a) simple network similar to that of Fig. 13.3; (b) simple feedback network with sum of out-degrees equal to one.

In matrix terms, this is

$$\frac{\partial S}{\partial t} = QS$$

$$Q = \begin{bmatrix} -0.25 & 0 & 0 \\ 0 & -0.50 & 0 \\ 0.25 & 0.50 & -0.67 \end{bmatrix} \quad S(0) = \begin{bmatrix} 1 \\ 2 \\ 0 \end{bmatrix}$$

This system has a negative spectral radius, $\rho(Q) = -0.25$, so it should find a finite fixed-point solution rather than blowing up. Indeed, all nodes converge to zero, but not before responding according to the curves shown in Fig. 13.7. These response curves show that this simple network converges to zero, due to the dampening effects of the inhibitor loop and the depletion of states S_1 and S_2. Nodes S_1 and S_2 decline exponentially from their initial values of 1 and 2, respectively; node S_3 rises sharply from zero to 1.25, and then declines to zero.

The mass kinetics network of Fig. 13.6a is stable and dampens the perturbations at nodes S_1 and S_2 over time. Program *BioNet.jar* can be used to illustrate the response shown in Fig. 13.7, and gives estimates of attractor values for the given initial condition. This example supports the linear systems theory of dynamic networks. But how was matrix Q determined?

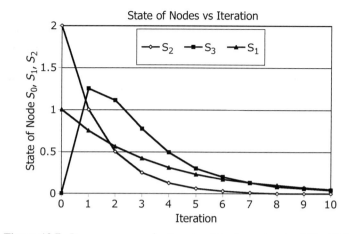

Figure 13.7 Response curves for the mass kinetics network of Fig. 13.6a.

The input portion of the state equation is W^TS, where W^T is the transposed adjacency matrix. For the example in Fig. 13.6a, adjacency matrix W and its transpose W^T are

$$W = \begin{bmatrix} 0 & 0 & \frac{1}{4} \\ 0 & 0 & \frac{1}{2} \\ 0 & 0 & -\frac{1}{3} \end{bmatrix}$$

$$W^T = \begin{bmatrix} 0 & 0 & 0 \\ 0 & 0 & 0 \\ \frac{1}{4} & \frac{1}{2} & -\frac{1}{3} \end{bmatrix}$$

The output portion of the state equation is equal to the sum of absolute values of columns of W^T, out_j. These column sums are bounded by 100% to preserve conservation of mass. We subtract out_j from the diagonals of W^T to obtain Q:

$$\text{out}_j = \sum_i \left| w_{i,j}^T \right|$$

$$\text{OUT} = \begin{bmatrix} \sum_i \left| w_{i,1}^T \right| & 0 & \cdots & 0 \\ 0 & \sum_i \left| w_{i,2}^T \right| & \cdots & 0 \\ 0 & 0 & \cdots & 0 \\ 0 & 0 & 0 & \sum_i \left| w_{i,n}^T \right| \end{bmatrix}$$

$$Q = W^T - \text{OUT}$$

$$\frac{\partial S}{\partial t} = QS(t) = [W^T - \text{OUT}]S(t)$$

Stability of a mass kinetic network is determined by the condition of matrix Q. If $\rho(Q) < 0$, the network converges to a fixed point, or repeats states contained within a *limit cycle*. In either case, the state of one or more nodes may oscillate rather than follow a smooth response curve as shown in Fig. 13.7. For example, consider the mass kinetic network of Fig. 13.6b, and compute W, W^T, Q, and then $\rho(Q)$:

$$W = \begin{bmatrix} 0 & 0 & 1 \\ 0 & 0 & 1 \\ \frac{2}{3} & \frac{1}{3} & 0 \end{bmatrix}$$

$$W^T = \begin{bmatrix} 0 & 0 & \frac{2}{3} \\ 0 & 0 & \frac{1}{3} \\ 1 & 1 & 0 \end{bmatrix}$$

$$\text{OUT} = \begin{bmatrix} -1 & 0 & 0 \\ 0 & -1 & 0 \\ 0 & 0 & -1 \end{bmatrix}$$

$$Q = W^T - \text{OUT} = \begin{bmatrix} -1 & 0 & \frac{2}{3} \\ 0 & -1 & \frac{1}{3} \\ 1 & 1 & -1 \end{bmatrix}$$

Since $\rho(Q) < 0$, this network converges, but not smoothly. Instead of seeking an attractor value and staying there, each node oscillates between values. This network is bistable because the oscillations neither increase nor decrease in amplitude. Instead, the node's states fall into a *limit cycle*, repeating the following sequences, indefinitely:

$$S_1: \quad 0,2,0,2,\ldots.$$
$$S_2: \quad 0,1,0,1,\ldots$$
$$S_3: \quad 0,3,0,3,\ldots$$

This limit cycle is a *tipping point*—a delicate dividing line between stable fixed-point attractors and unstable oscillations that eventually blow up. If we change parameters only slightly, the network finds an attractor on either side of the limit cycle. For example, if the sum of output weights from S_3 to S_1 and S_2 is less than 1.0 (e.g., $w_3 = 0.6$, $w_4 = 0.30$), the network finds a stable fixed point at $S_1 = 0.95$, $S_2 = 0.47$, and $S_3 = 1.58$. On the other hand, if the sum of the output weights exceeds 1.0, the network blows up. For example, if $w_3 = 0.75$ and $w_4 = 0.35$, then the sum of output weights from S_3 is 1.1.

13.4.2 Bounded Mass Kinetic Networks

Expression networks are relatively new and unexplored models of protein interaction in biology. The relationship between mass kinetics and network models is even less developed. But perhaps we can gain some insight into possible connections between network science and metabolic processes by speculating on the role of network stability in biology. However, the reader is cautioned that this section is pure speculation and not backed up by biology.

We know that the ability of a dynamic network to synchronize and arrive at a stable fixed point is related to its spectral radius, among other things.[1] If the spectral radius is negative and bounded by zero, the network will find a finite fixed point. In some cases, we need additional conditions to hold, also, as in the Kirchhoff network. Generally, the spectral radius must be less than zero to guarantee that a dynamic network will not blow up. However, is there virtue in even lower values of spectral radius, especially as it pertains to the mass kinetics network described above? Are biological networks with lower spectral radius somehow more "fit" than networks with higher spectral radius?

Consider the following simulations of random and scale-free mass kinetics networks with $n = 50$ nodes and $m = 100$ links ($\Delta m = 2$ for the scale-free network). In each case, generate a network using the *ER* or *BA generative procedure*, but with weighted and directed links. Spectral radius is determined by both directedness and weight of links, as well as degree sequence. Assuming that the direction of links is determined by the ER and BA generators, the only remaining factors to vary are weights and topology. Therefore, analyze the resulting spectral radius as a function of weights and class of network.

Figure 13.8 shows the results of 10 simulations using program *BioNet.jar* to generate random and scale-free networks with different link weight allocation patterns. Spectral radius is averaged and plotted as shown, along with its plus-and-minus standard deviation value. In the first category (weights $= 1$), all links are assigned a weight of one. In the second category (sum OUT $= 1$), all links are assigned a value equal to $1/\text{node}$ [tail].out_degree, where node[tail].out_degree is the out-degree of the anchor or tail node corresponding with the link. Similarly, the third category (Sum IN $= 1$) assigns weights such that the sum of all incoming links to a node is one. Finally, random weights in the interval [0,1) are assigned to all links in the random weights category.

If we believe that networks with lower spectral radius are more stable—and therefore, more fit—then Fig. 13.8 suggests a ranking, as follows:

Scale-free (weights $= 1$): Most stable

Scale-free (Sum OUT $= 1$):

Random (Sum OUT $= 1$):

---

[1]"Other things" include reinforcing feedback loops.

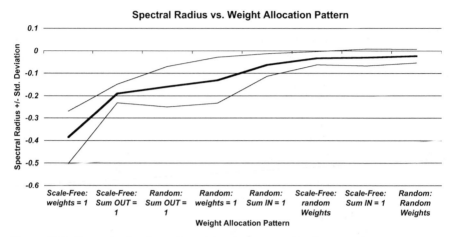

Figure 13.8 Spectral radius for random and scale-free mass kinetics networks versus category of link weight allocation.

Random (weights = 1):
Random (Sum IN = 1):
Scale-free (random weights):
Scale-free (Sum IN = 1):
Random (random weights): Least stable

These simulation results are not conclusive evidence of the virtue of scale-free networks versus random, because of the similarity of spectral radius for both scale-free and random networks when their output link weights sum to one. It appears that adhering to a conservation of matter law by bounding the output from each node to 100% is more critical to lowering spectral radius than degree sequence. Two of the three lowest spectral radius results involved scale-free topologies, and two relied on the "OUT = 1" constraint.

The pairing of network science with metabolic and protein science is an exciting new area of investigation, with many unanswered questions. We have only scratched the surface with this introductory chapter. The answers are left as an exercise for the reader!

13.5   EXERCISES

13.1. What is the attractor value of node S_3 in Fig. 13.3, when the expression network's initial state is $[2, 5, 0]^T$?

13.2. What is the final state of the Boolean network equivalent of the expression network in Fig. 13.3, when its initial state is $[1, 0, 0]^T$?

13.3. What are the values of all eigenvalues of the network in Fig. 13.3 if it is treated as a protein expression network? What if it is treated like a mass kinetics network?

13.4. Is the mass kinetics network of Fig. 13.6b stable for $w_3 = \frac{3}{4}$ and $w_4 = \frac{1}{4}$? If so, what are the network's attractors?

13.5. Build a logic table for the Bi-Fan motif in Fig. 13.1a and show that it is equivalent to a logical OR gate when treated like a Boolean network; that is, the outputs, C,D, are obtained by the simple OR operation: $C = A$ OR B; $D = A$ OR B.

BIBLIOGRAPHY

Adamic, L. A., The small world web, in *Research and Advanced Technology for Digital Libraries, Lecture Notes in Computer Science 1696*, S. Abiteboul and A.-M. Vercoustre, eds, Springer-Verlag, New York, 1999, 443–452.

Adamic, L. A. and B. A. Huberman, Power-law distribution of the World Wide Web, *Science* **287**:2115 (2000).

Adamic, L. A., R. M. Lukose, A. R., Puniyani, and B. A. Huberman, Search in power-law networks, *Phys. Rev. E* **64**(4):046135 (2001).

Adamic, L. A., R. M. Lukose, and B. A. Huberman, *Local Search in Unstructured Networks*, Wiley-VCH, Verlag, Berlin, 2002.

Albert, R., H. Jeong, and A.-L. Barabasi, Diameter of the World Wide Web, *Nature* **401**:130–131 (1999).

Albert, R., H. Jeong, and A. L. Barabasi, The Internet's Achilles' heel: Error and attack tolerance of complex networks, *Nature* **406**:378–382 (2000).

Albert, R. and A.-L. Barabasi, Statistical mechanics of complex networks, *Rev. Mod. Phys.* **74**:47–97 (2002).

Albert, R., Scale-free networks in cell biology, *J. Cell Sci.* **118**:4947–4957 (The Company of Biologists) (2005).

Albert, R., Network inference, analysis, and modeling in systems biology, the plant cell online, www.aspb.org, *Am. Soc. Plant Biol.* 1–12 (Nov. 2007).

Al-Mannai, W. and T. Lewis, Minimizing network risk with application to critical infrastructure protection, *J. Inform. Warfare* **6**(2):52–68 (Aug. 2007).

Amaral, L. A., A. Scala, M. Barthelemy, and H. E. Stanley, Classes of small-world networks, *Proc. Natl. Acad. Sci. USA* **97**(21):11149–11152 (2000).

Network Science: Theory and Practice. By Ted G. Lewis
Copyright © 2009 John Wiley & Sons, Inc.

Atay, F. M., T. Biyikoglu, and J. Jost, Synchronization of networks with prescribed degree distributions, *IEEE Trans. Circuits Syst. I* **53**(1):92–98 (2006).

Bagnoli, F. and M. Bezzi, Small world effects in evolution, *Phys. Rev. E* **64**:021914 (2001).

Ball, F. G., D. Mollison, and G. Scalia-Tomba, Epidemics with two levels of mixing, *Ann. Appl. Prob.* **7**(1):46–89 (1997).

Barabasi, A.-L., R. Albert, and H. Jeong, Emergence of scaling in random networks, *Science* **286**:509–512 (1999).

Barabasi, A.-L., E. Ravasz, and T. Vicsek, Deterministic scale-free networks, *Physica A* **299**(3–4):559–564 (2001).

Barabasi, A.-L., *Linked: The New Science of Networks*, Perseus Publishing, Cambridge, MA, 2002.

Barabasi, A.-L., H. Jeong, Z. Neda, E. Ravasz, A. Schubert, and T. Vicsek, Evolution of the social network of scientific collaborations, *Physica A* **311**(3–4):590–614 (2002).

Barahona, M. and L. M. Pecora, Synchronization in small-world systems, *Phys. Rev. Lett.* **89**:054101 (2002).

Barnes, J. A., *Social Network*, Addison-Wesley, Reading, MA, 1972.

Barrat, A., Comment on Small-world networks: Evidence for a crossover picture, preprint 9903323 available from http://arxiv.org/abs/cond-mat/ (1999).

Barrat, A. and M. Weigt, On the properties of small-world network models, *Eur. Phys. J. B* **13**:547 (2000); available as *Condensed Matter/9903411*.

Barthelemy, M. and L. A. N. Amaral, Small-world networks: Evidence for a crossover picture, *Phys. Rev. Lett.* **82**:3180 (1999).

Bass, F. M., A new product growth for model consumer durables, *Manage. Sci.* **15**:215–227 (1969).

Bass, P. I. and F. M. Bass, *Diffusion of Technology Generations: A Model of Adoption and Repeat Sales*, Working Paper, Bass Economics Inc. (www.basseconomics.com), Frisco, TX, 2001.

Ben-Naim, E. and P. L. Krapivsky, Size of outbreaks near the epidemic threshold, *Phys. Rev. E* **69**:050901 (2004).

Bollobás, B., *Random Graphs*, Academic Press, New York, 1985.

Bollobas, B., O. Riordan, J. Spencer, and G. Tusnady, The degree sequence of a scale-free random graph process, *Random Struct. Algorithms* **18**(3):279–290 (2001).

Bonacich, P., Factoring and weighing approaches to clique identification, *J. Math. Sociol.* **2**:113–120 (1972).

Bristor, J. M. and M. J. Ryan, Applying the small world phenomenon to organizational buying, in M. Kochen, ed., *The Small World*, Ablex, Norwood, NJ, 1989, Chapter 4, pp. 87–99.

Broder, A., S. R. Kumar, F. Maghoul, P. Raghavan, S. Rajagopalan, R. Stata, A. Tomkins, and J. Wiener, Graph structure in the web, *Comput. Networks* **33**(1–6):309–320, (2000).

Burt, R. S., *Structural Holes: The Social Structure of Competition*, Harvard Univ. Press, Cambridge, MA, 1992.

Callon, M., The dynamics of techno-economic networks, in P. S. Rod Coombs and V. Walsh, eds, *Technological Change and Company Strategies: Economic and Sociological Perspectives*, Harcourt Brace Jovanovich, San Diego, 1992, pp. 72–102.

Chen, L.-C. and K. M. Carley, The impact of countermeasure propagation on the prevalence of computer viruses, *IEEE Trans. Syst. Man Cybernetics* (Part B: *Cybernetics*) 1–11 (2004).

Christensen, C. C., *The Innovator's Dilemma*, HarperCollins, 2003.

Coleman, J., *Foundations of Social Theory*, Belknap Press, 1990.

Collins, J. J., and C. C. Chow, It's a small world, *Nature* **393**:409–410 (1998).

Comellas, F., J. Ozon, and J. G. Peters, Deterministic small-world communication networks, *Inform. Process. Lett.*, **76**(1–2):83–90 (2000).

Das, R., M. Mitchell, and J. P. Crutchfield, A genetic algorithm discovers particle based computation in cellular automata, in Y. Davidor, H. P. Schwefel, and R. Manner eds, *Parallel Problem Solving in Nature, Lecture Notes in Computer Science*, Springer, Berlin, 1994, pp. 344–353.

Davidsen, J., H. Ebel, and S. Bornholdt, Emergence of a small world from local interactions: Modeling acquaintance networks, *Phys. Rev. Lett.* **88**(12):128701 (2002).

Dezso, Z. and A.-L. Barabasi, Halting viruses in scale-free networks, *Phys. Rev. E* **65**(5) (2002).

Dorogovtsev, S. N., J. F. F. Mendes, and A. N. Samukhin, Structure of growing networks with preferential linking, *Phys. Rev. Lett.* **85**(21):4633–4636 (2000).

Dorogovtsev, S. N., A. V. Goltsev, and J. F. F. Mendes, Pseudofractal scale-free web, *Phys. Rev. E* **65**(6):066122 (2002).

Dorogovtsev, S. N. and J. F. F. Mendes, Evolution of networks, *Adv. Phys.* **51**(4):1079–1187 (2002).

Dorogovtsev, S. N. and J. F. F. Mendes, *Evolution of Networks—from Biological Nets to the Internet and WWW*, Oxford Univ. Press, 2003.

Erdös, P. and A. Rényi, On the evolution of random graphs, *Publ. Math. Inst. Hungar. Acad. Sci.* **5**:17–61 (1960).

Erdos, P. and A. Renyi, On random graphs I, in *Selected Papers of Alfred Renyi*, Akademiai Kiadu, Budapest, Hungary, 1976 (1st publication in 1959), Vol. 2, pp. 308–315.

Erdos, P. and A. Renyi, On the evolution of random graphs, in *Selected Papers of Alfred Renyi*, Akademiai Kiadu, Budapest, Hungary, 1976 (1st publication in 1960), Vol. 2, pp. 482–525.

Eriksen, K. A. and M. Hornquist, Scale-free growing networks imply linear preferential attachment, *Phys. Rev. E* **65**(1):017102 (2002).

Euler, Leonhard (1707–1783), Koenigsberg Bridges Problem.

Faloutsos, M., P. Faloutsos, and C. Faloutsos, On power-law relationships of the Internet topology, *Proc. ACM SIGCOMM '99 Conf. Applications, Technologies, Architectures, and Protocols for Computer Communication in Cambridge, MA, USA*, ACM Press, New York, 1999, pp. 251–262.

Forman, C. and A. Goldfarb, *ICT Diffusion to Businesses*, http://www.andrew.cmu.edu/user/cforman/ICTDiffusion.pdf.

Foster, J., *From Simplistic to Complex Systems in Economics*, Discussion Paper 335, School of Economics, Univ. Queensland, St. Lucia QLD 4072, Australia, j.foster@economics.uq.edu.au, Oct. 2004.

Gabbay, M., The effects of nonlinear interactions and network structure in small group opinion dynamics, *Physica A* **378**:118–126 (www.elsevier.com/locate/physa) (2007).

Giaever, G., A. M. Chu, L. Ni, C. Connelly, L. Riles, S. Veronneau, S. Dow, A. Lucau-Danila, K. Anderson, B. Andre, et al., Functional profiling of the Saccharomyces ceravisiae genome, *Nature* **418**:387–391 (2002).

Gilbert, E. N., Random graphs, *Ann. Math. Stat.* **30**(4):1141–1144 (1959).

Girvan, M. and M. E. J. Newman, Community structure in social and biological networks, *Proc. Natl. Acad. Sci. USA* **99**(12):7821–7826 (2002).

Gleiss, P. M., P. F. Stadler, A. Wagner, and D. A. Fell, *Small Cycles in Small Worlds*, cond-mat/0009124, Working Paper 0-10-058, Santa Fe Institute, 2000.

Goh, K.-I., B. Kahng, and D. Kim, Spectra and eigenvectors of scale-free networks, *Phys. Rev. E* **64**(5):051903 (2001).

Granovetter, M. S., The strength of weak ties, *Am. J. Sociol.* **78**(6):1360–1380 (1973).

Guare, J., *Six Degrees of Separation: A Play*. Vintage, New York, 1990.

Hansen, M. T., The search-transfer problem: The role of weak ties in sharing knowledge across organization subunits, *Admin. Sci. Quart.* **44**:82–111 (1999).

Hayes, B., Graph theory in practice: Part I, *Am. Sci.* **88**(1):9–13 (2000).

Hayes, B., Graph theory in practice: Part II, *Am. Sci.* **88**(2):104–109 (2000).

Holland, J. H., *Emergence: From Chaos to Order*, Addison-Wesley, Reading, MA, 1998.

Holme, P. and B. J. Kim, Growing scale-free networks with tunable clustering, *Phys. Rev. E* **65**(2).026101 (2002).

Hong, H., M. Y. Choi, and B. J. Kim, Synchronization on small-world networks, *Phys. Rev. E* **65**:026139 (2002),

Huberman, B. A. and L. A. Adamic, Growth dynamics of the worldwide web, *Nature* **401**:131–132 (1999).

Hunter, J. and R. L. Shotland, Treating data collected by the small world method as a Markov process, *Social Forces* **52**:321–332 (1974).

Jeong, H., B. Tombor, R. Albert, Z. N. Oltvai, and A.-L. Barabasi, The large-scale organization of metabolic networks, *Nature* **407**:651–654 (2000).

Jeong, H., Z. Neda, and A.-L. Barabasi, Measuring preferential attachment for evolving networks, *Europhys. Lett.* **61**(4):567–572 (2003).

Jost, J. and M. P. Joy, Spectral properties and synchronization in coupled map lattices, *Phys. Rev. E* **65**(1):016201 (2002).

Jung, S., S. Kim, and B. Kahng, A geometric fractal growth model for scale-free networks, *Phys. Rev. E* **65**(6):056101 (2002).

Kephart, J. O. and S. R. White, Directed-graph epidemiological models of computer viruses, *Proc. IEEE Computer Society Symp. Research in Security and Privacy, May 20–22*, 1991, pp. 343–359.

Kermack, W. O. and A. G. McKendrick, A contribution to the mathematical theory of epidemics. *Proc. Roy. Soc. Lond. A* **115**:700–721 (1927).

Kim, B. J., C. N. Yoon, S. K. Han, and H. Jeong, Path finding strategies in scale-free networks, *Phys. Rev. E* **65**(2):027103, (2002).

Kleinberg, J. M., S. R. Kumar, P. Raghavan, S. Rajagopalan, and A. S. Tomkins, The Web as a graph: Measurements, models, and methods, in T. Asano, H. Imai, D. Lee, S. Nakano, and T. Tokuyama, eds, *Proc. 5th Annual Intnatl. Conf. Computing and Combinatorics,* Tokyo, *Lecture Notes in Computer Science*, Vol. 1627, Springer-Verlag, Berlin, 1999.

Kleinberg, J. M., Navigation in a small world, *Nature* **406**:845 (2000).

Kleinberg, J. M., The small-world phenomenon: An algorithm perspective, in STOC, *Proc. 32nd Annual ACM Symp. Theory of Computing*, Portland, OR, ACM Press, New York, 2000, pp. 163–170.

Kleinfeld, J., Six degrees of separation: Urban myth? *Psychol. Today* (2002).

Kogut, B. and G. Walker, *The Small World of Firm Ownership and Acquisitions in Germany from 1993 to 1997: The Durability of National Networks*, Wharton School, Reginald H. Jones Center Working Paper.

Korte, C. and S. Milgram, Acquaintance networks between racial groups: Application of the small-world method, *J. Personality Soc. Psychol.* **15**:101–108 (1970).

Krapivsky, P. L., S. Redner, and F. A. Leyvraz, Connectivity of growing random networks, *Phys. Rev. Lett.* **85**(21):4629–4632 (2000).

Kretzschmar, M. and M. Morris, Measures of concurrency in networks and the spread of infectious disease, *Math. Biosci.* **133**:165–96 (1996).

Kulkarni, R. V., E. Almaas, and D. Stroud, Evolutionary dynamics in the Bak-Sneppen model on small-world networks, available as *Condensed Matter/9905066* (1999).

Kulkarni, R. V., E. Almaas, and D. Stroud, Exact results and scaling properties of small-world networks, available as *Condensed Matter/9908216* (1999).

Kuramoto, Y., *Chemical Oscillations, Waves, Turbulence*, Springer-Verlag, 1984; republished by Dover Publications, 2003 (www.doverpublications.com).

Lago-Fernandez, L. F., R. Huerta, F. Corbacho, and J. Siguenza, Fast response and temporal coding on coherent oscillations in small-world networks, available as *Condensed Matter/9909379* (1999).

Laherrere, J. and D. Sornette, Stretched exponential distributions in nature and economy: "Fat tails with characteristic scales," *Eur. Phys. J. B* **2**:525–539 (1998).

Lai, Y.-C., A. E. Motter, and T. Nishikawa, *Attacks and Cascades in Complex Networks, Lecture Notes in Physics*, Vol. **650**, 2004, pp. 299–310. http://www.springerlink.com/.

Latora, V. and M. Marchiori, Efficient behavior of small-world networks, *Phys. Rev. Lett.* **87**(19):198701 (2001).

Latour, B., Technology is society made durable, in J. Law, ed., *A Sociology of Monsters*, Routledge, London, 1991.

Levene, M., T. Fenner, G. Loizou, and R. Wheeldon, A stochastic model for the evolution of the web, *Comput. Networks* **39**:277–287 (2002).

Lewis, T. G., *Critical Infrastructure Protection in Homeland Security: Defending a Networked Nation*, Wiley, Aoboken, NJ, 2006.

Li, X. and G. Chen, A local-world evolving network model, *Physica A* **328**:274–286 (2002).

Lin, N., The small world technique as a theory-construction tool, in M. Kochen, ed., *The Small World*, Ablex, Norwood, NJ, 1989, Chapter 2, pp. 231–238.

Liu, J., T. Zhou, and S. Zhang, Chaos synchronization between linearly coupled chaotic system, *Chaos Solut. Fractals* **144**:529–541 (2002).

Liu, J., General complex dynamical network models and its synchronization criterions, *Proc. 22nd Chinese Control Conf.*, Yichang, China, Aug. 10–14, 2003, pp. 380–384.

Liu, J., X. Yu, and G. Chen, Chaos synchronization of general complex dynamical networks, *Physica A* **334**:281–302 (2004).

Liu, J., X. Yu, G. Chen, and D. Cheng, Characterizing the synchronizability of small world dynamical networks, *IEEE Trans. Circuits Syst. I* **51** (2004).

Luczak, T., Phase transition phenomena in random discrete structures, *Discrete Math.* **136**(1–3):225–242 (1994).

Lundberg, C. C., Patterns of acquaintanceship in society and complex organization: A comparative study of the small world problem, *Pacific Sociol. Rev.* **18**:206–222 (1975).

Major, J., Advanced techniques for modeling terrorism risk, *J. Risk Finance* **4**(1) (Fall 2002).

Marchiori, M. and V. Latora, Harmony in the small-world, *Physica A* **285**(3–4):539–546 (2000).

Mathias, N. and V. Gopal, Small worlds: How and why, available as *Condensed Matter/0002076* (2000).

Mathias, N. and V. Gopai, Small worlds: How and why, *Phys. Rev. E* **63** (2001).

Medina, A., I. Matta, and J. Byers, On the origin of power laws in Internet topologies, *ACM Comput. Commun. Rev.* **30**(2):18–28 (2000).

Menezes M. Argollo de, C. F. Moukarzel, and T. J. P. Penna, First-order transition in small-world networks, *Europhys. Lett.* **50**(5):574 (2000).

Mihail, M., C. Gkantsidis, A. Saberi, and E. Zegura, *On the Semantics of Internet Topologies*. Technical Report GIT-CC-02-07, College of Computing, Georgia Institute of Technology, 2002.

Milgram, S., The small world problem, *Psychol. Today* **2**:60–67 (1967).

Mitzenmacher, M., A brief history of generative models for power law and lognormal distributions, *Internet Math.* **1**(2):226–251 (2004).

Molloy, M. and B. Reed, A critical point for random graphs with a given degree sequence, *Random Struct. Algorithms* **6**:161–180 (1995).

Monasson, R., Diffusion, localization and dispersion relations on "small-world" lattices, available as *Condensed Matter/9903347* (1999).

Montoya, J. M. and R. V. Solé, *Small World Patterns in Food Webs*, Santa Fe Institute Working Paper 00-10-059, 2000.

Moore, C. and M. E. J. Newman, Epidemics and percolation in small world networks, *Phys. Rev. E* **61**:5678–5682 (2000).

Moore, C. and M. E. J. Newman, *Exact Solution of Site and Bond Percolation on Small-World Networks*, Santa Fe Institute Working Paper 00-01-007, 2000.

Moukarzel, C. F. and M. Argollo de Menezes, Infinite characteristic length on small-world systems, available as *Condensed Matter/9905131* (1999).

Mukherjee, G. and S. S. Manna, Quasistatic scale-free networks, *Phys. Rev. E* **67**(1):012101 (2003).

National Research Council, Committee on Network Science for Future Army Applications, *Network Science*, Board of Army Science and Technology, National Academies Press, www.nap.edu, 2005.

Newman, M. E. J. and D. J. Watts, Scaling and percolation in the small world network model, *Phys. Rev. E* **60**(6):7332–7342 (1999).

Newmam, M. E. J., C. Moore, and D. J. Watts, Mean-field solution of the small world network model, available as *Condensed Matter/9909165* (1999).

Newman, M. E. J. and D. J. Watts, Scaling and percolation in the small-world network model, *Phys. Rev. E* **60**:7332–7342 (1999).

Newman, M. E. J. and D. J. Watts, Renormalization group analysis of the small world network model, available as *Condensed Matter/9903357* (1999).

Newman, M. E. J., C. Moore, and D. J. Watts, Mean-field solution of the small-world network model, *Phys. Rev. Lett.* **84**(14):3201–3204 (2000).

Newman, M. E. J., Models of the small world: A review, *J. Stat. Phys.* **101**:819–841 (2000).

Newman, M. E. J., Small worlds, the structure of social networks, *J. Stat. Phys.* **101**(3/4) (2000).

Newman, M. E. J., *The Structure of Scientific Collaboration Networks*, Santa Fe Institute Working Paper 00-07-037.

Newman, M. E. J., *Who Is the Best Connected Scientist? A Study of Scientific Co-Authorship Networks*, Santa Fe Institute Working Paper 00-12-064, 2000.

Newman, M. E. J., S. H. Strogatz, and D. J.Watts, Random graphs with arbitrary degree distributions and their applications, *Phys. Rev. E* **64**(2):026118 (2001).

Newman, M. E. J., The structure of scientific collaboration networks, *Proc. Natl. Acad. Sci. USA* **98**(2):404–409 (2001).

Newman, M. E. J., Clustering and preferential attachment in growing networks, *Phys. Rev. E* **64**(2):025102 (2001).

Newman, M. E. J., D. J. Watts, and S. H. Strogatz, Random graph models of social networks, *Proc. Natl. Acad. Sci. USA* **99**(Suppl. 1):2566–2572 (2002).

Newman, M. E. J., S. Forrest, and J. Balthrop, Email networks and the spread of computer viruses, *Phys. Rev. E* **66**(3):035101 (2002).

Newman, M. E. J., Mixing patterns in networks, *Phys. Rev. E* **67**:026126 (2003).

Newman, M. E. J., The structure and function of complex networks, *SIAM Rev. Soci. Industr. Appl. Math.* **45**(2):167–256 (2003).

Norton, J. H. and F. M. Bass, A diffusion theory model of adoption and substitution for successive generations of high-technology products, *Manage. Sci.* **33**(9):1069–1086 (Sept. 1987).

Pandurangan, G., P. Raghavan, and E. Upfal, Building low-diameter P2P networks, FOCS, *Proc. 42nd Annual Symp. Foundations of Computer Science,* Las Vegas, NV, IEEE Computer Society Press, Los Alamitos, CA, 2001, pp. 492–499.

Park, J., Evolving adaptive organizations, *Perspect. Business Innov.* **4**:59–64 (2000).

Pastor-Satorras, R. and A. Vespignani, Epidemic spreading in scale-free networks, *Phys. Rev. Lett.* **86**(14):3200–3203 (2001).

Paxson, V. and S. Floyd, Why we don't know how to simulate the internet, *Proc. 1997 Winter Simulation Conf., Atlanta, GA, ACM Press, New York*, 1997, pp. 1037–1044.

Pool, I. de Sola and M. Kochen, Contacts and influence, *Soc. Networks* **1**:1–48 (1978); reprinted in M. Kochen, ed., *The Small World*, Ablex, Norwood, NJ, 1989, Chapter 1, pp. 3–51.

Powell, R., *Defending Strategic Terrorists over the Long Run: A Basic Approach to Resource Allocation*, Institute of Governmental Studies, Univ. California, Berkeley, Paper WP2006-34, 2006.

Powers, M. R. and Z. Shen, *Colonel Blotto in the War on Terror: Implications for Event Frequency*, Fox School Working Paper, Temple Univ., 2005.

Price, D. J. de S., Networks of scientific papers, *Science* **149**:510–515 (1965).

Price, D. J. de S., A general theory of bibliometric and other cumulative advantage processes, *J. Am. Soc. Inform. Sci.* **27**:292–306 (1976).

Rapoport, A. and W. J. Horvath, A study of a large sociogram, *Behav. Sci.* **6**:280–285 (1961).

Redner, S., How popular is your paper? An empirical study of the citation distribution, *Eur. Phys. J. B* **4**(2):131–134 (1998).

Rosen, E., *The Anatomy of Buzz*, Doubleday-Random House, 2000.

Ryan, B. and N. C. Gross, The diffusion of hybrid seed corn in two Iowa communities, *Rural Sociol.* **8**:15–24 (1943).

Schumpeter, J. A., *Capitalism, Socialism and Democracy*, 1942.

Sedgewick, R. and P. Flajolet, *An Introduction to the Analysis of Algorithms*, Addison-Wesley, Reading, MA, 1996.

Simon, H. A., On a class of skew distribution functions, *Biometrika* **42**(3/4):425–440 (1955).

Solomonoff, R. and A. Rapoport, Connectivity of random nets, *Bull. Math. Biophys.* **13**:107–117 (1951).

Standish, R. K., Complexity and emergence, *Complexity Internatl.* **9** (2001).

Stevenson, W. B., B. Davidson, I. Manev, and K. Walsh, The small world of the university: A classroom exercise in the study of networks, *Connections* **20**(2):23–33 (1997).

Stoneman, P., *The Economics of Technological Diffusion*, Blackwell Publishers, Oxford, UK, 2002.

Strogatz, S., *SYNC: The Emerging Science of Spontaneous Order*, Hyperion, 2003.

Tadic, B., Adaptive random walks on the class of web graphs, *Eur. Phys. J. B* **23**(2):221–228 (2001).

Tadic, B., Dynamics of directed graphs: The world-wide web, *Physica A* **293**(1–2):273–284 (2001).

Tadic, B., Growth and structure of the world-wide web: Towards realistic modeling, *Comput. Phys. Commun.* **147**(1–2):586–589 (2002).

Tadic, B., Temporal fractal structures: Origin of power laws in the world-wide web, *Physica A* **314**(1–4):278–283 (2002).

Travers, J. and S. Milgram, An experimental study of the small world problem. *Sociometry* **32**:425 (1967).

Vazquez, A., R. Pastor-Satorras, and A. Vespignani, Large-scale topological and dynamical properties of the internet, *Phys. Rev. E* **65**(6):066130 (2002).

Vazquez, A. and M. Weigt, Computational complexity arising from degree correlations in networks, *Phys. Rev. E* **67**(2):027101 (2003).

Virtanen, S., *Properties of Non-uniform Random Graph Models*, Helsinki Univ. Technology, Laboratory for Theoretical Computer Science, Report FIN-02015 HUT, lab@tcs.hut, 2003.

Volchenkov, D. and P. Blanchard, An algorithm generating random graphs with power law degree distributions, *Physica A* **315**(3–4):677–690 (2002).

Vukadinovic, D., P. Huang, and T. Erlebach, On the spectrum and structure of internet topology graphs, in H. Unger, T. Bohme, and A. Mikler, eds, *Proc. 2nd Innatl. Workshop on Innovative Internet Computing Systems (IICS 2002)*, Khlungsborn, Germany, *Lecture Notes in Computer Science*, Vol. 2346, Springer-Verlag, Berlin, 2002, pp. 83–95.

Wagner, A. and D. Fell, *The Small World inside Large Metabolic Networks*, Santa Fe Institute Working Paper 00-07-041, 2000.

Walsh, T., Search in a small world, IJCAI'99, *Proc. 16th Intnatl. Joint Conf. Artificial Intelligence*, Stockholm, Sweden, Morgan Kaufmann Publishers, San Francisco, 1999, Vol. 2, pp. 1172–1177.

Walsh, T., Search on high degree graphs, IJCAI'01, *Proc. 17th Intnatl. Joint Conf. Artificial Intelligence*, Seattle, Morgan Kaufmann Publishers, San Francisco, 2001, pp. 266–274.

Wang, X. and G. Chen, Pinning control of scale-free dynamical networks, *Physica A* **310**:521–531 (2002).

Wang, X. and G. Chen, Synchronization in small-world dynamical networks, *J. Bifurcation Chaos* **12**(1):187–192 (2002).

Wang, X. and G. Chen, Synchronization in scale-free dynamical networks: Robustness and fragility, *IEEE Trans. Circuits Syst. I* **49**:54–62 (2002).

Wang, Z., D. Chakrabarti, C. Wang, and C. Faloutsos, Epidemic spreading in real networks: an eigenvalue viewpoint, *Proc. 22nd Intnatl. Symp. Reliable Distributed Systems,* Oct. 6–18, 2003.

Wang, Z., *Net Product Diffusion and Industry Lifecycle*, Univ. Chicago, Dept. Economics, Oct. 5, 2003, economics.uchicago.edu/download/Diffusion.pdf.

Wasserman, S. and K. Faust, *Social Network Analysis*, Cambridge Univ. Press, 1994.

Watts, D. J. and S. H. Strogatz, Collective Dynamics of "small world" networks, *Nature* **393**:440–442 (1998).

Watts, D., Networks, dynamics, and the small-world phenomenon, *Am. J. Sociol.* **105**:2 493–527 (Sept 1999).

Watts, D. J., *Small Worlds*, Princeton Univ. Press, Princeton, NJ, 1999.

Waxman, B. M., Routing of multipoint connections, *IEEE J. Select. Areas Commun.* **6**(9):1617–1622 (1988).

Weigt, M., Dynamics of heuristic optimization algorithms on random graphs, *Eur. Phys. J. B* **28**(3):369–381 (2002).

Wellman, B., J. Salaff, and D. Dimitrova, Computer networks as social networks: Virtual community, computer-supported cooperative work and telework, *Ann. Rev. Sociol.* **22**:213–238 (1996).

White, H. C., Search parameters for the small world problem, *Soc. Forces* **49**:259–264 (1970).

Yano, S. and E. Delfs, *The New Lanchester Strategy*, Lanchester Press, Sunnyvale, CA, 1990.

Yook, S. H., H. Jeong, A.-L. Barabasi, and Y. Tu, *Phys. Rev. Lett.* **86**:5835 (2001).

Yule, G. U., A Mathematical theory of evolution based on the conclusions of Dr. J. C. Willis, *Phil. Trans. Roy. Soc. Lond. B* **213**:21–87 (1925).

Yung, V. J. An exploration in the small world networks, available as *Condensed Matter/ 0004214* (2000/2001).

Zegura, E. W., K. L. Calvert, and S. Bhattacharjee, How to model an internetwork, *IEEE Infocom: The 15th Annual Joint Conf. IEEE Computer and Communications Societies*, San Francisco, IEEE Computer Society Press, Los Alamitos, CA, 1996, Vol. 2, pp. 594–602.

Zegura, E. W., K. L. Calvert, and M. J. Donahoo, A quantitative comparison of graph-based models for Internet topology, *IEEE/ACM Trans. Networking* **5**(6):770–783 (1997).

Zhang, H., A. Goel, and R. Govindan, Using the small world model to improve Freenet performance, *Comput. Networks* **46**(4):555–574 (2002).

Zhu, X., M. Gerstein, and M. Snyder, Getting connected: Analysis and principles of biological networks, *Genes Devel.* **21**:1010–1024 (2007).

Zipf, G. K., *Human Behavior and the Principle of Least Effort*, Addison-Wesley Press, Cambridge, MA, 1949.

ABOUT THE AUTHOR

Ted Lewis has extensive academic and private-sector experience as a member of the faculties of the University of Missouri—Rolla, University of Louisiana—Lafayette, Oregon State University—Corvallis, and the Naval Postgraduate School, Monterey, California. His industrial experience includes senior vice president of Eastman Kodak Company; President and CEO of Daimler Research and Technology, North America, Inc.; and Director of Research at the Oregon Advanced Computing Institute. As a member of the IEEE-Computer Society, Lewis had the privilege of serving as the Editor-in-Chief of *IEEE Software* and *Computer* magazines. He is the Wiley author of *Critical Infrastructure Protection: Defending a Networked Nation* and over 30 other books on computing and business.

INDEX

Network Science: Theory and Practice. By Ted G. Lewis
Copyright © 2009 John Wiley & Sons, Inc.

1,600